The Papers of
George Washington

The Papers of George Washington

Philander D. Chase, *Editor*

Frank E. Grizzard, Jr., and

Beverly H. Runge, *Associate Editors*

Robert F. Haggard, David R. Hoth, Edward G. Lengel,
Mark A. Mastromarino, and Christine S. Patrick, *Assistant Editors*

Presidential Series
10

March–August 1792

Robert F. Haggard and Mark A. Mastromarino, *Editors*

UNIVERSITY OF VIRGINIA PRESS

CHARLOTTESVILLE AND LONDON

This edition has been prepared by the staff of
The Papers of George Washington
sponsored by
The Mount Vernon Ladies' Association of the Union
and the University of Virginia
with the support of
the National Endowment for the Humanities and
the National Historical Publications and Records Commission.
The publication of this volume has been supported by a grant from
the National Historical Publications and Records Commission.

UNIVERSITY OF VIRGINIA PRESS

Printed in the United States of America on acid-free paper

First published in 2002

Library of Congress Cataloging-in-Publication Data
Washington, George, 1732–1799.
The papers of George Washington, Philander D. Chase, ed.

Presidential series vol. 10 edited by Robert F. Haggard and Mark A. Mastromarino.
Includes indexes.
Contents: 1. September 1788–March 1789—[etc.]—10. March–August 1792
1. United States—Politics and government—1789–1797. 2. Washington, George, 1732–1799—Correspondence. 3. Presidents—United States—Correspondence. I. Chase, Philander. II. Haggard, Robert F. III. Presidential series.
E312.72 1987b 973.4′1′092 87-410017
ISBN 0-8139-1103-6 (v. 1)
ISBN 0-8139-2101-5 (v. 10)

Frontispiece: Portrait of Washington by Archibald Robertson, 1792. (Sulgrave Manor, Sulgrave, United Kingdom.) Scottish artist Archibald Robertson (1765–1835) came to the United States in 1791 with a commission from the earl of Buchan to paint a portrait of George Washington (see Buchan to GW, 28 June 1791). Although Robertson claimed completion of this portrait in a letter to GW of 21 April 1792, the portrait was not sent to Buchan until the spring of 1793 (see Tobias Lear to GW, 9 Nov. 1793).

Contents

NOTE: Volume numbers refer to the *Presidential Series.*

Illustrations

Editorial Apparatus

Transcription of the documents in the volumes of *The Papers of George Washington* has remained as close to a literal reproduction of the manuscript as possible. Punctuation, capitalization, and spelling of all words are retained as they appear in the original document; only for documents printed in annotations has paragraphing been modified. Dashes used as punctuation have been retained except when a dash and another mark of punctuation appear together. The appropriate marks of punctuation have always been added at the end of a paragraph. When a tilde (~) is used in the manuscript to indicate a double letter, the letter has been doubled. Washington and some of his correspondents occasionally used a tilde above an incorrectly spelled word to indicate an error in orthography. When this device is used the editors have silently corrected the word. In cases where a tilde has been inserted above an abbreviation or contraction, usually in letter-book copies, the word has been expanded. Otherwise, contractions and abbreviations have been retained as written except that a period has been inserted after an abbreviation when needed. If the meaning of an abbreviation or contraction is not obvious, it has been expanded in square brackets: "H[is] M[ajest]y." Editorial insertions or corrections in the text also appear in square brackets. Angle brackets ⟨ ⟩ are used to indicate illegible or mutilated material. A space left blank in a manuscript by the writer is indicated by a square-bracketed gap in the text [ ]. Deletion of material by the author of a manuscript is ignored unless it contains substantive material, and then it appears in a footnote. If the intended location of marginal notations is clear from the text, they are inserted without comment; otherwise they are recorded in the notes. The ampersand has been retained, and the thorn transcribed as "th." The symbol for per (℘) is used when it appears in the manuscript. The dateline has been placed at the head of a document regardless of where it occurred in the manuscript. All of the documents printed in this volume, as well as omitted routine Washington documents and various ancillary material cited in the notes, may be found in the CD-ROM edition of Washington's Papers (CD-ROM:GW). The reports of Washington's farm managers at Mount Vernon, some of which have been printed in previous volumes of the *Presidential Series,* from now on will appear only in CD-ROM:GW.

During both of Washington's administrations, but particularly in the period shortly before and after his first inauguration, he was besieged with applications for public office. Many of the applicants continued to seek appointment or promotion. The editors have usually printed only one of these letters in full and cited other letters both from the applicant and in support of his application in notes to the initial letter. When Washington replied to these requests at all, the replies were generally pro forma reiterations of his policy of noncommitment until the appointment to a post was made. In such cases his replies have been included only in the notes to the original application and do not appear in their chronological sequence. These and other letters to or from Washington that, in whole or in part, are printed out of their chronological sequence are listed in the table of contents with an indication of where they may be found in the volumes.

Since Washington read no language other than English, incoming letters written to him in foreign languages were generally translated for his information. Where this contemporary translation has survived, it has been used as the text of the document, and the original version has been included in CD-ROM:GW. If there is no contemporary translation, the document in its original language has been used as the text.

During the early years of the new government, the executive sent out a large number of circular letters, under either Washington's name or that of one of his secretaries. Circular letters covered copies of laws passed by Congress and sent to the governors of the states. They also covered commissions and announcements of appointment for public offices sent to individuals after their nominations had been approved by the Senate. In both instances, the circulars requested recipients to acknowledge receipt of the documents. The circulars and the routine acknowledgments of these circulars, usually addressed to Washington but sometimes to one of his secretaries, have been omitted unless they contain material of other interest or significance. In such cases the letters are either calendared or printed in full. The entire text of the documents is available in the CD-ROM edition.

Individuals mentioned in the text in each series are usually identified only at their first substantive mention in the series. The index to each volume indicates where an identification appears in an earlier volume of the *Presidential Series.*

During Washington's first administration, he depended upon the services of several secretaries: both Tobias Lear and David Humphreys, who had been in his service at Mount Vernon, went with him to New York. Two of Washington's nephews also joined his secretarial staff: Robert Lewis of Fredericksburg joined the staff in May 1789, and Bartholomew Dandridge sometime in the spring of 1791. Thomas Nelson and William Jackson assumed secretarial duties in 1789; the former left Washington's service in November 1790, and the latter resigned in December 1791. Relatively few drafts in Washington's hand of letters from early 1791 have survived, and the sequence in which outgoing letters and documents were drafted and copied is often difficult to determine. In Record Group 59, State Department Miscellaneous Letters, in the National Archives, are numerous documents that appear to be the original retained copies of letters written by Washington shortly before he became president and in the first years of his first administration. Much of this correspondence is in the hand of Lear or Humphreys. In early 1791 letterpress copies of documents drafted by Lear in Philadelphia also began to appear. Occasionally the frequency with which the secretary's emendations and insertions appear suggests that the document was a draft prepared by him for Washington. More rarely Washington himself made changes and corrections to a document. On other occasions the documents appear to be simply retained copies either of his original draft or of the receiver's copy. For most of the letters found in Miscellaneous Letters, there are also letter-book copies in the Washington Papers at the Library of Congress. Some of the letters for this period probably were copied into the letter books close to the time they were written, but others obviously were entered much later. Occasionally Thomas Nelson's writing appears in the letter-book copies for the summer of 1789, as does Bartholomew Dandridge's, although Nelson did not join the staff until October and Dandridge was not employed until 1791. Finally, a few letter-book copies are in the handwriting of Howell Lewis, Washington's nephew, who did not assume his duties until the spring of 1792. When the receiver's copy of a letter has not been found, the editors have generally assumed that the copy in Miscellaneous Letters was made from the receiver's copy or the draft and have used it as the text, rather than the letter-book copy, and have described the document either as a copy or a draft, depending on the appearance of the manuscript.

Symbols Designating Documents

AD	Autograph Document
ADS	Autograph Document Signed
ADf	Autograph Draft
ADfS	Autograph Draft Signed
AL	Autograph Letter
ALS	Autograph Letter Signed
D	Document
DS	Document Signed
Df	Draft

DfS	Draft Signed
L	Letter
LS	Letter Signed
LB	Letter-Book Copy
[S]	Used with other symbols to indicate that the signature on the document has been cropped or clipped.

Repository Symbols and Abbreviations

Arch. Aff. Etr.	Archives du Ministère des Affaires Etrangères, Paris (photocopies at Library of Congress)
AU-M	University of Alabama Medical Center, Birmingham
CCC	Honnold Library, Claremont, Calif.
CD-ROM:GW	*See* "Editorial Apparatus"
CSmH	Henry E. Huntington Library, San Marino, Calif.
CSt	Stanford University, Palo Alto, Calif.
CtSoP	Pequot Library Association, Southport, Conn.
CtY	Yale University, New Haven
DLC	Library of Congress
DLC:GW	George Washington Papers, Library of Congress
DNA	National Archives
DNA:PCC	Papers of the Continental Congress, National Archives
DSoCi	Society of the Cincinnati, Washington, D.C.
MdHi	Maryland Historical Society, Baltimore
MH	Harvard University, Cambridge, Mass.
MHi	Massachusetts Historical Society, Boston
MHi-A	Adams Papers, Massachusetts Historical Society, Boston
N	New York State Library, Albany
NBuErHi	Buffalo and Erie County Historical Society, Buffalo, N.Y.
Nc-Ar	North Carolina State Department of Archives and History, Raleigh
NCH	Hamilton College, Clinton, N.Y.
NHi	New-York Historical Society, New York
NjMoNP	Washington Headquarters Library, Morristown, N.J.
NjP	Princeton University, Princeton, N.J.
NN	New York Public Library, New York
NNC	Columbia University, New York
NNGL	Gilder Lehrman Collection at the Pierpont Morgan Library, New York

NNMM	Metropolitan Museum of Art, New York
NNPM	Pierpont Morgan Library, New York
OCHP	Cincinnati Historical Society
OHi	Ohio State Historical Society, Columbus
OMC	Marietta College, Marietta, Ohio
PHi	Historical Society of Pennsylvania, Philadelphia
PPAmP	American Philosophical Society, Philadelphia
PPRF	Rosenbach Foundation, Philadelphia
PWacD	David Library of the American Revolution, Sol Feinstone Collection, on deposit at the American Philosophical Society
RG	Record Group (designating the location of documents in the National Archives)
RHi	Rhode Island Historical Society, Providence
ScHi	South Carolina Historical Society, Charleston
Vi	Library of Virginia, Richmond
ViHi	Virginia Historical Society, Richmond
ViLxW	Washington and Lee University, Lexington, Va.
ViMtV	Mount Vernon Ladies' Association of the Union
ViW	College of William and Mary, Williamsburg, Va.
Vt	Vermont State Library, Montpelier

Short Title List

American Book-Prices Current. *American Book-Prices Current.* 105 vols. to date. New York, 1895—.

Annals of Congress. Joseph Gales, Sr., comp. *The Debates and Proceedings in the Congress of the United States; with an Appendix, Containing Important State Papers and Public Documents, and All the Laws of a Public Nature.* 42 vols. Washington, D.C., 1834–56.

ASP. Walter Lowrie et al., eds. *American State Papers: Documents, Legislative and Executive, of the Congress of the United States.* 38 vols. Washington, D.C., 1832–61.

Barnby, *Prisoners of Algiers.* H. G. Barnby. *The Prisoners of Algiers: An Account of the Forgotten American-Algerian War, 1785–1797.* New York, 1966.

Bond, *Correspondence of Symmes.* Beverley W. Bond, Jr., ed. *The Correspondence of John Cleves Symmes, Founder of the Miami Purchase.* New York, 1926.

Brighton, *Checkered Career of Tobias Lear.* Ray Brighton. *The Checkered Career of Tobias Lear.* Portsmouth, N.H., 1985.

Buell, *Putnam Memoirs.* Rowena Buell, ed. *The Memoirs of Rufus Put-*

nam and Certain Official Papers and Correspondence. Boston and New York, 1903.

Calendar of Virginia State Papers. William P. Palmer et al., eds. *Calendar of Virginia State Papers and Other Manuscripts.* 11 vols. Richmond, 1875–93.

Candler, *Revolutionary Records of Georgia.* Allen D. Candler, comp. *The Revolutionary Records of the State of Georgia.* 3 vols. Atlanta, 1908.

Carter, *Territorial Papers.* Clarence E. Carter et al., eds. *The Territorial Papers of the United States.* 27 vols. Washington, D.C., 1934–69.

Caughey, *McGillivray of the Creeks.* John Walton Caughey. *McGillivray of the Creeks.* Norman, Okla., 1938.

Cohen, "Reuben Harvey." Sheldon S. Cohen. "Reuben Harvey: Irish Friend of American Freedom." *Quaker History* 88 (Spring 1999), 22–39.

Davis, *Earlier History of American Corporations.* Joseph Stancliffe Davis. *Essays in the Earlier History of American Corporations.* Harvard Economic Studies, vol. 16, nos. 1–4. 2 vols. Cambridge, Mass., 1917.

Decatur, *Private Affairs of George Washington.* Stephen Decatur, Jr. *Private Affairs of George Washington, from the Records and Accounts of Tobias Lear, Esquire, His Secretary.* Boston, 1933.

DHFC. Linda G. De Pauw et al., eds. *Documentary History of the First Federal Congress of the United States of America.* 13 vols. to date. Baltimore, 1972—.

Diaries. Donald Jackson and Dorothy Twohig, eds. *The Diaries of George Washington.* 6 vols. Charlottesville, Va., 1976–79.

Eckhardt, *Pennsylvania Clocks and Clockmakers.* George H. Eckhardt. *Pennsylvania Clocks and Clockmakers.* New York, 1955.

Eisen, *Portraits of Washington.* Gustavus A. Eisen. *Portraits of Washington.* 3 vols. New York, 1932.

Executive Journal. *Journal of the Executive Proceedings of the Senate of the United States of America.* Vol. 1. Washington, D.C., 1828.

Fields, *Papers of Martha Washington.* Joseph E. Fields, comp. *"Worthy Partner": The Papers of Martha Washington.* Westport, Conn., and London, 1994.

Ford, *Wills of George Washington.* Worthington Chauncey Ford, ed. *Wills of George Washington and His Immediate Ancestors.* Brooklyn, 1891.

Griffin, *Boston Athenæum Washington Collection.* Appleton P. C. Griffin, comp. *A Catalogue of the Washington Collection in the Boston Athenæum.* Cambridge, Mass., 1897.

Harris, *Thornton Papers.* C. M. Harris, ed. *Papers of William Thornton.* 1 vol. to date. Charlottesville, Va., 1995—.

Heads of Families (Maryland). *Heads of Families at the First Census of the United States Taken in the Year 1790* (Maryland). 1907. Reprint. Baltimore, 1965.

Heads of Families (Massachusetts). *Heads of Families at the First Census of the United States Taken in the Year 1790* (Massachusetts). 1908. Reprint. Baltimore, 1964.

Heads of Families (New York). *Heads of Families at the First Census of the United States Taken in the Year 1790* (New York). 1908. Reprint. Baltimore, 1966.

Heads of Families (Pennsylvania). *Heads of Families at the First Census of the United States Taken in the Year 1790* (Pennsylvania). 1908. Reprint. Baltimore, 1970.

Heads of Families (Rhode Island). *Heads of Families at the First Census of the United States Taken in the Year 1790* (Rhode Island). 1908. Reprint. Spartanburg, S.C., 1963.

Hening. William Waller Hening, ed. *The Statutes at Large; Being a Collection of All the Laws of Virginia from the First Session of the Legislature, in the Year 1619.* 13 vols. 1819–23. Reprint. Charlottesville, Va., 1969.

Higginbotham, *Daniel Morgan.* Don Higginbotham. *Daniel Morgan: Revolutionary Rifleman.* Chapel Hill, N.C., 1961.

JCC. Worthington C. Ford et al., eds. *Journals of the Continental Congress.* 34 vols. Washington, D.C., 1904–37.

Jefferson Papers. Julian P. Boyd et al., eds. *The Papers of Thomas Jefferson.* 29 vols. to date. Princeton, N.J., 1950—.

Jennings and Fenton, *Iroquois Indians.* Francis Jennings and William Fenton, eds. *Iroquois Indians: A Documentary History of the Diplomacy of the Six Nations and Their League.* Microfilm. 50 reels. Woodbridge, Conn., 1985.

Journal of the House. *Journal of the House of Representatives: George Washington's Administration, 1789–1797.* Ed. Martin P. Claussen. 9 vols. Wilmington, Del., 1977.

Journal of the Senate. *Journal of the Senate Including the Journal of the Executive Proceedings of the Senate: George Washington's Administration, 1789–1797.* Ed. Martin P. Claussen. 9 vols. Wilmington, Del., 1977.

JPP. Dorothy Twohig, ed. *Journal of the Proceedings of the President, 1793–1797.* Charlottesville, Va., 1981.

Kinnaird, *Spain in the Mississippi Valley.* Lawrence Kinnaird, ed. *Spain in the Mississippi Valley, 1765–1794.* 3 vols. Annual Report of the American Historical Association for the Year 1945. Washington, D.C., 1946.

Kite, *L'Enfant and Washington.* Elizabeth S. Kite. *L'Enfant and Washington, 1791–1792: Published and Unpublished Documents Now Brought Together for the First Time.* Baltimore, 1929.

Kline, *Burr Papers.* Mary-Jo Kline, ed. *Political Correspondence and Public Papers of Aaron Burr.* 2 vols. Princeton, N.J., 1983.

Knopf, *Wayne.* Richard C. Knopf, ed. *Anthony Wayne, a Name in Arms. Soldier, Diplomat, Defender of Expansion Westward of a Nation: The Wayne-Knox-Pickering-McHenry Correspondence.* Pittsburgh, 1960.

Laurens Papers. Philip M. Hamer et al., eds. *The Papers of Henry Laurens.* 15 vols. to date. Columbia, S.C., 1968—.

Ledger B. Manuscript Ledger in George Washington Papers, Library of Congress.

Ledger C. Manuscript Ledger in Morristown National Historical Park, Morristown, N.J.

Madison, *Notes of Debates in the Federal Convention.* James Madison. *Notes of Debates in the Federal Convention of 1787.* Reprint. New York, 1966.

Madison Papers. William T. Hutchinson et al., eds. *The Papers of James Madison.* [1st series.] 17 vols. Chicago and Charlottesville, Va., 1962–91.

Marcus and Perry, *Documentary History of the Supreme Court.* Maeva Marcus et al., eds. *The Documentary History of the Supreme Court of the United States, 1789–1800.* 6 vols. to date. New York, 1985–.

Miller, *Peale Papers.* Lillian B. Miller, ed. *The Selected Papers of Charles Willson Peale and His Family.* 5 vols. New Haven, 1983–88.

Miller, *Treaties.* Hunter Miller, ed. *Treaties and Other International Acts of the United States of America.* Vol. 2. Washington, D.C., 1931.

Moore, *History of Slavery in Massachusetts.* George Henry Moore. *Notes on the History of Slavery in Massachusetts.* New York, 1866.

Morris, *Diary of the French Revolution.* Beatrix Cary Davenport, ed. *A Diary of the French Revolution by Gouverneur Morris.* 2 vols. Boston, 1939.

Naval Documents. William Bell Clark et al., eds. *Naval Documents of the American Revolution.* 10 vols. to date. Washington, D.C., 1964—.

New York City Directory, 1792. William Duncan. *The New-York Directory, and Register, for the Year 1792.* New York, 1792.

Pa. Archives. Samuel Hazard et al., eds. *Pennsylvania Archives.* 138 vols. Philadelphia and Harrisburg, Pa., 1852–1949.

Papers, Colonial Series. W. W. Abbot et al., eds. *The Papers of George Washington, Colonial Series.* 10 vols. Charlottesville, Va., 1983–95.

Papers, Retirement Series. Dorothy Twohig et al., eds. *The Papers of George Washington, Retirement Series.* 4 vols. Charlottesville, Va., 1998–99.

Papers, Revolutionary War Series. W. W. Abbot et al., eds. *The Papers of George Washington. Revolutionary War Series.* 12 vols. to date. Charlottesville, Va., 1985—.

Pennsylvania in 1800. John D. Stemmons, ed. *Pennsylvania in 1800: A Computerized Index to the 1800 Federal Population Schedules of the State of Pennsylvania with Other Aids to Research.* Salt Lake City, 1972.

Pennypacker, *George Washington's Spies.* Morton Pennypacker. *General Washington's Spies on Long Island and in New York.* Brooklyn, 1939.

Philadelphia Directory, 1791. Clement Biddle. *The Philadelphia Directory.* Philadelphia, 1791.

Philadelphia Directory, 1794. James Hardie. *The Philadelphia Directory and Register.* Philadelphia, 1794.

St. Clair, *Narrative.* Arthur St. Clair. *A Narrative of the Manner in Which the Campaign against the Indians, in the Year One Thousand Seven Hundred and Ninety-one, Was Conducted, under the Command of Major General St. Clair. . . .* Philadelphia, 1812.

Schenck, *History of Fairfield.* Elizabeth Hubbell Schenck. *The History of Fairfield, Fairfield County, Connecticut from 1700 to 1800.* 2 vols. New York, 1905.

Sellers, *Peale's Museum.* Charles Coleman Sellers. *Mr. Peale's Museum: Charles Willson Peale and the First Popular Museum of Natural Science and Art.* New York, 1980.

1 *Stat.* Richard Peters, ed. *The Public Statutes at Large of the United States of America.* Vol. 1. Boston, 1845.

6 *Stat.* Richard Peters, ed. *The Public Statutes at Large of the United States of America.* Vol. 6. Boston, 1848.

Syrett, *Hamilton Papers.* Harold C. Syrett et al., eds. *The Papers of Alexander Hamilton.* 27 vols. New York, 1961–87.

Thomas, *Reminiscences.* Ebenezer Smith Thomas. *Reminiscences of the Last Sixty-Five Years, Commencing with the Battle of Lexington.* 2 vols. Hartford, 1840.

Trumbull, *Autobiography.* John Trumbull. *The Autobiography of Colonel John Trumbull.* Ed. Theodore Sizer. New Haven, 1953. Reprint. New York, 1970.

Turner, *Correspondence of the French Ministers.* Frederick J. Turner. *Correspondence of the French Ministers to the United States, 1791–1797.* 2 vols. American Historical Association for the Year 1903. Washington, D.C., 1904.

Walton, *Vermont Records.* E. P. Walton, ed. *Records of the Governor and Council of the State of Vermont.* Vol. 4. Montpelier, Vt., 1876.

Wright, *Bowles.* J. Leitch Wright, Jr. *William Augustus Bowles, Director General of the Creek Nation.* Athens, Ga., 1967.

The Papers of George Washington
Presidential Series
Volume 10
March–August 1792

From a Citizen of Georgia

Sir 1st March 1792.

Permit me a Member of the Community of the Free Citisens of the State of Georgia, to address you at this critical Period; The Lustre of the former Deeds executed by yr Magnanimity calls on every member of the Union to venerate and esteem you, and even to consider you as a Father to the People of the western World; but suffer me to imprecate you as a Parent fostering your dependant Children, to use your Influence to suspend the inhuman and unprofitable War heretofore carried on against the Tribes of Miami and other Indians to the Westward; as those people contend for the Gift of Nature, and yr Invasion has been justly reprobated by two Defeats remarkably signel;[1] for God's sake purchase the Lands from the native Proprietors, if the United States stand in need of them, as it most undoubtedly will be the cheapest Mode of acquiring them; but why so coveting as to wish for those extensive Countries at this time of Day, when our Territories are already so extensive, that we cant people them, and none but Land-Jobbers can be benefitted by such unreasonable Acquisitions, while the Union is disgraced & unnecessarily impoverished.

Pray turn yr Attention to the meserable Situation of my Fellow Citisens in Georgia you'll please recollect that in consequence of the power vested in you, a Treaty of Peace, was negotiated, by your Excellency, on the part of the United States & Colo. McGilvra on part of the savage Tribes, South & West of Georgia, which League, binding as far as writing cou'd compel, has been violated by the Savages, who have butcherd many innocent Families resting secure in consequence of the solemn Treaty engag'd in.[2]

At this moment one third of the Militia of our State is in marching Orders, & unhappily a respectable party has been lately cut off[.] Doubtless this is sufficient cause for resentment, if not for revenge, to kindle the blaze of War. & cruel to neglect us when murderd under sanction of Treaty, while the cause to the Northward is unecessary & unjust; as the People of Miami, have ever declar'd boldly that they wou'd not treat with you, &

therefore, no violation of Compact can be charg'd against them & why shou'd they? if they think it unnecessary; doubtless they are independant People, as we are, & have a right to consult their own Interest—The People of Georgia dare not, I suppose, demand, Aid from the Union but from in their present distresd Situation, are induc'd to implore it.

Sire Many considerate People, wish, you vested with an absalute *Negative* in the legislature of the Unitd States; fully convinc'd that many infurnal & ridiculous Laws hither to pass'd by that Body woud have met their proper Negative well assur'd if you alone was responsable to the People for the good or ill consiquence of the Laws enacted, their welfare, wou'd be more maturely considerd. This I considr a defect in the Constitution, & you may rely on it, when a full Representation takes place agreeable to the Census, the whole System of your funding Laws, with many others, will suffer a repeal; grounding their Right of reviewing those great subjects, as being affected when the People were not duely represented.

Was the President vested with an absalute negative, this Evil need not be dreaded, but 'till that Period; 'tis impossible that Stability & Permanence can be in any measures Congress may adopt.

Pray excuse the deviation to which I have been harried on by a croud of Ideas, fearing that Congress might neglect her Citizens acting on the defensive, against savage Enemies, regardless of every Bond of Treaty; & at the same time prosecute a War equally savage against the Miami Tribe, whose crimanality consists in a determination to defend their own Territory; & have from the beginning declard they will enter into no Negotiation or Treaty with you; & pray Sir, lay your hand on your Heart, & ask the question whether this self defence to free Men, can be accounted a fault—from Venerable Sir Your great admirer & well wisher

a Citizen of Georgia

AL, DNA: RG 59, Miscellaneous Letters. The author's handwriting bears some similarity to that of U.S. Senator William Few of Georgia.

1. For the defeat by northwestern Indians of a U.S. Army expedition commanded by Brig. Gen. Josiah Harmar in October 1790 and another under Maj. Gen. Arthur St. Clair in November 1791, see GW to Henry Knox, 19 Nov. 1790, n.3, William Darke to GW, 9–10 Nov. 1791, source note, and GW to the

U.S. Senate and House of Representatives, 12 Dec. 1791, n.1. The administration by this time already had begun preparations for yet another major military offensive against the Miami and the other hostile Indian nations of the Northwest (see Knox to GW, 26 Dec. 1791, n.2, GW to the U.S. Senate and House of Representatives, 11 Jan. 1792, n.2, and Knox to GW, 2 Mar. 1792).

2. For the Treaty of New York, which was signed on 7 Aug. 1790 by Alexander McGillivray and twenty-three other Creek chiefs, see GW to the U.S. Senate, 4 Aug. 1790, and enclosure, and Proclamation, 14 Aug. 1790, nn.4–5.

From Alexander Hamilton

Treasury Department March 1st 1792.

The Secretary of the Treasury has the honor to submit to the President of the United States the draft of a report on the subject of the Act concerning distilled Spirits.[1] There are one or two blanks in the draft, to the filling of which some additional examination & enquiry are requisite. The suggestions however to which they relate are true, as they stand, and the sense will be apparent. The Secretary sends the draft before they are filled to save time. He will wait upon the President on Monday for his commands respecting it.[2]

LB, DLC:GW.

For the background and early reactions to the Excise Act of March 1791 and the establishment of the excise service, see GW to the U.S. Senate, 4 Mar. (third letter), Executive Order, 15 Mar., GW to Hamilton, 15 Mar. (first letter), to David Humphreys, 20 July, Charles Pinckney to GW, 18 Aug., and GW to the U.S. Senate and House of Representatives, 31 Oct. 1791.

1. Hamilton apparently enclosed a draft of his report on the difficulties attending the execution of the Excise Act, which the U.S. House of Representatives had requested of him on 1–2 Nov. 1791 (see *Annals of Congress*, 2d Cong., 151–52).

2. For Hamilton's lengthy final report, which he signed on Monday, 5 Mar. 1792, and presented to the House the following day, see Syrett, *Hamilton Papers*, 11:77–106.

From Reuben Harvey

Respected Friend Cork [Ireland] March 1st 1792

Tho' I have often wish'd for an opportunity of communicating To The President of The United States my heart felt satisfaction that it has pleased our gracious Father to grant thee life & health for the great purposes entrusted to thy Care, yet I found an unwillingness to intrude or break in upon the important & numerous Concerns that daily attend thy time, Nor should I now take the liberty of adressing these few lines for thy perusal, was I not sorely distress'd at the unexpected & shocking disaster which befel your Army in the Miamis Country, the relation of which given by Genl St Clair to Secy Knox exceeds all relations of the kind that I have yet met, And seems as if written by a broken hearted dying Commander,[1] Indeed it's Contents seem to imply an impracticability for him, with an increas'd Force to stand against Indians, which I think is the first instance I've heard of where this savage Foe was so much to be dreaded in open ground, against Troops well provided with small Arms & Artillery; Till now I apprehended that Indians were only formidable in bushy woody Ground, in places of Ambush, or when vastly superior in Number, but alas, in the late Slaughter, they attack'd an Army under Arms in the open Field, & as far as we know suffer'd little or no loss themselves, which is altogether beyond my capacity to account for, And is very different from Braddock's defeat in 1755, he having incautiously march'd through woods & defiles, gave the Indians every advantage they could desire, notwthstanding (as I have heard) thy advice to him strongly enforced the necessity of having Partys on his Flanks. I hope thee'l forgive this freedom of expression, as it realy proceeds from my unabated *affection* for America, *which* has received a very painful Shock by the late Calamity. Before I conclude my letter, bear with me a little longer, just to let me say, that I have long lamented your not having the frontier Forts deliver'd up to you, according to Treaty; Is there not cause to suppose that The Possessors are not inimicable to your savage Enemys? I hope the Kentucky People have not acted improperly or unjustly, by taking any Land from the Indians, contrary to their inclination. With sincere good wishes for a continuance of thy Health I remain very respectf. Thy real Friend

Reuben Harvey

P.S. The 27th Ulto at 5 in the Evening a Fire broke out in our Parly House of Commons, & entirely consumed it—The Members were sitting.[2]

ALS, DNA: RG 59, Miscellaneous Letters.

During the Revolutionary War, Reuben Harvey (1734–1808), a Quaker merchant living in Cork, Ireland, had strongly protested the mistreatment of American prisoners of war held at nearby Kinsale and provided the captives with money and supplies. In consequence, the Continental Congress, at GW's behest, passed a resolution on 18 July 1783 expressing "the just sense" it entertained of "the services he has rendered during the late war, to American prisoners" in Ireland (*JCC,* 24:439–40). After the war Harvey continued to champion the American cause, particularly in the realm of trade, and he also engaged in a host of local philanthropic activities (see Cohen, "Reuben Harvey," 22–39).

1. GW's message to the U.S. Senate and House of Representatives of 13 Dec. 1791 and the documents it covered had been reprinted in a number of British newspapers by mid-February 1792 (see, for instance, *Dublin Journal,* 18 February). Harvey undoubtedly was referring to one of the enclosures, Maj. Gen. Arthur St. Clair's despondent dispatch from Fort Washington to Henry Knox of 9 Nov. 1791.

2. According to a British newspaper report, a malfunctioning stove started the fire at the Irish House of Commons that gutted the building and caused its dome to collapse. "The explosion of flame and smoke that followed," the report continued, "exhibited a scene that has not inaptly been compared to an eruption of Vesuvius." All of the Commons's legislative records were saved, however (*Times* [London], 6 Mar. 1792).

Thomas Jefferson's Memorandum of Conversations with Washington

[Philadelphia]

Conversations with the President. March 1. 1792.

1792. Feb. 28. I was to have been with him long enough before 3. aclock (which was the hour & day he received visits) to have opened to him a proposition for doubling the velocity of the post riders, who now travel about 50. miles a day, & might without difficulty go 100. and for taking measures (by way-bills) to know where the delay is, when there is any. I was delayed by business, so as to have scarcely time to give him the outlines. I run over them rapidly, & observed afterwards that I had hitherto never spoke to him on the subject of the post office, not knowing whether it was considered as a revenue law, or a law for the general accomodation of the citizens; that the law just passed seemed to have removed the doubt, by declaring that the whole profits of the office should be applied to extending the posts &

that even the past profits should be refunded by the treasury for the same purpose:[1] that I therefore conceived it was now in the department of the Secretary of state: that I thought it would be advantageous so to declare it for another reason, to wit, that the department of the treasury possessed already such an influence as to swallow up the whole Executive powers, and that even the future Presidents (not supported by the weight of character which himself possessed) would not be able to make head against this department. that in urging this measure I had certainly no personal interest, since, if I was supposed to have any appetite for power, yet as my career would certainly be exactly as short as his own, the intervening time was too short to be an object. my real wish was to avail the public of every occasion during the residue of the President's period, to place things on a safe footing. he was now called on to attend his company & he desired me to come and breakfast with him the next morning.

Feb. 29. I did so, & after breakfast we retired to his room, & I unfolded my plan for the post-office, and after such an approbation of it as he usually permitted himself on the first presentment of any idea, and desiring me to commit it to writing, he, during that pause of conversation which follows a business closed, said in an affectionate tone, that he had felt much concern at an expression which dropt from me yesterday, & which marked my intention of retiring when he should. that as to himself, many motives obliged him to it. he had through the whole course of the war, and most particularly at the close of it uniformly declared his resolution to retire from public affairs, & never to act in any public office;[2] that he had retired under that firm resolution, that the government however which had been formed being found evidently too inefficacious, and it being supposed that his aid was of some consequence towards bringing the people to consent to one of sufficient efficacy for their own good, he consented to come into the convention, & on the same motive, after much pressing, to take a part in the new government and get it under way. that were he to continue longer, it might give room to say, that having tasted the sweets of office he could not do without them: that he really felt himself growing old, his bodily health less firm, his memory, always bad, becoming worse, and perhaps the other faculties of his mind shewing a decay to others of which he was insensible himself, that this apprehension particularly oppressed him, that he found moreover his activity lessened, business therefore more irksome, and tranquillity & retirement become an irresistable passion. that however he felt himself obliged for these reasons to retire from the government, yet he should consider it as unfortunate if that should bring on the retirement of the great officers of the government, and that this might produce a shock on the public mind of dangerous consequence. I told him that no man had ever had less desire of entering into public offices than my self: that the circumstance of a perilous war, which brought every thing into danger, & called for all the services which every citizen could render, had induced me to undertake the administration of the government of Virginia, that I had both before & after refused repeated appointments of Congress to go abroad in that sort of office, which if I had consulted my own gratification, would always have been the most agreeable to me, that at the end of two years, I resigned the government of Virginia, & retired with a firm resolution never more to appear in public life, that a domestic loss however happened,[3] and made me fancy that absence, & a change of scene for a time might be expedient for me, that I therefore accepted a foreign appointment limited to two years, that at the close of that, Dr Franklin having left France, I was appointed to supply his place, which I had accepted, & tho' I continued in it three or four years, it was under the constant idea of remaining only a year or two longer; that the revolution in France coming on, I had so interested myself in the event of that, that when obliged to bring my family home, I had still an idea of returning & awaiting the close of that, to fix the aera of my final retirement; that on my arrival here I found he had appointed me to my present office,[4] that he knew I had not come into it without some reluctance, that it was on my part a sacrifice of inclination to the opinion that I might be more serviceable here than in France, & with a firm resolution in my mind to indulge my constant wish for retirement at no very distant day: that when therefore I received his letter written from Mount Vernon, on his way to Carolina & Georgia (Apr. 1. 1791.) and discovered from an expression in that that he meant to retire from the government ere long, & as to the precise epoch there could be no doubt,[5] my mind was immediately made up to make that the epoch of my own retirement from those labors, of which I was heartily tired. that however I did not beleive there was any idea in either of my brethren in the administration of retiring, that on the contrary I had perceived at a late meeting of the trustees of the sinking fund that the Secretary of the Treasury had developed the plan he intended to pursue, & that it embraced years in it's view.[6] he said that he considered the Treasury department as a much more limited one going only to the single object of revenue, while that of the Secretary of state embracing nearly all the objects of administration, was much more important, & the retirement of the officer therefore would be more noticed: that tho' the government had set out with a pretty general good will of the public, yet that symptoms of dissatisfaction had lately shewn themselves far beyond what he could have expected, and to what height these might arise in case of too great a change in the administration, could not be foreseen. I told him that in my opinion there was only a single source of these discontents. tho' they had indeed appear to spread themselves over the war department also, yet I considered that as an overflowing only from their real channel which would never have taken place if they had not first been generated in another department—to wit that of the treasury. that a system had there been contrived, for deluging the states with papermoney instead of gold & silver, for withdrawing our citizens from the pursuits of commerce, manufactures, buildings, & other branches of useful industry, to occupy themselves & their capitals in a species of gambling, destructive of morality, & which had introduced it's poison into the government itself. that it was a fact, as certainly known as that he & I were then conversing, that particular members of the legislature, while those laws were on the carpet, had feathered their nests with paper, had then voted for the laws, and constantly since lent all the energy of their talents, & instrumentality of their offices to the establishment & enlargement of this system: that they had chained it about our necks for a great length of time; & in order to keep the game in their hands had from time to time aided in making such legislative constructions of the constitution as made it a very different thing from what the people thought they had submitted to: that they had now brought forward a proposition, far beyond every one ever yet advanced, & to which the eyes of many were turned, as the decision which was to let us know whether we live under a limited or an unlimited government. he asked me to what proposition I alluded? I answered to that—the Report on manufactures which, under colour of giving *bounties* for the encouragement of particular manufactures, meant to establish the doctrine that the power given by the Constitution to collect taxes to provide for the *general welfare* of the U.S. permitted Congress to take every thing under their management which *they* should deem for the *public welfare,* & which is susceptible of the application of money:[7] consequently that the subsequent enumeration of their powers was not the description to which resort must be had, & did not at all constitute the limits of their authority: that this was a very different question from that of the bank, which was thought an incident to an enumerated power:[8] that therefore this decision was expected with great anxiety: that indeed I hoped the proposition would be rejected, believing there was a majority in both houses against it, and that if it should be, it would be considered as a proof that things were returning into their true channel; & that at any rate I looked forward to the broad representation which would shortly take place for keeping the general constitution on it's true ground, & that this would remove a great deal of the discontent which had shewn itself.[9] the conversation ended with this last topic. it is here stated nearly as much at length as it really was, the expressions preserved where I could recollect them, and their substance always faithfully stated.

Th: J.

ADS, DLC: Jefferson Papers.

1. For "An Act to establish the Post Office and Post Roads within the United States" of 20 Feb. 1792, see *Annals of Congress,* 2d Cong., 1333–41. Jefferson's "Plan for Expediting Postal Service" of 4 Mar. 1792 "proposed that there shall be one post a week passing along the main post road from North to South, at the rate of 100 miles a day. . . . Let this road be divided into stages of 25 miles each, as nearly as may be. . . . Let the hours for post-riding be from 3. aclock in the morning to 11. aclock at night, which gives 20. hours, allowing to every rider 5. hours to perform his stage of 25. miles. . . . Let every rider take a way-bill from the postmaster of the stage he leaves expressing the day, hour and minute of his departure . . . that delays may be traced" (*Jefferson Papers,* 23:192–93).

2. GW had announced his resolution to retire forever from public life in his Circular to the States of 8–21 June 1783 (LS, NNPM).

3. Jefferson's wife, Martha Wayles Skelton Jefferson (1748–1782), whom he had married in January 1772, died on 6 Sept. 1782.

4. For GW's appointment of Jefferson as secretary of state and Jefferson's

reluctant acceptance, see GW to the U.S. Senate, 25 Sept. 1789, to Jefferson, 13 Oct. 1789, 21 Jan. 1790, Jefferson to GW, 15 Dec. 1789, 14 Feb. 1790, and GW to James Madison, 20 Feb. 1790, n.1.

5. GW had written Jefferson on 1 April 1791 concerning the construction of federal buildings in Philadelphia: "The most superb edifices may be erected, and I shall wish their inhabitants much happiness, and that too very disinterestedly, as I shall never be of the number myself."

6. For Jefferson's continued disagreements with Alexander Hamilton while both were commissioners of the sinking fund, see Hamilton to GW, 12 April, nn.1–2.

7. For Hamilton's "Report on the Subject of Manufactures" of 5 Dec. 1791, see Syrett, *Hamilton Papers,* 10:1–340. The House read Hamilton's report on 5 Dec. and ordered it to lie on the table. On 23 Jan. 1792 the House decided to consider it further on the following Monday, 30 Jan., but it apparently did not do so (*Journal of the House,* 4:48, 82).

8. For the debate over the constitutionality of the Bank of the United States in the winter of 1791, see Edmund Randolph to GW, 12 Feb., and enclosures, Jefferson to GW, 15 Feb., GW to Alexander Hamilton, 16 Feb., James Madison to GW, 21 Feb., and Hamilton to GW, 23 Feb. 1791.

9. For the passage of "An Act for apportioning Representatives among the several States according to the First Enumeration" on 14 April 1792, following a presidential veto, see GW to the U.S. House of Representatives, 5 April, and note 1.

From Henry Knox

Sir. War-department March 1 1792.

I have the honor to submit a draft of a letter to general St Clair;[1] and also, a representation from Judge Putnam relative to the situation of Marietta[2]—If perfectly convenient, I will wait upon you to morrow morning, relative to these subjects, and some others, relative to the appointments of officers soon to be made. I have the honor to be Sir, with the highest respect, Your most obedient servt

H. Knox

LS, DLC:GW; LB, DLC:GW.

Northwest territorial governor Arthur St. Clair arrived in the federal capital of Philadelphia on 21 Jan. 1792 to defend his military reputation against the "bitter calumnies, gross misrepresentations, and vile falsehoods" that had arisen in the wake of his disastrous campaign against the northwestern Indians (see St. Clair, *Narrative,* vii; *Federal Gazette and Philadelphia Daily Advertiser,* 23 Jan. 1792). For the background to St. Clair's expedition and the major defeat of 4 Nov. 1791, see Knox to Tobias Lear, 25 Feb. 1791, n.1, GW to the U.S. Senate, 4 Mar. 1791 (second letter), to the Miami Indians, 11 Mar. 1791, Knox to GW, 14, 18 Mar. 1791 (first letter), n.2, 13 Oct. 1791, n.1, William Darke to GW, 9–10 Nov. 1791, GW to the U.S. Senate and House of Representatives, 12 Dec. 1791, n.1, Knox to GW, 22 Jan. 1792, n.2, and to Lear, 31 Jan. 1792, n.1.

1. On 24 Feb., St. Clair wrote GW a letter which apparently covered a draft (not found) of a second letter defending his performance as commander of the failed expedition. In the cover letter St. Clair notified GW that the enclosed "Letter is intended to be published . . . if there be any Sentiment in it, or any thing in the manner of expression that you disaprove of, you would be pleased to point it out that it may be suppressed or altered before it be too late" (see GW to Knox, 29 Feb., n.1). On 29 Feb., GW asked Knox to prepare a draft of his reply to St. Clair's letter. After receiving Knox's draft, which has not been found, GW forwarded it to Thomas Jefferson. For Jefferson's comments, see Jefferson to GW, 2 March. St. Clair's revised letter to GW bears the date 26 March. GW's revised response is dated 28 Mar. 1792. The correspondence between GW and St. Clair concerning the resignation of the latter's military commission was printed in the 14 April edition of the *Gazette of the United States* (Philadelphia) and in the 16 April issue of the *National Gazette* (Philadelphia); see St. Clair to GW, 26, 31 Mar., 7 April, and GW to St. Clair, 28 Mar., 4 April 1792.

2. The enclosed "representation" from Judge Rufus Putnam has not been identified. For Putnam's letters to GW since his arrival at Marietta, a new settlement in the Northwest Territory, see Putnam to GW, 20 Dec. 1790, 8 Jan., 28 Feb., and 26 Dec. 1791.

To Thomas Jefferson

[Philadelphia] Friday-Morning, 2d March [1792]

Be so good as to examine the enclosed draught of a letter to Genl St Clair, and make such alterations (with a pencil) as you shall judge proper; as letter and answer will, it is presumed, be handed to the public.[1] The bearer will wait to bring it back to me.

AL, DLC: Jefferson Papers.

1. Henry Knox's enclosed draft of GW's letter to Maj. Gen. Arthur St. Clair has not been found (see Knox to GW, 1 Mar., n.1). The correspondence between St. Clair and the president concerning the resignation of St. Clair's military commission was printed in the 14 April edition of the *Gazette of the United States* (Philadelphia) and in the 16 April issue of the *National Gazette* (Philadelphia); see St. Clair to GW, 26, 31 Mar., 7 April, and GW to St. Clair, 28 Mar., 4 April 1792.

From Thomas Jefferson

[Philadelphia] March 2. 92.

Th: Jefferson presents his respects to the President and returns him the letter to Genl St Clair.[1] the only passage about which he has any doubt is the following "it does not appear by any information in my possession, that your exertions were wanting to produce a different result either *in the previous preparations, or in the time of action.*"[2] Th: J: never heard a statement of the matter from Genl St Clair himself in conversation: but he has been told by those who have, that, from his own account it appears he was so confident of not meeting an enemy, that he had not taken the proper precautions to have advice of one previous to the action, and his manner of conducting the action has been pretty much condemned. if these criticisms be just, the only question is whether the above paragraph will not be so understood as to be exposed to them? Th: J. does not pretend to judge of the fact, and perhaps the expression may not bear the meaning he apprehends.

AL, DNA: RG 59, Miscellaneous Letters; AL (retained copy), DLC: Jefferson Papers; LB, DNA: RG 59, George Washington's Correspondence with His Secretaries of State; LB (photocopy), DLC:GW. Jefferson wrote on the bottom of his retained copy: "The above is verbatim, as nearly as I can recollect, the diction of a note I wrote to the President this morning, & forgot to take a copy of before it went out of my hands. but I think there will be found scarcely a word of difference, except perhaps in the quotation, the substance of which alone can be answered for."

1. Henry Knox's draft of GW's letter to Arthur St. Clair has not been found (see Knox to GW, 1 Mar. 1792, n.1).

2. This phrase was eliminated, as Jefferson suggested, from the letter that GW sent to Arthur St. Clair on 28 March.

From Henry Knox

Sir. War-department, March 2d 1792.

I have the honor respectfully to submit to your view the following facts and circumstances relative to the promotion shortly to take place in the first and second regiments, in order to enable you to make such determination as may best promote the public interests.

The idea is submitted that the Lieutenant Colonel Commandant will be promoted to a brigadier.[1]

If this promotion should take place, the office of lieutenant colonel commandant of the first and second regiments will both be vacant.

Major Hamtramck, the senior major, has been considered as an excellent disciplinarian—The only circumstances which appear to impair his right to promotion are—

First—His expedition against the Vermilion Towns in the fall of 1790, which did not appear to have such a result as to mark the commandant with any eclat, or as possessing uncommon talents. It has been alledged that the militia were disorderly, which is probably well founded.

Secondly. His retreat on the 4th of November last, when advanced seven miles from Fort Jefferson towards the army. It appears, on[2] hearing of the defeat he had a council with a few of his officers—detached an officer and forty men to meet the flying troops—and then returned, with the regiment under his command, to Fort Jefferson.[3]

It is to be understood, that the first regiment had not any provisions, and that there were none at the fort, and this is given as one of the execuses for this retreat.

It is to be considered, how far these two circumstances, in which Major Hamtramck is placed, indicate him as a proper person to be promoted to the command of the first regiment.

others will consist of nearly one thousand non commissioned and privates.

Major Zeigler is the second major—While the major's fitness as a captain, and even a major, is conceded, it is very questionable whether he has talents sufficient to command a regiment of the magnitude proposed—He has lately had some disagreement with Mr Hodgdon, the quarter master general, relatively to a payment which he ordered, and which Mr Hodgdon refused—The major has offered to resign.[4]

The major seems to have mistaken his situation greatly—By being in the accidental command of Fort Washington, he fancies himself the commanding general. An officer is arrested and a court martial is ordered, and sentences the officer to be cashiered—The officer fears the sentence of the court, and offers to resign, and the major accepts the commission. This he had no right to do, as the articles of war are explicit on the point, and which articles were in the major's possession.

Were the service to be bettered by the major's resignation, it might be well to accept it—But, the next in command is, major Call, who it is presumed cannot be promoted with the imputations against him.[5]

Hamtramck, Zeigler and Call, are all the majors in service, the majorities of the second regiment are all vacant.

If Hamtramck should be promoted, then there would be four vacant majorities to be filled in the first and second regiments.

The four oldest captains of the first regiment are—

Strong—a plain, brave, man, but without any considerable abilities.

Smith—brother to Col. William S. Smith—brave, but not very attentive.

Asheton—a plain, brave, man.

Beatty—a plain, modest, brave, man—brother to Col: Beatty.[6]

It is to be observed, that these officers are entitled to promotion, by the right of seniority, according to the principles fixed in 1786, and re-established since the present government.

The captains of the second regiment are older officers of the late war—But, having come into service under the Act of March 3d, 1791 are to be considered as junior in the present arrangement[7]—while the captains of the second acted seperately from the captains of the first, the disagreeable sensations occasioned by reversing the former rank, would not be so lively, as when those, who were formerly junior, shall be promoted over their heads in the same regiment—It is therefore submitted, that as many of the captains be promoted to majorities, in the new regiments, as may be consistently with the other general principles which will govern in the appointments.

While this arrangement will be a sort of accommodation, soothing to the captains of the second regiment, it is presumed that they will make as suitable majors as may elsewhere be found.

But, a difficulty will still remain, by major Zeigler not being promoted—All the officers who are retained by that circumstance will consider themselves as injured, and they will probably resign, and perhaps the captains of the second regiment, if, a new person should be brought in, over their heads—It will be perceived that this measure will affect every officer in both regiments, and in some sort, be a breach of an implied contract on the part of the public.

This circumstance is to be weighed and balanced against a commander being placed at the head of the regiment, whose heart should be sound and brave, but whose head and talents would not promise much.

L, NNGL: Knox Papers.

1. GW had appointed James Wilkinson lieutenant colonel in command of the 2d Infantry Regiment on 22 Oct. 1791 (see Henry Knox to GW, 22 Sept. 1791 [second letter], n.2).

2. The copyist of this letter mistakenly wrote "an" on the manuscript page.

3. For John Francis Hamtramck's diversionary expedition up the Wabash River in the fall of 1790 and his controversial actions during and shortly after St. Clair's defeat in November 1791, see Jefferson to GW, 29 Aug. 1790, n.1, William Darke to GW, 9–10 Nov. 1791, source note and note 4, and John Hurt to GW, 1 Jan. 1792.

4. Maj. David Zeigler (d. 1811) of the 1st Infantry Regiment was highly critical of Samuel Hodgdon's performance as quartermaster general during St. Clair's campaign (see St. Clair, *Narrative,* 206–11). On 29 Mar. 1792 Knox sent Tobias Lear "Major Zeigler's letter offering his resignation" for submission to the president and two letters from James Wilkinson on the subject (DLC:GW). The original letter of resignation has not been identified. GW's message to the Senate of 9 April states that Zeigler resigned on 5 March. Zeigler's letter to Wilkinson of 11 Mar. apparently covered his commission, which he relinquished in order to avoid serving under Hodgdon and to return to Pennsylvania to settle his accounts with that state (see copies of Zeigler to Wilkinson, 9, 11 Mar., NNGL: Knox Papers).

5. For a report of the intemperance of Maj. Richard Call (d. 1792), the commander of the federal troops in Georgia, see James Seagrove to GW, 5 July 1792. See also GW to Knox, 19 Aug. 1792.

6. For the promotions of captains David Strong, John Smith, and Joseph Asheton to the rank of major in the 2d Regiment and of Capt. Erkuries (Erskurius) Beatty as a major in the 1st Regiment in place of Zeigler, see GW to the U.S. Senate, 9 April. Beatty resigned his commission in November 1792.

7. For "An Act for raising and adding another Regiment to the Military Establishment of the United States, and for making farther provision for the protection of the frontiers," see 1 *Stat.* 222–24.

Deed to the Erie Triangle

[Philadelphia, 3 March 1792]

In the name of the United States!
To all, to whom these presents shall come.

Whereas by an act of congress, intituled an act "for carrying into effect a contract between the United States and the state of Pennsylvania,"[1] it was provided, that for duly conveying to the said state a certain tract of land, the right to the government and jurisdiction whereof was relinquished to the said state by a resolution of congress of the fourth day of September in the year one thousand seven hundred and eighty eight, and, whereof the right of soil has been sold by virtue of a previous resolution of congress of the sixth day of June in the said year,[2] the President of the United States be authorized, on fulfilment of the terms, stipulated on the part of the said state, to issue letters patent, in the name and under the seal of the United States, granting and conveying to the said state for ever the said tract of land, as the same was ascertained by a survey, made in pursuance of the resolution of congress, of the 6th of June 1788; Now Know Ye, that inasmuch as it appears by a certificate from the comptroller of the treasury, that the terms, stipulated On the part of the said state concerning the tract of land aforesaid, have been fulfilled, according to the true intent and meaning of the said contract; I do by these presents, in pursuance of the above-recited act of congress, grant and convey to the said state of Pennsylvania for ever the said tract of land, as the same was ascertained by the survey aforesaid, a copy whereof is herewith annexed.[3]

In testimony whereof I have caused these letters to be made patent; and have hereunto subscribed my name, and caused the seal of the United States to be affixed, at Philadelphia, this 3rd day of March in the year of our lord one thousand seven hundred and ninety two, and of the Independence of the United States of America sixteenth.

George Washington

By the President
Thomas Jefferson

Df, in Edmund Randolph's writing, DNA: RG 59, Miscellaneous Letters. Randolph endorsed the document's cover: "Rough deed to Pennsylvania. This deed has been Submitted to Mr [Alexander J.] Dallas, who approves it—It is therefore sent to Mr J[efferson] to be transcribed in form at his office, and presented to the Prest for Signature, according to what passed yesterday between Mr J. & myself. Will he see, if there be any error. E.R."

For the background to the sale of federal land in the Erie Triangle to the state of Pennsylvania, see Thomas Mifflin to GW, 15 Dec. 1791, source note. Dallas was Governor Mifflin's secretary.

1. GW had signed this act on 3 Jan. 1792 (see GW to the U.S. Senate and House of Representatives, 20 Dec. 1791, n.1).

2. For the two resolutions of the Confederation Congress, see *JCC,* 34:203, 499–500.

3. The survey, which may not have been enclosed in Randolph's draft, has not been found. Alexander Hamilton transmitted the official copy of it to Thomas Jefferson on 6 Mar. 1792 and asked that it be returned to the Treasury Department files after the secretary of state had copied it (*Jefferson Papers,* 23:228).

To the United States Senate and House of Representatives

United States [Philadelphia] March 3d 1792.

Gentlemen of the Senate, and of the House of Representatives.

I lay before you a copy of the return of the number of Inhabitants in the District of South Carolina, as made to me by the Marshal thereof; and the copy of a letter which accompanied said return.[1]

Go: Washington

DS, DNA: RG 46, Second Congress, 1791–1793, Records of Legislative Proceedings, President's Messages; LB, DLC:GW.

For GW's personal interest in the results of the U.S. census of 1790, see GW to Gouverneur Morris, 28 July 1791, n.3.

1. For Isaac Huger's accompanying letter to GW of 5 Feb. 1792 and the S.C. census return that it covered, see GW to the U.S. Senate and House of Representatives, 1 Nov. 1791, n.1. On 18 April, Lear informed Richard Harrison that GW had received the South Carolina return on 2 Mar. (DNA: RG 59, Miscellaneous Letters), one day after the expiration of the extension given to Huger in "An Act granting farther Time for making Return of the Enumeration of the Inhabitants in the District of South Carolina," which GW had signed into law on 8 Nov. 1791 (1 *Stat.* 226). Tobias Lear transmitted the South Carolina return to Thomas Jefferson earlier in the day, noting "The President is desireous of having a copy of the aggregate of each description of persons mentioned in the return from So. Carolina, to be laid before the House of Repre-

sentativs which meets today" (DLC: Jefferson Papers). Lear also forwarded to Jefferson, on 7 Mar., the census return made by Samuel McDowell, Jr., the federal marshal for Kentucky (DLC:GW).

From Alexander Hamilton

[Philadelphia] 4th. March 1792.

The Secretary of the Treasury has the honor to communicate to the President of the U: States certain resolutions of the Bank of the U: States, in answer to communications from the Treasury. He will ask the President's orders on Monday. the first resolution will particularly require attention.[1]

LB, DLC:GW.

For the background to the establishment of the Bank of the United States in late February 1791, see Edmund Randolph to GW, 12 Feb., and enclosures, Thomas Jefferson to GW, 15 Feb., GW to Alexander Hamilton, 16, 23 Feb., James Madison to GW, 21 Feb., and Hamilton to GW, 23, 24 Feb., and 27 Mar. 1791.

1. The enclosed resolutions have not been identified. The editors of the *Hamilton Papers* assume that they were destroyed in one of the Treasury Department fires of the nineteenth century, either in 1814 or 1833 (Syrett, *Hamilton Papers,* 11:74). The day on which Hamilton was to ask for the president's orders was Monday, 5 Mar. 1792.

To Thomas Jefferson

[Philadelphia] 11 Oclock—A.M. March 4th 1792.

The enclosed came by the Post yesterday. I send it for your perusal.[1]

Have you had any conversation with Mr Ellicot respecting the completion of the Survey, & lots of the Federal City?—If so, what was the result?—He ought, if he undertakes it, to proceed to that place immediately—so as to be there at the proposed meeting of the Commissionrs.[2]

The Engravers say *eight weeks* is the *shortest* time in which the Plan can be engraved—(probably they may keep it eight months).[3] Is not this misteriously strange!—Ellicot talked of getting you to walk with him to these People. The current in *this* City sets so strongly against the Federal City, that I believe nothing that *can* be avoided will ever be accomplished in it.

Are there any good Engravers in Boston? If so, would it not be well to obtain a copy (under some other pretext) and send it there, or even to London with out any one (even Ellicot's) being appris'd of it?[4] Yrs sincerely

Go: Washington

ALS, DLC: Jefferson Papers.

1. The enclosure may have been David Stuart's letter to GW of 26 Feb. concerning the progress of work in the Federal City and relations between Pierre L'Enfant and the commissioners for the District of Columbia.

2. Jefferson and GW composed an undated agenda (D, in the writings of Jefferson and GW, DLC:GW), probably between 1 and 6 Mar., for the next meeting of the commissioners, which was to take place at Georgetown on 11 Mar. (see Daniel Carroll of Rock Creek to Jefferson, 6 Mar., *Jefferson Papers,* 23:223). Jefferson suggested that the commissioners settle the matter of Daniel Carroll of Duddington's demolished house; consider dropping legal proceedings against Isaac Roberdeau; employ Andrew Ellicott to finish laying out the Federal City and discuss his past and future wages; hire a superintendent and other officers; advertise for plans for the public buildings; prioritize work projects for the 1792 construction season, including a bridge over Rock Creek, wharves, a canal, cellars and foundations for the presidential mansion and the Capitol, and the making of bricks and the collection of other construction materials; and set the rate of compensation for L'Enfant. Jefferson probably sent this agenda to GW after receiving GW's letter of 4 Mar., and GW made written comments on it before returning it to Jefferson, who used it to prepare his letter to the commissioners of 6 Mar. (see *Jefferson Papers,* 23:224–28). After Jefferson's comment on L'Enfant's compensation, GW added, "Quary Stone to be raised by Skilfull people," and he finished Jefferson's "Loan" subheading with the phrase "on the Security of the State of Maryland 4 or 500,000 dollars." GW then wrote: "The buildings, especially the Capitol, ought to be upon a scale far superior to any thing in *this* Country. The House for the President should also (in the design though not executed all at once) be upon a Commensurate scale. Measures, in my opinion ought to be taken for importing Highlanders & Germans as laborers—Mechanics also, if practicable. Carroll of Duddingtons Ho[use] ought not to be paid for by the Valuation rendered—but every material taken care of—& put up again (where they are not injured) in the manner they were before in a proper situation. Estimates &ca are sent to shew the views &ca of Majr LEnfant."

3. For the difficulties surrounding the engraving of Pierre L'Enfant's plan in Philadelphia, see GW to Tobias Lear, 2, 14 Oct., Lear to GW, 6, 9, 11 Oct., GW to David Stuart, 20 Nov., L'Enfant to GW, 21 Nov., and GW to L'Enfant, 28 Nov. 1791, 28 Feb. 1792. See also GW to the Commissioners for the District of Columbia, 6 Mar. 1792.

4. In the end Jefferson did arrange to have the plan engraved in Boston (see Jefferson to GW, 11 July 1792, n.3).

From John Belli

Honoured *President* Philadelphia. March 5th 1792

The letter I had the pleasure to carry from Mr McDowell to you,[1] was not of Sufficient magnitude to delever you in your own hands, consequently, destitude, of the opportunity of makeng you acquainted with my wishes—I now take the Liberty Sir, by this Present to Let you know I would be glad to have Some office in the Regular Army, if any adequate to my abilities Sould offer, my acquaintance in the western country for Some years passed, and the confidence I have acquired there, will enable me to obtain Supplies for the army on the very best terms, as to my capacities I appeal to Genl Knox Mr Brown[2] Maj. Howell[3] and Sundry other caracters of distinction in the city, and flatter me self will prove Satisfactory—excuse this freedom,[4] and believe me to be Honoured *President* Your very humbe & obt St

John *Belli*

ALS, DLC:GW.

John Belli owned land in Danville, Ky., before 1788 and served as paymaster for the Kentucky mounted volunteers that accompanied Lt. Col. James Wilkinson's expedition of August 1791 against the Indian villages along the L'Anguille (Eel) and Wabash rivers (see the Ky. Board of War to Henry Knox, 30 Aug. 1791, in Henry Knox to GW, 22 Sept. 1791, n.2).

1. This letter, which has not been identified, may have been written by Samuel McDowell, Jr., the federal marshal for Kentucky, from whom GW received a census return no later than 7 Mar. (see GW to the U.S. Senate and House of Representatives, 3 Mar., n.1).

2. Congressman John Brown of Virginia wrote GW from Philadelphia on 12 Mar., recommending "Mr John Billi of the District of Kentucky," who "has requested me to make known to you his desire to obtain some employment in the Army." Brown wrote: "From his acquaintance with Business, his long residence in Kentucky and knowledge of the resources of the Western Country in general, he has been induced to believe that he is qualified to discharge the duties of Deputy Quarter Master, with credit to himself, & advantage to the United States. Should he be honored with the appointment, & should Sureties for the due execution of the Trust be required of him, he will have it in his power to offer such as must be deemed unexceptionable. I beg leave to add that I have been acquainted with Mr Billi since the Year 1784 and cannot hesitate to recommend him as a Gentleman of Character, whose integrity, & punctuality in Business have, during that time been conspicuous" (DLC:GW).

3. Belli apparently is referring to Joseph Howell, Jr., the acting paymaster of the U.S. Army.

4. GW nominated Belli deputy quartermaster general on 9 April 1792.

When Belli's appointment was considered on 11 April, however, the Senate ordered that it be postponed pending further inquiry. The Senate resumed consideration of Belli's appointment on 16 April and confirmed it that day (see GW to the U.S. Senate, 9 April; *Executive Journal,* 1:117–20). Belli returned to Philadelphia in April 1793 with his military accounts, and he resigned his commission in November 1794 (see Knox to Anthony Wayne, 13 April 1793, in Knopf, *Wayne,* 217–19).

From Beale Gaither

Baltimore 5th March 1792.

The memorial of Beale Gaither To the President of the united States Humbly Sheweth that in November last he the Said Beale Gaither being a Subject of the unitd States presentd an Order petition together with a manuscript Containg nearly Or about an hundred & eighty pages at the door of the House of Representatives directd to the Congress which was by the doorkeeper immeadiately Conveyd to the Speaker whom you⟨r⟩ Humble memoralist Observd from the gallery to break the Seals & hand Or present the Sam⟨e⟩ to the Clerk which the Speaker Shortly receiv⟨ed⟩ from the Clerk & Rolling the Same in the Cover put the whole into his Table drawer your hum⟨ble⟩ memoralist having awaitd a fortnight without Seeing any Prospect of his petition Or manuscri⟨pt⟩ being brought forward notwithstanding your Humble memoralist Realy Conceivd he hea[r]d a member of the House of Representatives Call for his proceedings & the Clerk to apply for them which did not appear to your Humble memoralist to be attendd to by the Speaker but as your memoralist was in the gallery he humbly begs leave to refer your excellency to the clerk of the House of Representatives in this Case at the expiration of a fortnight your Humble memoralist presentd a memorial also directd to the Congress Humbly praying that if his petition Could not be Complyd with that it together with his manuscript might be returd in the Same manner Such had been presentd which was done two days after your humble memoralist had presentd the aforementiond memorial now wherein your humble memoralist Conceives the Speaker of the house of representatives has errd is as appears to your humble memoralist in assuming the full power of the whole Congress which your humble memoralist Conceives the governmt has neither inten'd nor given to any individual your humble memoralist as a Subject of the unitd States has Since been much dissattisfied and would Sooner have made his Case known to your excellency had not a Variety of Circumstances intervend which preventd him and your humble memoralist further begs leave to represent to your excellency that he Conceives from particular Circumstances that there are those who even deserve Banishment that are yet Continued in office Contrary to your excellencies wish Or desire and who as your Humble memoralist really Conceives are Subverting the laws & the Constituti⟨on⟩ and arbitraly Oppressing the Subjects Contrary to the Rights of men & Contrary to your excellencies Intention and as you⟨r⟩ Humble memoralist although a Subject of the unitd States and whose fore fathers have been Subjects of the State of maryland y⟨et⟩ as your memoralist is not at this period par⟨*illegible*⟩ Settled in any part of the unitd States therefore you⟨r⟩ memoralist humbly begs leave to Request that your excellencies determination may be publis⟨hed⟩ in the Baltimore advertiser from whence your Humble memoralist Conceives he ma⟨y⟩ have an Oppertunity of Observing the Sam⟨e⟩ And your humble memoralist Conceives it to be his indispensable duty ever to Conduct himself truly as a peaceable Subject and really as a well disposd & usefull Member of Society & is in duty bound to Pray.

AD, DNA: RG 59, Miscellaneous Letters.

In the 1790 U.S. census, Beale Gaither is listed as heading a household consisting of himself and five slaves in Montgomery County, Md. (*Heads of Families* [Maryland], 90). By the summer of 1793, Gaither had moved to Martinsburg, Va. (now W.Va.), and he wrote to GW from there on 8 Aug. 1793: "In november ninetyone I Presentd to the House of Representatives a manuscript Containing An hundred & eighty Pages treating mostly On Philosophical Subjects which falling into the hands of [Jonathan] Trumbull was by him Secreted a fortnight in march ninety two I wrote a Complaint to you which I lodgd in the Baltimore Post Office of late I have wrote An other manuscript Containing eighty six Pages also Philosophical which I Seald up together with An address bearing date the eighth of may And lodgd in the Post Office of this Place directd to you [*not found*] which I Orderd to be Sent to Philidelphia in my address I humbly Solicitd the favor of the Return of this manuscript As I wishd to Improve On it but hearing nothing from you Since I Am at a loss to know whether you have Receivd it Or not And if you have not Or if you have Sent it in Return As I have not got it I must And do Complain of the neglect of the Post masters it has been my misfortune to have been born with a Philosophical turn of mind and to have been bred to merchandize (divide the Attention

And Ruin the man) my misserable Reducd Circumstances keeps me in this wretched Place which lies Somewhat Remote And being a Plentifull Country appears to be the Reason of many wretchd & deformd and of the offcast of Society Resorting to it where the Vicious torture the wretchd & their Animal Creatures yelling & howling in Concert has oft thrown my Studious brain even into a State of the most distressfull Agitation as in fact the Inhabitants but too generally Rather appear to be Actuatd by the Instinct of Brutes than the faculties of men who by their misserable absurdities have almost broke my heart And well nigh driven me to a State of Insanity I do therefore most humbly beg for the love of God and in humanity to men that you may let me hear from you as Soon as Propriety and Convenience may admit And I trust in good hope And full Confidence that you will not at most Say worse to me than the Lord God Said unto Cain. Cain if thou doest well it Shall be well with the[e] [Gen. 4.7] And as Cain was a Barbarous murderer And I Am Only a broken merchant And as the Lord God was mercifull I do therefore most humbly trust in all good hope and full Confidence" (DNA: RG 59, Miscellaneous Letters). There is little reason to believe that GW responded to any of Gaither's letters.

To Thomas Jefferson

[Philadelphia, c.5–6 March 1792][1]

The catalogue of complaints, enclosed, is long.[2]

May not our loss of the Indian trade—the participation of it I mean—and the expence & losses sustain'd by the Indian War be set against Mr H—— list of grievances, in behalf of the B—— Merchants—as well as, by taking our Slaves away depriving us of the means of paying debts.[3]

AL, DLC: Jefferson Papers.

George Hammond, who was appointed Britain's minister plenipotentiary to the United States in the fall of 1791, had been instructed to induce the Americans to fulfill the provisions of the Treaty of Paris of 1783 regarding British creditors and American Loyalists, persuade Congress not to discriminate against British trade, offer British mediation in the war between the United States and the hostile Indians of the Northwest, and begin negotiating a commercial treaty (see George III to GW, 2 Sept. 1791, source note and note 1). Hammond had arrived in the U.S. capital on 20 Oct. 1791.

1. Jefferson endorsed this undated letter as having been received on 6 Mar., but the entry in his Summary Journal of Public Letters appears to be under 5 Mar. (DLC: Jefferson Papers).

2. On 15 Dec. 1791 Jefferson had written Hammond suggesting that they "begin by specifying, on each side, the particular acts which each considers to have been done by the other in contravention of the treaty" of Paris (*Jefferson Papers,* 22:409–12). GW's enclosure was the detailed enumeration of griev-

ances that Hammond had sent to the secretary of state on 5 Mar. 1792 and that Jefferson apparently had forwarded to the president (ibid., 23:196–220).

3. Jefferson's lengthy reply to Hammond's list of complaints against the Americans of 5 Mar. was not completed until 29 May 1792 (see *Jefferson Papers,* 23:551–613).

Tobias Lear to Thomas Jefferson

Dear Sir, [Philadelphia] Monday Evening 5th March 92

Upon submitting the enclosed note from Mr Bache to the President, he desired I would send it to you, that if you thought it right for him to be furnished with the letter wh. he requests it might be done.[1] Should you determine in the affirmative & not have a copy of the translation at hand—I will have a copy of the note left with the President—sent to Mr B.

The President has been informed that upon receiving the translation of the letter today in the Ho. of Representatives, a motion was made for a committee to be appointed to draft an Answer; but was dropped at that time, upon a suggestion that it might be improper for the Ho. to take it up, as it wd undoubtedly be answered by the President—This motion was founded upon the letters being directed *To the United States of N.A.*—The President wishes you would look at the cover of the letter & see what the direction is there.[2]

The Person who brot Mr B.'s note to me is the bearer of this to you—thus if you should judge it proper to furnish him with a copy of the letter he might take it with him[3]—With true respect & perfect esteem I am Dear Sir, Yr mos. Ob. ser.

Tobias Lear.

ALS, DLC: Jefferson Papers.

1. The enclosed note from Benjamin Franklin Bache, editor of the *General Advertiser* (Philadelphia), has not been identified; it apparently requested a copy of Louis XVI's letter to GW of 19 Sept. 1791.

2. Louis XVI's letter was addressed to "nos très chers grands amis et alliés les Etats unis de l'Amérique Septentrionale." For congressional action on the letter, see GW to the U.S. Senate and House of Representatives, 5 Mar. 1792, n.2.

3. Although the translation of Louis XVI's letter was not printed in Bache's newspaper, it did appear on 8 Mar. in the *National Gazette* (Philadelphia), edited by Philip Freneau, Jefferson's clerk for foreign languages in the Department of State.

To the United States Senate and House of Representatives

United States [Philadelphia] March 5th 1792.

Gentlemen of the Senate, and of the House of Representatives.

Knowing the friendly interest you take in whatever may promote the happiness and prosperity of the French Nation, it is with pleasure that I lay before you the translation of a letter which I have received from His most Christian Majesty,[1] announcing to the United States of America his acceptance of the Constitution presented to him in the name of his nation.[2]

Go: Washington

DS, DNA: RG 46, Second Congress, 1791–1793, Records of Legislative Proceedings, President's Messages; LB, DLC:GW.

1. On 2 Mar. 1792 Jean-Baptiste, chevalier de Ternant, the French minister to the United States, presented to GW the receiver's copy of Louis XVI's letter of 19 Sept. 1791. At GW's request Thomas Jefferson translated it and then prepared a message to Congress to cover his translation. The letterpress copy of Jefferson's draft of the message (DLC: Jefferson Papers) is printed in *Jefferson Papers,* 23:221n.

2. As both the Senate and the House had tabled GW's message after receiving it (*Annals of Congress,* 2d Cong., 100, 434–35), GW set Jefferson to work drafting a reply to the king. GW signed the letter on 10 Mar. and showed it to Ternant preparatory to sending it to France (see Jefferson's Memoranda of Consultations with the President, 11 Mar.–9 April, DLC: Jefferson Papers). On that same day, however, James Madison and the friends of the French Revolution in the House passed a resolution "That this House has received, with sentiments of high satisfaction, the notification of the King of the French, of his acceptance of the Constitution presented to him in the name of the Nation: And that the President of the United States be requested, in his answer to the said notification, to express the sincere participation of the House in the interests of the French Nation, on this great and important event . . . And their wish that the wisdom and magnanimity displayed in the formation and acceptance of the Constitution, may be rewarded by the most perfect attainment of its object, the permanent happiness of so great a People." The House then appointed Madison, Thomas Tudor Tucker, John Francis Mercer, John Vining, and John Page to a committee to wait on GW with its resolution. Two days later the Senate postponed consideration of a motion that GW "be requested to make known to the King of the French the satisfaction with which the Senate of the United States has received the official communication of his acceptance of a Constitution, which, it is their earnest wish, may establish, on a solid basis, the freedom and prosperity of the French nation, and the happiness and glory of the Monarch presiding over it." Resuming consideration of the matter on 13 Mar., the Senate passed the resolution after slightly amending its word-

ing (*Annals of Congress,* 2d Cong., 105–7, 456–57; see also Jefferson to GW, 13 Mar., and GW's Conversation with a Committee of the U.S. House of Representatives, 12 Mar. 1792, and source note). Because of the spate of congressional activity, GW did not send his response to Louis XVI until 14 March.

To the Commissioners for the District of Columbia

Gentlemen, Philadelphia March 6th 1792.

Mr Jefferson, in a letter which he writes to you this day,[1] will enter fully into the points touched upon in your letters to me of the 21st of December, and of the 7th 9th 10 & 21st of January and Mr Johnson's letter of the 3d of february.[2] I shall therefore, do little more at present (being much pressed with other important public matters) than acknowledge the receipt of these letters, and state the reasons which caused me to delay writing to you 'till this time.

Until I received Mr Johnson's letter, the expectation of seeing him here, and conferring with him fully upon the several points mentioned in your letters, kept me from writing; and since that time the unsettled state of matters with respect to Major L'Enfant has put it out of my power to write to you in a manner that would be decisive or satisfactory.

Matters are at length brought to a close with Majr L'Enfant.[3] As I had a strong desire to retain his services in this business, provided it could have been done upon a proper footing I gave him every opportunity of coming forward and stating the mode in which he would wish to be employed, always, however, assuring him that he *must* be under the controul of the Commissioners. But after keeping open the communication with him as long as any reasonable means could be found of doing it, he chose to close it by declaring, that he could only act in a certain way—which way was inadmissable. His services, therefore, must be no longer calculated upon. Altho' his talents in designing, and the skill which he is said to possess in the execution of this kind of business, may occasion the loss of his services to be regretted; Yet I doubt upon the whole, whether it will be found in the end that his dereliction will be of real disservice to the undertaking; for so unaccommodating is his disposition that he would never suffer any interference in his plans, much less would he have been contented under the direction of the Commissioners. I am convinced, Gentlemen, that in your transactions with Majr L'Enfant, you must have suffered much from his temper; & if my approbatn of yr conduct in this business can afford you pleasure, you may be assured you have it. Even if I had no corrobaration of the fact, I should be persuaded, from what I have known of his disposition on the recent occasion, that there would scarcely be a possibility of acting harmoniously in concert with him.[4]

As Mr Jefferson has, in his letter, mentioned the particular objects to which your attention will probably be turned[5]—I shall only observe here, that I am impressed in, the strongest manner, with the necessity there is of carrying on this business with as much vigour as the nature of the thing will admit. It has been observed by intelligent & well informed men, (not however of the class most friendly to the measures)[6] that the whole success of the Federal City, depends upon the exertions which may be made in the ensuing season towards completing the object; for such is now the state of the public mind on this subject that it appears as it were in an equilibrium, and will preponderate either for or against the measure, as the progress of the thing may be: And there are not wanting those who, being interested in arresting the business, will leave no means unessayed to injure it. By the proposition for a loan which Mr Jefferson transmits to you, you will see what prospect you have of funds in addition to those to be depended upon from the two states.[7] And in your exertions, Gentlemen, to make the best of these, I have the fullest confidence.

It is impossible to say with any certainty when the plan of the City will be engraved.[8] Upon Major L'Enfant's arrival in this place, in the latter part of december, I pressed him in the most earnest manner to get the plan ready for engraving as soon as possible. Finding there was no prospect of obtaining it thro' him (at least not in any definite time) the matter was put into Mr Ellicott's hands to prepare about 3 weeks ago: He has prepared it; but the engravers who have undertaken to execute it, say it cannot certainly be done in less than 2—perhaps not under three months. There shall, however, be every effort made to have the thing effected with all possible dispatch. with great esteem I am Gentn Yr Most Obedt Servt[9]

Go: W——n

DfS, in Tobias Lear's hand, DLC:GW; LB, DLC:GW. For the insertions in the draft in GW's writing, see notes 6 and 9.

1. For Thomas Jefferson's letter to the D.C. commissioners of 6 Mar. 1792, see *Jefferson Papers,* 23:224–28.

2. Thomas Johnson's letter to GW of 3 Feb. 1792 has not been found.

3. For the background to the dispute between Pierre L'Enfant and the D.C. commissioners, see L'Enfant to GW, 21 Nov. 1791, editorial note.

4. Crosshatch symbols in the draft before the next two paragraphs apparently indicate that their order was to be reversed by the copyist preparing the receiver's copy. The order is reversed in the letter-book copy.

5. Jefferson and GW had earlier drawn up a draft agenda for matters to be discussed at the next meeting of the D.C. commissioners. Jefferson apparently relied on the agenda in preparing his letter to the commissioners of this date (see GW to Jefferson, 4 Mar. 1792, n.2).

6. GW inserted this parenthetical expression above the line in the draft.

7. Jefferson enclosed in his letter to the D.C. commissioners of 6 Mar. a contract with Samuel Blodget, Jr., for the loan of $500,000 and draft advertisements for designs of the Capitol and the presidential mansion. GW wrote in pencil on the latter in response to Jefferson's note at the bottom of the page requesting "the President . . . to make the above what he thinks it should be": "I see nothing wanting but to fill the blanks—& that I presume the Comrs will do—unless, after the words 'destination of the building' is added 'and situation of the ground' for I think particular situation wd require parlr kind or shaped buildings" (DLC: District of Columbia Papers). Jefferson incorporated GW's suggestions into the draft advertisement (see ibid., 225–28).

8. For the difficulties surrounding the engraving of Pierre L'Enfant's plan in Philadelphia, see GW to Tobias Lear, 2, 14 Oct., Lear to GW, 6, 9, 11 Oct., GW to David Stuart, 20 Nov., L'Enfant to GW, 21 Nov., and GW to L'Enfant, 28 Nov. 1791, 28 Feb. 1792. For the sending of the plan to Boston to be engraved, see GW to Jefferson, 4 Mar., and notes 3 and 4, and Jefferson to GW, 11 July 1792, n.3.

9. The complimentary closing and signature in the draft are in GW's handwriting.

From John Hurd

Boston March 6th 1792

Presuming on the Candor with which Your Excellency receives Applications from persons of all Denominations—I take the Liberty with modest diffidence, to address you, & request the favor, that among the Number of Candidates for Official Business by Appointmts from Congress, I may have liberty to offer myself and beg your Indulgence to make Mention of the Circumstances & Situation I was in, previous to, & during great part of the late War.

A few years before the Commencemt of Hostilities I had officiated as private Secretary to Governor Wentworth in New Hampshire and Deputy Surveyor of His Majestys Woods—and after several years Services under him By his recommendation remov'd into the Coho'os Country on Connecticut River, where in a then new establishd County, I was honord wth several public Employments, pardon my mentioning the particulars—viz.

Receiver General of His Majesty's Quit Rents for the province of N:H.—Register of Deeds in the County, County Treasurer, first Justice of the Court of Common pleas, with a Commission of Colonel in the Militia—The Emoluments of all which were as good as £200 Sterling p. an[nu]m. But as I took the side of my Country from principle early in the Contest, notwithstanding a near Connection & Friendship with Governor Wentworth, I freely resignd all Employmt under the British Governmt, & was chosen by the people of Haverhill (Coho'os) to attend the first Convention at Exeter; from whence I was deputed one of the Committee to go down to Portsmouth being known to be well acquainted there, and demand of all the public Officers, the public Money they had on hand; and did actually receive out of the Treasury upwards of sixteen hundred pounds in Gold & silver, which I deliver'd into the hands of Treasurer Gilman at Exeter, and it was of eminent Service at that Juncture to send abroad for a supply of Gunpowder—this was effected while one of the British Frigates lay in the River, and Governor Wentworth at Fort William & Mary, who having Intelligence of what the Committee was doing sent two of his most intimate Friends to the Treasury, Doctor Rogers of the Council & Mr McDonough his private Secretary, the same Gentleman who now resides in Boston as British Consul, to be Evidences of the Fact—and the Barge Men of the Frigate with an Officer were also at hand to watch our Motions, offering his Services to the Treasurer, who however declin'd making any Stir, and sufferd us to carry off the money—From this time I must of Course have bid Adieu to all Expectations from the British Government.[1]

I was often employd in the public Service, and among several Others residing on that Frontier pointed at by the Enemy, and frequently in danger of being carried off into Canada by scouting parties; was also assisting to General Bayley, Colonel Bedel and General Hazen when by Yr Excellency's Orders he was cutting a Road towds Canada & making a Diversion in that Country.[2]

The Circumstances of my Family oblig'd me to remove from thence to Boston my native place in 1779 where I have since resided in the Employment of an Assurance Broker—my two only Sons that I then had, I sent into the Army, one of sixteen years old was at Saratoga at the Capture of General Burgoine, and afterwards out in a privateer Captain of Marines, the other was in the Service an Ensign in Colonel Henry Jackson's Regimt the last three years of the War, & died soon after the Close in a Consumption hasten'd on by the fatigues of the Service, being of a slender Constitution.[3]

In the year 1783 I married the Widow of Doctor Isaac Foster who was Director General of the Hospitals for the Northern Department, a Gentleman, I presume well known to your Excellency from the time of your being at Cambridge in this State, and the greatest part of the War[4]—he was suppos'd to have left a Sufficiency for the support of his Widow & Children by the Security he had to receive from the public—But the Necessities of the family were such as obligd us to part with the most of them at a time when they were at the lowest Ebb of Depreciation—I had the Misfortune to loose my Wife in the year 1786 who left on my hands three of the Doctor's Children with three young ones we had together—their little Fortune being cheifly in public Securities almost exhausted, and my own property lying principally in the back Lands in N: Hampsh: where I before resided and necessarily expended very considerable Sums, but to little purpose as the Value of those Lands have turnd since the War, & having sufferd much by the Depreciation of public Securities before the new federal Government was establishd, reduces me to the Necessity of making this late application to Your Excellency for some public Employmt in an Official way—I do not look for, nor expect any great Things, a decent support being pretty far advancd in Life, woud be quite satisfactory—my Character while in New Hampshire was well known to several Gentlemn now in Congress, Mr Langdon of the Senate & Judge Livermore, also to several from this state Mr Goodhue, Mr Gerry & Mr Ames—and in particular the Vice President, to whom I had the honor of writing on the subject, last year and if your Excellency thinks proper, beg to be refer'd to him[5]—I am sensible, Sir, you may be troubled with many solicitations in this way, & it hurts my feelings to take up so much of your time at this interesting Juncture—If from the relation of my particular Circumstances, & the Sacrifice I made of my several Offices under the former Government by adhering to the Interest of my Country, You think I merit any Claim, whatever Commands you may honor me with shall be executed with the strictest Integrity & punctuality, and I will with the utmost gratitude acknowledge the favor, being most respectfully your Excellency's very obedient humble Servt

John Hurd

ALS, DLC:GW.

John Hurd (1727–1809), the son of Boston goldsmith Jacob Hurd, graduated from Harvard College in 1747. After his marriage in 1755 to Elizabeth Foster (d. 1779) of Boston, he traveled widely from Nova Scotia to New Hampshire filling commissions for various Boston merchants. As early as 1763 he became interested in the frontier lands of the Coös region. While transacting land business in Portsmouth, N.H., Hurd came to the notice of royal governor John Wentworth (1737–1820), who made him his private secretary. The Hurds had at least two children by early 1773, when they moved to Haverhill in Grafton County, N.H.; Hurd was subsequently appointed to several county offices and served on the county court. He married Mary Russell Foster (c.1749–1786) in 1783 and had three children by her. Hurd married his third wife, Rebecca Leppington Hurd (c.1751–1836), in June 1790. She wrote Abigail Adams in July 1790 and again eight years later, asking her to support Hurd's applications to John Adams for federal office (see Rebecca Leppington Hurd to Abigail Adams, 26 June 1798, MHi-A).

1. On 8 June 1775 the fourth N.H. provincial congress appointed a committee to seize the funds in the royal treasury. Treasurer George Jaffrey of Portsmouth handed over £1,516 in specie to the provincial committeemen despite the presence in Portsmouth Harbor of the royal frigate *Scarborough,* which sailed for Boston with Governor Wentworth and his family in August 1775. Thomas McDonough, who had, in addition to his service as Wentworth's private secretary, held the offices of N.H. deputy auditor and receiver of quitrents before the American Revolution, served in the Royal Navy for five years before immigrating to Britain in 1780. He returned to New England in the fall of 1790 as British consul for Massachusetts, Rhode Island, New Hampshire, and Connecticut.

2. Col. Moses Hazen was sent north in the summer of 1779 to build a road from Newbury, Conn., to within thirty miles of the Canadian border in preparation for a renewed American military effort in that direction. Jacob Bayley (1728–1815) served as a brigadier general in the N.H. militia and was a Continental deputy quartermaster general during the Revolutionary War. For his efforts to build a road to Canada in 1776, see *Papers, Revolutionary War Series,* 2:602–3, 3:363–64, 512, 4:306–7, 399, 5:97–98, 6:571–72, 584–85. Timothy Bedel (c.1737–1787) rose from captain to colonel of the N.H. Rangers in 1775. After being cashiered in the summer of 1776, he was appointed a colonel in the N.H. militia, and he served in that capacity until 1781.

3. Hurd's eldest son, Jacob Hurd (1761–1812), was a private with the New Hampshire troops during the Revolutionary War. His brother, Ensign John J. Hurd, Jr. (d. 1784), was in the 9th Massachusetts Regiment from June 1781 to January 1783, when he transferred to the 2d Massachusetts. Henry Jackson (1747–1809) of Boston was colonel of one of the Sixteen Additional Continental Regiments from 1777 to 1781, when he became colonel of the 9th Massachusetts Regiment. Jackson commanded the 4th Massachusetts Regiment during 1783, and he was brevetted a brigadier general in September 1783.

4. Isaac Foster (d. 1781) of Massachusetts, who had been a volunteer surgeon at the Battle of Bunker Hill in 1775 and a hospital surgeon in 1776, served as deputy director general of the hospital in the eastern department from April 1777 until October 1780.

5. Hurd wrote a similar letter to John Adams from Boston on 17 Mar. 1790 soliciting "any opening either in this State, New Hampshire, or either of the New States" (MHi-A). The letter-book copy of Adams's reply of 5 April 1790 states that the vice-president had "an agreable recollection" of Hurd's private character from their "former personal acquaintance" but that he was unable to help him in the present instance: "the office I hold is totally detached from the executive authority, and confined to the legislative; which renders it very improper for me to intermeddle in appointments to offices; except in cases where the President or some of his ministers of State in their several departments, have occasion to ask my opinion of matters of fact. If this should ever happen in your case Sir, my report will certainly be much in your favor" (MHi-A). Hurd acknowledged Adams's letter on 17 April and admitted that "being unknown to the supreme Executive, I had not Resolution eno' to make my Application to the President himself" (MHi-A). Upon the death of loan officer Nathaniel Appleton in Boston in 1798, Hurd applied to President Adams for the vacancy (Hurd to Adams, 26 June 1798, MHi-A), but he received neither that nor apparently any other federal appointment. Edward St. Loe Livermore (1762–1832) was appointed U.S. district attorney for New Hampshire in 1794 and associate justice of the state supreme court in 1797. He later served as a Federalist member of Congress from Massachusetts from 1807 to 1811.

To John Jay

My dear Sir, Philadelphia Mar. 6th 1792.

Your favor of the 27th of Jany came safely to hand (but not by Judge Cushing)[1] as did your letter of the 23d of September for which I thank you.

It is with pleasure I congratulate you on the increase of your family and the restoration of health to Mrs Jay—both of wch events we have heard.[2]

Mr B——'s motion, alluded to in your letter of the 27th of Jany, is only the prelude, *I* conceive to what is intended to follow as occasions shall present themselves.[3]

I am persuaded your goodness will excuse my not having acknowledged the receipt of your letters of the above dates at an earlier period. Many matters of a public nature have pressed upon me—some of them not very pleasant ones.

My best wishes, in which Mrs Washington cordially unite, are presented to Mrs Jay and yourself—and with affectionate esteem & regard I am always Your Obedient Servant

Go: Washington

ALS, NNC: Jay Collection; LB, DLC:GW. GW marked the addressed cover of the receiver's copy "(Private)."

1. William Cushing (1732–1810), who before the Revolutionary War had served as a private attorney, land company lawyer, and occasional land speculator in his native Massachusetts, joined the new state Superior Court of Judicature in 1775. Upon John Adams's resignation in February 1777, Cushing was named chief justice. In addition to his duties on the Massachusetts high court, Cushing served in the state's constitutional convention in 1779, was elected vice-president of the convention called to ratify the U.S. Constitution in 1788, and voted as a federal elector in the first presidential election. In September 1789 GW appointed Cushing to the U.S. Supreme Court. While Jay traveled overseas on his mission to Great Britain in 1794 and 1795, Cushing, as senior associate justice, served as acting chief justice. Although GW wished to promote him to chief justice in January 1796, Cushing refused on the grounds of ill health. He continued to serve as an associate justice, however, until his death at the age of 78 in September 1810.

2. Sarah Livingston Jay (1756–1802), whom Jay had married in 1774, recently had given birth to their fifth child, a daughter (see John Jay to GW, 27 Jan. 1792, n.1). Since February, Jay had been a candidate in the increasingly bitter New York gubernatorial election, attempting to unseat the incumbent, George Clinton.

3. On 16 Jan., in the midst of the Senate debate concerning GW's ministerial appointments, Aaron Burr of New York had presented a motion arguing that no reason then existed for the dispatch of a U.S. minister to The Hague (see *Executive Journal,* 1:96–98; see also GW to the U.S. Senate, 22 Dec. 1791, and the Controversy over Diplomatic Appointments to Great Britain, France, and the Netherlands, 3 Jan. 1792, editorial note).

From Mirbeck

Cap français [Saint Domingue]

Monsieur Le Président le 6 mars 1792.

J'ai l'honneur d'envoyer, à Votre Excellence, quelques imprimés, qui vous instruiront de l'etat actuel de la partie française dela Colonie de st Domingue.[1]

Je la prie d'en agréer l'hommage; c'est un tribut que Je Suis enchanté de Rendre aux talents et aux Vertus d'un grand homme qui fait, depuis longtems, mon admiration et celle du Monde. Je suis avec les Sentimens que Votre Excellence a inspirés à l'univers entier Monsieur le Président Votre très humble et très obeissant Serviteur.

de Mirbeck
Commissaire national-civil, délégué
par le Roi aux Iles françaises
de l'Amérique Sous le Vent.

LS, DNA: RG 59, Miscellaneous Letters.

Frédéric-Ignace de Mirbeck (1732–1818) was an attorney in Lorraine before moving in 1774 to Paris, where he became a consulting barrister to Louis XVI. In 1791 the National Assembly appointed him to head a civil commission to investigate the recent slave insurrection in Saint Domingue and to restore political order there. After clashing with the colonial assembly, Mirbeck and the other commissioners returned to France in April 1792 (see Nathaniel Cutting to Thomas Jefferson, 13 April, in *Jefferson Papers,* 23:413–17).

1. The enclosed pamphlets have not been identified but may have included Mirbeck's published letter of February to Saint Domingue's colonial assembly, a copy of which Nathaniel Cutting sent to Jefferson on 1 Mar. (see ibid., 177–79).

From Josiah Parker

Sir Philadelphia 6th March 1792

No applicants for commissions in the Army have been made to me from the District of Virginia I represent or should have presumed to have made them known to you. to day I have received letters requesting I would take the liberty to Name Henry Beverly Towles, son of Colo. Olliver Towles of Spotsilvania as a candidate for a Lieutenancy. I know nothing of the young gentleman but he is warmly recommended to me as a sensible good young man. his being a Lieutenant in the late expedition in the Livies under Colo. Darke may be some recommendation to him.[1]

Mr Isaac Younghusband Son of Mr Younghusband of Richmond is allso recommended. I know him to be a Young Man of talents and have no doubt but will make a good Officer. he Solicits an ensigncy.[2]

Captn Saml Tinsley of Richmond has again written me he appears Solicituous to obtain a commission, his being an officer in the late war may be a recommendation to him.[3]

Lemuel Riddick who I formerly recommended and lately appointed Surveyor at Suffolk, was very desirous of a Commission & I still think [if] he had an appointment in the Army he would accept of it & I am flattered into a belief if he was he would do honor to it.[4]

Perhaps this ought properly to be directed to the Secretary of War but as I have an objection to troubling that Officer You will please excuse this trouble, and believe me with every respect & esteem Your most Obedient servant

J. Parker

ALS, DLC:GW.

1. GW appointed Henry Beverly Towles (d. 1794), son of Col. Oliver Towles (1736–1825), a lieutenant of infantry in the U.S. Army (see GW to the U.S. Senate, 14 Mar. 1792). Towles was assigned to the 4th Sub-Legion under Maj. Gen. Anthony Wayne in September 1792 and was killed in the Battle of Fallen Timbers on 20 Aug. 1794.

2. Isaac Younghusband (d. 1794), son of Isaac Younghusband of Richmond, was a lawyer in Henrico County, Va., before GW appointed him an ensign in the 2d Infantry (see GW to the U.S. Senate, 9 April 1792). Later this year Younghusband was assigned to the 2d Sub-Legion, and he was promoted to lieutenant in January 1793.

3. Samuel Tinsley (c.1756–1833) served throughout most of the Revolutionary War as a captain in a Virginia state regiment. GW appointed him a first lieutenant of infantry (see GW to the U.S. Senate, 14 Mar. 1792), and in September 1792 he was assigned to the 3d Sub-Legion. Tinsley was promoted to captain in February 1794 and transferred to the 1st U.S. Infantry in November 1796.

4. Parker had recommended Riddick in a letter to GW of 19 Dec. 1791. For Riddick's appointment as port inspector at Suffolk, Va., see GW to the U.S. Senate, this date.

From Two Frenchmen

[6 March 1792][1]

Two frenchmen who came to America to establish themselves upon the lands which they purchased of the Scioto Company, and who have remained there one year, not being able to obtain possession of their purchase, and having consumed their funds, implore the bounty of your Excellency to put them in a situation to return to their own Country.

One of the Supplicants is he whom M. Le Marquis de lafayette has deigned to recommend to his Excellency.[2] He hopes that such a respectable recommendation will be serviceable to him, and he will retain in his heart a grateful recollection of his Excellency who will releive him from the distress in which he is now involved.[3]

Translation, in Tobias Lear's hand, DNA: RG 59, Miscellaneous Letters; AL, DNA. RG 59, Miscellaneous Letters. The French text of the original receiver's copy appears in CD-ROM:GW.

One writer of this letter was probably either M. de Tavernol or M. de Rocher, who arrived together in America in November 1790 (see William Short to Thomas Jefferson, 22 Aug. 1790, in *Jefferson Papers,* 17:410–13). For the background to the Scioto Company and its unsuccessful French settlement in the Ohio Country, see Louis Le Bègue de Presle Duportail to GW, 10 Feb. 1790, source note. The collapse of William Duer's speculations sealed the fate of the Scioto Company, which no longer could send provisions to its settlers. The French minister to the United States wrote to his new superior from Philadelphia in mid-March 1792 that only 100 of the original 1,000 French emigrants remained at the settlement, and they awaited only the return of good weather to leave. The daily arrival of these destitute countrymen at Philadelphia distressed him because he did not have the means to assist them. In consequence, he requested permission to allow free passage home for the most deserving of them (see Ternant to Claude-Antoine de Valdec de Lessart, 13 Mar., in Turner, *Correspondence of the French Ministers,* 94–97).

1. Tobias Lear docketed the receiver's copy: "From The two frenchmen who applied to the President to assist them in returning to france—March 6th 1792."

2. In his letter to GW of 23 Aug. 1790, Lafayette recommended its bearers, "two Gentlemen, one of them an Artillery officer [Tavernol], who are Going to Settle on the Banks of the famed Scioto" as "Entitled to Regard."

3. The correspondents wrote to GW again on 8 Mar. 1792, apparently after meeting with him. Lear's translation of this letter reads: "The two french men to whom his Excellency has already had the goodness to render an essential service & to draw them from the distress in which they were involved, take the liberty of signifying their gratitude to him, and presenting their humble thanks. As his Excellency had the goodness to have them informed that he would contribute towards facilitating their return to france; they think it proper to inform his Excellency that in a few days the french ship Le jeune Eole will sail for Havre de Grace, and that the price of each passenger is 192 livres tournois. The supplicants beseech his Excellency to assist them in obtaining a passage—Assuring they shall never cease to remember that it is to his Excellency they owe the happiness of seeing their native Country again & liv-

ing in the midst of their families" (DNA: RG 59, Miscellaneous Letters; the French text of the original receiver's copy appears in CD-ROM:GW). The *Jeune Eole,* master J. B. Freehon, which had been waiting at Russell's wharf for the opening of the Delaware River, cleared Philadelphia by 13 Mar. (see *Dunlap's American Daily Advertiser* [Philadelphia], 8, 10, 13 Mar. 1792).

To the United States Senate

United States [Philadelphia]
March 6th 1792.

Gentlemen of the Senate,

I lay before you the following Report which has been submitted to me by the Secretary of State.[1]

"The Secretary of State having received information that the Merchants and Merchandize of the United States are subject in Copenhagen and other ports of Denmark to considerable extra duties, from which they might probably be relieved by the presence of a Consul there;

"Reports to the President of the United States; That it would be expedient to name a Consul, to be resident in the port of Copenhagen: That he has not been able to find that there is any citizen of the United States residing there: That there is a certain Hans Rudolph Saaby, a Danish subject and merchant of that place, of good character, of wealth and distinction, and well qualified and disposed to act there for the United States, who would probably accept the commission of Consul; but that that of Vice-Consul, hitherto given by the President to foreigners in ports where there was no proper American citizen, would probably not be accepted, because in this, as in some other ports of Europe, usage has established it as a subordinate grade.

"And that he is therefore of opinion, that the said Hans Rudolph Saaby should be nominated Consul of the United States of America for the port of Copenhagen, and such other places within the allegiance of his Danish Majesty as shall be nearer to the said port than to the residence of any other Consul or Vice-Consul of the United States within the same allegiance.[2]

Th: Jefferson
January 10th 1792."

Gentlemen of the Senate,

With a view to relieve the Merchants and Merchandize of the United States from the extra duties to which they are or may be subjected in the Ports of Denmark, I have thought it for the interest of the United States that a Consul be appointed to reside at Copenhagen—I therefore nominate Hans Rudolph Saaby, a Danish subject and merchant of Copenhagen, to be Consul for the United States of America at the port of Copenhagen, and for such other places within the allegiance of his Danish Majesty as shall be nearer to the said port than to the Residence of any other Consul or Vice Consul of the United States within the same allegiance.[3]

Go: Washington

DS, DNA: RG 46, Second Congress, 1791–1793, Records of Executive Proceedings, President's Messages—Executive Nominations; LB, DLC:GW.

1. A letterpress copy of Thomas Jefferson's original report to GW of 10 Jan. 1792 is in DLC: Jefferson Papers.

2. Hans Rudolph Saabye had written GW on 5 Aug. 1789 to solicit the office of U.S. consul general in Denmark.

3. After receiving and reading this message on 6 Mar., the Senate ordered it to lie for consideration. When the nomination was taken up again the following day, the Senate confirmed Saabye's appointment (see *Executive Journal*, 1:100–101, 105). Tobias Lear wrote the secretary of state that day to inform him that the Senate had concurred and that a vessel would sail for Copenhagen within a few days (DNA: RG 59, George Washington's Correspondence with His Secretaries of State).

To the United States Senate

United States [Philadelphia]

Gentlemen of the Senate, 6th March 1792

As it will require time to ascertain suitable characters, for the commissioned Officers of the Troops about to be raised, I shall occasionally make such nominations as shall appear to be proper.

I now nominate the persons named in the list accompanying this Message,[1] for the commissioned Officers of twelve Companies, intended to be raised upon the frontiers of Pennsylvania and Virginia.[2]

Go: Washington

DS, DNA: RG 46, Second Congress, 1791–1793, Records of Executive Proceedings, President's Messages—Executive Nominations; LB, DLC:GW.

1. The enclosed list of nominations is printed below.

2. After reading GW's message this day, the Senate ordered it to lie for consideration. When it was taken up again the following day, the Senate confirmed all of the listed appointments (see *Executive Journal,* 1:101–2, 105). Tobias Lear immediately informed Henry Knox of the Senate's concurrence (Lear to Knox, 7 Mar., DLC:GW).

Enclosure
Nominations of Commissioned Officers

[Philadelphia, 6 March 1792]

Pennsylvania.

Captains	
*Edward Butler	Allegany County
*John Guthrie	Westmorland
*Richard Sparks[1]	Allegany.
*William Faulkner	Washington.
Uriah Springer	Fayette
John Cook	Northumberland.
Lieutenants	
*William Smith	Washington.
*John Cummings	Westmorland.
*Samuel Vance[2]	Fayette.
*Nathaniel Huston	Washington.
William Steedman	Northumberland.
*Daniel T. Jennifer	Allegany.
Ensigns	
Robert Purdy[3]	Mifflin
John Kelso	Dauphin.
Robert Lee	Northumberland.
John Steele	Cumberland.
David Hall	Westmorland.
Reason Beall[4]	Washington.

Virginia.

Captains	
Benjamin Biggs	Ohio County.
*John Crawford	Ohio
Thomas Lewis	Bottetourt.
William Lewis	Wythe.

Hugh Caperton	Green-briar
*James Stephenson[5]	Berkley.
Lieutenants	
*James Glenn	Berkley.
Robert Craig	Russell.
William Clark	Louisville, Kentucky.
John Boyer[6]	Bottetourt.
*Benjamin Lockwood	Ohio.
Benjamin Strother	Culpepper.
Ensigns	
Patrick Shirkey	Bottetourt.
Archibald Gray	Green-briar
Stephen Trigg	Kentucky.
James Hawkins	Bottetourt.
Baker Davidson	Bath.
Hugh Brady[7]	Ohio.

Go: Washington

DS, DNA: RG 46, Second Congress, 1791–1793, Records of Executive Proceedings, President's Messages—Executive Nominations; LB, DLC:GW. At the bottom of the list appears the footnote: "Those with this mark * served with reputation in the levies last year."

1. Richard Sparks (d. 1815), who had been a captain of the levies of 1791, served as a captain in the U.S. Army until 1806. He was promoted to major in July 1806, lieutenant colonel in December 1807, and colonel in July 1812. Sparks was honorably discharged from the army in mid-June 1815.

2. Samuel C. Vance (d. 1830) was promoted to captain in July 1797, and he served as deputy paymaster general from July 1799 until April 1802.

3. Robert Purdy was promoted to lieutenant in April 1793 and to captain in March 1799. Although he resigned from the army in 1803, Purdy returned to the service in 1809 with the rank of lieutenant colonel. He was promoted to colonel in August 1812, and he was honorably discharged from the army in mid-June 1815.

4. Reason (Reazin) Beall (d. 1843) served as an ensign in the U.S. Army from March 1792 until January 1794. In 1812 Beall was a brigadier general of the Ohio volunteers.

5. James Stephenson (1764–1833) resigned his commission as a captain in the U.S. Army in December 1792. He served in the Virginia house of delegates 1800–1803 and 1806–7 and was a Federalist congressman 1804–5, 1809–11, and 1822–25.

6. John Boyer (Bowyer) was promoted to captain in January 1799, major in December 1808, lieutenant colonel in July 1812, and colonel in March 1814. He retired from the U.S. Army in June 1815.

7. Hugh Brady (d. 1851) was promoted to lieutenant in February 1794. After resigning from the army in October 1795, he returned to the service as a captain in 1799–1800. In July 1812 Brady became a colonel in the U.S. Army, and ten years later he was brevetted a brigadier general. Brady was promoted to major general in May 1848.

To the United States Senate

United States [Philadelphia]
Gentlemen of the Senate, March the 6th 1792.

Appointments were made during the recess of the Senate, to carry into effect the act passed at the last Session of Congress, for repealing the duties heretofore laid upon distilled spirits, and laying others in their stead.[1] And as these appointments must expire at the end of your present session, I nominate the following persons to be Inspectors of the Surveys and Ports annexed to their names respectively.[2]

Inspectors of Surveys.

Districts.	Names of Inspectors.	No. of Survey.
Massachusetts.	Jonathan Jackson	2.
	Leonard Jarvis	3.
Pennsylvania	James Collins	2.
	Edward Hand	3.
	John Neville[3]	4.
Maryland	Philip Thomas	2.
Virginia	Drury Ragsdale	1.
	Edward Stevens	2.
	Mayo Carrington	3.
	Thomas Newton Jr	4.
	Edward Smith	5.
	James Brackenridge[4]	6.
	Thomas Marshall	7.
North Carolina	James Read	1.
	John Daves	2.
	Thomas Benbury	3.
	John Whitaker	4.
	Joseph McDowell the younger of Pleasant Garden[5]	5.
South Carolina.	Benjamin Cudworth	2.
	Silvanus Walker	3.

Inspectors of Ports.

Districts.	Ports.	Names of Inspectors.
New Hampshire.	Portsmouth	Thomas Martin.
Massachusetts.	Newbury Port	Michael Hodge
	Gloucester	Samuel Whittemore
	Salem	Bartm Putnam.
	Beverly	Josiah Bachelor
	Ipswich	Jeremiah Staineford
	Marblehead	Samuel R. Gerry
	Boston	Thomas Melvile.
	Plymouth	William Watson.
	Barnstable	Joseph Otis.
	Nantucket & Sherburne	Stephen Hussey
	Edgartown	John Pease.
	New Bedford	Edward Pope
	Dighton	Hodijah Baylies
	York	Richard Trevett
	Biddeford & Peperelborough	Jeremiah Hill
	Portland & Falmouth	James Lunt
	Bath	William Webb
	Wiscasset	Francis Cook
	Penobscott	John Lee
	Frenchman's Bay	Melatiah Jordan
	Machias	Stephen Smith
	Passamaquody	Lewis Fredk Delesdenier
Rhode Island.	Newport	Daniel Lyman
	Providence	William Barton
	North Kingston	Daniel E. Updike
	East Greenwich	Thomas Arnold
	Warren & Barrington	Nathaniel Phillips
	Bristol	Samuel Bosworth
	Pawcatuck River	George Stillman
	Patuxet	Zachariah Rhodes.
Connecticut.	New London	Nathaniel Richards
	Stonington	Jonathan Palmer Jr
	Middletown	Comfort Sage
	Newhaven	Jonathan Fitch
	Fairfield	Samuel Smedley.
Vermont	Allburgh	Stephen Keyes.
New York	New York	John Lasher
	Hudson	John C. Tenbrock
	Albany	Henry J. Bogert

	Sagg Harbour	Henry P. Deering.
New Jersey.	Perth Amboy.	John Halsted
	Burlington	John Ross
	Bridgetown	Eli Elmer
	Little Egg Harbour	Ebenezar Tucker
	Great Egg Harbour	Daniel Benezet Junr
Pennsylvania.	Philadelphia	William McPherson
Delaware	Wilmington	George Bush
	New Castle	["]
	Port Penn	["]
Maryland.	Baltimore	Robert Ballard
	Chester	Jeremiah Nichols
	Oxford	Jeremiah Banning
	Vienna	John Muir
	Snow Hill	John Gunby
	Annapolis	John Davidson
	Nottingham	George Biscoe
	Town Creek	Charles Chelton
	Cedar Point	John C. Jones
	St Mary's	Robert Chesley
	Lewellengsburg	Jeremiah Jordan
	George Town	James M. Lingan.
Virginia.	Hampton	George Wray
	Norfolk & Portsmouth	Daniel Bedinger
	Suffolk	Lemuel Reddick
	Smithfield	James Wells[6]
	Bermuda Hundred	Christopher Roan
	Petersburgh	James Gibbon
	Richmond	Zachariah Rowland
	Yorktown	Abraham Archer
	West Point	Alexander Moore
	Tappahannock	Hudson Muse
	Urbanna	Peter Kemp
	Port Royal	George Catlett
	Fredericksburg	William Lewis
	Yeocomico River	Vincent Redman
	Dumfries	Richard M. Scott
	Alexandria	Samuel Hanson
	Folly Landing	William Gibb
	Cherrystone	Nathaniel Wilkins
	South Quay	Thomas Bowne
North Carolina.	Wilmington	Thomas Callender
	Newburn	John Daves

	Beaufort	John Easton
	Swansborough	John McCullough
	Washington	Nathan Keais
	Edenton	Thomas Benbury.
	Hartford	James Murdaugh
	Bennett's Creek	John Baker
	Plymouth	Thomas Davis Freeman
	Windsor	William Benson
	Skewarky	Henry Hunter
	Murfreesborough	Hardy Murfree
	Plankbridge	Isaac Gregory
	Nixonton	Hugh Knox
	Indian Town	Thomas Williams
	Currituck Inlet	Samuel Jasper
	Pasquetank River-bridge	Edmund Sawyer
	Newbiggen Creek	Elias Albertson.
South Carolina.	Charleston	Edward Weyman
	Beaufort	Andrew Agnew
	Georgetown	Charles Brown.
Georgia	Savannah	John Berrian
	Sunbury	John Lawson, the Younger,
	Brunswick	Christopher Hillary
	St Mary's	James Seagrove.

I likewise nominate Richard Morris to be Supervisor of the District of New York; vice William S. Smith, resigned; And John Lawson the younger, to be Collector of the Port of Sunbury, in the State of Georgia; vice Cornelius Collins, deceased.

Go: Washington

DS, DNA: RG 46, Second Congress, 1791–1793, Records of Executive Proceedings, President's Messages—Executive Nominations; LB, DLC:GW.

After reading this message the Senate ordered it to lie for consideration. It was taken up on 7 Mar., when the Senate confirmed the Georgia appointments. The following day the Senate resumed consideration of the message and confirmed all of the remaining appointments (see *Executive Journal,* 1:102–6, 111). On 9 Mar., Lear sent Jefferson a list of the appointments confirmed by the Senate (DNA: RG 59, George Washington's Correspondence with His Secretaries of State).

1. GW is referring to "An act repealing, after the last day of June next, the duties heretofore laid on distilled spirits imported from abroad, and laying others in their stead; and also upon spirits distilled within the United States, and for appropriating the same" of 3 Mar. 1791 (*Annals of Congress,* 1st Cong., 2384–2405).

2. On 4 Mar., Alexander Hamilton sent GW a "List of appointments of Inspectors of the Revenue, which took place during the recess of the Senate, as well for Ports as Surveys," which GW incorporated into this message (DLC:GW).

3. John Neville (1731–1803), who had been appointed a lieutenant colonel in the Continental army in November 1776, was promoted to colonel in December 1777 and was brevetted a brigadier general in September 1783. In mid-July 1794, in response to Neville's attempts to serve processes issued by the U.S. district court at Philadelphia against distillers who had not registered the previous year, his house, Bower Hill, near Pittsburgh, was attacked and burned.

4. James Brackenridge (1763–1833) was a member of the Virginia house of delegates 1789–1802, 1806–8, 1819–21, and 1823–24 and a Federalist congressman 1809–17. He also served as a brigadier general during the War of 1812 and aided Thomas Jefferson in the founding of the University of Virginia.

5. In his letter to GW of 4 Mar. covering the list of interim appointments, Hamilton wrote: "The President will recollect that the Joseph McDowell who was truly contemplated is '*the younger*' of Pleasant Garden, though described in the Commission & in the List as '*the Elder*'" (DLC:GW). For the confusion over the two Joseph McDowells, see Tobias Lear to GW, 29 May 1791, n.3, and Hamilton to Lear, 24 Feb. 1792, in Hamilton to GW, 18 Feb. 1792, n.1.

6. On 30 June, Tobias Lear transmitted to Thomas Jefferson at GW's command "the Commissn of Jas Wells, late Surveyor of the Port of Smithfield in Virga & Inspector of the Revenue for the same. Mr Wells has not returned his Commissn of Surveyorship; but he resigns both Offices of course. The reason, his being elected a Representative to the Genl Assembly. The President desires that Commissions may be made out for Copland Parker to fill the places vacated by Mr Wells" (DNA: RG 59, Miscellaneous Letters).

From Brown & Francis

Dr Sir Providence March 7th 1792.

We are exceeding sorry to be under the Necessity of a moment of your Attention on a subject which we think there was no Occasion, that the Judge of the Federal Court Living at Newburn in North Carolina should have compell'd us to apply to you upon, but the Fact is that the said Judge is the Cause of withholding from Capt. Low (the Bearer) & as a Considerable Sum of Money & other property which was run away with according to the enclosed advertisement,[1] we being the Sole Owners of the Sloop & Cargo, & Capt. Low had a handsome adventure on board, the Money is now in the hands of the Collector at Newburn & the sugar &c. in the hands of a Mr Benjamin Cheney both of North Carolina who have utterly refused delivering the property, either to our power of Attorney, or to Capt. Lows, without special orders from the said Judge, and he would not deliver it without special directions from your Excellency, altho we see no reason why he should give you or us this unnecessary trouble, we must entreat you Dr Sir to give Capt. Low (the bearer) such Directions to the said Judge as you may think proper.[2] And you'll much Oblige, Sr, Your Most Obedient & Most Humble servts

Brown & Francis

P.S. We understand by Capt. Low that the Judge declined giving Orders for the delivery of our Property till the Pirate had his Tryal, suppose they Choose to defer it as they have done, he may never come to Tryal & of course we are deprived of the Cargo, as well as of the Vessell & all her stores, which they have already wasted in pretended expences. We believe the name of the Judge at Newburn is Sitgreaves.

Your much Esteemed Favor of the 7th January came duly to hand and are perfectly satisfied with the Contents thereof.[3]

L, DNA: RG 59, Miscellaneous Letters.

1. The enclosed advertisement has not been identified.

2. GW received this letter by 24 Mar., when Tobias Lear sent it to Edmund Randolph with the president's request that the attorney general report on it (DNA: RG 59, Miscellaneous Letters). Randolph's opinion, which Lear forwarded to Brown & Francis on 2 April (DNA: RG 59, Miscellaneous Letters), has not been identified.

3. On 7 Jan. 1792 GW wrote Brown & Francis that as a public figure he could not in clear conscience recommend the firm's current shipbuilding project to bankers in Amsterdam, as the firm had requested of him on 13 Dec. 1791.

From Andrew G. Fraunces

Sir Philadelphia March 7th 1792.

It has not been with a little hesitation that I have presumed to address you and to make a request which I fear may be considered an improper one; however I am encouraged to proceed from the knowlege I possess of the extreme goodness of your heart: On this ground I venture, buoyed with the hope that you will grant me the favor I ask, if I have been, or may be found to merit it.

Having since the year 1785 served the public, in the Treasury department, I have entirely devoted my attention to that business, nor thought of turning aside to any other, and flattered my self that by unremitted exertions in the duties of my station I might be found worthy at some future day, if opportunity offered, for public notice. I have waited patiently and I trust have pursued the plan I at first determined on—an opportunity seems now to present itself.

The report of a Committee of Congress on the Treasury department &ca I observe contemplates the abolishment of the office of the assistant, and substitutes in lieu thereof, two principal Clerks[1]—for one of those offices (if a law should be passed making such alteration in the department) I have petitioned the Secretary—*and now most humbly beg that you will honor me by mentioning me to him favorably*—I must notwithstanding, in justice to the public declare, that I do not wish the office I petition for, nor the favor I presume to ask of you—if I have not been found strictly attentive to their interests; and my knowlege of the business of the department, and my abilities are not sufficiently competent to the appointment.[2]

Permit me to say Sir—that from my infancy I have been taught to look up to you as the *father* of the rising generation—as a *child* then let me hope you will indulge me with the favor I ask—or if it is an improper request, to pardon it, and attribute it to an anxious desire, of, as well as making myself useful and conspicuous in the station in which providence has placed me—as to the maintaining and providing for the education of a family which the same providence has committed to my care. I have the honor to be with all possible respect, and the truest attachment Your most obedient and most humble servant

Andrew G. Fraunces

ALS, DNA: RG 59, Miscellaneous Letters.

1. "An Act making alterations in the Treasury and War Departments," which GW signed on 8 May, abolished the office of assistant to the secretary of the treasury and in its place created the office of commissioner of the revenue. It also authorized two principal clerks for the secretary of the treasury, each with an annual salary of $800. Finally, the act lifted the prohibition on Treasury Department clerks from carrying on any outside trade or business (see 1 *Stat.* 279–81).

2. Fraunces, who was not promoted to one of the two principal clerkships, became involved in a bitter dispute with the secretary of the treasury following his dismissal from the Treasury Department in March 1793 (see GW to

Hamilton, 3 Aug. 1793, Hamilton to GW, 9 Aug. 1793; see also Fraunces to Hamilton, 16 May 1793, introductory note, Hamilton to Jeremiah Wadsworth, 3 Sept. 1793, and Tench Coxe to Hamilton, 18 Dec. 1793, in Syrett, *Hamilton Papers,* 14:460–71, 26:713–14, 719–23).

To Thomas Jefferson

[Philadelphia, 7 March 1792][1]

The enclosed,[2] sent for Mr Jeffersons perusal, corrobates the idea held out in the communication of Mr H——d.

G.W.

ALS, DLC: Jefferson Papers.

At the bottom of the letter, Jefferson wrote: "Extract from [Samuel] Kirkland's letter [to Henry Knox], dated Kanandaiqua Feb. 25. 1792. 'The British at Niagara, hold out this idea, that the U.S. will not be able to refund the confiscated Tory estates—therefore a new boundary line must be made betwixt the two powers, & that this line will probably be from the Genesee to the Ohio, & that their Ambassedor mister Hammond is sent over to negociate the business. this is talked of as a serious matter at the garrison & it's vicinity.'" Kirkland's incomplete draft of his letter of 25 Feb. does not give the addressee and contains textual variations. It adds, furthermore, that the probable new boundary will extend to the junction of the Ohio and Mississippi rivers and notes that the British later "shall erect a fortress at Grand River—& another opposite to Detroit—where the Indians shall be encouraged & protected—this latter is indian report—the former, is talked of as a serious matter at Niagara & its vicinity" (NCH: Kirkland Papers).

Jefferson wrote in a memorandum on 11 Mar. 1792: "a few days after, came to hand Kirkland's letter informing us that the British at Niagara expected to run a new line between them & us, and the reports of [Peter] Pond & [William] Stedman [Steedman], informing us it was understood at Niagara that Capt. [Charles] Stevens [Stevenson] had bn sent here by [John Graves] Simcoe to settle that plan with Hammd. hence Hamilton's attack of the principle I had laid down, in order to prepare the way for this new line" (Jefferson's Memoranda of Consultations with the President, 11 Mar.–9 April 1792, DLC: Jefferson Papers).

For the background to Anglo-American relations and Hammond's communication to Jefferson of 5 Mar. 1792, see GW to Jefferson, c.5–6 Mar., source note and note 2.

1. Jefferson endorsed this letter as having been received on 7 March.

2. The original enclosure has not been found.

From Thomas Jefferson

Sir, Philadelphia. March 7th 1792.

Immediately on the passage of the Act providing the means of intercourse between the United States and foreign Nations,[1] I desired the bankers of the United States in Amsterdam, to raise an account with the Secretary of State of the United States, to be confined to the objects of that Act,[2] and requested them and our Ministers abroad to make up their accounts from July to July annually, and furnish me with them, that I might enable you to lay before Congress, regularly, the account of those expenditures which the law requires. It was not till yesterday that I received the General Account of the bankers for the first year, by a vessel from Amsterdam, which seems to have had four or five months passage:[3] nor have I yet been able to get all the particular accounts, which would be necessary to give a satisfactory view of this branch of expenditure. I therefore, for the present, enclose the General Account only, expressing this caution that the balance therein stated, is only that which had not yet been drawn out of their hands, though, at that moment, there were existing demands for a great part of it. I have reason to be tolerably confident that the measures for having the particular, as well as the General Account kept and forwarded to me regularly, will, in the course of this second year, get so far into effect, as that I may be sure of enabling you, at the next session of Congress to lay before them a complete statement of the application of this fund, general and special, to the 1st of July next ensuing, and, when once under regular way, the annual communication to the legislature may be afterwards constantly made.[4] I have the honor to be, with the most profound respect and attachment, Sir, Your most obedient and most humble servant

Th: Jefferson

LS, DNA: RG 46, Second Congress, 1791–1793, Records of Legislative Proceedings, President's Messages; LS (letterpress copy of second copy), DLC: Jefferson Papers; LB, DLC:GW; LB, DNA: RG 59, Domestic Letters.

1. GW signed "An Act providing the means of intercourse between the United States and foreign nations" on 1 July 1790. It authorized the president to draw from the treasury up to $40,000 annually to support "such persons as he shall commission to serve the United States in foreign parts, and for the expense incident to the business in which they may be employed." The act also

provided that "the President shall account specifically for all such expenditures of the said money as in his judgment may be made public, and also for the amount of such expenditures as he may think it advisable not to specify, and cause a regular statement and account thereof to be laid before Congress annually, and also lodged in the proper office of the treasury department" (1 *Stat.* 128–29).

2. For the secretary of state's letter to the American bankers at Amsterdam, see Jefferson to Willink, Van Staphorst & Hubbard, 5 Aug. 1791, in Jefferson to Willink, Van Staphorst & Hubbard, 11 May 1791 (second letter), source note, *Jefferson Papers,* 20:393–94. See also Jefferson to Willink, Van Staphorst & Hubbard, 23 Jan. 1792, ibid., 23:60–61.

3. The enclosed letter from Willink, Van Staphorst & Hubbard to Jefferson of 24 Oct. 1791 and the "General" statement of account with the United States that it covered are printed in *Jefferson Papers,* 22:228–31.

4. GW laid this letter and its enclosures before Congress on 9 Mar. 1792.

From Thomas Jefferson

[Philadelphia] Mar. 7. 1792.

Th: Jefferson presents his respects to the President and sends him his report on the subject of commerce with Spain, & the form of a message to the Senate.[1] a second copy is now making out for the President's own use, so that he may send in the one now inclosed to-day, assured of receiving the other the moment it is finished.[2]

AL, DNA: RG 59, Miscellaneous Letters; LB, DNA: RG 59, George Washington's Correspondence with His Secretaries of State; LB (photocopy), DLC:GW.

1. Jefferson's enclosed "report on the subject of commerce with Spain" is printed below as a separate document.

2. GW submitted this letter and its enclosure to the Senate this day.

Enclosure
From Thomas Jefferson

[Philadelphia] March 7th 1792.

The Secretary of State having understood from communications with the Commissioners of his Catholic Majesty, subsequent to that which he reported to the President on the 22d of Decembr last, that though they considered the navigation of the Missisippi as the principal object of negociation between the two Countries, yet it was expected by their Court that the conferences would extend to all the matters which were under negociation on the former occasion with Mr Gardoqui, and particularly to some arrangements of Commerce[1]—is of opinion that to renew the conferences on this subject also, since they desire it, will be but friendly and respectful, and can lead to nothing without our own consent, and that to refuse it, might obstruct the settlement of the questions of navigation and boundary: and therefore Reports

To the President of the United States the following Observations and Instructions to the Commissioners of the United States appointed to negociate with the Court of Spain a treaty or convention relative to the navigation of the Missisippi; which observations and instructions he is of opinion should be laid before the Senate of the United States, and their decision be desired, Whether they will advise and consent that a treaty be entered into by the Commissioners of the United States with Spain conformable thereto.[2]

After stating to our Commissioners the foundation of our rights to navigate the Missisippi, and to hold our Southern boundary at the 31st degree of latitude, and that each of these is to be a sine quo non, it is proposed to add as follows.

On the former conferences on the navigation of the Missisippi, Spain chose to blend with it the subject of commerce; and accordingly specific propositions thereon passed between the negociators.[3] Her object then was to obtain our renunciation of the navigation, and to hold out commercial arrangements, perhaps as a lure to us. Perhaps however she might then, and may now really set a value on commercial arrangements with us, and may receive them as a consideration for accommodating us in the navigation, or may wish for them to have the appearance of receiving a consideration. Commercial arrangements, if acceptable in themselves, will not be the less so if coupled with those relating to navigation & boundary. We have only to take care that they be acceptable in themselves.

There are two principles which may be proposed as the basis of a commercial treaty, 1st that of exchanging the privileges of native citizens, or 2d those of the most favoured Nation.

1st With the nations holding important possessions in America, we are ready to exchange the rights of native citizens, provided they be extended through the whole possessions of both parties; but the propositions of Spain made on the former occasion (a copy of which accompanies this)[4] were, that we should give their merchants, vessels and productions the privileges of native merchants, vessels and productions, thro' the whole of our possessions, and they give the same to our's only in Spain and the Canaries. This is inadmissible because unequal: and as we believe that Spain is not ripe for an equal exchange on this basis, we avoid proposing it.

2d Though treaties which merely exchange the rights of the most favoured nations are not without all inconvenience, yet they have their conveniencies also. It is an important one that they leave each party free to make what internal regulations they please, and to give what preferences they find expedient to native merchants, vessels and productions. And as we already have treaties on this basis with France, Holland, Sweden & Prussia, the two former of which are perpetual, it will be but small additional embarrassment to extend it to Spain.[5] On the contrary we are sensible it is right to place that nation on the most favoured footing, whether we have a treaty with them or not; and it can do us no harm to secure by treaty a reciprocation of the right.

Of the four treaties beforementioned, either the French or the Prussian might be taken as a model; but it would be useless to propose the Prussian, because we have already supposed that Spain would never consent to those articles which give to each party access to all the dominions of the other; and without this equivalent, we would not agree to tie our own hands so materially in War as would be done by the 23d article, which renounces the right of fitting out privateers, or of capturing merchant vessels. The French treaty therefore is proposed as the model. In this however the following changes are to be made.

We should be admitted to all the dominions of Spain to which any other foreign nation is, or may be admitted.

Art: 5. being an exemption from a particular duty in France, will of course be omitted as inapplicable to Spain.

Art: 8. to be omitted as unnecessary with Morocco, and inefficacious and little honorable with any of the Barbary powers; but it may furnish occasion to sound Spain on the project of a convention of the powers at war with the Barbary states, to keep up by rotation, a constant cruise of a given force on their coasts, 'till they shall be compelled to renounce for ever, and against all nations, their predatory practices.[6] Perhaps the infidelities of the Algerines to their treaty of peace with Spain, though the latter does not chuse to break openly, may induce her to subsidize *us* to cruise against them with a given force.

Art: 9 & 10. concerning fisheries to be omitted as inapplicable.

Art: 11. The first paragraph of this article respecting the Droit d'Aubaine to be omitted, that law being supposed peculiar to France.[7]

Art: 17. giving asylum in the ports of either to the armed vessels of the other with the prizes taken from the enemies of that other, must be qualified as it is in the 19th article of the Prussian treaty, as the stipulation in the latter part of the article "that no shelter or refuge shall be given in the ports of the one to such as shall have made prize on the subjects of the other of the parties", would forbid us in case of a war between France and Spain, to give shelter in our ports to prizes made by the latter on the former, while the first part of the article would oblige us to shelter those made by the former on the latter: a very dangerous covenant, and which ought never to be repeated in any other instance.

Art: 29. Consuls should be received at all the ports at which the vessels of either party may be received.

Art: 30. concerning free ports in Europe & America. Free ports in the Spanish possessions in America, and particularly at the Havanna, are more to be desired than expected. It can therefore only be recommended to the best endeavours of the Commissioners to obtain them. It will be something to obtain for our vessels, flour, &c: admission to those ports during their pleasure. In like manner if they could be prevailed on to re-establish our right of cutting log wood in the bay of Campeachy, on the footing on which it stood before the treaty of 1763, it would be desireable, and not endanger to us any contest with the English, who by the revolution treaty are restrained to the South Eastern parts of Yucatan.[8]

Art: 31. The *act* of ratification on our part may require a twelvemonth from the date of the treaty, as the Senate meets regularly but once a year, and to return it to Madrid for *exchange* may require four months more.

The treaty must not exceed [ ] years duration, except the

clauses relating to Boundary and the navigation of the Missisippi, which must be perpetual and final. Indeed these two subjects had better be in a separate instrument.

There might have been mentioned a third species of arrangement, that of making special agreements on every special subject of commerce, and of settling a tariff of duty to be paid, on each side, on every particular article; but this would require in our commissioners a very minute knowledge of our commerce, as it is impossible to foresee every proposition of this kind which might be brought into discussion, and to prepare them for it by information and instruction from hence. Our commerce too is as yet rather in a course of experiment, and the channels in which it will ultimately flow are not sufficiently known to enable us to provide for it by special agreement; nor have the exigencies of our new Government as yet so far developed themselves, as that we can know to what degree we may or must have recourse to commerce, for the purposes of revenue. No common consideration therefore ought to induce us as yet to arrangements of this kind. Perhaps nothing should do it, with any nation, short of the privileges of natives in all their possessions foreign and domestic.

It were to be wished indeed that some positively favourable stipulations respecting our grain, flour and fish could be obtained, even on our giving reciprocal advantages to some of the commodities of Spain, say her wines and brandies. But

1st If we quit the ground of the *most favoured nation* as to certain articles for our convenience, Spain may insist on doing the same for other articles for her convenience, and thus our Commissioners will get themselves on the ground of a *treaty of detail,* for which they will not be prepared.

2d If we grant favour to the wines and brandies of Spain, then Portugal and France will demand the same; and in order to create an equivalent, Portugal may lay a duty on our fish and grain, and France a prohibition on our whale oils, the removal of which will be proposed as an equivalent.

Thus much however as to grain and flour may be attempted. There has not long since been a considerable duty laid on them in Spain. This was while a treaty on the subject of commerce was pending between us and Spain, as that court considers the matter. It is not generally thought right to change the state of things pending a treaty concerning them. On this consideration, and on the motive of cultivating our friendship, perhaps the Commissioners may induce them to restore this commodity to the footing on which it was on opening the conferences with Mr Gardoqui on the 26th day of July 1785. If Spain says, "do the same by your tonnage on our vessels", the answer may be, "that our foreign tonnage affects Spain very little, and other nations very much, whereas the duty on flour in Spain affects us very much, and other nations very little; consequently there would be no equality in reciprocal relinquishment, as there had been none in the reciprocal innovation; and Spain by insisting on this, would in fact only be aiding the interests of her rival nations, to whom we should be forced to extend the same indulgence." At the time of opening the conferences too, we had as yet not erected any system: Our government itself being not yet erected; Innovation then was unavoidable on our part, if it be innovation to establish a system: we did it on fair and general ground, on ground favourable to Spain: but they had a system, & therefore innovation was avoidable on their part.

Th: Jefferson

DS, DNA: RG 46, Second Congress, 1791–1793, Records of Executive Proceedings, President's Messages—Foreign Relations; DS (copy), DNA: RG 59, Miscellaneous Letters; DS (letterpress copy of copy), DLC: Jefferson Papers; AD (letterpress copy; incomplete), DLC: Jefferson Papers; copy, DNA: RG 59, Reports of the Secretary of State to the President and Congress; LB, DLC:GW.

For the background to the negotiation of a commercial treaty between Spain and the United States, see Thomas Jefferson to GW, 22 Dec. 1791 (first letter), Memorandum of Thomas Jefferson, 4 Jan., and GW to the U.S. Senate, 11 Jan. 1792. See also Jefferson to GW, 18 Mar. 1792.

1. For the expansion of the number of topics to be considered in the treaty with Spain, see Jefferson's Memorandum of Conversation with José de Jaudenes, 27 Dec. 1791, Jefferson to Jaudenes and José Ignacio de Viar, 25, 26 Jan., and Jaudenes and Viar to Jefferson, 25, 27 Jan. 1792, all in *Jefferson Papers,* 22:459, 23:66–68, 76, 78–81. Although Jefferson had undoubtedly informed GW of Spain's intention to expand the scope of the negotiations, when the president nominated William Short and William Carmichael as treaty commissioners he did not inform the Senate of the change (see GW to the U.S. Senate, 11 Jan. 1792).

2. GW submitted Jefferson's report to the Senate this day.

3. Jefferson is referring to the long but ultimately fruitless negotiations conducted by John Jay and the Spanish plenipotentiary Diego Maria de Gardoqui in 1785–86 (see James Monroe to GW, 20 Aug. 1786, and note 2).

4. At the bottom of the last page of Jefferson's report is written: "add from

Wait Vol. 10 pages 108–9 'Articles proposed' &c." The copy of the "Articles proposed by Don Diego Gardoqui to be inserted in the Treaty with the United States" that GW presented to the Senate reads: "1. That all commercial regulations affecting each other shall be founded in perfect reciprocity. Spanish merchants shall enjoy all the commercial privileges of native merchants in the United States; and American merchants shall enjoy all the commercial privileges of native merchants in the Kingdom of Spain, and in the Canaries and other Islands belonging & adjacent thereto. The same privileges shall extend to their respective vessels, and merchandize consisting of the manufactures and productions of their respective Countries.

"2. Each party may establish Consuls in the Countries of the other (excepting such Provinces in Spain, into which none have heretofore been admitted, vizt Bilboa and Guipusca) with such powers and privileges as shall be ascertained by a particular Convention.

"3. That the bona fide manufactures and productions of the United States (Tobacco only excepted, which shall continue under its present regulations) may be imported in American or Spanish vessels, into any parts of his Majesty's European Dominions and Islands aforesaid, in like manner as if they were the productions of Spain. And on the other hand, that the bona fide manufactures and productions of his Majesty's Dominions, may be imported into the United States in Spanish or American vessels, in like manner as if they were the manufactures and productions of the said States. And further that all such duties and imposts, as may mutually be thought necessary to lay on them by either party, shall be ascertained and regulated on principles of exact reciprocity, by a tariff, to be formed by a Convention for that purpose, to be negociated and made within *one* year after the exchange of the ratification of this Treaty; and in the mean time, that no other duties or imposts shall be exacted from each others merchants and Ships, than such as may be payable by natives in like cases.

"4. That in asmuch as the United States, from not having mines of Gold and Silver, may often want supplies of specie for a circulating medium, his Catholic Majesty as a proof of his good will, agrees to order the masts and timber which may from time to time be wanted for his royal navy, to be purchased and paid for in specie, in the United States; Provided the said masts and Timber shall be of equal quality, and when brought to Spain, shall not cost more than the like may there be had for, from other Countries.

"5. It is agreed that the Articles commonly inserted in other Treaties of Commerce for mutual and reciprocal convenience, shall be inserted in this; and that this Treaty and every Article and stipulation therein shall continue in full force for [ ] years, to be computed from the day of the date hereof" (DNA: RG 46, Second Congress, 1791–1793, Records of Executive Proceedings, President's Messages—Foreign Relations).

5. For the texts of the treaties of amity and commerce with France (6 Feb. 1778), the Netherlands (8 Oct. 1782), Sweden (3 April 1783), and Prussia (10 Sept. 1785), see Miller, *Treaties*, 2:3–34, 59–90, 123–50, 162–84.

6. Jefferson long had been interested in the creation of an international convention against the Barbary corsairs (see Jefferson to GW, 12 July 1790 [first letter]).

7. For the complaints of American merchants about the *droit d'aubaines*, the French law by which the property of any deceased foreigner was confiscated by the state to the exclusion of any heirs at law, see GW to Jefferson, 26 July 1790.

8. American woodcutting rights at Campeche on the Yucatan Peninsula were not reestablished by the treaty between the United States and Spain of October 1795 (ibid., 318–45).

From Joseph Phillips, Sr.

Sir Maidenhead New-Jersey 7th March 1792.

I beg leave to offer my services as an Engineer, tolerably well versed in that business; and would go in that character [(]if wanted) to the Westward the ensuing Campaign. I would not at this time have attempted to divert the attention of the illustrious President of the United States, from contemplation on the more important interests of the Union; to such a very small object as myself; had I had any the least personal acquaintance with the Secretary of War: And I beg that this unfavorable circumstance alone, may be admitted as an apology for the obtrusion.

I have written notwithstanding, to General Knox more fully on this subject, and could not repress my vanity, which I am afraid will appear too conspicuous, by an inclosure to him, of a very polite note of approbation, signified to me by order of His Excellency the Commander in Chief, in the year 1776 by Rob. H. Harrison Secretary in regard to some Works proposed to be erected.[1]

I shall be happy in an appointment, as above; It is the first I ever sollicited, and if I succeed, it will (I believe) be the last effort, I shall ever make in a Military Character, and must suffice, my lack of service. I have a son, now with the Army in that Country.[2] I have the honour to be Your most devoted, faithful humble & most obedt servt.

Jos. Phillips.

ALS, DLC:GW.

Joseph Phillips, Sr., of Hunterdon County, N.J., served as an engineer at Fort Pitt and in the West Indies during the French and Indian War. On 14 June 1776 he was commissioned major of the militia regiment raised in Hunterdon and Somerset counties. In August 1776 Phillips was promoted to lieutenant colonel, and following the death of his commanding officer at the Battle of

Long Island, he became colonel of the regiment. Phillips was appointed colonel of the 1st Regiment of Hunterdon County militia in March 1777.

1. Phillips wrote GW in October 1776 requesting permission to reinforce existing batteries and erect new ones opposite Fort Washington, N.Y., in order to annoy enemy shipping on the Hudson River. Robert Hanson Harrison informed Phillips of GW's approval of the plan and gratitude for the "generous motives which Induced you to lay the measure before him" (see Harrison to Phillips, 12 Oct. 1776, in Phillips to GW, c.12 Oct. 1776, n.1).

2. Phillips did not receive a military appointment, but his son Joseph Phillips, Jr., also of New Jersey, who was a surgeon's mate in the levies during Arthur St. Clair's ill-fated campaign against the Indians in 1791, was reappointed on 11 April 1792. The younger Phillips was promoted to surgeon in June 1796, and he was honorably discharged from the U.S. Army in early June 1802.

To the United States Senate

United States [Philadelphia]

Gentlemen of the Senate, March 7th 1792.

I submit to your consideration the report of the Secretary of State which accompanies this,[1] stating the reasons for extending the negotiation proposed at Madrid to the subject of commerce, and explaining, under the form of instructions to the Commissioners lately appointed to that Court, the principles on which commercial arrangements with Spain might, if desired on her part, be acceded to on ours: And I have to request your decision, whether you will advise and consent to the extension of the powers of the Commissioners as proposed, and to the ratification of a treaty which shall conform to those instructions, should they enter into such a one with that Court.[2]

Go: Washington

DS, DNA: RG 46, Second Congress, 1791–1793, Records of Executive Proceedings, President's Messages—Foreign Relations; LB, DLC:GW; copy, DLC: Jefferson Papers.

1. For Jefferson's accompanying report, see the enclosure to Jefferson to GW, 7 Mar. 1792 (second letter).

2. The Senate read this message and its accompanying papers later on this date and referred them for consideration to a committee comprised of George Cabot, Robert Morris, and John Langdon. On 15 Mar., Cabot presented the committee's report, which the Senate ordered to lie on the table. The next day, after resuming consideration of the report, the Senate resolved "(two-thirds of the Senators concurring therein,) 'That they advise and consent to the extension of the powers of the Commissioners, as proposed, and that they

will advise and consent to the ratification of such treaty as the said Commissioners shall enter into with the Court of Spain, in conformity to those instructions.'" The Senate then ordered its secretary, Samuel A. Otis, to present this resolution to GW (*Executive Journal,* 1:106–10, 115). On 16 Mar., Tobias Lear by GW's command transmitted to Jefferson a copy of the Senate's resolution (DLC: Jefferson Papers).

From Alexander Hamilton

[Philadelphia] 8th March 1792.

The Secretary of the Treasury has the honor to submit to the President a letter which he has drafted in answer to one from the Minister Plenipotentiary of France, and which contains such Ideas as have appeared to him compatible with the Law, with the state of the Treasury and with a liberal attention to the conjuncture.[1] He will wait on the President this evening for his orders, as Mr Ternant appears urgent.[2]

LB, DLC:GW.

On 3 Mar. 1792 Jean-Baptiste, chevalier de Ternant, had asked Thomas Jefferson for "a supply of four hundred thousand dollars on account of reimbursements due from us to France, to be applied to relieve the distresses of the colony of St. Domingo." Jefferson replied on 7 Mar. that Ternant should apply to Alexander Hamilton at the Treasury Department (*Jefferson Papers,* 23:191, 231–32). Ternant wrote Hamilton the following day (see Syrett, *Hamilton Papers,* 11:113–14). For the slave uprising on the island of Saint Domingue, see Samuel Wall to GW, 16 Sept. 1791, and note 1, and Charles Pinckney to GW, 20 Sept. 1791, and note 1.

1. The enclosure was a draft of Hamilton's letter to Ternant of 8 Mar. 1792, the ALS of which reads: "I have the honor of your letter of this date, communicating the copy of one to you from the Secretary of State in answer to your application of the 3d. instant.

"Assuring you of the pleasure I shall feel, in executing the views of the President, relatively to the accommodation, which is desired, in as efficacious a manner, as the state of our public resources compared with our public exigencies will admit—I am to inform you that you can have from the Treasury of the United States, on account of your Government the following advances viz 100,000 Dollars immediately, a like sum on the first of June, a like sum on the first of September and a like sum on the first of December next. Provision will be made for the punctual payment of these several sums at the Bank of the United States.

"It would be more agreeable, if it were practicable to stipulate shorter periods for these advances, but considering the extra-demands, which the operations on foot for the defence of our Western frontier will add to the ordinary demands for the current service, it does not appear adviseable to promise earlier payments.

"If however in the progress of things, it shall be found compatible with the general arrangements of the Treasury, to anticipate the periods which have been mentioned, it will without fail be done.

"It remains more to explain the principles on which these advances, consistently with the authority vested by law in the President, can be made.

"From the instructions which have been given to Mr. [William] Short, from the known progress of his operations, and from some passages in a letter which I have received from him of the 12th of November last—I conclude with certainty, that he has discharged all the arrears of interest and installments of principal due to France to the end of the year 1791.

"The sums now agreed to be furnished therefore will be an anticipation of so much *hereafter to become due.*

"The law, which makes provision for the reimbursements to France, contemplates the payment of whatever sums should have *actually become due,* unconditionally, but restrains the discretion of the Executive as to payments, by anticipation, with this condition—that they 'can be effected upon terms *advantageous* to the United States.'

"It is clear then, adopting the most liberal construction of this condition, that such payments can only be made upon terms which will involve *no loss* to the United States.

"The fund, from which must arise the advances proposed to be made, is a part of the sums borrowed abroad, pursuant to the law which has been referred to.

"These monies have been borrowed at an interest of five per Cent, with charges amounting to four per Cent, and are to be reimbursed in six equal yearly installments, the first at the end of ten years. The time between the receipt of the money in Amsterdam from the lenders, and the placing of it in the Treasury of the United States, cannot be stated at less than six months, during which time an interest has been paid by the United States, for which they have not been compensated by the use of the money. As the money was drawn from Amsterdam by bills of exchange, which were sold upon a credit the transfer was effected at *par,* while private bills, upon that place were at the times of the sales considerably below par in our market.

"The United States will consequently avoid loss, and no more, if the advances which shall be made, are so liquidated, as to include an indemnification for the charges of the loan and the interest of the money during the time lost in transferring it from Amsterdam to the United States. The quantum of such an indemnification will be merely matter of calculation upon the data above stated.

"If however instead of an allowance for the six months interest, you prefer as a rule the rate of exchange between the United States and Amsterdam you are at liberty to make the option.

"The sums, which have been mentioned will of course only operate as payments, from the respective times; when they shall be actually paid, so as *thenceforth* to arrest the progress of interest on *equal sums* of the Debt to France.

"The intrinsic par of the metals will be the standard of computation, for converting dollars into livres.

"When it is considered, that the indemnification, which is sought, is in compliance with an express law, it is hoped that it will obviate all impression of a too minute attention to pecuniary advantage in a case, which is certainly not of great magnitude, and on an occasion, which it is felt claims a liberal treatment.

"When also it is considered, that the United States sustained a heavy loss in the first instance, upon their negociations in relation to the aids which constituted their debt to France—on a considerable proportion of not less than 40 per Cent—that by the terms of their contract they are obliged to repay that debt at Paris and consequently were subjected to whatever loss might have been incident to a state of exchange disadvantageous to them—that they in the present case wave the benefit of a state of Exchange highly advantageous to them, and, renouncing gain from that circumstance, are content with merely not suffering loss; it is relied upon, that the terms which have been suggested will appear to you not only equitable but liberal.

"Nevertheless, as it is the wish of the President, to obviate all embarrassment on your part and to put the matter upon a footing perfectly satisfactory to your Government and Nation, I am instructed by him to inform you, that if it will be more agreeable to you, he will refer the question of indemnification to a future adjustment with your Court and will cause the necessary instructions for that purpose to be sent to our minister Plenipotentiary there [Gouverneur Morris]" (Syrett, *Hamilton Papers,* 11:114–17). Hamilton sent a second copy of his letter to Ternant to GW on 19 April.

2. Ternant wrote Hamilton again on 10 Mar. (see Hamilton to GW, 19 April, n.1). The secretary of the treasury responded on 11 Mar. that "six and a half ℔ Ct. is the *utmost* extent of the requisite imdemnification," and on 12 Mar. he wrote that upon the application of the French consul general, "A warrant on the Treasurer has in course been executed" (ibid., 125–26, 128–29). See also Hamilton to GW, 19 April 1792.

To Thomas Jefferson

Dear Sir, [Philadelphia] Thursday Morning [8 March 1792][1]

I do not recollect whether any notice has ever been taken in your letter to the Commrs of Mr Johnsons suggestion of bringing the Canal navigation to the City—The ascertainment of the practicability ought by all means to be encouraged.[2] Yours

G.W.

ALS, DLC: Jefferson Papers.

1. Jefferson apparently was mistaken when he endorsed this letter as having been received on 7 Mar., as GW dated it "Thursday Morning," 8 March.

2. In his letter to the commissioners for the District of Columbia of 6 Mar.,

Jefferson had mentioned the canal as a possible undertaking for the current work season (see *Jefferson Papers,* 23:224–28). After receiving GW's letter Jefferson wrote privately on 8 Mar. to commissioner Thomas Johnson: "You formerly hinted the expediency of bringing the navigable canal from the little falls down to Washington. The President thinks the practicability of this should be properly examined into, as it would undoubtedly be useful" (ibid., 236–37).

To David Stuart

Dear Sir, Philadelphia March 8th 1792.

In a short letter which I wrote to you by the last Post, I promised a lengthy one by the Post of tomorrow;[1] but such is my present situation that I must pass by some things & be more concise on others than I intended.

That Mr Johnsons health did not permit him to come to this City as he proposed & was expected, is matter of exceeding great regret,[2] as many things relative to the Federal district—the City—and the public buildings might have been more Satisfactorily arranged; and delays avoided; but as there is no contending against acts of Providence we must submit, as it becomes us so to do, and endeavor to recover the time lost, in the best manner we can.

That the Commissioners have had more than a little trouble & vexation with Majr L'Enfant, I can readily conceive (if your representation of the fact had been wanting) from the specimens he has given of his untoward temper since his arrival in this City—And I can as easily conceive that in proportion to the yieldings of the Commissioners his claims would extend. Such upon a nearer view, appears to be the nature of the Man!

Every advantage will be taken of the Majors deriliction. A vigorous counter action therefore is essential. If he does not come forward openly to declare it, *his friends* and the *enemies* to the *measure,* will do it for him, that he found matters we⟨re⟩ likely to be conducted upon so pimping a s⟨cale⟩ that he would not hazard his character, ⟨or⟩ reputation on the event under the controul he was to be placed. It is even said (but nothing has appeared yet) that he means to publish this to the world. The half friends to the New City (if this is not allowing them more than their due) ⟨under⟩take to predict that, it now stands in equilibrio. that a feather will turn the Scale either way. If say they the matter is pushed with vigor, and upon a plan commensurate to the design, & the public expectation, the permanent Seat of the Government will be fixed on the Potowmack. On the other hand, if inactivity and contractedness should mark the steps of the Commissioners of that district, whilst action, on the part of this state is displayed in providing commodious buildings for Congress &ca the Government will remain where it now is. That exertions will be made by this State to effect the purpose, there can be no doubt. A late message from the Governor to the Assembly proposing a ⟨certain⟩ grant of money for the erection of the house designed for the President is one, among other instances which have occurred.[3]

It would have been very agreeable to me, that you should have shewn the copies of the letters I had written to Major L'Enfant, declaratory of the Subordinate part he was destined to act under the Commissioners. It does not appear to have been so understood by the Proprietors, from the sentiments expressed by Mr Walker (while he was in this City) for when he was told in what explicit language Major L'Enfant was given to understand this, he seemed quite surprised. You did me no more than justice when you supposed me incapable of duplicity in this business—I have had but one idea on the subject from the beginning—nor but one design, and that was to convince the Major[4] of the subordinate part he was destined to act in it—I was obliged, as you have seen, to use stronger & stronger language as I found his repugnance encreased 'till he was told, in even harsh terms, that the Commissioners stood between him and the P—— of the U. States and that it was from them that he was to receive directions.

The doubts, and opinion of others with respect to the permanent seat has occasioned ⟨no change⟩ in my sentiments on the subject. They have always been, that the plan ought to be prosecuted with all the dispatch the nature of the case will admit—and that the public Buildings in size—form—and elegance shou'd look beyond the present day. I would not have it understood from hence that I lean to extravagance. A chaste plan sufficiently capacious & convenient for a period not *too* remote, but one to which we may *reasonably* look forward, would meet my idea in the Capitol. For the Presidents House, I would design a building which should also look forward, but execute no more of it at present than might suit the circumstances of this Country when it shall be first wanted. A Plan comprehending more may be executed at a future period when the wealth, population & importance of it shall stand upon much higher ground than they do at present.

How, and when you will be able to obtain plans of such buildings is with yourselves to decide on. No aid I am persuaded is to be expected from Major L'Enfant in the exhibition—rather, I apprehend, opposition & a reprobation of every one designed by any other however perfect.

The part, which Mr Walker by your letter to me, & another from Mr Johnson to Mr Jefferson, appears to have acted, surprises me exceedingly[5]—his interest in ⟨the City,⟩ & the discernment with which he seems to have viewed the measure, in the early stages of it, would have led me to have drawn a different conclusion. The calumnies which seem to have been traced to him and the Major are more to be despised than to be regarded or resented. More than once you will remember I have given it to you as my opinion, that it would be by side blows and indirect attack that attempts would be made to defeat the Law. To sow the Seeds of dissension—jealousy and distrust—are among the means that will be practiced—There is a current in this City which sets so strongly against every thing which relates to the Federal district that it is next to impossible to stem it. To this cause is to be ascribed the backwardness of the engraving. Danger from them is to be apprehended; and, in my opinion, from no other. The best antidote against them is perseverance, & vigorous exertion on the part of the Commissioners; and good temper, and mutual forbearance with one another, on the part of the proprietors; for who are so much interested in the success, & progress of the measure as they?

I see no necessity for diminishing the Square allotted for the Presidents House, &ca at this time. It is easier at all times to retrench, than it is to enlarge a square; and a diviation from the plan in this instance would open the door to other applications, which might perplex, embarrass and delay business exceedingly; and end, more than probably, in violent discontents.

Where you will find a character qualified in all respects for a Superintendant, I know not; none present themselves to my view; yet, one must be had. A better than Mr Ellicott for all matters, at present, cannot be had. No one I presume, can lay out the ground with more accuracy, lay out the squares, and divide them into lots better. He must understand levelling also perfectly, and has, I suppose competent skill in the conducting of water. Beyond these, your opportunities to form an opinion of him must exceed mine. Whether he is a man of arrangement—is sober, & Industrious—are matters unknown to me. I believe he is obliging—and he would be perfectly Subordinate. What he asks, five dollars a day (if sundays are included) seems high, but whether a fit character can be had for less I am unable to say.[6]

The Plan of the City having met universal applause (as far as my information goes)—and Major L'Enfant having become a very discontented man, it was thought that less than from 2500 to 3000 dollars would not be proper to offer him for his services: instead of this, suppose five hundred guineas and a lot in a good part of the City was to be substituted? I think it would be more pleasing, and less expensive.

I have never exchanged a word with Mr Roberdeau since he came to this place, consequently, am unable to relate, what his expressions have been, or what his ideas are; he lives with, and more than probably partakes of the sentiments of Majr L'Enfant; unless the dismission of the latter may have worked a change in them, which, not unlikely, is the case with both; as I can hardly conceive that either of them contemplated the result of their conduct.

Although what I am going to add may be a calumny, it is nevertheless necessary you should be apprised of the report that Colo. Deakins applies the public money in his hands to speculative purposes; and is unable, at times, to answer the call of the workmen, an instance has been given. There are doubts also of the sincerity of Mr Frans Cabot. Of both these matters you are to judge from the evidence before you. I have nothing to charge either with, myself: these hints are disclosed in confidence, to place you on your guard.

The idea of importing Germans and Highlanders, as Artizans and labourers, has been touched upon in the letter from Mr Jefferson to the Commissioners[7]—It is, in my opinion worthy of serious consideration in an œconomical point of view, & because it will contribute to the population of the place. The enclosed extract of a letter from General Lincoln to Mr Lear is sent, that you may see the prospect in that Quarter.[8] The General is a candid undesigning man, in whose word much confidence may be placed; and having been in this City, & lately returnd from it, has had opportunities of making the remarks which are contained in the extract.

I began with telling you, that I should not write a lengthy letter, but the result has contradicted it. It is to be considered as a private letter, in answr to yours of the 26th Ulto; but it may under that idea be communicated to your associates in Office—They, & you, must receive it, blotted & scratched as you find it, for I have not time to copy it. It is now ten oclock at night (after my usual hour for retiring to rest) and the mail will be closed early tomorrow morning.[9] Sincerely & affectionately I am—Yours

Go: Washington

ALS (letterpress copy), DLC:GW; LB, DLC:GW. The mutilated text is supplied within angle brackets from the letter-book copy.

1. GW had written to Stuart on 7 Mar.: "By the Post on friday—whi⟨ch⟩ in its usual course will reach George To⟨wn⟩ on Monday, I will write you (if I can) more fully for I am exceedingly pressed—this only serves to acknowledge the receipt of your letter of the 26th Ult. and to assure you of the sincere est. & regard with which I am—Dr Sir Yr Obedt Servt" (ADfS, owned [1983] by Mr. Thomas J. Budnik, Alexandria, Va.; LB, DLC:GW).

2. Ill health prevented Thomas Johnson from attending the February session of the Supreme Court in Philadelphia (see David Stuart to GW, 26 Feb. 1792).

3. For the buildings that the state of Pennsylvania was constructing for the use of the federal government, perhaps in an attempt to keep the U.S. capital in Philadelphia, see Thomas Jefferson to GW, 27 Mar. 1791, and note 5, and GW to Jefferson, 1 April 1791. For the Pennsylvania legislature's decision to build a presidential mansion in Philadelphia, see Tobias Lear to GW, 21 Sept. (first letter), n.7, 25, 30 Sept., and GW to Lear, 26 Sept. 1791. Gov. Thomas Mifflin had notified the Pennsylvania assembly on 25 Feb. 1792 that in his effort "to obtain a satisfactory plan and estimate of the expense of a suitable building" for the president he had found that the construction "will require a greater sum than remains of the appropriated fund." If the assembly should "be disposed to augment the appropriation, permit me to suggest, that the tax on pleasurable carriages being principally paid by the citizens of Philadelphia, might, with some propriety, perhaps, be applied to an object which is to be peculiarly ornamental to the city" (*Pa. Archives,* 4th ser., 4:223–24).

4. GW apparently added the remainder of this sentence to the letterpress copy after the original impression had been made.

5. For Thomas Johnson's letter to Thomas Jefferson of 29 Feb. 1792, see *Jefferson Papers,* 23:164–67.

6. A marginal note at this point in the letterpress copy reads: "⟨*Illegible*⟩ will be a ⟨*illegible*⟩."

7. For Jefferson's letter to the D.C. commissioners of 6 Mar., see ibid., 224–28.

8. Although the enclosed extract has not been identified, a draft of Benjamin Lincoln's letter to Tobias Lear dated "Boston Feby 1792" is located at MHi. In it Lincoln writes that "Since my return hom[e] I have heard much about the federal City and that there is a secret influence constantly at work to counter act the intentions of the late Congress" to move the capital of the United States from Philadelphia to the federal district. Lincoln did "not beleive that to be the wish of this State [Massachusetts] though it is manifestly so of others—I should be more anxious on this occasion than I now am did I not beleive that it was in the power of the friends of a removal to make the matter certain by proper exertions—Preperations must certainly be made for the reception and accomodation of Congress should this be omitted the opposers to the measures would be furnished with new and incontestable argument in support of their doctrine." Lincoln believed that there was never a more "favourable moment to lay a sure foundation for the accomplishment of an object so interesting to the general Government"; that "This from every view of the matter is the time when the public should come forward with spirit if they do, in an exact ratio, as they advance in these preperations the hopes of their opposers must dwindle"; that consideration should be given to the "augmentation of the number" of commissioners; and that "This is the moment for making entreaty for men and materials." Lincoln concludes that "If after all it should be said that we are not in possession of the means to pursue this business with vigour I cannot persuade my self as it is an object of so much importance to Virginia & Maryland but that an application to them for a loan of a certain sum would succeed a small sum now will do much more than a large sum will do hereafter" (MHi: Lincoln Papers).

9. GW sent this letter under cover of a letter to the D.C. commissioners dated 9 Mar., in which he wrote: "The enclosed is an answer to a private letter from Doctr Stuart, It relates as his did wholly to the Affairs under your direction—and may therefore be opened by either of the Comrs but by no other, as there are some confidential communications to them *alone*" (ADfS, DLC: GW; LB, DLC:GW).

From Thomas William Ballendine

Sir— Dumfries [Va.] the 9th of March 1792

Under expectation that appointments are now going on of Officers for the war against the Indians I offer myself for such an one as it may be judged I am capable of doing justice to my active

Service as a Soldier is yet to learn, and as an Officer too but as I apprehend the Duty of a Captain to one desirous of being taught is but little more difficult than that of an Ensign, a Captain I would wish to be appointed & one either in the Foot or Cavalry—It has been my Lott to get the little of my hardly earned Knowledge by Experience & that I may know how to value justly the Worth of Soldiers fighting for their Country it seems to me best to know what it is to do so. If others recruit their men with the Bounty allowed I can do it either in this or the Back Country. Your Most humble Servant

Thos Wm Ballendine

ALS, DLC:GW.

Thomas William Ballendine, who had attended the College of William and Mary in 1779 and 1780 and had been a member of Phi Beta Kappa, apparently did not receive a military appointment from GW.

From Alexander Hamilton

Treasury Departt 9th Mar. 1792.

The Secretary of the Treasury has the honor respectfully to enclose to the President of the United States a Petition to the President from Samuel Davis of the State of Rhode Island & Providence Plantations, together with the papers from the files of the Treasury relative thereto.[1] These last are transmitted with the Petition at the request of the honorable Mr Bourne of that State, who has applied in behalf of the Petitioner.

LB, DLC:GW.

1. The enclosures have not been identified. Capt. Samuel Davis, the master of the schooner *Sally,* had illegally landed two bales of cotton in Tarpaulin Cove on the south shore of Naushon Island in the Elizabeth Islands of Massachusetts's Buzzards Bay in July 1791. After a jury at Salem, Mass., in early September had been unable to agree on a verdict, the case was referred to the Massachusetts circuit court, before which Davis pleaded guilty to false swearing in November and was sentenced to jail until he paid a fine of $50. According to the State Department memorandum book (DNA:PCC, item 187), GW issued Davis a pardon on 21 June 1792. For more information about the case, see Benjamin Lincoln to Hamilton, 29 July, 9 Sept. 1791, and Hamilton to Lincoln, 7 Oct. 1791, in Syrett, *Hamilton Papers,* 8:583–84, 9:194–95, 293.

Thomas Jefferson's Memorandum of a Meeting of the Heads of the Executive Departments

[1]792. Mar. 9. A Consultation at ⨀.[1]
present H[amilton] K[nox] & J[efferson].

1. Subject. Kirkland's letter. British idea of a new line from Genesee to Ohio. see extract on another paper.[2]

deputation of 6. nations now on their way here.[3] their dispositions doubtful. Street, a Connecticut man, a great scoundrel coming with them. ¼ of the nation agt us. other ¾ qu.

agreed they should be well treated, but not overtrusted.

Pond's report. Stedman's report. these two persons hd bn to Niagara, where they had much conversation with Colo. Gordon, commandg officer.[4] he sd he had relation of St Clair's defeat from a sensible Indn who assured him the Indns had 50. killed & 150. wounded. they were commanded by Simon Girthy, a renegado white from Virginia or Pennsylvania. He sd the Indns were right, that we shd find them a powerful enemy, they were improving in war, did you ever before hear, says he of Indns being rallied 3. times? (this rallying was nothing more than the returns on the 3 charges with bayonets made by our troops, which produced a correspondent retirement of the Indns but not a flight.) that we should never have peace of the Indns but thro' the mediation of Britain. that Britn must appt one Comm[issione]r the U.S. one, the Indns one: a line must be drawn, & Britn guarantee the line & peace. Pond says the British have a project of settling 1000 fam[ilies] at the Illinois. that Capt. Stevenson, who was here some time ago, & who came over with Govr Simcoe, was sent here to Hammond to confer about these matters. (Stevenson staid here 5. days & we know was constantly with Hammond)[5] Colo. Gordon refused to let Pond and Stedman go on. they pretended private business, but in reality had been sent by the President to propose peace to the North Wn Indns.

H[amilton] doubts Pond's truth & his fidelity, as he talks of a close intimacy with Colo. Gordon.

J[efferson] observes that whether Pond be faithful or false, his facts are probable, because not of a nature to be designedly communicated if false. besides they are supported in many points from other quarters.

It seems that the English exercise jurisdiction over all the country South of the Genisee, & their idea appears, to have a new line along that river, then along the Allegeney to Fort Pitt, thence due West or perhaps along the Indn lines to the Missisipi, to give them access to the Mississippi. H[amilton] here mentd that Hammond in a conversation with him had spoke of settling our incertain boundary from the lake of the wood *due West to the Missi.*, by substituting from the lake of the wood *in a streight line to the head* of the Missi.

Agreed unâ voce never to admit British mediation.

H[amilton] proposed that a summary statement of all the facts we are possessed of relative to the aid by the British to the Indns be made & delivered to Pinkney to form a representation on it to the C[our]t of London.

J[efferson] observed it wd be proper to possess mister Pinkney of all facts, that he m[us]t at all times be able to meet the Brit. Min. in conversation, but that whether he shd make a representation or not, in form, dependd on another questn Whether it is better to keep the negociation here, or transfer it there? for that certainly any proceedg there wd slacken those here & put it in their power gradually to render them the principal. the Pr[esident] was of opn the negociation shd be kept here by all means.

Shall any thing be said here to Hammond. J[efferson]. no. there is no doubt but the aids given by subordinate officers are with secret approbation of their court. a feeble complt to Hammond then will not change their conduct, & yet will humiliate us.

Qu. proposd by Pr[esident]. shall a person be sent to the N. Western Indns by the way of Fort Pitt & Vincennes to propose peace? K[nox] observed that such a person cd at this season be at Vincennes in 25. days & recommended one Trueman, & that he shd from Ft Washington take some of the Indn prisoners as a safeguard.[6] agreed nem[ine] con[tradicente] but the person to be further considd of.

Qu. shall a 2d deputation be procured from the Indns now expected here, to go to same place on same object. H[amilton]. no. it will shew too much earnestness. J[efferson]. no for same reason, & because 2 deputations independt of each other might counterwork each other. Pr[esident]. no for the last reason.[7]

J[efferson] proposed taking a small post at Presque isle. 1. to cut off communication betw. 6. natns & Westn Indns. 2. to vindicate our right by possession. 3. to be able to begin a naval preparation. H[amilton] contra. it will certainly be attacked by Eng. & bring on war. we are not in a condition to go to war—K[nox] as usual with H[amilton]. Pr[esident]. whenever we take post at Presq. isle it must be by going in great force, so as to establish ourselves completely before an attack can be made, & with workmen & all materials to create a fleet instanter: & he verily beleives it will come to that.[8]

Brant says he has resigned his Eng. commission & means to become entirely an Indn & wishes to head & unite all the Indns in a body.

The Pr[esident]'s answer to St Clair's letter of resignation considered.[9] it was drawn by Knox. the passage was now omitted to which I objected in my note to the Pr[esident] of Mar. 2. K[nox] wished to insert something like an approbation of all his conduct by the Pr[esident]. I said if the Pr[esident] approvd all his conduct it wd be right to say so. Pr[esident] sd he hd always disapprovd of two things 1. the want of information. 2. not keepg his army in such a position always as to be able to display them in a line behind trees in the Indn manner at any moment. K[nox] acquiesced, & the letter was alterd to avoid touching on any thing relative to the action, unless St Clair shd chuse to retain a clause acknolegg his zeal that day.

The future commander talked of.[10]

Pr[esident] went over all the characters, viz. Morgan. No head. health gone. Speculator.

Wayne. brave & nothing else. deserves credit for Stony pt but on another occasion run his head agt a wall where success was both impossible & useless.

Irwin. does not know him. has formd a midling opinion of him. H[amilton]. he never distingd himself. all that he did during war was to avoid any censure of any kind.

Wilkinson. brave, enterprising to excess, but many unapprovable points in his character.

Lee. a better head & more resource than any of them. but no economy, & being a junior officer, we shd lose benefit of good seniors who wd not serve under him.

Pinkney. sensible. tactician. but immersed in business, has refused other appointments & probably will refuse this or accept with reluctance.

Pickings. Genl Pinkney recommends him for Southern command if necessary. sensible, modest, enterprising, & judicious. yet doubtful if he is equal to commd of 5000. men. wd be an untried undertaking for him.

J[efferson] mentd Sumpter. K[nox] intimated he must be commander in chief or nothing. incapable of subordination.

nothing concluded.

Qu. proposed. shall we use Indns agt Indns & particularly shall we invite the 6. natns to join us. K[nox] agreed there were but 36. of them who joined the enemy last year, & that we cd not count on more than the Cornplanter & 200 to join us. J[efferson] agt employing Indns. dishonorable policy—he hd rathr let 36. take the other side than have 200. on ours. H[amilton] disliked employing them. no dependance—barbarians, treach. K[nox] for employing 500.

Pr[esident]. they must be employed with us or they will be against us. perhaps immaterial as to 6. nations but material as to Southern. he would use them to scour round the army at a distance. no small parties of enemy could approach thro. them to discover our movements. He wd notwithstanding take same precautions by our own men, for fear of infidelity. expensive, discontented, insubordinate. Conclusion. they shall not be invited, but to be told that if they cannot restrain their young men from taking one side or the other, we will receive & employ them.

AD, DLC: Jefferson Papers. Jefferson noted at the foot of the document that it was "written this 10th of Mar. 92." In his Summary Journal of Public Letters, he referred to the memorandum as "Notes of consultation on our affairs with Gr. Br. in the North, on our war & conferences with Indians—characters of General officers" (DLC: Jefferson Papers).

1. Jefferson's symbol indicates that the meeting took place at the presidential mansion in Philadelphia.

2. For Jefferson's extract of Samuel Kirkland's letter to Henry Knox of 25 Feb. 1792, see GW to Jefferson, 7 Mar. 1792, source note.

3. For the administration's invitation to the leaders of the Six Nations to visit Philadelphia, see Timothy Pickering to GW, 21 Mar., n.1.

4. For the unsuccessful mission of Peter Pond and William Steedman, see Henry Knox to GW, 9 Jan. 1792, n.1.

5. John Graves Simcoe (1752–1806), who during the Revolutionary War had commanded the Queen's Rangers, rising to the rank of lieutenant colonel, and had been captured along with Lord Cornwallis at Yorktown, Va., in 1781, entered Parliament in 1790. Upon the division of Canada in 1791, Simcoe was appointed the first lieutenant governor of Upper Canada. In the fall of 1794,

he was transferred to the recently captured island of Saint Domingue and given the rank of major general. Simcoe returned to England in 1797, where, as a lieutenant general, he continued to serve in the British army until his death in 1806. Charles Stevenson of the 5th Regiment served as one of Simcoe's aides during his tenure in Upper Canada.

6. For the peace mission of Capt. Alexander Trueman, who was promoted to major on 9 April, see Knox to GW, 1 April 1792, n.2.

7. GW apparently changed his mind about sending a deputation of Iroquois on a peace mission to the hostile Indian nations of the Northwest (see Israel Chapin to Knox, 17 July, enclosed in Knox to GW, 7 August).

8. For the president's reluctance to risk war with Britain by moving militarily against the northwestern posts retained by the British in defiance of the Treaty of Paris of 1783, see GW to Knox, 13 Aug. 1792. On 11 Mar., Jefferson wrote, as "another proof" of Alexander Hamilton's communicating with British minister George Hammond: "at one of our consultations about the first of Dec. I mentd that I wished to give in my report on Commerce, in which I cd nt avoid recommendg a commercial retaliation agt Gr. Br. H[amilton] opposed it violently; & among other arguments observed that it was of more importance to us to have the posts than to commence a commercial war, that this & this alone wd free us from the expence of the Indn wars, that it wd therefore be the height of imprudce in us while treating for the surrender of the posts to engage in any thing which wd irritate them, that if we did so, they wd naturally say 'these people mean war, let us therefore hold what we have in our hands.' this argument struck me forcibly, & I said 'if there is a hope of obtaining the posts, I agree it wd be imprudent to risk that hope by a commercial retaliation. I will therefore wait till mister Hammond gives me in his assignment of breaches, & if that gives a glimmering of hope that they mean to surrender the posts, I will not give in my report till the next session.' now Hammond had recd my assignment of breaches on the 15th of Dec. and about the 22d or 23d had made me an apology, for not having been able to send me his counter-assignment of breaches, but in terms which shewed I might expect it in a few days. from the moment it escaped my lips in the presence of Hamilton that I wd nt give in my rept till I shd see Hammond's counter-complaint & judge if there were a hope of the posts, Hammond never said a word to me on any occasion as to the time he should be ready. at length the Presidt got out of patience & insisted I shd jog him. this I did on the 21st of Feb. at the President's assembly, he immediately promised I should have it in a few days and accordingly on the 5th of Mar. I recd them" (Jefferson's Memoranda of Consultations with the President, 11 Mar.–9 April 1792, DLC: Jefferson Papers).

9. For the drafting of a reply to Maj. Gen. Arthur St. Clair's letter of resignation, see Knox to GW, 1 Mar., GW to Jefferson, 2 Mar., Jefferson to GW, 2 Mar., and GW to St. Clair, 28 Mar. 1792.

10. For GW's undated notes on the candidates for the command of the new military force authorized by Congress, see his Memorandum on General Officers, this date.

Memorandum on General Officers

[Philadelphia, 9 March 1792][1]

The following list contain the names of all the General Officers now living, & in this Country, as low as *actual* Brigadiers inclusively. Except those who it is conjectured would not, from age, want of health, & other circumstances come forward by any inducements that could be offered to them—& such as ought not to be named for the important trust of Commander in Chief.

Major General Lincoln. Sober, honest, brave and sensible, but infirm; past the vigor of life—& reluctantly (if offered to him) would accept the appointment.

Majr Genl Baron de Steuben[.] Sensible, Sober & brave; well acquainted with Tactics & with the arrangement & discipline of an Army. High in his ideas of Subordination—impetuous in his temper—ambitious—and a foreigner.

Majr Genl Moultree. Brave, & it is believed accommodating in his temper—Served the whole of last War; & has been an Officer in the preceeding one, at least had been engaged in an Expedition against the Cherokees; having defeated them in one or two considerable actions. What the resources or powers of his mind are—how active he may be—and whether temperate or not, are points I cannot speak to with decision, because I have had little or no opportunities to form an opinion of him.

Brigadier (but by Brevet Majr General) McIntosh. Is old and inactive; supposed to be honest and brave. Not much known in the Union, and therefore would not obtain much confidence, or command much respect; either in the Community or the Army.

Majr General (by Brevet) Wayne. More active & enterprizing than judicious & cautious. No œconomist it is feared. Open to flattery—vain—easily imposed upon—and liable to be drawn into scrapes. Too indulgent (the effect perhaps of some of the causes just mentioned) to his Officers & men. Whether sober—or a little addicted to the bottle, I know not.[2]

Majr Genl (by Brevet) Weedon. Not supposed to be an Officer of much resource though not deficient of a competent share of understanding; rather addicted to ease & pleasure; & no enemy it is said to the bottle; never has had his name brot forward on this acct.

Majr Genl (by brevet) Hand. A sensible & judicious man; his

integrity unimpeached; and was esteemed a pretty good Officer. But, if I recollect rightly, not a very active one. He has never been charged with intemperance to my knowledge; His name has rarely been mentioned under the present difficulty of chusing an Officer to commd, but this may, in a great measure, be owing to his being at a distance.

Majr Genl (by brevet) Scott. Brave, & means well; but is an Officer of inadequate abilities for extensive command; &, by report, is addicted to drinking.

Majr Genl (by Brevet) Huntington.[3] Sober, sensible, and very discreet. Has never discover'd much enterprize; yet, no doubt has ever been enter[t]ained of his want of spirit, or firmness.

Brigadier General Wilkenson. Is, *by brevet* Senr to those whose names follow—but the appointment to this rank was merely honorary. and as he was but a short time in Service, little can be said of his abilities as an Officer. He is lively, sensible, pompous and ambitious; but whether sober, or not, is unknown to me.[4]

Brigadier General Gist. Little has ever been said of his qualifications as a General Officer. His activity, & attention to duty is somewhat doubtful; tho' his spirit, I believe, is unimpeached.

Brigadier General Irvine. Is sober, tolerably sensible and prudent. It is said he is an œconomist; and supported his authority whilst he was entrusted with a seperate command. But I have no recollection of any circumstance that marks him as a decidedly good, or indifferent Officr.

Brigadier General Morgan. Has been fortunate, & has met with eclat. Yet there are different opinions with respect to his abilities as an Officer. He is accused of using improper means to obtain certificates from the Soldiers. It is said he has been [(]if the case is not so now) intemperate; that he is troubled with a palpitation which often lays him up. And it is not denied that he is illiterate.[5]

Brigadier General Williams. Is a sensible man, but not without vanity. No doubt, I believe, is entertained of his firmness—and it is thought he does not want activity; but it is not easy, where there is nothing conspicuous in a character, to pronounce decidedly upon a Military man who has always acted under the immediate orders of a superior Officer; unless he had been seen frequently in Action. The discipline, interior œconomy & police of his Corp is the best evidence one can have of his talents in this line and of this, in the case of Genl Williams I can say nothing; as he was appointed a Brigadier after he left the Northern to join the Southern Army. But a material objection to him is delicate health (if there has been no change in his Constitution)—for he has gone to the Sweet Springs two or three years successively in such bad health as to afford little hope of his ever returning from them.[6]

Brigadier General Rufus Putnam. Possesses a strong mind—and is a discreet man. No question has ever been made (that has come to my knowledge) of his want of firmness. In short, there is nothing conspicuous in his character—And he is but little known out of his own State, and a narrow circle.[7]

Brigadier Genl (by brevet) Pinckney. A Colonel since Septr 16th 1776; but appointed a Brigadr by brevet at the close of the War, *only*. In this Gentleman many valuable qualities are to be found. He is of unquestionable bravery—Is a man of strict honor, erudition & good sense: and it is said has made Tactic's a study—But what his spirit for enterprize is—whether active or indolent; or fitted for arrangement, I am unable to say—never having had any opportunity to form a judgment of his talents as a Military character. The capture of Charleston put an end to his Military Services; but his junr Rank, and being little known in this part of the Union, are the two considerations most opposed to him, particularly the latter, as it is more than probable his being a prisoner prevented his promotion; which ought not to be any bar to his ranking as a Brigadier from the time that others of his standing as a Colonel, were promoted.

The above, and foregoing, closes the list of *all the General Officers* who as has been observed from age—want of health—disinclination, or peculiar circumstances, can be brought into view; from whom to chuse an Officer to command the Troops of the U.S.

If from either of the three Major Generals, which have been mentioned; or from those made so by *brevet,* the Commander of the Troops should be taken, no junior Officer can decline serving on the score of Rank; although he may desire, and have had expectations of being—first in command—himself.

Under this idea, and upon the principle of distribution, the arrangement of the Commanding Officer, and those next in grade to him, may be placed in the following points of view.

Commander
Lincoln or Moultree.

Under either of these Major Generals might serve as Brigadiers

Wayne unless by being a Majr Genl by brevet—& seeking the command himself—he should recoil at it.

Morgan for one of the above reasons would also revolt—viz.—command—or Williams—or Darke.

Wilkinson

Pickens

Brooks[8]

If Pennsylvania gives the Commanding Officer, and he is of the Rank (by brevet) of Majr Generl; the above arrangement is equally applicable on the principle of distribution, & as unexceptionable on the score of rank. But if, in the first case, Wayne, Morgan and Williams refuse to serve, and in the Second, the two last do it, unless it be as Commander; then some others, junr in dates of Commission, or of inferior rank, must be resorted to.

If upon a full view of characters, and circumstances, General Pinckney should be deemed the most eligable for the command; it would be a fruitless attempt, & a waste of time to propose to those Officers who have been his Seniors, to engage again subordinately; especially if they have been his seniors in the line of *Colonels*: and here I would draw a line which I think is a just one—and that is—that his Colonels, & not his Brigadrs Commission, ought to decide his Rank as a Generl Officer—because it would be hard upon him to suffer in it on acct of his captivity; when motives of policy and not of demerit, suspended (as may fairly be presumed) his promotion during that period: but why, when it did take place, Rank was not (to a certain antecedant date) restord I am unable to conceive.

If this be fair reasoning (and I really think it is) neither Morgan nor Williams would have ground to object against serving under Pinckney. but as it is more than probable they will look to what is, rather than to what ought to be; a difficulty would be made on the subject of Rank—especially if there is any derilliction in them to the Service in any other character than that of Commanding it—and therefore it would be expedient perhaps to look for Officers of Junr Rank—& in that case may come in as—

Brigadiers

Wilkenson—whose rank is very questionable
Darke—or Howard
Willet[9]—or Smith
Brooks.

If Governor Lee should be prefered to the Command, then Officers of lower grades than any that have been mentioned, in the preceeding pages must be sought after, as all of those are greatly his Seniors, & their being, in my opinion but little ground to hope that either the Military talents which he has displayed in the course of the War, or his present dignified Station, would reconcile any of them to act a subordinate part; except it be Wilkenson; who, as has been observed before, from having been but a short time in Service, & quitting it at an early period of the War, would have but little or no cause to complain. As also Pickens, who has never been in the Continental line. The arrangemt wd then be in this case—

Govr Lee Commander

Brigadrs

Wilkenson
Pickens

ADf, N.

Soon after St. Clair's defeat in November 1791, the administration began preparing another major military offensive against the hostile Indian nations of the Northwest (see Henry Knox to GW, 26 Dec. 1791, n.2, GW to the U.S. Senate and House of Representatives, 11 Jan. 1792, n.2, and Knox to GW, 1 Mar. 1792, source note).

1. GW apparently prepared this document sometime on or before 9 Mar. 1792, when he discussed military appointments with his department heads (see Thomas Jefferson's Memorandum of a Meeting of the Heads of the Executive Departments, 9 Mar.; see also GW to Jefferson, 10 March).

2. On 1 April, Knox sent GW a letter from Anthony Wayne, whose disputed election to Congress had been nullified by a unanimous resolution of the House of Representatives on 16 Mar. (see Wayne to GW, 13 Mar., n.2). GW wrote Knox on 4 April to ask whether Wayne had yet decided to accept the commission of major general if it was offered to him. The president nominated Wayne to that rank three days later (see GW to the U.S. Senate, 9 April 1792).

3. Jedediah Huntington (1743–1818), who had been a colonel in the Lexington Alarm in 1775 and commanded one of Connecticut's regiments during the first two years of the Revolutionary War, was promoted to brigadier general in May 1777. He served in that capacity until the close of the conflict. Huntington later helped draw up the Institution of the Society of the Cincinnati, and he presided over the Connecticut branch of the society during the 1780s.

4. GW apparently later asked the secretary of war for further information about James Wilkinson, for on 24 Mar., Knox wrote Tobias Lear that Wilkinson had never served as a colonel (DLC:GW). GW nevertheless nominated Wilkinson a brigadier general on 9 April (see GW to the U.S. Senate, 9 April).

5. Gossip surrounding Morgan's purchase of depreciated military certificates from his soldiers first arose toward the end of the Revolutionary War. Whether his intention was to aid his troops by purchasing the securities from men who desperately needed the money or his motivations were less charitable has never been definitively established. Although proof of impropriety is lacking, Morgan's purchase of the certificates did place him "in a position susceptible of criticism" (Higginbotham, *Daniel Morgan,* 176). GW apparently asked Knox for further information about Morgan, for the secretary of war on 24 Mar. wrote Lear: "I cannot at this moment ascertain the Colonels Rank of Daniel Morgan but I beleive it was the 1 Jany 1777" (DLC:GW). GW nominated Morgan a brigadier general on 9 April, after attempting to ascertain whether Morgan would accept the commission or not. Morgan did not, and Knox sent Lear on 5 May Morgan's letter of declination (DLC:GW; see also GW to Thomas Jefferson, 30 Mar., 4 April, and GW to the U.S. Senate, 9 April 1792).

6. After unsuccessfully attempting to discover whether Otho Holland Williams would accept a commission as brigadier general, GW nominated him on 8 May (see Knox to GW, 8, 12 May, and GW to the U.S. Senate, 8 May [second letter]). Williams declined the commission for health reasons (see Williams to GW, 13 May).

7. GW nominated Rufus Putnam a brigadier general after Marinus Willett declined his commission (see GW to the U.S. Senate, 3 May [third letter]).

8. GW placed asterisks before the names of Andrew Pickens and John Brooks and noted that "If Lincoln commands, Brooks cannot be appointed and if Moultree commands, the same will happn to Pickens." John Brooks, who was serving as federal marshal for Massachusetts, replied conditionally to the secretary of war's apparent query whether or not he would accept a commission as brigadier general. At 3:00 P.M. on 3 May, Knox sent Lear a letter "just received from Genl Brooks—the time he requires seems to be the principal difficulty. Will you please to submit it to the President—It is necessary I should answer it this evening, therefore please to return it to me" (DLC:GW). GW nominated Brooks a brigadier general on 9 April, but Brooks declined the commission (see GW to the U.S. Senate, 9 April, and Knox to GW, 20 May).

9. After receiving a letter of Marinus Willett's from Knox on 1 April, GW nominated Willett a brigadier general (see Knox to GW, 1 April, and GW to the U.S. Senate, 9 April). Willett declined the commission, however (see Willett to GW, 15 April, n.1).

To the United States Senate and House of Representatives

United States [Philadelphia] March 9th 1792.

Gentlemen of the Senate, and of the House of Representatives.

I now lay before you a General Account rendered by the Bankers of the United States at Amsterdam of the payments they had made between the 1st of July 1790 and 1791 from the fund deposited in their hands for the purposes of the Act providing the means of intercourse between the United States, and foreign Nations, and of the balance remaining in their hands; together with a letter from the Secretary of State on the subject.[1]

Go: Washington

DS, DNA: RG 46, Second Congress, 1791–1793, Records of Legislative Proceedings, President's Messages; retained copy (letterpress copy), DLC: Jefferson Papers; LB, DLC:GW; copy, DNA: RG 233, Second Congress, 1791–1793, Records of Legislative Proceedings, Journals.

1. For the enclosed letter from the secretary of state to GW and the account of Willink, Van Staphorst & Hubbard that it covered, see Jefferson to GW, 7 Mar. 1792 (first letter). Both the Senate and the House of Representatives read and tabled GW's message and its accompanying papers after receiving them (*Annals of Congress,* 2d Cong., 104, 452).

From Samuel Hanson

Sir Alexandria [Va.] March 10th, 1792

It is not without considerable hesitation & reluctance that I have formed the resolution of troubling you with the concerns of an Individual, by soliciting your relief in a case of official persecution under which I am labouring.

About 6 Weeks ago I submitted a part of my Grievances to the Secretary of the Treasury;[1] but, not having been favoured with a reply from that Gentleman, I hope I shall be excused in appealing to yourself, as the last Resort.

Sir, it appears that Mr Lee, from resentment of my information to you of his neglect of duty, is determined to harass and incommode me, as much as possible, in the execution of mine. In confirmation of this charge, I enclose a Copy of his official Letter to me of 9th January last.[2]

with respect to the Assistant-Measurer of Vessels, I beg leave to state that; upon my request, he appointed one about 18 Months ago, without the smallest objection—that this Person was always paid by me—and performed the duty with fidelity and accuracy, untill the said 9th Jany last, when Mr Lee thought proper to revoke the appointment, without any Complaint against the Assistant. I immediately addressed the Secretary upon the Subject. His reply was as follows: "The Collector has authority to appoint one; and, if you are willing to be at the Expence of such Assistance, and recommend a fit Person, as no doubt you will, I presume the Collector will appoint him. This Assistant to the Surveyor is only contemplated when his other duties shall render one necessary; and therefore you will perceive he is left to be agreed with and compensated by the Surveyor out of his fees for Admeasurement."[3]

A Copy of this passage I enclosed to Mr Lee, hoping and expecting he would, upon that Authority, reinstate my Assistant. But, instead of doing so, he writes to me as follows: "Whenever it shall be necessary, I shall appoint a Person to measure each and every Vessel that cannot be measured by yourself Conveniently with your other official duties."

Thus, Sir, Mr Lee reserves to himself the right of determining the necessity for my Employing an Assistant. I am far from wishing any accommodation not granted to other Surveyors. If it be said that at the great Ports the encreased number of Vessels renders an Assistant necessary, I presume my claim to the same indulgence will not be weakend by the consideration of the small proportion of business at this Port; since that Circumstance obliges me to call in the Aid of a private Employment to procure that Subsistance which my public one alone would be far from affording.

with regard to the 4th Article of Mr Lees instructions, contained in his Letter, I beg leave to ask whether it will not be sufficient to see that the deliveries of goods be conformable to the *Permits* for landing them; the Permits being Transcripts of the Entries? If it should be thought otherwise—and that my duty requires me to attend at the Custom-House, after the discharge of each Vessel—it is evident that the performance of this Article of my duty must occasion the omission of some other one, since I can not be at two places at one time.

Sir, I beg leave to represent to you that never has it been more necessary for me to have an assistant-Measurer than at this moment—for never has the press of business been greater, upon the Surveyor—And, yet Mr Lee is not here to make the Appointment, tho' he were inclined to do it. He has been absent about 3 Weeks; and I am well informed means to be very little at this Port till next Winter. Upon this head I beg the favour to be informed whether the Acts of his Deputy, during these his Absences, which are neither *occasional* nor *necessary,* be valid? And whether I ought to pay regard to, or Act upon, any documents signed by his Deputy in these Cases?

I presume that the obligation upon all the Port-Officers is the same. If so, with the utmost deference I submit whether, whilst I am so confined as never to have been absent 3 Working Days at any one time since my Appointment, and not 40 days in all—it is proper that Mr Lee (a much more important Officer) should leave the Port for 6 & 8 Weeks together, and, upon the whole, be absent 9 months out of the 12? That the Service suffers both by his Absence, and neglect, even when here, I can prove.

I request the favour that my duties may be precisely defined—that, if the appointment of an Assistant-Measurer be warranted by Law, Mr Lee may be directed to make it—and that the power of harassing and incommoding me, may be taken out of his Hands.

If my duties must be performed in the manner directed by Mr Lee in his instructions (the result of 2½ years Enquiry & deliberation—for, so long has he been in office) it is very evident I must be under the necessity of quitting either my public Employment, or my private one—(both, being too much for any one Man to go through)—tho both together furnish, as is well known, a very scanty Subsistence.[4] Relying on your wonted indulgence & benevolence to excuse the length, & freedom, of this Address, I remain, with perfect respect & Esteem, Sir your much-obliged and obedt Sert

S. Hanson of Saml

ALS, DNA: RG 59, Miscellaneous Letters.

1. Hanson's letter to Alexander Hamilton, which must have been written before 18 Jan. 1792, has not been identified (see Hamilton to Charles Lee, 18 Jan., n.3, in Syrett, *Hamilton Papers,* 10:522–23).

2. Hanson had written GW on 14 Oct. 1791 about Charles Lee's excessive absences from his post as collector of the port of Alexandria. The enclosed copy of Lee's letter to Hanson of 9 Jan. 1792 reads: "Having revised the Laws of Congress respecting such matters as concern the Custom-House department, it appears to me that every duty assigned to you as Surveyor of this district ought to be performed by yourself, unless occasional and necessary absence or Sickness shall in certain cases render it impossible.

"I refer you to the 6th & 7th Sections of the Collection Law, and the 3d 27th & 28th Sections of the Coasting Law as parts which relate to the duties of your office. The former law requires that you should 1st Superintend and direct all the Inspectors, Weighers, Measurers and Gaugers within this District[;] 2d That you should ascertain the proof of distilled Spirits[;] 3d That you should visit and inspect the Vessels which arrive within this District, and empowers you to put on board each of them one or more Inspectors[;] 4th That you should examine whether the Goods imported in any Ship or Vessel, and the deliveries thereof are conformable to the Entries of such goods and the permits for landing them.

"These two last Articles of your official duty are inseparably connected in their performance, & necessarily require you to inspect the Entries and my Books.

"The measurement of Vessels ought to be made by yourself, unless in any particular case another person be authorized to do it, which in future I shall forbear to do, unless in such special cases where the measurement cannot be conveniently made by you, upon acct of the press of other business.

"The hours of doing business in my Office are from 9 O'Clock in the morning 'till 3 O'Clock in the after-Noon, and will continue so till the 1st day of April, and according to this disposition you will regulate your official intercourse with me.

"In future it is expected you will conform to the instructions contained in this Letter" (DNA: RG 59, Miscellaneous Letters).

3. This letter has not been identified.

4. Alexander Hamilton's draft of Tobias Lear's reply to Hanson of 21 April reads: "I am directed by the President of the U.S. to acknowlege the receipt of your letter of the 10th of March and to give you the following answer. The law appears to contemplate the surveyor where there is one at a Port, as the person who is ordinarily to perform the service of measuring Vessels, and it may be inferred that the exercise of the power given to the Collector to appoint persons for the purpose is intended to be auxiliary and occasional only. Under this view of the matter and as the power of appointment is expressly vested in the Collector, there does not appear to be propriety in a special interposition to produce the arrangement you desire, contrary to his judgment of what the public service requires" (DNA: RG 59, Miscellaneous Letters).

To Thomas Jefferson

[Philadelphia]

My dear Sir, Saturday Morning [10 March 1792][1]

I was informed last Night by Mr Izard that a Comee of three, of which he was one, were to be with me on Monday Morning upon the Subject of the Algarene business. The Senate do not know how to get money for the purpose without the Agency of the Reps. & they are afraid to make the Comn.[2]

I wish you to consider this matter—& if not before, to let me see you by half-after 7 Oclock on Monday Morng.[3]

Genl Knox is to be with me on the appointments of the Officers at ten to day & will keep me employed most of the day—the forenoon I mean. Yrs &ca

G.W.

ALS, DLC: Jefferson Papers.

For the background to the captivity of a number of American sailors at Algiers and attempts to secure their release, see Mathew Irwin to GW, 9 July 1789, GW to Irwin, 20 July 1789, Isaac Stephens to GW, 23 Sept. 1789, Matthew Whiting to GW, 25 Oct. 1789, Conversation with Thomas Jefferson, 23 Mar. 1790, Jefferson to GW, 12 July, 28 Dec. 1790, and 7 Mar. 1792, enclosure, James Simpson to GW, 25 Aug. 1790, GW to the U.S. Senate, 22 Feb. 1791, Hannah Stephens to GW, 9 Dec. 1791, and Richard O'Bryen to GW, 8 Jan. 1792.

1. Jefferson endorsed this letter as having been received on 10 Mar. 1792.

2. For GW's meeting with senators Ralph Izard, Rufus King, and Robert Morris, see Conversation with a Committee of the U.S. Senate, 12 March.

3. Jefferson met with GW on 11 Mar. according to the secretary of state's Memorandum of a Conference with the President on a Treaty with Algiers of that date: "Consulted verbally by the President on whom a committee of the Senate (Izard, Morris & King) are to wait tomorrow morning to know Whether he will think it proper to redeem our Algerine captives & make a treaty with the Algerines on the single vote of the Senate without taking that of the Represent.

"My opinions run on the following heads.

"We must go to Algiers with the cash in our hands.

"where shall we get it?—by loan?—by converting money now in the treasury?

"probably a loan—m[igh]t be obtd on the Presid.'s authority but as this cd nt be repd without a subseqt act of legislature, the Represent. m[igh]t refuse it.

"so if convert money in treasury, they may refuse to sanction it.

"The subseqt approbation of the Sen. being necessary to validate a treaty they expect to be consulted before hand if the case admits.

"so the subseqt act of the Repr. being necessary where money is given—why shd nt they expect to be consulted in like manner where the case admits?

"a treaty is a law of the land. but prudence will point out this difference to be attended to in making them, viz.

"where a treaty contains such articles only as will go into execution of themselves, or be carried into execution by the judges, they may be safely made:

"but where there are articles which require a law to be passed afterwds by the legislature, great caution is requisite.

"e.g. the Consular convention with France required a very small legislative regulation. this convention was unanimously ratified by the Senate, yet the same identical men threw by the law to enforce it at the last session—& the Repr. at this session have placed it among the laws which they may take up or not at their own convenience, as if that was a higher motive than the public faith.

"therefore against hazarding this transaction without the sanction of both houses.

"The Pres. concurred. The Senate express the motive for this proposition to be a fear that the Repr. wd not keep the secret. he has no opinion of the secrecy of the senate. in this very case mister Izard made the communication to him setting next to him at table on one hand, while a lady (mistress Mclane) was on his other hand and the Fr. minister next to her, and as mister Izard got on with his communication, his voice kept rising, & his stutter belting the words out loudly at intervals, so that the minister might hear if he would. he sd he hd a great mind at one time to have got up in order to put a stop to mr Izard" (DLC: Jefferson Papers).

To John Armstrong

(Private)

Dear Sir, Philad. March 11th 1792

I am persuaded that no one will be more ready than yourself to make the proper allowances for my not having sooner acknowledged the receipt of your friendly letter of the 23d of December, as you there express a conviction that the pressure of my public duties will allow me but very little time to attend to my private correspondences.[1] This is literally the truth, and to it must be imputed the lateness as well as the brevity of this letter.

The loss of the brave Officers and men who fell in the late unfortunate affair to the westward, is, I hope, the only one which the Public sustain on the occasion, that can not be readily repaired. The loss of these is not only painful to their friends; but is a subject of serious regret to the Public. It is not, however, our part to despond; we must pursue such measures as appear best calculated to retrieve our misfortune, and give a happy issue to the business. I am sure there never was a people who had more reason to acknowledge a divine interposition in their affairs than those of the United States; and I should be pained to believe that they have forgotten that agency which was so often manifested during our Revolution—or that they failed to consider the omnipotence of that God who is alone able to protect them.

Your friendly wishes for my happiness and prosperity are received with gratitude—and are sincerely reciprocated by Dear Sir, Your affectionate & obed. Servt

Go: Washington

LB, DLC:GW.

1. Armstrong's letter of 23 Dec. 1791 from Carlisle, Pa., reads: "Nothing but my Sensibility of that pressure of mind you must Sustain from a multiplicity of publick concerns has prevented a much earlier acknowledgment of your very Satisfactory & Obligeing favour with which I was honored in february last. but having always presumed on writing your Excellency a few lines (at certain intervals) my design at present is only to touch the disaster & late loss of our troops in the West—and with you Sir, sincerely condole & regret the hard fate, of so many good Soliders & Citizens, who from their attitude & order of battle had but a small chance to secure e⟨i⟩ther life or honor! poor [Richard] Butler & perhaps other worthy men still alive when the Camp was abandoned—who could doubt, who knows the abilities of the first officers of that Army, that the only successful mode of copeing with Indians in a forrest, had not been preconcerted over & over long before that day—the partial or momentary advantage gain'd by the flanking partys only as I apprehend with Screwed baionets, would easily discover the error of the former Arrangement, but alas it was then too late either to devise a new One, or change the Old for a better. placeing the Militia in a body over the brook, permit me to say, was an unwarrentable Step, where two or three small picquets would have served a better purpose. It seems probable, that too much attachment to regular or military rule, or a too great confidence in the Artillary (which it seems formed part of the lines which had a tendency to render the troops Stationary) must have been the motives which led to the adopted Order of Action, I call it adopted because the General does not speak of having intended any other—whereby we presented a large & visible Object perhaps in close Order too, to an enemy near eno. to destroy, but from their known modes of action, comparatively invisible, whereby we may redily infer that 500 Indians were fully sufficient to do us all the injury we have Sustained, nor can I conceive them to have been many more; but tragical as the event hath been, we have this consolation, that during the action, our Officers And troops, discovered great bravery—and that the loss of a battle is not always the loss of the cause—In vain however may we expect success against our present adversaries without taking a few lessons from them, which I thought Americans had learned long ago; the principles of their military action are rational & therefore often Suc-

cessful, we must in a great degree take a similar method in order to counteract them.

"As the best of men are liable to mistakes, shall we lay all the blame of this heavy misfortune to the score of natural causes & our half surprized & mangled Army? no verily, for if we do, the last error will be greater than the first—no Sir, the people at large on behalf of whom the Action was brought on, are more essentially to blame and lost the battle! an infatuating Security seemed to pervade the minds of all men amongst us, we pondered not sufficiently the nature & importance of the Object, our lips declared there was no danger—our Creeds announce the universal Superintendance of the Deity, that the events of time & things, are in his hands—we say the Shields that defend the earth, Solely belong to him—and yet on this Occasion we either forgot or impiously neglected him! and I confess myself one of the guilty number—there were no publick adresses made to God on this Occassion, and too probably, but few private ones either. hence it appears that he went not forth with our Army, but was in very deed against us—wisdom appeared to forsake the wise (or those that ought to have been so) and the men of might could not find their hands. whether this *defect* & others of a Similer nature, may be the radical cause of our misfortunes or not, is best known to God, but reflexion carries us to that quarter & strongly presents them in that view.

"You See, very dear Sir, that whether modeish or otherwise, whether right or wrong—I have no hesitation in commiting myself to you—and am with all the Consideration & regard I am capable of—invariably Yours" (DLC:GW).

Conversation with a Committee of the United States House of Representatives

[Philadelphia, 12 March 1792][1]

The President informed the Committee that the request of the House of Representatives, contained in the Resolution now handed to him, should be complied with.[2] And added, that the letter from the King of France having been communicated to the House merely as a piece of information, and there being a Vessel to sail immediately for France he had answered the letter. But, upon learning that this Resolution had been passed in the House, the Secretary of State had been desired to get back the answer, which was already on board the Vessel, that another might be written, communicating the sentiments of the House agreeably to their request.[3]

LB, DLC:GW.

Sometime before 9 A.M. on 12 Mar., GW wrote to Thomas Jefferson: "The P—— would be glad to see Mr Jefferson immediately, and requests him to bring the Copy of the P——t's letter to the French King with him" (AL, DLC:

Jefferson Papers). Jefferson later this day described their meeting: "Mar. 12. 92. sent for by the Presidt & desired to bring the letter he had signed to the k. of France. went. he said the H. of Repr. had on Saturday [10 Mar.] taken up the communication he had made of the king's letter to him, and come to a vote in their own name, that he did not expect this when he sent his message & the letter, otherwise he would have sent the message without the letter as I had proposed. that he apprehendd the legislature wd be endeavoring to invade the executive. I told him I hd understood the house had resolved to request him to join their congratulations to his on the completion & acceptance of the constitution on which part of the vote there were only 2. dissentients ([Robert] Barnwell & [Egbert] Benson) that the vote was 35. to 16 on that part which expressed an approbation of the wisdom of the constitution: that in the letter he had signed I had avoided saying a word in approbation of the constitution, not knowing whether the King in his heart approved it. why indeed says he I begin to doubt very much of the affairs of France. there are papers from London as late as the 10th of Jan. which represent them as going into confusion. he read over the letter he had signed, found there was not a word which could commit his judgment about the constitution, & gave it me back again—this is one of many proofs I have had of his want of confidence in the event of the French revolution. the fact is that Gouverneur Morris, a high flying Monarchy-man, shutting his eyes & his faith to every fact against his wishes, & believing every thing he desires to be true, has kept the President's mind constantly poisoned with his forebodings. that the President wishes the revolution may be established I believe from several indications. I remember when I recd the news of the king's flight & capture, I first told him of it at his assembly. I never saw him so much dejected by any event in my life. he expressed clearly on this occasion his disapprobation of the legislature referring things to the heads of departments" (Jefferson's Memoranda of Consultations with the President, 11 Mar.–9 April 1792, DLC: Jefferson Papers).

At 10:00 A.M. on 12 Mar., GW sent Tobias Lear to Jefferson "to ask what answer he shall give the committee, & particularly whether he shall add to it that 'in making the communication it was not his expectation that the house should give any answer.' I told mister Lear that I thought the house had a right, independantly of legislation, to express sentiments on other subjects. that when these subjects did not belong to any other branch particularly they would publish them by their own authority; that in the present case which respected a foreign nation, the Pres. being the organ of our nation with other nations, the house would satisfy their duty if instead of a direct communication they shd pass their sentiments thro' the President. that if expressing a sentiment were really an invasion of the Executive power, it was so faint a one that it would be difficult to demonstrate it to the public, & to a public partial to the French revolution, & not disposed to consider the approbation of it from any quarter as improper. that the Senate indeed had given many indications of their wish to invade the Executive power. the Represent. had done it in one case which was indeed mischeivous & alarming, that of giving orders to the heads of the executive departments without consulting the Pres. but that the late vote for directing the Sec. of the Treasy to report ways & means, tho' carried, was carried by so small a majority & with the aid of members so notoriously under a local influence on that question, as to give a hope that the practice would be arrested, & the constnl course be taken up, of asking the Pres. to have information laid before them. but that in the prest instance, it was so far from being clearly an invasion of the Executive, & wd be so little approved by the genl voice that I cd not advise the Pres. to express any dissatisfaction at the vote of the house. & I gave Lear in writing what I thought should be his answer" (Jefferson's Memoranda of Consultations with the President, 11 Mar.–9 April 1792, DLC: Jefferson Papers). Jefferson's written answer to GW of 12 Mar. 1792 reads: "Verbal answer proposed to the President to be made to the Committee who are to wait on him with the resolution of the 10th inst. congratulatory on the completion & acceptance of the French constitution. That the President will, in his answer, communicate to the king of the French, the sentiments expressed by the H. of representatives in the resolution which the committee has delivered him" (DLC: Jefferson Papers).

1. A committee of the U.S. House of Representatives, composed of James Madison, Thomas Tudor Tucker, John Francis Mercer, John Vining, and John Page, had been appointed on 10 Mar. to convey a resolution to the president, but it did not do so until two days later. On 13 Mar., Tucker "reported that the committee had discharged the duty assigned to them" (*Annals of Congress,* 2d Cong., 457–58).

2. For the House resolution of 10 Mar., see GW to the U.S. Senate and House of Representatives, 5 Mar., n.2.

3. Later this day Lear wrote Jefferson: "The President intended that T. Lear should have left the enclosed Resolution with the Secretary of State, that he might take the sentiment therein expressed to be inserted in the reply to the King of the French" (DLC: Jefferson Papers). For the English translation of GW's final reply to Louis XVI, which covered copies of the congratulatory resolutions of the House and Senate, see GW to Louis XVI, 14 Mar. 1792. See also Jefferson to GW, 13 March.

Conversation with a Committee of the United States Senate

[Philadelphia] March the 12 [1792]

On this day a Committee of the Senate, consisting of Mr King, Mr Morris and Mr Izard waited upon the President of the United States to confer with him on the subject of a treaty between the United States and Algiers, and the redemption of the American Captives at that place.

A Committee of the Senate had reported to that Body a Resolution on the subject abovementioned. But it being apprehended that if it should be known abroad, that the United States were about entering into a treaty with the Algerines, those European Nations which are interested in the Mediterranean trade, would throw every obsticle in the way, and perhaps totally defeat the object. As much secrecy as the nature of the thing will admit would therefore be necessary for making arrangements to carry this business into effect. A difficulty arises. Money is wanting; and the Constitution of the U.S. does not permit any money to be drawn from the Treasury but in consequence of an appropriation made by law. To obtain such appropriation the matter must be brought before the House of Representatives, the doing of which will hazard a discovery and a defeat of the object.

The Committee, therefore, wished to know from the President whether he would feel himself authorized to draw money from the Treasury, without a previous appropriation, to carry this matter into effect, relying upon the readiness of the House of Representatives to sanction the thing after the treaty should be made known to them, and the causes for not desiring an appropriation previous to an application of the money. The Constitution having given to the President and two thirds of the Senate the power of making treaties, which, by becoming the law of the land, the House of Representatives, *when made,* are *virtually* bound to make such appropriations of money as may be necessary for carrying them into effect—otherwise the power of making treaties would be nugatory.

But the plain and simple question in this case is, as no Treaty does exist; no provision is made for the expences of one, or for the redemption of our Citizens in Captivity; and as neither of these purposes can be effected without a considerable advance; whether the President will hazard himself by drawing on the Treasury, or borrowing such a sum as shall or may be deemed adequate without a previous communication with the other branch of the Legislature?

The President replied, that it was a subject upon which he would wish to consider well before he gave an opinion—and that, at any rate, it would be necessary for him to know from the Secretary of the Treasury the state of the Treasury before he could decide anything upon the matter.

LB, DLC:GW.

For the background to this meeting, see GW to Thomas Jefferson, 10 March.

To the United States Senate

⟨United States [Philadelphia]
March 12th 1792.

Gentlemen of the Senate,

I now nominate the persons whose names are contained in the following lists for appointments in the Squadron of Cavalry, and also for appointments and promotions in the battalion of Artillery.

Go: Washington.

Appointments for the Cavalry.

Major	Michael Rudulph	at present a Captain in the 1st Regt
Captains	John Watts[1]	Virginia
	John Craig	Pennsylvania
	Lawrence Manning[2]	South Carolina
	John Stake	New York.
Lieutenants	Robert MisCampbell	South Carolina.
	William Winston	Virginia
	William Aylett Lee	do
	William Davidson	Maryland
Cornets	Leonard Covington[3]	Maryland
	Carleton Fleming	Virginia
	Solomon Van Renselaer[4]	New York
	James Taylor	Pennsylvania.⟩

The Battalion of Artillery.

Information of the arrangement, as it stood 3d November 1791.

Captains

James Bradford
Henry Burbeck
Joseph Savage (excepted, who resigned 15th October 1791)
Mahlon Ford

Lieutenants

Dirck Schuyler[5]
John Peirce
Moses Porter[6]
Edward Spear
Daniel McLane
Abimael Youngs Nicoll

George Ingersoll
Staats Morris

Surgeon's Mate

Nathan Hayward.

Promotions & Appointments.

Promoted		
Henry Burbeck	Major Commandant	vice Ferguson killed 4th Nov: 1791.
	Captains	
John Peirce		vice Savage resigned 15th October 1791.
Moses Porter		vice Burbeck promoted 4th November 1791.
Daniel McLane		vice Bradford killed 4th November 1791.
	Lieutenants.	
George Demlar		vice Spear killed 4th November 1791—promoted from an Ensigncy in the 2d regt to rank from 5th March 1791[7]
Appointed.		
Joseph Elliot		vice Peirce promoted S. Carolina.
Peircy Pope		vice Porter promoted Virginia.
Ebenezer Massey		vice McLane promoted Maryland.

Go: Washington

DS (incomplete), DNA: RG 46, Second Congress, 1791–1793, Records of Executive Proceedings, President's Messages—Executive Nominations; LB, DLC: GW. The DS at the DNA contains only the section of this document concerning the battalion of artillery. The missing text is supplied within angle brackets from the letter-book copy.

The Senate tabled this message when it was received on 12 March. The next day the Senate postponed considering the nominations, after ordering "That the Secretary of War report to the Senate a list of the officers on the Military establishment, specifying their respective rank, and the date of their commissions." Upon receiving the Senate's order, Knox submitted it to the president (see Knox to Lear, 13 Mar., DLC:GW). GW apparently told Knox to provide the requisite report to the Senate, which the secretary of war did on 14 March.

The Senate approved all of the nominations that day, except the one for Demlar. On 16 Mar., after receiving GW's message of the previous day which corrected the date of Demlar's rank (see note 7), the Senate also approved his nomination (see *Executive Journal,* 1:112–16). In letters of 15 and 17 Mar., Lear informed Knox of the Senate's concurrence with GW's nominations of 12 Mar. (both DLC:GW).

1. John Watts (1752–1830), who had risen to the rank of captain in the Continental dragoons during the Revolutionary War, declined the offered commission, a decision which Henry Knox forwarded to Tobias Lear on 5 May 1792 (DLC:GW). In 1799–1800, however, Watts served as a lieutenant colonel of light dragoons.

2. Although Lawrence Manning, who had served in Henry Lee's Legionary Corps during the Revolutionary War and had been wounded at the Battle of Eutaw Springs in September 1781, declined his commission, he held the rank of lieutenant colonel in the U.S. Army from 1813 to 1815.

3. Leonard Covington (d. 1813) was promoted to lieutenant in October 1792 and captain in July 1794. Covington resigned his commission in September 1795, but he returned to the service as a lieutenant colonel of light dragoons in January 1809, later rising to the rank of brigadier general in August 1813. He died from wounds received at the Battle of Chrystler's Field on 11 Nov. 1813.

4. Solomon Van Rensselaer (d. 1852) was promoted to lieutenant in September 1792, captain in July 1793, and major in January 1799. Having been honorably discharged from the U.S. Army in June 1800, Van Rensselaer returned to the service as a lieutenant colonel of N.Y. volunteers in 1812.

5. The letter-book copy includes the following note concerning Dirck Schuyler: "In Arrest, and disqualified for promotion, upon various grounds."

6. Moses Porter (d. 1822), who had been a second lieutenant in the Continental artillery during the Revolutionary War, was appointed a lieutenant in the U.S. Army in October 1786, and he was promoted to captain in November 1791, major in May 1800, and colonel of light artillery in March 1812. Porter was brevetted a brigadier general in September 1813 for his distinguished service in the campaign of that year.

7. GW informed the Senate on 15 Mar.: "Understanding that the rank of George Demlar, nominated for a Lieutenant of Artillery is, in the list transmitted to the Senate, stated to take place from the 5th of march *1791*. This was a clerical mistake entirely, as it was intended that his rank should take place under the Act of 5th of march *1792*" (LB, DLC:GW).

From Aaron Burr

Philada 13 Mar. 1792

An Opinion has for sometime prevailed that peace with the Indians is attainable; That the War has arisen from a belief: that this Government seek to disposses them of their Lands, and will cease whenever these misapprehensions are removed. Unfortunately it does not appear that we have since the commencement of hostilities conveyed to them any direct assurances of our wishes and designs towards them.

The late attempt to negociate thro' Col. Proctor at the very time when hostile expeditions were Authorized by Government and actually executed by the Kentucky Militia, could not have tended to conciliate or undeceive.[1]

If therefore the measure should be deemed in itself desireable or it should be thought not unimportant to engage more firmly the public opinion in favor of the Measures of Government; any Intimation which shall indicate a mode of access to the Indians cannot be unacceptable.

The six Nations especially those of them who are resident within the United States are known to be well disposed towards us and hitherto at Peace with the Miamis and their Allies[.] Many Individuals of these friendly Savages preserve a free intercourse with the hostile Tribes and would chearfully assist in bearing a Message or conducting Messengers[.] I am credibly informed that Brant has offered his services in this way.

Again

The Stockbridge Indians, remnant of a Moheaqunck Tribe have lately left their former residence and Joined that part of the six nations who are within the United States: They claim affinity with the Miamis, and visit them as relations; many among them may be relied on either to carry messages or conduct Agents.[2]

Thro' either of these channels it is presumed communications may be made to the Nations now at war with us. I can if necessary point out characters who are known to many of the above mentioned friendly Indians who possess their confidence and in whom they confide.

Aaron Burr

ADS, DNA: RG 59, Miscellaneous Letters. Although this document was not addressed to any particular person, the fact that it was deposited in the files of the State Department led the editors of the Burr Papers to suggest that it originally was submitted to Thomas Jefferson (Kline, *Burr Papers,* 1:101–3). The docket in the writing of Tobias Lear, which reads "From Colo. Aaron Burr Respecting an intercourse with the Western Indians 13 March 1792," however, suggests that the president viewed the document and that it probably was intended for him.

1. For the failure of Col. Thomas Proctor's peace mission to the Miami and Wabash nations in the spring of 1791, see Knox to GW, 30 May 1791, n.7.

2. The remnant of the Stockbridge Indians moved from western Massachusetts to New York after the Revolutionary War and settled on a tract adjacent to the Oneida reservation granted them by the state of New York in the Treaty of Fort Schuyler in 1788. Stockbridge sachems arrived at Philadelphia this day with leaders of the Six Nations in response to the administration's invitation (see Timothy Pickering to GW, 21 Mar. 1792, n.3). GW eventually authorized an Iroquois peace mission to the hostile northwestern Indians (see Israel Chapin to Knox, 17 July, enclosed in Knox to GW, 7 August).

From Thomas Jefferson

[Philadelphia] Mar. 13. 92.

The Secretary of State incloses to the President the letter to the King of France with the alteration he proposes for incorporating the vote of the house. if the President approves it, he will be so good as to return it in time to be written at large to-day, signed & sealed.[1] Th: J. thinks the copy of the resolution delivered the President with the signature of the Speaker will be the proper one to send. he therefore incloses him the informal copy in exchange for it.

AL, DNA: RG 59, Miscellaneous Letters; LB, DNA: RG 59, George Washington's Correspondence with His Secretaries of State; LB (photocopy), DLC:GW.

For the background to this letter, see Louis XVI to GW, 19 Sept. 1791, GW to the U.S. Senate and House of Representatives, 5 Mar. 1792, and Conversation with a Committee of the U.S. House of Representatives, 12 Mar. 1792.

1. Tobias Lear informed Jefferson this day of the president's approval of the draft letter, and Lear sent Jefferson the original resolution of the House of Representatives signed by Speaker Jonathan Trumbull. Lear added: "As it is possible that the Senate may come forward with a Resolution on this occasion; the President asks, if it would not be best to delay preparing the letter to the King as long as can be done with security to the present opportunity, in order to comprehend the sentiments of the senate if they should be expressed! The Resolution of the House is dated the 10th—the letter will therefore be dated the same, or a subsequent day" (DLC: Jefferson Papers). For the Senate's congratulatory resolution, see GW to the U.S. Senate and House of Representatives, 5 Mar., n.2. GW's reply to Louis XVI, which covered copies of both congressional resolutions, is dated 14 March.

From Joseph Wanton Rhodes

Walpole State Massachusetts

May it please Your Excellency, March 13th 1792

Although I have not the honor of being personally known to you yet I humbly wish the motive that induces me to this freedom of address may plead my Apology. In the early part of my life I was educated in the Medical line and received diaplomas from the Proffessors of medecine in the City of Philadelphia. For several years I was engaged in the different branches of my proffession, but at length a series of indisposition interupted my practice: it is some time since that my health has been reestablished, but my attempts although successfull in a degree have been inadequate by reason of an encreasing family of little ones who look up to me for support. That philanthrophy to the world; and patronage to many which are the striking features of your Excellencys character emboldens me to ask your assistance. However painfull the task on my part to surmount that diffidence (being unknown to your Excellency) in making this application, yet from the sentiments which flow from your pen I derive this pleasing hope that I ask it from one whose heart is neve⟨r⟩ more greatly awakened to all the feelings of tender sensibility than when an oportunity occurs to releive those characters that misfortune has depressed.

Should there be any vacancy in point of Office in the civil department at this or any future period, although out of the medical Line, or assistance in any other way which your Excellency might think proper to confer, wo'd be received with the most lively gratitude—An inofensive line of conduct has ever been my aim from which I claim no merit. should you require any further testimony of my moral Character than the enclos'd,[1] I fell myself so happy in that particular as to be able to give you the fullest satisfaction.

May Heaven continue to shower down on you its choicests blessings and the supreme architect of the universe in his spiritual Lodge for ever preserve you in his holy keeping, is the prayer of your devoted and Obedient serv't[2]

Joseph W. Rhodes

ALS, DLC:GW.

1. The enclosure has not been identified.

2. GW never appointed Rhodes (c.1752–1793) to any federal office.

From Robert Rutherford

Dear Sir Berkeley County, Virga March 13th 1792

My very good friend and neighbour Colo. Darke intending to wait on you, I could not forgo the pleasure of presenting my sincere good wishes, for your health and perfect happiness, and as you well know the spartan virtues of my friend, it becomes unnecessary to enlarge on the innate and Very amiable, quality's of his heart and mind. I Indeed sympathize Very tenderly with him on the death of his sons, as that of his youngest was followed by the death of his eldest son, a few days after his return home and who left a small family.[1] My own tears can never cease to flow while I breath this vitol air for the Loss of a most dutiful endearing & innocent Daughter at Norfolk in June last.[2] but these are Vicessitudes in the nature of things and we must submit.

The fatal Surprize and Slaughter of the troops (a battle it could not be termed) was very unfortunate, and by the fall of so many brave officers and men, is truly distressing. but to loos sight of this important business untill the Indians will Seriously treat for peace, would, in my opinion, be a tacit consession of fear and an acknowledgement, that every exertion, to repel their more than cruel ravages, has been wrong, and surely it is an Idea replete with insensibility, and betrays a very selfish mind to urge that the united power is not to protect so respectable and extended a frontier, the uniform rule of every wise Goverment.

I have been surprized by arguments in support of repressing the people within the old settlements, as there is something very selfish and Contracted in such reasoning. for to Say to many thousands of good Citizens, you shall remain with your posterity on the spot where you first drew breath, destitute of Lands or property, meerly to Labour on the Land of others for a very scanty subsistance, is tyrannical absurd. as it is only by the prospect of acquiring Lands on easy terms, that men with their family's and others will brave the dangers of the Atlantic, while this is the very seed time as it were of the American people, when peace and plenty await them, except this Indian war which will no doubt be shortly done away, as every exertion has been made since your administration for this desirable end, but the supine inattention of former measures, had suffered things to fall into such a train that it is very difficcult to restore them to order.

I donot mean to defend the mode of settling imprudently and in haste in every part of the widely extended, united territory, for the emolument of Company's, as such a proceeding would be pregnant with evil.

Perhaps the Indians might be reduced to a disposition for peace by recruiting Three Regiments as near the fronteirs as possible to serve for one year, if not sooner discharged, and to consist of about 600 men each with a Captain Two Lieutenants an Ensign 8 Serjeants and 4 Corporals to every 100. Rank & file. Half of each Regiment to be Horse men properly armed, as such, exclusive of their Rifles. The other half to Carry good Rifles, Hatchets, and light wooden spears pointed with steel. such a body of men would protect & plant the regular troops in garrissons where it might be judged necessary, and having these several garrissons, for retreat & supply's, would Carry terror amongst the ill disposed tribes. The regular troops need not be so numerous. The Horsemen might supply their own Horses to be paid for if lost, and as a man by long possession sets a peculiar value on this useful annimal, the owner would be more Careful of his Horse than if he were public property.

The chickasaws in the spring 1788 lost a chief of note & his son at the Clinch River on the Trace from Cumberland to the Holston in what was, termed, the Lawyers defeat.[3] Being stimulated by this injury, they had some Warriors on the unfortunate Expedition under Genl St Clair, and it is probable a respectable number of these might be engaged to act.

One Hundred and Fifty good men in proper Boats on the Ohio would be in abled to discover where parties of the enimy might Cross to give intelligence to the Inhabitants & often to detach parties by land to persue those of the Indians, with effect, not suspecting this mode of persuit.

A Colonel McMullen or McMillen well known at Kentucky and Colo. Darke Could recruit Regiments of the above description and very shortly with some proper person on the frontier of Pensilvania for the third.[4] All these to choose their own officers & to admit none but the most popular and proper, and to receive no man who had not been accustomed to the woods & of a ferm Constitution. Men imbodied in this manner would act with Vigour, united by common interest in defense of what would be most dear to them and intimately acquainted from early youth with many affinities, still more endearing.

If Colo. Darke Cannot serve, as by the Loss of his sons, his Domestic concerns loudly demand his attention, there is a son or two of the late General Lewis, altogether proper for such a duty.[5]

These Regiments commanded by a person in whom they could place entire confidence (as much depends on this, & a long acquaintance) would be exceeding formidable. Generals Morgan or Scott I have thought of perhaps the former possessing an uncommon strength of mind and full of stratagem might be prefered.[6]

I have presumed so far, on the goodness of your heart as to offer a few things, to your far superior judgement, and beg pardon for having thus in the fulness of my mind, given you the trouble of this letter, and please to observe, that I donot wish to detain you from the great multiplicity of your momentous engagements to answer things of this nature. May you with good Lady Continue to enjoy, uninterruptedly, every choice temporal blessing, is the unfeigned wish of Dear Sir Your Very affectionate And Most Obt Hble Sert

R. Rutherford

ALS, DLC:GW.

1. Lt. Col. William Darke and his son Capt. Joseph Darke were both wounded at St. Clair's defeat in November 1791; Joseph Darke later died of his wounds (see Darke to GW, 9–10 Nov. 1791). Two other sons, John and Samuel, also died in early adulthood.

2. Rutherford's youngest daughter, Margaret, had died unmarried at the age of 19.

3. Rutherford may be referring to the killing by Creek Indians of the brother and nephew of the Chickasaw chief Piomingo while they were on their way to a council with the Cherokee on the French Broad River in early June 1789 (see Alexander McGillivray to Esteban Rodríguez Miró, 24 June 1789, in Caughey, *McGillivray of the Creeks,* 238–40).

4. Rutherford may be referring to Col. James McMillan (McMullin, McMullen; 1733–1799) of Clark County, Ky., who emigrated from Scotland before

the Revolutionary War and served as a soldier on six trans-Ohio expeditions during the conflict. He moved permanently to Kentucky in 1792 and apparently served as a private on Maj. Gen. Anthony Wayne's expedition against the northwestern Indians in 1794.

5. Andrew Lewis, Sr. (1720–1781), commanded a company of the Virginia troops surrendered by GW to the French at Fort Necessity in 1754. He served on the frontier throughout the French and Indian War as major of GW's Virginia Regiment and led the Virginia forces against the Indians in the victory at Point Pleasant in 1774. Lewis was appointed a brigadier general at the beginning of the Revolutionary War but, disappointed that he had not been promoted to major general and claiming ill health, he resigned his commission in 1777. Three of his sons were referred to as colonels at this time: Andrew, Jr. (1759–1844), of Greenbrier County; Thomas, of Kanawha County; and Samuel (d. 1810), of Botetourt County, all in Virginia.

6. For GW's opinions of Daniel Morgan and Charles Scott, see his Memorandum on General Officers, 9 Mar. 1792.

From John Wade

Fort Washington [Northwest Territory]

Sir March 13th 1792

Flattered by the Honor you conferred upon me, in appointing me to an Ensigncy in the first Regiment, in the Service of the United States, and conscious that implicit obedience to the Commands of a Superior officer, is one of the first principles of a Soldier, I have made it my study so to conduct myself as to merit approbation, and I pride myself in the opinion of having in some measure met it—Honor and ambition Sir—are leading traits in military life, my attachment to that life, Joined to a sincere wish not to disappoint the friendly anxiety of the Gentlemen who so kindly interceded for my present appointment, have stimulated me to obtain as speedily as possible a Knowledge of Tactics, the little progress I have made is pleasing to me, and leads me to hope, that by perseverance and attention, I shall not reflect discredit upon my friends—a prevalence of Report furnishes me with an Expectation, that an Augmentation to the existing military establishment, will probably take place, At so early a period of my advancement in the army, a solicitation for promotion may be deemed presumption, but sanctioned by the attention of the present Commanding Officer of this Territory, and flattered by his good wishes, I am induced to solicit of your Excellency—(should my Expectations be realized) to confer upon me such superior rank to what I now hold, as you may in your better Judgment think me deserving of—In aid of this request—should an opportunity offer—I beg your Excellency to refer yourself to Major Genl St Clair, whom, I had the Honor to serve last Campaign or to Lieut. Col. Commdt Wilkinson for my Conduct since I have had the pleasure of being commanded by him. It is my ardent wish, not only to meet but merit promotion. Your Excellency will pardon this tresspass on your more important moments, and impute it to the ambition of a young Soldier who wishes to come forward, Justified by the Auspices of his Commanding officers. I have the Honor to be with the highest respect your Excellencys most Obedient Humble Servt

Jno. Wade Ensn
1st U.S. Regt

ALS, DNA: RG 59, Miscellaneous Letters.

John Wade of Elizabethtown, Pa., who had been appointed an ensign in the U.S. Army on 4 Mar. 1791, was promoted to lieutenant in April 1792 (see GW to the U.S. Senate, 9 April 1792) and to captain in December 1794. Wade resigned his commission in January 1802.

From Anthony Wayne

Sir Philadelphia 13th March 1792

I took the liberty to put into your hands (in the course of last summer) a letter from James Seagrove Esqr. mentioning the alarming emigration from *Georgia* into *East Florida* in consequence of a Proclamation of the Spanish Governor, and as I can not find it among my papers, may I request the favor, that you will please to direct, one of your Gentlemen, to make a search for it.[1] my reason for this request is, in order to shew the cause of the difference of the number of Voters, at the late Election for a member to Congress, compared with the enumeration of the Inhabitants of Camden County—the legality of which Election is disputed by Genl Jackson.[2]

I will do myself the honor to attend at the levee as soon as Congress adjourn, when I shall be happy to receive that letter if it can be found, will you have the goodness to pardon this freedom, & to believe me to be with every sentiment of Esteem sir Your most Obt & very Hume Sert

Anty Wayne

ALS, DNA: RG 59, Miscellaneous Letters.

1. James Seagrove's letter to Wayne has not been identified. For the increased emigration from the southernmost states after Spain liberalized its settlement policies in East Florida, see Thomas Jefferson to GW, 2 April 1791, n.3, and Charles Pinckney to GW, 18 Aug. 1791, n.5.

2. In January 1791 Wayne had defeated his friend James Jackson for the congressional seat of Georgia's First District. That summer Jackson accused Wayne's campaign manager, Savannah mayor Thomas Gibbons (1757–1826), of replacing the duly charged magistrates with his own friends as election judges and falsifying voting lists in at least one precinct. In a second precinct Wayne received more votes than there were eligible voters. Judge Henry Osborne of the state superior court knowingly certified the spurious returns. Wayne took his seat on 1 Nov. 1791 at the opening of the first session of the Second Congress, but two weeks later, on 14 Nov., Jackson petitioned the House of Representatives, formally contesting Wayne's election. On 16 Nov. the petition was referred to a standing committee on contested elections, which reported on 21 November. A Committee of the Whole House considered the report on 24 and 25 Nov. and resolved to hold a trial on 6 Feb. 1792, which would give Wayne time to collect his evidence. The House apparently granted Wayne two postponements, the first until 27 Feb. and the second until 12 March. On that day the House refused the request of Wayne's counsel for a further delay and began the examination of Jackson's evidence. On 16 Mar. the House unanimously resolved "That ANTHONY WAYNE was not duly elected a Member of this House." Wayne, who was never personally implicated in the election fraud, managed by another parliamentary maneuver to delay the inevitable outcome for a further week, when his noncertification was confirmed and a new election called on 21 Mar. to fill the empty seat. Neither Jackson nor Wayne ran again. John Milledge (1757–1818) was elected to represent Georgia's First District and took his seat on 22 Nov. 1792 (*Annals of Congress,* 2d Cong., 145, 150, 176, 194, 200, 210–11, 428–29, 458–72, 477–79, 670, 723). Milledge served in the House of Representatives in 1792–93, 1795–99, and 1801–2. In 1802 he was elected governor of Georgia, and between 1806 and 1809 he held a seat in the U.S. Senate.

From John Armstrong

Sir Carlisle [Pa.] 14th March 1792

Whatever may have been the constructions of others respecting the designs of Government, in marching an Armed force into the West; I shall in the present state of things reduce all other conjectures into the idea of *Peace,* viewing it with it's natural consequences not only as the primary Object of the publick measures, but that whereby the farther concerns of the Union in that country may with greater facility be accomplished. this peace we presume, from the recent triumphs of the natives & the irritations they may be Supposed to derive from british traders—must be preceded or purchased by *War,* in order to impress their minds with that conviction & temper that is essential to a serious treaty or an honorable peace.

How or by what means this conviction or dispossition, may most probably be effected appears to be a leading question—we have said it must be by War, but as this may be essayed in different modes, the question recurs to that which hath the most elligible appearance? in order to offer some answer to it, the probable effects of such modes of proceduer as we apprehend most likely to be pursued, requires a distinct consideration.

Suppose the first to be that already attempted, by marching in force to the Miam⟨i⟩ Villages or farther; this force estimated at not less than four thousand men, moving in good Order—on this hypothesis some Gentlemen have seemed to please themselves with a decisive Action & an early period to the war, but without book—the proba⟨bili⟩ty rather is, that no general Action will then happen, or if it should, the enemy will not ke⟨ep⟩ the field long enough to receive the necessary mortification, but rather reserve the⟨ir⟩ resentment for our Succeeding Convoys, our frontiers, or both—they are not idiots without some advice beside their own: their alternatives & optional power superc⟨ede⟩ the necessity of a decisive action, leaving it totaly contingent. however, say we have no⟨t⟩ gained a local possession wheresoever we chuse, the hostile enemy will immediately m⟨arch⟩ off, but they are neither defeated, conciliated, nor humbled; as far from a temper to trea⟨*mutilated*⟩ when we began, altho' we have incured an heavy expence.

Suppose another mode of proceduer, to be that of the rendezvouse of the troops ⟨at⟩ Fort Washington & the other Posts now in possession of the Federal Govt from thence by appointed partys make as many excursions into the Indian country as possible for the destruction of their towns & produce, together with such other damages as on similar occass⟨i⟩ons have been known to fall within our power. this method of business tends to the immediate & inevitable embarrassment of the enemy, and is capable not only of comparative Secrecy, variation & dispatch, but also of improvement beyond what ha⟨s⟩ yet been experienced amongst us—and applys more directly to the nature & circumstances of the enemy in question than any other—the natural consequenc⟨e⟩ wherof, is to excite fear, murmerings & depression, amongst the Squaws, Old Men and Children, which at length through their Counselors must have its operation toward peace, on the reluctant warriors themselves—preparing them to treat & listen to such terms of accomodation, as altho' we may not call them permanent, will not only yield quiet on the frontiers, but give access to the Federal Government in Erecting One or more buildings at pleasure.

But should these two different ways of proceeding be contrasted, and with respect to bringing on a treaty & the latter appear the most elligible, a farther question will yet arise—namely—whether from the Villages, or from the posts now in possession, may this desultory method of depredations on their Towns be carried on with the greatest apparent facility? from anything I can derive from the Map & having but little other information, this question altho' an important one, is not easily Solved—at present the Villages from their proximity to the hostile towns has a manifest advantage, but were our troops in possession of that Spot, these towns would suddenly be evacuated; where they would sit down is uncertain, whether in equal reach of the one place or the other—but when we know a little better where these Villagers now are, and their strength, they may possibly be considered as objects of a little chastisement before they have time either to collect their Allies or to abandon their present residence. By extending the contrast mentioned above to the preparatives necessary to each, much Saving of expence will readily appear, as considerably fewer troops may be competant to the latter, than can be thought so to the former; to which must be added the differance of transportation, together with comparative risque—or Safety of the successive Convoys—the latter mode too, supposes a number of the troops to remain in Garrison for domestick defence & improvement in discipline, wherby ⟨*mutilated*⟩ need should require the frontiers may be aided with more dispatch than the former can ⟨p⟩ossibly admit. On the whole, were it not for the important consideration of the necessary con⟨v⟩oys, these two modes would bear but little comparison, it being only in the first instance that the latter calls for any; there being nothing formidable in a direct march to the primary

Object even with three thousand men, but better prepared than the last—yet is the common maxim still to be regarded—"not to make more haste than good speed," and altho' I am unwilling to risque a peremtory or decided opinion in favour of either of those modes—yet when hesitations of some & opposition of others to any ofensive measures shall, together with some pain respecting the treasury & publick debt are taken into the question joined to the probable effects of either as mentioned above, the latter appears to claim a preference, as the necessary calculations will make more evident. for in this case, it is neither predilection for, nor mere possession of any particular Spot, (I mean in the first instance) that can secure—or comprehend the designs of Governt unless it is apparent that from such Spot above all others, the hostile temper of the enemy may with greater facility & more certainty be reduced. but against such local advantage, whether real or imaginary, must be placed the length of transportation & greater risque of suseeding Convoys, which must always remain until a disposition to treat is obtained—how far the influence of some friendly Indians may go to that purpose we cannot tell, but must first, appear in Arms & make some use of them too. I am ashamed of the want of perspicuty & brevity, as well as of the blots of this letter, which I can neither Copy nor correct if it go by this post, but happy in the confidence that the Simplicity of my meaning will be understood, therefore shall add no further appollogy than that with great truth I have the honor to be Your Excellencys Obedt humble Servt.

John Armstrong

ALS, DLC:GW.

From the Commissioners for the District of Columbia

Sir George-Town 14th March 1792

We have to acknowledge the receipt of your several dispatches to us by the last Post[1]—We regret you should have had any occasion to experience the untowardness of Majr LEnfants Temper—But without it, you could not have been so sensible of the very great disquietude which he has given us—As we were sincerely desirous, of retaining him as long as it was practiable, we cannot but lament the perverseness, which made it at length impossible.

When such was his temper, we are free to acknowledge, that we think we shall be better without him—We beg leave to assure you that we feel ourselves fully compensated by your approbation of our conduct for the troubles and dirty reports with which we have been Assailed—No diligence nor attention on our part will be wanted, to CounterAct the ill effects which the enemies to the permanent Seat, may prophecy from his dismission—It is not our intention to take up your time with a long Letter having written as fully to Mr Jefferson as the short time we have yet had to attend to the objects he has pointed out to us will permit at present[2]—We cannot conclude without assuring you that we cannot but consider the report respecting Colo. Deakins as perfectly groundless—We know on the contrary, that he more than once the last Summer when we were disappointed in our expectations from Virginia, advanced Money himself, no Complaints have even yet been made to us of our orders on him not being punctually paid—We have heard of the Suggestion you mention respecting Mr Cabot—How far this be true we cannot judge—We trust it has no better foundation than the jelouscy and reports which has of late unfortunately prevailed in George Town. We are Sir &c.

Dd Stuart
Danl Carroll

LB, DNA: RG 42, Records of the Commissioners for the District of Columbia, Letters Sent, 1791–1802. The commissioners apparently returned to GW as an enclosure to this letter Pierre L'Enfant's letter to GW of 22 June 1791 (see L'Enfant to GW, 22 June 1791, source note).

1. See GW to the Commissioners for the District of Columbia, 6 Mar. 1792.

2. The commissioners also wrote Thomas Jefferson on this date (see the Commissioners of the Federal District to Jefferson, 14 Mar. [second letter], *Jefferson Papers,* 23:278–80).

To Thomas Jefferson

[Philadelphia] Wednesday Afternoon 14th Mar. 1792

At the time Mr Jeffersons letter to the President was put into his hands, he was so much engaged as hardly to find time to read it.[1] The general purport of it, however, he well recollects was agreeable to him but whether the following ideas if they are not already substantially expressed, might not with propriety be conveyed, Mr Jefferson will judge of, and act accordingly.

That no farther movement on the part of Government, can ever be made towards Majr L'Enfant without prostration, *which will not be done.* That the P—— thinks himself insulted in the answer given to his Secretary, who was sent to him for the *express* purpose of removing some of his *unfounded* suspicions—viz. "that he had already heard enough of this matter."[2]

No farther overtures will *ever* be made to this Gentn by the Government; in truth it would be useless, for in proportion as attempts have been made to accomodate what *appeared* to be his wishes, he has receded from his own ground. If therefore his conduct should chan⟨ge⟩ and a reinstatement of him is desire⟨d⟩, the *only* way to effect it is by a direct application to the Commissioners.

AL, DLC: Jefferson Papers. For the background to this letter, see Pierre L'Enfant to GW, 21 Nov. 1791, editorial note, GW to Jefferson, 26, 28 Feb., L'Enfant to GW, 27 Feb., and GW to L'Enfant, 28 Feb. 1792.

1. This letter has not been positively identified. GW possibly is referring to Jefferson's letter to George Walker of this date, which the secretary of state may have submitted for the president's approval (see Jefferson to Walker, 14 Mar., *Jefferson Papers,* 23:283).

2. For Tobias Lear's visit to L'Enfant sometime between 17 and 22 Feb. 1792, see GW to Jefferson, 26 Feb., n.2. See also Jefferson to L'Enfant, 27 Feb., and the editorial note to "Fixing the Seat of Government" (*Jefferson Papers,* 20:70 n.202, 23:161).

To Thomas Jefferson

[Philadelphia] Wednesday [14 March 1792] ½ past 6 Oclock[1]

The P—— put Mr J——n's suggestions, respecting the Post Office, into the hands of the Postmaster Genl yesterday & requested him to be here at half past Seven (Genl Knox being soon after) this Morning. If Mr J—— is at leisure the P—— would be glad to see him here at the sametime, on that business.[2]

AL, DLC: Jefferson Papers.

1. The entry under this date in Jefferson's Summary Journal of Public Letters (DLC: Jefferson Papers) reads: "G.W. to Th: J. on the proposal to increase rapidity of Post office."

2. For the secretary of state's suggestions for expediting the postal service, see Thomas Jefferson's Memorandum of Conversations with Washington, 1 Mar. 1792, n.1. Postmaster General Timothy Pickering on 22 Mar. apparently prepared a cost estimate of postal routes as a result of the meeting of this date (see GW to Jefferson, 25 Mar., n.5; see also Jefferson to Pickering, 28 Mar., *Jefferson Papers*, 23:347–48).

To Louis XVI

[Philadelphia, 14 March 1792]

Very great, good, and dear Friend and Ally.

I receive as a new proof of friendship to the United States, the letter wherein you inform me that you have accepted the Constitution presented to you in the name of your nation, and according to which it is henceforth to be governed.[1] On an event so important to your Kingdom, and so honorable to yourself, accept the offering of my sincere congratulations, and of the Sentiments of the Senate and Representatives of the United States expressed in their resolutions now enclosed.[2]

We have watched, with the most friendly solicitude, the movements of your nation for the advancement of their happiness: we have regarded this great spectacle with the feelings natural to those who have themselves passed through like perils, and with sincere satisfaction, we have seen this second occasion proclaim your majesty, a second time, the friend and patron of the rights of mankind.

That yourself, your family and people, under the edifice which you have now completed, may repose at length in freedom, happiness and safety, shall be our constant prayer; and that God may ever have you, great and dear friend and Ally in his safe and holy keeping.

Written at Philadelphia, this fourteenth day of March 1792, and of our Independence the sixteenth. your faithful friend and Ally

George Washington.

By the President
Thomas Jefferson.

Copy (letterpress copy), DLC: Jefferson Papers; LB, DNA: RG 59, Credences; French translation, Arch. Aff. Etr., Cor. Polit., Etats Unis, 36.

For the background to this letter, see GW's Conversation with a Committee of the U.S. House of Representatives, 12 Mar., and Jefferson to GW, 13 Mar. 1792, n.1.

1. Louis XVI's letter was dated 19 Sept. 1791.

2. For the enclosed resolutions of the Senate and House of Representatives, see GW to the U.S. Senate and House of Representatives, 5 Mar. 1792, n.2.

To William Moultrie

Dear Sir, Phil. 14th Mar. 1792.

I have the pleasure to acknowledge the receipt of your letters of the 28th of november, and 29th of December, and to inform you that the plants which you had the goodness to send me, arrived safe at Norfolk (the ice not permitting the vessel to reach Baltimore) where they are put into the hands of a Gentleman, who will forward them to Mount Vernon by the first opportunity.[1]

Were I not assured of the pleasure which you take in obliging me, I should be at a loss how to express my acknowledgments for the kind attention which you have shewn to my wishes in sending these plants. But you have not, however less of my thanks from the circumstance of my knowing your goodness.

I am persuaded that Lord Wycombe will not consider Charleston as among the least agreeable of the places he has visited in the United States.[2] The acknowledged hospitality and politeness of its inhabitants can not fail of making proper impressions upon the respectable foreigners who may visit that city.

The unfortunate affair to the westward is, I hope, more to be regretted on account of the loss of those brave Officers and men who fell on the occasion, than of any other serious influence it may have on our public Affairs. We are, happily, in a situation to repair every other loss, but that of lives.

I shall give you the trouble of presenting me to the recollection of the Ladies in the circle in which you move—and that you would be assured of the sincere esteem and regard with which I am Dr Sir, Your most ob. Serv.

Go: Washington

LB, DLC:GW.

1. For Moultrie's letter of 28 Nov. 1791, see GW to Moultrie, 8 Nov., n.2. For the misadventures of the plants he sent GW from Charleston, S.C., see GW

to Otho Holland Williams, 7 Feb. 1792, n.2. See also Williams to GW, 22 Mar., and GW to Moultrie, 5 May 1792.

2. GW's letter to Moultrie of 8 Nov. 1791 introduced John Henry Petty, Earl Wycombe, son of the marquis of Lansdowne. For Wycombe's American tour, see GW to Lansdowne, 7 Nov., n.2.

To the United States Senate

United States [Philadelphia] 14th March 1792.
Appointments for twelve companies of Infantry.

	Captains.	Lieutenants.	Ensigns.
Vermont.	William Eaton	James Underhill	Charles Hyde
New York	Isaac Guion	Robert Cochran[1]	Nanning I. Vischer.
New Jersey	*Zebulon Pike	*John Read	*John Polhemus.
Pennsylvania	*Jacob Slough	*Robert Thompson	*John Paine[2]
Delaware	James Wells	*Maxwell Bines (Pennsylva)	*William Diven (Pennsylvania.)
Maryland	*Henry Carberry	*Benjamin Price	Campbell Smith.
	*William Buchannen	*Henry DeButts	*William Pitt Gassaway.
	*William Lewis	*Joseph Gough	Charles Wright.
Virginia	*Nicholas Hannah.	*William McRea[3]	*Aaron Gregg.
	*Joseph Brock	*Henry B. Towles	*Peter Grayson.
	John Heth	Samuel Tinsley	Peter Marks
North Carolina	Joseph Kerr[4]	Thoms E. Sumner	Samuel Davidson.

Gentlemen of the Senate.

I nominate the above-named persons for the commissioned officers of twelve companies—This nomination will complete the company officers of the additional troops, according to the arrangement which will hereafter be made, in pursuance of the powers vested in me by law.[5]

Go: Washington

DS, DNA: RG 46, Second Congress, 1791–1793, Records of Executive Proceedings, President's Messages—Executive Nominations; LB, DLC:GW.

A note at the end of the list reads: "Those marked with * served with reputation in the levies last year."

1. Cochran's given name was actually Samuel (see GW to the U.S. Senate, 8 May [second letter]).

2. John Paine resigned his ensign's commission in October 1792. He served as a brigadier general of Kentucky volunteers in 1812–13.

3. William MacRea (McRea; d. 1832), who had served as a lieutenant in the levies of 1791, was promoted to captain in October 1794, and he was honor-

ably discharged from the army in November 1796. MacRea returned to the service as a captain in June 1798. He was promoted to major in July 1800, lieutenant colonel in April 1814, and colonel in April 1824.

4. GW inserted this name in his own writing.

5. The Senate received GW's message from Tobias Lear on this date, read it, and ordered it to lie for consideration. The next day consideration of the nominations was again postponed. On 16 Mar. the Senate resolved to advise and consent to the appointments and ordered that the president be so informed (*Executive Journal,* 1:114–16). Tobias Lear notified Henry Knox of the Senate's concurrence on 17 Mar. 1792 (DLC:GW).

Letter not found: to Otho Holland Williams, 14 Mar. 1792. Williams wrote GW on 22 Mar.: "The receipt of your obliging letter of the 14th Instant gave me very great pleasure."

From Caleb Brewster

Sir Fairfield in Connecticut March 15. 1792

I have presumed upon your Excellency's known love of Justice, and upon the generous interest you take in the misfortunes of your old faithful military servants, to address to your Excellency the following representation; and I hope that the peculiar circumstances of my case & the unusual Sufferings that have attended my situation will be received as an apology for thus soliciting your Excellency's aid & support—I will, with your leave, submit to your Excellency a simple and short detail of the facts on which I ground this application.

In the year 1777 I was honored with a commission of Captain in the line of the State of New York and was placed on a detached service, commanding an armed boat for the purpose of cruizing in the Long Island Sound, and for the more important service of obtaining & conveying intelligence from the Enemy. Under this commission I acted till the close of the late war—Of the services I rendered in this capacity your Excellency who was acquainted with the details of these secret operations at that period, is a competent Judge[1]—Early in the war, on the shore of Long Island from an exertion of bodily labor in carrying the boat I commanded into a place of safety & concealment, I recieved a dangerous & incurable rupture which has ever since been subject to the painful & inconvenient application of those modes of local support which are common in such cases—On the 7th of December 1782 while in the aforesaid service in a bloody engagement with two armed boats of the Enemy I received a wound by a ball thro. my breast[2]—With this wound I languished & was confined two years & a half under distressing chisurgical operations & a most forlorn hope of cure. The nature of these wounds together with the impairing of my constitution by the long continuance of my confinement have rendered me incapable of any labour that requires a considerable exertion & have reduced me to the melancholy condition of an invalid for life. These are the facts on which I claimed a place on the invalid list of the United States. Of the truth of them there is ample & abundant evidence in detail from the Vouchers now in the possession of the Hon. Aaron Burr of the Senate of the United States. Having thus stated to your Excellency the merits of my situation as they existed before any application was made for public relief, I intreat your Excellency's attention to a short account of the means I have used to obtain it. At an early day I applied to Col. Richard Platt & Col. Richard Varrick authorised by the State of New York to hear & examine the claims of invalids of the New York line of the late army and produced to them my evidence & vouchers, but they refused to recommend and report me as a proper object of relief solely on the ground of A law of their state enacting that none should be placed upon the Pension list of New York, who were residents within any other State and as I was then an inhabitant of the State of Connecticut I came within the operation of this clause of exclusion. I next sollicited relief from the State of Connecticut and met here with the same ill success on the ground of my being an Officer of the line of the State of New York and not entitled to compensation according to the laws of Connecticut. In this distressing dilemma I laboured for several years under the embarrassments resulting from my personal Disability, and the enormous expences I had incurred in my long & dangerous indisposition. Early after the assembling of the Congress of the United States under the new constitution I presented a petition to Congress praying relief as an invalid of the United States and at their last session in the City of New York I obtained a resolve in my favour providing for the reimbursements of the expences I had incurred on account of my wounds; and also an allowance of half pay for life, under the express condition of my returning & giving up to the United States the commutation notes I recd in common with all the officers who had served on the continental establishment.[3] These had long since been expended at the depriciated rate of three shillings in the pound to support the expences I mentioned above & to support myself & Family. On the Credit however of this resolve & of an eventual settlement at the treasury, I procured Final settlement securities at the enhanced price of thirteen shillings & six pence in the pound and applied at the office of the Auditor of the Treasury for an adjustment in Execution of the above resolve but the Auditor refused such an adjustment unless I should deliver the identical certificates which has been issued to me in my own name. This was utterly impracticable. Despairing of relief I replaced the securities I had procured of my Friends & came home—In the course of the last winter I made another application at the Treasury and met with the same success as before—But was then informed that a bill was depending before Congress which was probably calculated to remove the embarrassment & restraint under which the treasury had acted in doing me justice.[4] As this bill is designed to embrace my subject if not to provide for me expressly & as it is to pass the examination & decision of the President in its passage to a law, I humbly intreat your Excellency to take my distressed case into his benevolent consideration and lend such a favorable notice to my unfortunate situation as will ensure me that Justice which I have long sought & hitherto sought in vain. I am with profound respect Your Excellency's most obedt & Most humble Servant

Caleb Brewster

ALS, DNA: RG 59, Miscellaneous Letters.

A descendant of *Mayflower* passenger William Brewster, Caleb Brewster (1747–1827) was born at Setauket, N.Y., and had sailed on a whaler to Greenland and on a merchant ship to London before the Revolutionary War. Upon his return to America in 1776, he accepted a commission as an ensign in the 4th New York Regiment. Appointed a first lieutenant in the 2d Continental Artillery in January 1777, Brewster was promoted to captain lieutenant in June 1780, and he served until June 1783. Brewster became first mate of the federal revenue cutter for New York in 1796, and he acted as its commander after the death of Capt. Patrick Dennis early in 1798. Brewster resigned that August when he was denied promotion on account of his political views. He later reentered the cutter service, became a commander, and served until his retirement in 1816 (see Brewster to Henry Dearborn, 27 April 1801, DNA: RG 59, Applications and Recommendations for Public Office; *DHFC,* 7:400; Pennypacker, *General Washington's Spies,* 285, 287).

1. Brewster's invaluable contributions to the Continental war effort while serving under Benjamin Tallmadge (1754–1835), chief of GW's intelligence service during the Revolutionary War, consisted of delivering secret dispatches from GW's spies in New York City; providing intelligence on the strength, movements, and positions of the British army; destroying their stores; harassing and capturing enemy boats in Long Island Sound; and discomforting Loyalists in Connecticut and on Long Island (see GW to Brewster, 8 Aug. [ADfS, DLC:GW], 11 Aug. 1778 [copy, DLC:GW], 23 Feb. 1781 [LS, in private hands], 7 May 1782 [copy, DLC:GW], 10 June 1784 [LB, DLC:GW], and Brewster to GW, 27 Aug., 15 Sept. 1778, 14 Feb., 30 July 1781, all in DLC:GW; Pennypacker, *General Washington's Spies,* 37–38, 91–94, 116, 191). For GW's certificate of 10 June 1784 attesting to Brewster's "fidelity, judgment & bravery" in those operations, see GW to Brewster, 10 June 1784, n.2.

2. On 7 Dec. 1782 three armed whaleboats under Brewster's command engaged a similar number of enemy boats in Long Island Sound off Fairfield, Connecticut. William Wheeler wrote in his journal that Brewster held his fire until his boat was within 150 feet of the lead British boat, when he "poured in a broadside & then another, & boarded" (quoted in Schenck, *History of Fairfield,* 2:398). Brewster was wounded by a rifle ball through his shoulder, and in the hand-to-hand fighting that followed he sustained back injuries from a steel gun rammer wielded by the captain of the British vessel. Four other members of his crew were wounded, one mortally. Brewster's second boat, armed with a swivel gun, captured another enemy boat, but the third British vessel escaped (Tallmadge to GW, 8 Dec. 1782, DLC:GW; see also GW to Tallmadge, 10, 26 Dec. 1782, both Df, in DLC:GW). Three months later Brewster's exertions as commander of a sloop out of Fairfield that engaged and captured another British armed vessel exacerbated his wounds and incapacitated him from further military service (Pennypacker, *General Washington's Spies,* 286–87; see also Report of the Secretary of War on the Petition of Caleb Brewster, 21 June 1790, delivered to Congress on 23 June, *DHFC,* 7:416–17).

3. When Brewster's petition was presented to the U.S. House of Representatives on 13 April 1790, it was referred to the secretary of war, "with instruction to examine the same." Henry Knox's favorable report of 21 June was presented to Congress on 23 June, when it was ordered to lie on the table. The House resolved on 28 June to place Brewster on the pension list, and his case was referred to the committee preparing the disabled soldiers and seamen bill, which reported on 16 July. The House read, debated, and amended the bill on 17 and 19 July and agreed to it on 28 July, when it was sent to the Senate, which read it on 29 July and amended it on 6 Aug. before returning it to the House (*DHFC,* 3:365, 474 n.102, 479, 7:405–6, 416–17, 420, 422). GW signed "An Act for the relief of disabled soldiers and seamen lately in the service of the United States, and of certain other persons" on 11 Aug. 1790. Section 2 reads: "*And be it further enacted,* That Caleb Brewster . . . be allowed three hundred forty-eight dollars and fifty-seven cents, the amount of his necessary

expenses for sustenance and medical assistance, while dangerously ill of his wounds, including the interest to the first of July, one thousand seven hundred and ninety. And that the said Brewster be allowed a pension equal to his half pay as lieutenant, from the third of November, one thousand seven hundred and eighty-three, he first having returned his commutation of half pay" (6 *Stat.* 4). A payment to Brewster of $348.57 was authorized on 21 Dec. 1790 (see Alexander Hamilton's Report on the Receipts and Expenditures of Public Monies to the End of the Year 1791, 10 Nov. 1792, in Syrett, *Hamilton Papers,* 13:105).

4. The House passed an engrossed bill to ascertain and regulate the claims to half-pay and invalid pensions on 26 Jan. 1792, when it was sent to the Senate. The Senate read it for the first time the same day and amended the bill upon its third reading on 29 February. The House received the amended bill on 2 Mar. but did not consider it until the next day. On 3 Mar. the House notified the Senate of its rejection of the amendments, and a joint committee was appointed two days later. On 14 Mar. the Senate informed the House that it insisted on its amendments and also proposed a new one. Two days later the House agreed to all the Senate amendments (*Annals of Congress,* 2d Cong., 77–78, 96–97, 337, 433–35, 470, 472). On 23 Mar. 1792 GW signed "An Act to provide for the settlement of the Claims of Widows and Orphans barred by the limitations heretofore established, and to regulate the Claims to Invalid Pensions," which, among other things, enacted "That any commissioned officer, not having received the commutation of half pay, . . . shall be entitled to be placed on the pension list of the United States, during life" (1 *Stat.* 243–45).

From Lafayette

My dear General. Paris March the 15th 1792.

I have been called from the army to this Capital for a conference between the two other generals, the ministers, and myself, and am about returning to my military post. The coalition between the continental powers respecting our affairs is certain, and will not be broken by the Emperor's death; but, altho' warlike preparations are going on, it is very doubtful whether our neighbors will attempt to stifle a flame so very catching as that of liberty is.[1]

The danger for us lies with our state of anarchy, owing to the ignorance of the people, the number of non-proprietors, the jealousy of every governing measure, all which inconveniences are worked up by designing men, or aristocrats in disguise; but both extremes tend to defeat our ideas of public order. Do not believe, however, my dear General, the exagerated accounts you may receive, particularly from England. That liberty and equality will be preserved in France, there is no doubt. In case there was, you well know that I will not, if they fall, survive them. But you may be assured that we will emerge from this unpleasant situation either by an honorable defense, or by internal improvements. How far this constitution of ours insures a good government has not been as yet fairly experienced. This only we know, that it has restored to the people their rights, destroyed almost every abuse, and turned French vassalage and slavery into national dignity, and the enjoyment of those faculties, which nature has given and society ought to insure.

Give me leave, my General, to you alone to offer an observation respecting the late choice of the American ambassador. You know I am personally a friend to Gouverneur Morris,[2] and ever, as a private man, have been satisfied with him; but the aristocratic, and indeed counter-revolutionary principles he has professed, unfitted him to be the representative of the only nation, whose politics have a likeness with ours, since they are founded on the plan of a representative democracy. This I may add, that, surrounded with enemies as France is, it looks as if America was preparing for a change in this government, not only that kind of alteration, which the democrats may wish for and bring about, but the wild attempts of aristocracy, such as the restoration of a noblesse, a house of Lords, and such other political blasphemies, which, while we are living, cannot be reëstablished in France. I wish we had an elective senate, a more independent set of judges, and a more energetic administration. but the people must be taught the advantage of a firm government, before they reconcile it to their ideas of freedom, and can distinguish it from the arbitrary systems, which they have just got over. You see, my dear General, I am not an enthusiast of every part of our constitution, altho' I love its principles, which are the same as those of the United States, excepting heredity in the president of the executive, which I think suitable to our circumstances. But I hate every thing like despotism and aristocracy, and I cannot help wishing the American and French principles were in the heart and on the lips of the American ambassador to France. This I mention *for you alone,* and only for the case when arrangements suitable [ ][3]; and yet I beg this hint of mine, may never be mentioned to any body. Give me leave, my dear general, to add the tribute of praise which I owe to Mr Short for the sentiments he has professed, and the esteem he has acquired in this country. I wish this gentleman was personally known to you.

There have been changes in the ministry. The King has chosen his council amidst the most violent popular party, the Jacobin club, a Jesuitic institution, more fit to make deserters from, than converts to our cause. The new ministers, however, being unsuspected, have a chance to restore public order, and say they will improve it. The Assembly are uninformed, and too fond of popular applause; the King slow, and rather backward in his daily conduct, altho now and then he acts fully well; but, upon the whole, it will do, and the success of our revolution cannot be questioned.

My command extends on the frontiers from *Givet* to *Bitche.* I have sixty thousand men, a number that is increasing now, as young men pour in from every part of the empire to fill up the regiments. This voluntary recruiting shows a most patriotic spirit. I am going to encamp thirty thousand men, with a detached corps of about four or five thousand in an intrenched camp. The remainder will occupy the fortified places. The armies of marshalls Lukner and Rochambeau are inferior to mine, because we have sent many regiments to the Southward, but in case we have a war to undertake, we may gather respectable forces.

Our *Emigrants* are beginning to come in. Their situation abroad is miserable, and in case even we quarrel with our neighbors, they will be out of the question. Our paper money has been of late rising very fast. Manufactures of every kind are much employed. The farmer finds his taxes alleviated, and will feel the more happy under our constitution, as the Assembly are going to give up their patronage of one set of Priests. You see, my dear general, that altho we have many causes to be as yet unsatisfied, we may hope every thing will bye and bye come to rights. Licentiousness, under a mask of patriotism, is our greatest evil, as it threatens property, tranquility, and liberty itself.

Adieu, my dear general. My best respects wait on Mrs Washington. Remember me most affectionately to our friends, and think sometimes of your respectful, loving and filial friend

Lafayette.

Sparks transcript, MH.

1. For the military appointments of Lafayette, Rochambeau, and Baron Luckner, which were occasioned by the war crisis between France and Austria, see Gouverneur Morris to GW, 27–31 Dec. 1791, n.3, and Lafayette to GW, 22 Jan. 1792. Marie Antoinette's brother, Holy Roman Emperor Leopold II (b. 1747), died on 1 Mar. 1792 and was succeeded by his son Francis II (1768–1835), who was more susceptible to the influence of the Austrian war party.

2. The copyist, Jared Sparks, marked this name with an asterisk and noted at the bottom of the page: "Mr Morris had been appointed Minister Plenipotentiary to France on the 12th of January." For GW's controversial appointment of Gouverneur Morris, see GW to the U.S. Senate, 22 Dec. 1791, source note, and GW to Morris, 28 Jan. 1792.

3. At this place in the manuscript Sparks originally wrote "to ⟨*illegible*⟩ I wish might in future"; he then struck out the phrase and inserted "(blank)" above the line.

From Alexander Hamilton

Treasury Departt March 16th 1792

The Secretary of the Treasury has the honor to submit to the President the draft of a report[1] on the subject of *ways & means* for carrying into execution the Military bill.[2]

He will wait on the President tomorrow morning for his Orders; as it is interesting there should be no avoidable delay.

LB, DLC:GW.

1. The enclosed draft of Hamilton's Report Relative to the Additional Supplies for the Ensuing Year has not been found, but the final version, which he signed and dated this day and presented to the U.S. House of Representatives on 17 Mar., is in DNA: RG 233, Second Congress, 1791–1793, Records of Legislative Proceedings, Reports and Communications Submitted to the House.

On 8 Mar. after intense debate, the House had passed by a vote of 31 to 27 a resolution requesting the secretary of the treasury to give his opinion of the best mode for raising the additional funds that would be required to undertake a new military expedition against the hostile northwestern Indian nations (*Annals of Congress,* 2d Cong., 437–52). In his report of 16 Mar., Hamilton rejected using the interest in the Bank of the United States to which the government was entitled or adding to the public debt and favored temporarily increasing duties on imported goods. Hamilton estimated that such a measure would provide an additional $523,000 and suggested the passage of a law authorizing a temporary loan for that amount (see Syrett, *Hamilton Papers,* 11:139–49). The House considered Hamilton's report on 5–6 April and debated a resulting bill on 17–21 April, which it passed on 21 April and sent to the Senate two days later. The Senate amended the bill on 26 April and returned it to the House the following day (*Annals of Congress,* 2d Cong., 127, 129–32,

538–39, 541, 558–62, 566–72). GW signed "An Act for raising a farther sum of money for the protection of the frontiers, and for other purposes therein mentioned" on 2 May (see 1 *Stat.* 259–63).

2. For "An Act for making farther and more effectual Provision for the Protection of the Frontiers of the United States," which GW signed on 5 Mar., see GW to the U.S. Senate and House of Representatives, 11 Jan., n.2; 1 *Stat.* 241–43.

From Benjamin Hawkins

sir, Senate Chamber 16 march 1792

As I make it a rule to give my assent to all military nominations without enquiry, and shall continue to do so, so long as a military Judge shall be President of the United States; I hope it will not be deemed indelicate in me to offer the opinion of an individual, which has resulted from reflections on the conversation I had last evening with you.

Colo. Lee as a military man certainly possesses a degree of enterprise caution and foresight not excelled by any of his contemporaries of equal rank. He has a comprehensive mind, he has gained his experience in a sort of partisan Warfare the best of all others for qualifying a man to command against Indians.

It may be objected to him that he was not of the rank in the late army to entitle him to the command. To this I shall only repeat what I said in the Senate on the case of Demler that the President had exclusively the right to nominate, and the fitness of his character, not the rank of the man, was the only enquiry to be made in the Senate;[1] And that if the Senate did not possess a contrary proof, the nomination should be conclusive in favour of the person nominated. There is perhaps on the score of rank, this further to be said of Colo. Lee, that his present standing in society is an exalted and dignified one.[2] He commanded I believe genl Pickens at the Siege of Augusta altho' the latter was of superior rank.[3] I have the honor to be most respectfully sir your most obediant servt

Benjamin Hawkins

ALS, DLC:GW.

1. For the Senate's confirmation of the appointment of George Demlar, see GW to the U.S. Senate, 12 Mar. 1792, n.7.

2. Henry Lee had been elected governor of Virginia in November 1791. For

GW's opinion of Lee's abilities as a leader, see Thomas Jefferson's Memorandum of a Meeting of the Heads of the Executive Departments, 9 Mar., and Memorandum on General Officers, 9 March.

3. In May and June 1781, Lee commanded forces under Andrew Pickens and Elijah Clarke at the successful siege of British forts Grierson and Cornwallis at Augusta, Georgia.

From Thomas Jefferson

[Philadelphia] 16 Mar. 1792. Sends GW "two letters just recd from Colo. Humphreys."[1]

AL, DNA: RG 59, Miscellaneous Letters; LB, DNA: RG 59, George Washington's Correspondence with His Secretaries of State; LB (photocopy), DLC:GW.

1. The enclosures were two letters from the U.S. minister to Portugal, David Humphreys, which the secretary of state had received this day: a dispatch of 23 Dec. 1791 containing information on Brazil, passing along the Portuguese ambassador to Spain's hint that the Spanish government favored negotiations with the United States, and announcing the arrival at Gibraltar in early December of Thomas Barclay, the U.S. consul to the court of Algiers, and a letter of 24 Dec. in which Humphreys copied an extract from Barclay's letter to him of 8 Dec. stating that Barclay would soon depart for North Africa (see *Jefferson Papers,* 22:434–35).

Tobias Lear to Henry Knox

United States [Philadelphia] 16 Mar. 1792. Transmits by GW's command a representation to the president from the county lieutenants and field officers of the District of Kentucky.[1]

ALS (letterpress copy), DLC:GW; LB, DLC:GW.

1. The enclosure has not been found, but it was probably similar in nature to the request of a council of militia officers in Harrison County, Va., for authorization to raise additional scouts and defensive forces to protect their frontier settlements (see Benjamin Wilson to GW, 29 Feb. 1792).

From William Hamilton

The Woodlands [Philadelphia County, Pa.]
17th March 1792

Dear Sir

I will with great pleasure forward you on Monday whatever is in my power of the kinds of plants you desire & will prepare them in the best manner for the voyage.[1]

The time being short, I am uncertain at what time of the day they may be ready. You need not therefore send for them. I will have them deliver'd at your House in the course of it. With the most perfect respect & sincerest regard I am dear Sir Your most obedt humble servt

W. Hamilton

ALS, DLC:GW.

William Hamilton (1745–1813), a wealthy patron of the arts who lived at The Woodlands, a large, handsome estate on the Schuylkill River near Gray's Ferry, imported and propagated a large variety of plants. GW, who had dined with Hamilton on several occasions during the spring and summer of 1787 at another one of Hamilton's estates near Philadelphia, Bush Hill, along with his wife, Martha, visited Hamilton at The Woodlands on 19 May 1792 (*Diaries,* 5:160, 165, 181, 238–39, 244; Decatur, *Private Affairs of George Washington,* 259).

1. An undated "List of Plants, from Mr Hamilton's" probably accompanied the plants that Hamilton delivered to GW on Monday, 19 March:

		no. of plants
No. 1.	Spanish chesnut; bears very large Fruit	2.
2.	Bladder Senna, with yellow Flowers (grows 10 or 12 feet high.)	
3.	Laburnum; call'd Ebony of the alps (12 or 15 feet high)	4.
4.	Roan tree, or Mountain ash—bears beautiful clusters of red fruit	4.
5.	Flowering Raspberry	8.
6.	Twice bearing Raspberry (the fruit excellent)	12.
7.	Pyracantha, or Evergreen Thorn	2.
8.	white flowering Lilac	6.
9.	Manna ash from Italy	2.
10.	Junipers	2.
11.	Willow with variegated leaves	2.
12.	Paper Mulberry of Japan	4.
13.	English white Thorn—the sort used for hedges	1.
14.	St Peters wort (grows 3 or 4 feet high)	4.
15.	Hypericum: shrub St Johns wort (4 feet high)	6.
16.	Spirea frutex	4.
17.	Dwarf Syringa or Mock orange, with double flowers	4.
18.	Rose Acacia	15.
19.	Double flowering Almonds	3.
20.	Willow with Bay leaves	2.
21.	English Laurel	1.
22.	Spanish broom, & white broom, 1 plant of each	2.
23.	Double flowering Bramble	5.
24.	Common Broom	24.
25.	Dwarf American Laurel	12.
26.	Rhododendron or Mountain Rose Laurel	4.

		Cuttings
27.	True Osier, or Basket willow	
28.	Flowering, or Palm	Do
29.	Bay leafed	Do
30.	Variegated	Do

(DLC:GW).

From L. Hoopstad & Co.

Sir! Rio Demerary[1] March 17, 1792

as Merchants in a Extensive trading Country, under the protection of a Sovereign, trading largely, with the Subjects of the united States of America, we take the Liberty to Address ourselves, by this Opportunity.

we have been Informed that it has pleased your Excellency to Sent to the Consignation of Mr T. Brandon Merchant in the River Suriname in the year 1787. a few barrels of flour, & to sell the same to the best advantage.[2]

this Encourage us, to Recommend ourselves in your Excelly Attention in Case it should be Agreable to your Exc. to sent Any to this Country.

this Government has given all Encouragement to the Merchants of the U.S. of America, & still Continue the same nothing discourage this Commerce, the dutys & Expences of Clearing In & out are so Triffling that 200 Dollars, will not be Required for a Vessel of 200 Tun Burthen. this Colony is the only one, at present who is under the Protection of the sovereign there High Migthtinesse for the States of Holland.

We Shall be greatly Honoured With your Excellency Command in Case our House of Commerce, Shall be able to be of any Service.[3] We have the Honour to be With due Respect Sir Your Excellcy most Obed. & Hbl. Servants

L. Hoopstad & Co.

L, DNA: RG 59, Miscellaneous Letters. The addressed cover appears to bear a postmark of Boston, 11 April.

1. Demerara, a 200-year-old Dutch colony along the Demerara River on the Atlantic coast of South America, was occupied by the British from 1796 to 1802. Ceded to Great Britain in 1815, it became part of British Guiana.

2. In 1786 GW had sent twenty-five barrels of flour to Samuel Branden (Brandon), a merchant operating in Surinam, in payment for a jenny that GW had requested for breeding with his jackasses (see John Fitzgerald to GW, 7 Feb. 1786, n.1).

3. No evidence has been found that GW conducted any business with the firm.

From Henry Knox

[Philadelphia] 17 Mar. 1792. Communicates a letter from Gen. Charles Cotesworth Pinckney that Ralph Izard had just delivered to the War Department.[1]

ALS, DLC:GW; LB, DLC:GW.

1. The enclosed letter from Charles Cotesworth Pinckney, who had been brevetted a brigadier general at the close of the Revolutionary War, has not been identified.

From Gouverneur Morris

Dear Sir, London 17 March 1792

I had the Honor to write to you on the fourth of last Month. Two Days after, I was informed that you had nominated me as Minister to the Court of France, but the latest Advices from America, which come down to the tenth of January, shew that the Senate had not then made their Decision.[1] Be that Decision what it may, I shall ever gratefully esteem and acknowlege this Mark of Confidence from the Person in the World whose good opinion I consider as most estimable.

In my Letter of the fourth, I gave you a Picture of the french Ministry, and a View of the Measures pursued by different Parties, including the Mission of the bishop d'autun.[2] As *he* has now got back to Paris it may be well to communicate the Results. His Reception was bad for three Reasons. First that the Court looks with Horror and Apprehension at the Scenes acting in France, of which they consider him as a prime Mover. Secondly, that his Reputation is offensive to Persons who pique themselves on Decency of Manners & Deportment. And lastly because he was so imprudent, when he first arrived, as to propogate the Idea that he should corrupt the Members of Administration; and afterwards by keeping Company with leading Characters among the Dissenters and other similar Circumstances he renewed the Impression made before his Departure from Paris that he meant to intrigue with the discontented. His public Reception however furnishes no Clue to decide on the Success of his Mission; because the former might have been very bad and the latter very good. The Fact however is that he could offer Nothing worthy of their Acceptance, and that what he asked was of a Nature not to be granted. This Offer was confined to a Cession of Tobago, a Demolition of the Portes of Cherburgh, & an Extension of the commercial Treaty. He asked a strict Neutrality in Case of War with the Emperor. Now you will observe that no Court would prudently treat with France in her present Situation, seeing that no body can promise in her Name otherwise than as Godfathers and Godmothers do at a Christening, and how such Promises are kept every Body knows. Convinced of this, the Bishop never told his Errand to Lord Gower, the British Embassador at Paris, who mentioned that Circumstance to me as extraordinary, but yet as so far agreable in that he was glad not to have been called on for Letters of Introduction.[3]

Respecting Tobago, I must make a Digression. It is now a long Time since it was mentioned to me, in Paris, that some of the Colonists of St Domingo had come hither to make overtures to Mr Pitt. Since that Period I learnt that the french Ministry were in Possession of Documents to prove, not only that he fomented the Disturbances in France, but that he was in deep Intrigues with Regard to that Colony. The particular Proofs were not shewn to me; so that I cannot speak positively. Neither can I vouch for what I have learnt further on that Subject within this Month, but I am assured that it is Mr Pitts Intention to bring about if he can the Independence of St Domingo. Mr Clarkson, the great Negro Advocate,[4] is mentioned to me as his agent for their Business at Paris; and the Conduct of a Part of the Assembly in opposing Succor to that Island seems corroborative of such Idea. This then being the Case, or supposing it to be so, the Offer of Tobago was too trifling to attract Mr Pitts notice, even if unconnected with other Circumstances. By the bye my Informant tells me also that Mr Pitt means to coax us into the Adoption of his Plan respecting St Domingo. And I learn from another Quarter that he means to offer us his Mediation for a Peace with the Indians.[5] If all this be true, his Game is evident. The Mediation is to be with us a Price for adopting his Plans, and with the Indian Tribes a Means of constituting himself their Patron and Protector. It may be proper to combine all this with the late Division of

Canada, and the present Measures for military Colonization of the upper Country, and above all with what may come from Mr Hammond.[6] I return to St Domingo. If such be Mr Pitt's Scheme, altho we shall not I presume engage in or countenance it, yet the Success will be *entirely* for our Advantage, and a meer preliminary to Something of the same Sort which must happen to Jamaica at the first Change of wind in the political world. The Destruction of the Port of Cherbourg is no present Object with the british Ministry, because they suppose it will be ruined by the Elements before it can be compleated, and because the french Marine is (from the want of Discipline) an Object more of Contempt than apprehension. The profferd Extension of the Commercial Treaty amounts to Nothing, because at present every Part of France is open to contraband Commerce, and because there is little Reason to beleive that the Stipulations in a Treaty now made would be of any long Duration. Thus it happens that neither of the Objects offered were worthy of Notice. But the Neutrality required was of a most important Nature. By leaving the Austrian low Countries exposed to french Invasion, it would have been a Violation both of antient and of recent Treaties. Nor is this all, for (as I have already had occasion to remark) the Annexation of those Provinces to the french Monarchy would prove almost, if not altogether, fatal to Great Britain. And when we consider that they are almost in Revolt already, and that it is in fact their Interest to become one with France, there is some Reason to suppose that an Union might have been effected in Case of a War with the Emperor. So much then on the Ground of Good Faith and good Policy, but there is still a further Cause which as the World goes may be equal in its Operation to all others. It seems to be a moot Point whether it is the british or the prussian Cabinet which directs the other. Perhaps there may be a little of both, but be all that as it may, this much is certain that neither feels disposed to counteract the Views of its Ally in any open manner. Now putting aside the personal Feelings which naturally agitate the Sovereign of this as well as of Other Kingdoms in Regard to the french Revolution, it is notorious that, from the very Dawn of it, Agents were employed to foment a Spirit of Revolt in other States; particularly in Prussia. The King of Prussia therefore feels for the french Revolutionists all the Enmity of a proud passionate and offended german

Prince. Add to this that the Elector of Hanover, as such, cannot wish for a Change in the Government of Germany.[7] If therefore it had been the Interest of Great Britain to establish a free Constitution in France (which it certainly is not) I am perfectly convinced that this Court would never have made a single Effort for the Purpose.

I stated to you in my last the french Ministry as being extremely disjointed.[8] It was too much so for any durable Existence, besides which the Members took effectual Means to precipitate each others Ruin. Mr de Narbonne wished to get into the Office of foreign Affairs. This was desirable to him (it is said) on many accounts but particularly so because it gives the Command of large Sums without Account. Whatever may have been his Motives, the following seems to have been his Conduct. He stood forth the Advocate of all violent Measures. This would naturally have excited Suspicions with thinking Men, but not so with the Assembly. He associated himself to the Partizans of Democracy, and while by this Means he secured himself against their Clamors, he took great Care of his pecuniary Affairs. This at least is affirmed to me, and with the addition that he had the Imprudence to pay off his Debts altho it is notorious that his Estate, which is in St Domingo, is among those which are laid Waste. It is further asserted, that in order to quiet the Clamors of Contractors who had given him money and found themselves in the Road to Ruin he agreed to compensate the Depreciation of the Assignats. In order to remove a great Obstacle to his Proceedings he joined in the Intrigues against Mr Bertrand, and at the same Time fostered other Intrigues against Mr Delessart with a View of getting his Place. The Proofs of all these things are said to be in the King's Hands. Mr Delessart's Conduct I have already in Part communicated.[9] I must add that, afterwards, imagining that Brissot de Warville and Condorcet[10] were omnipotent in the Assembly he violated his Engagements made with the Triumvirate, and wrote some Dispatches conformably to the Views of those two Gentlemen. In Consequence of this it was resolved to displace him, and they were looking out for a Successor. The person applied to was actually deliberating whether he should or should not accept, at the Moment when Brissot brought about his Impeachment and Arrest. In this same Moment Mr de Narbonne was dismissed, and with him was to go Monsieur de Gerville. The Chevalier de Grave succeeds Mr de Narbonne.[11] When I left Paris he was attached to the Triumvirate. He does not want for Understanding, but I think it almost impossible that he should succeed. Monsr Bertrand against whom an Address from the Assembly was at length carried, has I find resigned. There is Something at the Bottom which I cannot discover, without being on the Spot, but you may rely on it he goes out with the full Confidence of the King and Queen.

My Informations from Paris were previous to the News of the Emperor's Death, which has probably occasioned the violent Proceedings against poor de lessart, by removing the Fears of those who (in the Midst of all their big Words) were confoundedly frightened. What may be the Consequences of this Event it is impossible to determine, or even to conjecture. Much, very much, depends on the personal Character of his Successor which I am not yet acquainted with.[12]

It is supposed, by some here, that Mr Pitt is not strong in the Cabinet at present, altho the Majority in Parliament was never more decisive, and this is said to arise from his refusing to ask Money for Payment of the Prince of Wales's Debts which the King it is said was desirous of, and which his Minister declined *with some offensive Expressions.* Mr Pitt's Friends insist on the other Hand that the whole Story is false from Begining to End.[13] For my own Part, I do not think he will be turned out, because I beleive him to be a very cunning Fellow; and altho he has conducted foreign Affairs but poorly, he manages all the little Court and parliamentary Intrigues with consummate Address. Farewell my dear Sir, I am ever truly yours

Gouvr Morris

ALS, DLC:GW; LB, DLC: Gouverneur Morris Papers. The franked addressed cover of the receiver's copy is postmarked New York, 4 June.

1. For GW's controversial appointment of Morris, see GW to the U.S. Senate, 22 Dec. 1791, source note, and to Morris, 28 Jan. 1792. The Senate confirmed Morris's appointment on 12 Jan. (*Executive Journal,* 1:96). Morris received GW's letter of 28 Jan. and an official notification of his appointment on 6 April 1792 (see Morris to GW, that date).

2. For the London mission of Charles-Maurice de Talleyrand-Périgord, the bishop of Autun, see Morris to GW, 4 Feb. 1792, and note 10.

3. George Granville Leveson-Gower (1758–1833) was Britain's ambassador in Paris from 1790 until August 1792.

4. Thomas Clarkson (1760–1846), the famed antislavery agitator and

writer, had spent six months in France during the last half of 1789 in an attempt to convince the French government to suppress the slave trade. He apparently did not return to the Continent at this time.

5. GW and his department heads agreed that they would never accept British mediation between the United States and the hostile Indian nations of the Northwest (see GW to Thomas Jefferson, c.5–6 Mar., source note, and Jefferson's Memorandum of a Meeting of the Heads of the Executive Departments, 9 March).

6. For the background to George Hammond's mission to the United States, see GW to Thomas Jefferson, c.5–6 Mar. 1792, source note.

7. Frederick William II (1744–1797), a nephew of Frederick the Great, reigned as king of Prussia from 1786 until 1797. King George III of Great Britain was also the elector of Hanover.

8. Morris had last written GW on 4 Feb. 1792.

9. For Morris's earlier comments on Valdec de Lessart's conduct, see Morris to GW, 4 Feb. 1792.

10. The liberal, anticlerical philosophe Marie-Jean-Antoine-Nicolas de Caritat, marquis de Condorcet (1743–1794), represented Paris in the French Legislative Assembly at this time.

11. Pierre-Marie, marquis de Grave (1755–1825), served as minister of war from March until May 1792.

12. For the succession of Francis II as Holy Roman Emperor upon the death of his father, Leopold II, see Lafayette to GW, 15 Mar. 1792, n.1.

13. George, Prince of Wales (1762–1830), the eldest son of George III, served as regent from 1811 to 1820 and as king from 1820 to 1830.

To Charles Pinckney

Dear Sir, Philada March 17th 1792.

I have the pleasure to acknowledge the receipt of your letters of the 8th of January and their duplicates. That of a public nature, on the subject of a proposed application from yourself to the Governor of East Florida, for the redelivery of certain fugitives charged with having forged the Indents assumed by the U. States will be answered by the Secretary of State.[1] To your private favor I shall now reply. And in the first place, let me beg your acceptance of my thanks for the remembrance of, and kind attention to my wishes in sending the box of seeds, which I have received by Captain Ort.[2]

I am flattered by the regret which you express at having been absent from Charleston during the stay of Lord Wycombe in that City, & being thereby deprived of an opportunity of paying the attention which you wished to that Nobleman to whom I had given a letter for you; and am glad that his intention of returning among you, after having visited the Floridas, will permit you to do it.[3]

I must say that I lament the decision of your legislature upon the question of importing Slaves after March 1793—I was in hopes that motives of policy, as well as other good reasons supported by the direful effects of Slavery which at this moment are presented, would have operated to produce a total prohibition of the importation of Slaves whenever the question came to be agitated in any State that might be interested in the measure.[4]

Our misfortune at the westwards is certainly a circumstance much to be regretted: but it affords consolation to know, that every public loss on that occasion may be readily repaired, except that of the lives of the brave Officers and men, who fell in the conflict.

I believe with you, that the absence of the Cherokee chief's from their Nation at so critical a moment, was a fortunate event; and I trust they have received such impressions here as will not fail to have a happy influence in their nation with regard to us.[5]

If in the course of our military arrangements, it should be found compatible with the plan which it is proposed, to adopt, to require the services of Genl Pickens, I shall not be unmindful of your recommendation of that Gentleman; and from his talents, knowledge and influence, should look for the best effects. But I most sincerely join with you in hoping, that the war with the Indians may not extend so far to the southward, as to render your frontiers an object of immediate defence. I beg my best respects may be presented to Mrs Pinckney—and to Colo. Laurens, when you see him—with very great esteem and regard—I am Dr Sir, Your most obedt humble servant

Go: Washington.

LB, DLC:GW.

1. On 1 April, Thomas Jefferson sent Pinckney a copy of his report to GW of 22 Mar. proposing that the United States negotiate an extradition convention with Spain (see *Jefferson Papers,* 23:360–61).

2. A Captain Art commanded the ship *Delaware* from Charleston, S.C., which arrived in Philadelphia on 11 Mar. (see *Dunlap's American Daily Advertiser* [Philadelphia], 12 Mar. 1792). GW probably personally requested plants and seeds for Mount Vernon from Pinckney when the president was in Charleston in early May 1791 during his Southern Tour (see Pinckney to GW, 8 Jan. 1792 [first letter], n.4).

3. For John Henry Petty, earl Wycombe, son of the marquis of Lansdowne, and his tour of America, see GW to Lansdowne, 7 Nov. 1791, n.2. GW wrote a letter introducing Wycombe to Pinckney on 8 November.

4. The two-year ban on the importation of slaves into South Carolina which was passed by the state legislature in 1791 continued to be renewed until 1803 (see Pinckney to GW, 8 Jan. 1792 [first letter], n.2). The "direful effects of Slavery" to which GW is referring were undoubtedly the slave uprising of August–September 1791 in Saint Domingue and the resulting murder or exodus of members of the planter class from the French Caribbean colony (see Samuel Wall to GW, 16 Sept., n.1, Pinckney to GW, 20 Sept., n.1, and Ternant to GW, 22, 24 Sept. 1791).

5. For the visit of the Cherokee chiefs to Philadelphia between December 1791 and February 1792, see Henry Knox to GW, 17 Jan. 1792, source note.

From George Taylor, Jr.

Sir, Philadelphia March 17th 1792.

Being much flattered by the confidence reposed in me by you, while I was employed in your recording Secretary's Office, and the notice you have honored me with since that period, permit me to enclose the copy of a letter I have just now written to Mr Jefferson, and as far as may be consistent, to solicit the favor of your Influence and Support, in obtaining the object of it.[1] I have the honor to be with the most profound respect, Sir, Your most obedient and most humble servant

Geo. Taylor Jr

ALS, DNA: RG 59, Miscellaneous Letters.

1. In the enclosed copy of the letter of application for the chief clerkship of the State Department that Taylor wrote to Thomas Jefferson on this date, he states:

"1st That in the years 1779, –80, and part of –81, I served as an Assist. Quarter master in the State of New York.

"2. That in 1781 and part of –82 I served as principal Assistant to the Agent of that State.

"3. That in 1782—and –83 I served as a Clerk to the recording Secy to His Excellency General Washington, and had the honor to be made choice of by the General in a letter to him, which he shewed me, as the person, out of the 3 then for some time employed, who *alone* should record his *own private letters*; letters the matter of which at this day I conceive to be secrets of high importance.

"4th That I have had the honor to be appointed a Clerk in the office of your predecessor, Mr [John] Jay, upwards of 7 years ago—and that of being continued by you, on his recommendation.

"To the above I would beg leave to add that I have studiously endeavored to qualify myself for executing the duties of the Office with accuracy & dispatch, and that I have found my salary an inadequate support for my family" (DNA: RG 59, Miscellaneous Letters). Taylor received the desired appointment on 1 April.

Joseph Davenport's Proposal

[Mount Vernon,
Propositions from J: Davenport— 18 March 1792]

Joseph Davenport proposes continuing with the President of the United states one year after the expiration of the present year, on the following terms—His wages to be seventy two pounds pensylvania Curry pr year finding himself Bord with out any of the perquisites now allowed him by the President except the use of two Cows—the House he now occupies and firewood as usual—he relinquishes the raising of Geese keeping a Horse and every other privilege that his present agreement entitles him to & that he will attend the mill without assistance except in the time of manufacturing and when the mill does not require His attendance he will be imployed in the Coopers Shop pay the strictest attention to keeping the Mill in the Best order.

Df, in the writing of George Augustine Washington, DLC:GW.

For the gristmill at Mount Vernon that GW had built on Dogue Run in 1770–71 and in which he had installed laborsaving machinery in 1791, see GW's Cash Accounts, August 1770, n.9, Tobias Lear to Oliver Evans, 29 Aug. 1791, and GW to Anthony Whitting, 4 Sept. 1791, n.3; see also editorial note, 8 Feb. 1771, *Diaries,* 3:7.

Joseph Davenport (d. 1796) operated the mill at Mount Vernon from the summer of 1785 until his death (see Robert Lewis & Sons to GW, 5 April 1785, and GW to Clement Biddle, 8 April 1798, n.3). An account with Alexandria inspector Alexander Smith, 19 Mar. 1792–25 June 1793, shows that Smith examined 190 barrels of GW's flour on 19 Mar. 1792 and 314 in June 1793 (DLC:GW). A state law to inspect Virginia exports of flour and bread, which was passed on 23 Nov. 1787 and amended on 10 Dec. 1788, appointed thirty inspectors at towns, ports, and other sites to regulate the quantity and quality of flour and bread and the size and manufacture of casks, to record millers' and bakers' brands, and to receive and save manifests of the gross, tare, and net weights of the products (see Hening, 12:515–20, 692–93).

From Thomas Jefferson

[Philadelphia] Sunday Mar. 18. 1792.

Th: Jefferson having received information that a vessel sails from New York for Amsterdam *about Wednesday,* is endeavoring to get ready the necessary papers for Messrs Short & Carmichael, to go by tomorrow's post.[1] he beleives it impossible; but in order to take the chance of it, he troubles the President to sign the Commission to-day, which mister Taylor now carries to him for that purpose.[2]

AL, DNA: RG 59, Miscellaneous Letters; LB, DNA: RG 59, George Washington's Correspondence with His Secretaries of State; LB (photocopy), DLC:GW.

1. The "necessary papers" that Jefferson was preparing included copies of his instructions to William Carmichael and William Short (see Jefferson to GW, 7 Mar. [second letter], and GW to the U.S. Senate, 7 Mar.), a letter covering their commission (see Jefferson to Carmichael and Short, 18 Mar., *Jefferson Papers,* 23:292–93), and a detailed report on negotiations with Spain, along with supporting documentation, to guide the commissioners. On 11 Mar., Jefferson reported: "I delivd to the Presid. my report of Instructions for Carmichl & Short on the subjects of navigation, boundary & commerce; & desired him to submit it to Hamilton. H[amilton] made several just criticisms on difft parts of it. but where I asserted that the U.S. had no right to alienate an inch of the territory of any state he attacked & denied the doctrine" (Jefferson's Memoranda of Consultations with the President, 11 Mar.–9 April 1792, DLC: Jefferson Papers). Hamilton's undated notes on Jefferson's report of instructions to the treaty commissioners and Jefferson's written comments on Hamilton's notes are both in DLC:GW, and they are printed in *Jefferson Papers,* 23:179–83, and Syrett, *Hamilton Papers,* 11:68–73. Jefferson incorporated eight of Hamilton's ten suggestions into his final report of this day, which is divided into three sections. Section I of the report reviews the history of the boundary between the United States and Spain's North American possessions; Section II justifies America's right to the free navigation of the Mississippi River and to deposit goods somewhere near its mouth; and Section III includes the text of Jefferson's report to GW of 7 Mar. (DLC: Jefferson Papers). The report is printed and extensively annotated in *Jefferson Papers,* 23:296–317.

2. The commission for Carmichael and Short to settle outstanding differences between the United States and Spain was signed by GW and Jefferson on this date, according to a similarly signed and dated duplicate (ViW: William Short Papers). The unsigned commission was delivered to GW by State Department clerk George Taylor, Jr., who might also have delivered at the same time his own letter to GW of 17 March. Jefferson forwarded this day the commission, along with the other papers for Carmichael and Short, to Henry Remsen, Jr., for transmittal to the American bankers at Amsterdam, who were

instructed to deliver them personally to Short (see Jefferson to Remsen, 18 Mar., and Report on Negotiations with Spain, 18 Mar., source note, both in *Jefferson Papers,* 23:295, 313).

To Samuel Potts

Sir, Philad. 18th Mar. 1792

Your letter of the 31st of October, on the subject of a Legacy left by Mr[s] Savage to Mrs Bomford, has been received;[1] and shall be transmitted to the Revd Mr Fairfax, whose avocations not being of the constant and indispensible nature that mine have been and still are, have given him better opportunities of attending to the Affairs of the late Mr[s] Savage than I have had; his knowledge of the situation of that business is therefore much more accurate than mine. You will see by the enclosed copy of a letter which I wrote to Mrs Bomford on the 6th of January 1790, that it has been totally out of my power to pay any attention to the Affairs of Mrs Savage since the year 1775, and that I have referred her to Mr Fairfax, to whom I must likewise beg leave to refer you. I am Sir, Your most obedt Servant

Go: Washington.

LB, DLC:GW.

1. The letter, which GW forwarded to Bryan Fairfax on 19 March, has not been found. For Sarah Bomford and the background to GW's involvement in the settlement of the estate of Margaret Green Savage, see Henry Lee and Daniel Payne to GW, 24 April 1767, n.1, GW to Savage, 28 June 1768, 27 Jan. 1772, Peter Trenor to GW, 8 Nov. 1786, n.1, GW to Fairfax, 6 April 1789, n.3, Trenor to GW, 29 Jan. 1790, and Fairfax to GW, 7 Feb. 1790.

To Bryan Fairfax

Dear Sir, Philadelphia, March 19th 1792.

I enclose you a letter which I have received from a Mr Samuel Potts, on the subject of a Legacy left to Mrs Bomford by the late Mr[s] Savage.[1]

It is unnecessary to detail to you, my dear Sir, the causes which have put it out of my power to pay any attention to the Affairs of Mrs Savage since the year 1775. You know them well. And I can only assure you that they still exist, and in a stronger degree, if possible, than heretofore. I must, therefore, as I have before mentioned to you, rely upon your endeavours to have every thing relative to that unfortunate womans Affairs brought to a close as speedily as the nature of the case will admit: and as you must have a much better knowledge of the present situation of them than I can have, I have referred Mr Potts (as I before did Mrs Bomford herself) to you for information on the subject; not doubting but you will give him all the satisfaction in your power relative to the business.

Mrs Washington joins her best wishe[s][2] for yourself, Mrs Fair fax[3] and your family, to those of, Dear Sir, Your affte & hble Servant

Go: Washington.

LB, DLC:GW. The LS of this letter, which was offered for sale in 1980 by B. Altman, has not been found (*New York Times,* 10 Feb. 1980).

For the background to this letter, see the documents cited in GW to Samuel Potts, 18 Mar. 1792, n.1.

1. Samuel Potts's letter to GW of 31 Oct. 1791 has not been found.

2. The copyist mistakenly wrote "wished."

3. Jane (Jenny) Dennison (Donaldson) Fairfax, Bryan Fairfax's second wife, died in 1805.

Henry Knox to Tobias Lear

Dear Sir. [Philadelphia] March 19th 1792.

Will you be so good as to inform the President of the United States, that French Peter, who was in France with the Marquis, died last night, and that he will be buried to morrow[1]—This event will prevent, according to their customs, their waiting on the President until thursday[2] 12 o'clock. I am Dear Sir, Yours

H. Knox

LS, DLC:GW; LB, DLC:GW.

1. The *Pennsylvania Gazette* (Philadelphia) reported on 28 Mar. the death in Philadelphia on Monday, 19 Mar., of Peter Otsequette (Jaquette), "one of the principal sachems of the Oneida Nation of Indians . . . [who] was educated in France; he accompanied M. de la Fayette to that country on his return from the United States."

2. Knox is referring to Thursday, 22 Mar. 1792.

From John Carroll

Baltimore 20th March 1792

The subscriber has the honour of stating, that the President in opening the present session of Congress, was pleased to express a sentiment, suggesting the propriety of introducing a system of conduct towards the Indians within, and contiguous to the United States, *corresponding with the mild principles of religion and philanthropy*;[1] that experience has shewn, how much this would contribute to put a period to those cruelties and devastations, which have distressed so often the frontier inhabitants of these States; that a few of those Indian tribes having received formerly some instruction in the principles and duties of Christianity, their manners became more gentle, their warfare less savage, and a strong attachment was formed in their minds towards the nation, to whose provident care they were indebted, for enabling the ministers of religion to subsist amongst them; that at present, some worthy and respectable clergymen are willing and desirous of devoting themselves to the charitable employment of reviving and continuing amongst those Indians the lessons of religion and morality, which were deliver'd to them formerly; that a proposal so benevolent in its object, and promising so much advantage to the United States, was warmly encouraged by the subscriber, who flattered himself, that these charitable men would find some provision for their subsistance, during their dangerous and painful employment, in the produce of a body of land near the Kaskaskias, of which the Seminary of Quebeck conceived itself to be the undoubted owner, and for the cession of which, for the purpose stated in this memorial, some correspondence has subsisted between a member of the Seminary and the Subscriber: that an Act of Congress, passed last session, founded, no doubt, on reasons of right and justice, has disposed otherwise of that land;[2] so that now, no means are left for the support of so meritorious and useful an undertaking, unless the wisdom and benevolence of Congress should deem it advisable to make for a few years, a small allowance for the necessary subsistance of clergymen employed in disseminating the principles of Christianity amongst the natives of the Western Territory; and to make them a grant equivalent to the lands heretofore held near the Kaskaskias, which in a short time may supply all their necessities.

That the President and Congress may be more sensible of the advantages contemplated in this memorial, the Subscriber has the honour of subjoining two original letters, received some time since, one from, and the other relating to the Indians situated at the Eastern extremity of these states;[3] and he relies, with entire confidence, on the wisdom, sound policy, and regard for public happiness, which have distinguished the proceedings of the general government.

J. Carroll.

ADS, DNA: RG 59, Miscellaneous Letters.

1. In his first address to the Second Congress, GW said that "A System corrisponding with the mild principles of religion and philanthropy towards an unenlightened race of men, whose happiness materially depends on the conduct of the United States, would be as honorable to the national character as conformable to the dictates of sound policy" (GW to the U.S. Senate and House of Representatives, 25 Oct. 1791).

2. On 3 Mar. 1791 GW signed "An Act for granting lands to the Inhabitants and settlers at Vincennes and the Illinois country, in the territory northwest of the Ohio, and for confirming them in their possessions." Section 7 reads in part: "That a tract of land at Kaskaskia, formerly occupied by the Jesuits, be laid off and confirmed to St. Jam Beouvais [Jean-Baptiste St. Gemme Bauvais], who claims the same in virtue of a purchase thereof" (1 *Stat.* 221–22). For the background to this provision, see Extracts from the Report of the Governor of the Territory of the United States North-west of the Ohio, c.17 Feb. 1791, n.5, enclosed in Thomas Jefferson to GW, 17 Feb. 1791.

3. The enclosures have not been identified. In his reply to Carroll of 10 April, GW noted that he had returned them to Carroll's cousin, U.S. Senator Charles Carroll of Carrollton.

To the United States Senate and House of Representatives

[Philadelphia, 20 March 1792]

Gentlemen of the Senate, and of the House of Representatives,

The several Acts which have been passed relatively to the military establishment of the United States, and the protection of the Frontiers, do not appear to have made provision for more than one Brigadier General.[1] It is incumbent upon me to observe, that with a view merely to the organization of the troops designated by those Acts, a greater number of Officers of that grade would in my opinion be conducive to the good of the public service. But an increase of the number becomes still more desireable, in reference to a different organization which is contemplated, pursuant to the authority vested in me for that purpose, and which, besides other advantages expected from it, is recommended by considerations of œconomy.

I therefore request that you will be pleased to take this subject into your early consideration, and to adopt such measures thereon as you shall judge proper.[2]

Go: Washington

DS, DNA: RG 46, Second Congress, 1791–1793, Records of Legislative Proceedings, President's Messages; copy, DNA: RG 233, Second Congress, 1791–1793, Records of Legislative Proceedings, Journals; LB, DLC:GW.

1. GW signed congressional acts establishing and organizing the army of the United States and providing for frontier defense on 29 Sept. 1789, 30 April 1790, 3 Mar. 1791, and 5 Mar. 1792 (1 *Stat.* 95–96, 119–21, 222–24, 241–43).

2. On this date the U.S. Senate committed GW's message to Aaron Burr, James Gunn, and Benjamin Hawkins to consider and report on it, and the House of Representatives on 21 Mar. appointed a committee of three for similar purposes. On 22 Mar. the Senate committee reported a bill to supplement "An Act for making farther and more effectual Provision for the Protection of the Frontiers of the United States" of 5 March. The supplemental bill passed the Senate on 23 Mar., and the House read it twice and committed it the same day. On 24 Mar. the House amended and passed it, and the Senate approved the amended bill on 26 Mar. (*Annals of Congress,* 2d Cong., 110, 112–13, 477, 481–83). On 28 Mar., GW signed "An Act supplemental to the act for making farther and more effectual provision for the protection of the frontiers of the United States," which authorized the president, by and with the advice and consent of the Senate, to appoint up to four brigadier generals "as may be conducive to the good of the public service" (1 *Stat.* 246). For GW's nomination of four additional brigadier generals, see GW to the U.S. Senate, 9 April.

From Thomas Jefferson

[Philadelphia, c.21 March 1792][1]

Th: Jefferson presents his respects to the President, and sends for his perusal a letter he has prepared for the Commissioners, which will inform him also of mister Blodget's ideas. in the mean time Blodget will be preparing the necessary papers.[2]

Th: J. has at length been able to see Dr Wistar about the big bones. they are at his house, always open to inspection. the

Doctor is habitually at home at two oclock: if the President would rather go when he is not at home, the servants will shew the bones. Th: J. did not intimate to the Doctr who it was that wished to see them, so that the President will fix any day & hour he pleases on these premises, & Th: J. will have the honor to attend him.[3]

AL, DNA: RG 59, Miscellaneous Letters; LB, DNA: RG 59, George Washington's Correspondence with His Secretaries of State; LB (photocopy), DLC:GW.

1. Tobias Lear docketed the cover of the receiver's copy "March—1792 (private)." A second writer later wrote "28" over Lear's dash. A third person wrote at the top of the letter: "file March 28. 1792." Jefferson, however, must have written it sometime before GW's apparent reply of this day.

2. Jefferson's enclosed letter to the commissioners for the District of Columbia of 21 Mar. concluded that "The temporary check on the price of public paper, occasioned by Mr. [William] Duer's failure, induces Mr. [Samuel] Blodget [Jr.] to think it will be better to postpone for a few days the opening of the loan proposed, as he thinks it important that the present panic should be so far over, as to enable him to get it through at once, when proposed" (*Jefferson Papers,* 23:320–21). For Blodget's proposed loan to finance projects in the Federal City, see GW to the Commissioners for the District of Columbia, 6 Mar. 1792, n.7.

The financial panic in New York City following the collapse of William Duer's project to corner the government bond market did not subside until May 1792. Duer's overextension of credit proved fatal to his reputation and to his far-flung speculations when his first payments to the government fell due after the price for securities had peaked in late January and declined over the next five weeks. He was forced to suspend payments on 9 Mar., the day after the Bank of New York stopped extending him credit. Duer's financial situation was further complicated by the Treasury Department's decision to recover $200,000 from Duer's long-overdue accounts stemming from war contracts and his service as secretary to the Board of Treasury, a move instituted on 12 Mar. by U.S. comptroller Oliver Wolcott, Jr., who wished to secure the government's claims on Duer's assets before he fell into bankruptcy. Duer was committed to the city prison on 23 Mar., as much for his own safety against mobs of his creditors who had invested their all in his scheme as for his own fiscal mismanagement. Duer's partner, New York speculator Alexander Macomb, was forced to suspend payments on his loans on 12 April. He entered debtors' prison a week later, where he remained until February 1793 (see Duer to Alexander Hamilton, 12 Mar., Hamilton to Duer, 14, 23 Mar., Robert Troup to Hamilton, 19 Mar., Philip Schuyler to Hamilton, 25 Mar., and William Seton to Hamilton, 9 April 1792, all in Syrett, *Hamilton Papers,* 11:126–27, 131–32, 155–58, 170–72, 186–90, 257–58; "The Panic of 1792" in Davis, *Earlier History of American Corporations,* 1:278–315). Jefferson and other opponents of Hamilton's funding system made much political capital out of the panic, and the secretary of the treasury was forced to shore up government securities to restore public confidence in the administration's fiscal policies (see Hamilton to GW, 12 April, n.1, Jefferson to GW, 23 May [second letter]).

3. Dr. Casper (Caspar) Wistar (1761–1818), who had received medical degrees from the University of the State of Pennsylvania in 1782 and the University of Edinburgh in 1786 and who resided at 138 High Street in Philadelphia in 1792, was a professor of chemistry at the College of Philadelphia and, later, a professor of anatomy at the University of Pennsylvania. Wistar also served as curator, vice-president (1795–1815), and president (1815–1818) of the American Philosophical Society. In 1794 Henry Wansey wrote in his journal that Wistar, "I am told, has collected a vast variety of huge bones of this animal [mammoth], which he is endeavouring to systematise" (Miller, *Peale Papers,* 2:97).

To Thomas Jefferson

[Philadelphia]

Dear Sir, Wednesday Afternoon [21 March 1792]

To morrow I shall be engaged all day—but will, in the course of it, fix a time to view the Big bones at Doctr Wisters.

I hope Mr Blodget does not begin to hesitate concerning the loan?—And I hope the Commissioners, when they are about it, will build a Stone bridge and a compleat one, over Rock Creek—it will be the cheapest in the end.[1] Yrs sincerely

Go: Washington

ALS, DLC: Jefferson Papers.

1. Jefferson added in a postscript to his letter to the commissioners for the District of Columbia of this day: "The President thinks the bridge over Rock creek should be of stone, and that it will be the cheapest in the end" (*Jefferson Papers,* 23:320–21). The commissioners contracted with Baltimore builder Leonard Harbaugh to build a sixty-foot multiarched stone bridge that rose twenty feet over Rock Creek. The foundation stone of the Federal Bridge, the first permanent structure built by the commissioners, was laid with celebration on 4 July 1792, and the bridge was completed in early 1793. By that June, however, the central arch had begun to crumble as the bridge's piers settled three feet. The commissioners decided to convert the bridge into a wooden drawbridge in the autumn of 1794 (see GW to David Stuart, 8 April, Stuart to GW, 18 April, and GW to Lear, 30 July 1792).

From Gouverneur Morris

Dear Sir London 21 March 1792

Yesterday I was informed that the Senate had agreed to your Nomination of diplomatic Servants.[1] If I know my own Heart this

Intelligence is far less agreable to me on my own Account than on that of the Public. I am sure that a Rejection, from whatever Cause it may have arisen, would have been attributed to Disunion in our Councils.

I find that the King of France has appointed to the Office of foreign Affairs a Monsieur Demouriez and that it is considered as a Sacrifice to the Jacobins.[2] He is a bold determin'd Man. I am not acquainted with him personally, but I know that he has long been seeking a Place in the Administration and was, about six Months ago, determin'd if appointed one of the Ministers to destroy at the Peril of his Life the *jacobin* and all other Clubs, and to effect a Change in the Government. How far he may have changed his Opinions since, I really cannot tell, but I mention this to you *now* because When I know more I can refer to this Letter and say that *by coming into Office he has not changed his Sentiments* if he persists in those his antient Determinations. If not, I will tell you that *he is more prudent than was supposed.* And these Words will in either Case mean nothing more than is here set down for them. The King consulted him (as I was told by his confidential friend in the Middle of last October) on the State of Affairs when Monsr de Montmorin went out, but the high toned Measures he proposed were not adopted. I am my dear Sir, with most sincere Esteem & Respect yours

Gouvr Morris

ALS, DLC:GW; LB, DLC: Gouverneur Morris Papers.

1. Morris wrote William Short on 22 Mar. that "A gentleman of my Acquaintance has received a Letter by the Packet which mentions that the Senate have approved the Nominations made by the President in the diplomatic Line" (Morris, *Diary of the French Revolution,* 2:391). Morris did not receive the secretary of state's official letter of 23 Jan. with his credentials and instructions and GW's private letter of 28 Jan. concerning the appointment until 6 April (see Morris to GW, 6 April; Morris, *Diary of the French Revolution,* 2:396).

2. Charles-François du Périer (Duperrier) Dumouriez (1739–1823) served as French minister of foreign affairs from 17 Mar. until 16 June 1792, when he resumed his military career. He was responsible for the French victories at Valmy and Jemappes and the invasion of Belgium and Holland during the fall of 1792. Following his defeat at the Battle of Neerwinden on 18 Mar. 1793, Dumouriez was denounced as a traitor and summoned to Paris. To save himself from execution, he deserted to the Austrians and eventually immigrated to England.

From Timothy Pickering

Sir, Philadelphia Wednesday Evening March 21. 1792.

The manner in which I have been employed to effect the present visit of the Chiefs of the Five Nations, renders me peculiarly interested that the negociations with them should conform with the direct object of the invitation. This object is indelibly impressed on my mind; it having been the main argument offered by me, to convince them of the real friendship of the United States. I feel interested in its accomplishment, because it involves the *good faith of the United States.* For, agreeably to my instructions; "I informed them how desirous you were that the Indians should have imparted to them the blessings of husbandry and the arts:" And I repeated to them your words—"That the United States will be true and faithful to their engagements."

Having assured them of the assistance of the United States to introduce among them the knowledge of husbandry and a few other important arts connected with it, I invited a small number of the principal chiefs to come to Philadelphia, after the last Corn Harvest, to negociate the plan for their introduction. The visit too, independently of its principal object, might make useful impressions. They delayed coming. The destructive defeat of our army took place. This sad event might *prevent* their coming. Good policy dictated a fresh invitation. And that it might not seem to flow from fear or discouragement—I thought the renewal of the invitation should appear to proceed wholly from me. The idea was liked by General Knox. I wrote a message to be sent by Mr Kirkland. As I recollect, the General informed me that it was approved by you.[1]

In the message I reminded them of my former invitation to come to the *Great Council Fire of the United States,* in order to fix the time and manner of introducing among them the knowledge of farming—of smith's & carpenter's work—of spinning & weaving—and of reading and writing: these being the arts I had before expressly mentioned.

I added—"That I was impatient for their arrival, that they might receive strong proofs, that the words I spoke to them were true—that they came from my heart—and that the United States are faithful to their engagements."

The invitation was confined to *this single object.* Permit me, therefore, to express my opinion, That until the entire arrangement relative to it be formed, to their full satisfaction—no other object should be brought into view. But this being adjusted; with such strong proofs before them of the candor—the truth—the justice & the liberality of the United States—they will be convinced that we are *really their friends*: and thus they may be led to entertain a belief that we are heartily disposed to be *the friends* of the *other tribes* now in arms against us: and impressed with this belief—they may listen to overtures to become mediators between us. But if the latter be proposed in the first instance—the natural order of things will be reversed; and, I fear, every object of their visit defeated.

If the secretary of war had asked me a single question on the subject, I should freely have suggested to him these ideas. This evening I chanced to hear that he (doubtless not adverting to the terms of the invitation) is preparing a speech, to be delivered tomorrow, in which the disposition of the Five Nations to become mediators, is to be sounded.[2] I have therefore thought it *my duty,* without loss of time, to submit them to your consideration. I have no desire to appear in the matter: having nothing in view but to prevent a *serious mischief.*

There is an additional reason for the caution here suggested, which I beg leave to mention.

Last Thursday,[3] when the Indians gave me their formal answers to my invitation, they stated many causes of their delay. Among other things they told me that Brant had been the means of detaining them. "Brant, (said they) who knows as much as white people know, told us that the real design of the invitation was not *on* the paper—but *behind* it." That is the *avowed object* of the invitation was merely *ostensible*: while the *real object* was *kept out of sight.*

There is another reason, which I ought not to conceal. Indians have been so often deceived by White people, that *White Man* is among many of them, but another name for *Liar.* Really, Sir I am unwilling to be subjected to this infamy. I confess I am not indifferent to a good name, even among Indians[.] Besides, they recieved, and expressly considered *me,* as "*your Representative*["]; and my promises, as the promises of ["]*The Town Destroyer.*" Sir, for your honour & the honour & interest of the United States, I wish them to *know* that *there are some white men who are incapable of deceiving.*

I acknowledge sir, that my feelings have been excited: and if I have expressed myself in a stile unusual in addressing you, I trust you will ascribe it to the true cause—the interesting situation in which I stand. With great respect I am sir, Your most h'ble & obedt servt

T.P.

ADfS, MHi: Timothy Pickering Papers; copy, written and signed by Pickering, DLC: Hamilton Papers. Pickering notes on the draft that he sent this letter to the president on "Thursday Morning," 22 March. Pickering forwarded the copy in DLC to Hamilton on 8 May 1792 (see Syrett, *Hamilton Papers,* 11:372–78).

1. On 2 May 1791 Henry Knox had instructed Pickering, among other things, to invite Joseph Brant "to repair to this place [Philadelphia], when the President of the United States shall be present, together with such other important characters as you may judge proper" when he met with the Iroquois near Newtown (Elmira), N.Y. (*ASP, Indian Affairs,* 1:166). For the July 1791 meeting between Pickering and the Iroquois at Newtown, see Knox to GW, 17 Aug. 1791, n.1. For Pickering's renewed invitation of 19 Dec. 1791 and Samuel Kirkland's and Secretary of War Knox's unsuccessful efforts to induce Brant to make the trip to the U.S. capital at this time, see GW to Knox, 25 Feb. 1792, source note and note 1. Joseph Brant finally visited Philadelphia in June 1792, three months after his fellow chiefs arrived (see Knox to Tobias Lear, 16 June, GW to Gouverneur Morris, 21 June 1792).

2. Knox wrote Tobias Lear on 22 Mar.: "I enclose you, in order to be submitted to the President of the United States, the draft of a speech to the deputation of the five nations of indians now in this city." Lear replied to Knox the next day: "As the President will give the Speech now in his possession to the Indians, he wishes to have another copy prepared for him to keep" (both letters are in DLC:GW). For the copy of the speech made by the clerk of Congress, see GW to the Five Nations, 23 March.

3. The Iroquois chiefs arrived in Philadelphia on 13 March. They gave their "formal answers" to Pickering's invitation two days later, on Thursday, 15 Mar. 1792. For more on their visit to the U.S. capital, see GW to the Five Nations, 23 Mar. 1792, and source note.

From Thomas Jefferson

[Philadelphia] Mar. 22. 1792.

The Secretary of state having had under consideration the expediency & extent of a Convention with Spain to be established for with respect to fugitives from the United states to their adjoining provinces, or from those provinces to the United States, Reports to the President of the United States the inclosed Analytical view of the motives & principles which should govern such a Convention, and the Project of a convention adapted thereto, which he is of opinion should be forwarded to messrs Carmichael & Short, with powers to treat & conclude thereon.[1]

Th: Jefferson

ADS, DNA: RG 59, Miscellaneous Letters; ADS (letterpress copy), DLC: Jefferson Papers; LB, DNA: RG 59, George Washington's Correspondence with His Secretaries of State; LB (photocopy), DLC:GW; copy, DNA: RG 59, Reports of the Secretary of State to the President and Congress.

For the administration's desire to sign a limited extradition treaty with Spain, see Jefferson to GW, 2 April, 7 Nov. 1791, GW to James Seagrove, 20 May 1791, and Charles Pinckney to GW, 18 Aug. 1791, 8 Jan. 1792 (second letter).

1. The enclosed "Project of a Convention with the Spanish provinces" reads: "Any person having committed Murder of malice prepense, not of the nature of treason, within the United States or the Spanish provinces adjoining thereto, and fleeing from the justice of the country, shall be delivered up by the government where he shall be found, to that from which he fled, whenever demanded by the same.

"The manner of the demand by the Spanish government, and of the compliance by that of the United States, shall be as follows. The person authorized by the Spanish government, where the Murder was committed to pursue the fugitive, may apply to any justice of the supreme court of the United States or to the district judge of the place where the fugitive is, exhibiting proof on oath that a Murder has been committed by the said fugitive within the said government, who shall thereon issue his warrant to the Marshal or deputy Marshal of the same place to arrest the fugitive and have him before the said district judge, or the said pursuer may apply to such marshal or deputy marshal directly, who, on exhibition of proof as aforesaid, shall thereupon arrest the fugitive, and carry him before the said district judge, and when before him in either way, he shall, within not less than [ ] days, nor more than [ ] hold a special court of inquiry, causing a grand jury to be summoned thereto, and charging them to inquire whether the fugitive hath committed a Murder, not of the nature of treason, within the province demanding him, and on their finding a true bill, the judge shall order the officer, in whose custody the fugitive is, to deliver him over to the person authorized as aforesaid to receive him, and shall give such further authorities to aid the said person in safe keeping and conveying the said fugitive to the limits of the United States as shall be necessary and within his powers; and his powers shall expressly extend to command the aid of the posse of every district through which the said fugitive is to be carried. And the said justices, judges, and other officers shall use in the premises the same process and proceedings, mutatis mutandis, and govern themselves by the same principles and rules of law as in cases of Murder committed on the high seas.

"And the manner of demand by the United States and of compliance by the Spanish government, shall be as follows. The person authorized by any justice of the Supreme court of the United States, or by the district judge where the Murder was committed, to pursue the fugitive, may apply to [ ].

"Evidence on oath, though written, and ex parte, shall have the same weight with the judge and grand jury in the preceding cases, as if the same had been given before them orally, and in presence of the prisoner.

"The courts of Justice of the said states and provinces shall be reciprocally open for the demand and recovery of debts due to any person inhabiting the one, from any person fled therefrom and found in the other, in like manner as they are open to their own citizens: likewise for the recovery of the property, or the value thereof carried away from any person inhabiting the one, by any person fled therefrom and found in the other, which carrying away shall give a right of civil action, whether the fugitive came to the original possession lawfully or unlawfully, even feloniously; likewise for the recovery of damages sustained by any forgery committed by such fugitive. And the same provision shall hold in favor of the representatives of the original creditor or sufferer, and against the representatives of the original debtor, carrier away or forger: also in favor of either government or of corporations as of natural persons: but in no case shall the person of the defendant be imprisoned for the debt, though the process, whether original, mesne, or final be, for the form sake, directed against his person. the time between the flight and the commencement of the action, shall be counted but as one day under any act of limitations.

"This convention shall continue in force [ ] Years from the exchange of ratifications, and shall not extend to any thing happening previous to such exchange" (DNA: RG 59, Miscellaneous Letters). On the verso of this document was an outline of "Heads of consideration on the establishment of Conventions between the United States and their neighbors for the mutual delivery of Fugitives from Justice," dated 22 Mar. 1792, which is printed in full in *Jefferson Papers,* 23:328–30. For GW's comments on the project, see GW to Jefferson, 25 March. Jefferson sent his final draft of the documents to the commissioners to treat with Spain on 24 April (see ibid., 453–54).

John Lamb to Tobias Lear

New York, 22 Mar. 1792. Requests Lear's "favor, in delivering the enclosed."[1]

ALS, DLC:GW.

1. The enclosure was Lamb's letter of this date to Martha Washington covering a receipt for two barrels of "Newtown Pippins" being shipped on the

New York packet, for which he begged her acceptance. On 10 Dec. 1790 he had sent the first lady three barrels of apples, along with some ginger and salmon (Fields, *Papers of Martha Washington,* 227, 236).

From Otho Holland Williams

(Private)

Dear Sir, Baltimore 22d March 1792

The receipt of your obliging letter of the 14th Instant gave me very great pleasure, as it gratified a wish to know that your plants were not lost; and that you had a prospect, ultimately, of receiving them safe at Mount Vernon.[1]

I have, for some time past, deliberated on the propriety of consulting you on a circumstance relative to our State Government; and if my mind could admit of an idea that any unworthy motive might possibly be ascribed as the inducement I should certainly have resolved on being silent.

Several persons are nominated, by different interests, as successor to Mr Plater in the Office of Governor of this State; but no one, as yet, seems to obtain a decided preference.[2]

The line of my public conduct has always been direct and decisive; and although I have never Assumed the lead in political controversy, neither have I at any time implicitly followed the dictates of any party. This conduct while it has rendered me more respectable in the opinion of the friends of the present forms of Government, makes me less exceptionable in the opinion of others. In consequence of which, and the persuasion of some respectable men I am induced to believe that I should be honored with an election to the office if I would accept the appointment.

But, my Dear Sir, the office is only temporary and is incompatible with that which I hold under the United States; and although the former may be deemed the most honorable, it is not, all circumstances considered, more profitable than the latter; which, although not permanent is nevertheless bestowed upon a better tenor, and is a convenient addition to the means of supporting my family.

The undeviating Respect, Esteem, Affection and Veneration which I have constantly manifested for your person and Character must give you the most perfect assurance that I think it *impossible* you should afford the least countenance to an indirect measure with a view to favor an individual to the prejudice of the public; and I flatter myself that you believe me incapable of wishing your condescension to a thing unworthy of the most exalted elevation of Character—I trust too, that you think I would not, on my own account, risque a proposition improper, or unjust; and in this confidence I beg leave to suggest to you that in the event of my being elected to the Office of Governor of this State, it would be a great inducement to my acceptance, if I could know that Mr William Smith, late of Congress, would be my successor in the Office of Collector for the port of Baltimore;[3] For although I could not possible participate with him the profits of the Office of Collector during my continuance in the other Yet, besides the pleasure of serving him, I could rely upon his liberality and friendship (at a proper time) for his making, in my favor, a vacancy in that Office which for the satisfaction of friends, and perhaps the gratification of ambition, I had relinquished to him. His qualifications for the discharge of its duties, and the respectability of his character leave me no room to apprehend any exception on his account.

My hesitation arose from the delicate nature of the subject which I have not mentioned, and will not mention, even to Mr Smith, without your approbation.[4] I am, Dear Sir, With the most perfect Esteem, respect and attachment; Your most obedient and most Humble Servant

O. H. Williams

ALS, DLC:GW.

1. GW's letter to Williams of 14 Mar. has not been found. For the plants that William Moultrie had sent from South Carolina, see GW to Moultrie, 8 Nov. 1791, n.2, 14 Mar., 5 May 1792, Moultrie to GW, 29 Dec. 1791, and GW to Williams, 7 Feb. 1792, n.2.

2. Three days after the death of Gov. George Plater in Annapolis on 10 Feb., acting governor James Brice issued a proclamation calling the Maryland legislature into session on 2 April to elect a successor to complete Plater's term. Williams was not nominated. The nominees were Thomas Sim Lee, Nicholas Carroll (1751–1812), and Benjamin Ogle (1749–1809), and Lee was elected.

3. Williams had married Mary Smith, the daughter of wealthy Baltimore merchant William Smith, in 1786. GW appointed Smith auditor of the United States on 16 July 1791, but Smith hesitated to accept the post and eventually declined it (see Hamilton to GW, 6 Oct. 1791, n.2).

4. After the gubernatorial election Williams again wrote GW, on 18 April, asking him "to cancel" the letter of this date and to erase its subject from his memory. GW replied sympathetically on 26 April, and he later attempted to appoint Williams a brigadier general. Although Williams declined his commission in the U.S. military because of ill health, he retained his collectorship until his death in 1794 (see GW to the U.S. Senate, 8 May [second letter], and Williams to GW, 13 May).

To the Five Nations

Philadelphia. 23d March 1792.

Speech of the President of the United States, to the Chiefs and Representatives of the five nations of Indians, in Philadelphia.

Sachems and Warriors of the Five Nations.

It affords me great satisfaction, to see so many of you, who are the respectable Chiefs and Representatives of your several tribes, and I cordially bid you welcome to the Seat of the government of the United States.

You have been invited to this place by Colonel Pickering, at my special request, in order to remove all causes of discontent: to devise and adopt plans to promote your welfare, and firmly to cement the peace between the United States and you, so as that in future, we shall consider ourselves as brothers indeed.

I assure, that I am desirous, that a firm peace should exist, not only between the United States and the five Nations, but also between the United States and all the natives of this land; and this peace should be founded upon the principles of justice and humanity as upon an immovable rock.

That you may partake of all the comforts of this earth, which can be derived from civilized life, enriched by the possession of industry, virtue and knowledge: And I trust, that such judicious measures will now be concerted, to secure to you and your children, these invaluable objects, as will afford you just cause of rejoicing while you live.

That these are the strong and sincere desires of my heart, I hope time and circumstances will convince you. But in order that our peace and friendship may forever be unclouded, we must forget the misunderstandings of past times. Let us now look forward, and devise measures to render our friendship perpetual.

I am aware, that the existing hostilities with some of the western Indians have been ascribed to an unjust possession of their lands by the United States. But be assured, this is not the case. We require no lands but those obtained by treaties, which we consider as fairly made, and particularly confirmed by the treaty of Muskingum in the year 1789.[1]

If the western Indians should entertain the opinion, that we want to wrest their lands from them, they are laboring under an error. If this error should be corrected, it would be for their happiness; and nothing would give me more pleasure, because it would open to both of us the door of peace.

I shall not enter into further particulars with you at present, but refer you to General Knox, the Secretary of War, and Colonel Pickering, who will communicate with you, upon the objects of your journey, and inform me thereof.

As an evidence of the sincerity of the desires of the United States, for perfect peace and friendship with you, I deliver you this white belt of Wampum, which I request you will safely keep.

Go. Washington.

LB, DNA: RG 233, Records of the Office of the Clerk, Records of Reports from Executive Departments; DS (extract), CSt. The extract, which consists of the document's final paragraph and GW's signature, might have accompanied the wampum belt.

For the background to this speech, see Timothy Pickering to GW, 21 Mar., nn.1–3. On 2 April Henry Knox sent GW the Indians' reply.

The following incomplete undated note appears under GW's name in the copy in the records of the clerk of the House: "On the 13th of March, a deputation of the five nations, consisting of fifty, arrived in Philadelphia. They were invited through the agency of Mr [Samuel] Kirkland, for the purpose of attaching them to, and convincing them of, the justice and humanity of the United States, and also to influence them to repair to the hostile tribes, in order to use their efforts to bring about a peace. These objects appeared to be effected, and they departed" (DNA: RG 233, Records of the Office of the Clerk, Records of Reports from Executive Departments). The rest of the note is printed in *ASP, Indian Affairs*: "to carry them into execution. Besides abundant presents, fifteen hundred dollars, annually, were stipulated to these Indians by the President and Senate of the United States, for the purpose of attempting to civilize them. . . . They arrived at Buffalo creek in the beginning of June, but, owing to their frequent counselling, and dilatory manner of conducting business, they did not set out from fort Erie for the hostile Indians until the middle of September, when they were accompanied by the firm friend of the United States, the Cornplanter. The result of their interference is not yet known, but may, with the determination of the hostile Indians, be daily expected" (1:229).

1. For the treaty signed on 9 Jan. 1789 by Arthur St. Clair and representatives of the Wyandot, Delaware, Ottawa, Chippewa, Potawatomi, and Sac nations at Fort Harmar on the Muskingum River, see St. Clair to GW, 2 May, n.4, GW to the U.S. Senate, 25 May, n.1, 17 Sept., n.1, and Proclamation on the Treaty of Fort Harmar, 29 Sept. 1789.

Charles Willson Peale to Tobias Lear

Museum[1] *[Philadelphia] 23 Mar. 1792.* Oblige me by using the enclosed cards at your leisure, and I will be pleased if my labors can contribute in the least to your amusements.[2] "I have now the prospect before me that by the assistance of Gentlemen of science, and by the Aid of a Generous Public to be enabled me to spend the remainder of my time in bringing the Museum into such perfection and Stability as to be in future highly useful as well as Entertaining. The plain is now laid to produce a Repository of subjects in Natural history which in a few years may become equal to any thing of the kind in Europe." Since leaving you, I thought that the donation of the Otahitian dress might be in your name.[3] Please inform me if I am permitted to publish this in my next list of communications to the Museum.[4]

ADfS, PPAmP.

1. Charles Willson Peale's museum was located at Philosophical Hall, opposite the library, on South Fifth Street. While presiding over the Federal Convention in 1787, GW had visited the museum at Peale's request to pose for a mezzotint. When Peale first printed the annual subscription list for tickets to the museum in January 1794, GW's signature headed the list (see the facsimile in Sellers, *Peale's Museum,* 72; see also *Diaries,* 5:173, 242; Peale to GW, 27 June 1790, source note).

2. The enclosures have not been identified but were probably tickets for admission to Peale's museum, which cost one shilling each in 1788.

3. GW had been presented the costume "by some gentlemen of Boston, adventurers in the first voyage made from thence to Nootka Sound, and the Otahitian Islands" (*Dunlap's American Daily Advertiser* [Philadelphia], 28 Aug. 1792; see also Thomas, *Reminiscences,* 1:42–43). For more on the expedition that left Boston in September 1787 and returned in the summer of 1790, see Estéban José Martínez to GW, 14 April 1792, n.1.

4. The list of the museum's recent acquisitions published by Peale in *Dunlap's American Daily Advertiser* on 28 Aug. 1792 says that the "long cloak and a cap, made of feathers, and very elegant" was "now deposited in this Museum for preservation and safe-keeping for the President."

To the United States Senate

United States [Philadelphia]
Gentlemen of the Senate. March 23d 1792.

At the conferrences which Colonel Pickering had with the five Nations at the painted post, the last year, ideas were then held out of introducing among them some of the primary principles of civilization.[1] In consequence of which, as well as more firmly to attach them to the interests of the United States, they have been invited to the seat of the general government.

As the representation now here, is respectable for its characters and influence, it is of some importance that the chiefs should be well satisfied of the entire good faith and liberality of the United States.

In managing the affairs of the indian tribes, generally, it appears proper to teach them to expect annual presents, conditioned on the evidence of their attachment to the interests of the United States—The situation of the five nations, and the present crisis of affairs would seem to render the extension of this measure to them highly judicious—I therefore request the advice of the Senate, whether an Article shall be stipulated, with the five nations, to the following purport.

To wit: "The United States, in order to promote the happiness of the five nations of indians, will cause to be expended ann[u]ally the amount of one thousand five hundred dollars, in purchasing for them clothing, domestic animals and implements of husbandry, and for encouraging useful artificers to reside in their Villages."[2]

Go: Washington

DS, DNA: RG 46, Second Congress, 1791–1793, Records of Executive Proceedings, President's Messages—Indian Relations; LB, DLC:GW.

For the background to this document, see Timothy Pickering to GW, 21 Mar., nn.1–2, and GW to the Five Nations, 23 March.

1. For Pickering's negotiations with the Five Nations in July 1791, which were moved from Painted Post, N.Y., to Tioga, Pa., see Henry Knox to GW, 17 Aug., nn.1–2, and Pickering to GW, 27 Aug. 1791.

2. After Tobias Lear delivered this message this day, the Senate ordered it to lie on the table. On 26 Mar., when the message was read, "It was thereupon Resolved, (two thirds of the Senate concurring) that they advise & consent to the Stipulation above recited," as an unidentified person wrote at the bottom of the receiver's copy. The secretary of the Senate, Samuel A. Otis, was then

ordered to lay this resolution before the president (*Executive Journal,* 1:116–17). GW and Thomas Jefferson signed and sealed the ratification of this article on 23 April (Jennings and Fenton, *Iroquois Indians*).

From Alexander Hamilton

[Philadelphia] 24th March 1792.

The Secretary of the Treasury has the honor to communicate to The President a letter which he has just received from Mr Short. It communicates the agreeable information of a Loan at four per Cent.[1]

LB, DLC:GW.

1. The enclosed letter of William Short to Hamilton was either that of 23 or 28 Dec. 1791, both of which announced the new loan completed at Amsterdam (see Syrett, *Hamilton Papers,* 10:403–4, 472–80).

To Thomas Jefferson

[Philadelphia] Saturday Afternoon [24 March 1792][1]

The Letters from Mr de Mirbeck[2] and Mr Vall-travers[3] to the P—— and from the Proprietors of the Federal City to Mr Walker,[4] he wishes Mr Jefferson to read & consider, that answers to, or proper notice of them, may result from it.

AL, DLC: Jefferson Papers.

1. Jefferson endorsed this letter as having been received on Saturday, 24 Mar. 1792.

2. The enclosed letter from Frédéric-Ignace de Mirbeck to GW is dated 6 Mar. 1792.

3. For the enclosed letter from Rodolph Vall-travers to GW of 30 Nov. 1791, see Vall-travers to GW, 21 July 1791, n.5. Jefferson replied to Vall-travers for the president on 2 April (see *Jefferson Papers,* 23:366–67).

4. For the enclosed letter from the proprietors of the federal district to George Walker of 9 Mar. protesting L'Enfant's dismissal, see Kite, *L'Enfant and Washington,* 168–69.

To Hannah Fairfax Washington

Dear Madam, Philad. 24th March, 1792.

Having lately received from Sir Isaac Heard a letter, with a sketch of a genealogical table of the family of Washington, I have taken the liberty to enclose copies of them to you, begging your assistance to enable me to comply with the request he has made (if among the Papers of my deceased relation there be any trace of this matter) that I will complete the sketch, by making the additions which are there wanting—or rather by filling up the blanks.[1]

As I have heretofore paid but little attention to this subject, and my present avocations not permitting me to make the necessary researches now, I am induced to ask your aid, presuming, as your late Husband's father was older than mine[2] you might, either from your own knowledge or a recurrence to documents, or tables in your possession, be able to complete the sketch, and thereby put it in my power to comply with the request of Sr Isaac Heard, which seems to be made with much earnestness, and to which an attention seems due, on account of his politeness. This must be my excuse for giving you the trouble of receiving and answering this letter as soon as you can make it convenient. I am &c.

Go: Washington.

LB, DLC:GW.

1. For the enclosed genealogical table and inquiries of Sir Isaac Heard, see Heard to GW, 7 Dec. 1791, nn.1–2.

2. John Washington, the father of Hannah's deceased husband, Warner Washington, was born in 1692. GW's father, Augustine Washington, was born in 1694 and died in 1743. Both were sons of Maj. Lawrence Washington (1659–1697/98).

To Thomas Jefferson

[Philadelphia] March 25th 1792.

The President of the United States has attentively considered the "Project of a Convention with the Spanish Provences" which was submitted to him by the Secretary of State, and informs him that the same meets his approbation.[1] The President, however, thinks it proper to observe, that in perusing the beforementioned Project some doubts arose in his mind as to the expediency of two points mentioned therein. The one relative to instituting a civil, instead of a criminal process against Forgerers; who, generally, if not always, are possessed of little property.[2]

The other, respecting the *unlimited* time in which a person may be liable to an Action.[3]

By expressing these quæries the President would not be understood as objecting to the points touched upon;[4] he only wishes to draw the Secretary's further attention to them, & if he should, upon reconsideration, think it right for them to stand upon their present footing the President acquiesces therein.[5]

AL, DLC: Jefferson Papers; Df (in the writing of Tobias Lear, with emendations in GW's hand), DNA: RG 59, Miscellaneous Letters; LB, DNA: RG 59, George Washington's Correspondence with His Secretaries of State; LB (photocopy), DLC:GW. The changes that GW made to the draft are given in notes 2, 3, and 5.

1. For Jefferson's projected extradition treaty with Spain, see Jefferson to GW, 22 Mar., n.1.

2. In Lear's draft GW added this clause above the line.

3. At this place in the draft, GW struck out the following two paragraphs: "In regard to the first, Altho' from a well intentioned principle of lenity a civil, instead of a criminal process might be desireable against persons accused of the high crime of forgery; Yet, might not instances occur in which, from the enormity of the crime or from some peculiar circumstances atten⟨ding it⟩ a criminal process would be highly proper, and that a serious detriment might accrue to the Government from having given up the *right* of instituting such a process?—And would not the recovery of damages against the culprit, in all cases, be inadequate to the injury sustained by the prosecuting party, and especially, as those who may be guilty of such crimes are generally persons destitute of sufficient property to make good the damages they have done?

"In regard to the second point. Would not a limitation of the time between the flight & the commencement of the Action (letting the time extend far enough to take in every supposeable case) be a piece of attention due to the *unfortunate* (for there may be some of that description among fugitives) by releiving them from solicitude & perhaps vexatious prosecutions after a certain period?—And would not such a limitation prevent an endless litigation, without depriving the Creditor of that right of prosecution to which he is justly entitled?"

4. In the copy of the proposed treaty that Jefferson sent to William Carmichael and William Short on 24 April, Jefferson heeded GW's suggestion of limiting the period of time, by altering the text to read: "If the time between the flight and the commencement of the action exceed not [ ] years, it shall be counted but as one day under any act of limitations" (see Jefferson to GW, 22 Mar., n.1.; *Jefferson Papers,* 23:331–32).

5. At this place in the draft, the following passage is deleted: "The Secy will receive herewith for his consideration an Estimate of the Post Master Genl for carrying the Mails, (which the President requests him to take into consideration)." GW apparently presented Timothy Pickering's expense estimate of 22 Mar. (DLC: Jefferson Papers) to Jefferson in another manner, as the secre-

tary of state commented on it in a letter to the postmaster general of 28 Mar. (see Jefferson to Pickering, 28 Mar., *Jefferson Papers,* 23:347–48).

From Arthur St. Clair

Sir, Philadelphia March 26th 1792

I beg leave to offer you my unfeigned Thanks for the honor conferred upon me by the Appointment to the command of the Army of the united States the last Campaign. Though that Campaign was unfortunate, I am not conscious that any thing within my power to have produced a more happy Issue, was neglected. As I was prompted, Sir, to accept that Command by no motives of either Ambition or Interest, but by a fervent Wish to be of Service to my Country, and a Belief, perhaps too fondly entertained that I could be so; that I am led to decline it in future proceeds neither from Disgust nor Disapointment.

Having been much afflicted with Sickness during nearly the whole of the Campaign, tho' I flatter myself the public Interests did not suffer by it; and although my Health is now tolerably restored, my Constitution has received a very severe shock, and I might not again be able to go through the weight of Business which necessarily follows the command of an Army.

Although Sir, I am myself persuaded that every thing was done, in the Course of the last Campaign, that could be done on my part, fully to answer the public Expectations, yet it is denied by some, doubted by many, and known to but few out of the Army—A Wish to rectify the public Opinion, and a Duty that, I conceive I owe to myself, induces me to request that an Enquiry into my Conduct may be instituted—When that is over I may hope to be permitted to resign the Commission of Major General which I now hold. Should the Result of the Enquiry be that, in any Instance, the Duties of my Station were neglected; or, that I did not improve every Hour, and every Opportunity to the best Advantage; or, that the Operations of the Army, after it was in a Condition to operate, were delayed one Moment in consequence of my illness, I shall patiently submit to the merited Censure.[1]

To whoever may be appointed my Successor, I shall be happy

Sir, to give every Light and information my Situation as General of the Army, or of Governor of the western Territory put in my Power to obtain, and to evince to you Sir, and to the World, that the Confidence you were pleased to repose in me was not misplaced. With every Sentiment of Gratitude, of Respect, and allow me add of Affection I have the honor to be Sir, Your most obedient Servant

Ar St Clair

ALS, DNA: RG 59, Miscellaneous Letters; ADfS, OHi: Arthur St. Clair Papers; ADf, OHi: Arthur St. Clair Papers.

For the background to this letter, see GW to the U.S. Senate and House of Representatives, 12 Dec. 1791, n.1, Henry Knox to GW, 22 Jan., n.2, 1 Mar. 1792, Knox to Tobias Lear, 31 Jan. 1792, n.1, GW to Thomas Jefferson, 2 Mar., and Jefferson to GW, 2 Mar. 1792. On 24 Feb. 1792 St. Clair submitted to GW a lost draft of this letter, which he asked the president to review before its intended publication. GW requested Knox and Jefferson to assist in drafting a proper reply (see GW to Knox, 29 Feb., n.1). St. Clair's letter of this date with other correspondence concerning the resignation of his commission as major general appeared in the 16 April issue of the *National Gazette* (Philadelphia) (see GW to St. Clair, 28 Mar., 4 April, and St. Clair to GW, 31 Mar., 7 April).

If this was the letter that Tobias Lear returned to St. Clair by GW's direction, then St. Clair did not send it until 28 Mar., when he put it under cover of a letter to Lear "with a request that it might be submitted to the President" (Lear to St. Clair, 28 Mar., DNA: RG 59, Miscellaneous Letters).

1. Newspaper accounts initially absolved St. Clair of blame for the humiliating defeat of 4 Nov. 1791. For instance, the report in *Dunlap's American Daily Advertiser* (Philadelphia) of 2 Jan. 1792 reads: "All accounts of the late action with the Indians reflect honour on the conduct of General St. Clair and his gallent troops." After St. Clair arrived at the capital on 21 Jan., however, he became involved in a newspaper controversy. On 10 Feb. *Dunlap's American Daily Advertiser* published an "*Extract of a letter from* COLONEL ———, *Commanding Officer of a Frontier County, to a Member of Congress—dated Lexington, January, 1792,*" in which Col. William Darke sharply criticized both St. Clair and GW's administration: "That the executive should commit the reputation of the government, the event of a war already irksome to the people, and safety of the frontier, to a man, who from the situation of his health, was under the necessity of travelling on a bier, seems to have been an oversight as unexpected as it has been severely censured. A general, enwrapped ten-fold in flannel robes, unable to walk alone, placed on his car, bolstered on all sides with pillows and medicines, and thus moving on to attack the most active enemy in the world, was to the people of Kentuckey a *Raree-shew* of a very tragi-comical appearance indeed." After discoursing on strategy, Darke condemned "the *farcical pagaentry* of dragging brass field pieces through an unexplored wilderness, to batter down the limbs of trees upon the enemy" as "an experiment too ridiculous

to deserve serious reflection," and he concluded "That an officer, commanding an army of near 3000 men, should suffer an enemy, capable of defeating him, to encamp within gun shot of his quarters, the night preceding the engagement, without acquiring the necessary information, is deemed an egregious error, an unwarrantable inattention, which calls aloud for public investigation."

Samuel Blair to Tobias Lear

Tuesday afternoon [27 March 1792][1]

Allow me, Sir, the liberty, which I now assume, of addressing the President of the United States through you in consequence of the unavoidable delay of an answer to his and Mrs Washington's invitation to Mrs Blair and myself to dine with them on Thursdy next.[2] The delay was owing to my not being able to procure an earlier information from Mrs Blair on the subject.

She is very sorry that it is not in her power, on account of the badness of the road from Germantown, to come into Town this week. She therefore requests that her apology may be made.

At the same time, allow me likewise to communicate through you my desire of being excused on the present occasion, partly on account of ill health,[3] & partly on other considerations, which render it inconvenient for me to do myself the intended honor on Thursday next. Your very respectful humble Servant

Saml Blair

ALS, NNGL.

Samuel Blair (1741–1818) graduated from the College of New Jersey in 1760 and held a pastorate in Boston before settling in Germantown, Pa., where he became rector of a Presbyterian church. He served as a chaplain in the Continental army during the Revolutionary War, retiring in the winter of 1780–81 due to ill health. When the federal government moved to Philadelphia in late 1790, Blair obtained a position as congressional chaplain, which he held for two years.

1. When this undated letter was printed in 1933, the editor supplied the date of 26 Mar. 1792, which was a Monday (Decatur, *Private Affairs of George Washington,* 258–59).

2. Susannah Shippen (1743–1821), the eldest daughter of prominent Philadelphia physician William Shippen, Sr., married Blair on 24 Sept. 1769.

3. Blair also had been unable to attend GW's birthday celebrations in February 1792 because he was confined to his bed (see William White to Lear, 21 Feb., in GW to Thomas Jefferson, 11 Feb., n.2).

From Benjamin Galloway

Sir, Annapolis [Md.] March 27th 1792.

I have taken the Liberty of making the following Communication, in confidence that it will be attributed to a proper Motive, though it should not eventually be productive of the desired Consequence—a Young Gentleman,[1] who served the United States in the Cavalry during the late War; who was afterwards honoured with an Appointment in your Family, and who now resides on the Eastern Shore of the State of Maryland, by a casual concurrence of unfortunate Circumstances, has sustained a considerable Loss of property, insomuch that he has it in contemplation to remove himself, an amiable Wife, and large young Family to the *Western Waters*—being *incapacitated to encounter the Difficulties* necessarily connected with such an Undertaking, the probable Consequences would be extremely distressful to himself and Family: I am perswaded Inclination will not be wanting in your Disposition, Sir, to make such provision for him as will enable him to continue in this Country, should a favourable Opportunity offer for so doing, by such an Appointment in the Service of his Country, as his Qualifications entitle him to fill, with Credit to himself and advantage to the Commonwealth—I am with perfect Consideration. Sir. Your Obedient & devoted Servt

Benjamin Galloway

ALS, DLC:GW. The addressed cover of the letter is postmarked Annapolis, 28 Mar. 1792.

Benjamin Galloway (1752–1831) of Anne Arundel County, Md., was a lawyer and planter who served in the lower house of the Maryland legislature in 1777, as state attorney general in 1778, and in various local judicial offices during the 1780s.

1. The "Young Gentleman" was probably William Shaw, who had served as GW's secretary between July 1785 and August 1786. Upon leaving GW's employ, Shaw had given GW the impression that he intended "to proceed to the Northward to embark at Philadelphia for the West Inds" (*Diaries,* 5:30). GW, who had often complained about Shaw's absences from Mount Vernon during his tenure as secretary, apparently never appointed Shaw to a federal office (see Thomas Montgomerie to GW, 21 June 1785, n.1; *Diaries,* 4:158–59). Shaw headed a household of six whites and two slaves in Kent County, Md., in 1790 (*Heads of Families* [Maryland], 84).

From William Archibald McCrea

Sir, Philadelphia March 27th 1792

The eminent Station of Supreme Magistrate, which your Excellency holds, in the Administration of the Government of this Country, naturally leads the Great & numerous People over whom you preside, to consider you as their, Friend, their Protector, & their Father. Appellations which Associate with themselves respectful Esteem, Gratefull Remembrance, & Filial Affection. Having been taught, from my early Youth, to contemplate you, as acting for your Country, in all the above mentioned beneficent Characters, I am the more emboldened to trouble you with the present Application, beleiving that your Goodness will excuse it, should you finally deem it inexpedient to comply with my request—The Necessity I am under to provide for my Family & the consciousness I feel that I could discharge the Duties of the Office of Treasurer of the National Mint,[1] have led me to make known my Situation, in hopes that if no Person better qualified to serve the Public appeared as a Candidate for that Office, that it might be conferred on me, in consideration of my peculiar Circumstances.

Your Excellencys Time is too Valuable for me to go into a minute Detail. I will therefore only mention some of the more important Occurrences of my Life, as the Grounds of my present Application.

I am now in the 27th Year of my Age, I was born at Newark in New Castle County in the State of Delaware. My Fathers Name was William McCrea a Merchant of that Place, who died when I was but six Months old—My Mother who is still living, after the Death of my Father, married Mr Job Ruston late of Chester County in the State of Pensylvania Deceased. By Her kind care & Attention, I received an Academical Education at Newark. After which I served a regular Apprenticeship to the Profession of Physick, under the Tuition of Doctr William W. Smith late of this City Deceased[.] Soon after I Married & Settled at Newark, in the State of Delaware with good Prospects—But I met with the Misfortune to have my House take Fire in the Night Time—The Fire was not discovered 'till a considerable part of the House was in Flames, when it was impossible to suppress it—By this heavy

Misfortune I lost my House, all my Furniture, almost the whole of the Cloathing of my Family, all my Books, Medicines, Shop, Furniture & in short the principal part of my Personal Estate—I was then advised to remove to Pencader in the same state. I did so—It was an unfortunate Step. The Vicinity was by no means equal to what I was led to expect—I therefore, a little more than two Months since, removed from the State of Delaware to this City, with my Family, in hopes of being able to find employment decently to support them, & in which I could derive greater Advantages from my Education, than at Pencader, beleiving that every Man ought to render himself as usefull to his Country, & as beneficial to Society as his Education & Circumstances will Admit.

I am at present out of Business, the Losses I have sustained as before mentioned, depressed my Situation in Life—But they have not lessened my Abilities, my Integrity, or my Zeal to serve the Public—It was an accidental Misfortune such as often commands Commiseration. I think I can satisfactorily discharge the Duties of the Office I Solicit, & I can produce ample sureties for my Fidelity in it, with recommendatory Testimonials of my Character, Conduct & Reputation in Life, which I expect to receive in a few Days from the State of Delaware, in Addition to those herewith communicated, & which I shall then beg leave Also to Submit to your Inspection.[2] Will your Excellency therefore forgive my troubling you with this Application?

Should I be Appointed to the Office, I will do every thing in my power that you may not have cause to regret it—Fidelity, Industry, & Attention to the Duties of it shall mark my conduct—It would add much to the Happiness of myself & Family; & their Gratitude & their Blessings would be incessant—If contrary to my expectations my conduct should not give satisfaction; on the least Intimation of it, however remote, from your Excellency, I would resign the Office without the least Hesitation. Permit me to beseech your Excellency to consider my Situation, & the Testimonials I shall produce, &, if you think it compatible with the Publick Good, to give me a Nomination to the before mentioned Office,[3] which will for ever oblidge, Your Excellency's most Obedient and most Humble Servt,

William A. McCrea

ALS, DLC:GW.

1. On 25 Oct. 1791 GW had informed Congress that "the disorders in the existing currency, and especially the scarcity of small change . . . strongly recommend the carrying into immediate effect the resolution already entered into concerning the establishment of a Mint." Six days later the Senate appointed a committee composed of Robert Morris, Rufus King, Ralph Izard, George Cabot, and John Henry to consider the subject and, if it thought proper, report a bill to the upper chamber. On 21 Dec. 1791 Morris presented "A bill establishing a Mint, and regulating the coins of the United States," which the Senate passed on 12 Jan. 1792 and sent on to the House for its concurrence. The House resolved itself into a Committee of the Whole on 24 Mar. to consider the Senate bill, which, after a bit of intrachamber negotiating, it passed in due course. GW signed "An Act establishing a Mint, and regulating the Coins of the United States" into law on 2 April 1792 (*Annals of Congress*, 2d Cong., 20, 52, 69, 483–90; for the text of the act, see ibid., 1351–56).

2. The recommendations "herewith communicated" were letters to GW from Nicholas B. Waters, dated 8 Mar. 1792, and Hugh McCulloch, dated 10 March. Waters certified that an "Acquaintance of ten Years, commencing during his Apprenticeship with the late Dr William W. Smith of this City, has afforded me many proofs of his good moral Character & Acquirements . . . I am well convinced he would discharge the Duties" of treasurer of the Mint, "or any other Office committed to his Care, with a Degree of Integrity which would reflect honor on himself & his respectable family Connections" (DLC:GW). Hugh McCulloch, also writing from Philadelphia, testified that he "had a long Acquaintance with [McCrea's] Family connexions, and some Acquaintance with him personlly" and mentioned McCrea's birth at Newark, Del., his father's early death, his mother's remarriage, and his education, apprenticeship, marriage, and move to Philadelphia. McCulloch concluded: "the family Connexions of Doctr McCrea are respectable & he has so far as I have been informed, Supported a good reputation for Morality Integrity & Fidelity to those by whom he has been employed, & should he be appointed to the above mentioned Office I fully believe he would discharge the duties of it with Integrity & to the satisfaction of his Country" (DLC:GW).

McCrea's application also was supported by several other recommendations and character references addressed to GW, including those of Congressman James Boyd of Chester County, Pa., dated 13 Mar., and Thomas Wattson, justice of the peace for New Castle County, Del., dated 29 March. Recommendations to GW from the Rev. John McCrery, 28 Mar., and William Thomson, rector of Newark Academy, 29 Mar., an undated one from James Black, Esq., of New Castle County, and a letter to GW from William Patterson (not found) were sent under cover of a letter to GW of 30 Mar. from Delaware governor John McKinly who wrote that McCrea's recommenders were themselves men of candor (all six extant letters are in DLC:GW). McCrea apparently delivered the letters from McKinly, McCrery, Thomson, Black, and Patterson to GW in person (see McKinly to GW, 30 Mar., DLC:GW). Alexander Hamilton sent GW at least one more recommendation of McCrea, written by Senator Theodore Foster of Rhode Island (see Hamilton to GW, 11 April, n.1).

3. GW appointed Tristram Dalton treasurer of the U.S. Mint in early May (see GW to the U.S. Senate, 3 May [second letter]). By that time McCrea, who had earlier been informed that he would not be a candidate for the position, had been offered a military commission as a surgeon's mate (see McCrea to GW, 9 April). McCrea served in that capacity until October 1795.

From Thomas Jefferson

Sir
Philadelphia Mar. 28. 1792.

I have the honor to inclose you two letters from Judge Symmes of Jan. 25th & 27th. his letter of Sep. 17. mentioned in the first of these was received by me Nov. 23. and after being laid before you, was answered Dec. 4.[1] the part of the answer respecting leave from you to come to Philadelphia was in these words. "the President does not conceive that the Constitution has given him any controul over the proceedings of the Judges, and therefore considers that his permission or refusal of absence from your district would be merely nugatory."

With respect to the escort for the judges on their circuits, you will be pleased to determine whether the good of the service will permit them to have one from the military, or whether that part of the letter shall be laid before the legislature to make regular provision for an escort. That part of the letter respecting jails, must, as I apprehend, be laid before the legislature.[2]

The complaint against Capt. Armstrong, in the letter of Jan. 27. coming formally from a judge, will require notice.[3] a civil prosecution in the courts of the Territory appears to me most proper. perhaps a formal instruction to the Governor as Commander in chief to put his officers on their guard against any resistance to civil process might have the effect of preventing future disputes. I shall have the honor of waiting on you to take your pleasure on these several subjects, & have now that of being with sentiments of profound respect & sincere attachment Sir Your most obedt & most humble servt

Th: Jefferson

ALS, DNA: RG 59, Miscellaneous Letters; ALS (letterpress copy), DLC: Jefferson Papers; LB, DNA: RG 59, George Washington's Correspondence with His Secretaries of State; LB (photocopy), DLC:GW; LB, DNA: RG 59, Domestic Letters.

1. The three letters from Judge John Cleves Symmes to the secretary of state have not been found by the editors of the *Jefferson Papers* (23:350n.). For Jef-

ferson's reply of 4 Dec. 1791, see ibid., 22:377–78. Symmes (1742–1814), who had served on the N.J. supreme court 1777–87 and in the Continental Congress 1785–86, was appointed a judge in the Northwest Territory in 1788.

2. No evidence has been found suggesting that GW laid these two matters before Congress.

3. This complaint probably concerned an incident that Symmes reported to Elias Boudinot and Jonathan Dayton two days earlier: "Captain John Armstrong, who commands, for the present, at Fort Hamilton, has, within a few days past, ordered out of the purchase some of Mr. [John] Dunlap's settlers, at Colerain, against whom he has a pique. He threatens to dislodge them with a party of soldiers if he is not obeyed. The citizens have applied to me for advice, and I have directed them to pay no regard to his menaces, yet I very much fear he will put his threats in execution, for I well know his imperious disposition" (Bond, *Correspondence of Symmes,* 161). John Armstrong (1755–1816), a veteran of the Revolutionary War from Pennsylvania, was promoted to major in September 1792, and he resigned from the U.S. Army in March 1793.

To Arthur St. Clair

Sir, United States [Philadelphia] March 28th 1792.

Your knowledge of the Country North-west of the Ohio, and of the resources for an Army in its vicinity, added to a full confidence in your military character, founded on mature experience, induced my nomination of you to the command of the troops on the frontiers.

Your desire of rectifying any errors of the public opinion, relatively to your conduct, by an investigation of a Court of Enquiry, is highly laudable, and would be readily complied with, were the measure practicable. But a total deficiency of Officers, in actual service, of competent rank to form a legal Court, for that purpose, precludes the power of gratifying your wishes on this occasion.

The intimation of your readiness to afford your successor all the information of which you are capable, although unnecessary for my personal conviction, must be regarded as an additional evidence of the goodness of your heart, and of your Attachment to your Country. I am, Sir, with esteem and regard Your most Obedt Servt

Go: Washington

LS, CSmH; Df, DNA: RG 59, Miscellaneous Letters; LB, DLC:GW. The draft has a circled paragraph at the bottom of its last page: "While I accept your resignation, for the cause you state, I sincerely regret the occasion—I fervently hope, that your health may be perfectly re-established, and that you may enjoy uninterrupted happiness." It apparently was marked for deletion, as a different hand (Tobias Lear's) inserted the complimentary close and internal address line above it.

For the background to this letter, which served as GW's reply to St. Clair's letter of 26 Mar., see GW to the U.S. Senate and House of Representatives, 12 Dec. 1791, n.1, Henry Knox to GW, 22 Jan., n.2, 1 Mar. 1792, GW to Knox, 29 Feb., n.1, Knox to Tobias Lear, 31 Jan. 1792, n.1, GW to Thomas Jefferson, 2 Mar., and Jefferson to GW, 2 Mar. 1792. GW's letter was printed in the 16 April issue of the *National Gazette* (Philadelphia) with other correspondence concerning St. Clair's resignation of his commission as major general (see GW to St. Clair, 4 April, and St. Clair to GW, 26, 31 Mar., 7 April).

Tobias Lear to Matthew Clarkson

Sir, Philadelphia, March 29th 1792.

The President of the United States has received your letter of the 22d instant, expressing an intention of resigning the Office of Marshal for the New York District.[1]

While the President regrets the loss of your services to the public, he hopes the circumstances which have induced a resignation of your appointment, are such as will conduce to your personal happiness and prosperity. But, Sir, permit me to say, that I know it will not only be pleasing to the President, but releiving him from an addition to the weight of his important business at this moment, if you will continue to exercise the duties of your Office some little time longer, until he shall have time to turn his thought towards a proper character for your successor. But if this shou'd be incompatible with your views, the return of your Commission will be an evidence of it to the President, who must then fix upon another person immediately to fill the Office.[2] I have the honor to be, very respectfully, Sir, Your most Obedt Servt

Tobias Lear.
Secretary to the President
of the United States.

ALS (letterpress copy), DNA: RG 59, Miscellaneous Letters; LB, DLC:GW.

1. Clarkson wrote GW from New York on 22 Mar. 1792 to resign his "peculiarly gratifying" appointment because of unstated "particular circumstances" (DNA: RG 59, Miscellaneous Letters). GW had appointed Clarkson federal marshal of the New York district in the summer of 1791, when Congress was

not in session, and the Senate confirmed the appointment that November (see John Jay to GW, 13 Mar. 1791, n.1, and GW to the U.S. Senate, 31 Oct. 1791 [first letter], n.3).

2. Clarkson apparently continued to perform the duties of his office a little while longer, as GW did not name Aquila Giles to succeed him until May 1792 (see GW to the U.S. Senate, 3 May [second letter]). Lear forwarded Clarkson's returned commission to Thomas Jefferson on 7 June (DNA: RG 59, George Washington's Correspondence with His Secretaries of State).

From Francis Willis

Sir March 29th 1792

I venture on the liberty of enclosing you a copy of a paragraph contained in a letter to me from, Wm Sturges[1] now living in Charleston So. Carolina, in the year 82 when I was about to set of to Georgia, supposing that a new Country would hold out advantages to young men of strict morals and promising talents, I offered to take this young Gentleman with me (who is the son of my worthy neighbour The Revd Daniel Sturges) and do the best I could for him, he was about nineteen years of age, I got him in the Surveyor general's office early in 83, with a sallerey of Eighty pounds sterling per Annum, In April 84 I left the state and returned for my family, in my absence he left the office, oweing to some irregularities not of his but others that were unpleasent to him, since which he has been generally residing in Charleston and Surveying in that state, with tolerable success, the whole of his conduct while under my eye and since as far as I have any knowledge of it serves to impress me with hope almost equal to confidence that he will continue to immitate his amiable father, who is now my neighbour in Georgia, doing as well as might be reasonably expected.

I would not take the liberty in many cases and such as I have several times refused to trouble you with, and indeed one of my own, where I wish for an Ensigncy for one of my Sons,[2] but this is peculiar. The old and worthy Clergeman and his family and this young Gentn in particular, have been long before we left Virginia and ever since accustomed to command my attention and friendship and always to deserve that of every one, I hope Sir this is a sufficient apology for the freedom I have taken; with respect to the propriety of my furnishing the materials required, contained in the map of the Federal City now in the possession of the house of Representatives, is an additional reason for this communication.[3] I am Sir with the most perfect sentiment⟨s⟩ of respect and Attachment your most obedient and very Humble Servt

Frans Willis

ALS, DLC:GW.

1. The enclosed extract reads: "To be brief it is to request of you, that you would be so good as to send me by the first opportunity (if in your power to obtain it) a Plan of the Federal City? as descriptive in a rough manner as possible of the natural and artificial marks (viz.) Rivers, Creeks, Branches, Springs, Marshes, Eminencies &Ca agreeable to the designation and arrangement of—the Gentleman who superintended the laying it out—I forgot his name—I think if you could oblige me in this instance, and I could have time to complete some number of copies before any printed ones are extant that I could dispose of them here to pretty good advantage.

"It is very apposite in my line of business, and will afford me agreeable imployment when the season will not admit of my being active in the field; You know that I have a natural turn as well as fondness, for amusements of that kind which would be hightened by the idea of emolument.

"I wish our good President when he is dispensing his favors, would think of the son of a venerable old acquaintance; who I beleive posseses as many virtues as ever did the patriarchs, Abraham Isaac and Jacob, and who will be bold to say that he inherits a patrimony of his Father which he hopes will ever remain in-tact and unalienable—namely honesty, and a small share of natural ingenuity[.] I have the vanity to think, that had I the honor of his acquaintance, he would not think me altogether an object unworthy his attention in that way. If you could venture to recommend me to him (in which generous act I think my friend Mr [Abraham] Baldwin would not be backward in joining his interest) you would be infinitely obliging a friend, whose conduct I flatter myself would always evince to you, that you had not served him unworthily; I would prefer some appointment in the Geographical or surveying department, in which I am the most conversant; such as laying out and describing boundaries &ca, in the prosecution of which, would endeavour to deduce some Topographical essays, which perhaps may not be void of some utility. Between you and me, I could mention another good it would be promotive of. It would enable me to dispence with the exigences of business in seasons unfavorable to health in our torrid climate, as well as increase that inspiration excited in me by a sense of his inimitable virtues, to attempt an ode to his praise every anniversary of his birthday, which has been my constant practice since I ventured on the back of Pegasus and which my freinds tell me are not to be classed among the meanest of the kind. I do not mention this as anything recommendatory of myself; neither do I think, that any such paltry allurements can possibly bias that Great Man (abstracted from more necessary qualifications for public service) in the disposal of his appointments" (DLC:GW). William Sturges (born c.1763) was the son of the Rev. Daniel Sturges, the Anglican minister of Norbourne Parish at Charles Town, Va. (now W. Va.), from 1771 to 1786. William Sturges received a grant of 400 acres in Richmond County from the state of Georgia in September 1784 (Candler, *Revolutionary Records of Georgia,* 2:720). He apparently did not receive an appointment from GW.

2. None of Francis Willis's sons received an appointment in the U.S. Army during GW's tenure in office.

3. GW laid an unofficial copy of Pierre L'Enfant's plan of the Federal City before Congress on 13 Dec. 1791. For the reasons the president was unable to provide Congress with a more polished plan, see GW to Tobias Lear, 2 Oct., n.5, L'Enfant to GW, 21 Nov., editorial note, and GW to the U.S. Senate and House of Representatives, 13 Dec. 1791, source note.

To Thomas Jefferson

[Philadelphia] Friday Morning [30 March 1792]

The enclosed Instrumt does not accord with my recollection of Mr Blodgets proposed Loan[1]—and I confess I had much rather see a clear expression of the intention than to meet an explanation of it afterwards by one of the parties, to the contract.

The *number* of Lots to be Mortgaged I do not positively recollect—but sure I am one half were to be North of an East & West line from the Presidents House. I do not remember that the words "*valuable Lots*" were inserted in the proposition of Mr Blodget—& think the Mortgaged Lots were releasable by the substitn of other—If therefore the subsequent instrument should not place these matters in a very precise point of view, a foundation will be laid for much discontent, & probably disputes.

Did you see Mr White yesterday? and in that case what was his opinion respecting M——n's acceptance in the manner suggested?[2]

AL, DLC: Jefferson Papers.

1. The enclosure, apparently a draft of the loan warrants for the District of Columbia, has not been identified. For the proposed loan of Samuel Blodget, Jr., to finance projects in the Federal City, see GW to the Commissioners for the District of Columbia, 6 Mar., n.7, and GW to Jefferson, 21 Mar., 3 April.

2. Despite having misgivings, GW was considering naming Daniel Morgan a general officer of the new expedition against the hostile northwestern Indian nations (see Jefferson's Memorandum of a Meeting of the Heads of the Executive Departments, 9 Mar., and GW's Memorandum on General Officers, 9 Mar., n.5). GW had apparently asked Jefferson to obtain the opinion of Virginia congressman Alexander White on whether or not Morgan would accept a commission (see GW to Jefferson, 4 April).

From Henry Knox

Sir. War-department, March 30th 1792.

I have the honor to submit you, an order of a committee, to inquire into the failure of the late expedition.[1] As I do not conceive myself authorized to deliver these papers of myself, I beg your permission, that they may be laid before the committee, if you should see no impropriety therein, together with major general St Clair's letters; or such others, as the committee may request.[2] I have the honor to be Sir, with the highest respect, Your most obedient servt

H. Knox
secy of War

LS, DLC:GW; LB, DLC:GW.

1. As early as 2 Feb., Congressman John Steele of North Carolina made a motion that the House of Representatives appoint a committee to inquire into and report on the number of Indians currently in arms against the United States, "the causes of the delay of the Federal Army on the Ohio; the scarcity of provisions and forage; the quality of the powder; and such other causes as may have been, in the judgment of the committee, conducive to the late unfortunate defeat." This motion apparently was tabled, and on 27 Mar., William Branch Giles of Virginia introduced a resolution "That the President . . . be requested to institute an inquiry into the causes of the late defeat of the army under the command of Major General St. Clair; and also into the causes of the detentions or delays which are suggested to have attended the money, clothing, provisions, and military stores, for the use of the said army, and into such other causes as may, in any manner, have been productive of the said defeat." After debating the resolution's practicality and constitutionality and defeating a motion to commit it to a select committee, the House agreed to vote on it in two sections. The resolution that the president be requested to institute an inquiry was defeated by fourteen votes. The subsequent resolution that a House committee be appointed to investigate the cause of the expedition's failure passed by a vote of 44 to 10. Thomas FitzSimons was appointed chairman, and Giles, Steele, John Francis Mercer, John Vining, Abraham Clark, and Theodore Sedgwick were named to the committee (*Annals of Congress,* 2d Cong., 356, 490–94).

FitzSimons's order to Knox of 30 Mar. reads: "The Committee appointed to enquire into the causes of the failure of the late expedition under Major General St Clair, have directed me to transmit to you a resolution entered into by them this day. 'That the Secretary for the Department of War furnish this Committee with the official letters, received by him from the late General [Richard] Butler, while employed in the late expedition: And the official correspondence of the Quarter Master while employed in that service'" (DLC:GW). Revolutionary War veteran Samuel Hodgdon (1745–1824) served as quartermaster general of the U.S. Army from March 1791 until April 1792.

2. Thomas Jefferson wrote in a memorandum that after receiving Knox's letter of this day with its enclosed resolution, GW called a meeting of Knox, Jefferson, Alexander Hamilton, and Edmund Randolph on 31 Mar. "to consult, merely because it was the first example, & he wished that so far as it shd become a precedent, it should be rightly conducted. he neither acknoleged nor denied, nor even doubted the propriety of what the house were doing, for he had not thought upon it, nor was acquainted with subjects of this kind. he could readily conceive there might be papers of so secret a nature as that they ought not to be given up. we were not prepared & wished time to think & enquire." Randolph and the heads of the executive departments again met with the president on 2 April, when they "were of one mind 1. that the house was an inquest, & therefore might institute enquiries. 2. that they might call for papers generally. 3. that the Executive ought to communicate such papers as the public good would permit, & ought to refuse those the disclosure of which would injure the public. consequently were to exercise a discretion. 4. that neither the Committee nor House had a right to call on the head of a department, who & whose papers were under the Presidt alone, but that the Committee shd instruct their chairman to move the house to address the President." Jefferson noted that Hamilton "agr[ee]d with us in all these points except as to the power of the house to call on heads of departments. he observed that as to his department the act constituting it had made it subject to Congress in some points; but he thought himself not so far subject as to be obliged to produce all papers they might call for. they might demand secrets of a very mischeivous nature." He added in square brackets: "here I tho't he began to fear they would go to examining how far their own members & other persons in the government had been dabbling in stocks, banks &c. and that he probably would chuse in this case to deny their power, & in short he endeavd to place himself subject to the house when the Executive should propose what he did not like, & subject to the Executive when the house shd propose any thing disagreeable." Jefferson reported that the president and his department heads and the attorney general "finally agreed to speak separatim to the members of the committee & bring them by persuasion into the right channel it was agreed in this case that there was not a paper which might not be properly produced, that copies only should be sent, with an assurance—that if they should desire it, a clerk should attend with the originals to be verified by themselves" (Jefferson's Memoranda of Consultations with the President, 11 Mar.–9 April 1792, DLC: Jefferson Papers).

GW returned the enclosed resolution to Knox on 4 April and requested him to provide the House committee with the requisite papers. See also GW to Hamilton, 6 April (second letter).

From Peter Greene

May it please your Excellency, Boston 31st March 1792.

To pardon the liberty that I have presumed in the present occasion to offer myself to your Excellency, as a Major, to serve in one of the New Regiments against the Hostile Indians—should that office be Vacant—at the same time I must believe Your Excellency will be surprised that such liberty should be presumed, by one who is a stranger to Your Excellency—Sir, if it will not be presumption in me to inform Your Excellency that at the Age of 19 Years, I was appointed an Ensign in Colo. Hitchcock's Regiment at Prospect Hill, in the Year 1775,[1] and in September following I went thro' the Wilderness with Colo. Arnold, to Quebec, after the unfortunate attack upon that City, I was appointed Adjutant, of that Regiment, by Colo. Arnold, until that Corps returned Home—in the year 1777 I was appointed Officer of Marines on Board the Continental Ship, "Queen, of France"—in the year 1780 I was taken Prisoner of War, at Charleston S. Carolina under the Command of General Lincoln, and returned Home a prisoner on parole—and in the year 1787 when Daniel Shayes, Commenced a rebellion in the State of Massachusetts, I was appointed to Command a Company by Governor Bowdoin, and went out under the Command of General Lincoln, against Said Shayes.[2]

I now Sir, hold a Lieutenant Colonels, Commission, in the first Regiment of Millitia, in the County of Suffolk, in the town of Boston. I thought it my duty to acquaint Your Excellency, of these particulars as being a Stranger—Should your Excellency desire further information with respect to my Character, or Abilities, I would refer your Excellency, to Governor Hancock, or to the Hon. Thomas Russell Esqr.[3]—if your Excellency should think p[r]oper to Confer on me such an Office, I hope it will be in my power to give such satisfaction, as may be agreeable to Your Excellency, and the United States.[4] Being with great Respect Sir Your Excellency's Most Obedient & most Humble Servant

Peter Greene.

ALS, DLC:GW.

Peter Greene (Green) headed a Boston household consisting of five persons in 1790 (*Heads of Families* [Massachusetts], 187).

1. Col. Daniel Hitchcock (1739–1777) commanded a Rhode Island regiment until his death at Morristown, N.J., in January 1777.

2. Capt. Daniel Shays (1747–1825), who had served at the battles of Lexington, Bunker Hill, and Saratoga during the Revolutionary War, resigned from the service in October 1780. After leaving the army he moved to Pelham, Mass., where he was elected to the committee of safety and to the post of town warden. During the economic downturn of the mid-1780s, Shays led a rebel-

lion which aimed at lightening the tax burden, reducing the number of seizures for overdue debts, and increasing the amount of paper currency in circulation in Massachusetts. After several armed clashes the rebels dispersed. Shays and a number of the other leaders of the insurrection were condemned to death, but they were later pardoned.

3. During the Revolutionary War, Thomas Russell (1740–1796), a wealthy merchant from Charlestown, Mass., raised subscriptions in Boston for the Bank of North America and served as deputy agent of marine for New England. After the war Russell supported the adoption of the Constitution at the state ratifying convention, held various local offices, joined a number of philanthropic and learned societies, and continued to expand his vast business enterprises. No correspondence between GW and either John Hancock or Russell concerning Greene has been found.

4. GW apparently never appointed Greene an officer in the U.S. Army.

Tobias Lear to Thomas Jefferson

United States [Philadelphia] 31st March 1792.

By the President's command T. Lear has the honor to transmit to the Secretary of State, letters from Mr Seagrove, that the Secretary may take extracts therefrom for the purpose mentioned this day.[1]

The President wishes to know if the Copies of Mr Hammond's letter[2] which have been sent to the President were intended to be put into the hands of the Secretary of War to be transmitted by him to Mr Seagrove.[3]

Tobias Lear.
Secretary to the President
of the United States.

ALS, DLC: Jefferson Papers; ALS (retained copy), DNA: RG 59, Miscellaneous Letters; LB, DNA: RG 59, George Washington's Correspondence with His Secretaries of State; LB (photocopy), DLC:GW.

1. The enclosed "letters from Mr [James] Seagrove" have not been identified, but they probably included Seagrove's letter to Henry Knox of 14 Jan., which Jefferson extracted and sent to José de Viar and José de Jaudenes on 17 May 1792 (*Jefferson Papers,* 23:523; see also Knox to Tobias Lear, 29 Mar., DLC:GW).

2. "Mr Hammond's letter" was probably that which the British minister had sent to the secretary of state on 30 March. Having just received a communication from the British government, Hammond could assure the administration that Britain in no way encouraged or countenanced the operations of the adventurer William Bowles in the Creek country (see Hammond to Jefferson, 30 Mar., *Jefferson Papers,* 23:354). Jefferson replied to Hammond on 31 Mar.

that he immediately had laid Hammond's letter before the president "and I have it in charge from him to express to you the perfect satisfaction which these assurances on the part of your court have given him that Bowles, who is the subject of them, is an unauthorised impostor. The promptitude of their disavowal of what their candour had forbidden him to credit, is a new proof of their friendly dispositions, and a fresh incitement to us to cherish corresponding sentiments. To those we are led both by interest and inclination, and I am authorised to assure you that no occasion will be omitted on our part of manifesting their sincerity" (ibid., 357–58). For the background information concerning William Augustus Bowles and his intrigues against Alexander McGillivray in the Creek country from the summer of 1791 until Bowles's seizure by Spanish authorities in New Orleans in late February 1792, see the Secret Article of the Treaty with the Creeks, 4 Aug. 1790, source note, enclosed in GW to the U.S. Senate, 4 Aug. 1790, "John A. Dingwell" to GW, 12, 16 Aug. 1790, "Dingwell" to Knox or Lear, 17 Aug. 1790, the enclosures to Memorandum from Lear, 18 Aug. 1790, Knox to GW, 14 Nov. 1791, n.1, 26 Dec. 1791, n.1, and to Lear, 30 Nov. 1791, n.1.

3. Jefferson must have answered this query positively, as Lear later this day sent Knox two authenticated copies of Hammond's letter to Jefferson of 30 Mar., "one of which the President desires may be transmitted to Mr Seagrove and the other to Genl McGillivray, by the first opportunity" (DLC:GW).

From Arthur St. Clair

Sir, Philadelphia March 31st 1792

I have had the honor to receive your Letter of the twenty eighth instant. While I lament that Circumstances prevent an Investigation into my Conduct by a Court of Enquiry, I cannot but accquiesce in the Reasons you have assigned why it cannot take Place, And I beg leave to present my thanks for the Desire to have gratified me, had it been practicable, which you have been pleased to manifest.

In my Letter to you Sir, of the twenty-sixth, I expressed an Intention of retiring from the Army when the Enquiry should be over: The only Reason I had for wishing to retain my Commission until that time was, that if any misconduct should appear, in the Course of the Enquiry, I might be amenable to a Court Martial, which a Resignation would have precluded—The House of Representatives Sir, have directed an Enquiry into the Causes of the failure of the last Campaign to be made by a Committee of their own Body: The same Reason that influenced me when a Court of Enquiry was contemplated, operates now with equal Force; and therefor it may be proper that I should still retain my Commission; but, as it will soon be requisite that some Person be at the Head of the Army who is to continue to command it, it is necessary, Sir, that I should inform You explicitly, which I now do, of my fixed Resolution to resign the Moment that Enquiry is finished should no fault be found; that any Embarrassment which may exist, with respect to providing a Successor for me, may be removed.[1]

Be pleased to observe Sir, that my sole Object is to give Effect to public Justice, in the usual Way by a Court Martial, should it appear that, *in any manner whatsoever,* the Misfortunes of the last Campaign can be attributed to me—and it is the proper, and I believe the only Tribunal where military Crimes and Misconduct can be enquired into and punished; or, where an Officers Reputation, infinitely dearer than Life, can be vindicated. Should the public Service, however, require that another Officer of the same Rank with me be appointed immediately, I am ready to make the Resignation forthwith, notwithstanding that it may seem to proceed, and, at a distance, will be supposed to have arisen, from a Sense that the Volume of Calumny and Defamation, which is daily pouring from the Press into the public Ear, has too much foundation for me to meet it—that I shrink from the Consequences and chuse to shelter myself in a private Station: I am ready Sir, upon this Occasion, as I ever have been upon every other, to sacrifice every private and personal Consideration to the Public Good.[2] With every Sentiment of Respect I have the Honor to be Sir, Your most obedient Servant

Ar St Clair

ALS, DNA: RG 59, Miscellaneous Letters; ALS (copy), OHi: Arthur St. Clair Papers; ADfS, OCHP.

St. Clair's letter of this date was printed in the 16 April issue of the *National Gazette* (Philadelphia) with other correspondence concerning the resignation of his commission.

1. For the congressional inquiry into St. Clair's defeat, see Knox to GW, 30 Mar., source note.

2. GW informed St. Clair by letter on 4 April that his successor had to be appointed immediately. St. Clair resigned his commission on 7 April, and GW nominated Anthony Wayne as major general of the army two days later (see GW to the U.S. Senate, 9 April).

From Anonymous

Sir [March 1792][1]

I know you to be good—and you are great, independent of public opinion—I mean intrinsically great, if you were not possessed of that opinion. But you are possessed of it, and stand higher, beyond all comparison in the estimation of persons of every description than any man. The virtuous part of the community who have for years put everything to hazard to obtain a Government, likely to insure their happiness, woud therefore look up to you wth anxious hope, and implore your protection against the wicked artifices of a set of democratical incendiaries who are endeavouring to level the federal Edifice to the ground. They have unfortunately got the whole delegation from Virginia under their direction. For the aggrandizement of Mr Jefferson they are endeavouring to make you odious. I trust they will not succeed. If you wd exert yourself—they wd shrink into insignificance. Mr Hamilton is the object of Mr Jefferson's mortal aversion. He knows his superior merit and talents, and is indefatigable in his endeavors to compass his ruin. His emissaries are constantly at work to revile all his plans, and to withdraw from him the confidence of the Public, of wch he at present is most justly possessed. Two of the most impudent and inflammatory tools of the party are Giles,[2] and Mercer. It is said the latter is determined to plunge this Country into a quarrel wth England by insulting the British Minister. I do not believe you know that the National Gazette was established under the immediate patronage of Mr Jefferson and Mr Madison, and that Mr Freneau the Printer of it is a Clerk in the Secretary of State's Office wth a Salary as Interpreter.[3] Examine the productions wch appear in that Gazette. Is it proper that the Secretary of State should encourage the malevolent attacks wch are continually making against the Government? Be assured Sir that those Men are at the head of a most wicked Faction, chiefly composed of Virginians, but assisted by some other restless, ambitious Men. Their objects are to destroy Mr Hamilton, by making him odious in the public Eye, to place Mr Jefferson at the head of the Government, to make Mr Madison prime Minister, to displace the Vice President at the next Election, to lay this Country prostrate at the feet of France, to affront and quarrel wth England, to take advantage of the cry of the ignorant multitude in favor of Democracy, and thus to establish an absolute Tyranny over the minds of the populace by the affectation of a most tender regard to the rights of Man, and a more popular Government.

AL, DLC:GW. This unsigned, undated letter is in the same handwriting as those written to GW c.3 and c.20 Jan. 1792.

1. GW docketed the addressed cover: "Anonymous recd the latter end of March—1792."

2. William Branch Giles (1762–1830) served in the U.S. House of Representatives 1790–98 and 1801–3, in the Virginia house of delegates 1798–1800, 1816–17, and 1826–27, in the U.S. Senate 1803–15, and as governor of Virginia 1827–30.

3. Thomas Jefferson appointed the poet and editor Philip Freneau (1752–1832), a college classmate of James Madison's at the College of New Jersey, clerk for foreign languages at the State Department in August 1791. He served in that capacity until October 1793. From 31 Oct. 1791 to 26 Oct. 1793, Freneau published, with the encouragement of Madison and Jefferson, the strongly Antifederalist *National Gazette* in Philadelphia (see "Jefferson, Freneau, and the Founding of the *National Gazette*" in *Jefferson Papers,* 20:718–53, for a detailed treatment of the relationship between Jefferson and Freneau).

List of Plants from John Bartram's Nursery

[March 1792][1]

Catalogue of Trees, Shrubs & Plants, of Jno. Bartram.

Nos. Plants feet high

a[2] 1. Rhododendron maximum 2 grow from 5 to 10.

Evergreen, large maximum rose coloured blossoms. ["Mountain laurel," great laurel, rosebay]

E. d 2. Ulex europeus 2. 3 to 4.

Embellished with sweet scented flowers, of a fine yellow colour. [Furze]

a 3 Hypericum kalmianum 2 3 to 4.

Profusely garnished with fine Gold coloured blossoms. ["Shrub St. John's wort"]

4. H[ypericum]. Angustifolium 3. 3 to 6.

Evergreen; adorned with fine yellow flowers.

e 5. Taxus procumbens 1. 3 to 6.

Evergreen; of a splendid full green throughout the year—red berries. [Yew]

E 6. Buxus aureis [*aureus*] 1. 3 to 10.

Elegant, call'd gilded box.

E 7. Daphne mezerium [*mezereum*] 2. 1. to 3.
An early flowering sweet scented little shrub. [Mezereon, paradise plant]

8 Calycanthus floridus 5. 4 to 8.
Odoriferous, its blossoms scented like the Pine apple. ["Sweet Shrub of Carolina," Carolina allspice]

9. Berberis canadensis 3. 2. to 4.
Berries of a perfect coral red [barberry]

E. 10. Æsculus hippocastanum 2. 20, 40, to 50.
A magnificent flowering & shady *Tree.* [Horse chestnut]

11. Evonimus atrapurpurous 3. 6 to 8.
Its fruit of a bright crimson in the Autumn (*burning bush*). [*Euonymus atropurpureus*]

12. Fothergilla gardeni[i] 6. 2 to 4.
Early in blossom; flowers in spikes, white & delicate. [Dwarf fothergilla, dwarf witchalder]

13. Franklinia alatamaha 1. 3, 15 to 20
Flowers large, white & fragrant—native of Georgia. [Franklin tree]

14 Baccharis[3] 3. 4 to 6.
In autumn silvered over with white silky down.

15. Laurus estivalis [*æstivalis*] 1. 5 to 8.
Aromatic & beautified with coral red berries. [Bay tree]

16. Kalmia angustifolia (with the *Gaultheria* [*procumbens*], or mountain tea [wintergreen]) 1 to 2.
Evergreen; garnished with crimson speckled flowers. ["Thyme leav'd Kalmia," lambkill, sheep laurel]

17 Ilex angustifolia 1 3 to 6.
Evergreen, new. [Holly]

18. Dirca palustris 2. 2. to 3.
Early in bloom; singular—(call'd Leather wood). ["Leather Bark"]

19. Thuja occidentalis 4 15, 30, to 40.
A handsome evergreen *Tree;* beautiful foliage, & odoriferous. [American arborvitae, white cedar]

20. Zanthorhiza apiifolia 6. 1 to 3.
Singular flowers early: its root affords a splendid transparent yellow dye (call'd Yellow root, in Carola). [*Xanthorhiza simplicissima*]

21. Jeffersonia egrilla 1. 4 to 10
Foliage of deep splendid green, & embellished with a delicate plumage of white flowers (call'd Iron wood.)

22. Magnolia tripetala[4] 1. 8 to 15.
Foliage ample, expansive & light, plumed with large white flowers, which are succeeded by large crimson strobile. ["Umbrella Tree"]

23. Magnolia acuminata 1. 30, 80 to 100.
Erect with a pyramidal head, the dry strobile odoriferous. [“Cucumber Tree”]

24. Halesia tetraptera [or *carolina*] 1. 4, 10, to 15.
The flowers abundant, white, of the shape of little bells. [Carolina silverbell][5]

25. Viburnum opulifolium 1. 3 to 7.
of singular beauty in flower and fruit.

26 Viburnum Arboreum 2. 6, 10, 15.
very shewy in flower. fruit eatable.

27. Viburnum Alnifolium 2. 3 to 6.
handsome flowering shrub. [*Viburnum lantanoides;* hobble bush]

28. Cupressus disticha 1. 50, 80, 100.
stature majestic, foliage most delicate, wood of a fine yellow colour, odoriferous & incorruptible. [“Bald Cyprus”]

E. 29. Sorbus sativa[6] 1. 10, 15, 30.
Its fruit pear & apple shaped, as large & well tasted when mellow.

30. Carpinus ostrya 3. 10, 15. 20.
handsome form, dress becoming, fruit singular. (Hop tree).[7] [“Horn Beam”]

31. Sorbus aucuparia 2. 8, 15, 30.
Foliage elegant, embellished with umbells of coral red berries. [European mountain ash]

32. Acer striatum 1. 10 to 20.
singularly beautiful; the younger branches inscribed with silvery lines, or scrawls, on a dark purpleish green ground. [*Acer pensylvanicum;* striped maple, moosewood]

b 33. Acer glaucum 2. 30, 50.
beautiful foliage. spreading & shady—(Silver-leaf’d Maple).[8]

34. Acer sacharinum[9] 1. 50, 80, 100.
A stately Tree, in his native forests—(Sugar Maple)

E 35. Acer platanoides 2. 30, 50.
graceful stature, full of asscending branches, foliage & flower elegant, casts a grateful shade on the Lawn. [Norway maple]

e 36. Stewartia malachodendron 4 5 to 8.
Floriferous, the flowers large & white embellished with a large tuft of black or purple threads in their centre. [Silky stewartia or stuartia]

37. Clethra alnifolia 1. 3 to 6
Flowers abundant in spikes, exceedingly sweet scented. [“Clethra,” sweet pepperbush]

38. Styrax grandifolium 1 3 to 10.
a most charming flowering shrub, blossoms snow white & of the most grateful scent; (called Snow-drop tree). [Snowbell, storax]

E. b. 39. Philadelphus coronarius 2. 4, 6, 10.
a sweet flowering shrub, (call'd Mock Orange)

40. Philadelphus inodorus 1. 5, 7, 10.
his robe a silvery flower'd mantle.

e 41. Pinus Strobus 6. 50, 80, 100.
Magnificent! he presides in the evergreen Groves (white pine).

E. f 42. Pinus communis 2. 20, 40, 60.
a stately tree, foliage of a Seagreen colour, & exhibits a good appearance whilst young. (Scotch Fir).[10]

E 43. Pinus Larix 1. 40 to 60.
elegant figure & foliage. ["Larch Tree"]

E 44. Thuja orientalis 1 6 to 12
Foliage pleasing. [Oriental arborvitae]

45 Robinia villosa 4 1, 2, 3, 5, 6.
a gay shrub, enrobed with plumed leaves & roseat flowers. ["Peach Blossom Acacia"]

e 46. Pinus balsamea[11] 6. 20 to 40.
a tree of pleasing figure, delicate foliage, evergreen, & affords fragrant & medicinal balsam (Balm of Gilead Fir).

f. 47. Pinus abies virginiana 5. 50, 80, 100.
A Stately evergreen Tree, his foliage of delicate appearance; the wood useful and durable, & of great value (Hemlock Spruce).[12]

E 48. Cornus mascula [or *mas*] 1. 5, 8, 10.
flowers early, the fruit oblong of the size of a plum, of a fine crimson colour, and wholsome pleasant eating. [Cornelian cherry]

E. 49. Prunus cerasus, flore roseo 1 5, 10, 20,
more or less according to the stock; a very beautiful flowering tree, its blushing blossoms double—(double flowering cherry).

e 50. Prunus maritima 1 5 to 8,
flowers early, fruit of a dark purple sweet & pleasant eating. ["Beach or Sea-side-Plumb"]

f. 51. Prunus missisipi 1 6, 8, 10, 12.
Fruit of the largest size, oval; of a perfect deep crimson colour, possesses an agreeable taste, & affords an animating marmolade. ["Crimson Plumb"]

52. Prunus chicasa 1 6, 8, 10.
Early flowering, very fruitful; the fruit nearly round, cleft, red, purple, yellow, of an inticing look, most agreeable taste & wholsome. ["Chicasaw Plumb"]

e 53. Glycine frutescens 3.
A rambling florobundant climber; the blossoms in large pendant clusters, of a fine celestial blue, well adapted for covering arbors. [*Wisteria frutescens;* "Kidney Bean Tree," wisteria]

54 Æsculus pavia
[Red buckeye]

55. Æ. " " varietas 2. 6, 8, 10, 12, 15
their light & airy foliage, crimson & variegated flowers, present a gay & mirthful appearance; continually, whilst in bloom visited by the brilliant thundering Humingbird. *The root of this Tree is esteemed preferable to soap, for scouring & cleansing woolen Cloths.*

e. 56. Æsculus virginica 1 20, 40, 50
beautiful foliage Flowers pale yellow. [Yellow horse chestnut]

57. Æsculus alba 1 1, 4, 6.
The branches terminate with long erect spikes of sweet white flowers.

E. 58. Juniperus sabina 1 1 to 5
Evergreen. [Savin]

a 59. Evonimus americanus 1 4, 7.
evergreen, presents a fine appearance in Autumn, with crimson fruit. [*Euonymus americanus;* spindle tree]

E. f. 60. Prunus Laurus cerasus 1 10, 15, 20.
A beautiful evergreen tree of Europe; its green leaves are said to possess a dangerous deleterious quality. [*Prunus laurocerasus;* cherry laurel, English laurel]

61. Yucca filamentosa 2
beautiful ornamental evergreen [Adam's needle]

62. Yucca gloriosa[13]
flowering plants. [Spanish dagger]

c. 63. Myrica gale 4 2 to 4.
possesses an highly aromatic, and very agreeable scent. ["Bog gale," sweet gale, bog myrtle]

E. b. 64. Platanus orientalis 2 60, 80, 100.
a famous tree celebrated for the beauty of his foliage, expansion, and grateful shade he affords. [Oriental sycamore, oriental plane]

d. 65. Amorpha fruticosa 1. 4, 6 to 8.
[Bastard indigo]

66. Amorpha cærulia [*cœrulea*] 2. 2–4.
Foliage light and delicately pennated, garnished with flowers of a fine [Bastard indigo]

E. e. 67. Salix variegata 1 10 to 15.
Silver blotched willow.

68 Mespilus nivea 1 10 to 15.
An early flowering shrub, of uncommon elegance (Snowy mespilus). [Medlar]

69. Mesp. pubescens 2 2, 3, 4
Somewhat resembling the foregoing; but of less stature & the flowers not so large, nor of so clean a white: both produce very pleasant fruit.

70.	Mesp: pusilla	1	1 to 2½

flowers early, the blossoms white & abundant; exhibits a fine appearance.

71.	Mesp. prunifolia	1.	2, 4, 5.

Presents a good appearance, when all red with its clusters of berries. [*Aronia prunifolia;* chokeberry]

E. f. 72.	Colutia [*Colutea*] arborescens	3.	3, 6, 10.

exhibits a good appearance, foliage pinnated, of a soft pleasant green, colour, interspersed with the large yellow papillionacious flowers, in succession. [Bladder senna]

E. 73.	Rhus Italicum	1.	8 to 12.

[Sumac]

E. 74.	Mespilus pyracantha	4.	4, 8, 10.

a beautiful flowerg shrub, evergreen in mild seasons. [*Pyracantha coccinea;* firethorn]

75.	Itea virginiana [or *virginica*]	3.	3 to 6.

a handsome flowerg shrub. [Virginia sweetspire, Virginia willow, tassel-white]

76.	Cornus alba[14]	1.	3, 6

white berried swamp Dogwood.

77.	Prunus divaricata	2.	6, 8.

diciduous, flowers white in raumes [racemes], stems diverging & branches pendulous. [*Prunus cerasifera divaricata;* cherry plum]

78.	Hydrangia [*Hydrangea*] arborescens	3.	3, 5, 6.

Ornamental in shruberies, flowers white in large corymbes.

79.	Andromeda axil[l]aris	1.	1 to 3.

Evergreen. [Bog rosemary]

80	Acer pumilum	3.	4. 8.

handsome shrub for coppices, foliage singular, younger shoots red. [Dwarf maple]

E. 81.	Amygdalus persica, flore pleno	1.	8, 10, 12.

of great splendour & amiable presence. [*Prunus persica, flore pleno;* double-flowered peach]

e 82.[15]	Magnolia glauca	1.	3. 10. 15.

charming—the milk-white roseate blossom possesses an animating fragrance. [*Magnolia virginiana;* "Rose Laurel," sweet bay, swamp magnolia]

83.	Sambucus rubra	1	3, 5, 7.

early flowering and handsome; its coral red berries in large clusters, ripe abt midsummer. [*Sambucus canadensis;* American elder, sweet elder]

84	Rubus odoratus	3.	3 to 7.

foliage beautiful; flowers of the figure, colour & fragrance of the rose. [Flowering raspberry, thimbleberry]

f. 85. Rosa Pennsylvanica flor: pleno 2. 2 to 4
flowers monthly from May 'till Novembr [*Rosa palustris;* swamp rose]

86. Lonicera inodora 1 5, 10, 20
Twine's round, & ascends trees spreading its bloom over their boughs. [Honeysuckle]

b. 87. Ribes oxyacanthoides[16] 1 3, 5.
fruit small & smooth. ["Prickly Gooseberry"]

88. Populus balsamifera 1. 7. 15. 20.
foliage beautiful, its buds in the spring replete with an odoriferous balsam. [Balsam poplar]

E. f. 89. Crategus [*Cratægus*] aria 1. 20, 30.
foliage beautiful; silvered with white cottony down, underside. [Hawthorn]

90. Pt[e]lea trifoliata 2. 4 to 9.
singular, (call'd the foil tree) ["Trefoil Tree," hop tree]

91. Lonicera symphoricarpos 1. 2. 4.
singular; appears well in winter when garnished with clusters of red berries. ["Indian Currants"]

E. 92. Laurus nobilis 1. 10. 20. 30.
Sweet Bay, a celebrated Evergreen—leaves odoriferous. ["Red Bay," bay laurel, sweet bay]

e. 93. Rhus triphyllum 5. 3 to 7.
Singular early flowering shrub. ["Poison Oak," sumac]

E. 94. Citisus laburnum 1. 10. 15.
foliage delicate, embellished with pendant clusters of splendid yellow papillionacious flowers. [*Cytisus anagyroides laburnum, Laburnum anagyroides;* golden-chain]

E. 95. Periploca græca 2. 7 to 10.
climbing up trees & shrubs; flowers very singular. [Silk vine]

96. Hibiscus coccineus 1. 8 to 10.
a most elegant flowering plant; flowers large, of a splendid crimson colour. [Scarlet rosemallow]

97. Bignonia crucigera 1 40 to 50.
A climber, mounting to the tops of trees & buildings; flowers abundant. ["Cross Vine," trumpet flower]

98. Bignonia semper virens 2
A climber as famous, at least for the richness of his robe; flowers of a splendid golden yellow, & odoriferous; very proper for covering arbors &c. ["Yellow Jasmin"]

99. Betula (alnus) maritima[17] 2. 6, 10. 12.
singular; retains his verdure very late in the autumn. ["Sea side Alder"]

f. E. 100. Amygdalus pumila, flor: pleno 1 2 to 4
A most elegant flowering shrub; ornimental in vases for Court yards &c. [*Prunus pumila, flore pleno;* sand or dwarf cherry, dwarf double-flowering almond]

c. 101. Arundo donax 1. 5. 6. 8.
Maiden Cane.

e 102. Callicarpa americana 1. 3 to 6.
Very shewy & pleasing; the flowers of a delicate incarnate hue, & vast clusters of purple berries. ["Bermudas Mulberry," French mulberry, American beautyberry]

f. E. 103. Syringa persica 2. 3 to 5.
(Persian Lilac) elegant; its flexile stems terminate with heavy panicles of purple blossoms, of animating fragrance.

e 104. Mimosa virgata 1. 3. 5. 10.
Singularly beautiful in its plumed foliage—native of Pearl Island near the Misisipi.

E. 105. Punica granatum flor. plen: 1 3, 6, 10.
the figure & splendour of its flowers exceed description. [Pomegranate]

b. e. 106. Aristolochia sipho. 1
Climbs & spreads over trees & other supports, to a great height & distance: flowers of singular figure; its abundant large leaves, present it as a vine well adapted for covering arbors. [*Aristolochia macrophylla;* Dutchman's pipe]

The following letters in the margin, serve to explain the natural soil & situation of the Trees, shrubs &c.

a. rich, moist, loose or loamy soil, in shade of other trees.
b. rich deep soil.
c. wet moorish soil.
d. Dry indifferent soil.
e. A good loamy moist soil in any situation.
f. Any soil & situation.
E. Exoticks.

D, DLC:GW.

For ease of reading, all of the letters indicating the best type of soil for each plant have been moved in front of the plant's botanical classification, regardless of their original location on the manuscript page. Common names for each plant (when missing from the descriptive entry), modern classifications (if different), alternative classifications, and corrected spellings are given in square brackets. Common names in quotation marks are taken from Bartram's *Catalogue of American Trees, Shrubs, and Herbacious Plants: Most of Which Are Now Growing, and Produce Ripe Seeds in John Bartram's Garden, Near Philadelphia. The*

Seed and Growing Plants of Which Are Disposed Of on the Most Reasonable Terms (Philadelphia, 1784).

On 10 June and 2 Sept. 1787, GW had visited the famous botanical gardens on the west bank of the Schuylkill River three miles southwest of Philadelphia that John Bartram, Jr., had received from his father in 1771 (*Diaries,* 5:166–67, 183). For GW's attempt to obtain a list of plants available from that garden, see Tobias Lear to Clement Biddle, 2 Oct. 1789. The list of March 1792 describes the plants from Bartram's garden that arrived at Mount Vernon in early April 1792 (see George Augustine Washington to GW, 15 April 1792). For GW's reordering of the plants which had not survived, see Directive for John Christian Ehlers, 7 Nov. 1792.

1. The date of this document is taken from GW's docket on the cover, which reads, "List of Plants & Shrubs from Mr Bartram March—1792," and from his directions for his gardener John Christian Ehlers of 7 Nov. 1792, in which he refers to Bartram's "Catalogue of Mar: 92."

2. For the meaning of the letters that precede many of the plant names, see Bartram's explanatory list at the end of this document.

3. "Baccharis" is probably *Baccharis halimifolia,* the groundsel tree.

4. Bartram classifies this as "Magnolia Umbrella" in his 1784 catalog.

5. Bartram offered "Halesia or Silver Bells 2 varieties" in his 1784 catalog.

6. "Sorbus sativa" is probably *Sorbus domestica,* the service tree.

7. The hop hornbeam is classified as *Ostrya virginiana.* The hop tree is classified as *Ptelea trifoliate;* see item number 90 in the document. The American hornbeam is classified as *Carpinus caroliniana.*

8. *Acer saccharinum* is the classification for the silver maple, and *Acer saccharum glaucum* is the classification for a variant of the sugar maple. However, Bartram's catalog lists "Acer Glauca" as the "Silver leav'd Maple."

9. The correct classification for the sugar maple is *Acer saccharum,* while *Acer saccharinum* is the silver maple.

10. The Scotch pine is classified as *Pinus sylvestris.*

11. Bartram's catalog identifies the Balm of Gilead fir as "Pinus Abies Canadesis," but today it is classified as *Abies balsamea.*

12. Hemlock spruce is now classified under the genus *Tsuga.*

13. *Yucca gloriosa* and *Yucca filamentosa* are bracketed together on the manuscript page, indicating the purchase of two plants total.

14. Bartram classifies this tree as "Cornus Perlata" in his 1784 catalog.

15. An endnote at this point in the text explains: "Altho' a wet moorish soil, is the natural soil & situation of this charming flowering tree, (Magnolia glauca) yet, from experience we find it thrives equally well in the common soil & situation of flower gardens & shrubberies; & produces a greater abundance of flowers with a longer succession, & the blossoms equally fragrant."

16. Both Bartram and modern botanists classify this plant as *Grossularia canadenis.*

17. Bartram and modern botanists classify this tree as *Alnus maritima, betula.*

To Thomas Jefferson

[Philadelphia] Sunday Morng [1 April 1792][1]

The enclosed are sent for Mr Jeffersons perusal—The letter from Mr Knox the P. thinks was (the original) sent to Mr Jefferson before.[2]

AL, DLC: Jefferson Papers.

1. Jefferson's Summary Journal of Public Letters (DLC: Jefferson Papers) indicates that the secretary of state received a letter from GW written on Sunday, 1 April 1792, enclosing a letter of 27 Dec. 1791 from Gouverneur Morris.

2. Jefferson noted at the bottom of the page that one of the enclosures was a letter to GW "from Gouvernr Morris. Paris. Dec. 27. 91" (see Morris to GW, 27–31 Dec. 1791). The enclosed letter from Henry Knox has not been identified.

To Thomas Jefferson

[Philadelphia] April 1st 1792.

The President of the U. States has read, and approves the draught of the Secretary of States letter to the Govr of So. Carolina of this date.[1]

AL, DLC: Jefferson Papers; ADf, DNA: RG 59, Miscellaneous Letters; LB, DNA: RG 59, George Washington's Correspondence with His Secretaries of State; LB (photocopy), DLC:GW.

1. On 3 Mar., Tobias Lear transmitted to Jefferson "a letter from Governor [Charles] Pinckney, which the President wishes the Secretary to take into consideration and either answer it himself or report upon it to the President, if in his opinion either is necessary to be done" (DLC: Jefferson Papers). The letter was probably Pinckney's official one to GW of 8 January. Jefferson wrote GW on 1 April that he "has the honor to return to the President Governor Pinkney's letters, & to submit his answer to his perusel" (DNA: RG 59, Miscellaneous Letters). Jefferson apparently returned Pinckney's letters to GW of both 18 Aug. 1791 and 8 Jan. 1792. The letterpress copy of Jefferson's letter to Pinckney of 1 April, which was enclosed for GW's perusal, is printed in *Jefferson Papers,* 23:360–61. It explains current measures being taken to sign an extradition treaty with Spain and covers copies of Jefferson's "Project of a Convention with the Spanish provinces" and his "Heads of consideration on the establishment of Conventions between the United States and their neighbors for the mutual delivery of Fugitives from Justice," both of which the secretary of state had submitted to the president on 22 March. For further correspondence concerning the return of fugitive slaves and criminals from Spanish Florida to South Carolina and Georgia, see GW to Pinckney, 8 Nov. 1791 (first letter) and 17 Mar. 1792.

From Thomas Jefferson

[Philadelphia] April 1. 1792.

Th: Jefferson has the honor to present to the view of the President the subjects relative to Algiers, under their different aspects.[1] on further consideration, & paying special attention to the circumstances of the present moment, which render expence an obstacle perhaps to what would be the best plan, he suggests others which would not be eligible under other circumstances, or for any length of time.[2] if the President will be pleased to make his option of these plans, & determine whether to consult one or both houses, messages adapted to the case shall be prepared.[3]

AL, DNA: RG 59, Miscellaneous Letters; AL (letterpress copy), DLC: Jefferson Papers; LB, DNA: RG 59, George Washington's Correspondence with His Secretaries of State; LB (photocopy), DLC:GW.

1. Jefferson's enclosed "Considerations on the subjects of Ransom, & Peace with the Algerines," which he signed on this day, reads:

"I. The Ransom of our captive citizens, being 14. in number. for facts on this subject refer to the Reports of Dec. 28. 1790. on the same ransom, & on the Mediterranean trade, & to mister [William] Short's letter of Aug. 24. 91. sent to the Senate. the probable cost will be 1500. doll. for the common men, & half as much more for officers, adding presents, duties & other expences, it will be little short of 40,000 D. this must be ready money, & consequently requires a joint, but secret vote of both houses. an Agent must be sent for the purpose.

"II. Peace, how best to be obtained?

"1. by war: that is to say by constant cruizes in the Mediterranean. this proved practicable by the experiment of M. de Massiac [and] by the Portuguese cruises. the co-operation of Portugal, Naples, Genoa, Malta could possibly be obtained. but the expence would be considerable. Vessels mounting 100. guns in the whole would probably be wanting on our part. these would cost in the outset 400,000 Doll. & annually afterwards 125,000 Doll. it may be doubted if this expence could be met during the pres[en]t Indian war. if it could, it is the most honourable & efficacious way of having peace.

"2. by paying a gross sum for a peace of 50. years. respectable opinions vary from 300,000 to 1,000,000 Doll. as to the first cost. then are to follow frequent occasional presents. & with all this, the peace will not be respected, unless we appear able to enforce it. and if able to enforce, why not rely on that solely? that same question recurs here. to wit Are we able to meet this expence at present?

"3. by tribute annually. the Dutch, Danes, Swedes & Venetians pay about 24,000 D. a year. we might perhaps obtain it for something less. if for ten or fifteen thousand dollars a year, it might be eligible.

"4. by a tariff for the ransom of the captives they shall take from us. if low, this might do for the present. The Agent to be sent for the purpose of ransom, might be authorised to treat. but should also make himself acquainted with their coast, harbour, vessels, manner of fighting &c.

"On either of these plans a vote of the Senate will be requisite. on the 1st or 2d the Representatives should be consulted; & perhaps on the 3d or 4th. it will be best to bring it on by a message from the President" (DNA: RG 59, Miscellaneous Letters). Jefferson earlier had forwarded to GW proposals concerning an international convention against Mediterranean piracy (see Jefferson to GW, 12 July 1790, source note and note 8). For the "experiment" of Claude-Louis, marquis de Massiac, see Lafayette to Jefferson, c.6 Mar. 1786, source note, *Jefferson Papers,* 9:318–20.

2. For the administration's concern over funding peace with Algiers, see GW to Jefferson, 10 Mar., n.3, and Conversation with a Committee of the U.S. Senate, 12 Mar. 1792.

3. On 10 April, Jefferson sent GW a draft of the president's message to the Senate on purchasing peace with Algiers, which GW delivered on 8 May (third letter).

From Henry Knox

[Philadelphia] April 1. 1792

I submit two letters one from Genl Wayne and the other from Colonel Willet, and I have seen Colo. Burr relatively to the latter.[1] In the morning when I wait upon you I will detail, the business. I have directed Capt. Trueman to be in readiness to set off on tuesday.[2] I am Sir with perfect respect Your humble Sert

H. Knox

ALS, DLC:GW; LB, DLC:GW.

1. The enclosed letter from Anthony Wayne was probably that to Knox of this date, which reads: "I have seriously & maturely considered the *confidential* and friendly communication with which you honor'd me yesterday, and entertain the most greatful & lively sense of the favorable Opinion the *President* is pleased to express of my Military abilities—and of his very kind intention in my favour; But I shou'd be wanting in duty—not only to that great and good man—but to myself was I to accept of an Appointment in which its more than probable I shou'd be restrained from rendering that service to my Country—in a *subaltern station*—that my experience might otherwise afford, if subject only, to the Orders and advice of the *President* and yourself. I can not therefore think of Committing my Military Character (which is dearer to me than life) to the fortuitous events of A War—which I can not direct—and shou'd it be crowned with success—the Glory & honor will belong to an other—whilst on the Contrary—shou'd it be unfortunate, I must share in the disgrace, after giving up peace and ease—and relinquishing certain pleasing prospects in the

Civil line to which I am invited by my fellow Citizens. Be pleased to accept of my sincere thanks for the friendly part you have taken—and assure the President that I shall always be ready to serve him with my life and best services in a situation in which I cou'd use, and exert them to the best advantage & with effect. . . . I will do myself the honor to call upon [you] at 10. OClock if you will be at leasure" (NNGL: Knox Papers). The letter from Marinus Willett to Knox has not been identified.

2. For GW's proposal that a peace mission be dispatched to the hostile Indian nations of the Northwest and Knox's suggestion that Capt. Alexander Trueman be sent, see Thomas Jefferson's Memorandum of a Meeting of the Heads of the Executive Departments, 9 Mar. 1792. On 2 April, Knox sent Tobias Lear for submission to the president a proposed message to the western Indians, which was to be written on parchment and delivered with a wampum belt, and Knox's proposed instructions to Trueman (DLC:GW). The final copy of Knox's message to the hostile Indian nations, which apparently was approved by GW, is dated 4 April and reads: "Brothers: The President of the United States, General Washington, the Great Chief of the nation, speaks to you by this address. Summon, therefore, your utmost powers of attention, and hear the important things which shall be spoken to you concerning your future welfare; and after having heard and well understood all things, invoke the Great Spirit above to give you due deliberation and wisdom, to decide upon a line of conduct that shall best promote your happiness, and the happiness of your children, and perpetuate you and them on the land of your forefathers.

"Brothers: The President of the United States entertains the opinion, that the war which exists is founded in error and mistake on your parts. That you believe the United States want to deprive you of your lands and drive you out of the country. Be assured this is not so; on the contrary, that we should be greatly gratified with the opportunity of imparting to you all the blessings of civilized life, of teaching you to cultivate the earth, and raise corn; to raise oxen, sheep, and other domestic animals; to build comfortable houses, and to educate your children, so as ever to dwell upon the land.

"Brothers: The President of the United States requests you to take this subject into your serious consideration, and to reflect how abundantly more it will be for your interest to be at peace with the United States, and to receive all the benefit, thereof, than to continue a war which, however flattering it may be to you for a moment, must in the end prove ruinous.

"The desire of peace has not arisen in consequence of the late defeat of the troops under Major General St. Clair; because, in the beginning of the last year, a similar message was sent you by Colonel [Thomas] Procter, but who was prevented from reaching you by the same insurmountable difficulties. All the Senecas at Buffalo creek can witness for the truth of this assertion, as he held, during the month of April last, long conferences with them, to devise the means of getting to you with safety.

"War, at all times, is a dreadful evil to those who are engaged therein, and more particularly so where a few people engage to act against so great numbers as the people of the United States.

"Brothers: Do not suffer the advantages you have gained to mislead your judgment, and influence you to continue the war; but reflect upon the destructive consequences which must attend such a measure.

"The President of the United States is highly desirous of seeing a number of your principal chiefs, and convincing you, in person, how much he wishes to avoid the evils of war for your sake, and the sake of humanity.

"Consult, therefore, upon the great object of peace; call in your parties, and enjoin a cessation of all further depredations; and as many of the principal chiefs as shall choose, repair to Philadelphia, the seat of the General Government, and there make a peace, founded upon the principles of justice and humanity. Remember that no additional lands will be required of you, or any other tribe, to those that have been ceded by former treaties, particularly by the tribes who had a right to make the treaty of Muskingum in the year 1789.

"But, if any of your tribes can prove that you have a fair right to any lands, comprehended by the said treaty, and have not been compensated therefor[e], you shall receive full satisfaction upon that head.

"The chiefs you send shall be safely escorted to this city; and shall be well fed and provided with all things for their journey; and the faith of the United States is hereby pledged to you for the true and liberal performance of every thing herein contained and suggested; and all this is confirmed, in your manner, by the great white belt, hereunto attached.

"Captain [Alexander] Trueman, the bearer, will show you the treaties which the United States have made with the powerful tribes of Indians south of the Ohio—the Creeks, Cherokees, Chickasaws, and Choctaws. You will there have the most decisive proof of the justice and liberality of the United States towards the Indian tribes.

"At present, there is in the city of Philadelphia, a deputation of fifty of the principal chiefs of the Five Nations, to wit: The Oneidas, Tuscaroras, Onondagas, and Senecas. Were you to see, with your own eyes, the kind manner in which these chiefs are treated, you would never more think of lifting the hatchet against the United States, who are desirous of being your best friends.

"Come, then, and be convinced for yourselves, of the beneficence of General Washington, the Great Chief of the United States, and afterwards return and spread the glad tidings of peace and prosperity of the Indians to the setting sun" (*ASP, Indian Affairs,* 1:230).

Knox's final instructions to Trueman, dated 3 April and also apparently approved by the president, read: "Confiding in your judgment and abilities to execute the mission herein designated, I hereby request you, in the name of the President of the United States, to enter upon the duties thereof, with all possible despatch.

"You will, therefore, immediately repair to Pittsburg. I have herewith given you an order to Captain [Thomas] Hughes, to furnish you with an escort, and a boat to transport you to fort Washington. On your arrival at that place, you will disclose to Lieutenant Colonel-commandant [James] Wilkinson the object of your mission, and concert with him the proper means for carrying it into execution.

"I have directed him, in a letter herewith delivered to you, to afford you all possible facility in pursuance of your orders.

"I have also, herewith delivered to you a speech for the Western Indians, with which you will repair to the Miami village, accompanied by such Indians, men or women, or both, as shall be judged best by you and Lieutenant Colonel Wilkinson. This speech is also accompanied by a belt. It will be of the highest importance that you shall have an interpreter capable fully of explaining your ideas.

"You will observe that the speech is designed to effect a peace with the hostile Indians, on the terms of humanity and justice; your language must all, therefore, be to the same effect.

"As the confederacy of Indians is supposed to be extensive, it will require time to bring your negotiations to a favorable issue. Your patience, your fortitude, and your knowledge of the human character, will all be tested by the objects of your mission.

"It may be said on all occasions, and the issue will justify the assertion, that nothing is more desired than to remove all causes of discontent, and to establish a peace upon a firm foundation.

"But, that, in order to bring about an event so pregnant with happiness to the Indians, they must instantly abstain from all further hostilities, recall their parties if they have any out, as we shall do, and let every thing be settled amicably.

"If the chiefs of the hostile tribes can be induced to repair here, it is conceived the view of the population of the country, and the improvements of all sorts, will exhibit to their minds, in strong colors, the futility of their continuing the war. As a further inducement to repairing here, presents of clothing and silver ornaments may be stipulated. The Creek treaty, the treaty with the Cherokees, and the present manner in which the deputation of the Six Nations, now in this city, are treated, may be cited as strong proofs of the pacific and liberal intentions of the General Government.

"Impressed verbally, as you have been, of the importance of a peace being concluded with the hostile Indians, little more need be added. I shall only say, that it is an event most devoutly desired by the President of the United States, and the people generally. If you shall be the instrument of effecting it, much personal reputation and honor will be the result; besides which, I am authorized by the President of the United States, that your expenses, while in the employment, shall be supported by the public, and that you shall be liberally rewarded in a pecuniary manner.

"It will be important that you take with you some white, or other persons, to serve as messengers between you and the commanding officer, so that he may be informed, and through him, me, of your prospects, from time to time. If you should succeed, you will please to accompany the chiefs to this place; but if you should fail, you will join the army under the commanding officer, after stating in the most ample manner the progress and result of your proceedings" (ibid., 229–30). On 20 May 1792 Gen. James Wilkinson instructed Col. John Hardin to act in conjunction with Trueman (Michigan Pioneer and Historical Society, *Historical Collections* 24 [1895]: 414–16).

Letter not found: to George Augustine Washington, 1 April 1792. GW's nephew wrote him from Mount Vernon on 8–9 April: "Your favor of the 1st Inst. came to hand at the usual time."

From Thomas Jefferson

[Philadelphia] April 2. 1792.

Th: Jefferson—has the honor to return to the President the letters of Seagrove from which he has had an extract taken.[1]

He incloses also the names of three gentlemen who have expressed their *willingness* to serve in the Mint. the President knows them personally & will judge of their *fitness*.[2]

AL, DNA: RG 59, Miscellaneous Letters; LB, DNA: RG 59, George Washington's Correspondence with His Secretaries of State; LB (photocopy), DLC:GW.

1. See Tobias Lear to Jefferson, 31 Mar., n.1.

2. The undated enclosure reads: "Mr [Sylvanus] Bourne (late Consul at St Domingo) to be appointed to some office in the Mint. Mr [John] Dawson of Virginia wishes to be Director of the Mint. Colo. [David Salisbury] Franks to be Treasurer of do. he says he is able to give the security requisite" (DNA: RG 59, Miscellaneous Letters). For Dawson's application, see James Monroe to Jefferson, 2 April 1792, *Jefferson Papers,* 23:365.

From Henry Knox

[Philadelphia] 2 April 1792. Submits "the Indians reply to Your speech to Colonel Pickering."[1]

ALS, DLC:GW; LB, DLC:GW.

1. Although the enclosure has not been positively identified, it was probably a copy of Red Jacket's speech of 31 March. War Department clerk John Stagg, Jr.'s copy of the account of that day's meeting reads: "The Indians of the five nations present in this City, being assembled in their council room addressed to Colonel Pickering the following Speech. The Chief named Sau-goo-a-wathau (or Red Jacket) being the Speaker and having in his hands the large White belt delivered to them by the President at the close of his Speech on the [ ] instant now request the Attention of the President of the United States by his agent Colonel Pickering here present."

Red Jacket's speech reads: "A few days since when the American Chief had spoken to us, he gave us to understand that General Knox and Colonel Pickering should be the agents to negotiate with us on things which concern our welfare.

"Let me call for Your compassion, as you can put all down upon paper, while we have to labour with our minds, to retain and digest what is Spoken, to enable us to make an Answer.

"Brother, whose attention I have called as the Representative of the great chief of this Island, when, the other day, he welcomed us to the great council fire of the thirteen United States, he said it was from his very heart. He said it gave him pleasure to look round and see such numerous representation of the five Nations of Indians. And that it was at his Special request we had been invited to the Seat of the general Government to promote the happiness of our nation, in a friendly connection with the United States.

"He then told us that his love of peace did not terminate with the five Nations: but extended to all the nations of the Setting Sun; and that it was his desire that Universal peace might prevail in this Island.

"Brother Conneh-Sau-ty, (The Indian name of Col. Pickering) and I requested your compassion; on account of our different Situations, that I should notice only a few of the principle things in the president's Speech declared to us the other day, Three things I have mentioned of the introductory part of his Speech. What other reply can we, Your brothers of the five nations Make to that introductory part of the Speech than to thank him, and Say, that it has given a Spring to every passion of our Souls?

"Brother, The President again observed to us, that he wished our minds might all be disposed to peace, that a happy peace might be established between Your brothers of the five nations, So firmly that nothing might move it: that it might be founded as upon a rock. this Sentiment of your Chief has given joy to our hearts—to compare that peace to a *rock,* which is *immoveable.*

"The President further observed to us, that by our contriving to walk in the path of peace, and hearkening to his council, We might Share with you in all the blessings of civilized life: This also meets the Approbation of our minds and has the thanks of all your brothers of the five nations.

"He again observed to us, that if we attended to his council in this matter, our children and childrens children might partake in all the blessings which should rise out of this earth. This has taken hold of our minds, and even we who are grown up look forward, and anticipate its fulfilment.

"The President again observed to us, that what he had Spoken was in the Sincerity of his heart and that time and opportunities would give further evidence, that what he said was true: And we believed it, because we saw the words come from his own lips: and therefore they were lodged deep in our minds.

"The President of the thirteen fires, while continuing his Speech made also this remark. That in order to establish all his words for the best good of Your nation & ours—we must forget all the evils that were past, and attend to what lies before us, and take such a course as Shall cement our peace, that we may be as one.

"The President again observed, That it had come to his ears, that the cause of the hostilities now prevailing with the Western Indians, was their persuasion that the United States had unjustly taken away their lands. But he assured us this was not the case. That it was not the mind of any of his Chiefs to take any land on the whole Island without agreeing for it. He then mentioned a treaty at Muskingum, and he concluded that what land was given up at that treaty was fairly obtained.

"He also observed to us that it was his opinion that the hostile Indians were in an error, that they had missed the true path, whatever evil Spirit or whatever lies had turned them aside—he wishes they could be discovered, that they might be removed. He expressed a Strong wish that those obstacles to the extending of peace to the Westward, might be discovered; and he would use all his exertions to remove them; that peace might be extended to the whole Island.

"Towards the close of the Speech the President informed us that there were many things which concerned the future happiness of the five nations the concerting of which he should refer to you (pointing to Colonel Pickering) here present, and the Chief Warrior of the United States.

"And at the close he observed, that our professions of friendship and regard were commonly witnessed by some token: therefore in the name of the United States, he presented us with this white belt, which was to be handed down from one generation to another, as a confirmation of his words, and a witness of the friendly disposition of the United States towards the peace and happiness of the five confederated nations.

"(Red Jacket here laid aside the white belt received from the President; and taking up a belt of their own (which is annexed) proceeded as follows).

"Now let the President of the United States, possess his mind in peace, that we have made but a short reply to his address to us the other day; for the belt he gave us is deposited with us; and we have taken fast hold of it. What more can we say, than but to return our United thanks for his address in welcoming us to the seat of the great Council and for the advise he gave us, and our pleasure is increased that You, Conneh-Sau-ty [Timothy Pickering], are appointed to assist us in devising the means to promote and secure the happiness of the five nations.

"Brother! Now open Your ears, as the Representative of the great Council of the Thirteen United States in our present council—hear the words we may Speak. And all here present of the great Council (some members of Congress were present—of which the Indians had been informed) and our Brethren of the five nations, hear!—We consider ourselves in the presence of the great Spirit, the Proprietor of us all.

"The President, in effect, observed to us that we of the five nations were our own proprietors; were freemen and might speak with freedom, This has gladdened our hearts, and removed a weight that was upon them. And therefore You will hear us patiently while we speak.

"The President has in effect told us that we were freemen; the sole proprietors of the soil on which we live. This is the Source of the joy; which we feel—How can two brothers speak freely together, unless they feel that they are on equal ground.

"I observed to you Brother that our considering ourselves by Your own acknowledgment as freemen has given the joy to our hearts. that we might Speak in Character. Therefore, we join with the president in his wish that all the evils which have hitherto disturbed our peace, may be buried in oblivion. And this wish proceeds from our heart. Now we can Speak our minds freely as they are free from pressure.

"Now Brother, which you continue to hear in behalf of the United States let all here present also open their ears, while those of the five nations, here present Speak with one voice. We wish to see Your words verified to our Children & Childrens children. You enjoy all the blessings of this life: to you therefore we look to make provision that the same may be enjoyed by our Children. This wish comes from our hearts. but we add, that our happiness cannot be great if in the introduction of your ways, we are put under too much constraint.

"Brother! Appointed agent to converse with us upon the affairs of our peace, continue to hear—we Your brothers of the five nations believe that the Great Spirit let this Island drop down from above—we also believe in his Superintending over this whole Island. Tis he who gives peace and prosperity, and he also sends evil. But prosperity has been Yours—American Brethren—All the good which can spring out of this Island You enjoy. We therefore wish that we and our Children and our Children's children may partake with you in that enjoyment.

"Brother! I observed that the great Spirit might Smile upon one people and turn & frown upon another. This you have Seen who are of one colour and one blood. The King of England and you Americans Strove to advance your happiness by extending your possessions upon this Island, which produces so many good things. And while you two great powers were thus contending for those good things, by which the whole Island was shaken and violently agitated, is it Strange that the peace of us the five nations was Shaken and overturned? But let me say no more of the trembling of our Island. All is in a measure now quieted. Peace is now restored. The peace of us the five nations is now budding. But still there is some Shaking among the original Americans, at setting sun—and you the thirteen fires, and the King of England: Know what is our situation, and the causes of this disturbance now here You have an Embassador as we are informed, from the King of England. Let him, in behalf of the King, and the Americans adjust all their matters according to their agreement at the making of peace—and then you will soon see all things settled among the Indian-Nations, peace will be Spread far and near; Let the president and the Embassador use all their exertions to bring about this settlement (according to their peace) and it will make us all glad & we shall consider both as our real friends.

"Brother! You continue to hear, be assured we have Spoken from our very hearts and not from our lips only Let us therefore make this observation That when you Americans and the King made peace, he did not mention us and showed us no compassion notwithstanding all he Said to us, and all we had suffered. This has been the occasion of great sorrow and pain, and great loss to us the five nations. When you asked and he settled the peace between you two great nations, he never asked us for a delegation to attend to our Interests, Had he done this a settlement of peace among all the Western nations might have been effected. But the neglecting of this and passing us by unnoticed has brought upon us great pain & trouble.

"Brother! It is evident that we of the five nations have Suffered much in consequence of the Strife between You and the King of England who are one colour and one blood. Our chain of peace has been broken—Peace & friendship have been chased from us. But you Americans were determined not to treat us in the same manner as we had been treated by the King of England You therefore desired us at the reestablishment of peace to Sit down at our ancient fire places, and again enjoy our lands. And had the peace between You and the King of England been completely accomplished it would long before this time, have extended far beyond the five nations.

"Brother Conneh-Sau-ty [Timothy Pickering] you are specially appointed with General Knox to confer with us our peace and happiness. We have rejoiced in Your appointment and we hope that the great Warrior will remember that though a *Warrior* he is to converse with us about *peace*: letting what concerns *War* Sleep; and the *Counselling* part of his mind, while acting with us, be of *peace.*

"Brother! have patience and continue to listen: the President has assured us, that *he* is not the cause of the hostilities now existing at the Westward but laments it. Brother we wish You to point out to us of the five nations *What You think is the real cause.*

"Brother! Agent of the Thirteen United States in the present Council, we now publicly return our thanks to the president & all the Counsellors of the thirteen United States for the words which he has spoken to us. They were good, without any mixture. Shall we observe that he wished that if the errors of the hostile Indians could be discovered he would use his Utmost exertions to remove them? Brother You & the King of England are the two governing powers of this Island. What are we? You both are important and proud: and you cannot adjust your own affairs agreeably to Your declarations of peace. Therefore the Western Indians are bewildered—one says one thing to them and one says another. Were these things adjusted it would be easy to diffuse peace everywhere.

"In confirmation of our words we give this belt which we wish the president to hold fast in remembrance of what we have now Spoken.

"(He then delivered to Colonel Pickering the annexed belt)" (NBuErHi: Indians [Ogden Treaty], BOO-2).

To Thomas Jefferson

[Philadelphia] Tuesday—Ten Oclock 3d April 1792

The President has examined the enclosed—thinks it exactly conformable to the loan proposed by Mr Blodget—and approves of it accordingly.[1]

Mr Jefferson will request the Attorney General to draw (with care & caution) a Deed proper for the occasion.

AL, DNA: RG 59, Miscellaneous Letters.

1. The enclosure has not been identified, but for Samuel Blodget, Jr.'s loan proposal, see GW to the Commissioners for the District of Columbia, 6 Mar., n.7, and GW to Jefferson, 21, 30 Mar. 1792.

The First Presidential Veto, 3–5 April 1792

Editorial Note

Congress's presentation of "An Act for an apportionment of Representatives among the several States according to the first enumeration" to Washington for his approbation on 26 Mar. 1792 set the scene for the first presidential veto in U.S. history. Recognizing the controversial nature of the bill, which increased the U.S. House of Representatives to 120 members, gave the size of each state's delegation, and stipulated that congressional representation would be based on a ratio of one member for every 30,000 citizens, Washington called on Henry Knox, Alexander Hamilton, Thomas Jefferson, and Edmund Randolph in early April to give him their opinions about whether he should sign or veto the bill.

Secretary of War Knox and Secretary of the Treasury Hamilton opposed a presidential veto in this instance. Knox argued on 3 April that as the Constitution was unclear about how representatives were to be apportioned, Washington's decision should be based on whether the bill was equitable. In Knox's opinion it was (see Document I). Hamilton wrote Washington on the following day that although he had not yet read the bill, it seemed to him to be constitutional and, as important, "consistent with *equality.*" Both Knox and Hamilton believed that where the Constitution might be reasonably interpreted in two different ways and neither interpretation was contrary to the public good Congress should prevail and the bill be signed into law (see Document II).

Attorney General Randolph and Secretary of State Jefferson strongly disagreed. In separate letters dated 4 April, they argued that the bill was unconstitutional because it established the total number of representatives, 120, by dividing the aggregate of the federal census by 30,000. They contended that the Constitution required the choice of a common divisor—a number that would divide each state's population evenly—and the division of the population residing in each state by that number to establish the size of the House of Representatives. In addition, as the bill gave an additional member to each of the eight states with the largest fraction left over after dividing by 30,000, the number of representatives in those eight states illegally exceeded the stipulated one for every 30,000 (see Documents III and IV).

After careful consideration Washington concluded that Randolph and Jefferson were correct that the bill was "contrary to the common understanding of" the Constitution and "to what was understood at the time by the makers of it." Even so, he hesitated to veto the bill. Because "the vote for & against the bill was perfectly geographical, a Northern ag[ains]t a Southern vote," Washington "feared he should be thought to be taking side with a Southern party." Worried that "there would ere long be a separation of the union . . . [Washington] went home, sent for Randolph the Atty Genl desired him to get mister Madison immediately & come to me [Jefferson], & if we three concurred in opinion that he should negative the bill, he desired to hear nothing more about it but that we would draw the instrument for him to sign. they came. our minds had been before made up. we drew the instrumt. Randolph carried it to him & told him we all concurred in it. he walked with him to the door, and as if he still wished to get off, he said, '& you say you approve of this yourself?' 'yes, Sir,[']' says Randolph, [']I do upon my honor.'"[1] On 5 April the president returned the bill to the House of Representatives (see Document VI). After receiving Washington's veto message, Congress threw out the original bill and decided, on 10 April, to apportion representatives at "the ratio of one for every thirty-three thousand persons in the respective States."[2]

1. Thomas Jefferson's Memoranda of Consultations with the President, 11 Mar.–9 April, DLC: Jefferson Papers; *Jefferson Papers,* 23:264.

2. *Annals of Congress,* 2d Cong., 550.

I. From Henry Knox

Sir War department. April 3d 1792.

Agreeably to your directions as delivered to me this day by the Attorney General, I have endeavoured to take into consideration the expediency of your giving your approbation to the Act intituled "An Act for an apportionment of Representatives among the several states according to the first enumeration," the constitutionality thereof being doubted by some persons.

I might plead my inability to give an opinion on so important and doubtful a point, as not possessing that previous information more peculiarly resulting from a study of the Law, and from not having seen the merits of the question discussed in any of the debates of the house.

It is therefore with the highest diffidence I venture on the subject.

The point upon which the question turns is, whether the numbers of representatives shall be apportioned on the aggregate number of all the people of the United States, or on the aggregate numbers of the people of each state, notwithstanding several large fractions may exist in each state unrepresented.

It has been said that either construction may be deemed to be within the letter as well as the spirit of the constitution, if this opinion should be just, which I freely confess I am not qualified of myself at this time to decide, it would result that the assent of the President of the United States is to be governed by the political equity of the measure.

In this view of the case I find my mind less embarrassed with doubt; for although some smaller fractions may be unrepresented yet most of the large ones are comprehended—In the bill eight states each having a fraction of upwards of twenty five thousand are provided with a representative; whereas in the other seven states no one of which would have more than Twelve thousand eight hundred and sixty six—only one state that number, and the whole Seven states but little more than fifty thousand federal numbers unrepresented, provided all idea of virtual representation should be rejected according to the principle of the bill itself—but on the contrary were the fractions of the eight states possessing the largest fractions not considered upwards of Two hundred thousand federal numbers would be unrepresented.

As then the Senate and house of representatives have passed this Law (by small majorities indeed) and as the constitutionality is only doubted not proved but the equity of the measure apparent, it would appear rather a delicate measure for the President to decide the question contrary to the bill as passed.

If precedents are to be drawn from the conduct of the King of Great Britain in similar cases of doubtful laws, it would render the propriety of the President's disapprobation still more questionable. I have the honour to be Sir with perfect respect Your most obedient servant

H. Knox
secy of War

LS, DLC:GW.

II. From Alexander Hamilton

Philadelphia April 4 1792

The Secretary of the Treasury presents his respects to the President of the United States. He was informed, yesterday, by the Attorney General, that his opinion concerning the constitutionality of the Representation Bill was desired this morning. He now sends it with his reasons but more imperfectly stated than he could have wished—through want of time.[1] He has never seen the bill, but from the accounts he has had of it he takes it for granted that he cannot have misconceived its contents so as to cause any material error in the process of his reasoning.

AL, DLC:GW.

1. Hamilton's enclosed opinion of 4 April reads: "The President desires an opinion, whether the Act intitled 'An Act for an apportionment of Representatives among the several states according to the first enumeration' be constitutional, or not.

"It is to be inferred from the provisions of the Act—That the following process has been pursued.

"I The aggregate numbers of the United States are divided by 30000, which gives the total number of representatives, or 120.

"II This number is apportionned among the several states by the following rule—As the *aggregate* numbers of the *United States* are to the *total number* of representatives found as above, so are the *particular numbers of each state* to the number of representatives of such state. But

"III As this second process leaves a residue of Eight out of the 120 members unapportioned, these are distributed among those states which upon that second process have the largest fractions or remainders.

"As a ratio Of 30000 appears to have been adopted as a guide—The Question is whether this ratio ought to have been applied, in the first instance, to the aggregate numbers of the United States or to the particular numbers of each state.

"I am of opinion that either of these courses might have been constitutionally pursued—or in other words that there is no criterion by which it can be pronounced decisively that the one or the other is the true construction. Cases so situated often arise on constitutions and Laws.

"The part of the constitution in question is thus expressed—'*Representatives* and *direct taxes* shall be *apportioned* among the several states according to their *respective numbers.*'

"Tis plain that the same rule is to be pursued with regard to *direct taxes* as with regard to *Representatives.*

"What is the process which would naturally be followed in relation to the apportionment of direct taxes?

"Clearly this—The *total sum* necessary would be first ascertained.

"This total sum would then ⟨be⟩ *apportioned* among the several states by the following rule—viz.

"As the *aggregate* numbers of the United States are to the *whole sum* required so are the *particular numbers* of a *particular state* to the proportion of such state. Which is, so far, the exact process that has been followed by the Bill, in the apportionment of representatives.

"And hence results a strong argument for its constitutionality.

"If there had been no ratio mentioned in the constitution 'tis evident that no other course could have been well pursued. No doubt at least of the propriety of that which has been pursued could have been then entertained.

"Does the mention of a ratio necessarily alter it?

"The words of the constitution in respect to the ratio are these 'The number of representatives shall not exceed one for every 30000, but each state shall have at least one representative.'

"This provision may naturally be read and understood thus—'The whole number of the representatives of the United States shall not exceed one to every 30000 of the aggregate numbers of the United States; but if it should happen that the proportion of the numbers of any state to the aggregate numbers of the United States should not give to such state one representative—such state shall nevertheless have *one.* No state shall be without a representative.[']

"There is nothing in the form of expression to confine the application of the ratio to the *several* numbers of the states. The mode of expression equally permits its application to their joint or *aggregate numbers.* The intent of inserting it is merely to determine a proportional limit which the number of the house of representatives shall not exceed—This is as well satisfied by resorting to the collective as to the separate population of the respective states.

"There is therefore nothing in the last recited clause to controul or direct the sense of the first.

"If it be said that the further process which apportions the residue among the states having the greatest remainders is the circumstance that renders the bill unconstitutional because it renders the representation not *strictly* according *to the respective numbers* of the states it may be answered.

"That this is but a necessary consequence of the first principle.

"As there would commonly be left, by the first process, an unapportioned residue of the total number, to be apportioned, it is of necessity that that residue should be distributed among the several states by some rule and none more equal or defensible can be found than that of giving a preference to the greatest remainders.

"If this makes the apportionment not mathematically 'according to the *respective numbers* of the several states' so neither would the opposite principle of construction.

"Fractions more or less great would in this case also, and, in a greater degree, prevent a conformity of the proportion of representatives to numbers. The same objection would lie in this respect against both principles of construction; against that in the bill least.

"Upon the whole then, The Bill *apportions* the Representatives among the several states *according to their respective numbers*; so as that the *number of representatives* does not *exceed* one for every 30000 persons *each state having at least one member*. It therefore performs every requisition of the constitution; and it will not be denied that it performs this in the manner most consistent with *equality*.

"There appears therefore no room to say, that the bill is unconstitutional, though there may be another construction, of which the constitution is capable. In cases where two constructions may reasonably be adopted, and neither can be pronounced inconsistent with the public good, it seems proper that the legislative sense should prevail. The present appears to the Secretary clearly to be such a case" (DLC:GW; the mutilated word supplied within angle brackets is taken from MH: Sparks Transcripts).

III. From Thomas Jefferson

[Philadelphia] Apr. 4. 1792.

The Constitution has declared that "Representatives & direct taxes shall be apportioned among the several states according to their respective numbers," that "the number of representatives shall not exceed one for every 30,000, but each state shall have at least one representative; & until such enumeration shall be made, the state of New Hampshire shall be entitled to chuse 3. Massachusets &c.["]

The bill for apportioning representatives among the several states, without explaining any principle at all, which may shew it's conformity with the constitution, or guide future apportionments, says that New-Hampshire shall have three members, Massachusets 16. &c. we are therefore to find by experiment what has been the principle of the bill, to do which it is proper to state the federal or representable numbers of each state, and the members allotted to them by the bill. they are as follows.

Vermont	85,532	3
New Hampshire	141.823	5
Massachusets	475,327	16
Rhode island	68,444	2

Connecticut	235,941	8
New York	352,915	11
New Jersey	179,556	6
Pennsylvania	432,880	14
Delaware	55,538	2
Maryland	278,513	9
Virginia	630,558	21
Kentuckey	68,705	2
North Carolina	353,521	11
South Carolina	206,236	7
Georgia	70,843	2
	3,636,312	120

It happens that this representation, whether tried as between great & small states, or as between North & South, yeilds, in the present instance, a tolerably just result, and consequently could not be objected to on that ground, if it were obtained by the process prescribed in the Constitution. but if obtained by any process out of that, it becomes arbitrary, & inadmissible.

The Ist member of the clause of the constitution above cited is express that representatives shall be apportioned among the several states according to their *respective numbers.* That is to say, they shall be apportioned by some common ratio. for *proportion,* & ratio, are equivalent words; & it is the definition of *proportion among numbers,* that they have a *ratio common to all,* or in other words a *common divisor.* now, trial will shew that there is no *common ratio,* or *divisor,* which, applied to the numbers of each state, will give to them the number of representatives allotted in this bill. for trying the several ratios of 29. 30. 31. 32. 33. The allotments would be as follows:

	29.	30	31.	32.	33.	the bill
Vermont	2	2	2	2	2	3
New Hampshire	4	4	4	4	4	5
Massachusets	16	15	15	14	14	16
Rhode-island	2	2	2	2	2	2
Connecticut	8	7	7	7	7	8
New York	12	11	11	11	10	11
New Jersey	6	5	5	5	5	6
Pennsylvania.	14	14	13	13	13	14
Delaware	1	1	1	1	1	2
Maryland	9	9	8	8	8	9
Virginia	21	21	20	19	19	21

Kentuckey	2	2	2	2	2	2
North Carolina	12	11	11	11	10	12
South Carolina	7	6	6	6	6	7
Georgia	2	2	2	2	2	2
	118	112	109	107	105	120

Then the bill reverses the Constitutional precept, because, by it, "representatives are *not* apportioned among the several states according to their respective numbers."

It will be said that though, for taxes, there may always be found a divisor which will apportion them among the states according to numbers exactly, without leaving any remainder, yet, for representatives, there can be no such common ratio, or divisor, which, applied to the several numbers, will divide them exactly, without a remainder or fraction. I answer then, that taxes must be divided *exactly,* & representatives *as nearly* as the *nearest ratio* will admit; and the fractions must be neglected: because the constitution wills absolutely that there be an *apportionment,* or *common ratio*; & if any fractions result from the operation, it has left them unprovided for. in fact it could not but foresee that such fractions would result, & it meant to submit to them. it knew they would be in favor of one part of the union at one time, & of another at another, so as, in the end, to balance occasional inequalities. but instead of such a *single* common ratio, or uniform divisor, as prescribed by the constitution, the bill has applied *two ratios,* at least, to the different states; to wit that of 30,026 to the seven following R. Island, N. York, Pennsylvania, Maryland, Virginia, Kentuckey & Georgia, and that of 27,770 to the eight others, namely Vermont, N. Hampshire, Massachusets, Connecticut[,] N. Jersey, Delaware, N. Carolina, & S. Carolina, as follows:

divided by 30,026 give			and	divided by 27,770 give		
R. Island	68,444	2		Vermont	85,532	3
N. York	352,915	11		N. Hampshire	141,823	5
Pennylvania	432,880	14		Massachusets	475,327	16
Maryland	278,513	9		Connecticut	235,941	8
Virginia	630,558	21		New Jersey	179,556	6
Kentuckey	68,705	2		Delaware	55,538	2
Georgia	70,843	2		N. Carolina	353,521	12
				S. Carolina	206,236	7

and if *two* ratios may be applied, then *15* may, & the distribution become arbitrary, instead of being apportioned to numbers.

Another member of the clause of the constitution, which has been cited, says "the number of representatives shall not exceed one for every 30,000, but each state shall have at least one representative." this last phrase proves that it had in contemplation that all fractions or *numbers below the common ratio,* were to be unrepresented; & it provides specially that in the case of a state whose whole number shall be below the common ratio, one representative shall be given to it. this is the single instance where it allows representation to any smaller number than the common ratio, and by providing specially for it in this, shews it was understood that, without special provision, the smaller number would, in this case, be involved in the general principle.

The first phrase of the above citation, that "the number of representatives shall not exceed one for every 30,000" is violated by this bill which has given to 8. states a number exceeding one for every 30,000. to wit, one for every 27,770.

In answer to this, it is said that this phrase may mean either the thirty thousands *in each state,* or the thirty thousands *in the whole union,* & that in the latter case it serves only to find the amount of the whole representation: which, in the present state of population, is 120 members. Suppose the phrase might bear both meanings: which will Common sense apply to it? which did the universal understanding of our country apply to it? which did the Senate & Representatives apply to it during the pendency of the first bill, & even till an advanced stage of this second bill, when an ingenious gentleman found out the doctrine of fractions, a doctrine so difficult & inobvious, as to be rejected at first sight by the very persons who afterwards became it's most zealous advocates?—The phrase stands in the midst of a number of others, every one of which relates to states in their separate capacity. will not plain common sense then understand it, like the rest of it's context, to relate to states in their separate capacities?

But if the phrase of one for 30,000. is only meant to give the aggregate of representatives, & not at all to influence their apportionment among the states, then the 120 being once found, in order to apportion them, we must recur to the former rule which does it *according to the numbers of the respective states*; and we must take the *nearest common divisor,* as the ratio of distribution, that is to say, that divisor which, applied to every state, gives to them such numbers as, added together, come nearest to 120. this nearest common ratio will be found to be 28,658. and will distribute 119 of the 120 members, leaving only a single residuary one. it will be found too to place 96,648 fractional numbers in the 8. Northernmost states, & 105,582 in the 7. Southernmost. the following table shews it:

	Ratio of 28,858		fraction	
Vermont	85,532	2.	27,816	
N. Hampshire	141,823	4.	26,391	
Massachusets	475,327	16.	13,599	
R. Island	68,444	2	10,728	
Connecticut	235,941	8	5,077	
N. York	352,915	12	6,619	
N. Jersey	179,556	6	6,408	
Pensylvania	432,880	15	10	96,648
Delaware	55,538	1	26,680	
Maryland	278,513	9	18,791	
Virginia	630,558	21	24,540	
Kentuckey	68,705	2	10,989	
N. Carolina	353,521	12	7,225	
S. Carolina	206,236	7	4,230	
[Georgia][1]	70,843	2	13,127	105,582
	3,636,312	119	202,230	202,230

Whatever may have been the intention, the effect of rejecting the nearest divisor, (which leaves but one residuary member) And adopting a distant one (which leaves eight) is merely to take a member from New York & Pensylvania each, & give them to Vermont & New Hampshire.

But it will be said, "this is giving more than one for 30,000." true: but has it not been just said that the one for 30,000 is prescribed only to fix the aggregate number, and that we are not to mind it when we come to apportion them among the states? that for this we must recur to the former rule which distributes them according to the numbers in each state? besides does not the bill itself apportion among 7. of the states by the ratio of 27,770? which is much more than one for 30,000.

Where a phrase is susceptible of two meanings, we ought certainly to adopt that which will bring upon us the fewest inconveniencies. let us weigh those resulting from both constructions.

From that giving to each state a member for every 30,000 in that state results the single inconvenience that there may be large fractions unrepresented. but, it being a mere hazard on which states this will fall, hazard will equalize it in the long run.

From the other results exactly the same inconvenience. a thousand cases may be imagined to prove it. take one.

			fractions
1st	45,000	2	15,000
2d	45,000	2	15,000
3d	45,000	2	15,000
4th	45,000	2	15,000
5th	45,000	2	15,000
6th	45,000	2	15,000
7th	45,000	2	15,000
8th	45,000	1	15,000
9th	44,999	1	14,999
10th	44,999	1	14,999
11th	44,999	1	14,999
12th	44,999	1	14,999
13th	44,999	1	14,999
14th	44,999	1	14,999
15th	44,999	1	14,999
	674,993	22	

suppose 8 of the states had 45,000 inhabitants each, and the other seven 44,999 each, that is to say each one less than each of the others. the aggregate would be 674,993. & the number of representatives at one for 30,000 of the aggregate, would be 22. then, after giving one member to each state, distribute the 7. residuary members among the 7. highest fractions, & tho' the difference of population be only an unit, the representation would be the double. here a single inhabitant the more would count as 30,000. nor is this case imaginable only: it will resemble the real one whenever the fractions happen to be pretty equal through the whole states. the numbers of our census happen by accident to give the fractions all very small, or very great, so as to produce the strongest case of inequality that could possibly have occurred, & which may never occur again. the probability is that the fractions will generally descend gradually from 29,999 to 1. the inconvenience then of large unrepresented fractions attends both constructions: & while the most obvious construction is liable to no other, that of the bill incurs many & grievous ones.

1. if you permit the large fraction in one state to chuse a representative for one of the small fractions in another state, you take from the latter it's election, which constitutes real representation, and substitute a virtual representation of the disfranchised fractions: and the tendency of the doctrine of virtual representation has been too well discussed & appreciated by reasoning & resistance, on a former great occasion, to need developement now.

2. the bill does not say that it has given the residuary representatives *to the greatest fractions*; tho' in fact it has done so. it seems to have avoided establishing that into a rule, lest it might not suit on another occasion. perhaps it may be found the next time more convenient to distribute them *among the smaller states*; at another *among the larger states*; at other times according to any other crotchet which ingenuity may invent, & the combinations of the day give strength to carry; or they may do it arbitrarily, by open bargain & cabal. in short this construction introduces into Congress a scramble, or a vendue, for the surplus members, it generates waste of time, hot-blood, & may at some time, when the passions are high, extend a disagreement between the two houses to the perpetual loss of the thing, as happens now in the Pensylvania assembly: whereas the other construction reduces the apportionment always to an arithmetical operation, about which no two men can ever possibly differ.

3. it leaves in full force the violation of the precept which declares that representatives shall be *apportioned* among the states according to their numbers i.e. by some common ratio.

Viewing this bill either as a *violation of the constitution,* or as giving an *inconvenient exposition to it's words,* is it a case wherein the President ought to interpose his negative? I think it is.

1. the Non-user of his negative begins already to excite a belief that no President will ever venture to use it: & consequently has begotten a desire to raise up barriers in the state legislatures against Congress throwing off the controul of the constitution.

2. it can never be used more pleasingly to the public, than in the protection of the constitution.

3. no invasions of the constitution are so fundamentally dan-

gerous as the tricks played on their own numbers, apportionment, & other circumstances respecting themselves, & affecting their legal qualifications to legislate for the Union.

4. The majorities by which this bill has been carried (to wit of 1. in the Senate, and 2. in the Representatives) shew how divided the opinions were there.

5. the whole of both houses admit the constitution will bear the other exposition, whereas the minorities in both deny it will bear that of the bill.

6. the application of any one ratio is intelligible to the people, & will therefore be approved: whereas the complex operations of this bill will never be comprehended by them, & tho' they may acquiesce, they cannot approve what they do not understand.

Th: Jefferson

ADS, DLC:GW.

1. Jefferson mistakenly wrote "Virginia" at this place on the manuscript page.

IV. From Edmund Randolph

[Philadelphia] April 4. 1792.

The attorney general of the U.S. has the honor of reporting to the President of the U.S., on the representation-bill, as follows:

The points, which involve the question of constitutionality, are three:

1. to ascertain the process, by which the bill fixes the total number of representatives at 120:

2. to ascertain the process, by which the bill distributes that number among the states:

and 3. to try both of them by the standard of the constitution.

The bill does not announce in terms the principle of proceeding, either in the establishment of the total number of 120, or its apportionment among the states. Some principle, however, it must have; otherwise the omission would of itself be glaringly unconstitutional, as creating a precedent for leaving the number of the house of representatives, and the distribution of that number, at the mere will of each different congress. It must therefore be sought by calculation.

1. From calculation then it appears, that neither 30,000, the lowest constitutional limit, nor any higher number, if assumed

as the divisor of the fœderal numbers in each state, separately considered, will produce to each state such a number of representatives, as, when added together, shall amount to 120.

We then naturally turn to the aggregate fœderal number of the U.S.; to wit, 3,615,825; and the only divisor, which can draw 120 members from that number, is 30,000.

This too is the only mode, by which 120 members can be obtained by any act of arithmetic.

2. One hundred and twenty members are, in the next place, to be distributed.

Here too we are informed by calculation, that no common divisor, applied to the fœderal number in each state, will allot as many members, as the bill prescribes. Thirty thousand will fail with respect to eight out of fifteen states: a greater number how little soever above 30,000, will at least be as far from that result; and every number beyond a certain point would be farther and farther still. The other seven states have the exact number of representatives, which arises from a division of their fœderal numbers by 30,000. But, as 30000, taken as the divisor of the fœderal population in each state, gives 112 members; as the remainder of the 120 members is 8; and to each of the eight states, having the highest fractions, one member is added; it may be safely concluded, that congress distributed the 120 members in this form.

3. In trying this double process by the standard of the constitution, we must first determine, whether congress were at liberty to fix the total number of representatives, by dividing the aggregate fœderal population of the U.S., instead of the separate fœderal population of each state.

The following passages in the constitution are material on this head.

"Representatives and direct taxes shall be apportioned among the several states, according to their respective numbers."

"The number of representatives shall not exceed one for every 30,000; but each state shall have at least one representative, and until such enumeration shall be made, the state of New-Hampshire shall be intitled to choose three" &c.

Hence it is argued, that as in laying direct taxes the sum must be resolved upon, before *it* can be apportioned; so a number of representatives must be established, before *they* can be apportioned; and this number can be procured only from the aggregate fœderal population.

It is not doubted, that this number must be the effect of some rule; and in fact we find the constitution declaring it to be, "*according to their respective numbers*"; that is the numbers of each state.

Let it then be seen, how direct taxes and representatives can be in *proportion* to numbers; for "*proportion*" and "*apportion*" may be accepted on this occasion, as synonimous. Direct taxes may be apportioned according to numbers by the rule of three thus; as the whole population is to the sum required; so is a particular population of a state to the sum, to be paid by that state. Thro' this means every individual enters into the estimate; and not a cent is lost. But it is not so with representatives. For with what propriety can it be stated with respect to representatives, in a manner analogous to direct taxes? Can it be said, as the whole fœderal population is to the whole number of representatives; so is the particular number of representatives to the particular fœderal population of each state? It cannot be so contended for two reasons; first, because when the inquiry itself is, what shall the whole number of representatives be, it is false reasoning to assume that number as actually known already; and secondly, because, as representation is the deputation of one man to act for many, more than one must be combined in the account, before a representative can exist. Of course the constitution looked for a ratio as to representation; whereas it computed individuals in taxes; that is, numbers shall govern in both cases; but they govern each subject, acccording to its nature; so at least as not to beget an absurdity.

Could congress increase the house of representatives to 240 members? No. Why? Because they must not exceed one for thirty thousand. What 30,000?—of the *respective* numbers; namely, of each state. If aggregate or collective numbers had been contemplated, how much easier would it have been, and how much more proper, to have substituted other words which were so obviously at hand? It seems to have been designed to make up the total number of representatives, just as a stock in trade is created: each state is a contributor to it; and the contributions added together, furnish the whole. In this way the first house of representatives is composed under the constitution: New Hampshire is to have three &c.

Why are states to have any representatives, as states, if the aggregate fœderal population is to decide the number? It ought rather to have been said, in the constitution, that the boundaries of the states should not be an obstacle; but that the ratio should yield a member, wherever the numbers should be found to fill up that ratio.

This never was intended. Are not the states distinct in their rights of election? Can the numbers of one county even in the same state assist another county in procuring a member? Is it not repugnant to the spirit of the constitution, to tack the numbers of one state to those of another, for the purpose of procuring a member? Is it not unexampled, that New-York should with its numbers contribute towards a member for New Jersey; when an elector of the former can have no fellow-interest or sympathy with the electors of the latter; and, without a freehold in the latter, would probably be debarred of a suffrage therein?

The fractions, it is true, are very large in many of the states; but such fractions are familiar in practice. In some states representatives are according to a certain ratio of population; but the number above one integer, and not equal to another, has always been laid aside. In the management too of the national bank, many shares between two numbers, constituting a vote, are unrespected. If the fraction of one state can raise a member for another, it may often happen, that the balance, which the states wish to preserve among themselves, may be destroyed unexpectedly by their own act. What would the sensations of South Carolina be, if her blacks should cooperate in giving a member to Connecticut?

It is remarkable, that most of the advocates of the bill do themselves admit, that the constitution is susceptible of the construction abovementioned, as well as of their own.

The argument, deduced from the amendment, proposed to the constitution on the subject of representation, might be shewn to be inapplicable, even if it were admissible. But it is inadmissible; because the amendment has not as yet become the sense of the U.S. It is inapplicable. For altho' it has been observed, that without recurring to the aggregate fœderal population, it might happen that three millions of persons would not give one hundred members; the answer is full as strong, to reply, that congress would not be called upon to have one hundred members, unless one hundred times 30,000 should be contained in the separate fœderal populations of the several states. Indeed the amendment proves nothing either way.

In short, it is wonderful, that, after admitting the necessity of applying some ratio, and after perceiving, that the application of that ratio to the aggregate fœderal population, will produce such a number of representatives, as cannot be distributed by any ratio whatever, the friends to the bill should not have abandoned it upon their own principles.

Here lies the radical objection, and the violation of the constitution.

If it be not here, the attorney general must in candor own, that it is no where, in his opinion. For if the 120 members can be established, the subdivision cannot be executed in any other, or in any fairer manner. The ratio of 30,000 is carried thro' the particular, as well as the aggregate fœderal population, as far as it can; and the remaining eight members are distributed equitably.

This is the best judgment therefore, which the attorney-general has been able to form without longer premeditation. Whether the reasoning on the opposite side ought to weigh against the interposition of a negative, it is not for him to decide.

Edm: Randolph

ADS, DLC:GW.

V. Tobias Lear's Notes on the Opinions of the Cabinet

[Philadelphia, c.4 April 1792][1]

The opinion of the Secretary of State

declares the bill unconstitutional—for it does not apportion the Representatives among the states *strictly* according to their numbers.

It provides for fractions—which the Constitution never intended.

It leaves the derternination of apportioning the Representatives without any fixed principle—which may hereafter be productive of great evil, and admits of caballing & bargaining on the subjects.

Bill carried by a small majority—1 in Senate & 2 in the House.

The Whole of both Houses admit that the constitution will bear either to have the bill in its present state—or to have one for 30,000 in each state—leaving the fractions. But the minorities will not admit of the constitutionality of the present bill.

The Atty Genl of the U.S.

The Bill does not express the principle or rule by wh. the number of Representatives is ascertained—it is therefore to be sought by Calculation—which makes one to 30,000. taking the whole number in the U.S.—But it will be found that dividing the number in each state by 30,000, & there will be found 8 states that will have each a membr less than they now have, if divided according to the numbers in the states respectively.

The Constitution looks for a *Ratio* in Representation; but it computed individuals as to taxes. The bill destroys the distinction of states; for the Ratio yields to numbers.

The advocates of the bill admit that the Constitution is susceptible of another construction, as well as of their's.

A Ratio is applied to the aggregate population of the U.S. as produces a number that cannot be distributed by any ratio whatever—and in this lays the unconstitutionality of the bill.

The Secretary of the Treasury

has not seen the bill; but *presumes* that the process, for forming the result of the bill, has been in a certain way, which he mentions.

Thinks either the division of the aggregate number in the U.S. by 30,000, or the particular number in each state by that ratio would be constitutional.

If a direct tax shd be imposed, the only way of apportioning it among the several States would be that which has been pursued in the bill & therefore, it is consonant to the clause in the constitution respectg Representation & taxation.

That there would be a residue arising upon the whole, after dividing the numbers in each state by 30,000, & that it is but right that the states having the greatest fraction should receive the benefit resulting from dividing the *aggregate* number in the U.S. by 30,000.

The bill performs every requisite in the Constitution in a manner most consistent with equality.

Altho' the Bill cannot be said to be unconstitutional, yet there may be another construction of wh. the Constitution is capable. And where it may be taken in either sense, it is best to follow the legislative opinion.

The Secretary of War

It has been said that the Construction of the bill may be deemed within the letter, as well as the spirit of the Constitution—If that is the case, the assent of the President of the U.S. is to be governed by the political equity of the measure.

He approves the bill upon the principle of its giving a representation to the largest fractions.

The constitutionality of the bill being only doubted—not proved—it wd appear a delicate measure for the President to decide against the sense of the legislature.

AD, DLC:GW.

1. Lear apparently prepared these notes after GW had received the various written opinions of the attorney general and department secretaries. GW later docketed the document "Opinions of the Secretaries of State Treasury & War—& Attorney General Respecting the Representation Bill negatived by the President of the United States April—1792."

VI. To the United States House of Representatives

United States [Philadelphia] April 5th 1792.

Gentlemen of the House of Representatives

I have maturely considered the Act passed by the two Houses, intituled "An Act for an apportionment of Representatives among the several States according to the first enumeration;" and I return it to your House, wherein it originated, with the following objections.

First—The Constitution has prescribed that representatives shall be apportioned among the several States according to their respective numbers: and there is no one proportion or divisor which, applied to the respective numbers of the States will yield the number and allotment of representatives proposed by the Bill.

Second—The Constitution has also provided that the number of Representatives shall not exceed one for every thirty thousand; which restriction is, by the context, and by fair and obvious construction, to be applied to the seperate and respective numbers of the States: and the Bill has allotted to eight of the States, more than one for thirty thousand.[1]

George Washington.

Copy, DNA: RG 233, Second Congress, 1791–1793, Records of Legislative Proceedings, Journals; LB, DLC:GW.

1. The House of Representatives this day read the president's veto message, entered his objections into the House's journal, and resolved to reconsider the bill "in the mode prescribed by the Constitution of the United States" on the following day. When the House voted on the bill on 6 April, it was defeated 33 to 23. On Saturday, 7 April, the House appointed a committee to bring in a new bill to apportion representatives among the several states. This committee, which was composed of representatives John Laurance of New York, Joshua Seney (1756–1798) of Maryland, and Jeremiah Smith (1759–1842) of New Hampshire, reported a bill that same day, which was read twice. On 10 April the bill, which set "the ratio of one for every thirty-three thousand persons in the respective States, was read the third time and passed." The bill was signed into law on 14 April (*Annals of Congress,* 2d Cong., 539, 541–42, 549–50, 1359).

From Bryan Fairfax

Dear Sir April the 4th 1792.

Your Favor of the 19th of March I received in due time, and have written to Mr Potts, to inform him, that no Money had been received—that there had been a great Remissness in the Prosecution of the Suit—that a few days before I had received Your Letter I had been speaking to a Gentleman of the Law whom I engaged last Summer to join with the one who had been before employed in the Room of one who had entirely neglected it, and that since, I had spoke to him again and had enquired at the Clerk's Office. And that all that had been done was the bringing a new Suit in the district Court vs the Executors of Dr Savage's Security.

And after mentioning by way of Excuse for myself (for he

knew that You, Sir, could not attend to it) that when a Suit was commenced a man could further it only by employing a lawyer in it, and after speaking to him from time to time, upon finding nothing done, to employ a second, and afterwards a third, I owned that as Mr Savage's heir at Law was in these parts a year or two If I had a Scire facias served upon him I was informed it would have been of Service but that it did not occur to me.

Indeed it gives me Concern that there should be such Remissness under my Management especially as I believe & know that You depend on me to do as much in it or more than I would for myself. I might have applied to the Clerk's Office and have issued a Scire facias myself—But as I was acting for another, it would seem right that the Lawyer should issue such Process as was adviseable—& who could have thought that such continued acting under different hands would have followed—I might also have applied to them once in two or three months instead of doing it twice in a year. On applying at the Clerk's Office the other day Mr Wagener told me Nothing had been done it in the Suit since it came from Richmond—And he could let me have no Process without a transcript of the Record where by it was remanded, this I know I brot up with me—but into whose hands I put it I don't remember. However as Colo. Simms says he has brot a new Suit in the district Court it will render needless any further Process from this Court. One thing which hindered my more frequent Applications to the Lawyers was my not having money at Command at all times.

But, Sir, as I seem to be vindicating my Conduct and it might appear that I feared your Censure, and as you might thence from your wonted kindness be induced to write to me again, I beg that You will not give yourself that trouble, because I know that You know me, & I can rest secure in Your Friendship which I have always esteemed so much the more as I have been persuaded that no Person could deprive me of it, & that nothing but my own misconduct could effect it.

I observe that Mr Potts hints at the Money being advanced by the Trustees which is rather an unreasonable Expectation.[1] And I cant say that I was pleased with Mrs Bomford's Proposal in her last Letter wherein she offered to relinquish half of her demand to me if I would pay the remainder which was a little Reflection on my Integrity as If I had it in my Power to pay it—Indeed the delay has been so unusual that it seems incredible, which I consider as an excuse for her.

Mrs Fairfax joins with me in our Respects to Mrs Washington[2]—We had a Marriage last Week in our Family my Daughter being married to Mr Griffith the oldest Son of Dr Griffith.[3] I remain with great Respect & Esteem Dr Sir Yr affect. humble Servt

Bryan Fairfax.

ALS, DLC:GW.

1. Potts's "hints" were apparently made in his letter to GW of 31 Oct. 1791 (not found), which GW had forwarded to Fairfax on 19 Mar. 1792.

2. Fairfax's first wife, Sarah Cary Fairfax, had died around 1788. He currently was married to Jane (Jenny) Dennison (Donaldson) Fairfax.

3. David Griffith, the son of Bryan Fairfax's predecessor as rector of Fairfax Parish, Va., Dr. David Griffith, married Elizabeth Fairfax in the early spring of 1792.

To Thomas Jefferson

Dear Sir, [Philadelphia] Wednesday Morning [4 April 1792][1]

Am I right in understanding, as the result of the Conversation you had with Mr White, that it was his opinion Genl Morgan would serve under Officers superior to him in Rank in the Army about to be raised? I want to get the appointments closed, but wish to know, previously, whether this was Mr Whites opinion.[2] Yours sincerely

G. W——n

ALS, DLC: Jefferson Papers.

1. On the cover, Jefferson docketed the letter as having been received on 4 April 1792.

2. Jefferson replied later this day: "Th: J. presents his respects to the President. mister White beleived pretty decidedly that General Morgan would serve under any officers who had been his superiors except Genl St Clair, but at the same time he said he could not engage it positively" (DNA: RG 59, Miscellaneous Letters). Before the end of March, GW had asked Jefferson to inquire of Virginia congressman Alexander White whether he thought Daniel Morgan would accept a brigadier generalship. Although GW nominated him for that rank, Morgan declined the commission (see GW to Jefferson, 30 Mar., and to the U.S. Senate, 9 April).

To Henry Knox

Dr Sir [Philadelphia] Wednesday Morng [4 April 1792]

Has G—— W——ne decided yet?[1] Has any answer been prepared for G—— St ——[2] —I am anxious to have these matters closed.

Also for the departure of T——[3] and that the business with the Indians may be brought to a conclusion. Yrs always

G. W——n

ALS, CSmH.

1. Anthony Wayne earlier had informed the secretary of war that he would not accept a subordinate position in the new force being raised to subdue the hostile northwestern Indian nations. GW apparently was waiting to hear if Wayne was willing to command the military expedition (see Henry Knox to GW, 1 April, n.1).

2. Later this day Knox gave the president a draft of a response to Maj. Gen. Arthur St. Clair's letter to GW of 31 Mar. (see GW to St. Clair, 4 April).

3. For Capt. Alexander Trueman's peace mission, see Knox to GW, 1 April, n.2.

To Henry Knox

Sir, United States [Philadelphia] April 4th 1792.

You will lay before the House of Representatives such papers, from your department, as are requested by the enclosed Resolution.[1]

Df, in Tobias Lear's hand, DLC:GW; LB, DLC:GW.

1. Tobias Lear noted at the bottom of the draft: "(The papers aluded to are such as relate to the expedition under Genl St Clair—)." The enclosed resolution was undoubtedly that passed by the House of Representatives this day and presented to GW by Thomas FitzSimons and William Branch Giles: "Resolved, That the President . . . be requested to cause the proper officers to lay before this House such papers of a public nature, in the Executive Department, as may be necessary to the investigation of the causes of the failure of the late expedition under Major General St. Clair." Knox laid the relevant papers in his possession before the House on 9 April, and it immediately referred them to the investigative committee (*Annals of Congress,* 2d Cong., 536, 549). For the appointment of the House committee of inquiry into the failure of the St. Clair expedition, see Knox to GW, 30 Mar., source note.

To Arthur St. Clair

Sir. United States[1] [Philadelphia] April 4th 1792.

I have read and duly considered your letter of the 31st ultimo.

The reasons you offer, for retaining your commission, until an opportunity should be presented, if necessary, of investigating your conduct, in every mode prescribed by law, would be conclusive with me, under any other circumstances than the present.

But, the establishment of the troops allows only of one major general—you have manifested your intention of retiring, and the esential interests of the public require, that your successor should be immediately appointed, in order to repair to the frontiers.

As the house of representatives have been pleased to institute an enquiry into the causes of the failure of the late expedition, I should hope an opportunity would thereby be afforded you, of explaining your conduct, in a manner satisfactory to the public and yourself.[2]

Df, DNA: RG 59, Miscellaneous Letters; LB, DLC:GW.

For the background to this letter, which was printed in the *National Gazette* (Philadelphia) on 16 April with other correspondence between GW and St. Clair concerning St. Clair's resignation, see GW to the U.S. Senate and House of Representatives, 12 Dec. 1791, n.1, Henry Knox to GW, 22 Jan., n.2, 1 Mar. 1792, GW to Knox, 29 Feb., n.1, Knox to Tobias Lear, 31 Jan. 1792, n.1, GW to Thomas Jefferson, 2 Mar., and Jefferson to GW, 2 Mar. 1792.

1. The War Department clerk who apparently drafted this letter for Henry Knox for presentation to GW wrote "War department" in the dateline, which Tobias Lear struck out and replaced with "United States."

2. For the congressional investigation of St. Clair's defeat, see Knox to GW, 30 Mar., source note.

From Robert Dick

Sir, Bladensburgh [Md.] 5th April 1792

Your known goodness will, I hope, excuse the trouble of this letter, which I presume to write You in order to introduce to Your notice the bearer of it Mr James Oswald; who is a Son of George Oswald Esqre of Scotstown near Glasgow, and a partner in the business which I have conducted in Virginia and Maryland for many years. This Young Gentleman is Grand Nephew to Richard Oswald Esqre, the British Plenipotentiary in making the Peace of 1783. He has lately entered into the Navy, and having some time to spare, and a strong desire to see America, he has, with his Father's approbation, embraced the opportunity of coming in one of our Ships, in order to gratify it.[1]

The notice which you may be pleased to take of him will be a particular obligation confered on, sir Your Most Obedient & humble Servant

Robt Dick

ALS, DLC:GW.

Robert Dick, who had emigrated from East Lothian, Scotland, to the United States in the fall of 1788 in the hope of establishing himself as an agriculturalist, arrived in Bladensburg, Md., by mid-March 1789 (see Dick to GW, 15 Nov., 8 Dec. 1788, 14 Mar. 1789). He is listed in the U.S. census of 1790 as heading a household consisting of 4 white males, 5 white females, and 21 slaves in Prince George's County, Md. (*Heads of Families* [Maryland], 93).

1. George Oswald (c.1735–1819) was head of the tobacco firm of Oswald, Dennistoun, & Company of Glasgow and a partner in the Ship Bank. His uncle, Richard Oswald (1705–1784), was Lord Shelburne's agent in the negotiations with Benjamin Franklin at Paris in 1782 and was the chief British negotiator of the peace treaty ending the Revolutionary War.

From Tobias Lear

[Philadelphia]

My dear & honored Sir, Thursday Morning April 5th 1792.

It is my duty to releive you from suspence on the subject which you had the goodness to communicate to me yesterday, when I have no longer any hesitation in determining on it myself. Permit me, therefore, while my heart overflows with gratitude for this new instance of your kind attention to my welfare, to decline the acceptance of the appointment which you had the goodness to offer me.[1]

And let me, at the same time, beg, that you will not consider this determination as proceeding from the want of a due sense of your fr[i]endship. This additional proof of your concern for me, altho' grateful to my feelings, was not necessary to convince me of your regard, or to increase my attachment to, or veneration of yourself—These have been long fixed, and I trust indelibly so.

When you opened this business to me yesterday, I mentioned a resolution I had formed not to engage in any public employment. And in pursuance of this resolution, I should have had no hesitation to have declined at that moment the honor you intended me; but I conceived it to be a mark of respect due to your goodness to re-consider that resolution, and to reflect upon the offer you have made. I have done so—and the result of my reflection is an adherence to my former determination.

But were I not to explain the extent of this resolution you might justly impute to me the want of the first and noblest of virtues—I mean a love of my Country and mankind. When, therefore, I say, that I have resolved not to engage in any public employment, I mean that I shall not do it for the sake of providing a support for myself and those dependent upon me—nor *merely* with a view of advancing myself to posts of honor and becoming conspicuous. But if ever my Country should call for the personal or other services of its citizens, I will venture to say that no one will be found more ready than myself to hazard or sacrifice every private & personal consideration for the public good; Or if ever an occasion should offer (of which however there seems no probability) where I could render better or more essential service to my Country than another person, I should embrace it with alacrity, and I trust I should not be found insensible to the charms of honor and glory if earned by solid services to my Country or to Mankind.

Actuated by the principles here expressed, I have paid no court to any person—my mind has been independent, and I hope my sentiments, when expressed, have corresponded therewith. By this means I beleive I have offended some, and sure I am that I am less pleasing to many than I should have been, had I pursued a different course. But I hope and trust that I shall not fall in the estimation of the upright and virtuous whenever I am known to them.

Let me, my dear & honored Sir, beg your patience for a moment longer while I observe, that, in my present situation I consider myself as rendering no small service to the public, and in a way peculiarly delightful to my feelings. For such is the importance of your life and of your services to this Country, that the person who is so happy in his situation as to be able, by attention & assiduity, in any degree to alleviate the weight necessarily imposed upon you, is benefitting his Country, altho' his services do not attract the attention of the public. And if my conduct hitherto has merited your approbation my reward will be *complete*; for an invariable adherence to honor, integrity, disinterestedness and purity of views has insured the approbation of my own feelings. If in any instance you conceive I have not acted with propriety, I must rely upon your goodness & sincere friendship for me to point it out without reserve, and let me correct my error.

I am afraid I have already intruded too much on your busy moments, and will only beg permission, som⟨e⟩ time hence, when you are less embarrassed with public concerns than you are at present, to converse with you respecting my future pursuits in life. With the most disinterested attachment and sincere affection I have the honor to be my dear & honored Sir Your's

Tobias Lear.

ALS, DLC:GW; ADfS, owned by an anonymous donor.

1. The nature of the appointment GW offered Lear has not been determined.

From Edmund Randolph

Sir Philadelphia April 5. 1792

Both Mr Blair and Mr Wilson are now at Trenton.[1] I have never heard Mr Blair say a syllable upon the subject of the representation bill. Some days ago I met Mr Wilson in Sixth Street, and he stopped to ask me, whether Mr Blair had communicated to me an idea, which both of them entertained on a late law of the present session, requiring the judges of the circuit courts to hear applications of pensioners, invalids &c.[2] I informed him, that Mr Blair had not mentioned it to me; but that it was said in town, that they meant to refuse to execute the act. Upon his making a strong remark against its constitutionality, (but by the way I suspect that in this the judges, if they persist, will be found wrong) I observed, that doubts had been entertained by some discerning and respectable men as to the constitutionality of the representation bill. To this he replied, it can never come before me, as a judge, and therefore I will say that congress appear to have forgotten the source, from which representation flows. We immediately separated, without exchanging another word. I have the honor sir, to be with the most affectionate attachment and respect yr mo. ob. serv.

Edm: Randolph

ALS, DLC:GW.

1. GW apparently had earlier requested Randolph to consult with U.S. Supreme Court justices James Wilson and John Blair about the constitutionality of the Apportionment Bill.

2. For "An Act to provide for the settlement of the Claims of Widows and Orphans barred by the limitations heretofore established, and to regulate the Claims to Invalid Pensions," which GW signed on 23 Mar. 1792, and the protests of the U.S. Supreme Court justices against its provisions, see Caleb Brewster to GW, 15 Mar., n.4, U.S. Circuit Court Judges for New York to GW, 10 April, GW to the U.S. Senate and House of Representatives, 16, 21 April, and James Iredell and John Sitgreaves to GW, 8 June 1792.

To Alexander Hamilton

United States [Philadelphia] April 6th 1792.

In virtue of the last clause of "an Act for the relief of certain Widows, Orphans, Invalids & other persons," you will cause to be paid to Nicholas Ferdinand Westfall the sum of three hundred and thirty six Dollars out of the fund of Ten thousand Dollars appropriated for defraying the contingent charges of Government, by an Act passed on the 26th day of March 1790.[1]

G: Washington.

LB, DLC:GW.

1. Hamilton had written GW on 5 April that "an application has been made at the Treasury by the honorable Mr [Frederick] Muhlenburg of Pennsylvania in behalf of the Administratrix of Nicholas F. Westphal deceased, for the discharge of a Claim due to the Estate of her late husband in virtue of the last clause of 'An Act for the relief of certain widows, Orphans, Invalids and other persons'" (DLC:GW). The last clause of the act reads: "That there be granted to Nicholas Ferdinand Westfall, who left the British service, and joined the Army of the United States during the late war, one hundred acres of unappropriated land in the Western Territory of the United States, free of all charges, and also the sum of three hundred and thirty-six dollars, out of any money appropriated to the contingent charges of Government" (*Annals of Congress,* 2d Cong., 1350). Hamilton had enclosed a copy of the act and suggested "that this claim being payable out of the unexpended appropriations to the contin-

gent charges of Government, it appears to require a special order of the President" (DLC:GW). Westfall, who had worked as a Philadelphia schoolmaster following the Revolutionary War, recently had died (*Philadelphia Directory*, 1791, 140).

To Alexander Hamilton

Sir, United States [Philadelphia] 6. April 1792.

You will lay before the House of Representatives such papers from your Department as are requested by the enclosed resolution.[1]

G:W.

N.B. The papers alluded to are such as relate to the Expedition under Genl St Clair.

LB, DLC:GW.

1. For the enclosed resolution of 4 April of the House of Representatives requesting papers in the files of the executive departments for the House inquiry into the failure of St. Clair's expedition, see GW to Henry Knox, 4 April (second letter), n.1. For the appointment of the congressional committee of inquiry, see Knox to GW, 30 Mar., source note.

Letter not found: from Samuel McDowell, 6 April 1792. In his letter to McDowell of 20 Oct. 1792, GW mentioned "Your letter of the 6th of April."

From Gouverneur Morris

My dear Sir, London 6 April 1792

I receive this Instant your favor of the twenty eighth of January and I do most sincerely thank you for the Informations which you have been so kind as to communicate. Beleive me I know how to value the friendship by which they were dictated. I have always thought that the Counsel of our Enemies is wholesome, tho bitter, if we can but turn it to good Account & In order that I may not fail to do so on the present Occasion *I now promise you* that Circumspection of Conduct which has hitherto I acknowlege formed no Part of my Character. And I make the *Promise* that my Sense of Integrity may enforce what my Sense of Propriety dictates.

I have hitherto in my Letters communicated to you many Things which I should not willingly entrust to others, and in the Course of Events I may again possess Information which it might be well that you were acquainted with At the same Time it is I presume expected that the public Servants will correspond fully and *freely* with the Office of foreign Affairs. It might therefore be deemed improper, not to say *all,* in my Letters to that Office. I wish therefore you would give me your candid opinion on this Subject.[1] I should be extremely sorry to offend or to give Pain, but I cannot have the same unreserved Confidence in others that I have in you and my Letter of the fourth of February will shew that Cases may occur in which I am not even Master of it.

I was told Yesterday that Mr Dundas has said that the United States have asked for the Mediation of this Country to bring about a Peace with the Indians. He told the same Person (a Mr Osgood the new Chief Justice of the new Province of Upper Canada) that the treaty made long since by Sir William Johnson seemed to be the proper Ground on which *to fix a Boundary* between the United States & the Indian tribes.[2] I learn these facts in such a Way that I am confident of the Truth, and therefore submit them without any Comment to your Consideration.

An Express arrived last Night brings an Account of the Assassination of the King of Sweden the twenty sixth of last Month, at a Masquerade And thus another Crown falls on the Head of a young Sovereign.[3] Those who conceive the french Jacobins to be at the Bottom of a great King-Killing Project approach the Deaths of the Emperor[4] the King of Sweden and the Movements making against France from whence they infer that the King of Prussia should take Care of himself and be cautious of his Cooks and Companions. Such sudden Deaths in so critical a Moment are extraordinary but I do not usually beleive in Enormities and I cannot see how a Club can persue a Path of Horrors in which Secrecy is essential to Success.

The young King of Hungary has made such Reply to the peremptory Demands of France as to cool a little the Extravagance of Joy manifested on his Fathers Death. I am told that he is a Disciple rather of his Uncle Joseph than of his Father if this be so he will not long remain idle.[5] The Death of his Swedish Majesty will however make some Derangement in the Plan of Operations. How all these Things will end God only knows. I am my dear Sir very sincerely and affectionately yours

Gouvr Morris

ALS, DLC:GW; LB, DLC: Gouverneur Morris Papers.

1. GW gave his opinion in his reply to Morris of 21 June 1792.

2. William Osgoode (1754–1824), who had been appointed chief justice of Upper Canada in 1791, sailed for North America in April 1792. Osgoode became chief justice of Lower Canada in 1794 and served in that capacity until 1801. Sir William Johnson (1715–1774), British superintendent of Indian affairs from 1756 until his death, negotiated the Treaty of Fort Stanwix with the Iroquois in November 1768.

3. Gustav III (1746–1792) of Sweden was shot in the back during a masquerade ball at the Stockholm opera house on 16 Mar. by Jakob Johan Anckarström, a former army officer. The king died of his wounds two weeks later and was succeeded by his son Gustav IV (1778–1837).

4. Morris is referring to the recent death of the Holy Roman Emperor Leopold II.

5. Morris is referring to the newly elected Holy Roman Emperor, Francis II, his father, Leopold II, and his uncle Joseph II (1741–1790).

From John Lowrey

Sir, Philadelphia April 7th 1792

I feal a degree of defidence, in troubling your Excellency—but beg that your impartial candor Will pardon the following observations.

When a requisition from the general government to Raise troops for the protection of our fronteer brethren At the westward, my fealings being effected with their Unhappy sittuation, felt that impulse to leave my Private walks of life and step forth agreeable to The requisitions afore cited, in the capasity of a Quarter Master, in the Jersey Battallean of levies—in which I endeavoured to discharg the duties of my station with fidelity to the publick and to the satisfaction of the Individuals of the Corps—but the Operations of the Campaign was in a degree unfortunate—by which my private business being deranged, and I still wishing to Contobute my exertion in another trial of the fortune of War—did on my return from the westward signify to the secretary at war my wishes to be appointed again in the troops to be raised for that purpose.

I therefore would wish to signify to your Excellency if you can conveniently indulge me with an appointment in said troops agreeable to the recommendations of those Gentlemen who solicited in my favour. I am your Excellencys most obedient and very humble servant

John Lowrey

ALS, DLC:GW.

John Lowrey (Lowry; d. 1793) of Mendham, Morris County, N.J., served as a lieutenant in the levies under the command of Maj. Gen. Arthur St. Clair in 1791. GW named him an ensign on 9 April, and the Senate confirmed the nomination two days later. Lowrey was promoted to lieutenant in the 2d Sub Legion in February 1793, and he was killed in action against the Indians in the Northwest Territory on 17 Oct. 1793 (see GW to the U.S. Senate, 9 April; *Executive Journal,* 1:118–19, 133–34).

From Arthur St. Clair

Sir, Philadelphia April 7th 1792

I have had the honor to receive your Letter of the fourth instant.

Although I was very desirous Sir, to hold my Commission of Major General until the Enquiry by the Committee of the House of Representatives should be over, for the Reasons which I assigned, and which you are pleased to think have some Weight, yet the evident necessity of the Officers being appointed who is to command the Troops, in order to his repairing to the Frontiers, is certainly pressing, and ought to silence, with me, every Wish of a mere personal Nature; I do therefor Sir, now formally resign the Appointment of Major General.

I have never Sir, entertained a Doubt that an Enquiry into the Causes of the failure of the late Expedition, whether directed particularly to my Conduct, or to that Connected with other Causes that may have operated, in whatever way it might be conducted, would not prove honorable to me and satisfactory to the public, as far as I was connected with it; but setting, as I do, a due value upon the public Opinion, and desirous not to lose that Place in the Esteem of the virtuous and intelligent of my fellow Citizens which I have long held, You will not wonder that, under existing Circumstances, a Degree of Anxiety, not only that an Enquiry should be made, but that every thing, capable of being miscontrued, should be avoided on my Part. I will Own to You Sir, that the Desire of honest Fame has ever been the strongest Passion in my Breast—I have thought that I had merited it—and it is all I have to compensate me for the Sacrifice of a very independant Situation, and the best Years of my Life devoted to the public Service, and the faithful Application of my Talents, such as they were, in every Situation in which I have been placed, with a Zeal bordering upon Enthusiasm. I trust Sir, I shall yet enjoy it, while those who have attempted to disturb it will be forgotten, or remembered with Indignation, and in their Bosoms, if they have feeling, Sensations may arise something similar to what Milton has described to have seized upon Satan when he discovered our first Parents in Paradise.[1] With every Sentiment of Respect and Duty I have the honor to be Sir Your most obedient Servant

Ar. St Clair

ALS, DNA: RG 59, Miscellaneous Letters; ALS (copy), OHi: Arthur St. Clair Papers; ADfS, OHi: Arthur St. Clair Papers.

For the background to this letter, which appeared in the *National Gazette* (Philadelphia) on 16 April with other correspondence between GW and St. Clair concerning the resignation of St. Clair's commission, see GW to the U.S. Senate and House of Representatives, 12 Dec. 1791, n.1, Henry Knox to GW, 22 Jan., n.2, 1 Mar. 1792, GW to Knox, 29 Feb., n.1, Knox to Tobias Lear, 31 Jan. 1792, n.1, GW to Thomas Jefferson, 2 Mar., and Jefferson to GW, 2 Mar. 1792.

Although he resigned his military commission, St. Clair retained his civil appointment as governor of the Northwest Territory until his dismissal by President Thomas Jefferson in 1802. Politically and financially bankrupt, St. Clair then returned to the Ligonier Valley of Pennsylvania and unsuccessfully pressed Congress for a full remuneration for his past services. In 1812, six years before his death, St. Clair published by subscription a vindication of his 1791 military command: *A Narrative of the Manner in Which the Campaign against the Indians, in the Year One Thousand Seven Hundred and Ninety-One, Was Conducted, under the Command of Major General St. Clair, Together with His Observations on the Statements of the Secretary of War and the Quarter Master General, Relative Thereto, and the Reports of the Committees Appointed to Inquire into the Causes of the Failure Thereof: Taken from the Files of the House of Representatives in Congress.*

1. St. Clair apparently is referring to lines 386–92 of Book IV of Milton's *Paradise Lost*:

> Thank him who puts me loath to this revenge
> On you who wrong me not, for him who wrong'd.
> And should I at your harmless innocence

Melt, as I do, yet public reason just,
Honour and empire with revenge enlarged,
By conqu'ring this new world, compels me now
To do what else, though damn'd, I should abhor.

To Betty Washington Lewis

My dear Sister, Philadelphia April 8th 1792.

If your Son Howell is living with you, and not usefully employed in your own Affairs; and should incline to spend a few months with me, as a writer in my Office (if he is fit for it) I will allow him at the rate of Three hundred dollars a year, provided he is diligent in discharging the duties of it from breakfast until dinner—Sundays excepted.

This sum will be punctually paid him and I am particular in declaring beforehand what I require, and what he may expect, that there may be no disappointment, or false expectations on either side. He will live in the family in the same manner his brother Robert did. If the offer is acceptable he must hold himself in readiness to come on immediately upon my giving him notice.

I take it for granted that he writes a fair & legible hand, otherwise he would not answer my purpose; as it is for recording letters, and other papers I want him. That I may be enabled to judge of his fitness let him acknowledge the receipt of this letter with his own hand, and say whether he will accept the offer here made him, or not. If he does, & I find him qualified from the specimen he gives in his letter I will immediately desire him to come on which he must do without a moments delay, or I shall be obliged to provide another instead of him.[1]

Mrs Washington unites with me in best wishes, and love for you and yours and I am—My dear Sister Your most Affecte Brother

Go: Washington

ALS, owned (1997) by Ms. Julie Rinaldini, New York, N.Y.; LB, DLC:GW.

1. GW's nephew Howell Lewis (1771–1822), a son of Fielding and Betty Washington Lewis of Fredericksburg, Va., accepted this offer in his letter to GW of 24 April. He served the president as a recording secretary until July 1793, when GW sent him to take care of his affairs at Mount Vernon after the death of farm manager Anthony Whitting.

To David Stuart

Dear Sir, Philad. April 8th 1792.

The letter from the Commissioners to Mr Jefferson of the [ ] has been laid before me, and I have desired him to approve the Contract respecting the bridge over Rock-Creek:[1] but in future, it would be more agreeable to me, after a plan, or the principles leading to the measure, is approved, not to have the details or the execution suspended for a reference to me. Because, to judge properly of the matter must (in many instances) depend upon calculation; upon accustomed modes; established prices, and usages of different places; none of which my time and avocations will allow me to investigate with promptness; consequently the business must be delayed (if I take time for examination) or I must decide in the dark, if I do not.

This has actually been the case with respect to the Bridge above mentioned; for if I had been called upon to say what such a bridge wou'd cost, I should have guessed less than the contract price. And though the Items which form the aggregate, may contain no more materials than are indispensably necessary; and the prices of them, and rates of work, not more than usual; yet, from a want of knowledge in these matters, both appear high to me.

Not for this reason, but because you have jealous and ill-disposed people about you, my advice to you, is to act with caution in all your contracts: and I give it with the freedom of friendship, because it has been insinuated, before the contract was made, that sufficient notice had not been given; and of course you would have no competitors for the undertaking of the Bridge.

Did Major L'Enfant assign any reason for his rejection of the compensation which had been offered him? Has any person applied for the Office of Superintendant? A Mr Blodget has been recommended by some of the Proprietors; but except being pretty deeply interested in the City—having been a pretty considerable traveller in European Countries—and an observant man with some taste—it is said—I can say nothing of his qualifications for such a trust. How far he is a man of industry—arrangement, and integrity I know not—having a very slight acquaintance with him personally, and less knowledge of his abilities.[2]

There is such an intimate connection in political and pecuniary considerations between the federal district and the inland navigation of the Potowmac, that no exertions, in my opinion, shou'd be dispensed with to accomplish the latter. For, in proportion as this advances, the City will be benefited. Public and private motives therefore combine to hasten this work. My best wishes to Mrs Stuart and the family. I am your affte hble Servant,

Go: Washington

LB, DLC:GW. The apparent cover to the original receiver's copy of this letter is postmarked "9 AP," stamped "FREE," and addressed by GW to "David Stuart Esqr. George Town—Potomac or Hope Park Virginia" (ViMtV).

1. GW is probably referring to the commissioners' letter to Thomas Jefferson of 30 Mar., which covered a drawing of the proposed Rock Creek bridge by Leonard Harbaugh of Baltimore and a copy of the conditional contract made with Harbaugh on 29 March. This contract would become binding only after GW approved it (see *Jefferson Papers,* 23:350–52).

2. When Stuart replied to GW on 18 April, he enclosed Pierre L'Enfant's letter to the commissioners of 18 Mar. and impugned the motives of the proprietors who supported Samuel Blodget, Jr., for the post of superintendent.

Letter not found: to George Augustine Washington, 8 April 1792. In his letter to GW of 15–16 April, G. A. Washington informed his uncle: "I have received Your favor of the 8th."

From George Augustine Washington

Honor'd Uncle Mount Vernon April 8[–9]th 1792

Your favor of the 1st Inst. came to hand at the usual time.[1] just as I had seated myself late in the evening—(Sunday) and was about informing You that the Trees seeds &c. had not arrived, Capt. Cahart sent his Boat on shore with a part of the things You advised me of having shiped on bord his Vessel;[2] the rest the Mate who came on shore (for the Vessel did not come to anchor) informed were stowed away so that they could not be come at untill they arrived at Alexandria, and that they would be sent down but on reflection not chusing to depend on it shall if the weather will permit send up in the morning a Boat if not will have them carefully brought down in a Cart—what I have received is a Box containing the cutings—2 Tubs with trees from Batrams a small Box with seeds from Governor Pinckney[3]—the

Bundle of Mulberry trees & 3 fowl's—they appear to be in good order tho' I have not yet overhaul'd them—the Gardner will begin grafting in the morning tho' tomorrow is a holiday (Easter), as it is now very late and he fears too late for this business as the Scion on which he is to graft are very forward many of them almost in full leaf however as I am persuaded he is very judicious I do not dispair of many of them being propigated I shall delay no time in geting the trees &c. Planted and hope as I shall be very careful to dispose of them in a manner that will be satisfactory—the Ovals tho' they may be larger than it was Your intention they should be, yet I flatter myself You will not condemn me, as I have not exceed'd the lines You directed me to draw, which was from the Chesnut to where the Walnut stood, and from thence to the Willow on the mound, in the formation of those Ovals as all such improvements are to please the eye I thought it proper and hope you will also be of the same opinion that the space and form of the Ground should in a great degree be the government.

There was as I apprehend, a mistake about the wine which I told the Capt. at the time of his landing it I was satisfied was the case, as no mention was made of it by Mr Newton in his Letter to me I had it put away carefully—it was intended for Mr Norton of Winchester as I have been informed by Thompson of Alexandria to whose care it had been sent.

I had cutings of the weeping willow planted some time ago on the Mill race from the Mill untill the race enters the woods below where it is intended to take the water out of the old or present race by a new one and had last week willows planted on the cross ditch in Mill meadow on which the post and rail fence is and also had cutings of the willow and Lombardy poplar planted alternately a post a part on the Bank, which the fence is upon that divides the meadow at the Ferry from field No. 2 in which the Barn is—I wish the ditch You speak of ranging with the fence dividing field No. 1 from fields No. 2 & 3. at D: Run could have been done but there being so much business of that kind in the swamps that it could not be done in the fall and the severity of the winter prevented all business of that kind—as I purpose Banking with the Plows for this fence it will be quickly done—this method I am satisfied You will give a decided preference to, in all except swamp grounds that require absolutely ditching to discharge the water. Banking is done with great dispatch as the principal labor is performed by the plow—and ditching I am well satisfied will prevent the raising of hedges, as the bank is formed of such poor earth being taken from such a depth, that nothing will grow in it—but in Banking, the earth which forms it is collected from both sides and so near the surface that it is formed of a much better soil; and another advantage I can clearly discover that it will become much more speedily turfed over which secures the Bank from decay.

Mr Whiting seems to be more and more an enthusiast in favor of Cedar for hedges, he not only thinks they will form a secure and formidable fence, but that they will succe'd better and be less subject to injury from stock than any thing else.

We shall be in readiness and purpose begining to plant Corn as I mentioned in my last on Monday week the 16th Inst. but for some time past we have had as much cause to complain of too much rain as we had last spring of too little. the ground was very wet before and on Friday night we had a powerful rain which put the ground in such a situation that on saturday in many places the Horses as they were plowing appeared to be almost up to their knees,[4] and nothing but the season being so advanced coud justify plowing when the ground is in such a state—being anxious to get in the Buckwheat designed for manure in No. 7 at Dogue Run I frequently examin the field and did shortly before this heavy rain and found it so wet that I could with difficulty ride through it and on Saturday many parts of it was entirely coverd with water, it will not, admiting that there is no more rain be in order for some time, not untill we begin Planting Corn when it will be a great interuption to the Plows as it will require 28 plows 3 days to put in the seed or rather to plow the ground as it will be harrow'd in. Mr Whiting prefers replanting when it is too late to replant with Common Corn to use the early Corn, in preference to potatoes as they do not come of[f] soon enough for sowing wheat, when so late planted, and it is inconvenient geting them from the ground so dispersed as they must be—I have directed and shall see that Your directions respecting the Planting of the Corn & Potatoes at D: Run in No. 2 is done in the way You wish in this field the Plows are now listing.

The spring being wet has operated powerfully on vegitation for 10 days past it has been as rapid and moreso I think than I ever saw it—the Grass sown last fall at Dogue Run is very promising the bare spots which was in the Clover near the Overseers house and adjoining the New Ground was resown last fall and this spring again—the Timothy in the swamp part of the same ground promises to grow as much as can well grow upon the ground—the Timothy in the Mill meadow will be good except in some poor spots indeed I do not think much of that ground very strong—the New Clover Lot at the Mansion House is coming on much better than I expected and think it now promis's to yield a good burthen—I do not discover much of the seed that was sown on the Snow but this weather will I expect bring it on so that I shall be able to give some account of it shortly.

The New Quarter will I have no doubt be fully adequate to accomodate conveniently all the Negro's that You would wish or find necessary to be kept at the Mansion House for untill they are all brought together and under proper regulations it is in vain to attempt or at least to protect improvements.

I have been promised to have a skillful well diger sent to me that I may have his opinion on the situation for a well and if his reasons are plausible and such as I think can be relied on and favor the probability of coming at water in any reasonable distance—the situation opposite the center of the Green House will certainly be much preferable to any other.

I will enclose the Stercorary in the Manner You direct[5]—I have left Bars at the lower end of the fence runing from the Stercorary for the purpose of geting in timber to the house where the Carpenters work while it remains there which will answer to let in Horses when it is necessary to the spring, but this I think will seldom be necessary as water may be generally had near the lime kiln from a little stream that runs down that vall'y—and as the situation of the present Ice House is a very unfavorable one, and it will require so much repair that You will build a new one which in the way they are generally done will require as little expence and by removing it nearer the river much labor will be dispensed with in filling it.

I was so sure that you would approve of sowing the Lucern in broad Cast that I engaged 15 lb. of a Man near Alexa. who is in the Botanical line and wished to have got double the quantity but he had it not at this time—he says he expects from France in the course of the summer 2 or 300 wt but as it is not certain could wish to get abt 15 or 20 lb. more in time to sow in Augt.

You clearly understand the acct I have given respecting the two Whitings and least I should have erred in my representation of the business I read to Mr Washington the report I made you, and which was repeated in Your last letter, which he says was agreeable to his representation and that in his surrender of the Papers to Colo. Mercer his acct was credited for the full amount both of principal and interest of Mathew Whitings Bond of Berkley which bond was not given up to said Whiting because no part of the money was or ever has been pd and that the Bond is now in suit—I see that this Bond amounted by the copy of a list surrenderd to £47.15. with 5 Years Interest £11.18.9. Total £59.13. 9d.[6]

I mention'd about three or four weeks ago my intention of going up for Harriet the next day which I did and brought her down.

We have not as yet had much success in fishing no herrings of any consequence have been caught but we are daily expecting them the weather having been very precarious has I imagine delayed their coming up.

The report mentions the death of Billy at Muddy hole his death I much regreted because he was a promising Boy he was taken and died in 7 days he was quite well as they inform me and was suddenly taken with a pain in his back but was not ill for 2 or three days he then became senseless and speachless—I sent for the Doctr who came immediately to him but seemed to have no hopes of him but tried every thing he thought advisable—he stayed all night and visited him the next day—I was with him on Saturday and Whiting thought that he discoverd more sensibility than he had done but he could not be got to recieve any nourishment nor had not for several days—I sent up to the Doctr to inform him his situation but he died before the Messenger returned.[7]

I hope when the weather gets settled that I shall experience less of my complaints. I beg my Aunt to be assured that She and the Children always have my sincerest good wishes for their health and happiness—and that You will believe me to be with the most unbounded attachment Your truely affectionate Nephew

Go. A. Washington

P.S.—Monday—there fell last night a great deal of rain and the appearance of the weather to day is very unsetled.

ALS, DLC:GW.

1. GW's letter to G. A. Washington of 1 April 1792 has not been found.

2. William Carhart (Carheart), who was described as a "sea captain," lived at 105 Swanson Street in the Philadelphia suburb of Southwark in 1791 (*Philadelphia Directory,* 1791, 19).

3. For the seeds sent by Gov. Charles Pinckney of South Carolina and the trees forwarded from Philadelphia by John Bartram, see Pinckney to GW, 8 Jan. (first letter), n.4, GW to Pinckney, 17 Mar., and List of Plants from John Bartram's Nursery, March 1792.

4. G. A. Washington is referring to Friday, 6 April, and Saturday, 7 April 1792.

5. The stercorary, or manure enclosure, was an important innovation in GW's soil conservation program. Archaeological excavations at Mount Vernon have uncovered the foundations of the open-sided, cobblestone-floored structure, which measured about thirty-one feet by twelve feet. Its construction may have been influenced by an illustration, "The Plan of the Dung Pit," in Thomas Hale's *A Compleat Book of Husbandry* (London, 1758–59), which GW owned (see Griffin, *Boston Athenæum Washington Collection,* 96–97).

6. After receiving G. A. Washington's letter, GW apparently brought this matter to the attention of Attorney General Edmund Randolph, who informed GW that he considered the president "as no further connected with Mr John Mercer or Colo. Geo. Mercer's estate, than as to Whiting's bond" (Tobias Lear to John Rutherfurd, 18 April, source note).

7. William (Billy; c.1780–1792), a son of GW's slaves Will and Kate, died on Saturday, 7 April (see Anthony Whitting's Farm Reports, 1–7 April, DLC:GW; see also CD-ROM:GW).

From William Archibald McCrea

Sir, Philadelphia April 9th 1792.

It was with doubtfull though respectful Solicitude, that I took the Liberty to address your Excellency, on the 26th Ulto requesting an appointment to the Office of Treasurer of the Mint.[1]

Having since been informed that I could not have that Honor conferred on me, but that your Excellency has been pleased to signify a Willingness that I should have an appointment, in the line of my Profession, that of Surgeons Mate, in the Military Establishment of the United States, I therefore again Humbly beg leave to trouble you with this Letter.[2]

The Peculiarity of my Situation, occasioned by the Losses I

have sustained by the Burning of my House, my removal from Newark to Pencader, and my being thrown out of Business, as I Theretofore mentioned, induced me to think of Publick Employment.

Though there is great Desparity in the two Offices yet considering that I am now out of Business, that it is my Duty to provide for my Family, that this is a Business to which I have been Educated, and in which I feel a consciousness I can give satisfaction, and Humbly hoping, should my Conduct be such as to merit approbation & Confidence, as I intend it shall, that if a Vacancy should happen, by resignation or otherwise, which would give opportunity to my rising a grade higher, that your Excellency will favour me with your Patronage, as much as you shall think I merit it, I will, if favoured with the appointment, chearfully undertake to discharge the Duties of it, to the best of my Abilities, gratefully acknowledging your goodness in Patronizing me, and promising to do all in my pow'r to compensate it by a faithfull Discharge of my Duty. I am, Sir, with the Highest Sentiments of respectfull Esteem, Your Excellency's most Obedient and most Humble Servant

Wm Mc:Crea

ALS, DLC:GW.

1. McCrea's letter to GW applying for the office of treasurer of the U.S. Mint was dated 27 Mar. 1792.

2. GW appointed McCrea a surgeon's mate on this date (see GW to the U.S. Senate, 9 April).

To the United States Senate

United States [Philadelphia]
April the 9th 1792.

Gentlemen of the Senate,

I nominate the following persons for Appointments and Promotions in the Army of the United States.

Major General	Anthony Wayne	vice Arthur St Clair, who has resigned.
Brigadier General	Daniel Morgan[1]	Virginia.
Brigadier General	Marinus Willet	New York.
Brigadier General	John Brooks	Massachusetts

Brigadier General	James Wilkinson	Kentucky.
Adjutant General and Inspector	Winthrop Sargent	North Westn Territory
Deputy Quarter Master General	John Belli	Kentucky.

Appointment of six Majors, for the proposed third and fourth legionary Corps, three to each.

*Thomas Butler[2]	Pennsylvania
*Henry Gaither[3]	Maryland
*John Clark	Pennsylvania
*Henry Bedinger[4]	Virginia
Alexander Trueman	Maryland from Captn in the 1st Regt
William McMahon	Virginia

The Arrangements, Promotions and Appointments of Surgeons and Mates.

Richard Allison, promoted from the first Regiment, to be Surgeon on the General Staff.

For the four proposed legionary Corps.

Surgeons

John Elliott (already appointed)	
John Scott, promoted from Surgeon's mate.	
John F. Carmichael	ditto
Nathan Hayward	ditto

Surgeon's Mates

Elijah Tisdale (already appointed)	
*Charles Brown	Pennsylvania.
*James Woodhouse	ditto
*Joseph Philips	New Jersey
*William McCloskey	Pennsylvania
Frederick Dalcho	Maryland
James Mease	Pennsylvania
Theophilus Elmer	New Jersey

And for Garrisons on the Western and Southern frontiers, and for extra service.

William A. McCrea	Delaware.
Thomas Hutchens	Pennsylvania.
John Sellman	Maryland
George Balfour	Virginia

James Clayton	Delaware.
Thomas Farley	Massachusetts.

Promotions in the First Regiment of Infantry.

Major	
Erkuries Beatty	vice Zeigler resigned 5th March 1792.
Captains	
William Peters	vice Strong promoted November 4th 1791.
Jacob Kingsbury	vice Smith promoted December 28th 1791.
Ebenezer Denny	vice Ashton promoted December 29th 1791.
Thomas Martin	vice Rudulph promoted March 5th 1792.
Thomas Pasteur	vice Beatty promoted March 5th 1792.
Mark McPherson	vice Truman promoted March 5th 1792.
Lieutenants	
[ ][5]	vice Peters promoted November 4th 1791.
James Clay	vice Kingsbury promoted December 28th 1791.
Daniel Britt	vice Denny promoted December 29th 1791.
Hamilton Armstrong	vice Thompson resigned January 10th 1792.
Bartholomew Schomberg	vice Martin promoted March 5th 1792.
Bernard Gains	vice Pasteur promoted March 5: 1792.
John Wade	vice McPherson promoted March 5th 1792.

Promotions in the Second Regiment of Infantry.

Majors	
David Strong	vice Heart killed November 4th 1791.
John Smith[6]	vice Trescott resigned, December 28th 1791.
Joseph Ashton	vice Burnham, resigned, December 29th 1791.
Captains	
Bazaleel Howe	vice Kirkwood, killed November 4th 1791.
Daniel Bradley	vice Phelon killed, November 4th 1791.
John Platt	vice Newman killed November 4th 1791.
Lieutenants	
John Tillinghast	vice Howe promoted November 4th 1791.
Daniel Tilton Junr	vice Bradley promoted November 4th 1791.
Samuel Andrews	vice Platt promoted November 4th 1791.
John Bird	vice Warren, killed, November 4th 1791.
Micah McDonough	vice Heth, promoted March 5th 1792.

Appointments of Ensigns to fill the Vacancies in the First and Second Regiments of Infantry.

Andrew McClary	New Hampshire
Samuel Drake	Connecticut
Daniel Bissell[7]	ditto
*John Marschalk[8]	New Jersey
*William Marts	ditto
*Lewis Bond	ditto
*John Lowrey	ditto
Robert Hunter	ditto
Peter Shoemaker	Pennsylvania
William Marcus Mills	ditto
Jacob Kreemer	ditto
John Michael	ditto
*Felix Long	ditto
*Samuel B. Turner	Maryland
*John Whistler	ditto
Isaac Younghusband	Virginia
Henry Montfort	Georgia
William Temple Payne,	late of North Carolina.

Captains

*William Powers	Pennsylvania vice Guthrie, appointed 8th March 1792, and who declines.
William Lowder	Virginia vice Biggs, appointed 8th March 1792, and who declines.

Ensign

Hartman Leitheizer	Pennsylvania vice Kelso, appointed 8th March 1792, and who declines.

Go: Washington

DS, DNA: RG 46, Second Congress, 1791–1793, Records of Executive Proceedings, President's Messages—Executive Nominations; LB, DLC:GW.

Upon the receipt of this message on this date the Senate postponed considering it until 11 April. On that date the Senate resolved to advise and consent to the appointment of GW's nominations of 9 April "except James Wilkinson, postponed generally, and John Belli postponed for further enquiry" (DLC: GW; *Executive Journal,* 1:117–19). Lear transmitted a copy of the Senate's resolution to Henry Knox on 11 April by the president's command (DLC:GW). The following day the secretary to the Senate, Samuel Allyne Otis, wrote Lear: "Understanding from General Knox that the President did not perfectly understand the vote of Senate on the nomination of General Wilkinson, I take the liberty to communicate to you a copy verbatim of the Journal of Yesterday"

(DLC:GW). On 16 April the Senate resolved to advise and consent to the nominations of Wilkinson and Belli and ordered Otis to inform the president of its decision (ibid., 120). That same day GW's secretary Bartholomew Dandridge transmitted a copy of the Senate's resolution to Knox by the president's direction (DLC:GW).

1. On 5 May, Henry Knox sent Tobias Lear for submission to the president letters from Daniel Morgan and John Watts declining their commissions (DLC: GW). On 8 May, GW appointed Otho Holland Williams and William Winston, respectively, in their places (see GW to the U.S. Senate, 8 May 1792 [second letter]).

2. An endnote on the manuscript says: "Those marked thus * served with reputation in the Levies last year." Thomas Butler (d. 1805) of Pennsylvania, who had risen to the rank of captain in the Continental army during the Revolutionary War, served as a major in the levies of 1791. He accepted this appointment as a major in the U.S. Army, and he was promoted to lieutenant colonel in July 1794 and colonel in April 1802.

3. Henry Gaither (c.1751–1811) of Maryland, who had served throughout the Revolutionary War and had been brevetted a major in September 1783, was a major in the levies of 1791. He accepted this appointment as major in the U.S. Army, and he was promoted to lieutenant colonel in October 1793.

4. Bedinger's first name was George, not Henry (see GW to the U.S. Senate, 8 May 1792 [second letter]).

5. Keyed to this point on the manuscript is the footnote: "reserved for John Morgan, if acquitted of the charges for which he is arrested." For Morgan's court-martial, see Knox to GW, 28 July, n.8.

6. John Smith (d. 1811) of Massachusetts, who had served as a second lieutenant during the latter years of the Revolutionary War, was appointed a captain in the U.S. Army in October 1786. Although Smith resigned his commission as major in October 1793, he returned to the service as a lieutenant colonel in 1799–1800 and in 1809.

7. Daniel Bissell (d. 1833) of Connecticut was promoted to lieutenant in January 1794, captain in January 1799, lieutenant colonel in August 1808, colonel in August 1812, and brigadier general in March 1814. Bissell retired from the U.S. Army in June 1821.

8. Marschalk's first name was Andrew, not John (see GW to the U.S. Senate, 8 May 1792 [second letter]).

From Hannah Fairfax Washington

Dear Sir Virginia Fairfield Apr: 9th 1792:

As soon as I receiv'd the honor of Your Letter,[1] I search'd over every old paper in my possession, but cou'd find nothing that cou'd give any information relative to the subject required, further than the Will of Laurence Washington (Your grand father; also the grand father of my deceas'd Husband) the abstracts of which You inclos'd me.[2] I found the Will of Mrs Warner, Your great grand mother, but as that did not relate to the family otherwise than the marriage of the said Laurence to Mildred Warner, her Daughter, I shall not inclose it.

I was not willing to give over my enquiries so soon, which was the reason I did not answer Your favor last Week, but was waiting for information from an Old acquaintance of the familys, when my grand Son War: Wash: call'd at Mr Herberts in his way to Philada & mention'd Your request to me, when that Gent: recollected an old Book written by Your Brother Laurence (now in his possession) from which, He took several memorandoms, & inclosed them to me, which I have copied & sent You.[3] It plainly appears from those accounts, that John, was the name of Your great, grand father, that He, & his Brother Laurence, were the two first of the Name ever in Virginia. The inclos'd do not mention any where the Marriage of the first Laurence, but He certainly did marry & had a Son, (if no more) by the name of John, who was cousin German to Laurence, Yr grand Father; & twice mention'd in his Will, by the name of his Cousin John, Senior, of Stafford County. I suppose Yr Brother thought it immaterial to mention the Marriages of any of the family, but the direct descendents of his grt grand Father, but You might find out from the Old records, & Wills, deposited in Westmoreland or Cumberland County, if You wish to know who He married.

Present my Affect: Compts & best regards, to my dear, & valuable old friend, Mrs Washington, & accept the sincere good wishes, & ardent prayers, for Your health & happiness, of Dear Sir Your most Affect: & oblig'd Hble Serv:

H: Washington

Please to return me the old will when perus'd.[4]

ALS, DLC:GW.

1. GW had written his cousin on 24 Mar., enclosing genealogical queries about the Washingtons made by Isaac Heard (see Heard to GW, 7 Dec. 1791).

2. For the text of Lawrence Washington's will of 11 Mar. 1698, see Ford, *Wills of George Washington,* 33–38.

3. The enclosed "Memorandum from Lawrence Washington's Book," which is in Hannah Washington's handwriting, includes two insertions that GW subsequently added in pencil. Those insertions appear within square brackets in the following transcription of the text: "John, & Laurence Washington [In 1657 (from the No. of England, either Yorkshire or Lancashire)] came into

Virginia during the usurpation of Oliver Cromwell, & settled at Bridges Creek [in Westmoreland County] on Potowmack. John was employed as General against the Indians in Maryland, & as a reward for his services was made a Colonel, & the parish wherein He lived, was call'd after him. He married Ann Pope, & left issue two Sons, Laurence & John, & one Daughter Ann, who married Major Francis Wright. Laurence married Mildred Warner, Daughter of Colo: Augustine Warner, of Gloucester County, by whom He had two Sons, John & Augustine, & one Daughtr named Mildred. John married Catherine Whiting of Gloucester Coty where He settled, & had many Children.

"Augustine married Jane Butler, the Daughter of Calib Butler of Westmorland, Apr: 20th 1715: by whom He had two Sons Laurence, & Augustine, & one Daughter Jane, who died when a Child. Jane Wife of Augustine, died Nov: 24th 1728: Augustine then married Mary Ball, March 6th 1729: by whom He had issue, George born Febru: 11th 1732: Betty born June 20th 1733: Samuel born Novbr 16th 1734: John born Janry 13th 1735/6: Charles, May 1st 1738: Mildred June 21st 1739: who died Oct: 28th 1740. Augustine moved to prince William Co. in the year 1734.

"Augustine departed this life Apr: 12th 1743: Aged 49: Yrs & was buried at Bridges Creek, in a Vault with his Ancestors.

"Laurence, Son to Augustine & Jane Washington, married July 19th 1743: Ann, eldest Daughter of the Honble William Fairfax Esqr., by whom He had issue, Jane, born September 27: 1744: who died Janry 1744/5: Fairfax, born Augst 22: 1747: who died in October 1747: Mildred, born Sepbr 28th 1748: who died in [ ] 1749: Sarah, born Novbr 7th 1750: who died in [ ] 175[ ].

"Augustine, Son of Augustine & Jane Washington, married Ann, Daughter & coheiress of William Aylett of Westmoreland Co: by whom He had issue" (DLC:GW).

4. GW enclosed the will in his letter to Hannah Washington of 20 May 1792.

To John Carroll

Sir, Philadelphia April 10th 1792

I have recd, & duly considered your memorial of the 20th ultimo, on the subject of instructing the Indians, within and contiguous to the United States, in the principles & duties of Christianity.

The war now existing between the United States and some tribes of the Western Indians prevents, for the present, any intercourse[1] of this nature with them. The Indians of the five nations are, in their religious concerns, under the immediate superintendance of the Revd Mr Kirkland; And those who dwell in the eastern extremity of the U.S. are, according to the best information that I can obtain, so situated as to be rather considered as a part of the inhabitants of the State of Massachusetts than otherwise,[2] and that State has always considered them as under its immediate care & protection. Any application therefore relative to these Indians, for the purposes mentioned in your memorial, would seem most proper to be made to the Government of Massachusetts. The original letters on this subject, which were submitted to my inspection, have been returned to Charles Carroll, Esq. of Carrolton.

Impressed as I am with an opinion, that the most effectual means of securing the permanent attachment of our savage neighbors is to convince them that we are just, and to shew them that a proper & friendly intercourse with us would be for our mutual advantage, I cannot conclude without giving you my thanks for your pious & benevolent wishes to effect this desireable end upon the mild principles of Religion & Philanthropy. And when a proper occasion shall offer I have no doubt but such measures will be pursued as may seem best calculated to communicate liberal instruction & the blessings of society to their untoutered minds. With very great esteem & regard I am Sir.

Df, in Tobias Lear's hand, DNA: RG 59, Miscellaneous Letters; LB, DLC:GW.

1. In the letter-book copy, this word reads "interference."

2. At this place on the manuscript, Lear wrote and then struck out the phrase: "Their constant intercourse with their civilized Neighbours has ⟨*illegible*⟩."

From Bartholomew von Heer

Philadelphia April 10th 1792.

The Memorial of Bartholomew Van Heer, formerly Captain of an independent Corps of Light Dragoons

Most respectfully sheweth

That Your Memorialist, about a Year ago, took the Liberty, to apply to Your Excellency for a Captain's Commission in the light Dragoons, if any should be raised; which was not done at that time:[1] That some time ago, when Your Memorialist understood, that some Companies of light Dragoons were to be raised, he again presented a Memorial to the Honorable the Secretary of War, in which application he hath not been, as yet, successful.

Having now been informed, that some of the Gentlemen, who have been appointed Captains of the Cavalry, now to be raised for the Service of the United States, have declined or are about to decline, he humbly begs Leave to renew his Application to Your Excellency under whose eyes he hath had the honor to command an independent Troop of light Dragoons, during the late War; and where, as he flatters himself, he has done his Duty as a brave and faithful Officer. He has no Calling, no Trade, whereby he could maintain himself having been brought up solely to the Use of Arms, and he hath met with various Misfortunes, which have reduced his Situation in Life: But he flatters himself to have it yet in his Power to be useful to his Country, if he should be so happy as to be employed in the Service thereof, and therefore humbly prayeth:

That Your Excellency will be pleased to take his Case into Consideration, and, in Case the before mentioned Vacancies should take Place, to appoint him to the Command of one of the Companies of Cavalry, to be raised for the Service of the United States.[2] And Your Petitioner as in Duty bound shall ever pray &ca

Bartholomew Von Heer

LS, DLC:GW.

1. No previous applications from Heer to GW dating from the early 1790s have been found.

2. GW did not offer Heer a military commission at this time.

Thomas Jefferson's Memorandum on a Treaty with Algiers

[Philadelphia] Apr. 10. 1792.

If the President should enter into a Provisional convention with the government of Algiers for a sum not exceeding 40,000 dollars, will the Senate advise & consent to it's ratification, the government of Algiers being made clearly to understand that we are not to be bound by the treaty until it shall be ratified?

If this sum appears too high, what lower limit would the Senate approve?

If the President should enter into a Provisional treaty of peace with the government of Algiers at an expence not exceeding

[ ] dollars to be paid on the ratification, & [ ] dollars payable annually afterwards, during it's continuance, will the Senate advise & consent to the ratification, the government of Algiers being made clearly to understand that we are not to be bound by the treaty until it shall be ratified?

If these sums appear too high, what lower limits would the Senate approve.[1]

AD, DLC:GW. The cover is mistakenly docketed "July 22d 1790."

On 9 April, Jefferson wrote in a memorandum: "The Presidt hd wished to redeem our captives at Algiers, & to make a peace with them on paying an annual tribute. the Senate were willing to approve this, but unwilling to have the lower house applied to previously to furnish the money. they wished the President to take the money from the treasury or open a loan for it. they thought that to consult the Representatives on one occasion would give them a handle always to claim it, & would let them in to a participation of the power of making treaties which the constitution had given exclusively to the President & Senate. they said too that if the particular sum was voted by the Represent. it would not be a secret. the President had no confidence in the secrecy of the Senate, & did not chuse to take money from the treasury or to borrow. but he agreed he would enter into provisional treaties with the Algerines, not to be binding on us till ratified here. I prepared questions for consultation with the Senate, & added that the Senate were to be apprised that on the return of the provisional treaty, & after they should advise the ratification, he should not have the seal put to it till the *two* houses should vote the money. he asked me if a treaty stipulating a sum & ratified by him with the advice of the Senate would not be good under the constitution & obligatory on the Repres. to furnish the money? I answered it certainly would, & that it would be the duty of the representatives to raise the money: but that they might decline to do what was their duty, & I thought it might be incautious to commit himself by a ratification with a foreign nation, where he might be left in the lurch in the execution it was possible too to concieve a treaty which it wd nt be their duty to provide for. he said that he did not like throwing too much into democratic hands, tha[t] if they would not do what the constitution called on them to do, the government would be at an end, & must *then assume another form.* he stopped here, & I kept silence to see whether he would say any thing more in the same line, or add any qualifying expressions to soften what he had said. but he did neither.

"I had observed that wherever the agency of either or both houses would be requisite subsequent to a treaty to carry it into effect, it would be prudent to consult them previously if the occasion admitted. that thus it was we were in the habit of consulting the Senate previously when the occasion permitted, because their subseqt ratification would be necessary. that there was the same reason for consulting the lower house previously where they were to be called on afterwards, & especially in a case of money, as they held the purse strings &

would be jealous of them. however he desired me to strike out the intimation that the seal would not be put till both houses should have voted the money" (Jefferson's Memoranda of Consultations with the President, 11 Mar.–9 April 1792, DLC: Jefferson Papers).

1. GW presented a modified version of this document to the U.S. Senate on 8 May 1792.

From James Mease

May it please your Excellency Philadelphia April 10th 1792

I have taken the liberty of addressing you on a subject of some importance, with regard to myself; and hope it will not be thought intruding on that time, which I well know is occupied with the consideration of much more weighty concerns, or be thought too arrogant, as what I have to offer is meant with the greatest humility and respect.

A few weeks since I applied to the Hble the secretary of war, for the post of a Surgeon in the hospital department, which I understood was to be a part of the medical establishment, in the army intended for the Westward; and accompanied the application with the certificate of my attendance, on the practice of the physicians & Surgeons, of the Pensylvania hospital; for three years and four months, referring him, at the same time, to that, given to me; with the rest of the candidates, last year; respecting our qualifications as surgeons, and also to the particular one, concerning myself, from my late preceptor Doctor John Jones, which were granted me on a wish that I expressed of entering the army; But on a more mature deliberation I was induced to relinquish the scheme, chiefly at the desire of Dr Jones, under whose care I thought I could obtain much more surgical knowledge than by accepting the commission of Surgeons mate.

The Secretary at War was likewise informed by Drs Shippen, & Hutchinson of my qualifications as a surgeon, and also of my having passed the examination for a degree of Doctor in Medecine, in the University of this City. I was greatly surprised therefore, on hearing yesterday evening, from several quarters, of my being in the list of those nominated for *Surgeons mates,*[1] By this I am put on a footing with some of those who began the Study of medecine one year and a half later than myself, and who had neither the opportunities, nor advantages with myself, except being under the direction of a physician.

If, after nigh one year being spent, in New York, in devoting my time almost solely, to acquiring the rudiments of our profession, or the preperation & Composition of medecines; three years close attendance on the practice of the Pensylvania hospital; near a year longer, under the care of a private physician, part of the same time under Dr Jones for the express purpose of learning surgery; and after being thought worthy by the Medical professors of a doctors degree, which I shall take in about three weeks, & recieving a liberal education, from our College; The secretary at War has thought fit to represent me as only qualified for a surgeon's mate; I would rather wish to decline accepting the commission.

I will urge as arguments in my favour, but would mention, the circumstances of my father, having been a citizen, of this place, for nigh forty years; his loosing a handsome independant property by joining in the late struggle for liberty, with two of my uncles; and my wishes to relieve the former, from the expense of maintaining me, which is a principal motive of my desire of entering the army; nor lastly, the circumstance of some young men being appointed to surgeon's posts, who were in Great Britain during the whole war, none of whose family lived in this Country; and who have not had the recommendations, that I have brought forward. With the greatest respect and humility, I beg leave to subscribe myself your Excellency's obedient servant

James Mease

ALS, DNA: RG 59, Miscellaneous Letters.

James Mease (1771–1846), the son of shipping merchant John Mease of Philadelphia, received a bachelor of arts degree from the University of the State of Pennsylvania in 1787 and a master's degree in 1790. In 1792 Mease was a member of the first class to graduate from the medical department of the newly created University of Pennsylvania. Having published in 1790 his first paper on rabies, in the *American Magazine,* he quickly became the leading American authority on the subject. Although afflicted with yellow fever during the epidemic of 1793, Mease survived and served as resident physician of the health office for the port of Philadelphia from 1794 to 1797. In 1800 he married Sarah Butler (c.1772–1831), a daughter of U.S. Senator Pierce Butler of South Carolina. Mease was actively involved in various Philadelphia learned societies, and he was elected to the American Philosophical Society in 1802.

1. For Mease's appointment as a surgeon's mate, see GW to the U.S. Senate, 9 April. The president accepted Mease's declination of the commission, and

on 3 May, he appointed Joseph Andrews of Massachusetts as a surgeon's mate in Mease's place.

From Gouverneur Morris

My dear sir, London 10 April 1792

There is an Idea in your Letter of the Twenty eighth of January which upon second thought I find it my Duty to examine because altho it cannot now affect me yet it may perhaps have some Influence on Mr Pinckney's Mission. At any Rate I wish you to be perfectly well acquainted with the leading Features of the british Administration. The Thing I allude to is the Cause which has been assigned for the Reserve I experienced in Negotiating with this Court. One leading Point I cannot investigate because the Death of my friend Monsieur de la luzerne has seald his Lips forever. But I very seriously doubt whether he repeated what I said to him and this for the plainest Reason on Earth. He was very apprehensive lest in the derang'd State of french Affairs We should call on his Court to support our application. He had made himself perfectly Master of their Sentiments respecting the Treaty and therefore told me at once that they would not give up the Posts. Knowing this therefore, it was clearly his Interest to appear unacquainted with the Demand and as to a Treaty of Commerce he knew not one syllable on the Subject. As to the Allegation of Intimacy with the opposition it is totally false. I saw none of them except Mr Fox and him but twice in my Life and one of those Times at a Ball. In fact knowing a little of the suspicious Disposition by confidential Communications which the french Embassador made to me respecting his own Situation and Transactions I purposely avoided the Oppositionists and went but rarely to see even Mr & Mrs Church from that Cause.[1] As to the Hauteur I beleive the Complaint to be in one Sense founded. You know Sir that it was not necessary to insist that they should actually appoint a Minister before we did. Time however has shewn that in this Instance at least I judged rightly. If I would have listen'd to Overtures derogatory to the Honor and Interest of my Country I should have been held very highly. And the mortal Sin was that I did not listen to such Overtures. You will recollect Sir that the Duke of Leeds offered to make his Communications to you thro me when I last saw him which I declin'd. At that Moment therefore their Reserve had not proceeded from the Causes now assign'd. Mr Burgess repeated this Offer in the End of December. At a subsequent Period they form'd the Plan of getting a Minister from America whom they supposd they would gain by their Attentions and they hop'd to make the stronger Impression on him by shewing that they were the Causes of his Elevation and my Depression. You have disappointed them and that will operate well.

I have already taken up more of your Time than I expected but this Subject is important and I must pursue it. During the Armament against Spain the Marquis del Campo who valued his Place very highly and was desirous of holding it if possible preserv'd a most profound Silence to every Body but this Court and we know the ridiculous Event of his Negotiations which must have been more successful if he had acted with the Sense and Spirit which the Occasion call'd for. *He* is a great Favorite at this Court.[2] The next Armament which Mr Pitt engaged in was against the Empress and every Art was used to coax Count Woranzow into a Conduct which might subserve Mr Pitts Views. But the firm Russian was too wise and too honest to become either Creature or Dupe. They then attempted to bully him as well as his Mistress and he treated both with Contempt. The Consequence of his Conduct was the compleat Success of his Sovereign and Mr Pitt finding him too well fix'd at his own Court to be shaken by his Intrigues has again had Recourse to a complimentary and apologetical Conduct. During the Course of that Armament the enclos'd Pamphlet was publish'd under the Counts Inspection and Direction. You will collect from it some useful Information. The british Ministry knowing the truth of what is therein asserted, and still more of what is insinuated, shrunk from the Controversy.[3] By the bye I was astonish'd to find that they had strongly supported the King of Prussia's attempt to possess himself of Dantzig.[4] I was not so much surprizd the other Day to find that Mr Pitt had asserted roundly in the House of Commons that he had not stimulated the Turk to War. There is not a Cabinet in Europe but what knows the contrary and many of his Hearers too.[5] I am ever yours

Gouvr Morris

ALS, DLC:GW; LB, DLC: Gouverneur Morris Papers.

1. John Barker Church (1748–1818), a member of Parliament and follower of Charles James Fox, had come to America during the Revolutionary War, and through his influence with Lafayette, he received an appointment as commissary to the French forces in the New World. In 1777 he had eloped with Angelica Schuyler (1756–1814), a daughter of Gen. Philip Schuyler, making him a brother-in-law of Alexander Hamilton.

2. Morris apparently had a low opinion of the longtime Spanish ambassador to the Court of St. James, Bernardo, marquis del Campo. On 4 Mar. 1792 Morris wrote in his diary that he had learned of "the absurd Manner in which the Marquis del Campo conducted the Negotiation about the Nootka Sound Affair." In his entry for 8 April 1792, Morris wrote that he had heard Campo referred to as "a Tool" of the British administration and "that he kept entirely secret from the French Embassador all his Proceedings" (Morris, *Diary of the French Revolution,* 2:374, 410). For a discussion of the Nootka Sound crisis, see Alexander Hamilton to GW, 8 July 1790, source note.

3. Count Semen Romanovich Vorontsov (Woronzow; 1744–1832) served as Russia's ambassador in London from 1785 to 1806. On 8 April Vorontsov told Morris that "for a long Time he believd him [Pitt] to be an honest, candid Man but he had at last detected him in seriously asserting on his Honor Things absolutely false. That the British Government have spread over all Europe the most unfavorable Impressions respecting America. . . . He mentions the Insolence of Mr. Pitt's Menaces to him and the Meanness of his subsequent indirect Apologies" (ibid., 410). Following the deposition and assassination of Peter III in 1762, Catherine the Great (1729–1796) became tsarina of Russia. The enclosed pamphlet has not been identified.

4. Danzig (Gdansk, Poland) had been seized in 1772 by Frederick the Great of Prussia. The city was officially incorporated into Prussia in 1793.

5. Morris is referring to the Russo-Turkish war of 1787–92. During that conflict Russia gained control of the lower Dniester and Danube rivers, and under the provisions of the Treaty of Jassy of January 1792, the Turks were forced to cede to Russia their possessions on the Black Sea from the Kerch Strait westward to the mouth of the Dniester River.

From Samuel Allyne Otis

Sir Philadelphia April 10th 1792

As my present employment is laborious in addition to the disagreeable circumstance of responsibility to *numbers* instead of one, I, by the advice of some friends take the liberty of soliciting the appointment to be Treasurer of the Mint; and if you think it expedient, the honor of your nomination to that office.[1] I am Sir With profund respect Your most humble Servt

Sam. A. Otis

ALS, DLC:GW.

1. GW nominated Tristram Dalton treasurer of the U.S. Mint, not Otis, who continued serving as secretary to the U.S. Senate until 1814 (see GW to the U.S. Senate, 3 May [second letter]).

From the United States Circuit Court Judges for New York

Sir, New York 10th April 1792.

As we could not in our opinion convey the enclosed extracts from the Minutes of the Circuit Court now setting here to the Congress of the United States in so respectful and proper a manner as thro' the President, we take the liberty to transmit them to you and to request the favor of you to communicate them to that honorable Body.[1] We have the honor to be, with perfect respect, Sir, Your most Obedient Servants

John Jay
Wm Cushing
Jas Duane

Copy, in the handwriting of Tobias Lear, DNA: RG 46, Second Congress, 1791–1793, Records of Legislative Proceedings, President's Messages; LB, DLC:GW.

For the background to the Invalid Pensions Act, see Caleb Brewster to GW, 15 Mar., n.4.

1. GW presented both the letter and its enclosure to Congress on 16 April. See also U.S. Circuit Court Judges for Pennsylvania to GW, 18 April, GW to the U.S. Senate and House of Representatives, 21 April, and James Iredell and John Sitgreaves to GW, 8 June.

Enclosure
Extracts of the Minutes of the United States Circuit Court for New York

At a stated Circuit Court of the United States held for the District of New York at the City of New York on Thursday the fifth day of April One thousand seven hundred and ninety two, at ten of the Clock Ante Meridiem.

Present The Honorable John Jay Esquire Chief Justice of the United States. The Honorable William Cushing Esquire One of the Associate Justices of the Supreme Court of the United States.

The Honorable James Duane Esquire Judge of the District of New York.

The Court proceeded to take into consideration the following Act of the Congress of the United States—Vizt

"An Act to provide for the settlement of the claims of Widows and Orphans barred by the limitations heretofore established, and to regulate the claims to Invalid Pensions."

(Here follows the Act, verbatim.)

The Court was thereupon unanimously of opinion and agreed

That by the Constitution of the United States the Government thereof is divided into *three* distinct and independent branches, and that it is the duty of each to abstain from, and to oppose encroachments on either.

That neither the *legislative* nor the *executive* branches, can constitutionally assign to the *judicial* any duties but such as are properly judicial, and to be performed in a judicial manner.

That the duties assigned to the Circuit Courts by this Act, are not of that description, and that the Act itself does not appear to contemplate them as such; inasmuch as it subjects the decisions of these Courts made pursuant to those duties, first to the consideration and suspension of the Secretary of War, and then to the revision of the Legislature; Whereas by the Constitution neither the Secretary at War nor any other executive Officer, nor even the Legislature are authorized to sit as a Court of Errors on the Judicial Acts or opinions of this Court.

As therefore the business assigned to this Court by the Act, is not judicial, nor directed to be performed judicially, the Act can only be considered as appointing Commissioners for the purposes mentioned in it, by *Official* instead of *personal* descriptions.

That the Judges of this Court regard themselves as being the Commissioners designated by the Act, and therefore as being at liberty to accept or to decline that Office.

That as the Objects of this Act are exceedingly benevolent, and do real honor to the humanity and justice of Congress; And as the Judges desire to manifest on all proper occasions, and in every proper manner their high respect for the national Legislature, they will execute this Act in the capacity of Commissioners.

That as the legislature have a right to extend the Session of this Court for any term which they might think proper by law to assign, the term of five days as directed by this act ought to be punctually observed.

That the Judges of this Court will as usual during the Session thereof adjourn the Court from day to day or other short periods, as circumstances may render proper, and that they will regularly between the Adjournments proceed as Commissioners to execute the business of this Act, in the same Court Room or Chamber.

A true extract from the minutes
Robt Troup, Clerk

Copy, in the handwriting of Tobias Lear, DNA: RG 46, Second Congress, 1791–1793, Records of Legislative Proceedings, President's Messages; LB, DLC:GW.

From Alexander Hamilton

[Philadelphia] April 11th 1792.

Mr Hamilton presents his respects to the President. Herewith are testimonials in favor of two Candidates for the Office of Treasurer of the Mint, Wm A. McCrea who has been mentioned by Mr Foster of the Senate,[1] and James Abercrombie who is recommended by a number of respectable characters.[2]

LB, DLC:GW.

1. Senator Theodore Foster wrote directly to GW on 2 April from Philadelphia that McCrea was "a Gentleman Suitable for filling the Office of Treasurer of the National Mint . . . I am well acquainted with Doctr McCrea, and am fully convinced of his Merit. of his Integrity, and his Abilities to discharge the Duties of the Office of Treasurer of the Mint, and as I beleive, he would make a good and faithful Officer, I could not resist the Inclination I felt, to serve him, as much as was in my Power, by recommending him to the Patronage of your Excellency, being willing to pledge myself and Property for his Fidelity and Good Conduct" (DLC:GW). For other recommendations of McCrea, see McCrea to GW, 27 Mar., n.2.

2. James Abercrombie (1758–1841) graduated from the College of Philadelphia in 1776 and prepared for the Episcopalian ministry under the Rev. (later Bishop) William White (1748–1836) until 1780. He then decided to pursue a mercantile career. He was elected a member of the Philadelphia common council in 1792, and he became an officer of the Bank of the United States. After his unsuccessful attempt to obtain a position at the U.S. Mint, Abercrombie was ordained a deacon in St. Peter's Episcopal Church in December 1793 and became assistant minister of it and Christ Church in June 1794. Neither McCrea nor Abercrombie was appointed by GW, who nominated Tris-

tram Dalton as treasurer of the U.S. Mint (see GW to the U.S. Senate, 3 May [second letter]; see also McCrea to GW, 9 April).

From Thomas Jefferson

[Philadelphia] Thursday[1] Apr. 11. [1792]

Th: Jefferson has the honor to send for the perusel of the President some letters from mister Barclay received yesterday.[2] he has received no letter from mister Short, nor any other person in France.

AL, DNA: RG 59, Miscellaneous Letters; LB, DNA: RG 59, George Washington's Correspondence with His Secretaries of State; LB (photocopy), DLC:GW.

1. The eleventh of April 1792 was a Wednesday.

2. The enclosures were Thomas Barclay's three dispatches from Gibraltar giving news of affairs in Morocco and on the Iberian Peninsula, all of which were received at the State Department on 10 April (see Barclay to Jefferson, 16 Jan., 23 and 24 Feb. 1792, in *Jefferson Papers,* 23:46–47, 144–45).

From William Gordon

My Dear Sir St Neots [England] April 12. 1792.

Though I rejoice whenever I receive a letter from You, & think myself highly honored by it; yet I would by no means call off your attention from the important business of the United States. Your excellency's safe return from the southern tour was matter of thankfulness, especially considering the danger you was once in upon the water.[1]

Not considering the distance & other circumstances, I viewed your letter of March as being in answer to mine of Jany, whereas I now perceive that mine was not rec'd at the time of your writing. The bill you forwarded was duly paid, & the account balanced.[2] My good wishes & prayers, for present & future happiness, you will always have, unless the decays of nature destroy my retentive faculties. There is not a day passes, but what I remember you.

The only intelligence I can probably communicate, is, that the methods pursuing by parliament in lowering the bounties on the shipping engaged in the whale fishery, will I apprehend prove highly injurious to that fishery, wherein it does not comprehend the spermaceti fishery. A particular friend of mine, who was once in the Virginia trade, & who knows you personally, you having been on board his vessel a long while back, for he has left off the sea near upon thirty years, & who is at present concerned in the whale fishery with success, & has a vessel out upon a years voyage in the spermaceti employ, commanded by an American, & navigated much upon American conditions; assured me, that tho' he & some others had succeeded yet the trade for the capture of the common-whale had not answered at large, & that if the bounty was diminished, the trade must necessarily decline, for that it could be no other than a losing one, considered in the aggregate. I can rely upon his integrity & capacity. In looking over the terms & conditions you had declared for regulating the buildings in the city of Washington I observed that the wall of no house was to be higher than forty feet to the roof—& that the eves of the houses were allowed to project over the wall into the street.[3] It reminded me, of what was done in many of the new buildings in G. Britain. The partition wall was carried about 18 inches above the roofs on each side, that so in case of fire, the communication of it from roof to roof might be hindered. The front wall was carried about the same height above the bottom of the roof, by which means in case of fire in the lower rooms, a person might escape out of the garret window & remain in safety, by means of the wall, till a ladder could be raised to assist his coming down: or if there were houses adjoining might escape with ease into one or other of them. The wall above the eves afforded the opportunity of conveying the water off, by the aid of gutters & so down spouts, without incommoding passengers.

You will admit the goodness of my intention as an excuse for my mentioning these particulars. Mrs Gordon joins in most fervent regards to Self & Mrs Washington with Your Excellency's sincere & affectionate friend

William Gordon

ALS, DLC:GW.

1. Gordon probably is referring to GW being stranded on a sandbar in the Severn River on the night of 25–26 Mar. 1791 before reaching Annapolis (see GW to the St. John's College Faculty, 26 Mar. 1791; *Diaries*, 6:100–102).

2. William Gordon had written to GW on 31 Jan. 1791. No letter from GW to Gordon dated March 1791 has been found, but in his letter of 19 July 1791, in which he claimed payment for Gordon's *History of the Rise, Progress, and Estab-*

lishment, of the Independence of the United States of America, GW indicated that he had written Gordon on 9 Mar. 1791 (see also GW to Gordon, 25 Feb. 1791).

3. For GW's proclamation of 17 Oct. 1791 for regulating the construction of buildings and the improvement of lots in the Federal City, see Proclamation, 17 Oct. 1791, n.1.

From Alexander Hamilton

[Philadelphia] 12th April 1792.

The Secretary of the Treasury has the honor to communicate to the President a resolution of the Trustees of the Sinking Fund as of this morning.[1] A particular piece of urgent business prevents personally waiting on the President with it. It is very much to be desired that the resolution may receive the immediate decision of the President. It is upon the same principles with the last.[2]

LB, DLC:GW.

1. On this day the commissioners of the sinking fund, Hamilton, John Adams, Thomas Jefferson, and Edmund Randolph, empowered the secretary of state "to expend, in the purchase of stock, a further sum, not exceeding two hundred thousand dollars, on the principles of the resolution of the 15th day of August, 1791." The trustees' resolution of that date had authorized the purchase of "between three and four hundred thousand dollars" of "Funded stock, bearing a present Interest of six per Centum, at twenty shillings in the Pound. Funded Debt bearing an Interest of three per Centum at twelve shillings in the Pound, and Deferred Debt at twelve shillings and six pence in the Pound." That resolution also says that "any Surplus of the said Purchase Money or the whole as the case under the preceeding circumstances may be, be applied in the first instance to the purchase of the three pCents and the deferrd Debt as far as they can be obtained, and afterwards to the purchase of funded Stock of six per Cent" (Syrett, *Hamilton Papers,* 9:67–68). Jefferson, however, dissented from "so much of the above resolution as relates to the purchase of three per cent. and deferred stock" (ibid., 11:272).

2. On 4 April the commissioners of the sinking fund had authorized the purchase of $100,000 worth of 3 percent and deferred stock at 5 percent interest. Jefferson dissented from the estimated value of both the 3 percent and the deferred 6 percent stock (ibid., 224–25).

From William Hull

Sir, Philadelphia April 12th 1792.

If Genl Brooks should accept, as he doubtless will, the Appointment of Brigadier General, the Office of Marshall in the district of Massachusetts will become vacant[1]—In that case, I take the liberty to express my wish for that Appointment—I am, with the highest respect, your most obedt Servt

William Hull

ALS, DLC:GW.

1. The federal marshal for Massachusetts, John Brooks, declined the military commission for which GW nominated him on 9 April (see Henry Knox to GW, 20 May).

From St. Hilaire

Mr President, 12 [April][1] 1792

I have made a voyage to Philadelphia expressly to have the honor of seeing you; but having learned that I cannot have an audience before tuesday,[2] I have thought it my duty to send you a letter with which I have been charged for you. Shall I presume to beg your Excellency to have regard to the recommendation of the sister of the unfortunate Mauduit?[3] I have not perhaps the talents which you knew in him; but I am certain I shall have the same zeal for the service of the United States if I should have the honor of being employed by them. If your Excelleny will deign to cast a favourable regard on my request, and speak a word in my favor to Mr Morris, my acknowledgement will end only with the profound respect with which I am, your Excellency's most humble & Obedt Servt

L: D. st hilaire
formerly Captain in the Regiment of
Besançon,[4] of the Corps of Royal Artillery.

Translation, in Tobias Lear's hand, DNA: RG 59, Miscellaneous Letters; ALS, DNA: RG 59, Miscellaneous Letters. The French text of the ALS appears in CD-ROM:GW.

For the background to this letter, see Mauduit Du Botderu to GW, 23 Dec. 1791.

1. Although both St. Hilaire's letter and Lear's translation are dated 12 May, Lear's docket on the receiver's copy indicates that the ALS was written on 12 April. Internal evidence supports the validity of Lear's docket. As GW was on 12 May on his way to Mount Vernon for a two-week visit, St. Hilaire could not possibly have arranged for a meeting with him on the following Tuesday.

2. St. Hilaire is referring to Tuesday, 17 April.

3. For the killing of Thomas-Antoine Mauduit Du Plessis, the commander of the French garrison at Port-au-Prince and brother of Jeanne-Thomasse-

Emilie Mauduit Du Botderu, on the island of Saint Domingue in March 1791, see Desbrosses to GW, 22 Mar. 1791, n.1. No written recommendation of St. Hilaire has been identified.

4. In his translation Tobias Lear mistakenly transcribed this word as "Besauçon."

Letter not found: from James Seagrove, 12 April 1792. On 21 April, Seagrove wrote to GW from Rock Landing, Ga.: "My last letter to you was from Savannah under date of the 12th Inst."

From Thomas Jefferson

Sir Philadelphia Apr. 13. 1792.

I have the honor to lay before you a communication from Mr Hammond Minister Plenipotentiary of his Britannic Majesty covering a clause of a statute of that country relative to it's commerce with this, and notifying a determination to carry it into execution henceforward.[1] Conceiving that the determination announced could not be really meant as extensively as the words import, I asked and received an explanation from the Minister, as expressed in the letter & answer herein inclosed:[2] and, on consideration of all circumstances, I cannot but confide in the opinion expressed by him, that it's sole object is to exclude foreign vessels from the islands of Jersey & Guernsey. the want of proportion between the motives expressed & the measure, it's magnitude & consequences, total silence as to the Proclamation on which the intercourse between the two countries has hitherto hung, & of which, in this broad sense, it would be a revocation, & the recent manifestations of the disposition of that government to concur with this in mutual offices of friendship & good-will, support his construction. the Minister moreover assured me verbelly that he would immediately write to his court for an explanation & in the mean time is of opinion that the usual intercourse of commerce between the two countries (Jersey & Guernsey excepted) need not be suspended. I have the honor to be with sentiments of the most profound respect & attachment, Sir, your most obedient & most humble servant

Th: Jefferson

ALS, DNA: RG 59, Miscellaneous Letters; ALS (letterpress copy), DLC: Jefferson Papers; LS, DNA: RG 46, Second Congress, 1791–1793, Records of Legislative Proceedings, President's Messages; LS (letterpress copy), DLC: Jefferson Papers; LB, DNA: RG 59, George Washington's Correspondence with His Secretaries of State; LB (photocopy), DLC:GW.

Jefferson sent a draft of his letter to GW to Hammond this day "in a friendly way," informing him that GW would probably lay the matter before Congress. Hammond replied, also on this day, that its contents were an accurate exposition of his views (*Jefferson Papers,* 23:417–18). GW immediately transmitted Jefferson's letter and its enclosures to Congress.

1. George Hammond's letter to Jefferson of 11 April 1792 reads: "I have received by a circular dispatch from my Court, directions to inform this Government that, considerable inconveniences having arisen from the importation of Tobacco in foreign vessels into the Ports of his Majesty's Dominions, contrary to the Act of the 12th Charles 2d Chap. 18. Sect. 3d (commonly called the navigation Act) it has been determined in future strictly to inforce this clause, of which I take the liberty of enclosing to you a copy" (DNA: RG 46, Second Congress, 1791–1793, Records of Legislative Proceedings, President's Messages). The enclosed copy of section 3 of the 1660 Navigation Act reads: "And it is further enacted by the authority aforesaid that no goods or Commodities whatsoever of the growth production manufacture of Africa, Asia or America, or of any part thereof which are described or laid down in the usual maps or charts of those places be imported into England Ireland or Wales Islands of Guernsey and Jersey or Town of Berwick upon Tweed in any other Ship or Ships Vessel or Vessels whatsoever but in such as do truly and without fraud belong only to the people of England or Ireland Dominion of Wales or Town of Berwick upon Tweed or of the lands Islands Plantations or Territories in Asia Africa or America to his Majesty belonging as the proprietors and right owners thereof and whereof the Master and three fourths at least of the mariners are English under the penalty of the forfeiture of all such goods and Commodities and of the Ship or vessel in which they were imported with all her Guns Tackle furniture ammunition and apparel one moiety to his Majesty his heirs and successors and the other moiety to him or them who shall seize inform or sue for the same in any Court of Record by Bill Information Plaint or other action wherein no Essoin [excuse for non-appearance in court] Protection or wager of Law shall be allowed" (DNA: RG 46, Second Congress, 1791–1793, Records of Legislative Proceedings, President's Messages).

2. The enclosed copy of Jefferson's letter to Hammond of 12 April reads: "I am this moment favored with the letter you did me the honor of writing yesterday, covering the extract of a British Statute forbidding the admission of foreign Vessels into any Ports of the British Dominions with goods or commodities of the growth, production or manufacture of America. The effect of this appears to me so extensive as to induce a doubt whether I understand rightly the determination to inforce it, which you notify and to oblige me to

ask of you whether we are to consider it as so far a revocation of the Proclamation of your Government regulating the Commerce between the two Countries, and that hence forth no articles of the growth, production, or manufacture of the United States are to be received in the Ports of Great Britain or Ireland in vessels belonging to the Citizens of the United States?" (DNA: RG 46, Second Congress, 1791–1793, Records of Legislative Proceedings, President's Messages).

The enclosed copy of Hammond's reply to Jefferson of 12 April reads: "In answer to your letter of this day, I have the honor of observing, that I have no other instructions upon the subject of my communication than such as are contained in the circular dispatch, of which I stated the purport in my letter dated yesterday. I have however no difficulty in assuring you, that the result of my personal conviction is, that the determination of his Majesty's Government to inforce the clause of the Act of Navigation (a copy of which I transmitted to you) with respect to the importation of commodities in foreign vessels, has originated in consequence of the many frauds, that have taken place in the importation of Tobacco into his Majesty's Dominions, in foreign vessels, and is not intended to militate against the Proclamation or Order of the King in Council, regulating the commercial intercourse between Great Britain and the United States, which, I have every reason to believe, still exists in full force, as I have not had the most distant intimation of its being revoked" (DNA: RG 46, Second Congress, 1791–1793, Records of Legislative Proceedings, President's Messages).

To the United States Senate

United States [Philadelphia]

Gentlemen of the Senate, April 13th 1792.

I nominate David Rittenhouse, of Pennsylvania, to be Director of the Mint.[1]

Go: Washington

DS, DNA: RG 46, Second Congress, 1791–1793, Records of Executive Proceedings, President's Messages—Executive Nominations; LB, DLC:GW.

1. The Senate received this message from Tobias Lear this day and ordered it to lie for consideration after reading it. On 14 April the Senate considered the nomination and resolved to consent to the appointment (*Executive Journal*, 1:119–20). Lear informed Jefferson on 14 April of the Senate's concurrence (DNA: RG 59, George Washington's Correspondence with His Secretaries of State), and Rittenhouse's commission as director of the U.S. Mint was filled out that day (DLC:GW).

To the United States Senate and House of Representatives

[Philadelphia] April 13. 1792.

Gentlemen of the Senate, and of the House of Representatives:

I have thought it proper to lay before you a communication of the 11th instant from the Minister Plenipotentiary of Great Britain, to the Secretary of State relative to the commerce of the two Countries, together with their explanatory correspondence, and the Secretary of State's letter to me on the subject.[1]

Go: Washington

DS, DNA: RG 46, Second Congress, 1791–1793, Records of Legislative Proceedings, President's Messages; LB, DLC:GW.

1. For the enclosures, see Jefferson to GW, 13 April, nn.1–2. Both the Senate and the House of Representatives received GW's message this day and ordered it to lie on the table (*Annals of Congress,* 2d Cong., 122, 556).

From Henry Voigt

Philadia April 13th 1792.

The Petition of Henry Voigt of the City of Philadelphia Clock and Watchmaker Humbly sheweth

Your Petitioner begs leave to represent to Your Excellency that he is well acquainted with all the different parts for Coining of Money—that he in his Younger days for several Years worked in the Mint of Saxe Gotha in Germany and has gone through all the various Branches belonging to the same—that he not only knows how to use every Engine belonging to a Mint, but is able to make every one himself in all its parts Compleat (except engraving the Dies)—and even has made some Improvements in the Machinery whereby a Considerable Expence was saved.

Your Petitioner further begs leave to represent that in the late Revolution from a Zeal to serve his Country in her distress, he manufactored Gears and Gunlocks for the Army of the United States—and erected and Carried on a Wire Manufactory to accomodate his Country with that Article for making Wool and Cotton Cards—and introducing several useful Machines for the purpose of expediting manufactoring of Cards—but that when Importation took place Your petitioner's Manufactory was ruined and reduced him to straightened Circumstances from a state of Contentment and easy living.

These Circumstances have emboldened Your Petitioner hereby to solicit Your Excellency to appoint him to an Office in the Mint of the United States.

Your Petitioner from a Conviction of giving Satisfaction humbly solicits Your Excellency to appoint him Chief Coiner of the Mint of the United States.[1] And as in Duty bound will ever pray &ca

Henry Voigt

ADS, DLC:GW.

Henry Voigt (Voight; 1738–1814) moved to Philadelphia shortly after closing his wire mill in Reading, Pa., in 1780. He associated himself with steamboat designer John Fitch in 1786–87 and entered into formal partnership with him in 1792 to manufacture steam engines, a project which proved to be unsuccessful. Voigt lived at 149 North Second Street, Philadelphia, in 1791 (see Fitch and Voigt to GW, 26 Feb. 1790; Eckhardt, *Pennsylvania Clocks and Clockmakers,* 195).

Voigt enclosed recommendations of this date from David Rittenhouse, former congressman Timothy Matlack (1730–1829), and the Philadelphia steelmaker John Nancarrow (all in DLC:GW). Rittenhouse wrote: "I have long been acquainted with Mr Voight's superior abilities as a Mechanic, and know that they are not confined to the Watch-making business, in which he excells, but that he is capable of executing works of the greatest force. His Wire Mill and Steam Engine, both of which I have seen at work with Much satisfaction, may be given as proofs of his talents as well for planning as for Execution."

1. Voigt was temporarily appointed chief coiner in July 1792, and GW made the appointment permanent on 28 Jan. 1793. Voigt served in the position until his death (*Executive Journal,* 1:127; see also Rittenhouse to GW, 9 July 1792, in GW to Thomas Jefferson, that date, n.1).

From Abraham Baldwin

sir Philadelphia 14th April 1792

Among the candidates who may be offered to your notice as proper persons to be nominated to the office of Treasurer of the mint, I take the liberty of recommending Mr Joel Barlow.[1]

By a letter which I have just received from him dated in London on the 13th of Jany, I am informed that he would be on his return to this country by the last of March. There can be little doubt of his arrival here in the course of a few weeks. An early and intimate acquaintance with him have given me such knowledge of his principles and integrity, that I wish to [be] considered as giving assurance of them which can be received from me with the greatest respect. I have the honour to be, sir your most Obedient humble servant

Abr. Baldwin

ALS, DLC:GW.

1. Joel Barlow sailed for Europe in May 1788, and while he was there he became agent in France for the Scioto Company. Barlow did not return to the United States until 1804 (see Rochambeau to GW, 31 Jan. 1789, and Alexander Hamilton to GW, 28 Aug. 1790, n.1).

From William Hull

Sir Philadelphia April 14th 1792.

Pursuant to the directions of the Officers of the Massachusetts line of the late American Army, I enclosed for your information all the papers which had any relation to the object of my Agency, to Congress.[1]

I feel it now a duty incumbent upon me to transmit a Copy of a circular address to the Officers of the different [states],[2] which will explain the motives which have induced me, not to attempt a Consideration of the subject the present Session, and the further Measures, which I have proposed for the Attainment of the Object of our reasonable Wishes.

It will be a peculiar happiness to the Officers of Massachusetts, if the Measures they are pursuing should meet with the Approbation of him, who was their illustrious leader in War, and is their great exemplar in peace. I have the honor to be with the highest respect, your most obedt and very humble Servt

William Hull

ALS, DNA: RG 59, Miscellaneous Letters.

1. The enclosed papers included a printed circular of 28 Feb. from a committee of Mass. officers to the officers of the other American states; a letter to Hull of 5 Mar. from the same committee of Mass. officers; an undated petition from the former officers of the Massachusetts line to Congress; and a printed copy of the memorial that the Mass. officers had presented to Congress over Benjamin Lincoln's signature (all in DNA: RG 59, Miscellaneous Letters).

The printed circular of 28 Feb. to the officers of the other American states announces the committee's intention to "prosecute their memorial" to Congress "on the subject of compensation for the losses sustained by them and the soldiers who served during the [Revolutionary] war"; that Hull had been appointed our "Agent to Congress to attend to and explain the nature of our application"; and "that, if you should think it expedient to adopt correspondent measures, our attempt may receive the aid of your advice and assistance." The letter written to Hull by the committee of Mass. officers on 5 Mar. appoints him their agent and asks him "to prove" to Congress "that the obligations of the Government are as yet undischarged, that their promises to the army remain as yet uncomplied with." It also instructs Hull to keep the committee informed of what he was doing in Philadelphia and to ask his brother officers from other states for their assistance and advice. The undated petition of the officers of the Massachusetts line to Congress decries "the losses sustained by your memorialists, & the Soldiers beforementioned in consequence of the manner in which they were compensated by the Government of the United States for their services in the field" and informs Congress of the appointment of Hull as the officers' agent. The printed copy of the undated "Memorial presented by the Officers" of Massachusetts to Congress and signed by Benjamin Lincoln argues that "in consequence of the resolutions of Congress, recommending to the several states to provide payment for the troops raised in them respectively for their services, until the expiration of the year 1780, they received promissary notes from the state of Massachusetts for the arrears of pay due to them within that period. And although the time has expired in which the principal of the said notes became due, they have received but an inconsiderable part either of principal or interest, five years of interest being now due on a certain description of them. From the commencement of January 1781, to the termination of the war, their accounts were settled by a Commissioner appointed from Congress. This Commissioner issued certificates ascertaining the ballances due to them respectively, and declaratory of an interest of six *per centum* to be annually paid thereon. . . . From the imbecility of the Confederation no funds have been established to support the credit of their certificates; and they have been left to take their value from publick opinion."

2. Hull's circular to the officers of the other American states, which he signed and dated this day at Philadelphia, announces his attendance "at the seat of government from the 20th of March to the present period"; that "I have it in particular command from the officers of Massachusetts, to request a co-operation of the officers of your line, at the opening of the next session of Congress"; that "the claim of the army is not chimerical, but founded in the clear and eternal principles of justice"; and that he was confident that, in addition to monetary compensation, "Congress will be disposed to make a liberal grant of land in the western territory" (DNA: RG 59, Miscellaneous Letters).

From William Jackson

Sir, Philadelphia, April 14th 1792.

As some appearances in the conduct of Mr Otis make an explanation of his application to you, as that application regards me personally, necessary—I pray permission to wait upon you for that purpose.[1]

A most earnest desire that whatever related to myself should be justly understood by you, Sir, is the influencing cause of this request—and I am confident that the conversation with which you may be pleased to honor me, will result in removing from your mind every idea unfavorable to the honor and delicacy of him who is with the most respectful and sincere attachment, Sir, your grateful obedient Servant

W. Jackson

ALS, DLC:GW.

1. For the application of Samuel Allyne Otis for the office of treasurer of the U.S. Mint, see Otis to GW, 10 April. Jackson, who had been an unsuccessful candidate for Otis's position as secretary to the Senate in 1789, wrote GW during the summer of 1790 that Otis wished to "receive an appointment in Massachusetts"; that few senators would regret his departure; and that in the event of Otis's resignation, he would probably succeed him (Jackson to GW, 31 July 1790). As Otis did not resign, Jackson continued to serve as GW's secretary until early 1792.

From Estéban José Martínez

Most excellent Sir Havana. 14 April. 1792.

Supposing that Y[our] E[xcellency] is acquainted with the services which I rendered to the Bostonian expedition commanded by Capt. John Kendrick[1] at the time when I was commander in chief of another on the North West coast of America, I take the liberty of troubling Y. E. to the end that interposing your influence with Congress, they may distinguish me with the order of Cincinnatus, for which I shall be very thankful to your Excellency.

I leave this place for Madrid the end of the present month I mention it to Y. E. that you may lay me your commands which I shall obey with pleasure. God preserve you &c.

Stephen Joseph Martinez

Translation, in Thomas Jefferson's handwriting, DSoCi; ALS, DSoCi. The Spanish text of the ALS appears in CD-ROM:GW.

Estéban José Martínez Fernández y Martínez de la Sierra (1742–1798) was a native of Seville, Spain, who studied at that city's Seminario de San Telmo before embarking on a naval career. Between 1776 and 1788 Martínez sailed on a series of voyages to Spanish California and earned a reputation as the commander most familiar with the region and route. In 1788 he led an expedition from San Blas on the western coast of Mexico to explore the Russian fur trade settlements in Alaska and to formalize Spanish claims to the Nootka Sound region, which he had first visited in 1774. In 1789 Martínez was ordered to occupy Nootka with a military garrison, map the adjacent coastline, and take possession of as much nearby territory as possible. His seizure of two English vessels that summer precipitated an international crisis that almost led to an Anglo-Spanish war (see Hamilton to GW, 8 July 1790, source note).

1. John Kendrick, Sr. (c.1740–1794), of Cape Cod, Mass., was a whaler and coastal trader who commanded privateers during the Revolutionary War. In September 1787 he led a trading expedition to the Pacific Northwest and China sponsored by Boston merchant Joseph Barrell and five other investors, who put up $50,000 to outfit two ships, the *Columbia Rediviva,* captained by Kendrick, and the *Lady Washington,* captained by Robert Gray. The expedition set out in September 1787 and rounded Cape Horn safely, but it had to put in at the Island of Juan Fernández off Chile, where the Spanish commander, who was led to believe that the vessels were personally owned by GW, was later relieved of his command for letting the Americans proceed. Kendrick reached Nootka Sound in September 1788, and in March 1789 he erected Fort Washington at Mawina Cove, seven miles up the sound, on land he later purchased from an Indian chief. Martínez and his expedition arrived off Nootka on 5 May, and shortly thereafter he arrested a British trader who was operating under the Portuguese flag and seized his ship and crew. Martínez began building a schooner at Mawina, purchasing materials from Kendrick, who had set up a forge there. Martínez seems to have left the American traders alone as they had apparently persuaded him that their stay was temporary and that they had no intention of encroaching upon Spanish rights, unlike their British and Russian counterparts. Kendrick later cooperated in the capture of another British trader, and when the *Columbia Rediviva* and *Lady Washington* sailed from Nootka in July 1789, they were escorted out of the sound by Martínez's launch. Kendrick was also granted permission to return the following season.

From Marinus Willett

Sir New York 14th April 1792

A report has reached me in a way I cannot doubt that I am on a nomination for Brigadier General.[1] I feel myself truly sensible of the honor of this nomination. It is a fresh Instance of the estimation in which I stand with you and of course very flattering to me. The repeated Instances I have experienced of your regarde are convincing evidences of your readiness to promote my welfare. It is therefore with regret I observe myself named for an office which as things are at present circumstanced would in all probability opperate to my disadvantage. The same desire to serve my Country which early took place in my breast still remains there. Yet when I reflect on the situation I am in and the kind of service this appointment would require from me I am led to decline engaging in it and flatter myself this measure will not be disproved of by you.

I am at present in the enjoyment of an office which while it lasts will be eaqual to all my wants—On account of its being limited if any thing more permanent which would not detach me too much from my famaly presented itself I should be happy in the receipt of it—The present offer would Introduce me into a business of a disagreeable nature. It has been my uniform opinion that the United States ought to avoid an Indian war. I have generally conceived this to be our proper virtuous and wisest pollicy—The reasons assigned for the necessaty of the present Indian war have never brought conviction to my mind. From my knowledge and experience of these people I am clear it is not a difficult thing to preserve peace with them—That there are bad people among them there is no doubt and that those bad men will at times do acts which deserve punishment is very clear, But I hold that to go to war is not the right and proper way to punish them.

Most of the Indians I have had knowledge of are conceited and vain, by feeding their vanity you create their good opinion. This in time procures their esteem and affection, when this becomes the case they are susseptable of almost any impressions—They are Credulous yet susspicious—They think a great deal and have in general good notions of right and wrong—They frequently exhibit proofs of greatfull minds—Yet they are very revengfull and tho they are not free from Chicane—and Intrigue—If their vanity is properly humored and they are dealt Justly by it is not a difficult matter to keep them in their rational Capacities straight; and by degrees encompass every reasonably measure with them.

The kind of Intercourse I have had with those people, The treatment I have myself and known others to receive from them has produced in me an advocate for them.

To fight with them would be the last choise of my mind, and yet Sir, I declare from the experience I have had, I view them a people easy to beat when brought to action—When in small parties they scatter themselves along a frontier they have always been found exceeding Injurious troublesome and Dangerous—This kind of warfare is thus fast and in it they become truly tremendious—But when they attempt any thing in large bodies I have found it notwithstanding their great dexterity in the wilderness and the advantage they usually have in taking positions they are easily beat.

In wood marches where troops are exposed to attacks from Indians much circumspection is requisite as well with respect to the mode and line of march of the troops at large—as in having small parties and single men extended far on the flanks, in front and in rear—But when ever a serious attack is made which usually is furious and generally severe, An Instuntanious charge with Huzaing sufficient to overcome the noise the Indians make will never fail to repell them—And this stroke repeated and pursued will I am well convinced ever effect a victory, And yet victories over Indians are generally paid for, But Defeats are terrible.

The honor however of fighting and beating Indians is what I do not asspire after—If in anyways I could be instrumental in effecting and maintaining peace with them, it would be to me an immence gratification—With sentiments of the purest veneration and respect—I have the honor to be Sir Your most Obedient and very humble Servant

Marinus Willett

ALS, DNA: RG 59, Miscellaneous Letters.

1. For GW's nomination of Willett as a brigadier general, see GW to the U.S. Senate, 9 April 1792. Willett had been GW's emissary to the Creek Indians in the summer of 1790. From 1792 to 1794 he served as sheriff of New York City and County.

From Friderici

Sir, Surinan 15th April 1792

The Sieur David Nassy, a native of this place, of a family whose Ancestry were the first settlers of one part of the Colony, a man well informed, and a man who has no fault, except that of being unfortunate, if that can be called one, has begged me to have the honor of remitting by him these lines to your Excellency.[1]

Reiterated disappointments which he has not deserved—infirm health, and the desire of living in a Country where, without regarding the difference of Religion in Individuals, personal merit is attended to, have led him to a determination of going to reside in the United States under the government of your Excellency. If he can there find himself happy, it will give me great pleasure on account of the Interest which I take in him, and more particularly if this should be the means of obtaining the p[r]otection of your Excellency by drawing your Attention. It is at least a subject worthy of his regard that I have the honor to recommend him. I have the honor to be with as much respect as veneration Sir Your Excellency's most Obedt & humble Servant

[Friderici][2]

Translation, in Tobias Lear's hand, DLC:GW; ALS, DLC:GW. The French text of the ALS appears in CD-ROM:GW.

Lt. Col. Juriaen François de Friderici (1751–1812) served as governor-general of Surinam from the early 1790s to 1802.

1. This letter was delivered by David de Isaac Cohen Nassy (1747–1806), a descendant of the David Nassy who had founded the Sephardic Jewish community in Surinam in 1664. Nassy immigrated to the United States in 1792, and he settled in Philadelphia, where he was elected a member of the American Philosophical Society. A physician and a writer, Nassy involved himself in the medical controversy surrounding the yellow fever epidemic of 1793. He reluctantly returned to Surinam in 1795, claiming that its climate was more congenial to his constitution than that of Pennsylvania. Before his departure Nassy paid his respects to the president and offered GW his "Services, [i]f I can render you any at Surinam, Where I have the happiness to possess Much the Confidence of the Governor" (see Nassy to GW, 2 Mar. 1795, DLC:GW).

2. Tobias Lear, who apparently translated this letter, misread the signature as "Triversie," but he correctly docketed the translation as being "From The Governor of Surinam."

From George Augustine Washington

Honor'd Uncle Mount Vernon April 15[–16]th 1792

I have received Your favor of the 8th[1] and it affords me pleasure that the Canada Gentlemen left Mount Vernon satisfied with their reception, it being my wish that every person coming here may have their curiocity gratified and be convinced of my disposition towards civility—at the time those Gentlemen were here Fanny the Children and myself were well, but have latterly been much afflicted with the head ach and since Friday[2] very severely and pains all over me owing to cold which generally effects me in this way last night I sufferd a good deel and was unable to leave my bed untill late to day I hope it will pass off tho' I am at this time very unwell—The weather since I wrote You last has been very disagreeable indeed[3]—the sun has seldom been seen during that time—Rains have been very frequent and often very hard which has occasion'd much interuption to business, plowing particularly which at this season is of great consequence has been almost entirely stoped for a week and the ground is now as wet as it can well be. yesterday the wind got to the north blew brisk and very cold last night there was a smart frost and had the wind lulled entirely there would probably have been a very severe one nothing I believe is killed but every thing appears chilled by it—tomorrow we had fixed on for begining our Corn planting but the interuption of the weather and the state of the ground will prevent it but I do not now expect admiting that the weather should be favorable to begin generally, sooner than the last of the week or the begining of the next.

Spanish brown will I think answer very well for painting the Roof of the Green House and the wings to it for white lead which if the principal paint in forming a slate color is very expensive I think there is in the store half as much Spanish brown as will be wanting for the purpose mentioned and the further quantity that may be required may perhaps be obtained on as good terms in Alexandria as in Philadelphia and Oil also of which a good deel will be wanting but of this I will inform myself the first time I go to Alexandria which will be tomorrow if I am well enough which I at present have little expectation of—if it should appear best to get it from Philadelphia will endeavour to make an estimate of the quantity of Paint and oil that may be required. there is some of the kind of sand You mention but I do not think near enough but more if it is Your desire shall be obtained but it appears to me that in the course of another year or two at most that the North front and the ends of the House must be done over and that it might be best to do the whole at the same time—the East front does not look so white but it has a much better Coat than the No.—speaking of painting reminds me of the dining room which is really not decent and ought to be painted before You come home—the chimney smokes in such a manner that it distroys the room the color is rather a gloomy one but supose on acct of the firniture you would have it of the same.

Mahony is about the Births in the last appartment in the Quarter now the Doors and windows are then to be done to make a finishing Mahonys time expires the 15th of May at which time he goes away.[4] a number of gates both for utility and appearance are wanting—Corn houses at every plantn before the time for housing Corn must be built. there is none at Dogue Run and Muddy hole that at the Ferry is not large enought—the present one at the River Plantn will require much repair—and a new one built.

The body of snow which remain'd upon the Piaza during winter and the frequent rains this spring has roted the roof so entirely as to put it beyond repair—the shingles are so decayed that they break through with the weight of a man except immediately upon the Rafters—there are many large holes in different parts of the Roof—which with the decay of the shingles which induced me to conclude when I was able to examin it that nothing short of an entire new Roof would be wanting but contrary to my expectation the joist Rafters and Cieling appeared quite sound I looked through several parts of the Roof and could discover no decay of any consequence and Green went in between the Roof and Cieling and could discover none and thinks none will be found of much consequence—it is a job that ought not to be delayed for the longer it is the greater difficulty will attend it but shall wait Your directions before I proceed to make preparations for it—Green seems to doubt the practicability of making a tight roof with shingles tho' I think if it can be done I had as soon trust it to him as any one for he is very capable—Copper or Lead appears to me to be the only secure covering that can be given it either will be very expensive—Green thinks Copper will be the best and cheapest and that he can put it on—Mr Whiting thinks a tight roof may be made of 3 feet shingles showing not more than 6 Inches but Green seems to doubt it—the repairs that this house will require in a very few years will be costly.

Had the winter and Spring but been tolerably favorable the Meadow at the Mill & the Swamp at the Ferry and Frenches would before this time have been in fine order but I have no doubt as I am satisfied You will make allowances for the weather and will recollect the situation You left them in that You will be pleased at the situation You will find them which will be very pleasing to me—there is yet much work to do in the swamp part of the Ferry and Frenches but do not dispair getg it in order in time for the early Corn—the grounds adjoining will be planted with Common—the whole of the Mill Meadow was designed for the early Corn.

The Wheat at Muddy-hole looks much better than it could be expected indeed very well some parts of No. 3 is thin but looks thriving No. 7 is really except in some spots, very good—the spots which I mentiond in some of the fields to be injured by wet have had no opportunity of recovering there having been so much rain latterly tho I do not think the whole would amount to more than 5 or 6 acres mostly in No. 6 at Frenches and No. 6 at D: Run—The Mill field is very good wheat except a little along the uper part of the post and Rail fence going to Mr Washingtons—You may rest assured that particular care shall be taken to ascertain with certainty the experiment of wheat made in No. 6 at D: Run. I am still of Your opinion and shall not be convinced but by facts that the thickest wheat will not be the most productive—As soon as the ground gets a little drier I will get about planting the honey locusts and there are many things of this kind and some other matters that I wish much to accomplish but the hurry of plantn business and fishing will I fear render it impossible—the weather particularly the last weak has been very unfavorable for Fishing on Saturday I was at the landing about 150,000 herring had then been caught[5]—more I believe than had been caught at any of the other landings—the quantity mention'd are the whole that have been caught.

It is the lot runing from the Gum spring Road up to the Barn which is broke up and sown with Oats & Clover—taken from field No. 5.

I hope the trees and shrubs You sent will the most if not the whole of them live tho they were advanced and many of those which were confind in the Boxes came out in a very tender state but they were plantd on Wednesday and Thursday when the ground was very wet and rainy the whole time which was favorable[6]—if the trees and shrubs succeed the Ovals will I think be very ornamental—the 6 ovals recd nearly 300 of the shrubs which were nearly the whole sent—the Gardner seems to have very little expectation of the cutings succeeding—he says vegitation had advanced entirely too far for grafting.

16th I intended yesterday had I been better to day to have gone to Alexandria but I continue so much indisposed that I am not able my present feelings give me cause to apprehend a billious attack. I shall try abstinence for a few days which perhaps may remove it—it arises from cold which the weather has exposed every one to—I beg that my Aunt and the Children may be assured of my tenderest regard and Mr & Mrs Lear and Mr Dandridge of my good wishes—and that I am with the warmest attachment Your sincerely affectionate Nephew

Go. A. Washington

P.S. The posts around the Circle are the most of them entirely rotten—if they cannot be had in Philadelphia I must endeavour to get the best I can here.[7]

ALS, DLC:GW.

1. GW's letter to G. A. Washington of 8 April has not been found.

2. G. A. Washington is referring to Friday, 13 April.

3. G. A. Washington had last written GW on 8–9 April 1792.

4. Thomas Mahony had worked on the Mount Vernon estate as a house carpenter and joiner since 1786 (see Farm Reports, 3–9 Jan. 1790, n.4).

5. G. A. Washington is referring to Saturday, 14 April.

6. GW apparently had ordered the plants from John Bartram in Philadelphia sometime in March (see List of Plants from John Bartram's Nursery, March 1792, and G. A. Washington to GW, 8–9 April 1792). G. A. Washington had them planted on Wednesday, 11 April, and Thursday, 12 April 1792.

7. G. A. Washington wrote the following note in the left margin of the last page of the manuscript: "the dimensions of the Roof of the Piaza is 98 feet by 20—I mention it least you should wish it."

From Marinus Willett

Sir New York April 15th 1792

The Inclosed copy of a letter I did myself the honor to address you yesterday previous to my receiving from the Minister of war an account of my being appointed Brigadier General in the army of the United States;[1] I most humbly beg leave to refer you to it for my reasons for not engaging in the service to which that appointment would call me.

It will afford me great satisfaction to hear that the Gentleman who is going out against the Indians goes with as pasific a disposition as the nature of the case will possibly admit, and that as the only thing to be required is peace—he may be the happy instrument of procuring it. I am Sir With the greatest sincerty Your most obedient and very humble Servt

Marinus Willett

ALS, DNA: RG 59, Miscellaneous Letters.

1. On 12 April, Henry Knox drafted a letter to Willett informing him of his appointment and mentioning "that the acceptance of [Daniel] Morgan is doubtful. . . . if he should decline then you would be second in command" of the military expedition under Maj. Gen. Anthony Wayne (NNGL: Knox Papers).

From Joseph Bloomfield

Sir, Burlington [N.J.] April 16: 1792.

I take the liberty of Offering myself to Your notice as a candidate for the Office of Treasurer of the mint.

Whether in the course of my services in the army, I was so fortunate as to be known, and shall now be so happy as to be recollected by You Sir, I do not know, but those services will at least be proofs of my zeal for the American cause and revolution.

The appointment of Attorney-General for New-Jersey where I reside, which I at this time hold, and have held for Nine Years, is in some degree an evidence of the confidence which is reposed in me by the legislature of the state. The very severe drudgery attendant upon the duties of that Office, and upon my professional pursuits, has reconciled me to the determination of relinquishing both.

The Members in Congress from New-Jersey, are, I presume, for the most part Acquainted with my situation, my circumstances and more particularly with my character in those respects which more immediately qualify the person for a trust of such a nature as the one in question.[1] I have the honor to be Sir, with the most perfect respect Your most Obedt servt

Joseph Bloomfield.

ALS, DLC:GW.

Joseph Bloomfield (1753–1823), who was born in Woodbridge, N.J., studied law under Attorney General Cortlandt Skinner and was admitted to the bar in 1774. The following year he was commissioned a lieutenant in the New Jersey Light Infantry. Bloomfield became a captain in the 3d New Jersey Regiment in February 1776, and he was promoted to major in November 1776. He served as deputy judge advocate general of the Continental army from 1776 until his resignation in October 1778. Bloomfield fought at the battles of Brandywine and Monmouth, and he was wounded at Brandywine. He was elected state attorney general of New Jersey in 1783 and reelected in 1788. After changing his politics to Jeffersonian republicanism, Bloomfield served as governor of New Jersey 1801–12 and as a member of Congress 1817–21.

1. GW appointed Tristram Dalton, not Bloomfield, treasurer of the U.S. Mint on 3 May (see GW to the U.S. Senate, 3 May [second letter]).

From Henry Knox

Sir. War-department, April 16th 1792.

I have the honor to submit you a private letter from General Wilkinson, to Colonel Biddle with a view to exhibit the opinion he entertains of Hodgdon[1]—The more I reflect on the state of the quarter master's department, the more anxious I am, that a successor to Hodgdon should be immediately appointed. After the most diligent search, in quest of a suitable person for the office who is acquainted with the characters and resources of the western country together with other proper qualifications, I cannot find any one so competent in my judgment on the whole as James O'Hara.[2] I have the honor to be, Sir, with the highest respect, Your very humble Servt

H. Knox
secy of War[3]

LS, DLC:GW; LB, DLC:GW.

1. The enclosure was probably Gen. James Wilkinson's letter from Fort Washington to Clement Biddle of 13 Mar., which reads: "I have duly received your favor of the 10th Ultmo & the doubts which that Letter conveys of General St Clairs continuance in Command, fill me with anxiety, for I anticipate that should a new Hand be appointed from the atlantic, He will come out with Ideas of false practice, false Opinions, an Ignorance of the Country in which he is to Act, & of the Enemy against whom he Acts—To foretel the Issue does not require a Spirit of divination—But whatever may be the arrangement, I have no doubt that I shall fulfil the duties of my Station, the hopes of my Friends, & the expectations of my Country.

"Hitherto my Command has been an unpleasant one, for I found this Garrison, torn & agitated by the most violent, indecent & invidious factions, I urged the propriety & the necessity of conciliary Conduct, but my Council was disregarded & my Overtures rejected—Majr [David] Zeigler on the one part & Col. [Samuel] Hodgdon the other, each had their adherents & were inflexible—I at once determined to leave these Gentlemen to their own direction, and to preserve the public Interests & Military Order—previous to my arrival the Major on Grounds which I conceive disgraceful to common sense had proffered a resignation to the Secy of War, & in consequence demanded of me permission to retire—I agreed to his request because I found he hourly fanned the flames of discontent & dissatisfaction, & informed Him he should have a short leave of absence to wait on the Secy of War—But having received on the 8th Inst. an order from the Secy of War, which required a vigorous exertion & finding at that time that the command of the 1st Regt would in case of the Majors absence devolve on an Ensign, I informed Him I was under the necessity of retracting the Permission, & that he must hold Himself in readiness for Command—he replied to me & heard the Order, the detail Issued, and the order for the March of the Detachment, when to my Surprize He refused duty & sent me his Commission; I remonstrated against his Conduct in the most amicable terms & with the most friendly admonition, but found Him as obstinate as a German Boor, & finally have consented that he should quit Service—He will ascend the Ohio with Capt. [Jonathan] Hask[e]ll who is detached to Muskingum, & from thence will push to Philadela under the delusive Idea, that He will there be able, by the influence of his Friends & ex parte representation, to destroy Hodgdon, He is a most insensible Blockhead, as seditious as any old Sargent, & destitute of every Ray of duty beyond the police of a Company & the Minutiæ of the parade—I suspect withal that He wants veracity & sincerity, and altho, he lives in my Family free of expence, & that we preserve the best appearances, I have some cause to suspect, that he is Enemical to me, because I will not gratify his resentment by putting Hodgdon into the Guard House—and I make this communication to you that you may be enabled to correct any Misrepresentation, which may come from Him.

"Our Friend [Josiah] Harmar since his unfortunate propensity to drink, has introduced & established the most disgraceful & pernicious habits in the 1st Regt, acting without check, restraint, or controul, he has sacraficed every thing to the capricious will of his officers, and I found them as petish & impatient as indulged Children—Hodgdon is an irritable, unaccommodating Character, & does not in my opinion possess comprehension, Capacity or resource for the office he fills, but at the same time, he is a Man exact in his Accounts, scrupulously tenacious of the public property, & I verily beleive possessing great Integrity—As the head of an important department, He is intitled to protection & respect, & has received it from me—my propriety of conduct in this Instance, has given much offence to a Capt. [Mahlon] Ford of the Artillery, a Gentleman of waspish, testy humour—The Capt. a few Days since, when officer of the Day, in violation of every principle of his Duty, & of military subordination & dicipline, made an outrageous & indecent attack upon Hodgdon, at the threshold of my Quarters, & in the face of the Soldiery—for this unofficerlike Conduct, I have put Him in arrest & shall bring Him before a general Court Martial, so soon as the public Service permits, in the mean time the Capt. continues to denounce the heaviest vengeance against poor Hodgdon, who has this day applied to me for protection—these are disagreable occurrences, but I shall not suffer them to interfere one Moment with the public good" (NNGL: Knox Papers). Apparently enclosed in Wilkinson's letter was

Samuel Hodgdon's letter to Wilkinson of 13 Mar. soliciting his protection from Captain Ford, who had continued to make threats against him (NNGL: Knox Papers).

2. For an identification of James O'Hara and his appointment as quartermaster general, see GW to the U.S. Senate, 17 April, n.1.

3. The title and signature are in Knox's writing.

From Henry Lee

Richmond, 16 April 1792. Transmits a "copy of a letter sent to me by Colonel Arthur Campbell of the county of Washington as it may perhaps convey information useful to you."[1]

LB, Vi: Executive Letter Book.

1. The original enclosure has not been found, but it was most likely Arthur Campbell's letter to Lee of 2 Mar. 1792 that reports: "Some indication of resistence seems to be given in the S. W. Territory to permitting the Inhabitants between what is called Henderson and Walker's Line becoming Citizens of Virginia, agreeably to the late Act of Assembly." It also covered an extract from a letter dated near Chota, Southwest Territory, 1 Feb., written by an unidentified officer who, Campbell says, "has often given intelligence that has turned out to the advantage of the Publick" (*Calendar of Virginia State Papers,* 5:479–80). The extract reads: "It is with difficulty that intelligence, (to be relied on,) can be had from the Cherokees at present. The Traders both in and out of the Towns, do all in their power to conceal the murders and robbery of the Indians, and has carefully instructed them the necessity of secrecy in such matters. However, some avenues are yet open thro' which I receive information. Some Indians have among the frontier Inhabitants favourites, whom they call Comrades, and to whom they will with freedom tell whatever they know.

"Major —— is a Comrade to the Chief of [T]ellico, who is one of the most friendly Indians in the Nation. He has lately informed the Major that 20 Warriors from the Town of Nicojac & Crow Town was at the defeat of our Army over ye Ohio, that two of them were slain, one a Chief of small note. Another Indian informed John —— of little River Settlement, that 60 Indians of the Chiccamogga Towns were in the battle, and that he saw them at Estanala with several scalps and a great deal of plunder.

"The mischief done in Washington at Mockison Gap, last fall, was done by a party of Cherokees, who lived in a Town at the mouth of Hiwassee. The party that did the mischief in the beginning of the Winter on ye Kentucky road was Cherokees, Commanded by a fellow called Red-Bird Bowles, commonly called Colo. Bowles, who went to England some years ago with Moses Price and some Indian Chiefs; is returned, and resides now among the upper Creeks, and who is endeavoring to engage them in a war with the United States, and that they were preparing to make a stroke in the Spring. M. Gillivray had departed for Pensacola greatly vexed with the conduct of the Creeks for listening to Bowles.

Little satisfaction can be got from the Indians respecting the business they went to England. Moses Price says the King of England advised them to live in peace with the United States. But it is curious that the King of England should be at so much trouble and expence for no other purpose but to advise the Indians to be at Peace. Bennet Bellow a few days ago, appeared at Knoxville in a Coat appearingly to be one of the Uniforms of the officers of ye Federal Regiment" (ibid., 480–81).

To the United States Senate and House of Representatives

United States [Philadelphia] April 16th 1792.

Gentlemen of the Senate, and of the House of Representatives,

I lay before you a copy of a letter from the Judges of the Circuit Court of the United States held for the New York District; and of their opinion and agreement respecting the "Act to provide for the settlement of the claims of Widows and Orphans barred by the limitations heretofore established, and to regulate the claims to Invalid Pensions."[1]

D[S], DNA: RG 46, Second Congress, 1791–1793, Records of Legislative Proceedings, President's Messages; copy, DNA: RG 233, Second Congress, 1791–1793, Records of Legislative Proceedings, Journals; LB, DLC:GW.

For the background to this document, see Caleb Brewster to GW, 15 Mar. 1792, n.4, and the U.S. Circuit Court Judges for New York to GW, 10 April.

1. The enclosures were the letter to GW of 10 April from the U.S. circuit court judges for New York and their opinion on the unconstitutionality of the Invalid Pensions Act. The House of Representatives received GW's message this day (*Annals of Congress,* 2d Cong., 557).

To the United States Senate

United States [Philadelphia]
April 17th 1792.

Gentlemen of the Senate,

I nominate James O Hara,[1] of Pennsylvania, to be Quarter Master General of the Army of the United States, vice Samuel Hodgdon.

Go: Washington

DS, DNA: RG 46, Second Congress, 1791–1793, Records of Executive Proceedings—Executive Nominations; LB, DLC:GW.

Tobias Lear delivered this message to the Senate on 18 April. On the next day the Senate considered the nomination, advised and consented to the appointment, and ordered that the president be so informed (*Executive Journal*, 1:120). Lear wrote Henry Knox on 19 April informing him of the Senate's concurrence with O'Hara's nomination (DLC:GW).

1. James O'Hara (c.1752–1819), a native of County Mayo, Ireland, attended the Jesuit College of St. Sulpice in Paris before becoming an ensign in the British Coldstream Guards in 1770. After resigning his commission he immigrated to Philadelphia in 1772 and soon settled at Pittsburgh. His backcountry excursions as an employee of the traders Devereaux Smith and Ephraim Douglas introduced him to Indians and frontier lands, the latter of which he began to purchase. During the Revolutionary War, O'Hara was a captain in the 3d Virginia Regiment, and he served with George Rogers Clark in the Ohio Country. In 1781 O'Hara was appointed commissary of the general hospital at Carlisle, Pa., and during the last years of the war, he served under Gen. Nathanael Greene as an assistant quartermaster. After opening a general store in Pittsburgh in 1784, O'Hara began supplying the U.S. Army as a government contractor. As a presidential elector in 1789, he cast his vote for GW. O'Hara played an active role in Maj. Gen. Anthony Wayne's 1794 expedition, during which he negotiated with the Indians, inspected forts, and traveled extensively to purchase food and clothing. He resigned his commission as quartermaster in May 1796 but remained active as a government contractor until 1802.

From Henry Knox

Sir [Philadelphia] 18. April 1792

I respectfully submit to you the speeches delivered to Colo. Pickering yesterday, which he has just sent me[1]—by which it woud appear that further hopes of obtaining (by general consent) any of their number to go to the Miami Village would be delusive—Capt. Hendricks would go almost alone but one or two others of no great Importance may be persuaded to go with him.[2]

If Colo. Willet will go, Hendricks and the others may accompany him. I submit the enclosed letter to Willet[3]—If he still declines he will be silenced forever—If you should please to approve I will transmit it—I am Sir most respectfully yr hble Servt

H. Knox

ALS, DLC:GW; LB, DLC:GW.

For the background to the visit to Philadelphia of the chiefs of the Five Nations, see Timothy Pickering to GW, 21 Mar. 1792, n.1.

1. The enclosed speeches have not been identified. In an undated letter to Tobias Lear that was delivered sometime in April 1792, Knox enclosed other

papers from Pickering for submission to the president (DLC:GW). On a Monday morning in April, possibly 16 April, Pickering wrote Lear: "I had just rolled up the inclosed papers to send to Genl Knox, which I supposed he would hand to the President, when I recd a note that the President desired to see me relative to the Indians. I will wait on him in an hour; and send the inclosed for his inspection in the meantime" (DLC:GW).

2. Capt. Hendrick Aupaumut (1757–1830) was a sachem of the Mohican village of New Stockbridge on Oneida Creek in central New York. Born in Stockbridge, Mass., he learned to read and write English there, and he served with the Mohican company in the Continental army during the Revolutionary War. Aupaumut was baptized by Samuel Kirkland in March 1787 and undertook a peace mission to the hostile northwestern nations in the summer of 1791. He traveled to the Northwest on a second peace mission in the summer of 1792, but Marinus Willett did not accompany him (see note 3; see also Timothy Pickering to Israel Chapin, 14 May 1792, NHi: O'Reilly Papers; Knox's instructions to Aupaumut, 8 May 1792, *ASP, Indian Affairs,* 1:233).

3. Knox apparently enclosed his letter to Willett of this date. Knox's draft of the letter, which is marked "private and confidential," reads: "It was with regret I read your letter of declinig the acceptance of the commissn of a brigadier Genl. But only you have the right to be perfectly master of your own conduct.

"The President of the United States has shewed me your letter of the 14th instant wherein you express your ideas of an Indian War—Be assured that nothig can be more disagreable to him and the government—That the present hostilities originatd in the War with Great Britn and that they while intensive continued increasig from then to Now Until they became too enormous to be longer overlooked by Governmt cannot be doubted by every honest and impartial man who will attend to the evidence But notwithstandg the past it is the desire of the President of the United States to terminate it without the further effusion of blood—Preparatory overtures have been made to the Indians who are to have A Great council at the miami Village the next month.

"But a person of character intelligence and address is required to be presen[t] at that Council in behalf of the U.S., to unfold in terms which the Indians will comprehend.

"1st That we require no lands but those which we conceive to have been fairly purchased of those tribes who had a right to sell.

"2dly That if any of the tribes Can shew just rght to any lands they Claim by virtue of the last treaty they Shall be liberaly compensatd for such right.

"3dly That we are not only willing to be at peace with all the Natns but to impart to them such of the blessings of Civilization as will serve their chilldren and serve ⟨*illegible*⟩ to perpetuate them in the land of their forefathers.

"4thly It is conceivd were they convinced of the truth of those sentiments that peace must be the consequence—But the difficu⟨lty⟩ Is to find a suitable charater[.] You have been applied to and decli[ned]—It would however appear from your letter to the President that you would seem still to be desirous of being of service to your Country in this time.

"I am authorized to assure You that if you will still undertake the mission without further preparatory Measures I can assure you there will be but little personal hazard (although that would not be [a] consideratn with you) that You would render Your Country a most acceptable service—That if you succeed of what I should flatter myself You will have the glory thereof, besides being most liberally compensated in a pecuniary way while Hendricks Superint[en]d[s] to your subsistence.

"If you should incline to undertake this affair, notwithstanding time would [not] to be lost resting here—The way woul[d] be by Pittsburg down to Fort Washington[.] every frie[n]dly assistance would be offered you—Capt. Hendricks and perhaps and others of the Indians here pres[en]t might accompany you[.] Besides their are women present at Fort Washington, and proba[b]ly friendly Wabash Indians who would ⟨*illegible*⟩ You.

"Permit me to urge your Compliance with this invitatn to perform the mission, and that you would more t[r]uly and explic[i]tly inform me of your Determination" (NNGL: Knox Papers).

Tobias Lear to John Rutherfurd

Sir, Philadelphia April 18th 1792.

I had the honor to lay before the President the letter which you left with me yesterday for that purpose,[1] and to communicate to him the ideas which you expressed respecting the deed for a certain tract of land formerly purchased by Edward Snickers—and have now the pleasure to convey to you the President's observations on the subject.

When Colo. *George* Mercer (not *James,* as mentioned in the letter left with me) was in England he took up money there from two persons, for which he mortgaged his estate in Virginia. His brother James Mercer, having been left by George in charge of his estate, with a full power of Attorney as James supposed respecting the management of it, found it necessary, to answer some purposes relative thereto, to give a Mortgage also on the estate, not knowing what his brother had done in England.

The Mortgagees in England pressing him for their money—George Mercer sent a power of Attorney to George Mason, George Washington and John Tayloe[2] to sell his estate; but when it was found that there were three mortgages upon the estate, and a dispute arose whether the last that was made in England, or that made by James should have the preference, it was at length determined by consent of parties, and was so decreed by the High Court of Chancery, that Washington & Tayloe (Mason having refused to act) should sell the Estate, and the money arising therefrom be made liable to the further order of the Court to be paid to those claims which might in the issue be found to have the preference, or to discharge all of them if the estate should produce enough for that purpose. The President (then Colo. Washington) and Colo. Tayloe, the Attornies of George Mercer, were authorized by the Court, as they before had been by George Mercer and his Mortgagees to sell the estate on twelve months credit. The land in Frederick County (relative to which you wish information) was divided into lots and advertised for sale in November 1774, on the Credit aforesaid, to the highest bidders, giving bond and good security. James Mercer, alledging that he was a Creditor of his brother's, became a purchaser of some of the lots by way of securing himself, and Edward Snickers (the President *beleives*) was likewise a purchaser. But Snickers, if he did purchase *any*, did not purchase from the Attornies the whole of the land mentioned in the letter left with me. James Mercer afterwards sold to Snickers some of the lots which he had purchased, which, with Snickers' purchase (if he made any in his own name) at the public sale, made up the whole quantity held by Snickers.

According to the conditions of the sale the money was to be paid in November 1775—and in cases where bond and approved security were not given at the sale deeds were withheld.

In may 1775 the President went to Philadelphia as a Delegate to Congress from Virginia—from whence he went to Cambridge and took the command of the Army which it is well known so occupied his time as to leave no room for private business. He therefore wrote to Colo. Tayloe, and requested that he would take the sole management of Colo. Mercer's affairs upon himself, for situated as he was it was impossible for him to pay any further attention to them, nor would he be any longer responsible.[3] Having thus put the management of the business altogether out of his hands, he declined, before every application that was made to him, having any agency in it. Colo. Tayloe dying, and the President not being able or willing to renew his agency in this business, a decree of the High Court of Chancery was obtained to put all the papers & matters relating to Colo. George Mercer's Estate into the hands of his brother John Mercer, (at present a Representative in Congress from Maryland) he giving Bonds to do & perform all those things which had been required by the former decree to be done by the Attornies aforementioned. Colo. John Mercer will, therefore be able to give any information that may be wanting relative to the business, as he has all the papers in his hands.

The President's memory will not permit him to say with certainty, what quantity of the land Snickers bought from the attornies, if any; or what from James Mercer. But the President recollects his having applied to him, he thinks in the year 1778 at Camp, in order to obtain deeds; but as he had long before given up the whole business to Colo. Tayloe, he declined doing any thing in it.[4]

The President further adds, that, so far as his memory serves him, he does not think that Snickers ever had deeds for any part of that land. And under the present circumstances of the case, and considering the length of time since he has had any agency in the business, the President declines doing anything in this matter, unless it shall appear *absolutely necessary* for him to ⟨*illegible*⟩, and, in the opinion of the best judges, that he shall not be liable to any inconvenience therefrom hereafter. Should these two points be established, the President will chearfully and with pleasure comply with your wishes.

I have thought it necessary to enter thus fully into the matter that you might have all the information relative to it that the President possesses. You will therefore pardon the length of this letter. I have the honor to be, with great respect & esteem, Sir, Your most Obedt Servt

Tobias Lear.

P.S. The letter which you left with me is enclosed herewith.

ALS, privately owned by an anonymous donor.

For the background to GW's involvement with George Mercer's estate, see Statement concerning George Mercer's Estate, 1 Feb. 1789, source note.

On 19 April, Edmund Randolph wrote GW "to inform him, that his inquietude about the securityship is groundless. The inclosed letter contains a copy of Mr [John Francis] Mercer's bond; and is therefore sent, that the President may deposit it, if he thinks proper, among his private papers. Mr R. will in future consider the President, as no further connected with Mr John Mercer or Colo. Geo. Mercer's estate, than as to Whiting's bond, of which he will obtain an explanation. He will press Mercer in behalf of Fearon, to adjust the business; and will inform both him and Mr [Edward] Montague, that the President's responsibility ended with the execution of the bond" (DLC:GW). GW did retain the enclosed letters in his private papers.

The letter from Robert Fearon (or Hearon) to Randolph, dated Petersburg, Va., 9 April 1792, merely covered a copy of a bond of 14 Nov. 1782 in the chancery suit of *Richard Gravatt et al. v. John Francis Mercer* that reads: "Know all men by these presents that we John Francis Mercer William Fitzhugh and Charles Carter of the County of Stafford are held and firmly bound unto Edmund Pendleton George Wythe and John Blair Esquire Judges of the High Court of Chancery in the Sum of ten thousand Pounds to be paid to the said Edmund Pendleton George Wythe and John Blair Esquires and their Successors to the which payment will and truly to be made we bind ourselves and each of us our and each and every of our heirs Executors and Administrators jointly and severally firmly by these presents Sealed with our Seals and dated this Sixteenth Day of November one thousand seven hundred and Eighty two.

"The Condition of the above obligation is such that whereas the above bound John Francis Mercer is appointed by the High Court of Chancery receiver of the Effects under the Sale of the Estate of George Mercer agreeable to an Interlocutory Decree of the former General Court between Richard Gravatt and others Plaintiffs against the said John Francis Mercer and others Defendants in the Person of his Excellency General Washington the former Receiver If therefore the said John Francis Mercer shall faithfully account for and pay all such Monies and Effects as may come to his Hands in Virtue of his Appointment by the said High Court of Chancery according to the future Decree of the Court as well in the Suit of the said Gravatt and others against the said John Francis Mercer as of the said John Francis Mercer against the said Gravatt and others then this Obligation to be void otherwise to remain in full Force and Virtue." The original document, of which the enclosure was a copy made by chancery court clerk Peter Tinsley, was signed and sealed by Mercer, Fitzhugh, and Carter in the presence of John Beckley and Charles Hay. Pendleton and Wythe signed their approval of Fitzhugh and Carter being securities for the plaintiff in the bond (DLC:GW).

1. The letter, which Lear returned to Rutherfurd (see postscript), has not been found.

2. John Tayloe (1721–1779), who after 1758 lived at Mount Airy on the Rappahannock River in Richmond County, Va., was a member of the Ohio Company and served on the Virginia council during the 1750s.

3. See GW to John Tayloe, 11 Dec. 1775.

4. On 29 May 1779 GW wrote Lund Washington: "Mr Snickers is here with some Deeds for Colo. [George] Mercers land for me to execute—I have refused to resume a business which I formally relinquished (as you know by Letter which passed through your hands) three years ago—indeed, without a single paper to refer to, I could not with propriety & common prudence go into a business of this kind even if I had time & inclination to do it, but there has been such miserable inattention & mismanagement on the part of Colo. Tayloe to whom I transferred the business that I should choose to look a little about me before I do any thing relative to that Estate" (ALS, ViMtV).

From David Stuart

Dear Sir, Hope Park [Fairfax County, Va.] 18th April 1792

Your favor of the 8th instant, I recieved during our meeting at G:etown last week: but the affairs of the Fœderal City, and Potomac Company made it so busy a week, that I had really no leasure before now, to answer it. I shall allways think myself highly honored by your friendly observations, and endeavour to profit from them—Perhaps, we may have carried our caution too far, in thinking it necessary to obtain your sanction to the contract for a bridge over Rock creek. But, we were not singular in the doubts we entertained, respecting our right to dispose of the money entrusted to us, to any purposes without the limits of the City. Several of the Proprietors suggested the same to us; and it is probable, if it was not known, that you had been consulted on the subject, you would have recieved a regular complaint respecting our conduct—It is certain, that even now, those whose interests lie towards the Eastern branch are much dissatisfyed with the marked preference shewn to G:etown, by the bridge & causeway. We have allways, before we entered into any contracts, made it a point to consult those who were well acquainted with the business; for which we were about to contract. In considering the costs of the bridge, you must observe, that the Undertaker is subject to frequent interruptions in the prosecution of his work, from high & unusual tides—to even great risque of having his work injured, before he is properly prepared against accidents—The notice was however shorter, than could have been wished. But still, Mr Herbaugh was not without two active competitors, who were anxious to have undertaken the bridge, but were discouraged by the low estimate he sent in as it appeared to them.[1]

Inclosed is a copy of Major L'Enfant's letter to us, declining our offers.[2] The only application yet made to us, for the office of Superintendant, has been, by Mr Clarke of Annapolis[3]—His terms were ten pr Cent on the expenditures—We declined his offer without entering into any explanation with him, concerning such extraordinary wages. Will it not be best, to wait till the plans of the buildings are exhibited, before we make any engagement with anyone? Mr Blodget appeared to me from my short acquaintance with him last Fall, to be an ingenious sensible man. He is I believe a man of taste and observation too, but I think the office of Superintendant requires something more than taste, and a general superficial knowledge of architecture. Mr Blodget cannot I expect pretend to more than this—Whether he is even so far qualifyed as this, or not, was I will venture to say, no consideration with the Proprietors who recommended him. A great part of these gentlemen have lately speculated much in Purchases of lands in the City—Their situation will not permit them to hold these long in their possession. They bought with the professed intention of selling out in a short time, for a high price, and very fiew of them look so far forward, as the ultimate success of the City, for the establishment of their fortunes. Mr Blodget being celebrated as a great Speculator, and having great acquaintance with this class of people, would answer well their selfish and temporary views—Tho' he may be very well qualified in every respect, I think this is the only point of view in which those who recommended him, have considered him. My conjecture is much confirmed by an extraordinary confession of Mr Stoddert's to Mr Carroll & myself—Speaking of L'Enfant's dismission, he said, his only reason for wishing him to be continued a little longer, was, that he had speculated a good deal in the City, and wished to sell out to advantage—that the high opinion concieved of L'Enfant might enable him to do it—that afterwards, he should have been well enough pleased with his dismission, having never considered him as well fitted for the execution of the business—I think he must have been off his guard, in giving such an explanation of his motives, for wishing to retain L'Enfant. He and his Partners, (tho' they may not allways appear) may be considered, as the prime movers of every thing which is so far matured, as to reach you. I cannot upon the whole, help thinking, that there are fiew of the Proprietors whose opinions deserve to be noticed; being the chief of them, most intent on such measures which may ensure present gain, without any consideration of their future tendency.

The completion of the navigation of the Potomac, is certainly a most important object. We gave directions at our late meeting, for a very considerable increase of lands. A good part of the canal at the lower Falls is walled, and Coll Gilpin thinks the whole may be done by the last of August. A call of eight pr Cent is made, to enable us to proceed with vigor. Matarials are ordered to be preparing for the locks. The river between the two falls, as soon as the waters have fallen sufficiently, will be attacked. It is our wish that Smith should visit the James river locks—we have accordingly written to him on the subject, requesting he would[4]—I think a full meeting of the Company in August, would be desirable; when I think it would be well to make another call for money.

At our Election on monday last, for members to the Assembly,[5] Coll Mason was present, and appeared quite transported at your having rejected the Representation bill. He seems now to think, every thing will go on well; and prophecies the happiest effects from this salutary check—It gives equal satisfaction to all I have yet heard mention it. I am Dr Sir, with the greatest respect Your Affectionate Servt

Dd Stuart.

ALS, DLC:GW.

1. For Leonard Harbaugh and his bridge over Rock Creek, see GW to Thomas Jefferson, 21 Mar. 1792, n.1.

2. The enclosed copy of Pierre L'Enfant's letter to the commissioners of 18 Mar. reads: "I this Day received your favor of the 14th Instant informing me you have ordered *five hundred Guineas* to be paid to me by Messrs Cunningham & Nesbit of Philadelphia, which sum you mention as intended for compensation—adding to it a Lot in the City—without enquiring of the principle upon the which you rest this offer[.] I shall only here testify my Surprise thereupon & in testimony of my intention to decline accepting of it, I hasten expressing to you my wish & request that you will call back your Order for the money & not take any Trouble respecting the Lot" (DLC:GW).

3. Joseph Clark (Clarke) had presented his plans for public buildings and proposals for the Federal City to GW at Mount Vernon in November 1790 (see Alexander Contee Hanson to GW, 2 Aug. 1790, n.1).

4. James Smith had been appointed manager of the Potomac River Company in 1788 (see GW to George Gilpin, 29 May 1788, n.3).

5. Stuart is referring to Monday, 16 April 1792.

From the United States Circuit Court Judges for Pennsylvania

Sir. Philadelphia, the 18th April, 1792.

To you it officially belongs to "take care that the Laws" of the United States "be faithfully executed." Before you, therefore, we think it our duty to lay the sentiments, which, on a late painful occasion, governed us with regard to an Act passed by the Legilature of the Union.

The People of the United States have vested in Congress all *legislative* Powers "granted in the constitution."

They have vested in one supreme Court and in such Inferior Courts as the Congress shall establish "the *judicial* Power of the United States."

It is worthy of remark, that, in Congress, the *whole* legislative Power of the United States is not vested. An important part of that power was exercised by the People themselves, when they "ordained and established the Constitution."

"This Constitution" is "the supreme Law of the Land."

This Supreme Law "all judicial Officers of the United States are bound by oath, or affirmation, to support."

It is a Principle important to Freedom, that, in Government, the *judicial* should be distinct from, and independent of the legislative Department.

To this important Principle the people of the United States, in forming their Constitution, have manifested the highest Regard.

They have placed their *judicial* Power, not in Congress, but in "*Courts.*" They have ordained that the "Judges" of those Courts "shall hold their Offices during good Behaviour," and that, "during their continuance in Office, their Salaries shall not be diminished."

Congress have lately passed an Act "to regulate," among other Things, "the claims to invalid Pensions."

Upon due consideration, we have been unanimously of opinion, that, under this act, the Circuit Court held for the Pennsylvania District could not proceed.[1]

1. Because the Business directed by this act is not of a judicial nature: It forms no Part of the Power vested, by the Constitution, in the Courts of the United States. The Circuit Court must, consequently, have proceeded *without* constitutional authority.

2. Because, if, upon that Business, the Court had proceeded, its *Judgments*—for its *Opinions* are its *Judgments*—might, under the same Act, have been revised and controuled by the Legislature and by an Officer in the executive Department. Such revision and controul we deemed radically inconsistent with the Independence of that judicial Power, which is vested in the Courts, and consequently, with that important Principle which is so strictly observed by the Constitution of the United States.

These, Sir, are the Reasons of our conduct. Be assured, that though it became necessary it was far from being pleasant. To be obliged to act contrary either to the obvious Directions of Congress or to a constitutional Principle, in our Judgment equally obvious, excited Feelings in us, which we hope never to experience again.[2] We have the Honour to be, with the most perfect consideration and Respect, Sir, Your most obedient and very humble Servants,

James Wilson
John Blair
Richard Peters

Copy, DNA: RG 46, Second Congress, 1791–1793, Records of Legislative Proceedings, President's Messages; LB, DLC:GW.

For the background to the protest of the federal judges against the Invalid Pensions Act, see Caleb Brewster to GW, 15 Mar. 1792, n.4, the U.S. Circuit Court Judges for New York to GW, 10 April, enclosure, and GW to the U.S. Senate and House of Representatives, 16 April.

1. On 13 April, William Haburn (Haburne), a Revolutionary War veteran from Virginia, presented a memorial to the House of Representatives "setting forth that he had applied yesterday to the Judges of the Circuit Court in this city to be put on the pension list pursuant to a late law of Congress; and that the Court having refused to take cognizance of his case, he was obliged to apply to Congress for relief. . . . This being the first instance in which a court of justice had declared a law of Congress to be unconstitutional, the novelty of the case produced a variety of opinions with respect to the measures to be taken on the occasion. At length a committee of five was appointed to inquire into the facts contained in the memorial, and to report thereon" (*Annals of Congress,* 2d Cong., 556–57). On 18 April the committee's report was read and tabled.

2. GW laid this document before Congress on 21 April.

From Otho Holland Williams

Dear Sir Baltimore 18th April 1792

If my letter, of the 22d ultimo, has been the cause of *the least* displeasure to you it will prove a source of lasting regret to me. A regret which I shall feel the more sensibly as the object of my proposal was, in my own estimation, too inconsiderable to have induced the smallest risque of your disapprobation.

Your silence, My Dear Sir, and my own reflections induce the apprehension that some impropriety may have appeared to you of which I was unconscious.

If my apprehension is not founded in error I wish, not that you would give yourself The trouble, or me the pain, of shewing me my fault; but that you would have the goodness to cancel the letter, and obliterate from your memory every trace of an incident which, whatever it may be, while it is remembered by you will not fail to inflict on me the severest regret and mortification.[1]

With the most reverential respect and Esteem, and allow me to add, with the sincerest affection, I am, Dear Sir Your most Obedient, and Most Humble Servant

O. H. Williams

ALS, DLC:GW; ADfS, MdHi: Otho Holland Williams Papers. The cover of the receiver's copy is marked "Private."

1. GW replied to Williams on 26 April.

From John Hall

May it please the President Philada 19 April 1792.

By the Law for establishing a Mint of The United States I find a Treasurer will be requisite.[1]

I am encouraged by Several of my friends to apply to your Excellency for that appointment and would beg leave to refer to their recommendations for my sufficiency to fullfil the duties of the office.[2] For myself I can only promise my best exertions, diligence & fidelity, should I be so happy as to be honoured with the appointment, and am with the greatest respect, Yr Excellency's Mo. Obt hble Servt

Jno. Hall.

ALS, DLC:GW.

The writer of this letter was probably John Hall (1729–1797) of The Vineyard in Anne Arundel County, Md., a lawyer, slaveholder, and landowner. He served as a delegate to the Continental Congress in 1775, in the lower house of the Maryland legislature 1762–85, and in the state senate 1786–96.

1. For "An Act establishing a Mint, and regulating the Coins of the United States," which GW signed on 2 April, see William McCrea to GW, 27 Mar. 1792, n.1. Section 3 of the law states that "The Treasurer shall receive from the Chief Coiner all the coins which shall have been struck, and shall pay or deliver them to the persons respectively to whom the same ought to be paid or delivered: he shall moreover receive and safely keep all monies which shall be for the use, maintenance and support of the mint, and shall disburse the same

upon warrants signed by the Director." The treasurer of the Mint was to receive an annual salary of $1,200 and was to be bonded for $10,000 (see 1 *Stat.* 246–51).

2. GW received two certificates recommending Hall. The first was signed in Philadelphia on 18 April by Thomas Hartley, William Vans Murray, William Findley, Joshua Seney, and others; the second, dated at Philadelphia on 19 April, was signed by Thomas McKean, Clement Biddle, and others (both in DLC:GW). GW nominated Tristram Dalton treasurer of the U.S. Mint, not Hall (see GW to the U.S. Senate, 3 May [second letter]).

From Alexander Hamilton

Treasury Department April 19. 1792

The Secretary of the Treasury has the honor to transmit to the President a copy of his letter of the 8. of March to the minister Plenipotentiary of France, on the subject of an advance of money, and another of the minister's answer;[1] in order that the President may be pleased to cause the necessary instructions to be sent through the proper department to the minister Plenipotentiary of the United States, at the Court of France.[2]

LB, DNA: RG 59, Instructions to Diplomatic Officers, Instructions, 1785–1906; copy (letterpress copy), DLC: Jefferson Papers.

For the background to this document and its enclosures, see Hamilton to GW, 8 Mar. 1792, source note.

1. For Hamilton's enclosed letter to Ternant of 8 Mar., see Hamilton to GW, 8 Mar., n.1. The enclosed copy of Ternant's reply of 10 Mar. reads: "I have received the letter you have taken the trouble to write to me in answer to that which I had the honor to address to you the day before yesterday. After the assurances you give me of the full repayment of the demandable part of the debt of the United States to France, and the necessity under which the law respecting this debt lays your Government to anticipate the reimbursement in consideration of the favorable conditions offered, I cannot do otherwise than accept the sum which you are willing to advance, and to agree to the terms proposed for carrying the same into effect.

"As to the indemnification, necessary to prevent all risk on the part of the United States, I prefer, if it should meet the approbation of the President, that this particular should be settled at Paris, on the grounds, or the alternative, mentioned in your letter. In consequence whereof I will transmit this letter to the Court, and in the mean time inform them of the obliging readiness with which the government of the United States has listened to the requisition I made in favor of St Domingo. It remains for me to request of you, Sir, to cause to be paid the 400,000. dollars to M. [Antoine-René-Charles Mathurin] de la Forest, or his order, and to anticipate the latter payments as fast as the Treasury arrangements will permit" (DNA: RG 59, Instructions to Diplomatic Officers, Instructions, 1785–1906).

2. On 28 April, Thomas Jefferson sent instructions and a copy of the correspondence between Hamilton and Ternant to Gouverneur Morris (see *Jefferson Papers,* 23:467–69).

From Betty Washington Lewis

My Dear Brother [Fredericksburg, Va.] April the 19: 1792

I receivd yr letter of the 8th of April and am under great obligations to you, for the kind proposials there in Contain'd—Howels absence from Town at this time prevents his acknowledging—your kindness with his own hand I shall send an express of immediately with yr letter to him, and you may expect an answer in less than a Fortnight.[1]

Howell my Dear Brother is a Boy of very Slender Education—his Fathers Death at so Early a Period has been a great disadvantage to him, left without any Person of Age and Judgement[2]—to examine his improvements he has been entirely left to him Self—and of Course not very well informd, However he has an exceeding Good disposition and the employment you have design'd for him not difficult, I hope when you see a letter from him it will answer your Expectations, However you will be the best Judge. with sincere love to My Sister Yr Self & Family I am Dear Brothe. Your Affctionate Sister

Betty Lewis

ALS, PWacD.

1. Howell Lewis's letter of acceptance, written to GW at Fredericksburg on 24 April, reads: "I should have done myself the pleasure of replying to your letter on its receipt by my Mother, but was at that time engaged in her business in Frederick; I consider myself extremely favour'd by your proposal of a birth in your family & shall chearfully accept it provided my probation is deemed satisfactory—I lament that I have not been more attentive to the improvement of my writing tho hope that I shall soon be qualified to do the business for which you mean to enploy me" (ALS, owned [1997] by Ms. Julie Rinaldini, New York, N.Y.). Howell Lewis joined GW's staff in mid-May (see Betty Washington Lewis to GW, 14 May).

2. Fielding Lewis died in January 1782, when his son Howell was 10 years old.

From John Francis Valley

Philadelphia April 19th 1792

The Petition and Representation of John Francis Vallee Most respectfully Sheweth

That your Petitioner is a native of France and being Attached to the cause of America in the late contest with great Brittain in the year one thousand seven hundred and Eighty One left his native Country and came over to America in the Capacity of a Soldier in the Legion of French Troops commanded by the Duke Lozun.

That your Petitioner being influenced by a zelous regard for the rights and liberties of this Country Engaged in the Battle that was fought at York Town in Virginia against Cornwallis when and where he unfortunately got wounded—That your Petitioner afterwards was reduced to the necessity of leaving the Army being in a great measure rendered incapable in doing Military duty and afterwards setled in the City of Philadelphia and purchased a House with the remains of his Fortune which shortly afterwards was unavoidably burned by accident.

Thus, your Petitioner is now circumstanced—wounded in with many others in obtaining liberty sovereignty and independence to this Country—having a Wife and Family to support—is reduced to the necessity of applying to the President—whose benevolence friendship and humanity is well known and Experienced both by Frenchmen and Americans especially to those who have been so unfortunate as your now Petitioner—and humbly solicits that the President would grant him an Office in such Publick Station as by him may be deemed proper—and your Petitioner engages should he be favour'd an appointment in any Public station he will discharge every duty that may be enjoined on him incidental thereto with fidelity and integrity and always conduct himself to the perfect satisfaction of the President—for whose prosperity health and long life no Frenchman can have a more ardent wish for than your Petitioner.

John fr. valley

DS, DLC:GW.

John Francis Valley (Jean-François Vallée; Veillée) was probably one of the sixteen troopers in the legion commanded by Armand-Louis de Gontaut, duc de Lauzun (1747–1793), who were wounded during a cavalry engagement on

3 Oct. 1781 at Gloucester Point, Va., across the York River from Yorktown. After Valley moved to Philadelphia, he opened a boardinghouse on Fourth Street, which was probably the building that he mentions as having burned. Valley, who was living in a boardinghouse on Cherry Street in 1794, lived in Philadelphia throughout the 1790s (*Philadelphia Directory,* 1794, 157; *Pennsylvania in 1800,* 628). He apparently never received a federal appointment from GW.

From Samuel and Sheppard Church

May it please your Excellency Philada 20th Apl 1792

The enclosed[1] was received a few days past ℘ the Aeriel Capt. Carson from Cadiz who saw the unfortunate writer in a Prizon in that place where he had been carried from the Havannah in the Island of Cuba,[2] he had written to Mr Carmichael but had not received any answer altho a longer time had elapsed than necessary for that purpose.

We pray your Excellency to give directions that application may be made to the Spanish Government for his release from Confinement,[3] which will be thankfully acknowledged by the unhappy prizoner and Yr Excellencys Mo. Hble Serts

Saml Church
Sheppard Church

LS, DNA: RG 59, Miscellaneous Letters.

Samuel Church was a Philadelphia merchant who owned property in Southwark (*Heads of Families* [Pennsylvania], 212–13; *Philadelphia Directory,* 1791, 21).

1. The enclosure was a letter that the Churches' brother John Church had written GW from Havana sometime in October 1791. It reads: "I arriv'd here in a Spanish ship in the Year 1787 from St Augustine—two years I follow'd the Business of a Goldsmith (to which I. wass bred.) with proffitt to myself & satisfaction to my Employers—at the Arrival of Dr Lewis, las Cassas [Luis de Las Casas], the present Govr here—some person who Expected to Obtain a pension for his Villany, lodg'd an Information with the Govr that I had been drawing planns of the Forts & fortifications of this place—I. wass hurried to a Dungeon and after two Weeks Confinement wass Examin'd by the Govr—the planns were—A ground plott of the City of Philadelphia—another of the Wharfs &c.—these were what I. had drawn and no Other—neither had I. Capacity or Inclination to draw any other—these I. had Drawn the year before and had given as a play thing to an Old Dotag'd Man—After being confind one Month, I. wass Order'd on board the ship Providence, Oliver Bowen Master for America—in Conversation with Bartholomew Crawford the Interpreter he told me that the Govr and every other person wass well Convinc'd of my

Innocence and that I. wass only order'd off the Island for the present as it wass expected an Approaching Warr—but that the Govr had no Objections to my Returning and even reside here if I thought proper—this Induc'd me to return Mate of the same ship with a Cargo of Negroes to this City—a small dispute Ariseing between the Captn and myself I. left the ship and Engag'd my passage in a small Vessel Bound to Charleston—but being detain'd selling their Slaves longer than I. expected, I. wass solicited by Captn Cook (of the schoonr Appelucia) to go his Mate to Pensacola & from thence to Philada—it being Necessary for me to Appear before the Govr for a pasport he ask'd me if I. wass not the person who wass prisoner here last Year—I. answer'd I. wass—he then Charg'd me with Returning contrary to his orders and Immediately order'd me to pison where I. have been Confin'd since the Month of August—I have sent a Memorial to the Govr Informing him of my being Ignorant of his Orders and that the Interpreter had Inform'd me very Different—I. wrote to McNamarra Russel Esq. Commanding his Brittannic Majesties Ship Diana who happend to put into this port Informing him of my Situation—who Accordingly Demanded me of the Govr and Recd for Answer that I. wass an American Subject and that he wou'd Keep me in prison as long as he thought Proper" (DNA: RG 59, Miscellaneous Letters).

2. GW also received from John Church, probably sometime after 24 April, another letter, written at "Cadiz Prison" and dated 22 Feb. 1792. It reads: "The ways of Heaven are dark and Intricate Puzzeld in Mazes and perplexd in Errors the mind searches for them in Vain Sir [Joseph] Addisson [*Cato* 1.1.49–51] puts the Above words into the mouth of Cato who wass Labouring under a Complication of woes for his Suffering Country—I make use of them because they express my Situation the best of any in the English Language. I am very Sensible that my Sufferings are and have been in a great Measure because I happen to be an American Subject had I been a Brittish Subject I shou'd have been sent on board his Majesties Ship Dianna at the Havanna—and at my Arrival here had I been a Brittish Subject I shou'd only have been Confin'd to the house of the Consul. Thou great Omnipotent Being. above the thoughts of all Supremely Wise. what is it that I have done to have incurr'd thy divine Displeasure by being punish'd in such an Eminent Degree. had my whole life been one Continu'd Scene of Wickedness methinks my punishment has Already been more than sufficient—but I bow with submission to thy Divine Will not knowing when the regular Confusion will end—I leave your Excellency to Judge my feelings and Situation Labouring under Sickness the Horrour ⟨of⟩ a Spanish Prison and what is worse than all the rest to be Suspected being a Spy—on my Arrival here the Brittish Consul wass Applied to Know wether or not he wou'd be Security for my Appearance when Call'd for—in which case I shou'd not be sent to Jail. he Replied that as my case wass of a very Delicate Nature and as he had done several Acts of Kindness for the Americans and had wrote sev⟨eral⟩ times to Mr Carmichael on the Subject, yet that Mr Carmichael had not the common politeness to return him an Answer—Mr [Keyran] Welch [Welsh] mercht of this place Inform'd me that a few months ago he Brought into this Country from Congress a packett of Letters—these he Immediately forwarded to Madrid—Mr Carmichael had not been so polite as to

Acknowledge the Receipt of them though fully convinc'd they had been receiv'd—But how will your Excellency be Surpriz'd when I Inform you that I have wrote two Letters To his Excellency Wm Carmichael at Madrid fully Informing him of my very Delicate Situation and at the same time sent him Copies of what I wrote your Excellency from the Havana—at the same time Earnestly requesting him Immediately to Interest himself in my behalf that if he wou'd write to the Brittish Consul on this Occasion I might at least be Bail'd to the Consuls House—yet as I said before how will you be Surpriz'd when he never Deign'd to return an Answer—I make this Complaint against Mr Carmichael as I very severely Suffer a Confinement in this Jail either through his Pride or Indolence—thus I am left alone by Mr Carmichael without council or advice on this so very trying an Occasion—Left to my own Meditations but Concious of my Innocence I defy the World.

"⟨*mutilated*⟩ Excellency will se[e] the propriety of Appointing an Agent or Consul in this City happy for me had there been one on my Arrival in this place I shou'd not have been sent to Prison—the Brittish Vice Consul in this City has in Conversation with me pointed out the Necessity there wass of Congress Appointing a Consul here—that frequently the Americans on their comeing here Involve themselves in Difficulties and then when in that Situation Apply to the Brittish Consuls for their Asstance—I cannot passover in Silence the Obligations I am under to Mr David Porter of this City (formerly in the service of the United States first in the 12th Virginia Regt afterwards Captn in the 3d Pensylvania Regt commanded by Colnl [Thomas] Craig) 'tis to his Kind Attention and Assiduities that the Brittish Consul has agreed to become Security for my Appearance when calld for that I may be Liberated from this Jail. I do not Attempt to dictate to your Excellency but if any person here be Appointed as a Servt of the publick I know of no person who stands in so Deserveing a light—Oh! Liberty thou sacred priviledge of Americans—And may thou ever remain so—may Savage Tyranny and Ambition never Destroy thy sacred fruits—in the same manner that I have been dragg'd to Spain wou'd the Americans have been Dragg'd to Great Brittain on the most frivilous pretences and like me have been Depriv'd of a Trial by their peers of the Vicinage or perhaps any trial at all—Pardon me sir for writeing so freely to you but tis a Subject that Awakens all my feelings and I feel for once happy that I wass one of the first that ⟨ever⟩ arm'd to Assert the Rights of my Country and rescue it from Destruction—To Conclude—it Appears highly probable that I shall be kept prisoner untill your Excellency either writes to this Court or sends some person to Demand my Liberty and if that is Denied may my Country in Vengance draw that Fatal sword that is the Scourge of Tyranny and never return it to its Scabbard untill the Southern World enjoy the sweets of Liberty

"'Till the freed Indians in their Native groves
Reap their own fruits and woe [woo] their sable loves
Then stretch thy Reign fair Peace from Shore to Shore
Till conquest cease and slavery be no more.' Pope"

(DNA: RG 59, Miscellaneous Letters; poetry paraphrased from Alexander Pope's "Windsor Forest," ll. 405–8).

3. On 24 April, Thomas Jefferson wrote Samuel and Sheppard Church: "The President has referred to me your letter, covering that of John Church, dated from the Havanna Oct. 91. It does not appear from these papers of what country he had been a citizen. It is presumable he was not of the United States because engaged in a traffic unauthorized by the laws of the United States. His application to the Commander of a British ship of war induces a conjecture that he had been a British subject. But having settled as a Goldsmith at the Havanna, and there carried on his trade two years, and appearing to have been of St. Augustine before that, he had made himself a Spanish subject, was liable to their laws, was charged and found guilty of an offence against their government, by the competent authority of the country, and is now under punishment for that offence. Were he a citizen of the U.S. we should be bound to respect the judgment pronounced on him by the regular authority of the country, till it's injustice should be proved palpably. But having made himself a Spanish subject, we have no more right to enquire into that judgment than the court of Spain would have to do the same with respect to the criminals now in our jails. I am sorry therefore to be obliged to give it as my opinion, that it is a case in which this government ought not to interfere" (*Jefferson Papers,* 23:455).

From Abijah Hart

Sir, New Haven 21st April 1792

The establishment of a national Mint presents me an opportunity of petitioning your Excellency for the Office of Treasurer in that Department—Being disengaged from other Business, my wish will be to serve my Country, in that way, by faithfully discharging the Duties of my Station, so long as I may preserve the Confidence of the Public. My Character I submit to my friend the Hon. J. Hillhouse Esq.[1] & shall gratefully acknowledge every public Favour. I am Sir, with the most perfect esteem your obedient and most humble Servant

Abijah Hart

ALS, DLC:GW.

For discussions of the establishment of the U.S. Mint and the position of treasurer, see William McCrea to GW, 27 Mar., n.1, and John Hall to GW, 19 April 1792, n.1.

By the time Hart next wrote GW, in the spring of 1796, he was a New York City merchant engaged in trade with Portugal (see Hart to GW, 13 June 1796, DNA: RG 59, Miscellaneous Letters). GW nominated Tristram Dalton treasurer of the U.S. Mint in May 1792, not Hart (see GW to the U.S. Senate, 3 May [second letter]).

1. James Hillhouse (1754–1832), a graduate of Yale College who had served

in a military capacity during the Revolutionary War, was a member of the Connecticut state house of representatives 1780–85, the state council 1789–90, the U.S. House of Representatives 1791–96, and the U.S. Senate 1796–1810.

From Henry Knox

Sir [Philadelphia] Saturday 4 oClock P.M. 21 April [1792]

I have the honor respectfully to submit a draft of a proposed letter to Governor Blount, of which, the clerk has just finished a copy.[1]

Genl Putnam left this City, this Morning, to return early in the next week. I am Sir Most respectfully Your obedient Servant

H. Knox

Dr Allen will be in readiness to return on Monday. He is getting Clothes made and his accounts are to be settled.[2]

ALS, DLC:GW; LB, DLC:GW.

1. The enclosed draft of a letter from Knox to Southwest Territory governor William Blount has not been identified. Knox had received a letter from Blount, written at Knoxville and dated 20 Mar. (Carter, *Territorial Papers,* 4:129–30), on 14 April, and he had transmitted it to Tobias Lear the same day for submission to the president (DLC:GW). Lear apparently returned this letter to the secretary of war on 15 April with GW's request that Knox report his opinion on the steps that needed to be taken (DLC:GW).

The letter that Knox sent to Blount on 22 April, which GW apparently approved, reads: "I have the honor to enclose you a duplicate of my letter to you of the 31st ultimo acknowledging the receipt of yours of the 2d ultimo by Mr [David] Allison, and containing some general principles relative to the militia you may judge expedient to call into service, for the defensive protection of such parts of your government as are exposed to the incursions of hostile Indians—and also containing the approbation of the President of the United States, for the proposed conference with the Chickasaws and Choctaws at Nashville on the first day of June next.

"Having on the 13th instant received your letter of the 14th of the last month, I shall now reply to it, and the one of the 2d of the same month.

"But previously thereto, I take occasion to state, That it is the most ardent desire of the President of the United States, and the general government, that a firm peace should be established with all the neighbouring tribes of Indians on such pure principles of justice and moderation, as will enforce the approbation of the dispassionate and enlightened part of mankind.

"That it is the intention of the President of the United States, that an adherence to this desire as to a well founded maxim, shall be the leading feature in the administration of Indian affairs while he is at the head of the government.

"That he shall lament, exceedingly all occasions which shall either suspend or impede the operations of those principles, which he considers essential to the reputation, and dignity of the Republic.

"That in pursuance of these ideas he endeavoured that a genuine state of their situation, and of the general dispositions of the United States upon this subject should be brought home to the minds of the western Indians before any co-ercion was attempted.

"That although the essays to this end were then ineffectual, yet it has been his directions that similar intimations should be continued.

"That therefore, every effort is making in order to impress the hostile Indians with their past errors—That the United States require nothing of them but peace, and a line of conduct tending to their own happiness.

"That all which has past shall still be buried in oblivion provided that they will immediately agree to a treaty of peace, in which they will obtain all they can possibly desire and relinquish nothing; for we demand none of their lands.

"That we are not sensible the hostile Indians, that is, the Miami and Wabash Indians, have any just claim to lands comprehended in the former treaties—But notwithstanding, if they can show they possess a fair right to any of those lands they shall receive a liberal compensation for the same.

"It is presumed if these sentiments could be fully impressed on the minds of the hostile Indians (and measures are taking for that purpose) that the establishment of tranquility on the frontiers would be the probable consequence.

"But if the hostile Indians should, after having these intentions of the government laid fully before them still persist in their depredations on the frontiers, it will be considered as the dictates of humanity to endeavour to punish with exemplary severity so incorrigible a race of men in order to deter other tribes in future from a like conduct.

"I have been thus particular in detailing to you these sentiments in order that you may lay them before the assembled nations at the proposed conference in full and strong terms.

"It will therefore be only in the result of the hostile Indians continuing in their hostility that the aid of the southern Indians would be required—But as this result will be known and as the commanding general will be directed to communicate it to you by expresses, while you are at the conference—You will of course proceed in obtaining the number mentioned in the letter to general Pickens, which is enclosed open for your perusal and consideration.

"The President of the United States being very favorable impressed with the character of general Pickens, is greatly desirous, if the war must proceed, that he should command the Indians combined with other troops.

"You will therefore please immediately to forward the letter to general Pickens, first sealing it—and upon receiving his answer, you will transmit it to Richmond by express, whence it will arrive by the stages as soon as by express.

"Mr Allison has been detained for the arrival of the spring ships—But he has now provided all the goods you requested as pr Invoice herein enclosed, excepting the rifles which unfortunately cannot be obtained here without taking those which are designed for the rifle Corps.

"If Mr Allison can obtain the number requested in the southern district, he is requested so to do.

"He will embark with the goods for Richmond on the 25th instant.

"Besides the Goods, which amount to Eight thousand, one hundred and ninety one dollars, eleven cents; he is charged with the sum of Two thousand dollars to pay for the provisions and other expences of the treaty as stated in your estimate: together with the sum of seven hundred and fifty dollars, contingencies of the treaty.

"In addition, he is charged with the sum of Three thousand dollars, for to pay the expence of transportation to Richmond and thence to your government.

"He is also charged with the further sum of Three thousand dollars, for to pay the Levies, who served in the campaign under general [Arthur] St Clair.

"I am anxious to hear of the safe arrival of Mr [Leonard] Shaw with you, and that they have gone forward into their nation continuing in that grateful state of mind in which they departed from this place.

"I flatter myself the manner of their treatment here, and the impressions of good designed by the United States for their, and the other friendly nations, will be received by joy by all the well disposed Cherokees—and will of course put to the route the ill disposed and bloody minded.

"We have in this city at present a numerous delegation of the principal Chiefs of the five nations, who have been invited to make this visit in order to prevent their being influenced to war, by the hostile Indians and their emissaries—They will return in a few days apparently well satisfied and have engaged to repair to the Miami village in order to influence the Indians in that quarter to peace.

"I am commanded by the President of the United States, to whom your letters are constantly submitted, to say with respect to your remarks upon the Line at Littleriver, that you will be pleased to make a liberal construction of that article, so as to render it entirely satisfactory to the Indians, and at the same time as consistently as may be with the treaty [of Holston]—and to observe, that he is satisfied with your sentiments on that subject.

"It is submitted to you, as the late depredations by the Cherokees must in some degree have interrupted that harmony and confidence, which ought to have flowed from the treaty of Holstein—whether, it will not be for the public interest to invite a few of the Chiefs of the Cherokees, to be present at the proposed conference at Nashville.

"And it were to be wished that Mr [Alexander] McGillivray's affair with [William Augustus] Bowles would permit him also to attend,—Provided you should be convinced of his cordiality to the post at Bear's creek, and the employment of some Creeks.

"You would then have an opportunity perhaps of talking over the whole affair relatively to Bear's creek, which the Chickasaws relinquished as a trading post, by the treaty of Hopewell.

"If this could be established by the general and open consent of all the tribes, it would be well—But it is to be apprehended that starting a new object at the mouth of Duck river [i.e., establishing a post there], would have the effect to excite suspicions and jealousies and unhinge any confidence they may have—That at this crisis the risque of injury would far over balance any advantages, and therefore the attempt ought not to be made.

"The distance from Duck river to Nashville is not more than fifty or sixty miles—and although not quite as convenient as at the mouth Duck river, yet the difference is not so great as to require any hazard of bad consequences from the attempt.

"General [James] Robertson has from his situation, character and other circumstances, incurred expences on account of the Indians, for which he has petitioned Congress—The petition is referred to me—Although general principles of equity seem to support the claim, more especially coming from a man of his character, yet it is extremely difficult to establish a general principle by law, to compensate such unauthorized advances without fixing dangerous precedents.

"The object of my mentioning this is, that in future, and until further arrangements, the President of the United States will consent that General Robertson be considered as temporary agent for the Chickasaws, with an appointment at the rate of Four hundred dollars per annum—you will therefore please to administer to him the oath of office which you yourself have taken.

"It is to be observed that the law authorizing such appointments has not yet passed, and that therefore this appointment can only at present have a temporary aspect.

"He will in future distribute such things, and perform such duties for the conciliation of the Choctaws, Chickasaws and others, as you shall from time to time direct.

"The business of the proposed conference will be interesting to the United States. I am happy it will be managed by you in person, as I am satisfied the government may rest with great confidence, in your exertions, as well as abilities to execute its wishes.

"The great object in managing Indians, or indeed any other men however enlightened is to obtain their confidence. This cannot be done but by convincing them of an attention to their interests—Deeply convinced of this general disposition of their protectors, they will be yielding in smaller matters.

"The Indians have constantly had their jealousies and hatred excited by the attempts to obtain their lands—I hope in God that all such designs are suspended for a long period—We may therefore now speak to them with the confidence of men conscious of the fairest motives towards their happiness and interest in all respects—A little perseverance in such a system will teach the Indians to love and reverence the power which protects and cherishes them. The reproach which our country has sustained will be obliterated and the protection of the helpless ignorant Indians, while they demean themselves peaceably, will adorn the character of the United States.

"It is the special direction of the President of the United States, that there be a *full* representation of the Chickasaws and Choctaws, and that all who shall be assembled shall have impressed on their minds clearly and strongly, the dispositions of the general government towards the *hostile tribes particularly,* as well as to all the *tribes generally*.

"You will find in the letter to General Pickens, that it is the desire of the President that the total of the Indians to be employed, should not exceed Five hundred warriors; and if the arrangement could be so made, that these should be taken in such proportions from the Creeks, Cherokees, Choctaws and Chickasaws as you shall judge proper. The number so constituted, would induce them to consider the war as a common cause, as well among one another as with the United States. It must be understood however, that the number of Five hundred is not be considered as an ultimatum, but only as a general idea to govern the number to be employed.

"It will be necessary that you should intimate to General Pickens, that you are in confidence made acquainted with the letter to him, and that you should also know the tenor of his answer.

"If the Indians should object joining our troops on account of not being well armed, you may assure them they shall be well supplied at Fort Washington with smooth bored muskets, but they cannot be promised Rifles.

"Any subordinate arrangement of characters which you shall judge proper to accompany them will be confided to your discretion—and also the nature of the rewards for their services, which however must not exceed the pay of the troops—with rations they will be abundantly provided. I am—&c.

"N.B.—In the duplicate transmitted by Mr Allison, the blanks were filled as above inserted—and the following added closing the letter.

"Instead of the sum of seven hundred and fifty dollars mentioned in this letter for contingencies of the Treaty, a warrant has been issued for this consideration for one thousand dollars.

"The sum of two thousand dollars is now advanced for the provisions at the Treaty, any excess of this sum will be paid on the final adjustment of the accounts" (Carter, *Territorial Papers,* 4:137–42).

David Allison (d. 1798), the deputy paymaster of federal troops and county militia in the Southwest Territory since 1790, had arrived in Philadelphia at the end of March carrying a letter from Blount to Knox dated 2 March. While in the capital he collected goods for Blount's upcoming treaty with the Choctaws and Chickasaws (see Knox to Blount, 31 Mar., ibid., 131–32).

2. Dr. Deodat Allen returned to western New York to deliver Knox's invitation to Joseph Brant and instructions to Israel Chapin, who had been appointed temporary deputy agent to the Five Nations (see Knox to Chapin, 23 April, in *ASP, Indian Affairs,* 1:231). Allen accompanied Brant to Philadelphia in June 1792, and he served in 1793 as a surgeon in the Ontario County, N.Y., militia (see Knox to GW, 22 April, n.2, and GW to Gouverneur Morris, 21 June 1792, n.5).

From Leonard Marbury

Sir Frederica [Saint Simons Island, Ga.] April 21st 1792

Mr Hamilton whom I sent to the upper Creeks in Jany last, has Just return'd with the pleasing Accts of the friendly disposition of that Nation, and their intention to have set out the 15th Instant in order to run the Line, he also brings us the Certainty & Particulrs of the taking of Bowles, by the Spaniards at St Marks, I have desired him to wait on your Excellency, and give the Particulars, he is a young Man of Truth, and may be depended on.[1]

I take the liberty of droping a few hints, relative to the mode of managing the Southern Tribes, in Order to preserve a Peace on which in a great measure depends the existence of this State. If they should meet your Excellency's approbation, and be found useful I shall feel myself happy.

First I conceive, the most essential means of Securing their Friendship, is by securing their Trade, and if Possible Wresting it out of the Hands of Panton Leslie & Co. who has for many Years supply'd them,[2] and has ever been invetirate Enemies to Our States, and has to my knowledge been in a great Measure the Cause of keeping the Indians at War with us, and indeed the little Trade at this time Carried on from Georgia is rather injurious, as the small Stores on our Frontiers are generally Calculated to draw down a few Hunters, which are induced to sell their Skins & Horses, they then get intoxicated and Quarrel with the Whites, and on leaving the settlements are almost sure to Steal Horses in order to Carry home whatever they may Purchase, they are generally follow'd by Parties of the Whites, little, if any better than themselves, and are in Turn rob'd of all they have, and indeed our People frequently begin by Stealing their Horses, in which case they are sure to make reprisals. This being the Case I think it would be better to keep the Indians and Whites as far seperate as Possible.

When the Trade of those Nations were Carried on entirely from this Country, the Merchant supply'd the Trader, who had, by giving Bond & Security for his Conduct, a Licence for a Particular Town, and dare not under a heavy Penalty Trade in any other, or buy a single skin in the Woods, or any where out of his Town, or dare a Mercht buy any thing of an Indian unless in a Town for which he had Licence, then the Indian was obliged to return to his home before he could dispose of his Hunt, or Horse, and of Course had no inducement to go into the settlement unless with an Intention of Stealing, which put the Inhabitans on their Guard, and any Inhabitant Trading with an Indian otherways than by a Licence as above; was subject to the Penalty of One Hundred Pounds sterling for every offence.

It might be good Policy to grant a priviledge to some Person to import Goods for that Trade, clear of duty, as no beginner can stand in Competition with a House so ever establish'd, as that of Panton Leslie & Co. unless they can import on equal Ground with them; but I conceive it woud be the Int. of the Public to take the whole into their own Hands and Confine the Trade to themselves; fit out a Trader to each Town, who shall be accountable for his Conduct. And when an Indian does any Mischief, and on demandg, Satisfaction is refus'd, Stop the Trade of the Town he belongs to, untill satisfaction is given. Or if hereafter the Creeks appear inclin'd for War, I make no doubt, but the Chocktaws, and Chickasaws, May be induced to fall on them, which wd effectually secure us.

As there are a Number of White Men among the Indians of Infamous Characters, such as cannot be reclaimd & brot over to our Intt ought to be remov'd by some means or other, as they are either Stealing themselves, or encouraging the Indians to Steal from Georgia & Cumberland and sending the Stolen property to West Florida. I am with due esteem your Excellencys most Humble Servant

Leod Marbury.

ALS, DNA: RG 59, Miscellaneous Letters.

Leonard Marbury (c.1749–1796) was born in Prince George's County, Md., and moved to Georgia in the early 1770s. He served as a deputy surveyor for St. Paul's Parish in 1772, and he was a member of the second Georgia provincial congress in 1775 and a lieutenant colonel in the state cavalry during the Revolutionary War. Marbury also was a delegate to the state constitutional convention of 1789, and he represented Glynn County in the Georgia legislature in 1791. By 1794 he had moved to East Feliciana Parish in Spanish West Florida. While visiting New Orleans in 1796, Marbury contracted yellow fever and died.

1. Marbury wrote on the cover of this letter that it was being delivered to GW "by Mr Hamilton." For a discussion of the administration's difficulties in getting Alexander McGillivray to run the boundary line between the United States and the Creek territory and of McGillivray's chief rival, William Augustus Bowles, who had been captured by the Spanish in February 1792, see Henry Knox to GW, 14 Nov., source note and note 1, 26 Dec. 1791, n.2, and Knox to Tobias Lear, 30 Nov. 1791, n.1, 17 Feb. 1792, n.1.

2. For a discussion of the firm of Panton, Leslie, & Co., see Knox to GW, 6 July 1789, n.1, and Secret Article of the Treaty with the Creeks, 4 Aug. 1790, source note, enclosed in GW to the U.S. Senate, that date.

From Elizabeth Willing Powel

Dear Sir [Philadelphia] April 21st 1792

I have taken the Liberty to send you a Pamphlet[1] which is, at this Time, a Subject of much public Animadversion, and I have done it under the Impression that, from a Consciousness of the Rectitude of your own Conduct, you will read it without Emotion, and that you wish to collect the Sentiments of Mankind with Respect to our public Measures & public Men; and, further, as I have ever thought the highest Compliment that cou'd be paid to the Magnanimity of a great & good Man by a Friend was to treat him with Candor, which, according to my Ideas, cannot be done if his Friend conceals from him Strictures that, however remotely, may affect him.

This Pamphlet appears to have been written either by an imprudent Friend of Mr H. or by an Enemy to the Government who wishes to create Disgust between the Heads of the great Departments. If you have already perused it be so good as to return me the Pamphlet if not keep it as long as you wish.[2] I am Sir with Sentiments of Respect & Esteem Your affectionate Friend

Eliza. Powel

ALS, DLC:GW.

1. The enclosure was *Strictures and Observations upon the Three Executive Departments of the Government of the United States* . . . (Philadelphia, 1792) by "Massachusettensis," whom the editors of the modern edition of Thomas Jefferson's papers have identified as Sir John Temple, the Massachusetts-born British consul general in the United States (see Henry Remsen, Jr., to Thomas Jefferson, 11 April 1792, source note, in *Jefferson Papers,* 23:401–3). The pamphlet lavishes praise on Alexander Hamilton's financial policies as secretary of the treasury and criticizes the supposedly pro-French policies of Secretary of War Henry Knox and Secretary of State Thomas Jefferson, claiming that they would disrupt American trade with Great Britain. For other attacks on Jefferson, see Anonymous to GW, 3, 20 Jan., and March 1792.

2. GW returned the pamphlet to Powel on 23 April.

From Archibald Robertson

New York April 21st 1792

Sir Mr James Renwicks No. 92 William Street[1]

Agreeable to your desire, I have the honor to intimate that the picture for the Earl Buchan being finished,[2] I mean to take the opportunity of a Ship that sails from this soon for Scotland to transmit it to his Lordship, any commands you may have for his Lordship, I shall be happy to have the honor to forward.[3] I remain Sir with the highest respect Your Most Obdt Hble Servt

Archibald Robertson

ALS, DLC:GW.

1. New York City merchant James Renwick headed a household of eight people at 92 William Street until at least 1795 (*Heads of Families* [New York], 119; *New York City Directory,* 1792, 125).

2. For more information about Robertson and the portrait of GW that he was painting for the earl of Buchan, see Buchan to GW, 28 June 1791, n.3, GW to Buchan, 1 May 1792, and the frontispiece to this volume. By 11 Jan. 1792 Robertson had completed a miniature watercolor-on-ivory life portrait of GW, from which he executed the larger oil painting for Buchan. Contrary to Robertson's claims in his letter of this date, he did not send the larger portrait to Buchan until the spring of 1793 (see Tobias Lear to GW, 9 Nov. 1793).

3. On 1 May, Lear forwarded to Robertson GW's letter to Buchan of that date. Lear's cover letter to Robertson says that GW had commanded him to "acknowledge the recet of your letter to him of the 21st ultimo—and to thank you for your polite attention in giving him information of an opportunity of writing to Earl Buchan. The enclosed letter for his Lordship the Presidt commits to your care & profits by your obliging offer to forward it. The Picture which you have taken for the Earl the President hopes will be satisfactory. Your knowledge of the size to correspond with others of his Lordships collection has undoubtedly enabled you to accommodate it to his wishes. And if you will be so good as to transmit to me the amount of the Picture I will have it paid to you immediately" (DNA: RG 59, Miscellaneous Letters).

From James Seagrove

Sir Rocklanding on the Oconee [Ga.] 21 April 1792

My last letter to you was from Savannah under date of the 12th Inst.[1] agreeably to what I then wrote I have returned to this place where I found my Interpreter just got back from General McGillivray with a letter in reply to mine of the 25th Ulto. For your information I now enclose you extracts from his two last letters to me, by them you will be informed of his intention of com-ing down to meet me, he seems in good humour with me and I hope to keep him so.[2]

My Interpreter tells me, that there remains much confusion in the Nation, it seems some of Bowles associates or partners have sent large packets of Letters, directed to Genl Bowles, which they say is from his friends on the other side of the great Water, and that all that Bowles promised them was on the point of being realized, and that though Bowles is now in the hands of the Spaniards, yet in forty days he will return to them again.[3]

There is a villain of the name of Wellbanks, who came with Bowles, who spreads those stories, and I believe fabricates those letters—I hope General McGillivray will be able to lay hands on him and his letters and will make an example of him to the Indians and all future adventurers.[4]

It is reported (and I believe with truth) that two men are lately killed by the Indians about fifty Miles above this place, this is said to be done by a party of the Cowettas in revenge for two of their people, which were murdered by the Georgians some Months past. Frequent applications having been made by the Indians to the Government of this State for redress by punishing the perpetrators, but not being able to get satisfaction in that way, they gave notice that they should retaliate, which I believe they have done as I have advice from the King of the Cowettas & Cussetas that the relations of the deceased Indians were out to take revenge, which they could not longer prevent.

These are unpleasant matters, but we may look for such events taking place frequent, whilst there is not energy in the Governt of this State to punish such wretches as those who wantonly killed the Indians that occasions the death of the innocent persons aluded to above.

Martin Johnston the principal in murdering a Cowetta Indian some time past near this place now lives near the shoals of great Ugechee about thirty miles from hence undisturbed.

Whilst the people of this Country will shelter such wretches as Johnston among them they ought not to wonder at the Indians revenging themselves on the innocent whilst they protect the Guilty.

When General McGillivray and the Chiefs come here I shall do all in my power to please them and get our business forwarded. I am sorry to find so great a number of the valuable Officers about to leave this place at so critical a juncture, when great discretion and strict dicipline may become more necessary—when we have to do with drunken Indians, it would be fortunate that we had sober Officers: I must say I am not pleased by the appearance of matters at this Station—but as you will soon see Major Rudolph Captains Mills and Porter, you will have opportunity of being fully informed from those Gentlemen.[5]

I shall do myself the honor of writing you by Major Rudolph in about six days[6] and am &c.

This Letter I have entrusted to Serjeant Torry of Captain Burbecks Company who goes forward I understand in hopes of promotion I have known him ever since his first arrival in this Country and my opinion of him is that he is a most deserving Young man.[7]

Copy, DLC:GW.

1. Seagrove's letter to GW of 12 April has not been found.

2. The enclosed extracts have not been identified.

3. For more information about William Bowles, who was not released as promised by the Spanish officials at New Orleans but sent to Spain by way of Cuba, see Secret Article of the Treaty with the Creeks, 4 Aug. 1790, source note, enclosed in GW to the U.S. Senate, 4 Aug. 1790, Minutes of Creek Council, 2 Mar. 1789, source note, enclosed in Memorandum from Tobias Lear, 18 Aug. 1790, Henry Knox to GW, 14 Nov. 1791, n.1, and Henry Lee to GW, 16 April 1792, n.1.

4. George Wellbank (died c.1794) apparently first met Bowles in New York during the Revolutionary War, when Wellbank was apprenticed to James Rivington, the editor of the *Royal Gazette.* Wellbank accompanied Bowles to the Creek country from the Bahamas in 1788, and after Bowles was imprisoned in New Orleans, Wellbank oversaw the St. Marks, Fla., property and warehouse of Panton, Leslie & Company that Bowles had captured in January 1792. Wellbank retired to Usachees on the Chattahoochee with Bowles's personal belongings and papers after a party of Creeks under McGillivray's brother-in-law took over the warehouse at St. Marks later in 1792. Wellbank subsequently lived among the Chickamaugas near Lookout Mountain, and in 1793 he went to Detroit and Niagara to obtain British assistance (see Robert Leslie to William Panton, 30 Jan. 1792, Alexander McGillivray to Arthur O'Neill, 12 May 1792, and McGillivray to William Panton, 28 Nov. 1792, all in Caughey, *McGillivray of the Creeks,* 305–6, 322, 346–49; see also Wright, *Bowles,* 66, 69–70, 147–48).

5. For Seagrove's further report on the drunkenness of Maj. Richard Call, see Seagrove to GW, 5 July 1792. For previous complaints about Call's conduct as commander of the federal troops in Georgia, see Knox to GW, 9 July 1791. Michael Rudolph (1758–c.1795), who had risen to the rank of captain in the light dragoons during the Revolutionary War, was appointed a captain in the U.S. Army in June 1790, and he was promoted to major in March 1792 and to adjutant and inspector of the army in February 1793. Rudolph resigned from the service in July 1793. John Mills (d. 1796), who had served as a captain during the Revolutionary War, became a captain in the U.S. Army

in March 1791, and he was promoted to major in February 1793 and adjutant and inspector of the army in May 1794. He retired from the army in February 1796 because of ill health, just a few months before his death.

6. The next letter from Seagrove to GW that has been found is dated 5 July 1792.

7. Knox wrote Anthony Wayne on 12 Oct. 1792 that Daniel Torrey's name would be submitted to the president for a promotion. GW nominated him a cornet on 22 Feb. 1793, and the Senate approved his appointment the next day. Torrey was killed in action against the Indians at the Battle of Fort Recovery in the Northwest Territory on 30 June 1794 (see Knopf, *Wayne,* 114–16, 346; GW to the U.S. Senate, 22 Feb. 1793 [first letter]; *Executive Journal,* 1: 134). Henry Burbeck (1754–1848), who had served in the Continental artillery throughout the Revolutionary War and been brevetted a major at the close of the conflict, was appointed a captain in the U.S. Army in October 1786, and he was promoted to major effective 4 Nov. 1791, lieutenant colonel in May 1798, colonel in April 1802, and brevet brigadier general in July 1812. Burbeck was honorably discharged from the service in June 1815.

To the United States Senate and House of Representatives

United States [Philadelphia] April 21st 1792.

Gentlemen of the Senate, and of the House of Representatives,

I lay before you the Copy of a Letter[1] which I have received from the Judges of the Circuit Court of the United States held for the Pennsylvania District, relatively to the "Act to provide for the settlement of the Claims of Widows and Orphans barred by the limitations heretofore established, and *to regulate the claims to Invalid Pensions.*"[2]

Go: Washington

DS, DNA: RG 46, Second Congress, 1791–1793, Records of Legislative Proceedings, President's Messages; copy, DNA: RG 233, Second Congress, 1791–1793, Records of Legislative Proceedings, Journals; LB, DLC:GW.

1. For the enclosure, see the U.S. Circuit Court Judges for Pennsylvania to GW, 18 April 1792.

2. The House of Representatives read this message and its enclosure when they were received this day. The Senate did not receive them until 23 April, when "The Message and papers were read, and ordered to be put on file" (*Annals of Congress,* 2d Cong., 127–28, 572–73).

From Henry Knox

[Philadelphia, 22 April 1792].[1] Submits "Doctor Allens report,[2] Brandts Letter to Kirkland,[3] and a recommendation of Genl Chapin handed to me by Mr Elsworth."[4]

ALS, DLC:GW; LB, DLC:GW.

1. Tobias Lear docketed the cover of this letter: "From The Secretary of War 22d April 1792." On this day GW dined with twenty-two of the visiting chiefs from the Five Nations, their interpreter, and Samuel Kirkland (see Knox to Kirkland, 21 April, NCH: Samuel Kirkland Papers).

2. This report may have been Dr. Deodat Allen's letter to Kirkland, which Kirkland forwarded to Knox in mid-February 1792 (see Kirkland to Knox, 13 Feb. 1792, NCH: Samuel Kirkland Papers). Allen had been employed by Kirkland since early that month in delivering letters to and from the Mohawk chief Joseph Brant.

3. This enclosure was probably the letter that Brant wrote to Kirkland from Fort Niagara, N.Y., on 4 Feb., which Kirkland forwarded to Knox nine days later (see Kirkland to Knox, 13 Feb., NCH: Samuel Kirkland Papers). It reads: "Your long Epistle of the 3d ult. I six days agone received & the one of the 25th ult. by Docter Allen, I yesterday was favoured with. You'll perceive if it would have been impossible for me to have met you at the Genesee the 20th ult. agreeable to your proposal (not having recd yours untill eight days after the time you limited) even would circumstances have permitted, for this instant I must relinquish the thought of visiting your seat of government & great warrior President Washington. but shall probably 'ere long perform my promise, & make the tour I much wish for, the pleasure of being accompanied by so worthy a friend will add to the satisfaction & the information I shall receive from one so well calculated, & so willing to commucate to the unlightend as your self. Am particularly happy to hear that you are settled to your satisfaction in the Oneida Country & that you mean still to persevere in good works the accomplishing which will require patience and perseverance both of which I must say you are remarked for, since your general government has founded the Establishment & are anxious of suceeding in civilization. I have no doubt of their success, it may at first seem a difficult task particularly so to those who may be set over us unacquainted in any wise with our manners or Customs, but this is a circumstance easily surmounted, as there may always be found some well acquainted with us, with whom our Pastors might advise if themselves were uninformed—As the plan for this Civilization has been drafted by you (so well acquainted with us[)], & approved of your government as the Patrons of this good work, the assistance that will be rendered I suppose will enable you to begin the undertaking in person, with your usual alacrity, spirit & perseverance, there can be no doubt but the end intended will be answered. The good effects you mention that the Creeks & Cherokees begin to feel from the establishment will be an incentive to persue th[i]s great, this praiseworthy work, the accomplishing which must ever redound to the credit of the U.S. & mark the first Promoter with the highest public applause: The secret pleasing satisfac-

tion that the undertaker, will be afforded, in reflecting on the good works in which he will be daily employed, must be such as none but those in a similar pursuit, will be able to judge of, if doing good deeds will render a person fit for the Kingdom of Heaven, accomplishing this Xinlike desireable business of civilization *must,* & will render his (or their[)] names famous to posterity; should you be enabled to persue your intention, you shall find every assistance that I can any ways afford & shall ever be happy whenever opportunity may serve, to join my poor Endeavor, with yours in forwarding wt we both seemingly wish for. You assure me of personal safety & good usuage, should I be able to visit your seat of Government, This I doubt not, The invitation coming from a Superintendt of Indn Affrs—who acts by public Authority. we must certainly know that the Faith of your Nation is pledged for our good treatment. but without your friendly assurances I should be no ways apprehensive (though without any kind of invitation) of venturing myself amongst you, & have no doubt of meeting with many friends.

"Relative to what agreements were made at Newtown Council, as I was not there, the business being then transacted without me I should suppose that those who were there active, & acquainted with the business that passed, wd be the most proper people now to attend in order to settle what further arrangements may be necessary. Those people are more pointedly mentioned in your superintendents invitation, had I reced so particular a message to have attended at the last Treaty, & likewise at the one now intended to be held, I should no doubt have done myself the pleasure of being amongst them. Should there be any other business to be done at this treaty than at these hitherto, some mention ought to be made of what is intended that we might be prepared. The present situation of affairs require that a candid & just statement of facts be made on behalf of our Indian Tribes, in order that the people of the *United States* & us might understand each other fully. This has never yet been the case, those of our people who have attended your councils being swayed by private interested motives so long as they can get their own ends answered, care little of what becomes of our Confederacy in General. Troubling you longer on this Subject is needless, as I wrote you my opinion very fully last winter & have only now to say, that your Superintendants proposal of introducing Agriculture, & the mechanic Arts &c. was to have been considered of by the different nations, whose deputies were present when the proposal was made, Fish carrier great sky &c. &c. propose holding a council at Buffaloe Creek, [(]whenever our Runner returns) where they request my attendance, if you could make it convenient to yourself I should be very happy in meeting you, we might then have the pleasure of explaining matters personally & perhaps to the satisfaction of each other.

"I can not think of accompanying some of these who I dare say will agreeable to invitation go down, differing widely in opinion from each other, this would in some manner make my jaunt perhaps disagreeable, & must further say that the invitation to me was rather, in my opinion in a cool kind of stile (such as even wd circumstances admit of my now attending) my honor would forbid it. I am extremely sorry to be for the present deprived of the pleasure of visiting your President, who I dare say is as fine a looking man as you describe him to be, & might in the foreigners opinion (you mention) been a much finer man than either the King of England, or King of france—I have had the honour to be introduced to the King of England—a finer man than whom I think it wd be a truly difficult task to find. No doubt but you have long ee'r this heard of the unfortunate affair in the miamis Country, the consequence being what I expected, when I last wrote you. Steps may perhaps now be taken towards an accommodation which I much wish for" (NCH: Samuel Kirkland Papers).

4. The enclosed recommendation of Israel Chapin forwarded to Knox by U.S. Senator Oliver Ellsworth has not been identified. GW appointed Chapin temporary deputy agent to the Five Nations on either this day or 23 April (see Knox to GW, 21 April, n.2).

From Gabriel Peterson Van Horne

Sir, Baltimore 22nd April 1792

Sensable of the important Conerns, which Surround the President, I feel a diffidence in Offering this Address; But impression which Arise, from a regard for the General welfare, are the *motives* which *dictate,* And will I trust, plead an Appology.

Facility, and dispatch of Public intelligence, being an Object of Considerable importance; I beg leave To Suggest the propriety of such Arrangements, as will at least Effect a *more speedy,* and Competant establishment On the *Great soarce* of Communication, between the City of Philadelphia, and Richmond.[1]

The System now in practice require 5 days to Compleat a Tour—the Same returning Admitts of 10 Days for Answering Letters, or dispatches—Enclosd therefore, is Submitted, principles perfectly *practicable,* which will Accomplish the Distance in *4 Days*—Answers in *Eight.*

Objections may Arise from the habits of *indulgence* with The Citizens of Philadelphia—the detention of the Public Mails In that City Twenty One Hours, (and confind to a late Hour in the Morning) greatly *Embarrass* Expedition—This Circumstance of Detention, admits Expresses to *Anticipate,* the intelligence of the Public Mails, to the Disadvantage of the Community; & the Injury of the Revanue, and its *requisite* recoursces.[2] Permit me Sir, to Subscribe myself, Your Most Obedient, and Obliged Servt

Gabriel P. Van Horne

ALS, DNA: RG 59, Miscellaneous Letters.

GW often relied on the services of Baltimore stagecoach owner Gabriel Peterson Van Horne (see GW to Tobias Lear, 31 Oct. 1790, n.2).

1. Van Horne enclosed an undated document containing the propositions: "For Conveying the Mails from Philadelphia to Richmond in 4 Days—To arrive in Philadelphia at 5 Oclock P.M. and Closd at 12 Oclock P.M. the same Evening—Arriving in Richmond at 5 Oclk P.M. and Closd at 10 the same Evening.

"Mails Leaving Philadelphia and Richmond on Mondays Wednesdays and Frydays

"Returning Tuesdays Thursdays and Saturdays

"Progress

"The first Days Stage will Start from Philadelphia, and Richmond; and arrive the same Day at Bush Town and Fredericksburgh. the Second Day to the City of Washington—The third, to Bush Town and Fredericksburgh—the fourth to Philadelphia & Richmond—Making the City of Washington and George Town The Centre Post between Philad. and Richmd.

"This Establishmt to Continue from Ap[ri]l 1t to December 1t in Each Year" (DNA: RG 59, Miscellaneous Letters).

2. Tobias Lear replied to Van Horne for the president on 17 June, writing that the proposed arrangement "is now under consideration, and that, if, on a view of all circumstances attending it, it shall be thought practicable & conducive to the public good, it will be carried into effect" (DNA: RG 59, Miscellaneous Letters).

From Alexander Hamilton

[Philadelphia] 23 April 1792. Submits "the enclosed communications respecting an instance of misconduct in the Collector of Newbury Port."[1]

LB, DLC:GW.

1. The enclosures have not been identified. Stephen Cross, the collector for the port of Newburyport, Mass., was immediately removed from office (see Cross to Hamilton, 18 Oct. 1792, Syrett, *Hamilton Papers,* 12:590), and on 3 May, GW appointed Edward Wigglesworth to "supersede" him (see GW to the U.S. Senate, 3 May [first letter]).

To Elizabeth Willing Powel

Dear Madam, Philadelphia April 23d 1792.

I pray you to accept my Compliments and thanks for having favored me with the perusal of the enclosed "Strictures &ca"[1]—

And an assurance that the sentiments and charges therein contained, have not given me a moments painful sensation.

It is to be regretted, however, that the Author, if his object was to convey *accurate* information to the public mind had not devoted a *little* of the time and pains he appears to have employed in writing *this* Pamphlet in the investigation of facts. Had he done this, he would, or might have found, many of his Charges as unsupported as the "baseless fabric of a Vision."[2] With very great esteem, regard & Affection I have the honr to be Dear Madam Your Obedt & obliged

Go: Washington

ALS, ViMtV; LB, DLC:GW.

1. For the enclosed pamphlet, see Powel to GW, 21 April 1792, n.1.

2. GW apparently is quoting Prospero from Shakespeare's *The Tempest* 4.1.151.

From Alexander Hamilton

Treasury Department, 24 April 1792. Submits a contract for oil between the superintendent of the Delaware lighthouse and Joseph Anthony & Son of Philadelphia, the terms of which are not unfavorable to the United States, as they have not changed from the previous two years. Nothing better had been offered after an advertisement for proposals was published, and it is understood that the wardens of Philadelphia had purchased a part of the same cargo at an equal price.[1]

LB, DLC:GW.

1. A copy of the enclosed contract signed on 23 April by superintendent William Allibone and Joseph Anthony & Son in the presence of Robert Bulley, Jr., is in DNA: RG 26, Lighthouse Deeds and Contracts, vol. A, 17. It says that the firm would deliver to the Cape Henlopen lighthouse at least 1,600 gallons of the best strained spermaceti oil at the rate of 3s. 7d. Pennsylvania currency per gallon. Tobias Lear wrote Hamilton on 25 April informing him of GW's approval of the contract (DLC:GW).

From William Darke

Tavern 23 Miles from Phild. on the Lancaster Road
[c.25 April 1792][1]

Sir

I wanted much to have Seen you before I left the City but Judging you were much ingaged in business of Grate importance, did not wish to intrude I wanted to know who would Command the Army the ensuing Campain—as I am informed Genl St Clear has Resigned and in Cause Judg Some other will Soon be apointed—I writ to you from fort washington about the 8th of Novr in which Letter I mentioned Captain Snoden not being Calculated for the army,[2] I had bean informed by Some officers that his behaviour in the action, was Not as Good as was expected, and as I did not Se him during the time of the action, had Some doubts myself I have Since bean inform by Several officers that he behaved Like a Soldier and that his Refusing to Let any wounded officer Rides his horse on the Retreat, was excuseable as he Could not walk on account of a wound he had Receiv'd in the Service Last war with the birtish, in Concequence of which wound he Cannot Travle on foot, but would be Glad of an apointment in the Horse.[3] Ensign Turner who was taken by the Indions the 4th Novr is desierous of Serving in the army, I Should think his father would much Rather he Stai'd at home I would be Glad to Serve the young man but perhaps it would Serve him best to Send him to his parents, who I am informed are Rich and have no other Son So that I know not what to Say for him[4]—Should you think me worthy of any apointment in the army I should want To know who I was to be Commanded by.[5] Have the Honor to be your obt hume Servt

Wm Darke

ALS, DLC:GW.

1. GW docketed the cover of this letter: "From Colo. Wm Darke no date recd April 25th 1792." Darke possibly was writing from the Admiral Warren Tavern (also known as Ashton's Ferry), which was located twenty-three miles from Philadelphia at Whiteland, Chester County, Pennsylvania.

2. See Darke to GW, 9–10 Nov. 1791.

3. Snowden did not receive a military appointment from GW at this time.

4. Edward D. Turner (c.1762–1811) of Boston, Mass., who had returned to Philadelphia in the spring of 1792, was promoted to lieutenant in July 1792 and became paymaster for the 2d Sub-Legion. Made a captain in November 1793, he served as a brigade inspector from 1799 to 1802. After resigning his commission in November 1805, Turner became a planter and judge in LaFourche Parish, Louisiana Territory (see Henry Knox to Anthony Wayne, 20 July 1792, and Wayne to Knox, 30 Mar. 1793, both in Knopf, *Wayne,* 34–44, n.63, 208–13; see also *Columbian Centinel. Massachusetts Federalist* [Boston], 30 Nov. 1811).

5. Darke did not receive an appointment from GW at this time.

Message to the Five Nations

[Philadelphia, 25 April 1792]

My Children of the Five Nations—

You were invited here at my request, in order that measures should be concerted with you, to impart such of the blessings of civilization, as may at present suit your condition, and give further desires to improve your own happiness.

Colonel Pickering has made the particular arrangements with you, to carry into execution these objects, all of which I hereby approve and confirm.

And in order that the money necessary to defray the annual expences of the arrangements which have been made should be provided, permanently, I now ratify an article which will secure the yearly appropriation of the sum of one thousand five hundred dollars: for the use and benefit of the five nations, the Stockbridge Indians included.[1]

The United States having received and provided for you as for a part of themselves will I am persuaded be strongly and gratefully impressed on your minds, and those of all your tribes.

Let it be spread abroad, among all your villages and throughout your Land that the United States are desireous, not only of a general peace with all the Indian Tribes, but of being their friends and protectors.

It has been my direction, and I hope it has been executed to your satisfaction, That during your residence here you should be well fed, well lodged, and well cloathed, and that presents should be furnished for your wives and Families.

I partake of your sorrow on account that it has pleased the great Spirit, to take from you two of your number by death, since your residence in this City.[2] I have ordered that your tears should be wiped away according to your custom and that presents should be sent to the relations of the deceased.

Our Lives are all in the hands of our Maker, and we must part with them whenever he shall demand them, and the survivors must submit to events they cannot prevent.

Having happily settled all your business and being about to return to your own Country I wish you a pleasant journey, and that you may safely return to your families after so long a journey, and find them all in good Health. Given under my hand at the City of Philadelphia this twenty fifth day of April 1792.

Go. Washington.

Copy, NCH: Samuel Kirkland Papers; copy, DNA: RG 233, Second Congress, 1791–1793, Records of the Office of the Clerk, Records of Reports from Executive Departments.

For the background to this document, see Timothy Pickering to GW, 21 Mar., and GW to the Five Nations, 23 Mar. 1792.

On 23 April, Tobias Lear transmitted an apparent draft of this message to Henry Knox and requested him to incorporate proposed alterations and return the completed version, along with Timothy Pickering's official report of his proceedings with the Indians, to GW as soon as possible (DLC:GW). Two days later Knox sent GW a revised final copy of the message and the instructions that he had sent to superintendent Israel Chapin that day (NCH: Samuel Kirkland Papers). On 28 April, Knox sent Lear "Colo. Pickerings *last words*" for submission to the president (DLC:GW).

1. For GW's ratification of the annuity for the Five Nations, see GW to the U.S. Senate, 23 Mar., n.2.

2. One of the two Indians who died in Philadelphia, Peter Ojekheta, an Oneida chief, was interred with full military honors on 24 Mar. in the burial ground of the Second Presbyterian Church. The Seneca chief Karontowanen (Kalondowea), or Big Tree, died on 19 April after a short illness and was interred in the Friends burial ground two days later (see *Independent Gazetteer, and Agricultural Repository* [Philadelphia], 24 Mar., 28 April 1792).

From John Francis Mercer

Sir Philadelphia Apl 25. 1792.

I take the liberty of presenting to your notice for an appointment which I understand is not yet filled—Treasurer of the Mint—Mr Andrew Skinner Ennals,[1] Merchant of Baltimore Town—a long course of years passed in the active scenes of mercantile life have established this Gentlemans reputation for exactitude & punctuality in a very uncommon degree—his respectability in business is equalled by the extent of personal friendships which his merits have secur'd him & a very numerous family connexion which woud give weight to most appointments that coud be confered on him, Mr Henry particularly—Mr Carrol & all the Maryland Delegation & Mr Rupet from Delaware will all I am persuaded feel pleasure in coroborating the representation I have made of this Gentlemans merit. with every Sentiment of respect & attachment I am Sir Yr mo: Obt hble

John F. Mercer

ALS, DLC:GW. This letter is mistakenly docketed "28th April 1792."

For the background to the establishment of the U.S. Mint and the position of treasurer, see William McCrea to GW, 27 Mar., n.1, and John Hall to GW, 19 April 1792, n.1. GW nominated Tristram Dalton treasurer of the U.S. Mint in May 1792, not Ennalls (see GW to the U.S. Senate, 3 May [second letter]).

1. On 18 Feb. 1791 Andrew Skinner Ennalls had applied to GW for a position in the excise service, but he did not receive an appointment.

From Samuel Chace

Most Dear and Respectable Sire Providence April 26. 1792

Pray permit the address of your Servant who wishes every happiness to your Excellency. I Samuel Chace father in law to Majr William Blodget Son of John Chace Esqr. a Gentleman native of Barbadoes who married Honorably in Newport Anno 1713 and was a magistrate there much respected many years.[1] A Church warden With Godfrey Malbone Esqr. the elder—They together with greatest zeal and exertion had built that noble edifice the Episcopal Church in that Town. Being left at my Hon'd Fathers death Anno 1738 I was kindly taken care of by my hond Uncle Danl Updike Esqr. King's attorney or attorney General for the then Colony[2] till Anno 1742: then being twenty years old he Kindly assisted me to Credit in a good Store of goods in which being attentive I soon paid for them and went into navigation with Governor Hopkins Judge Jenckes and other respectable Characters here[3]—were concerned in upwards twenty sail of vessels, but in the French and Spanish war by various ways and means lost my property.

When prosperous I entertained gratis all Gentlemen travellers passing thro' Providence—In Anno 1754 I went to Philadelphia on a party of pleasure and was by good letters To Mr Franklin an invited guest at his house to dine with other Gentlemen, and I was his Deputy Post Master near ten years, and had the honor of his company to dine at my house. I have been honor'd in acquaintance in New York with many first Characters there and in Boston with Governors Shirley—Pownall—and Hutchinson, and with them dined by invitation—as also with very many first Merchants there where I was in good credit and trade for upwards thirty years—and have dined at sixteen different Gentlemens tables in Sixteen days there—Also at Portsmouth dined with the Elder Govr Wentworth and afterwards for a week with the principal Gentlemen of that Town—Sed Tempora Mutantur nos mutamur in illis.[4]

In Anno 1774 I was obliged to open house for boarding and had the pleasure of seeing at that time your excellency Genl of our armies at our house by invitation of Mr Blodget, and I then lodged all your life guard with pleasure gratis.[5] When Genl Sullivan commanded here and we a garrison'd Town the Marquis Fayette visited him and us often upon business of importance, and we had as visitors and many of them lodgers—Genls Lee—Gates—Steuben—Lyncoln—How—Bailey—and Spensor—with Brigadiers Huntingdon Douglas—Glover—The Duke de Lauson—Starke—Varnum and Cornal.

I was honor'd in my early days in our Episcopal Church here—made a Warden anno 1743—and so—many times after, and ever since one of the Vestry and as a psalmodist to this day, in which I serve gratis. Mr Blodget served on our Organ for some years—my son Doctr John Chace succeeded him and served gratis near twenty[6] years—he is very lately deceased to my great discomfort.[7] When he married about 13 years since, I had with him and wife then attending the ceremony Twelve children reckoning my own and sons and daughters in law all men and women in full health rejoicing on the occasion—It has pleased God to take them almost all away since save only one daughter—one daughter in law—with Blodget and Malcolms 2 sons in Law—I have served this Colony and state as a justice of the peace from Anno 1754 to this year 1792—and held Commissions under nine different Governors—Being the eldest I've served as Coroner twenty three years—and as Notary Public twenty years past.

My house which has covered us near fifty years having suffered in trade, I was obliged to mortgage and that is now call'd for, so must I be deprived of not only a covering, but being no longer a free holder must of course lose the little offices also—Alas who is sufficient for such trials without the interposition of Gods great and peculiar mercy and grace!

May I not with the great Chaldean Job cry out pity me Oh

my friends, for the heavy hand of affliction by Gods permission is upon me.[8] My children as many as his and my property all gone—what can I do without some friendly assistance at seventy years of age—Oh the ways of God are unsearchable and past finding out—I see no way to keep up my spirits—my dignity—my power of doing good of which I have been formerly possessed.

Could I be so happy as to meet your excellencys pity and compassion under these my distressed circumstances how happy should I be—Oh! I beg your blessing as Esau of old begged of his father Jacob—saying hast thou not reserved a blessing for me—Bless me even me also O my father[9]—With prayers for Gods blessing upon your most important Person, I rest your humble faithful Servant.

L, RHi.

1. Samuel Chace (b. 1722) was the eldest son of Capt. John Chace (d. 1738) and Anne Arnold Chace. He married Freelove Lippitt (c.1720–1801) in 1743, and the couple had ten children, including a daughter, Ann (Anne) Phillis, who married Maj. William Blodget (1754–1809). Blodget served as one of Maj. Gen. Nathanael Greene's aides-de-camp between 1776 and 1779.

2. Godfrey Malbone, Sr., was a prominent Newport merchant who outfitted privateers for the Royal Navy and served as a militia colonel during the 1740s and 1750s. Daniel Updike (c.1693–1757) served as attorney general for the colony of Rhode Island from 1722 to 1732 and from 1743 until his death. Updike's first wife, Sarah Updike, was the daughter of Gov. Benedict Arnold.

3. Stephen Hopkins (1707–1785) was a member of the Rhode Island general assembly 1732–52 and 1770–75, chief justice of the court of common pleas in 1739, chief justice of the superior court 1751–54 and 1773, and colonial governor 1755, 1756, 1758–61, 1763, 1764, and 1767. He also served in the Continental Congress 1774–76 and was among the signers of the Declaration of Independence. Judge William Jenckes (1675–1765) had been the first chief justice of the court of Providence, Rhode Island.

4. The following translation appears in the margin: "But the times ⟨are altered⟩ and ⟨we are⟩ altered with them." Chace is referring to Massachusetts governors William Shirley (1694–1771), Thomas Pownall (1722–1805), and Thomas Hutchinson (1711–1780) and Gov. Benning Wentworth (1696–1770) of New Hampshire.

5. Chace probably is referring either to GW's stay at Providence in April 1776 on his way to New York or his visit in March 1781 (see GW to Nicholas Cooke, 6 April 1776).

6. "Ten" was later written in above this word.

7. John Chace of Providence, R.I., headed a household of six persons in 1790 (*Heads of Families* [Rhode Island], 34).

8. Chace is quoting roughly from Job 19:21.

9. Chace is quoting from Genesis 27:34. Jacob was Esau's brother; Isaac was their father.

To Betty Washington Lewis and Sarah Carlyle Herbert

Dear Sister & Dear Madam, Philad. April 26th 1792.

Mr James Robardet,[1] who has taught my two Grand children dancing, proposes going into your part of the Country to establish a School, if he should meet with sufficient encouragement, and has requested that I would give him a line of recommendation to some of my friends. Mr Robardet's attention to my grand children, and the progress which they have made under his instruction, induce me to recommend him on these accounts from my own knowledge: He has likewise kept a dancing School in this City the winter past—in which I am informed he has given much satisfaction, and his conduct has been marked with decency & propriety, so far as I have heard.

G.W.

LB, DLC:GW.

Sarah (Sally) Carlyle Herbert was the wife of Alexandria, Va., merchant William Herbert and a frequent visitor to Mount Vernon.

1. James Robardet apparently moved from New York City to Philadelphia sometime in the early 1790s and gave dance lessons to Eleanor Parke Custis and George Washington Parke Custis.

To Otho Holland Williams

(Private)

Dear Sir, Philadelphia April 26th 1792

Your letter of the 18th Instt came duly to hand, as did the one to which it alludes.[1] To the latter I could make no reply for reasons which will (perhaps have) occurred to you. Sensible however, if you had not assured me of it, that you meant not to give me pain by the proposition therein contained, I can assure you that I feel none, and that, with the same esteem & regard I always professed to have for you, I remain Dear Sir Your Most Obedient and Affectionate Servant

Go: Washington

ALS, NjMoNP; LB, DLC:GW.

1. Williams's letter of 18 April alludes to his earlier letter to GW of 22 Mar. 1792.

Tobias Lear to Alexander Hamilton

United States [Philadelphia] 27 April 1792. Transmits by GW's command a letter from the supervisor of the District of South Carolina requesting a three-month leave of absence from his office.[1] "The President refers this request to the Secretary of the Treasury whose knowledge of the duties to be performed by the Supervisor will enable him to say whether it can be granted consistent with the good of the public service. If it can, the President observes, that he can have no objection to indulging the Supervisor."

LB, DLC:GW.

1. No such letter from Daniel Stevens of Charleston, S.C., supervisor of the revenue, to GW has been found.

Henry Knox to Tobias Lear

[Philadelphia] 27 April 1792. "I am unwilling to trouble the President with so many papers, but it seems necessary he should be acquainted with those what are now enclosed[1] from Mr Seagrove, and from Govr Blount."[2]

ALS, DLC:GW; LB, DLC:GW.

1. Knox had sent Lear on 26 April some unidentified papers to be submitted to the president (DLC:GW). The enclosures to this letter have not been identified, but the papers from William Blount might have been Blount's letter to Knox of 20 Mar. 1792 that covered various letters and reports concerning the growing discontent among the inhabitants of the five lower Cherokee towns (see Carter, *Territorial Papers,* 4:129–30).

2. Knox added the postscript "All quiet at Pittsburg and its neighbourhood" to the receiver's copy.

From Andrew Lewis, Jr.

Sir Russel County [Va.] April 27th 1792

I see amongst the appointments for the Companys of Rifflemen to be raised on the Frontiers of Virginia that my Brother Wm Lewis is appointed to the command of a Company, and am heartily Sorry that his Situation would not allow him to accept the appointment he some time past was left a Widower with two small Children—and was a few Days prior to his receiving his Instructions Married[1] no Doubt but the long Friendship that Subsisted between your Excellency and our Deceased Father was the occasion of his meeting with the appointment—I have heard of Severals refusing to take their appointments amongst whom is Mr Hawkins now in Actual Service as Lieutt in my Company rais'd for the Defence Frontiers of this State that with his bad State of Health obliges him to refuse—if in there rooms others are appointed I would take the Liberty of recommending Mr James Bryan of Montgomery County as Ensign[2] a young man of an exceeding good Character & I would be answerable for his conduct as an Officer and well used to that of useing a Riffle if appointed will assure his Serving & will forever acknowledge it as a Singular Favour confered on myself, I should have been happy to have Served on that Expedition if I could have been in the Horse Service. I have Sir the Honor to be your Excellency's mo. Obedt Servt

Andrw Lewis

ALS, DLC:GW.

1. For GW's appointment of officers for the frontier companies, see the enclosure to his second letter to the U.S. Senate of 6 March. William Lewis was a son of Brig. Gen. Andrew Lewis, Sr. (1720–1781), and Elizabeth Givens Lewis. In 1793 he accepted a captaincy in Lt. Col. William Russell's Ky. militia regiment. During Maj. Gen. Anthony Wayne's campaign, he commanded a company in Maj. William Price's battalion of mounted volunteers, which had been called into federal service in 1794 as part of Brig. Gen. Robert Todd's brigade. Lewis served until his discharge in 1796.

2. At GW's request Alexander Gibson was appointed in place of William Lewis (see Henry Knox to GW, 12 May 1792). No evidence has been found suggesting that GW ever appointed James Bryan an ensign.

From Elihu Palmer

Sir, Philadelphia April 27th 1792. Cherry Alley No. 13

A person unknown to you respectfully presumes to ask your attention to what follows: In addressing a character of such known & distinguished merit, I feel a diffidence suited to my humble situation; but still I hope you will condescend to hear my prayer. Possibly you may have heard of me thro' the channel of those religious prejudices, which a disclosure of opinions has excited in this city. Be this as it may, I beg leave to observe, that by a variety of circumstances, I am now in a state of poverty & distress;

and this, not by any fault of mine; but the effect of unavoidable events. I have a wife & one child to take care of. My object is to go into the practice of the Law in this state; but I must perish with want, if cannot obtain pecuniary assistance to support me for three or four months till I can obtain business. It is therefore with the utmost respect, that I presume upon your goodness to lay me under obligations of this kind. I do not suppose, that the extension of your beneficence to a private individual can add to the greatness of your character already established in the minds of a free & enlightened people; but the gratitude of my heart, the only compensation which I could give, would perpetuate the charitable deed. As you, Sir, are unacquainted with me, I send you enclosed my admission at the bar in Georgia, together with Judge Walton's recommendation.[1] I am, Sir, with the greatest esteem your very humble Servt

Elihu Palmer

ALS, DNA: RG 59, Miscellaneous Letters.

Elihu Palmer (1764–1806), a native of Canterbury, Conn., who graduated from Dartmouth College in 1787, served as minister of the Presbyterian Church at Newtown, Long Island, in 1788 and 1789, when he moved to Philadelphia and joined the Universalists. Palmer's liberal deism was too much even for them, and he outraged the community by proposing to preach against the divinity of Jesus Christ. After briefly studying law in western Pennsylvania, Palmer returned to Philadelphia in 1793. His wife died during the yellow fever epidemic of that year, and he himself lost his eyesight, after which he moved to Georgia and then New York, where he founded a deistical society.

1. The enclosed credentials of admission to the Georgia bar and the recommendation from George Walton have not been identified. On 9 May, Palmer wrote GW, requesting the return of the credentials and recommendation, "as I expect in a few days to make application for admission here; and as those papers will be very serviceable to me" (DNA: RG 59, Miscellaneous Letters). Palmer was admitted to the Philadelphia bar in June 1793.

To Thomas Jefferson

[Philadelphia] Saturday 'forenoon 28th April 1792

In strict confidence the President of the U.S. sends the enclosed letter for the perusal of the Secretary of State.[1] *No other person* has seen, or been made acquainted with the contents. It is necessary the Secretary should be informed of the circumstances related in the letter—'Tis possible, these politics may have contributed to the change in the Spanish Ministry. I wish Mr Short was, or soon would be, at that Court.[2] I think also Mr Morris should be urged to embrace every favourable moment to relieve this Country from the impositions laid by France on our (Tobacco) trade &ca.[3]

AL, DLC: Jefferson Papers.

1. The enclosure was Gouverneur Morris's letter to GW of 4 Feb. 1792, which describes the growing political power of the Jacobins and the resulting change in French foreign policy that occurred when Jean-Marie-Antoine-Claude de Valdec de Lessart succeeded Louis-Philippe, comte de Ségur, as foreign minister. The new ministry sent a diplomatic mission to Great Britain that proposed to cede France's Caribbean possessions as well as the Spanish-held island of Tobago in return for an alliance against the Holy Roman Empire and Prussia.

2. For the appointment of William Short and William Carmichael as commissioners to negotiate a treaty with Spain, see GW to the U.S. Senate, 11 Jan., and Jefferson to GW, 18 Mar. 1792. Short received his instructions in November 1792, left The Hague in mid-December, and arrived at Madrid in early 1793 (see GW to Jefferson, 29 June 1792, n.2).

3. For the background to the French trade restrictions and the administration's desire to negotiate a new commercial treaty with France, see Jefferson to GW, 18 Jan., 30 July 1791, n.1, Lafayette to GW, 7 Mar. 1791, n.1, Louis XVI to GW, 28 May 1791, n.2, and GW to Jefferson, 9 Dec. 1791, n.3.

From William Smith

Sir Philadelphia April 28th 1792

The American Revolution, in which you have sustained so glorious a Part, being one of the most important Events produced in the Annals of Time, and becoming every Day more important, with Respect to its Consequences in the Dissemination of the Principles of Liberty and Virtue among the Nations of the Earth, a faithful *History* of that Event, commencing from the Treaty of Paris in 1763, comprizing a State of the Colonies at that Time, the predisposing Causes of the *Revolution,* the Conduct of the War, the *civil* and *military* Characters of those who bore an illustrious Part in it, and in the Establishment of Peace, Liberty and Safety, under the present happy Constitution of the United States—such a History as this, founded on authentic Documents, drawn up with Impartiality and Judgment, in a truly *classical* Style, to abide the Test of Ages, is now become an interesting *Desideratum,* not only in America, but among mankind in general.

Some of the *Histories,* or Accounts, of the Revolution, which have been hitherto compiled from the Materials at Hand, to meet the Avidity of the Public, have much merit, and will be of considerable Use to any One who shall be thought worthy of the Confidence of *Government,* and be permitted to have Access to such of the State-Papers and Documents, as in the Wisdom and Discretion of the President, or of the Ministers and Heads of Departments, shall be deemed necessary and proper materials for rectifying Mistakes, and producing a more compleat History upon the Plan proposed above.

The Writer of this, for many Years before the Time, at which he proposes to commence this History, has not been an indifferent nor inactive Spectator of the Affairs of America, and has had abundant Opportunities of preparing materials for the Work, which He has long had in View; although his other Employments have not permitted him to make any considerable Progress in digesting and arranging them. But he has now a near Prospect of being relieved, in a manner not disagreeable to Himself, from a laborious Station which he has honourably sustained for near *forty* Years past; and hopes (after a few months to be spent in the Western Counties of this State in the Settlement of his *private,* and also some public Affairs) he shall be able to devote the Remainder of his Life, so long as it may please God to continue his Abilities, to a Review and Publication of some of his own Writings, Theological, Philosophical and Political; and therewith in the drawing up the History proposed above, if he can be so happy as to obtain the Countenance and Protection of the President of the United States, in the Prosecution of the Work.

He has communicated his Plan *only* to the Secretary of State and the Secretary of the Treasury; requesting their Recommendation to the *President*; and if thereupon, and the President's own Judgment of the Capacity and Integrity of the Writer, he shall be favored in his Request, he will faithfully engage that no Use shall be made of any Paper with which he may be entrusted, otherwise than shall be approved of by those Gentlemen, or the President Himself, so far as his & their other weighty Concerns may allow them Leisure to peruse the Sheets during the Progress of the Work. It will also be his Wish that until the Work shall be finish'd, it may not even be known to the Public that he is engaged in it. All which is humbly submitted

William Smith

ALS, DNA: RG 59, Miscellaneous Letters.

For more information about the Rev. William Smith, see Smith to GW, 21 Sept. 1789, source note. Two volumes of Smith's collected works (Philadelphia, 1802–3) were published before his death, but they contain mostly religious sermons and none of his historical writings.

On 8 May, Thomas Jefferson drafted and GW initialed the president's reply to Smith: "I learn with much satisfaction from your letter of April 28. that you propose to undertake a history of the American revolution, and shall with pleasure procure you any aids I can towards the faithful execution of the work. I will therefore desire the heads of the Executive departments to communicate to you such papers of useful information in their respective offices as they, in their discretion, shall think may be communicated with propriety" (DfS, DNA: RG 59, Miscellaneous Letters; LB, DLC:GW).

From Anonymous

Monday ½ past 9 Oclock

General Washington, Sir, [30 April 1792][1]

Amid'st the more important objects which call your Philanthophy into action on a general scale, may not an individual intrude with his embarrassments stated.

I have found it in vain to complain to trees, and to pour out where there is either a want of sentiment or ability, is equally fruitless: therefore I have resolved (perhaps improperly) to apply where there is both ability and benevolence; and if I am soliciting it in a channel over confined I must put up with the disappointment. Its the first instance I ever knew in my time or by tradition of one of our family's ever soliciting the aid of any Man of Station although they came as early as 1653 into this Country, and indeed its as painful to me as your Excellency may think it improper; but as the trains who depend solely (and in the supreme being) on my success in life are both numerous and helpless that silences all my pride, and further I can scarcely believe that the Author of all good, can intend that where he has implanted so great a prepenity to administer good as I have always felt that he intends I should yield to these miserable prospects which now lays before me, and are inevitable without speedy aid from some powerful Patron; miserable not on my own account for I had rather dig for life and ask only one blessing from heaven that is health; than to ask a favor from mortal, but when I consider how many must be made miserable by my fall I can do any thing to prevent ruin which Justice will Warrant; and did you know how dear those where to me who will be most effected (I am confident you would pardon any improper application, for inde[e]d it would take up many sheets to point out one half the miseries which would attend my Ruin, which I fear is too certain without pecuniary aid; and on procuring some Stock, which I have not a right to make an absolute sale of, I though[t] all difficulty was over in raising money: however I am much disappointed; for the Na. Bank will not loan a shilling as I have no paper already in; nor can I find a single person here nor in N. York that will do it: so being almost brought to dispair I have taken this great liberty of troubling your Excellency with the application of effecting a loan on a deposit of Stock; and if you choose to treat it with neglect as being an unbecoming freedom, you will please to commit this Scrawl to the flames; but if there is any disposition to aid me, I can in this City get a certificate shewing how far my Relations may be credited, in case there should be a disposition to honor me with an interview: however as treating this application with entire silence may perhaps be in your Excellencey's opinion the contempt it merits, from the improper nature of it; so it will perhaps save a mortification to the person, who had the enthusuism and folly & perhaps it may not be amiss to say, the unparrelled impudence, to send a Scrawl near two Years ago, addressed to the same person, on a like subject.[2]

P.S. If any attention is though[t] due, to this line; you will please to send out a line to your porter, and the bearer will call in about 20 minutes; please to direct what hour I shall wait on your Excellency to have any chat on the business in case application is not thought all together improper.

AL, DLC:GW.

1. Although this letter is docketed "May 1st 1792," the dateline indicates that it was written on Monday, 30 April.

2. For the author's earlier plea for assistance, see Anonymous to GW, 9 July 1790.

From Charles Carter of Ludlow

My Dear Friend Fredericksbg [Va.] April 30th 1792.

I am told Major Jackson is about to leave you, and that you have written to yr Nephew Howell Lewis to go up.[1] If you shou'd be in want of another, give me leave to mention to you my son Chs L. Carter;[2] he has had a good education, is well acquainted with the Greek & Latin languages, writes a good hand and very correct, as a specimen of which I have made him copy this Letter.[3]

The wheel of fortune has made it necessary, for me, to endeavor, to put my sons, in a way of getting their livelihood. my Eldest Son Walker, is bound in Philadelphia, to a Mr Hunter, a Coachmaker.[4] his master speaks well of him. my two youngst, are bound to Farmers. Colo. Meade, Mr Geo. Fitzhugh of Prince Wm[5] and if you can take this Boy I shall be happy. If he was not my Son, I shoud say more, but depend on the word, of a sincere Friend. the Boy will please you, in any instance. Mrs Carter joins in compliments to yr good Lady & Famly. I am with every sentiment of regard yr Affe Friend & Hble St

Chs Carter

LS, DLC:GW.

1. For William Jackson's departure from GW's official family and Howell Lewis's employment as recording secretary, see GW to Jackson, 26 Dec. 1791, n.1, and Betty Washington Lewis to GW, 19 April, n.1, and 14 May 1792.

2. Charles Landon Carter (1774–1832) had received a classical education from the Rev. Thomas Ryan and worked as an assistant to a Fredericksburg, Va., physician since November 1791 (see Charles Carter to Thomas Jefferson, 21 May 1791, and Elizabeth Chiswell Carter to Jefferson, 3 Nov. 1791, *Jefferson Papers,* 20:473–74, 22:256–57). Carter later completed his medical studies at the College of Philadelphia and served as mayor of Fredericksburg (see Jefferson to Charles Carter, 10, 31 July 1791, and Charles Carter to Jefferson, c.6 Aug. 1791, ibid., 20:613, 705, 22:3).

3. This paragraph is in the handwriting of Charles Landon Carter.

4. Walker Randolph Carter (born c.1772) began a two-year apprenticeship with Philadelphia coachmaker William Hunter in November 1791 after his earlier failure to obtain a clerkship at the State Department (see Jefferson to Elizabeth Chiswell Carter, 1 Oct. 1790, Elizabeth Chiswell Carter to Jefferson, 3 Nov. 1791, ibid., 17:551–52, 22:256–57).

5. Richard Kidder Meade (1746–1805), who had lived in Prince George County, Va., before the Revolutionary War, served as an aide-de-camp to GW with the rank of lieutenant colonel from 1777 until the end of the war.

After the war Meade purchased an estate in Frederick County, Va., which he called Lucky Hit.

From Alexander Hamilton

Treasury Department April 30. 1792

The Secretary of the Treasury has the honor respectfully to communicate to the President authenticated copies of the Contracts for the three last loans made in Europe; that for 6000000 of Florins at Amsterdam bearing date 14. of December 1791 at a rate of 5 ℔ Cent Interest that for 3000000 of Florins at Antwerp, at a rate of 4½ ℔ Cent Interest bearing date the 30th day of November 1791 and the last for 3000000 of Florins at Amsterdam at 4 perCent Interest bearing date the 24 of December 1791; of which respective contracts a Ratification by The President as heretofore is requisite.[1]

AL, DNA: RG 59, Bills of Exchange and Loan Ratifications.

1. For the various loans negotiated by the United States at Amsterdam and Antwerp, see Hamilton to GW, 10 April 1791, n.1, 14 April 1791, n.1, and 23 Jan. 1792, n.1; see also Hamilton to Thomas Jefferson, 26 Aug. 1791, William Short to Hamilton, 31 Aug., 8 Nov., n.4, 12 Nov., 23, 28, 30 Dec. 1791, in Syrett, *Hamilton Papers,* 9:111–12, 132–42, 479–82, 498–500, 10:403–4, 472–80, 485–90.

To the Earl of Buchan

My Lord, Philadelphia May 1st 1792.

I should have had the honor of acknowledging sooner the receipt of your letter of the 28th of June last, had I not concluded to defer doing it 'till I could announce to you the transmission of my portrait, which has been just finished by Mr Robinson (of New York) who has also undertaken to forward it.[1] The manner of the execution does no discredit, I am told, to the Artist; of whose skill favorable mention had been made to me. I was further induced to entrust the execution to Mr Robinson from his having informed me that he had drawn others for your Lordship and knew the size which would best suit your collection.

I accept with sensibility and with satisfaction, the significant present of the Box which accompanied your Lordships letter.[2]

In yielding the tribute due from every lover of mankind to the patriotic and heroic virtues, of which it is commemorative, I estimate, as I ought, the additional value, which it derives from the hand that sent it; and my obligation for the sentiments that induced the transfer.

I will, however ask, that you will exempt me from a compliance with the request relating to its eventual destination. In an attempt to execute your wish in this particular, I should feel embarrassment from a just comparison of relative pretensions, and should fear to risk injustice by so marked a preferenc⟨e⟩.[3] With sentiments of the truest esteem & consideration I remain, Your Lordships Most Obedient Servan⟨t⟩

Go: Washington

ALS, Meisei University, Tokyo, Japan; LB, DLC:GW; copy, MHi: Miscellaneous Collection.

1. See Archibald Robertson to GW, 21 April.

2. For a detailed description of the hinged wooden snuffbox constructed from the oak tree that had sheltered the Scottish leader William Wallace following his defeat at the Battle of Falkirk in 1298, see Buchan to GW, 28 June 1791, n.4.

3. Unwilling to choose "the man in my country, who should appear to merit" possession of the snuffbox "best," GW stipulated in his will of 9 July 1799 that it be returned to Buchan (see George Washington's Last Will and Testament, *Papers, Retirement Series,* 4:486). For information about what happened to the box subsequent to its return to Scotland, see Buchan to GW, 28 June 1791, n.4.

From Enoch Edwards

Philada May 1st 1792

Mr Clymer applied to me to procure for your Excellency a dutch Plough which I will with Pleasure immediately do, but I would wish to know whether you would prefer a Barr-Shear, or one made in the common Way, with a wooden Chip—the difference between the two is that the former runs much lighter than the latter, but there is a little more difficulty it getting it new laid & sharpned. the Bar is apt to spring a little on being heated, & will not fit on again unless the Smith has the Plough sent to him as well as the Shear, But if it is to be used on a Farm where there is a Smith there will be no Inconvenience. otherwise I would recommend the kind that has a Chip fited to it.

I also wish to know whether you would like to run after two horses or three as the Construction of it should be somewhat different.

I would just mention to your Excellency that I have a Harrow I think superior to any yet used in this country take all advantages together I think it quite equal to the plough. I will take the Liberty to send you a Draught of one of them, & if it should please you, will at any time direct one to be made for you under my immediate Inspection.

I am under the Necessity of going out of Town this afternoon & am therefore obliged to trouble you now for your Instructions.[1] I have the honor to be with due Respect your Excellencys obedt Srvt

En: Edwards

ALS, DLC:GW.

Enoch Edwards (1751–1802), who had been one of Dr. Benjamin Rush's first pupils, served as a surgeon during the Revolutionary War. After the war Edwards was a member of the Pennsylvania ratifying convention of 1787 and the state constitutional convention of 1789. In 1791 Gov. Thomas Mifflin appointed Edwards an associate justice of the Pennsylvania court of common pleas, a position he held until his death.

1. No written response to this letter from GW has been found, but on 17 May, Bartholomew Dandridge wrote GW from Philadelphia: "The day before yesterday, and just as Capt. [William] Carhart [Carheart] was about to sail from this place, a plough was left here by a man from Frankfort, who said it was made at that place for the president. Never having heard you or Mr Lear mention that such a one was to be received for you, & not knowing from whom it came, I was at a loss whether to take it or not: I therefore enquired of Mr [George] Clymer, who I supposed might know something about it, & he informed me that it was made by his direction & your desire, & came from a Doctr [Enoch] Edwards; in consequence of which I have sent it by Capt. Carhart to you, which I hope is right" (owned [1977] by Patterson Branch, Sr., Richmond, Virginia).

Letter not found: from John Greenwood, 1 May 1792. In his letter to Greenwood of 1 July GW referred to "Your letter of the first of May."

To Isaac Heard

Sir, Philadelphia May 2d 1792.

Your letter of the 7th of December was put into my hands by Mr Thornton; and I must request you will accept my acknowledgments, as well for the polite manner in which you express your wishes for my happiness, as for the trouble you have taken in making genealogical collections relative to the family of Washington.

This is a subject to which I confess I have paid very little attention. My time has been so much occupied in the busy and active scenes of life from an early period of it that but a small portion of it could have been devoted to researches of this nature, even if my inclination or particular circumstances should have prompted the enquiry. I am therefore apprehensive that it will not be in my power (circumstanced as I am at present to furnish you with materials) to fill up the sketch which you have sent me, in so accurate a manner as you could wish. We have no Office of Record in this Country in which exact genealogical documents are preserved—and very few cases, I believe, occur where a recurrence to pedigree for any considerable distance back has been found necessary to establish such points as may frequently arise in older Countries.

On comparing the Tables which you sent with such documents as are in my possesion, and which I could readily obtain from another branch of the family with whom I am in the habits of corrispondence I find it to be just.[1] I have often heard others of the family, older than myself, say that our ancestor who first settled in this Country came from some one of the Northern Counties of England, but whether from Lancashire, Yorkshire or one still more northerly I do not precisely remember.

The Arms enclosed in your letter are the same that are held by the family here—though I have also seen, and have used as you may perceive by the Seal to this Packet a flying Griffen for the Crest.

If you can derive any information from the enclosed lineage which will enable you to complete your Table, I shall be well pleased in having been the mean to assist you in those researches which you have had the politeness to undertake, and shall be glad to be informed of the result—and of the ancient pedigree of the family—some of whom I find intermixed with the Ferrers &ca.[2]

Lawrence Washington, from whose Will you enclosed an abstract was my Grand father—the other abstracts (which you sent) do not, I believe, relate to the family of Washington in Virginia;

but of this I cannot speak positively. With due consideration—I am—Sir Your most Obedt Servt

Go: Washington

ALS, CSmH; ALS (letterpress copy), DLC:GW; LB, DLC:GW.

1. See GW to Hannah Fairfax Washington, 24 Mar., and her reply to GW of 9 April 1792.

2. Although Heard's researches were slowed considerably by a serious eye infection which beset him until at least the summer of 1796, he sent further genealogical information about the Washington family in his letters to GW of 9 Aug. 1793 and 10 July 1796 (both DLC:GW). The Ferrers family that GW mentions is possibly the family that included the prominent sixteenth-century English poet and politician George Ferrers (c.1500–1579).

Enclosure
Washington Genealogy

Philadelphia May 2d 1792

In the year 1657—or thereabouts, and during the Usurpation of Oliver Cromwell John and Lawrence Washington—Brothers Emigrated from the north of England, and settled at Bridges Creek, on Potomac River, in the County of Westmoreland. But from whom they descended the subscriber is possessed of no document to ascertain.

John Washington was employed as General against the Indians in Maryland, and as a reward for his services was made a Colonel; and the Parish wherein he lived was called after him.

He married Ann Pope, and left issue two Sons, Lawrence and John, and one daughter Ann, who married Major Francis Wright. The time of his death the subscriber is not able to ascertain—but it appears that he was Interred in a Vault which had been erected at Bridges Creek.

Lawrence Washington his eldest Son, married Mildred Warner, daughter of Coll Augustine Warner of Gloucester County, by whom he had two sons, John and Augustine, and one daughter named Mildred. He died in 1697 and was interred in the family Vault at Bridges Creek.

John Washington the eldest son of Lawrence and Mildred, married Catharine Whiting of Gloucester County, where he settled, died, and was buried. He had two Sons Warner and Henry, and three daughters, Mildred, Elizabeth and Catharine, all of whom are dead.

Warner Washington married, first—Elizabeth Macon daughter of Colo. William Macon of New Kent County, by whom he had one Son, who is now living and bears the name of Warner. His second wife was Hannah, youngest daughter of the Honble William Fairfax; by whom he left two Sons and five daughters—as follow—viz.—Mildred, Hannah, Catharine, Elizabeth, Louisa[,] Fairfax and Whiting. The three oldest of the daughters are married—Mildred to —— Throckmorton, Hannah to —— Whiting, and Catharine to —— Nelson. After his second marriage he removed from Gloucester and settled in Frederick County, where he died, in 1791, and was buried.

Warner Washington his son married —— Whiting of Gloucester, by whom he has many Sons and daughters—the eldest is called Warner and is now nearly, or quite of age.[1]

Henry, the other Son of John & Catharine Washington, married the daughter of Colonel Thacker of Middlesex County, and died many years ago, leaving one Son, Thacker, and two or three daughters.

Thacker Washington married the daughter of Sir John Peyton of Gloucester County & lives on the family estate, left to his Grandfather John at Machodac in the County of Westmoreland. He has several Children, but what are their Sex is not known to the Subscriber.

Mildred, daughter of John & Catharine of Gloucester was twice married, but never had a child—Elizabeth never was married—Catharine married Fielding Lewis by whom she had a son and daughter—John, the eldest, is now living—Frances died without issue.

Augustine, son of Lawrence and Mildred Washington, married Jane Butler, the daughter of Caleb Butler of Westmoreland April 20th 1715 by whom he had three Sons—Butler (who died young) Lawrence and Augustine, and one daughter Jane, who died when a child. Jane, wife of Augustine died Novr 24th 1728 and was buried in the family Vault at Bridges Creek.

Augustine then married [Mary] Ball March 6th 1730: by whom he had issue George Now President of the United States born February 11th (old style) 1732; Betty, born June 20th 1733; Samuel, born Novr 16th 1734; John Augustine, born Jany 13th 173[6];[2] Charles May 1st 1738; and Mildred June 21st 1739; who died Octr 28th 1740. Augustine departed this life April

12th 1743 Aged 49 years and was interred at Bridges Creek in the Vault of his Ancesters.

Lawrence, Son of Augustine and Jane Washington, married July 19th 1743 Ann, eldest daughter of the Honble William Fairfax of Fairfax County, by whom he had issue Jane, born Septr 27th 1744—who died Jany 1745—Fairfax born August 22d 1747 who died in Octr 1747—Mildred, born Septr 28th 1748 who died in 1749—Sarah, born Novr 7th 1750 who died in 175- —In 1752 Lawrence himself died aged about 34 and was interred in a Vault which he had caused to be erected at Mount Vernon in Fairfax County where he settled after he returned from the Carthagena Expedition and died.

Augustine, Son of Augustine and Jane Washington married Ann, daughter & Co heiress of William Aylett of Westmoreland County, by whom he had many children, all of whom died in their non-age & single except Elizabeth (who married Alexander Spotswood of Spotsylvania County, Grandson of General Spotswood Governor of Virginia, by whom she has a number of Children)—Ann (who married Burdet Ashton of Westmoreland, by whom she had one or two children & died young)—and William who married his cousin Jane, daughter of John Augustine Washington by whom he has four childn (names unknown to the Subscriber)—Augustine lived at the ancient mansion seat in Westmoreland County where he died and was interred in the family Vault.

George eldest son of Augustine Washington by the second marriage was born in Westmoreland County, and married Jany 6th 1759 Martha Custis, widow of Danl Parke Custis and daughter of John Dandridge—both of New Kent County. Has no issue.

Betty, daughter of Augustine & Mary Washington became the second wife of Fielding Lewis, by whom she had a number of Children—many of whom died young—but, five sons & a daughter are yet living.

Samuel, Son of Augustine & Mary was five times married. First to Jane, daughter of Colo. John Champe. 2d to Mildred daughter of Colo. John Thornton—3d Lucy daughter of Nathanl Chapman. 4th Ann daughter of Colo. Willm Steptoe and Widow of Willoughby Allerton—5th to a Widow Perrin. Samuel, by his second wife, Mildred, had issue one son, Thornton, who lived to be a man—was twice married and left three Sons. He died in, or about the year [ ] By his fourth Wife Ann he had three Sons, Ferdinand, George Steptoe, & Lawrence Augustine, and a daughter, Hariot. Ferdinand lived to be married, but died soon after leaving no issue; the other two sons, and daughter are living & single. Samuel had Children by his other wives, but they all died in their infancy. He departed this life, himself, in the year 1781 at Harewood in the County of Berkeley where he was buried.

John Augustine, son of Augustine and Mary, married Hannah Bushrod, daughter of Colo. John Bushrod of Westmoreland County, by whom he has left two Sons, Bushrod and Corbin—and two daughters, Jane and Mildred. he had several other Children, but they died young. Jane, his eldest child married (as has been before observed) William Washington, son of Augustine & Ann Washington and died in 1791 leaving four Children (names unknown to the Subscriber). Bushrod married in 1785 Ann Blackburn daughter of Colo. Thomas Blackburn of Prince William County—but has no issue. Corbin married a daughter of the Honble Richd Henry Lee, by whom he has three Sons (names unknown). Mildred married Thomas Lee, son of the said Richard Henry Lee. John Augustine died in Feby 1787 at his estate on Nomony in Westmoreland County & was there buried. Charles Washington, son of Augustine & Mary, married Mildred Thornton, daughter of Colonel Francis Thornton of Spotsylvania County, by whom he has four Children, George Augustine, Frances, Mildred & Samuel. George Augustine married Frances Basset, daughter of Colo. Burwell Basset of New Kent by whom he has had four Children, three of whom are living—viz.—Anna Maria, George Fayette, & Charles Augustine. Frances, married Colo. Burgess Ball by whom she has had several children. Mildred and Samuel are unmarried.

Mildred Washington, daughter of Lawrence & Mildred—& Sister to John & Augustine Washington married —— Gregory by whom she had three daughters, Frances, Mildred and Elizabeth, who married three brothers—Colo. Francis Thornton, Colo. John Thornton, and Reuben Thornton—all of Spotsylvania County. She had for her second husband Colo. Henry Willis, and by him the present Colo. Lewis Willis of Fredericksburgh.

The above is the best account the subscriber is able to give, at present, absent as he is, and at so great a distance from Virginia—and under circumstances too which allows no time for enquiry, of the family of Washington from which he is lenially descended.

The descendants of the first named Lawrence, and the second John, are also numerous; but for the reasons before mentioned, and from not having the same knowledge of them—and being moreover more remote from their places of Residence. And in truth not having enquired much into the names or connection of the lateral Branches of the family I am unable to give a Satisfactory account of them. But if it be in any degree necessary, or satisfactory to Sir Isaac Heard Carter Principal King of Arms, I will upon intimation thereof, set on foot an enquiry—and will at the sametime endeavor to be more particular with respect to the births, names, ages and burials of those of the branch to which the Subscriber belongs.

Go: Washington

ADS, CSmH; ADS (letterpress copy), DLC:GW; LB, DLC:GW.

GW also enclosed a one-page "geniological Table of the Family of Washington" for Heard's perusal (CSmH).

1. In the letter-book copy this clause reads: "is now nearly if not quite of age."

2. GW mistakenly wrote "1735" as the year of John Augustine Washington's birth.

Tobias Lear to Timothy Pickering

Dear sir, [Philadelphia] May 3d 1792

I enclose the translation of the letter which was transmitted to the Secretary of War by the Governor of New York—The translation was made yesterday in great haste, and if it should not be sufficiently clear, referrence had better be had to the original, in the possession of the Secy of War.[1]

The President wishes, in your conversation with Colo. Louis, that you would learn the precise time of holding the proposed Council at Buffaloe—and also that it may be impressed on Colo. Louis, if the deputation should go from Buffaloe to the Western Indians, that they would endeavour in the first instance to prevail upon the hostile indians to keep their warriors from committing depradations on our frontiers—as we shall restrain ours from making incursions into their Country. for unless this step is taken in the first instance all attempts at conciliation will probably be fruitless. With true respect & sincere regard I have the honor to be dear Sir Your most Obent St

T. Lear

ALS, MHi: Pickering Papers.

1. The enclosed translation of "the Message from the 7 nations of Canada" written at St. Louis on 24 Feb. 1792 reads: "We the Chiefs of the 7 Villages of lower Canada salute all our Brothers who compose the State of New York, and pray the Master of Breath (de la Vie) that he will preserve peace with all nations, and that the great Supreme Being will always render judgement unto all persons (Judicieux Vis-a-Vis touts personnes):

"Brothers We have received a letter from Governor George Clinton in answer to one which we addressed to you, by which we propose to you a treaty together, but the present circumstances will deprive us of that satisfaction, seeing that we are called to hold a Council with our Brothers the Chaivenons [Shawnee] and other savage Nations; it is our duty to attend punctually to endeavour to appease the troubles in this Country. We remember with pleasure that you recommended to us not to harken to the evil birds and not to lose the disposition Spirit (et de ne point perdre L'Esprit)—We will carefully guard ourselves on this head, and we beg you to do the like on your part, and to appease your Warriors as much as possible; for we desire nothing more than peace & harmony among all the nations, and we will not cease to implore the Great Master to assist us in æestablishing it—And we hope that you will take all care to render justice to whom Justice is due.

"Brothers After this arrangement, we will treat together at leisure, we only pray you not to let your people make any advances of settlements upon the lands which we claim, at least until we shall have treated together on this subject—And in full confidence that all these matters will be well arranged we wish you a good day, & that the Master of Breath may keep you in peace." Following twelve signatures, the message concludes: "You will receive this letter by Brothe[r] Louis Couque Lt Colonel, whom we have sent express to be the bearer of it—and pray he may meet with no delay" (MHi: Pickering Papers). Louis Cook (Atoyataghroughta; Atyatoghhanongwea; c.1740–1814), a Caughnawaga chief who had received a lieutenant colonel's commission in June 1779 for his support of the American cause, moved to Saint Régis, Canada, after the Revolutionary War. In October 1814 Cook died from injuries he received in a skirmish on the Niagara frontier near Buffalo, New York.

Timothy Pickering to Tobias Lear

Dear Sir, Philaa May 3d 1792.

I inclose the information given me by Colo. Louis.[1] The copy of the letter from his nation bears date the 24th of January. I sent to the war-office for the Original, which I found was dated

Feby 24th.[2] Bad travelling at the breaking up of winter and ten days sickness, Louis says have occasion so much delay in his journey. He is anxious to return. In great haste sincerely yours

T. Pickering

ALS, MHi: Pickering Papers.

1. Lt. Col. Louis Cook's information, which was written at Philadelphia on 3 May 1792, reads: "That 12 Indians came round, N. Side of Lake Erie from the Westward, as far as Taronto, on the North Side of Lake Ontario opposite Niagara, then six went back, not being used to Snow shoes. Six kept on, as far as the Mohawk Castle, 40 miles above Cataraqui. There 2 were left, & fo[u]r fearing the small pox, the message was carried to the Caughnawauga Indians by one Cayuga, who had had the Small pox.

"When the Caghnawaga Council was convened, the Cayuga Head Warrior addressed them in these words.

" 'Brothers I have come to your place. I am sent a messenger from the Shawanese, to you the seven tribes in Canada. Nevertheless brothers, be assured, that the principal nations at the Westward are concerned in this message. They invite you to hold a general council at Buffaloe Creek. To you Warriors I deliver the invitation strings (a large bunch of long strings). It is your part, from the Strength of your bodies, on any occasion, to carry the messages of the Sachems. Now Notify all your 7 tribes to repair to that place, with two prime counsellors & two head warriors from each nation. Pass by no one of your 7 tribes unnotified. And then also call upon all the Five Nations for like representation at that Council Fire.

" 'Brothers, At that place, I, the Shawanoe Nation, will meet you. There we will settle all our great national concerns: and if you are not yet fully ascertained of the real intentions of the Western Indians, I, the Shawanoe nation, will then inform you.

" 'The Western Indians have said, They will not listen to any *single* nation, until you, the 7 tribes, are in full council, & speak with one voice.'

" (*Here ends the Message by that Runner.*)

"After which, in private conference, I, (Colo. Louis) questioned the runner, to obtain his real sentiments of the disposition of the Western Indians; saying to him You must certainly know what their minds are; & you must know what occasions the war. Perhaps it is on account of land, that they will not listen to the voice of peace. Tell me the real truth. He answered—'As to land, it has but small influence in this affair. They say, as to that, it may easily be adjusted. But they say, they will not hearken to the voice of a *single* nation; altho' they may speak of peace, which is good. They desire in the first place, to have the complete voice of the 7 tribes in Canada & of the 5 nations, by their deputies. They are disposed to peace: but in order to that they want to bind themselves together in a peace for the good of *Indians,* which shall have no dependance on any *white people,* of any nation; nor ever oblige Indians to assist them, if in any future time they should quarrel. We Indians (said they) must all live in peace with one another; And when this business shall be finished, make proclamation, that we will never take part with any white people, in any future quarrel between them, And then we will entreat both sides, never more to ask our aid. Let us Indians live in peace.'

"I then told the Cayuga, If he had now related to me the real truth, without any disguise, I should attend to it—I would rise myself, & go to the place appointed for the Council Fire (at Buffaloe Creak). Otherwise, I would not meddle with it; but let every nation shift for themselves. To this he answered—'I have spoken nothing but the truth, the very truth.'

"(Here ended our private conference)

"After the first Council at Caughnauwaga, and the private pre conference, the Chiefs of the 7 nations thus replied to the Cayuga Runner.

"'Brother, Your message looks all right. We are inclined to embrace it, for the sake of diffusing peace, which is good. But how shall we undertake this? Unless we first send word to our brothers of the 13 Fires? altho' we of the 7 tribes live over the line, nevertheless they are our neighbours. Should we rise and go out, & take by the hand our brothers the Oneidas, Tuscaroras, Stockbridge Indians, Onondagas, Cayugas, Senekas to the end of the United House—then it may be toward the Sitting Sun, 'when there is Evil, what would the 13 Fires say to us? It is therefore expedient & friendly for us to acquaint them with this your message, & that we shall embrace it.'

"'Now Brothers (Say the Chiefs of the 7 tribes, addressing the 13 Fires) If you approve of this measure, and give us a word of encouragement, we will pursue it; and you shall hear from us.'

"(Colo. Louis adds. What ever shall be done in the council at Buffaloe Creek, we intend shall be agreed to by the Western Indians. And if we proceed, we will take them by the hand, and bring them down to the Great Council Fire of the U. States; for at no other place do we think a final peace can be established. The Caghnawagas & Oneidas will now afford great help in the Council at the Buffaloe, in laying the foundation for what shall finally be agreed on in the Great Council at the Westward.

"I am confident (says Louis) we shall carry our point and bring about a peace. And in order to effect this it was the Genl Opinion of the Caghnawagas, that no white people should be admitted into the Great Council at the westward. But at the Buffaloe they may be present as spectators; but not to intermeddle in the business).

"(The answer of the Cayugas Runner, as to the real cause of the war, not being satisfactory to T[imothy] P[ickering] he mentioned it to Colo. Louis; & asked—if the land be not the cause of the war, what do the Western Indians contend? He answered—The Shawanese are very angry, and they have drawn the other nations into the war. But now the Ottowas and others have said to the Shawanese—'You have undertaken to sell land, altho you did not own a foot. If the war goes on, we shall all lose our land and be ruined. Now you must send to the 7 nations in Canada, & the 5 nations, & hold a council; and we will hear their voice, for peace: but we will not hear the King, nor the 13 Fires, nor [Joseph] Brant.[']

"(Colo. Louis explained the situation of the Shawanese as to land, by comparing them to the Tuscaroras, who were permitted to reside among the 5 nations, but never were allowed to join in the sale of lands).

"To the Question of T.P.—Do not the western Indians complain of the 13 Fires, that they are grasping all their lands, quite to the Mississipi? He answered—They were not uneasy for their land, till Brant went among them, & told them that the U. States claimed the whole country.

"(He says, that as soon as he returns, the Chiefs of the 7 nations will set off, & send two runners in canoes to Oswego, to take the Oneidas by the hand, & so on thro' the 5 nations, till they reach Buffaloe and that they will not look at the King, because this is altogether *Indian* business.[)] It was the opinion of the 7 nations, that if peace were not now made, the United States would make such a strong war as would issue in the destruction of all the Indian nations. And Louis says also that the same is the *fixed opinion* of the Western Indians. And this is the reason why they want a general council.

"That so firm a peace may be made by the voice of all, that *Indians* may never more have war. This is the disposition of a great majority of the various nations of Indians. And if this intended council should not effect a peace, all will despair, & conclude to fight and die.

"Colo. Louis says, That Runners of the 7 nations were to set off as soon as the ice should be gone to the Western Indians, with this message 'Keep in your war parties, till we can meet together in council & see what we can do.'

"He supposes it will be the last of May before the Council can be held at Buffaloe Creek, which may last a fortnight. Then they will proceed to the Westward.

"Colo. Louis thinks it will not be adviseable for Capt. Hendrick [Aupaumut] to proceed to the Westward by the Quarter where the war is carried on. That the summer before last a Caughnawaga was sent with a message from Fort Pitt, The Hostile Indians took him prisoner—and, tho' they spared his life, because he was a Caughnawaga, they would not hear his message. He says Tis contrary to the custom of Indians to listen to any such messenger. runners with such messages must always go round, & come in at the back door" (MHi: Pickering Papers).

2. For "the Message from the 7 nations of Canada," see Lear to Pickering, this date, n.1.

To the United States Senate

United States [Philadelphia]

Gentlemen of the Senate, May the 3d 1792.

I nominate Edward Church of Georgia,[1] heretofore appointed but not received as Consul for the United States at Bilboa, to be Consul for the United States at the Port of Lisbon in the Kingdom of Portugal, and for such other parts within the allegiance of her most Faithful Majesty as shall be nearer to the said port, than to the residence of any other Consul, or Vice-Consul of the United States within the same allegiance.[2]

And, Elias Vanderhorst of South Carolina, now resident in Great Britain, to be Consul for the United States for the port of Bristol in the Kingdom of Great Britain, and for such other parts within the allegiance of his Britannic Majesty as shall be nearer to the said Port than to the residence of any other Consul or Vice-Consul of the United States within the same allegiance.[3]

Go: Washington

DS, DNA: RG 46, Second Congress, 1791–1793, Records of Executive Proceedings, President's Messages—Executive Nominations; Df (letterpress copy), in Thomas Jefferson's hand, DLC: Jefferson Papers. The draft in the Jefferson Papers is dated 24 Dec. 1791.

1. At this place in the draft, Jefferson identifies Edward Church as being "of Massachusets." Church, who had been born in the Azores, lived in Massachusetts from the late 1750s to the late 1780s. By 1789, however, he had moved to Georgia.

2. On 5 May, Tobias Lear wrote Jefferson that the Senate had that day concurred with Church's nomination (DNA: RG 59, George Washington's Correspondence with His Secretaries of State; see also *Executive Journal,* 1:122). Church served as U.S. consul to Portugal until June 1797 (ibid., 248).

3. Lear wrote Jefferson on 4 May that the Senate had that day concurred with Vanderhorst's nomination (DNA: RG 59, George Washington's Correspondence with His Secretaries of State; see also ibid., 121–22). Elias Vanderhorst (b. 1735) was a South Carolina merchant who had immigrated to England in 1772. For the background to his appointment, see Memorandum of Thomas Jefferson, 22 Dec. 1791.

To the United States Senate

United States [Philadelphia]

Gentlemen of the Senate, May the 3d 1792.

I nominate Tristram Dalton,[1] of Massachusetts, to be Treasurer of the Mint—Aquila Giles,[2] to be Marshal of New York District, vice Mathew Clarkson, resigned—and Edward Wigglesworth,[3] to be Collector of the Port of Newbury-Port, vice Stephen Cross, superseded.

Go: Washington

DS, in Tobias Lear's hand, DNA: RG 46, Second Congress, 1791–1793, Records of Executive Proceedings, President's Messages—Executive Nominations; LB, DLC:GW.

On 4 May, Lear wrote Thomas Jefferson that the Senate had that day concurred with the above nominations (DNA: RG 59, George Washington's Correspondence with His Secretaries of State; see also *Executive Journal,* 1:122).

1. On 25 Feb. 1791 Tristram Dalton had applied to GW for the position of postmaster general, and ten months later, on 26 Dec. 1791, he wrote GW to apply for the directorship of the U.S. Mint (both DLC:GW). Both applications were unsuccessful, however. On 9 May, Dalton wrote GW from Philadelphia: "Last evening I was honored with Official Information of my being appointed Treasurer of the Mint of the United States—and have signified to the Secretary of State my acceptance of the Trust. For this mark of Favor & Confidence I beg leave, Sir, to make my very grateful acknowledgments. My affairs in Massachusetts will demand my personal attendance there a few weeks. If the business of the Mint will permit my taking the present season for that purpose I shall be happy to be indulged with liberty to go in two or three days" (DNA: RG 59, Miscellaneous Letters).

2. On 25 May, Aquila Giles wrote GW from New York: "I with great gratitude acknowledge the Honour, which your Excellency, has been pleased to confer on me, by appointing me Marshal of this District—I flatter myself, that by a strict and punctual discharge of the duties of that Office, to confirm that confidence which your Excellency has been pleased to place in me" (DNA: RG 59, Miscellaneous Letters).

3. Earlier in the day Alexander Hamilton had written GW that "Colo. Wigglesworth's christian name is Edward," a fact that GW apparently had not known (DLC:GW). On 25 May, Wigglesworth wrote GW from Newburyport, Mass., that "The Secretary of the Treasury has transmitted me a Commission as Collector of the Customs for the district of Newbury Port which I with gratitude accept. I am ignorant to whom I am particularly indebted for such a favor unless your Excellency has been pleas'd to remember I once serv'd in the Army, and the only proper return I can make to those who have had the goodness to think of me, will be, to use my best endeavours, with diligence & fidelity to perform the several duties of my Office" (DNA: RG 59, Miscellaneous Letters). Edward Wigglesworth (1741–1826) had served as a colonel in the Massachusetts militia in 1776 and as colonel of the 13th Massachusetts Regiment from 1 Jan. 1777 to 10 Mar. 1779. Upon Wigglesworth's resignation the Continental Congress instructed GW to provide him with a certificate attesting to the value of his services to the American cause (*JCC,* 13:302). In the certificate, which is dated 19 Mar. 1779, GW wrote that Wigglesworth had "uniformly supported the Character of an attentive brave and judicious Officer" (Df, DLC:GW). Wigglesworth was replaced as collector at Newburyport, Mass., on 25 June 1795 (*Executive Journal,* 1:189).

To the United States Senate

United States [Philadelphia]

Gentlemen of the Senate, May the 3d 1792.

I nominate the following persons to fill vacancies which have taken place in the late military appointments—to-wit—

Rank.	*Names.*	*States.*
Brigadier General	Rufus Putnam	Territory of the United States North West of the Ohio—vice Marinus Willett, declined.
Captains of Cavalry	Jedediah Rodgers	New York—vice John Craig, declined.
	Henry Bowyer	Virginia—vice Lawrence Manning, declined.
Lieutt of Infantry	William Rickard	North Carolina vice Thos E. Sumner, declined.
Surgeons Mates	Joseph Strong	Connecticut—vice Theophilus Elmer, declined.
	Joseph Andrews	Massachusetts—vice James Mease, declined.
	John C. Wallace	Pennsylvania—vice John Woodhouse, declined.

Go: Washington

DS, in Tobias Lear's hand, DNA: RG 46, Second Congress, 1791–1793, Records of Executive Proceedings, President's Messages—Executive Nominations; LB, DLC:GW.

The Senate read GW's message on this day, and it considered and concurred with the president's military nominations on the following day (*Executive Journal,* 1:121–22). Tobias Lear informed Henry Knox of the Senate's concurrence on 4 May (DLC:GW).

To Andrew Hamilton

Sir, Philadelphia May 4th 1792.

I have had the pleasure to receive your polite letter of the 12th of December, together with a copy of "An Enquiry into the Principles of taxation,["] which accompanied it, & for which I must beg your acceptance of my best thanks.[1]

The subject of your book is certainly of the first importance to society; and those who undertake works of this nature upon the extensive scale that yours appears to be, are entitled to the thanks of the patriotic of every nation. In this country, where we are commencing a Government upon the experience of ages, it certainly behoves us to search into the "Principles of Taxation" and to avoid as much as possible the errors of other nations on this very important head: We must therefore receive with peculiar satisfaction any lights on the subject.

Your philanthropic wish "to see the world at large encreasing in knowledge, prosperity & happiness," is no less pleasing to me as a Citizen of the World, than your expressions of personal respect are deserving the acknowledgements of Sir Your Most Obt Servant

Go: Washington

LS, Scottish Record Office; Df, DNA: RG 59, Miscellaneous Letters; LB, DLC: GW. The LS includes Andrew Hamilton's docket, which reads: "4th May 1792 From George Washington Esqr. on receiving my Book."

1. Andrew Hamilton of Kinghorn, South Fifeshire, on the Firth of Forth, wrote his letter to GW of 12 Dec. 1791 at "Buccleugh place Edinburgh," Scotland. It reads: "Permit me to request your Acceptance of the Accompanying Copy of 'An Enquiry into the Principles of Taxation'—A Work, in which I have endeavoured, to exhibit the Practice, Point out the Errors, & gather into Distinct points of View the general Truths, which the Experience of Great Britain has exhibited, during the Course of a full Century in which her Statesmen have been engaged, in extracting a Revenue, from the general wealth of the Inhabitants. This Subject, you will allow, is in itself highly Interresting; but especially to a People, just beginning the Business of Taxation. You will see, that in this Department of Government, great Errors are to be avoided. And you know, much better than I can point out, how necessary, the proper Conduct of the Taxes may prove, to the future prosperity and Grandeur of the Empire over which you have now the Honor to Preside.

"My Local Distance, & the Situation I hold in my own Country, place me beyond the Imputation of any Motive in this address, but Veneration for your Character, & a desire to see, not one Country only; but the World at large, encreasing in Knowledge, Prosperity, & Happiness. . . . P.S. The Book was Published without my Name untill I should see how it was received by my fellow Citizens, and it is in Consequence of their approbation that I have taken the Liberty to give you this Trouble" (DLC:GW). A copy of Hamilton's book published in London in 1790 was in GW's library at the time of his death (Griffin, *Boston Athenæum Washington Collection,* 519).

Tobias Lear to Henry Knox

United States [Philadelphia] 4 May 1792. Returns by GW's command "the Instructions to Major Genl Wayne & a letter to Mr Seagrove, both of which meet the President['s] approbation."[1]

ALS (retained copy), DLC:GW; LB, DLC:GW.

1. War Department clerk Benjamin Bankson had transmitted Knox's proposed letter to James Seagrove to Lear on the previous day and had asked that it be submitted to the president (DLC:GW). Neither of the enclosures has been identified.

From John Lucas

Sir, Boston, 4th May 1792.

I take the liberty to communicate to you, for the purpose of perpetuating the evidence of a singular patriotic transaction of Elisha Brown, a poor man of this town, who in defence of liberty and the laws of his country, undauntedly stood alone as a *barrier* to our liberties,[1] "Agreeably to the Inscription, on the Monument," which I have the honor to forward to you, through the medium of General Knox, who was, at that time, in this place and, may, perhaps, confirm what I now relate.[2] We read, that "a poor wise man delivered a city; yet no man remembered that same poor wise man."[3] Brown's case I conceive to be analogous to this. My ardent desire, that every patriotic transaction, out of the common course, relative to our struggles for the rights of man, either of the poor or the rich, the wise or heroic, may have an equal chance to be transmitted to posterity, has constrained me to present the above mentioned Monument to the President of the United States and his Successor in Office.

That you may long live and see your country continue to prosper under your Presidency, is the sincere prayer of, Sir, Your most obedient And very humble servant,

John Lucas

LS, DLC:GW.

1. In October 1768 Elisha Brown (1720–1785) of Boston became a local celebrity through his refusal to allow Col. Campbell Dalrymple to use the manufactory house for the quartering of his regiment. Even after Gov. Francis Bernard had ordered Brown and his fellow tenants to evacuate the premises, the doors of the building remained closed to the British soldiers, and Brown hotly denied that Bernard had the right to dispossess him. After the standoff had lasted for several weeks, Dalrymple's men were lodged in Faneuil Hall (see Samuel Adams Drake, *Old Landmarks and Historic Personages of Boston* [Boston, 1900], 303). Reports of the incident were published in Massachusetts and in several other colonies; see, for example, *Boston-Gazette, and Country Journal,* 24 Oct. 1768; *Pennsylvania Gazette,* 13 Oct., 3, 24 Nov. 1768, 17 May 1770.

2. Lucas also wrote Henry Knox on 4 May: "You would oblige me to forward to the President of the United States the picture of Elisha Brown and the circumstance of his defending himself and Manufactory-House, when the British made an attempt, agreeably to the relation under the picture. This evidence is substantiated from the best information I can obtain. You may, perhaps, recollect the siege and circumstances. If you have any evidence to the contrary of what is related, I would not admit it into the Museum of the United States, or into any other. I have placed a Pyramid over his dust, in this place—describing &c. which I would brake down, were not the transaction founded on facts. Brown was left neglected by his Brother-patriots, and would have suffered, had not he possessed that conscious rectitude, which gave evidence to poor surrounding mortals, that he was more than a *man*—he was a *hero*—breathing his last, giving thanks to the Great first Cause, who gave his fellow men that *dear liberty* for which he dared to risque his life, (and when obtained) to defend, in full confidence of enjoying a blessed Immortality.

"If you can confirm the account, which I have given of Mr Brown, and it be admissible into some public Depository, I shall answer my wishes, if not, you will please to return it again" (NNGL: Knox Papers; because Lucas mistakenly wrote "1798" in the dateline, this letter is presently catalogued under 4 May 1798, not 1792). Although Knox forwarded Lucas's letter to GW, it has not been determined whether or not Knox confirmed Lucas's story.

3. Lucas is quoting from Ecclesiastes 9:15.

To Ségur

Sir, Philadelphia May 4th 1792.

I received with much satisfaction the information of your having made an acquisition in this Country, & of your intentions to take up your residence among us.[1] Your letter of the 30th of Sepr giving me this information, did not get to my hands 'till some time in the last month.

The United States opens, as it were, a new World to those who are disposed to retire from the noise & bustle of the old, & enjoy tranquility & security. And we shall always consider men of your character as among our most valuable acquisitions.

Our connection with France, formed in a gloomy & distressful hour, must ever interest us in the happinss of that nation. We have seen, with true commiseration, those outrages, inseparable from a Revolution, which have agitated the Kingdom, and we have not ceased our most fervent wishes that their termination may be as happy as their progress have been distressing. With great esteem I am, Sir, Yr most Obt Set

Df, in Tobias Lear's hand, DNA: RG 59, Miscellaneous Letters; LB, DLC:GW.

1. Ségur wrote to GW on 30 Sept. 1791 that he had long desired to become a citizen of the United States and that he had recently purchased an estate from Robert Morris called Eden Park in New Castle County, Delaware. Ségur never immigrated to America, however.

To James Madison

[Philadelphia] Saturday 5th May 1792

If Mr Madison can make it convenient to call upon the P—— between eight and nine this forenoon and spend half an hour it would oblige him.

If inconvenient, then at Six in the Afternoon.

AL, PWacD.

Madison's Conversations with Washington

5[–25] May 1792.

Substance of a Conversation with the President

In consequence of a note this morning from the President requesting me to call on him I did so; when he opened the conversation by observing that having some time ago communicated to me his intention of retiring from public life on the expiration of his four years, he wished to advise with me on the *mode* and *time* most proper for making known that intention. He had he said spoken with no one yet on those particular points, and took this opportunity of mentioning them to me, that I might consider the matter, and give him my opinion, before the adjournment of congress, or my departure from Philadelphia.[1] He had he said forborne to communicate his intention to any other persons whatever, but Mr Jefferson, Col. Hamilton, General Knox & myself, and of late to Mr Randolph. Col: Hamilton & Genl Knox he observed were extremely importunate that he should relinquish his purpose, and had made pressing representations to induce him to it. Mr Jefferson had expressed wishes to the like effect. He had not however persuaded himself that his continuance in public life could be of so much necessity or importance as was conceived, and his disinclination to it, was becoming every day more & more fixed;[2] so that he wished to make up his mind as soon as possible on the points he had mentioned. What he desired was to prefer that mode which would be most remote from the appearance of arrogantly presuming on his re-election in case he should not withdraw himself, and such a time as would be most convenient to the public in making the choice of his successor. It had, he said, at first occurred to him, that the commencement of the ensuing Session of Congress, would furnish him with an apt occasion for introducing the intimation,[3] but besides the lateness of the day, he was apprehensive that it might possibly produce some notice in the reply of Congress that might entangle him in further explanations.

I replied that I would revolve the subject as he desired and communicate the result before my leaving Philada;[4] but that I could not but yet hope there would be no necessity at this time for his decision on the two points he had stated. I told him that when he did me the honor to mention the resolution he had taken, I had forborne to do more than briefly express my apprehensions that it would give a surprize and shock to the public mind, being restrained from enlarging on the subject by an unwillingness to express sentiments sufficiently known to him; or to urge objections to a determination, which if absolute, it might look like affectation to oppose; that the aspect which things had been latterly assuming, seemed however to impose the task on all who had the opportunity, of urging a continuance of his public services; and that under such an impression I held it a duty, not indeed to express my wishes which would be superfluous, but to offer my opinion that his retiring at the present juncture, might have effects that ought not to be hazarded; that I was not unaware of the urgency of his inclination; or of the peculiar motives he might feel to withdraw himself from a situation into which it was so well known to myself he had entered with a scrupulous reluctance; that I well recollected the embarrassments under which his mind labored in deciding the question, on which he had consulted me, whether it could be his duty to accept his present station after having taken a final leave of public life; and that it was particularly in my recollection, that I then entertained & intimated a wish that his acceptance, which appeared to be indispensable, might be known hereafter to have been in no degree the effect of any motive which strangers to his character might suppose, but of the severe sacrifice which his friends knew, he made of his inclinations as a man, to his obligations as a citizen; that I owned I had at that time contemplated, & I believed, suggested as the most unequivocal tho' not the only proof of his real motives, a voluntary return to private life as soon as the state of the Government would permit, trusting that if any premature casualty should unhappily cut off the possibility of this proof, the evidence known to his friends would in some way or other be saved from oblivion and do justice to his character; that I was not less anxious on the same point now than I was then; and if I did not conceive that reasons of a like kind to those which required him to undertake, still required him to retain for some time longer, his present station; or did not presume that the purity of his motives would be sufficiently vindicated, I should be the last of his friends to press, or even to wish such a determination.

He then entered on a more explicit disclosure of the state of his mind; observing that he could not believe or conceive himself anywise necessary to the successful administration of the Government; that on the contrary he had from the beginning found himself deficient in many of the essential qualifications, owing to his inexperience in the forms of public business, his unfitness to judge of legal questions, and questions arising out of the Constitution; that others more conversant in such matters would be better able to execute the trust; that he found himself also in the decline of life, his health becoming sensibly more infirm, & perhaps his faculties also; that the fatigues & disagreeableness of his situation were in fact scarcely tolerably to him;[5] that he only uttered his real sentiments when he declared that his inclination would lead him rather to go to his farm, take his spade in his hand, and work for his bread, than remain in his present situation, that it was evident moreover that a spirit of party in the Government was becoming a fresh source of difficulty, and he was afraid was dividing some (alluding to the Secretary of State & Secy of the Treasury) more particularly connected with him in the administration; that there were discontents among the people which were also shewing themselves more & more, & that altho' the various attacks against public men & measures had not in general been pointed at him, yet in some instances it had been visible that he was the indirect object, and it was probable the evidence would grow stronger and stronger that his return to private life was consistent with every public consideration, and consequently that he was justified in giving way to his inclination for it.

I was led by this explanation to remark to him, that however novel or difficult the business might have been to him, it could not be doubted that with the aid of the official opinions & informations within his command, his judgment must have been as competent in all cases, as that of any one who could have been put in his place, and in many cases certainly more so; that in the great point of conciliating and uniting all parties under a Govt which had excited such violent controversies & divisions, it was well known that his services had been in a manner essential; that with respect to the spirit of party that was taking place under the operations of the Govt I was sensible of its existence but considered that as an argument for his remaining, rather than retiring, until the public opinion, the character of the Govt and the course of its administration shd be better decided, which could not fail to happen in a short time, especially under his auspices; that the existing parties did not appear to be so formidable to the Govt as some had represented; that in one party there might be a few who retaining their original disaffection to the Govt might still wish to destroy it, but that they would lose their weight with their associates, by betraying any such hostile purposes; that altho' it was pretty certain that the other were in general unfriendly to republican Govt and probably aimed at a gradual approximation of ours to a mixt monarchy, yet the public sentiment was so strongly opposed to their views, and so rapidly manifesting itself, that the party could not long be expected to retain a dangerous influence; that it might reasonably be hoped therefore that the conciliating influence of a temperate & wise administration, would before another term of four years should run out, give such a tone & firmness to the Government as would secure it against danger from either of these descriptions of enemies; that altho' I would not allow myself to believe but that the Govt would be safely administered by any successor elected by the people, yet it was not to be denied that in the present unsettled condition of our young Government, it was to be feared that no successor would answer all the purposes to be expected from the continuance of the present chief magistrate; that the option evidently lay between a few characters; Mr Adams, Mr Jay

& Mr Jefferson were most likely to be brought into view; that with respect to Mr Jefferson, his extreme repugnance to public life & anxiety to exchange it for his farm & his philosophy, made it doubtful with his friends whether it would be possible to obtain his own consent; and if obtained, whether local prejudices in the Northern States, with the views of Pennsylvania in relation to the seat of Govt would not be a bar to his appointment. With respect to Mr Adams, his monarchical principles, which he had not concealed, with his late conduct on the representation-bill had produced such a settled dislike among republicans every where, & particularly in the Southern States, that he seemed to be out of the question.[6] It would not be in the power of those who might be friendly to his private character, & willing to trust him in a public one, notwithstanding his political principles, to make head against the torrent. With respect to Mr Jay his election would be extremely dissatisfactory on several accounts. By many he was believed to entertain the same obnoxious principles with Mr Adams, & at the same time would be less open and therefore more successful in propagating them. By others (a pretty numerous class) he was disliked & distrusted, as being thought to have espoused the claims of British Creditors at the expence of the reasonable pretensions of his fellow Citizens in debt to them. Among the western people, to whom his negociations for ceding the Mississippi to Spain were generally known, he was considered as their most dangerous enemy & held in peculiar distrust & disesteem.[7] In this state of our prospects, which was rendered more striking by a variety of temporary circumstances, I could not forbear thinking that altho' his retirement might not be fatal to the public good, yet a postponement of it was another sacrifice exacted by his patriotism.

Without appearing to be any wise satisfied with what I had urged, he turned the conversation to other subjects; & when I was withdrawing repeated his request that I would think of the points he had mentioned to me, & let him have my ideas on them before the adjournment. I told him I would do so: but still hoped his decision on the main question, would supersede for the present all such incidental questions.

Wednesday Evening May 9. 1792 Understanding that the President was to set out the ensuing morning for Mount Vernon, I called on him to let him know that as far as I had formed an opinion on the subject he had mentioned to me, it was in favor of a direct address of notification to the public in time for its proper effect on the election, which I thought might be put into such a form as would avoid every appearance of presumption or indelicacy, and seemed to be absolutely required by his situation I observed that no other mode deserving consideration had occurred, except the one he had thought of & rejected, which seemed to me liable to the objections that had weighed with him. I added that if on further reflection I shd view the subject in any new lights, I would make it the subject of a letter tho' I retained my hopes that it would not yet be necessary for him to come to any opinion on it. He begged that I would do so, and also suggest any matters that might occur as proper to be included in what he might say to Congs at the opening of their next Session. passing over the idea of his relinquishing his purpose of retiring, in a manner that did not indicate the slightest assent to it.

Friday May 25. 1792 I met the President on the road returning from Mount Vernon to Philada, when he handed me the letter dated at the latter place on the 20th of May, the copy of the answer to which on the 21st of June is annexed.[8]

AD, DLC: Madison Papers.

1. Although Congress adjourned on 8 May, Madison did not leave Philadelphia until about 20 May 1792 (see *Madison Papers,* 14:310).

2. See Thomas Jefferson's Memorandum of Conversations with Washington, 1 Mar. 1792.

3. The next session of Congress was scheduled to begin on Monday, 5 Nov. 1792.

4. Madison's reply to GW is dated 20 June 1792 and was written in Orange, Virginia.

5. GW had made similar deprecating comments about his abilities to the secretary of state in late February 1792 (see Jefferson's Memorandum of Conversations with Washington, 1 Mar. 1792).

6. John Adams, as president of the Senate, on 15 Dec. 1791 cast the vote that upheld an amendment to the apportionment bill lowering the ratio of representation from one per 30,000 to one per 33,000 (*Annals of Congress,* 2d Cong., 49–50).

7. Madison is referring to the controversial negotiations conducted by John Jay and the Spanish plenipotentiary Diego Maria de Gardoqui in 1785–86 (see James Monroe to GW, 20 Aug. 1786, and note 2).

8. GW's letter to Madison of 20 May was written at Mount Vernon, not Philadelphia, and Madison's draft of GW's Farewell Address was dated 20, not 21, June 1792.

To William Moultrie

Dear Sir, Philadelphia May 5th 1792.

I have had the pleasure to receive your letter of last month, and the seeds you had the goodness to send me by Mr Pinckney.[1] The plants & trees which arrived at Norfolk, have reached Mount Vernon in pretty good order.[2]

My thanks and acknowledgements are due to you, my dear Sir, for the kind attention which you have paid to my wishes with respect to the seeds, plants &c. You must likewise accept of them for the detail which you have been so good as to give of the mode of carrying on a war against the Indians; the cloathing of the Troops employed in that service &c.

The first wish of the United States with respect to the Indians is, to be at peace with them all, and to cultivate a good understanding to our mutual benefit. As we have not been able to attain this without the effusion of blood, the next wish is, to pursue such measures as may terminate the hostilities in the speediest manner, & most for the honor & interest of the U.S. Observations, therefore, which are founded in experience, tending to effect this, cannot but merit the thanks and acknowledgements of those who have the management of public affairs.

I am much pleased to hear that the picture by Colo. Trumbull, gives so much satisfaction. The merit of this Artist cannot fail to give much pleasure to those of his Countrymen who possess a taste for the fine arts: and I know of no part of the U:S. where it could be put to a stronger test than in South Carolina.[3] With sincere regard, & best wishes for your health & happiness, Sir, Your Affte and Obedt Servt

Go: Washington

LS (photocopy), DLC:GW, ser. 9; Df, in Tobias Lear's hand, DNA: RG 59, Miscellaneous Letters; LB, DLC:GW.

1. Moultrie's letter to GW of April 1792 has not been found. Thomas Pinckney, who had been appointed U.S. minister to Great Britain in January 1792, apparently transmitted the seeds from Charleston, S.C., to Philadelphia while en route to his new position overseas.

2. For the plants that Moultrie sent GW from Charleston, S.C., see GW to Moultrie, 8 Nov. 1791, n.2, Moultrie to GW, 29 Dec. 1791, GW to Otho Holland Williams, 7 Feb. 1792, n.2, and Williams to GW, 22 Mar. 1792.

3. John Trumbull wrote in his autobiography that the "city of Charleston, S.C. instructed William R. Smith, one of the representatives of South Carolina,

to employ me to paint for them a portrait of the *great man,* and I undertook it *con amore* [in early 1792], (as the commission was unlimited,) meaning to give his military character, in the most sublime moment of its exertion—the evening previous to the battle of Princeton. . . . The result was in my own opinion eminently successful, and the general was satisfied. But it did not meet the views of Mr. Smith. He admired, he was personally pleased, but he thought the city would be better satisfied with a more matter-of-fact likeness, such as they had recently seen him—calm, tranquil, peaceful. . . . another was painted for Charleston, agreeable to their taste—a view of the city in the background, a horse, with scenery, and plants of the climate" (Trumbull, *Autobiography,* 170–71). The first portrait is on display at Yale University, and the second is located at the city hall in Charleston.

To Henry Merttins Bird

Sir, Philadelphia May 6th 1792.

I request you will accept my thanks for your polite attention in sending me the copy of Genl Lloyd's work which accompanied your letter of the 4th of February.

Mrs Washington joins me in Compliments to Mrs Bird and in acknowledgements for the kind offer of your & her services.[1] I am Sir, with esteem, Your most Obedt Servt.

Df, in Tobias Lear's hand, DNA: RG 59, Miscellaneous Letters; LB, DLC:GW.

1. Henry Merttins Bird wrote GW from London on 4 Feb. 1792: "My sincere attachment to the Interests of the United States, & my ardent desire to do all in my Power to promote their welfare must be my excuse for troubling you with this letter, accompanied by a work of General Lloyds lately republish'd, which I understand contains some hints, particularly relative to the use of the Pike, that may be of importance in an Indian War.

"I have heard the success of the Indians against General Sinclair's unfortunate Army much attributed to the use the Indians made of the Pike instead of the Bayonet, & I feel it my Duty as a friend to America to contribute every thing in my power to avert the repetition of so fatal a misfortune.

"I have too deep a sense of my own compleat ignorance of military affairs, & too high an opinion of the transcendant abilities you have so constantly display'd in the Art of war, to suppose that any hint from me on the subject can be of the least service, & I therefore hope that this letter will not subject me to a charge of presumption, but that it will be attributed to its right motives.

"If General Lloyds work shou'd in the smallest degree contribute to the success of the American Arms, it will greatly contribute to the happiness of Sir, Yr very obedt devoted & oblig'd humble Servt . . . Mrs [Elizabeth Ryan Manning] Bird unites with me in requesting you to offer our most respectful Compliments to Mrs Washington desiring her freely to command our Services in any thing in which it might be our good fortune to be of use to you or her in this Country" (DLC:GW). The enclosure was a copy of Henry Lloyd's *Political and Military Rhapsody on the Invasion and Defence of Great Britain and Ireland* (London, 1792), which was inventoried with GW's other books and pamphlets after his death (Griffin, *Boston Athenæum Washington Collection,* 521).

To Thomas Paine

Dear Sir, Philadelphia May 6th 1792.

To my friends, and those who know my occupations, I am sure no apology is necessary for keeping their letters so much longer unanswered than my inclination would lead me to do. I shall therefore offer no excuse for not having sooner acknowledged the Receipt of your letter of the 21st of July. My thanks, however, for the token of your remembrance, in the fifty copies of the "Rights of Man" are offered with no less cordiality than they would have been had I answered your letter in the first moment of receiving it.

The duties of my Office, which at all times (especially during the sitting of Congress) require an unremitting attention naturally become more pressing towards the close of it; and as that body have resolved to rise tomorrow, and as I have determined in case they should, to set out for Mount Vernon on the next day, you will readily conclude that the present is a busy moment with me[1]—and to that I am persuaded your goodness will impute my not entering into the several points touched upon in your letter. Let it suffice, therefore, at this time to say, that I rejoice in the information of your personal prosperity—and as no one can feel a greater interest in the happiness of mankind than I do, that it is the first wish of my heart that the enlightened policy of the present age may diffuse to all men those blessings to which they are entitled—and lay the foundation of happiness for future generations. With great esteem I am—Dear Sir Your most Obedt Servt,

Go: Washington

P.S. Since writing the foregoing I have receivd your letter of the 13th of February with twelve copies of your new Work which accompanied it—and for which you must accept my additional thanks.[2]

Go: W——n

ALS, in private hands; Df, in Thomas Jefferson's hand, DLC: Jefferson Papers; LB, DLC:GW.

1. The House of Representatives originally had resolved on 4 May to remain in session until "Thursday the tenth of May." However, after the Senate expressed its desire to adjourn on "Tuesday the eighth," the House agreed to recess on that date (*Annals of Congress,* 2d Cong., 136, 593). GW was not notified officially of that decision by a joint committee until 7 May (ibid., 137). GW set out for Mount Vernon on 10 May.

2. Paine's letter to GW of 13 Feb. 1792 has not been found. Although GW kept forty-three of the fifty copies of part 1 of *Rights of Man* that Paine had forwarded to him in July 1791, none of the twelve copies of part 2 sent to him in February 1792 remained in his possession at the time of his death (Griffin, *Boston Athenæum Washington Collection,* 523).

To Robert Sinclair

Sir, Philadelphia May 6th 1792.

I have received your letter of the 12th of December, in which you request information respecting Captain James MacKay, and likewise respecting the part of this Country which would be the most eligible for forming an establishment as a farmer or planter.[1]

The only information in my power to give you on the first head is, that my acquaintance with Captain MacKay commenced in the Army in the year 1754, when I commanded the troops w[hic]h were sent to prevent the encroachments of the french upon the western boundaries of the then Colononies. Captain Mackay then commanded an Independent Company either from Georgia or So. Carolina,[2] and was captured with me by an army of French & Indians at a place called the great Meadows. In 1755 he left the service, sold out, and went to Georgia. I heard nothing of him from that time 'till about 5 or 6 years ago, when he went, by water, from Georgia to Rhode Island on account of his health. On his return to Georgia, by land, he was seized either by the complaint for which he had gone to Rhode Island, or by some other disorder, and died at Alexandria (not at my house as your letter mentions). I was not informed of his being at Alexandria until after his death, which was a circumstance that I regretted much, not only on account of the regard which I had for him from our former acquaintance, but because I understood that he was then on his way to pay me a visit—and had expressed an anxious desire to see me before he died.[3] I do not know whether Captain Mackay left any family or not; for from the time of his qu[i]tting the service until his death, as I observed before, I knew nothing of him. I have, however, been informed that he was possessed of a handsome property in Georgia.[4]

On the second head of your enquiry I can hardly venture to give you an opinion. I do not, however, imagine that an establishment on the banks of the Mississippi would at this time be a very desireable one—and even the western parts of the U.S. lying on the waters running into the Mississippi, (which is perhaps as fertile a Country as any in the World) are now disturbed by the hostilities of some of the Indian tribes bordering upon them, and from that cause are at *this moment* unfriendly to new settlements. This evil will, however, I trust, be shortly removed and settlers sit down there in safety. I can observe generally, that the United States, from their extent, offer a variety of climate soil & situations that no Country in Europe can afford—and that in cheapness of land and in the blessings of civil & religious liberty, they stand perhaps unrivalled by any civilized nation on earth. To a person who intends to pursue the farming or planting business, and is possessed of the capital which you mention,[5] I should think some one of the middle states, from New York to Virginia, both inclusive, would hold out the best advantages—they are free from the inconveniencies peculiar to either extreme & unite most of the advantages of both—they afford to the farmer a ready market for his produce—the country is intersected by large & numerous Rivers, & the spirit which now prevails for improving Inland Navigation promises to secure a cheap & easy transportation from the most interior parts of the Country to the shipping ports.

Your idea of bringing over Highlanders appears to be a good one. They are a hardy industrious people, well calculated to form new settlements—and will in time become valuable citizens.

Before I close this subject I would observe, that many persons in Europe who have purchased land in this Country for the purpose of settling upon it themselves, have on their arrival & after examining their purchase been disappointed in their expectations respecting it. Exaggerations, if not misrepresentations are apt to be made of objects at so great a distance, and those who have lands for sale will naturally give them a gloss which perhaps a purchaser would hardly find. It would therefore be much more satisfactory to the purchaser & far more creditable to the Country, if those persons who wish to purchase land here & become settlers upon it themselves, would come into the Country[6] and purchase on the spot. They could then suit their taste in point of situation—have a variety to chuse from, & see & learn with truth all the circumstances necessary for them to know to become settlers.

When this method is pursued I am persuaded that every one who comes over with a view to establish himself here may do it much to his satisfaction, & if he has with him the means of purchasing, it can certainly be done on much better terms than it could be through an Agent. I am Sir Yr most Obet Sert.

Df, in Tobias Lear's hand, DNA: RG 59, Miscellaneous Letters; LB, DLC:GW.

1. On 12 Dec. 1791 Robert Sinclair "Esquire of ScotsCalder by the Bridgend of Halkirk Caithness N. Britain" (Scotland; born c.1755) wrote GW: "I beg leave to introduce myself to you as a Nephew of Capt. James Mackay of Strathy [Scotland; d. 1785] who I am acquainted was in the best habits with your excellency and who departed this life when on a visit to your house—What I intreat to know is what family he left and how to address them—Capt. Mackay left Britain with General [James] Oglthorpe as an adventurer when Georgia was first settled; It is full thirty years since my Mother—or any of his freinds in Scotland heard from him I addressed him a letter sometime ago which was returned me and this was the first Accounts I had of his death: When I wrote him I proposed settling in one of the Southern Colonies of America; might I trespas so far on your Excellencys time as to ask your approbation which is the most eligible of the Southern States to settle in for one above thirty six years of age unmarried possest of from five to six thousand pound Sterling that is to say in the farming or planting line and would it be adviseable to take indented Highlanders as servants across the atlantic; The settlement which would appear to me the most desireable would be along the Banks of the Mississippi from 32 to 36 Degrees N. Latitude if the same be inhabited by a civilized people.

"We are at present in Britain greatly alarmed about the fate of Lord CornWallis in the East Indies It is rumoured that he has met with a severe check from Tippoo Saib in attempting to Storm his Capital and that he was oblidged to retreat to Bangalore with considerable loss if this news proves true it will be the severest shock publick credit has got for this fifty years back and the present Ministry will lose their influence in both houses of Parliment" (DLC:GW). For more information about GW's relationship with Capt. James MacKay in 1754, see *Papers, Colonial Series,* vol. 1. For Lord Cornwallis's check outside the gates of Tippoo Saib's capital of Seringapatam in May 1791 during the Third Mysore War, see Thomas Jefferson to GW, 1 May 1791, n.2. Cornwallis resumed the offensive in the winter of 1791–92 and forced Tippoo to sue for peace in March 1792. In recognition of his services on the Indian subcontinent, Cornwallis was made a marquis in August 1792.

2. Between 1749 and 1755 MacKay commanded an independent company from South Carolina.

3. George Walton wrote GW from Savannah, Ga., on 11 June 1785 that James MacKay, a "worthy and respectable old gentleman, now makes a tour to the Northward; and I think principally to pay his respects to the man whom he has such just and honorable cause to remember." The obituary of MacKay in the *Virginia Journal and Alexandria Advertiser* of 1 Dec. 1785 says that he "Died: In this Town, on his way to Mount-Vernon."

4. Although the source of GW's information about MacKay's position in society has not been identified, he does seem to have died a wealthy man. Unknown to GW, MacKay had three daughters, two of whom were living at the time of their father's death (see William Harden, "James MacKay, of Strathy Hall, Comrade in Arms of George Washington," *Georgia Historical Quarterly* 1 [1917], 94, 97).

5. Sinclair says in his letter to GW of 12 Dec. 1791 that he possessed £5,000–£6,000 sterling (see note 1 above).

6. In the draft Lear first wrote and then struck out the phrase "& view the several parts of it before they purchased."

To Alexander Spotswood

Dear Sir, Philadelphia, 6th May 1792.

I made Mr Morris acquainted with the contents of your letter of the 14th of March, relative to your Son; and am informed by him, that if your son should be in Philadelphia, agreeably to your intention of sending him here, as mentioned in your letter, there is no doubt but many opportunities may occur of his making a voyage previous to the return of Captain Truxton from the East-Indies, which is expected to be sometime next Spring—or Summer; but Mr Morris observes, that it is impossible for him *now* to point the particular voyage or vessel in which he may be employed. When he is on the spot, opportunities of employment in his line will not be wanting, he thinks, if the skill, character and appearance of the applicant are approved. With great esteem and regard I am Dr Sir, Your most obedt Servant,

Go: Washington.

LB, DLC:GW.

For the background to Alexander Spotswood's attempt to obtain a berth for his second son, John Augustine Spotswood, with Capt. Thomas Truxtun in the

East India trade or, in the event of Truxtun's long absence, on one of Robert Morris's West India vessels, see Spotswood to GW, 4 Dec. 1791, and GW to Spotswood, 7 Feb. 1792, and note 2.

From Abraham Baldwin

Sir Philadelphia 7th of May 1792

If the office of Collector of St Mary's in Georgia is considered as vacant by the appointment of Mr Seagrove to superintend Indian affairs in that department, I beg leave to recommend John King Esqr. as a proper person to be nominated to the office of collector.[1]

I have been long acquainted with Mr King and have great confidence in his integrity and abilities. with the greatest respect I have the honor to be sir your obedient humble Servt

Abr. Baldwin

ALS, DLC:GW.

Abraham Baldwin (1754–1807) served in the Continental Congress in 1785, 1787, and 1788, in the U.S. House of Representatives 1789–99, and in the Senate 1799–1807.

1. The John King of this letter is possibly the man from Georgia of that name (c.1740–c.1803) who served as a soldier in the Continental army during the Revolutionary War and as one of the commissioners appointed by the Georgia general assembly to make a treaty with the Creek Indians in 1786. GW did not appoint King to a federal office, and James Seagrove retained his position as collector of St. Mary's in Georgia until February 1798 (see *Executive Journal,* 1:262).

To Alexander Hamilton

[Philadelphia, 7 May 1792]

For carrying into execution the provisions in that behalf made by the Act intitled "An Act for raising a farther sum of money for the protection of the Frontiers, and for other purposes therein mentioned," I do hereby authorise you the said Secretary of the Treasury to agree and contract with the President Directors & Company of the Bank of the United States; with any other body politic or corporate within the United States, or with any other person or persons, for a loan or loans to the United States of any sum or sums not exceeding in the whole Five hundred and twenty three thousand five hundred Dollars to be advanced & paid in such proportions and at such periods as you shall judge necessary for fulfilling the purposes of the said Act. Provided that the rate of interest of such loan or loans shall not exceed five per centum per annum, and that the principal thereof may be reimbursed at the pleasure of the United States.[1] And I hereby promise to ratify what you shall lawfully do in the premises.[2]

In testimony whereof I have hereunto subscribed my hand at the City of Philadelphia the seventh day of May in the year one thousand seven hundred and ninety two.

Go: Washington

LB, DLC:GW.

1. This letter is essentially a recapitulation of article 16 of this act (*Annals of Congress,* 2d Cong., 1369).

2. Hamilton returned to GW "a copy of the Authorisation which the President signed this morning" later this day (DLC:GW), and on 23 May, Hamilton sent a rough draft of an agreement to Thomas Willing, the president of the Bank of the United States (see Syrett, *Hamilton Papers,* 11:419). Two days later Hamilton and Willing signed a formal agreement, which reads: "Whereas the said President Directors and Company on the application of the said Secretary have consented to lend on account of the United States the aforesaid sum of Five hundred and twenty three thousand five hundred Dollars in conformity to the provision of the Act aforesaid.

"Now therefore these Presents Witness that it hath been agreed and it is hereby mutually agreed by and between the parties aforesaid as followeth to Wit.

"First that The said President Directors and Company shall advance lend and pay on account of the United States the aforesaid sum of Five hundred and twenty three thousand five hundred Dollars, or so much thereof as may be required in the following installments and at the following periods respectively, namely One hundred thousand dollars on the first day of June next, One hundred thousand dollars on the first day of July next, One hundred thousand dollars on the first day of August next One hundred thousand dollars on the first day of September next, and the residue of the said sum of Five hundred and twenty three thousand five hundred dollars on the first day of January next which several sums shall be paid to the Treasurer of the United States upon Warrants issued from the Department of the Treasury according to Law and shall bear an Interest at the rate of Five per Centum per annum to be computed upon each of the said sums from the time of passing the same to the credit of the said Treasurer.

"Secondly that the Interest upon so much of the Loan aforesaid as may be advanced prior to the first day of January next shall be paid upon the said day and that thenceforth until the reimbursement of the principal sum which shall have been advanced and lent as aforesaid, interest shall be payable half yearly, that is to say upon the first day of July and the first day of January in each year.

"Thirdly, That the surplus of the duties laid by the Act herein before mentioned shall pursuant to the true intent and meaning of the fifteenth Section of the said Act be well and truly applied, as the same shall accrue and be received to the reimbursement of the principal and interest of the monies which shall be advanced and lent as aforesaid and that until such reimbursement shall be completed, The Secretary of the Treasury for the time being shall cause half yearly returns of the amount of the said surplus to be laid before the said President Directors and Company for their information, as soon as may be after the expiration of each half year during the continuance of the said duties from the time of the commencement thereof until the said reimbursement shall be completed.

"Provided always that the whole or any part of the monies which shall have been advanced upon the loan together with all arrears of interest thereupon to the time of such reimbursement may at any time whatsoever at the pleasure of the United States be reimbursed paid off and discharged.

"And lastly—The said Secretary of the Treasury doth promise and engage That the President of the United States within two months from and after the date of these presents will in due form ratify and confirm the Agreement hereby made" (DNA: RG 59, Miscellaneous Letters).

On 1 June, Tobias Lear returned the agreement to Hamilton, informing him that it had been submitted to the president and that as the agreement had been "made conformably to instructions given by the President to the Secretary for that purpose, the President approves the same" (DLC:GW). On 5 June, Thomas Jefferson drafted GW's official ratification of the agreement between Hamilton and the Bank of the United States (Df, DNA: RG 59, State Dept., Bills of Exchange and Loan Ratifications).

Henry Knox to Tobias Lear

[Philadelphia] 7 May 1792. Asks Lear "to send me the Map of the tract to be reserved about fort Washington."[1]

ALS, DLC:GW; LB, DLC:GW.

1. On 12 April 1792 GW had approved "An Act for ascertaining the bounds of a tract of land purchased by John Cleves Symmes," which provided "That the President reserve to the United States such lands at and near Fort Washington as he may think necessary for the accommodation of a garrison at that fort" (*Annals of Congress,* 2d Cong., 1357). GW's land grant to Symmes of 30 Sept. 1794, in consequence, reserved "to the United States out of the said Tract the quantity of fifteen acres of Land for the accommodation of Fort Washington and the Garrison thereof including the space of Ground occupied by the said Fort to be located in such part of the said Tract and by such person as the President of the United States shall direct" (copy, ViLxW). The map that Knox requested be sent to him has not been identified.

To Thomas Pinckney

Dear Sir, [Philadelphia] Monday 7th May 1792

It has been discovered that, in the Card sent Mrs Pinckney and yourself to dine with me to day, Miss Elliot was not included. Be so good as to present Mrs Washington's compliments and mine to her, and request the favor of her Company also. I am—Dear Sir Your Obedient Servt

Go: Washington

ALS, ScHi.

Elizabeth (Betsey) Motte Pinckney (c.1761–1794) had married Thomas Pinckney in July 1779. The "Miss Elliot" referred to in this letter has not been identified.

From Frederick Folger

Sir Baltimore 8th May 1792

Seeing some provision has been made by the Legislature of the United States for the Support of Consuls in the States of Barbary;[1]

A number of respectable charactors in this town Encouraged me to Apply to your Excelleny for one of those Places—Should the Nomination not be filled up, & your Excelleny will pleas to notice my name as a Petitioner.

Recommendations of my Experience knoledge & Abilities Adequate to the Discharge of Such a Trust can be forwarded from here as soon as required.[2]

With the most profound respect & veneration I beg leav to Subscribe myself Your Excellency' Most Obedient & most devoted Servant

Fred. Folger

ALS, DLC:GW. Folger wrote a similar letter of application to Thomas Jefferson on this date (DLC:GW).

Capt. Frederick Folger (d. 1797) of Baltimore, a relative of Benjamin Franklin, had commanded the schooners *Felicity* and *Antelope* during the last years of the Revolutionary War. Folger did not receive an appointment from GW at this time, but on 2 Mar. 1797 GW nominated him U.S. consul for the port and district of Aux Cayes on the island of Saint Domingue. Upon learning of Folger's death later that year, President John Adams appointed a successor on 4 Dec. 1797 (*Executive Journal,* 1:228, 253).

1. Folger apparently is referring to a bill "concerning Consuls and Vice Consuls" which the U.S. Senate passed on 29 Nov. 1791. Section 5 of this bill reads: "That in case it be found necessary for the interest of the United States, that a consul or consuls be appointed to reside on the coast of Barbary, the President be authorized to allow an annual salary, not exceeding two thousand dollars to each person so to be appointed: *Provided,* That such salary be not allowed to more than one consul for any one of the States on the said coast" (*Journal of the Senate,* 4:37–38). The bill passed in the House on 10 April, and GW signed it into law four days later (*Journal of the House,* 4:177, 187).

2. On 31 May 1792 Maryland congressman Samuel Sterett (Sterrett; 1758–1833) wrote Secretary of State Jefferson that Folger was "an useful & respectable Citizen—During the late War he was distinguished for enterprise & activity, and he is again ambitious of serving his Country. Believing him to be worthy of confidence & capable in business, whether of a commercial or political Nature, I have no hesitation in" recommending him (DLC:GW).

From Henry Knox

Sir War department May 8th 1792

I have the honor to submit the military nominations[.][1] The post is in and no letters from General Williams.[2]

I beg leave again to submit Joseph Howell as Accountant to the Department of War and Caleb Swan as Paymaster to reside with the Army.[3] I have the honor to be with perfect respect Your most obedient servant.

H. Knox
secy of War

LS, DLC:GW; LB, DLC:GW.

1. For the list of nominations, see GW to the U.S. Senate, 8 May 1792 (second letter).

2. Knox had written Otho Holland Williams on 3 May to discover whether or not he would accept a commission as brigadier general in the U.S. Army. Although still waiting for an answer, GW nominated Williams on 8 May (see GW to the U.S. Senate, 8 May [second letter]). Williams declined his commission for health reasons, however (see Williams to GW, 13 May).

3. Caleb Swan (1758–1809) served as an ensign in the Continental army from 1779 to the end of the Revolutionary War and as paymaster of the U.S. Army from May 1792 until his resignation in June 1808.

To the United States Senate

United States [Philadelphia]
Gentlemen of the Senate, May the 8th 1792.

I nominate Tench Coxe,[1] of Pennsylvania, to be Commissioner of the Revenue—Joseph Howell, of Pennsylvania, to be Accountant to the Department of War—and Caleb Swan, of Massachusetts to be Paymaster of the Troops, to reside with the Army.[2]

Go: Washington

DS, in Tobias Lear's hand, DNA: RG 46, Second Congress, 1791–1793, Records of Executive Proceedings, President's Messages—Executive Nominations; LB, DLC:GW.

1. Tench Coxe (1755–1824) of Pennsylvania served as commissioner to the Federal Convention at Annapolis in 1786, a member of the Continental Congress in 1789, assistant secretary of the treasury from 1789 until the abolition of that post on 8 May 1792, commissioner of the revenue 1792–97, and purveyor of public supplies 1803–12.

2. The Senate consented to the appointment of Coxe, Howell, and Swan that same day (see *Executive Journal,* 1:124).

To the United States Senate

United States [Philadelphia]
Gentlemen of the Senate, May the 8th 1792.

I nominate the following persons for appointments and promotions in the Army of the United States.

Appointed Otho H. Williams, of Maryland, to be Brigadier General, vice Morgan, declined.

Cavalry

Promoted William Winston to be Captain, vice Watts, declined.

Tarleton Fleming to be Lieutenant, vice Winston, promoted.

Appointed John Webb Junr, of Virginia, to be Cornet, vice Fleming, promoted.

The following corrections in the names of former Appointments are requested to be made.[1]

Major	George M. Bedinger instead of *Henry* Bedinger.
Lieutenant	Samuel Cochran instead of *Robert* Cochran.
Ensign	Andrew Marschalk instead of *John* Marschalk.

Go: Washington

DS, in Tobias Lear's hand, DNA: RG 46, Second Congress, 1791–1793, Records of Executive Proceedings, President's Messages—Executive Nominations; LB, DLC:GW.

The Senate read, considered, and consented to GW's nominations on this day (*Executive Journal*, 1:123–24).

1. The mistakes had been introduced by GW in his messages to the Senate of 14 Mar. (Cochran) and 9 April (Bedinger and Marschalk).

To the United States Senate

[Philadelphia] May. 8. 1792.

If the President of the U.S. should conclude a Convention or treaty with the Government of Algiers for the ransom of the thirteen Americans in captivity there, for a sum not exceeding 40,000 dollars, all expences included, will the Senate approve the same? or is there any & what greater or lesser sum, which they would fix on as the limit beyond which they would not approve the ransom?

If the President of the U.S. should conclude a Treaty with the Government of Algiers for the establishment of peace with them at an expence not exceeding[1] twenty five thousand dollars paid at the signature, and a like sum to be paid annually afterwards during the continuance of the treaty would the Senate approve the same? or are there any greater or lesser sums which they would fix on as the limits beyond which they would not approve of such treaty?[2]

Df (letterpress copy), in Thomas Jefferson's hand, DLC: Jefferson Papers; LB, DLC:GW; copy, DNA: RG 233, Second Congress, 1791–1793, Records of the Office of the Clerk, Records of Reports from Executive Departments; copy, DNA: RG 46, Third Congress, 1793–1795, Records of Executive Proceedings, President's Messages—Foreign Relations.

For the background to this document, see the letters cited in GW to Thomas Jefferson, 10 Mar., source note, Conversation with a Committee of the U.S. Senate, 12 Mar., Jefferson to GW, 1 April, and notes 1 and 3, and Jefferson's Memorandum on a Treaty with Algiers, 10 April, and source note.

1. Jefferson left a blank at this place in the draft. The figure is supplied from the letter-book copy at DLC.

2. The Senate voted on this day to approve a treaty paying the government of Algiers $40,000 for the release of the American prisoners and $25,000 annually while the treaty between the United States and Algiers remained in effect (*Executive Journal,* 1:123).

To Alexander Hamilton

[Philadelphia, 9 May 1792]

For carrying into execution the provisions of the Eleventh section of the Act intitled "An Act to incorporate the subscribers to the Bank of the United States," I do hereby authorise you the said Secretary of the Treasury to subscribe by one or more subscriptions, on behalf and in the name of the United States, for such number of shares of and in the capital stock of the said Corporation as together shall amount to two Millions of Dollars, and the same to pay for out of any monies which shall have been or shall be borrowed by virtue of either of the Acts, the one intitled; "An Act making provision for the Debt of the United States," and the other intitled, "An Act making provision for the reduction of the public Debt": and I do further authorise you to borrow of the said Corporation for and on account of the United States an equal sum, namely, Two Millions of Dollars to be applied to the purposes for which the said monies shall have been procured, and to be reimbursable in Ten years by equal annual installments, or at any time sooner or in any greater proportions that the Government may think fit.[1] Provided that the interest on the said sum so by you to be borrowed, shall not exceed the rate of six per centum per annum, hereby empowering you to enter into and conclude with the said Corporation such contracts and Agreements as shall be necessary for fulfilling the purposes aforesaid, and promising to ratify whatever you shall lawfully do in the premises.[2]

In testimony whereof I have hereunto subscribed my hand at the City of Philadelphia the Ninth day of May in the year of our Lord one thousand seven hundred and ninety two.

G: Washington

LB, DLC:GW.

1. GW's letter to Hamilton to this point is essentially a recapitulation of section 11 of "An Act to incorporate . . ." of 25 Feb. 1791 (see *Annals of Congress,* 1st Cong., 2381).

2. On 11 June, Hamilton sent a draft of an agreement to the president of the Bank of the United States, Thomas Willing, for submission to the board of directors (Syrett, *Hamilton Papers,* 11:511–12). On 23 June, Hamilton submitted to GW in writing "the Draft of an Agreement concerning the subscription on behalf of the U. States to the Bank, agreeably to terms concerted with the Directors, in order that it may be considered by the President previous to it's execution. The Secretary will wait upon the President for his Orders on Monday morning" (DLC:GW). Having received GW's approval, Hamilton and Willing on Monday, 25 June, signed a formal agreement outlining the obligations of the respective parties. This document is printed in full in Syrett, *Hamilton Papers,* 11:560–63.

From Alexander Hamilton

Treasury Department, 9 May 1792. Transmits "a fair copy of the Draft approved by the President this morning respecting the Port of Entry & Delivery in the District of Vermont."[1]

LB, DLC:GW.

1. The enclosure says "that pursuant to the provision in that behalf made by the Act intitled 'An Act for raising a further sum of money for the protection of the Frontiers, and for other purposes therein mentioned' [of 2 May 1792] I have appointed, and by these presents do appoint the Island of South Hero in Lake Champlain to be the Port of Entry and Delivery within and for the District of Vermont" (LB, DLC:GW; see also *Annals of Congress,* 2d Cong., 1370).

From Alexander Hamilton

Sir, Treasury Department 9th May 1792.

I have the honor to send herewith an adjustment at the Treasury concerning the quantity of Acres in Warrants for army bounty rights, which ought to be deemed an equivalent for the 214,285, Acres of land mentioned in the second enacting clause of the Act intitled "An Act authorising the grant and conveyance of certain Lands to the Ohio Company of Associates";[1] and a Certificate of the delivery of the requisite quantity of Warrants in conformity to that adjustment.[2]

It is with regret I find myself required by Law to discharge an official duty in a case in which I happen to be interested as a party, and which is capable of being regulated by different constructions.[3]

Thus circumstanced I have conceived it proper to repose myself on the judgment of others; and having referred the matter to the accounting Officers of the Treasury, with the opinion of the Attorney General, which was previously obtained, I have governed myself by the determinations of those Officers.

I submit it nevertheless to the President whether it will not be adviseable to require as a condition to the issuing of the Grant that the parties give bond to pay any deficiency which there may be in the quantity of Warrants delivered, if the Legislature at the ensuing Session shall decide that the construction which has been adopted is not the true one, or to surrender the Letters Patent for the Tract in question.[4] With the highest respect, I have the honor to be &c.

Alexander Hamilton

LB, DLC:GW.

1. Section 2 of this act of 21 April 1792 empowered the president "by letters patent as aforesaid, to grant and convey to the said Rufus Putnam, Manasseh Cutler, Robert Oliver, and Griffin Green, and to their heirs and assigns, in trust, for the uses above expressed, one other tract of two hundred and fourteen thousand two hundred and eighty-five acres of land" provided that the above-mentioned individuals "or either of them, shall deliver to the Secretary of the Treasury, within six months, warrants which issued for Army bounty rights sufficient for that purpose, according to the provision of a resolve of Congress of the twenty-third day of July, one thousand seven hundred and eighty-seven" (*Annals of Congress,* 2d Cong., 1364; see also *JCC,* 33:399–401). For the dimensions of the tract, see Proclamation, 10 May 1792. For the earlier activities of the Ohio Company of Associates, see the Ohio Company Committee to GW, 13 June 1789, source note.

2. Hamilton's enclosure, a third letter to GW of this date, certified that Putnam, Cutler, Oliver, and Greene had delivered the warrants in question to the Treasury Department (DLC:GW).

3. Hamilton owned five and one-half shares in the Ohio Company.

4. For GW's decision, see Proclamation, 10 May 1792.

From Thomas Barclay

Gibraltar, 10 May 1792. Encloses "a letter which fell into my hands some Days ago, and which I beleive is from Algiers."[1]

ALS, DLC:GW.

1. The letter "from Algiers" that Barclay enclosed has not been identified.

To Giuseppe Ceracchi

Phila. May 10th 1792

The President of the United States presents his Compliments to Mr Ciracchi and with many thanks for his offer of the very elegant figures sent him, begs leave to restore them again to Mr Ciracchi.[1] His situation calling for uniformity of conduct in these cases, he relies that Mr Ciracchi will ascribe it in the presen[t][2] instance to its true motives, and accept the assurances the President now gives of the high sense he entertains of his talents & merit.

AL, MH; Df (letterpress copy), in Thomas Jefferson's hand, DLC: Jefferson Papers; LB, DLC:GW. Jefferson's draft, which is entitled "Sketch of Note to mr Ciracchi," is dated 12 Mar. 1792.

1. Ceracchi had sent the "very elegant" marble busts of Ariadne and Bacchus to GW in 1791. Although not wishing to own them, GW, as a favor to the artist, displayed the pieces at the presidential mansion for the next three years (see Ceracchi to GW, 31 Oct. 1791, source note).

2. GW mistakenly wrote the word "presence" on the AL; the correct word, "present," is found in both Jefferson's draft and the letter-book copy.

From William Preston

Sir Virginia, Montgomery County, May 10th 1792

Some Gentlemen who have been honored with the appointment of Captains of Volunteer Companies of Rifflemen not accepting their appointments, leaves a vacancy now to be filled.

Though I have not the smallest acquaintance with your Excellency yet I hope soliciting an appointment of this nature will not be taken amiss.

I am the third Son of the late Colo. William Preston, with

whom you formerly had an acquaintance from which acquaintance he formed an attachment for you worthy an honest mind;[1] by whose industry with a small addition of my own, my circumstances are not only comfortable but easy, yet I have from my infancy felt a fondness for a military life, in which I have some little experience in the Indian mode of Warfare living on the Frontiers, and only lament that my youth prevented my bearing a part with your Excellency in the late glorious Revolution between England and America.

Your Excellency I hope will pardon me for the Liberty I now take in Soliciting this appointment and at the same time referring you to the Honble John Brown and Andrew Moore Esquires for information of my abilities and integrity, and should I meet your approbation I hope I shall prove myself worthy the Appointment. I have the Honor to be Sir with Esteem your Mo. Obt Sert

William Preston

ALS, DLC:GW.

GW apparently appointed Preston to command one of the four rifle companies being raised on the southwestern frontier of Virginia (see Henry Knox to GW, 21 July 1792).

1. William Preston, Sr. (1729–1783), who had been a militia officer and a ranger captain on the Augusta County frontier during the French and Indian War, first met GW in 1756. In his capacity as surveyor of Fincastle County, Va., Preston had corresponded with GW in 1774–75.

Proclamation

[Philadelphia, 10 May 1792]

In the name of the United States. To all to whom these Presents shall come.

Whereas it hath been duly certified to me by the Secretary of the Treasury, in pursuance of the Act intituled "An Act authorising the grant and conveyance of certain lands to the Ohio Company of Associates" that Rufus Putnam, Manasseh Cutler, Robert Oliver, and Griffin Green have delivered to him warrants which issued for army bounty rights, sufficient for the purposes of the grant and conveyance of two hundred and fourteen thousand two hundred and eighty five acres of land; in the second section of the above recited act mentioned, according to the provision of a resolve of Congress of the twenty third day of July, one thousand seven hundred and eighty seven.[1]

Now Know Ye, that by virtue of the above recited Act, I do hereby grant and convey to the said Rufus Putnam, Manasseh Cutler, Robert Oliver, and Griffin Green and to their heirs and assigns one tract of land containing two hundred and fourteen thousand two hundred and eighty five acres to be located within the limits of the tract of one million five hundred thousand acres described in an Indenture executed on the twenty seventh day of October in the year one thousand seven hundred and eighty seven, between the then board of Treasury for the United States of America of the one part; and Manasseh Cutler and Winthrop Sergeant, as agents for the directors of the Ohio Company of Associates of the other part, and adjoining to the tract of land, described in the first section of the above recited act, and the form herein prescribed, as follows.[2]

Beginning on a line that has been surveyed and marked by Israel Ludlow (a plat or map whereof is filed in the Office of the Secretary of the Treasury)[3] as for the North boundary line of one million five hundred thousand acres expressed in an Indenture executed on the twenty seventh day of October one thousand seven hundred and eighty seven between the then board of Treasury for the United States of America of the one part and Manasseh Cutler and Winthrop Sergeant of the other part at a point which is and shall be established to be the North West corner of a tract of one hundred thousand acres granted to the said Rufus Putnam, Manasseh Cutler, Robert Oliver, and Griffin Green by letters patent bearing even date with these presents,[4] Thence running Westerly on the said line surveyed and marked as aforesaid to a point where the said line would intersect the West boundary line of the eleventh range of Townships if laid out agreeably to the Land ordinance passed the twentieth day of May one thousand seven hundred and eighty five,[5] Thence running South on the said Western boundary of the said eleventh range of Townships if laid out as aforesaid till it would intersect a Westerly continuation of the North boundary line of the third Township of the seventh range of Townships surveyed by the authority of the United States of America in Congress assembled, Thence running on a further Westerly continuation of the said

North boundary line of the said third Township to a point, station, or place, where the western boundary line of the sixteenth range of Townships would intersect or meet the same if laid out agreeably to the land Ordinance aforesaid, Thence running South on the said western boundary line of the sixteenth range of Townships if laid out as aforesaid to a point, station, or place, from which a line drawn due East to the West boundary line of a tract of nine hundred and thirteen thousand, eight hundred and eighty three acres granted to Rufus Putnam, Manasseh Cutler, Robert Oliver and Griffin Green by letters patent bearing even date with these presents will with the other lines of this tract as herein specified and described comprehend two hundred and fourteen thousand two hundred and eighty five acres, Thence running due East to the Western boundary line of the said tract of nine hundred and thiteen thousand eight hundred and eighty three acres, Thence running Northerly on the said Western boundary line to the Northwest corner of the said last mentioned tract, Thence running Easterly on the Northern boundary of the said last mentioned tract to the point where the same is touched or intersected by the Western boundary of the aforesaid tract of one hundred thousand acres, Thence Northerly on the said Western boundary of the said last mentioned tract to the place of beginning—To have and to hold the aforesaid tract of two hundred and fourteen thousand two hundred and eighty five acres of land to the said Rufus Putnam, Manasseh Cutler, Robert Oliver, and Griffin Green and to their heirs and assigns In Trust for the persons composing the said Ohio Company of Associates according to their several rights and interests and for their heirs and assigns as tenants in common, hereby willing and directing these letters to be made patent.[6]

Given under my hand and the Seal of the United States at the City of Philadelphia this tenth day of May in the year of our Lord one thousand seven hundred and ninety two and of Independance the sixteenth.

By the President Go: Washington.
Signed Th: Jefferson.

Copy, OMC. According to a notation at the bottom of the last manuscript page, this copy was made by Josiah Meigs on 20 Jan. 1819 at the "General Land-Office" in Washington, D.C.

1. For "An Act authorizing the grant and conveyance of certain lands to the

Ohio Company of Associates" of 21 April 1792, see *Annals of Congress,* 2d Cong., 1363–64. For Alexander Hamilton's certification of the delivery of the warrants to the Treasury Department, see Hamilton to GW, 9 May (second letter), n.2. For Congress's resolution of 23 July 1787, see *JCC,* 33:399–401. Robert Oliver (1738–1811) of Massachusetts, who became a captain in the Continental army in 1776, was promoted to major in November 1777 and was brevetted lieutenant colonel in 1783. Having moved to the Northwest Territory after the Revolutionary War, he was named a justice of the peace for Washington County in 1788 and was appointed a major in the county militia the following year. In 1797 Oliver was promoted to the rank of lieutenant colonel in the militia. Griffin Greene (1749–1804), a cousin of Nathanael Greene, served as a baker, paymaster, and deputy quartermaster during the Revolutionary War. An investor in the Ohio Company, Greene moved in 1788 to Marietta, Northwest Territory, where he became a justice of the peace. At the time of his death, Greene was Marietta's postmaster.

2. See the form prescribed in section 4 of the act of 21 April 1792 (*Annals of Congress,* 2d Cong., 1364).

3. For Israel Ludlow's presentation to Alexander Hamilton of "the whole of the survey of the Ohio and part of the Miami purchases, executed agreeably to instructions," see Ludlow to Hamilton, 5 May 1792, in Syrett, *Hamilton Papers,* 11:361–64. Israel Ludlow (1765–1804) of Morristown, N.J., had served as an assistant surveyor under the geographer of the United States, Thomas Hutchins (1730–1789), in the 1780s. During the 1790s Ludlow was "employed by the General Gove[r]nment for a number of years to conduct and compleat certain surveys and to ascertain the exterior lines or boundaries of the purchases made of the United States by the Ohio, the Scioto, & the Miami Company" (Ludlow to Timothy Pickering, 9 July 1796, DNA: RG 59, Miscellaneous Letters). In May 1800 President John Adams appointed Ludlow register of the land office at Cincinnati.

4. Section 3 of the act of 21 April 1792 empowered GW to convey an additional 100,000 acres to Putnam, Cutler, Oliver, and Greene provided that the grant became "void for such part thereof as the said Company shall not have, within five years from the passing of this act, conveyed in fee simple, as a bounty, and free of expense, in tracts of one hundred acres, to each male person not less than eighteen years of age, being an actual settler at the time of such conveyance" (*Annals of Congress,* 2d Cong., 1364).

5. For "An Ordinance for ascertaining the mode of disposing of Lands in the Western Territory" of 20 May 1785, see *JCC,* 28:375–81.

6. Hamilton wrote Secretary of State Jefferson on 12 May that he wished "the Patent for 214.285 acres when sealed & recorded to be delivered to the bearer The Rev Mr [Manasseh] Cutler." The patent was given to Cutler, who was in Philadelphia for a meeting of the board of directors of the Ohio Company, that same day (Syrett, *Hamilton Papers,* 11:396–97).

From Tench Coxe

Sir Philadelphia May 11th 1792

Having been informed by the Secretary of the Treasury, that you had been pleased to confide to me the office of the Commissioner of the Revenue,[1] I should have deemed it my duty immediately to have waited on you for the purpose of expressing my grateful sense of the honor confered upon me, and of respectfully informing you of my chearful obedience to your commands in this and every service in my power. But your departure for Virginia, which I understood was to take place in a few minutes, and an apprehension, that a personal performance of that act of duty and respect might at such a moment prove inconvenient to you, occasioned me to adopt this mode.

I humbly request you to believe, Sir, that I shall steadily endeavour, by an honest and assiduous exercise of the portion of ability with which providence has endowed me, to justify your confidence; and to make to you that return of *usefulness in my sphere,* which alone you desire from those to whom you dispense the public honors & emoluments. With unfeigned veneration for your person and exalted station—I have the honor to be Sir your most obedient & most humble Servant

Tench Coxe

ALS, DNA: RG 59, Miscellaneous Letters; ADfS, PHi: Tench Coxe Papers. It is evident from the large number of struck-out words in the draft at PHi that Coxe heavily edited this letter. All of his alterations are apparently stylistic, not substantive, however.

1. See GW to the U.S. Senate, 8 May (first letter), and notes 1 and 2.

William Pearce to Tobias Lear

Mr Lear Sir. Philadelphia May 11th 1792

I now have my Machinery &c. at Work, and should be glad to be informed when the President of the United States and his Lady, would be pleased to Honor me with their Company, to take a look at them.

Mrs Hamilton has likewise a desire to see them, when the President and his Lady, is pleased to fix the time, I will let her know, if it is agreeable to them.

Your answer by the bearer, if convenient will greatly oblige Sir Your obt hble Servant

Wm Pearce

P.S. Mr Hamilton & Mr Jefferson wishes to be there at the same time.[1]

ALS, NNGL.

For the background to William Pearce's immigration to the United States and his part in the invention of an improved double loom, see Thomas McCabe to GW, 21 July 1790, Thomas Attwood Digges to GW, c.28 April (letter-not-found entry), 1 July, 12 Nov. 1791, and GW to Thomas Jefferson, 12 July 1791, and note 3.

1. On 9 June 1792 the *Gazette of the United States* (Philadelphia) reported that "On Tuesday last [5 June] the PRESIDENT of the United States, and his Lady, attended by the Secretary of State, and the Secretary of the Treasury and his Lady, visited Mr. *Pearce's* Cotton Manufactory. The President attentively viewed the Machinery, &c. and saw the business performed in its different branches—which received his warmest approbation."

From Henry Knox

Sir, War department May 12. 1792

By the Pittsburg post it appears that all is quiet in that quarter.

I have the honor to submit the extract of a Letter from Governor Blount to Doctor Williamson dated April 14th 1792, boding trouble in that quarter.[1]

But I have but little doubt that upon the arrival of my letter and Mr Allison with the goods that tranquillity will be again restored.[2]

I also enclose the copy of a letter from James Seagrove dated the 24. April.[3]

You will probably have learned that General Williams has declined. It were to be wished Governor Howard would accept.[4]

Captain William Lewis of Bottetourt has also declined and agreeably to your orders Alexander Gibson is appointed.[5]

An Ensign in the same quarter by the name of Patrick Shirkey has declined, Mr Moore is to nominate a proper character to succeed him.[6] I have the honor to be with perfect Respect Your humble servant

H. Knox

LS, DLC:GW; LB, DLC:GW.

1. The enclosed extract of a letter from Gov. William Blount to Hugh Williamson, which was written at Knoxville on 14 April 1792, reads: "Thursday last was a week [5 April] an unlucky day, an Indian man passing peaceably from Colonel [James] Hubbards with four Squaws was fired on by two people he says Hubbards sons, one ball grazed his cheek and the other passed through his side not mortal—I have not yet been able to fix it on any particular persons. In the morning of the same day, Harper Ratcliffs wife and three children were killed in Stanly Valley which is on Clinch just below the Virginia line, five Indians were seen in the act by Ratcliff himself supposed to be [ ] the birch and his party and the same Evening a Number of Horses were taken from a station in Powells valley about twenty, And on the evening of the same day Thursday as the Head man of Hiwassa and other indians were encamped between Comberland mountain & Clinch they were fired upon, the Headman killed another wounded and the camp robbed of every thing they had. This is the account of the wounded man who reached Cayattee on the succeeding sunday night [8 April]—Immediately on hearing his account dispatched a Messenger over to Clinch to enquire who could have done it—and can hear nothing as to who did, but I am pretty sure it is by no people of this Territory and their is strong reasons to suspect that it was done by a part of those two companies Stationed on Clynch for the protection of the frontier of Russel County—I am also using my endeavours to find out the author of this damnable act. On thursday also the same day, I had ordered a company to be drafted in Hawkins County (being general muster day) to March on the 25th instant, for the defence of the frontiers of Cumberland under Captain [James] Cooper, which was done with great readiness, but all the unforeseen circumstances taking place, I shall order this company to range for the protection of the frontiers of Hawkins, and shall order another company to be raised to March to Cumberland, in some other county—I have order'd two to turn out in Miro district the whole four, for three months each.

"Yesterday arrived here three Chickasaws on their way for Philadelphia with a letter to the President from Piemingo [Piomingo; Mountain Leader]—I shall endeavor to turn them back; but its uncertain whether I can or not—They speak peace from the Chickasaws and Chactaws and say they will turn out 500 Men to assist the United States the next campaign—I shall immediately dispatch a Man to them to get them out as early as possible, and should have done it before, but . . . there were reasons to fear that they were hostile in which case there could have been no hope of success—If these Chickasaws do turn back it will be in consequence of my assuring them that a Treaty is to be held with them at Nashville and the Chactaws too in which I fully depend and if it is not, my reputation with them will be worse than General [Arthur] St Clair's, and that is bad enough. I depend much a Treaty is to be held—With these Chickasaws, came [James] Randolph Robertson, and Anthony Foster who inform that the scout sent out by General [James] Robertson over took a party of the Indians regained two horses wounded some Indians and lost two of their own party" (DLC:GW).

2. For the background to Governor Blount's conference with the Chickasaw

and Choctaw Indians at Nashville in the summer of 1792, see Henry Knox to GW, 21 April, n.1. Deputy paymaster David Allison, who had come to Philadelphia earlier in the spring to collect goods for the treaty, arrived at Knoxville on 31 May 1792 (see William Blount to Henry Knox, 2 June, in Carter, *Territorial Papers,* 4:154).

3. James Seagrove's letter to Secretary of War Knox of 24 April has not been identified.

4. For the recent offer of a brigadier generalship to Otho Holland Williams and his decision not to serve, see Knox to GW, 8 May, n.2, GW to the U.S. Senate, 8 May (second letter), and Williams to GW, 13 May, and the notes to that document. Former Maryland governor John Eager Howard also declined an appointment in the U.S. Army at this time. He continued to serve in the state senate until 1795.

5. For the reasons behind Capt. William Lewis's inability to serve in the military, see Andrew Lewis, Jr., to GW, 27 April. Alexander Gibson, who was appointed in Lewis's place, was a captain in the U.S. Army from 1792 to 1800 (see GW to the U.S. Senate, 19 Nov. [second letter]; *Executive Journal,* 1: 125–26).

6. Patrick Shirkey apparently continued serving in the U.S. Army until his resignation in January 1793, making it unnecessary for Andrew Moore to choose a replacement for him. For Shirkey's nomination, see GW to the U.S. Senate, 6 Mar., enclosure; ibid., 101–2, 105.

From Alexander Hamilton

Sir, Bristol [Pa.] May 13. 1792.

I left the City of Philadelphia this Morning on my way to Newark as I mention'd to you previous to your departure.[1] Nothing new had occurred.

Mr Belli was furnished with the requisite sum for the purchase of Dragoon Horses in Kentucke, in conformity to an arrangement, which I understand [from] the Secretary at War, was made pursuant to your direction. The Quarter Master General also has had an advance commensurate with the objects he is immediately to provide for; so that every thing is in proper train as far as pecuniary supply is concerned.[2] With the most perfect respect and truest attachment, I have the honor to be &c.

A: Hamilton

LB, DLC:GW.

1. On 16 May, Tench Coxe wrote GW from the revenue office at the Treasury Department that as Hamilton had "gone to New Jersey to attend an important meeting of the directors of the society for the promotion of useful

Manufactures in that State," he was forwarding to GW a letter (not identified) which had arrived "by the last Georgia Mail" (DNA: RG 59, Miscellaneous Letters). GW had left Philadelphia for Mount Vernon on 10 May 1792.

2. Quartermaster general James O'Hara, whose nomination had been confirmed by the Senate on 19 April, and deputy quartermaster general John Belli, who had received his commission three days earlier, both were acting under the "Act for making further and more effectual provision for the protection of the Frontiers of the United States" of 5 Mar. 1792 (see *Annals of Congress,* 2d Cong., 1343–46). Their task at this time was to ensure that the American forces at Pittsburgh and on the Ohio and Great Miami rivers were provisioned properly.

From Leonard Marbury

Sir, Frederica [Saint Simons Island, Ga.] 13th May 1792

I did myself the Honor to Write your Excellency on the 21t Ult. since then we have a Report of the death of General McGillivray,[1] shou'd this prove true I think it wou'd be advisable to have some Person among the Indians for a few Months in Order to prevail on the Chiefs to agree on some general Mode for the Regulation of their Conduct.

In my last I mention'd the manner in which the trade among the Indians had been generally conducted, but Omitted to inform that there was a stated Price for every Article thro' the Whole Nations and wou'd again Recommend the same Mode to be adopted in order to Prevent any imposition.

If the Report of McGillivrays death is well founded, I wou'd more strongly than ever Recommend that the United States take the Trade into their Own hands, as they may, by Importing the proper Indian Goods and selling them to the traders on an advance only sufficient to Pay Charges, put it out of the power of any Individual to take any Part of the trade. it wou'd also enable the traders in the different Towns to sell to the Indians much Cheaper than they have been able to Buy since the Commencement of the late War, and wou'd most effectually secure their friendship. Shou'd this plan be adopted I wou'd recommend the place for carrying on the Trade to be near the Confluence of the Rivers Oconie & Oakmulga.[2] I have the Honor to be with due Esteem Your Excellency's Most Humble Servant

Leod Marbury

ALS, DNA: RG 59, Miscellaneous Letters.

1. The report of Alexander McGillivray's death was premature. He died in February 1793 of what William Panton called "a Complication of disorders of Gout in the stomack attended with a perepneaumony" (see Panton to Francis Hector, baron de Carondelet, 16 Feb. 1793, in Caughey, *McGillivray of the Creeks,* 353).

2. The Oconee and Ocmulgee rivers join to form the Altamaha River a short distance north-northeast of Hazelhurst, Georgia.

From Otho Holland Williams

Sir Baltimore 13th May 1792

By a Note, received this morning from Mr Lear, I am requested to let you know "if I have received the notification of my appointment to the Office of Brigadier General; and whether I accept."[1]

I have not, Sir, received any Official Notice of such an appointment.

My answer to a private letter from the secretary of War, of which the inclosed is a copy, may in some measure, account for the delay; at the same time that it adduces some of the reasons which I beg may be received as my appology for not accepting.[2]

A propensity to the science of War, as a necessary means of public defence, and a desire of contributing to the service of my Country, had induced the contemplation of an appointment in the Army; and I had mentioned it to my friends previous to the receipt of General Knox's private letter; But the advice of my Physicians and the intreaties of all my friends united with the consideration of very great private inconvenience to make me wish that I might not receive that honor.

It is with real regret, Sir, that I am forced to decline the command to which it has been your pleasure to appoint me; and I feel perhaps more than is common upon such occasions as this is the first instance, of a great many, wherein my services have been required by my Country, either in a Military or a civil capacity, in which I have not obeyed the summons with alacrity and pleasure. I have the honor to be, with the most perfect respect, Sir, Your most Obliged, and most obedient, Humble, Servant.

O. H. Williams

N.B. Sunday[3] 10 o'Clock. I have this moment received an Official Notification from the Secretary at War, which I will answer immediately.

ALS, DNA: RG 59, Miscellaneous Letters; ADfS, MdHi: Otho Holland Williams Papers.

1. GW nominated Williams a brigadier general in the U.S. Army on 8 May, and the Senate confirmed the appointment that same day (see GW to the U.S. Senate, 8 May [second letter]; *Executive Journal,* 1:124). Tobias Lear's note to Williams of 13 May 1792 is located at MdHi: Otho Holland Williams Papers.

2. Williams enclosed a copy of his letter to Henry Knox of 6 May, which was written in response to Knox's "private letter" of 3 May and which reads in part: "I could not, at this time accept a command in the army even if the President were to think me worthy of commanding in chief.

"My health, for more than two Years, has been extremely precarious, and still requires the most attentive care. The happiness of my family, which is most dear to me, in case of my acceptance, must be for a time suspended if not sacrifised; and a charge in which my affections and integrity are engaged, a charge of a number of Orphan children and their estates, must be neglected. Under present circumstances I request to be excused for declining the honor proposed to be conferred on me" (DNA: RG 59, Miscellaneous Letters).

3. Williams's closing note was written on this same day, Sunday, 13 May 1792.

From Betty Washington Lewis

My Dear Brother May 14th 1792

You will receive this by Howell, who seems Very happy In the thought of becoming One of your family,[1] I sincerely wish he may be Equal to the task you desire for him, he has Promis'd me to Indeaver to Please, and by Close application to improve him self, it is with Infinite Pleasure to my self that he has a Prospect of geting in a Place where he may receive so much advantage to him self, his Fortune being very small there is little Prospect of happiness in this world without thay Can get into Busness of some sort.

I am Extrealy Obliged to you for your kind Invitation to Mount Vernon,[2] if it is in my Power shall do my self that Happiness if any thing should Prevent my Comeing, it would a'd infinate satisfaction to me to see you and my Sister here.[3] I am Dear Brother with sincere Love Your Affectionate Sister

Betty Lewis

ALS, MH.

1. For the background to Howell Lewis's employment as one of GW's secretaries, see GW to Betty Washington Lewis, 8 April, and Howell Lewis to GW, 24 April, which is printed as a note to Betty Lewis to GW, 19 April 1792.

2. GW's invitation to visit Mount Vernon has not been found.

3. Betty Washington Lewis lived at Kenmore, the Lewis family home in Fredericksburg, Virginia.

From Jean François Gergens

Mayence en Allemagne Sur Le Rhin le 15 de May 1792.

Excellence Monseigneur le Président!

Les merits, que votre Excellence S'â attiré toujours pour le bien d'humanité, le zèle noble et infatigable, dont vous avez gagné le vrai bien de vos frères; les plusieurs heures pleins de trouble, que vous avez Sacrifié pour la liberté de vos freres, et les differents dangers, que vous vous étes exposé pour defendre la liberté civile, et pour eloigner tout esclavage déshonorant l'humanité: Tous ces traits grands d'une ame noble, ne preuvent que trop, que votre Excellence dans votre carriere politique ne vive pas, que pour cela qui est bon et noble; et que vous gouvernez a present en paix cela, que vos talents mititairs ont bati. C'est cette humanité, ce Zele pour la fortune humaine, qui â pousse peut etre deja plusieurs allemands de probité, Sous le gouvernement Sage de votre Excellence tenter ses forces pour le bien de Ses freres. Par la meme raison ose aussi un jeune medecin, qui S'est assez préparé pour la medecine par les études de la philosophie et mathematique; qui par les etudes de la medecine, non Seulment en medecine, mais aussi en chirurgie et ⟨e⟩n accouchement s'est gagné les Sciences necessairs pour leur pratique; qu'il â prouvé deja dans un examen, et pratiqué dans des hopitaux. Celui ose de S'addresser a votre Excellence et a Congrés des etats unis; de demander en tout obeisance une avis favorable; Si Sous conditions appaisants un jeune medecin, qui a deja la permission de pratiquer Ses Sciences dans Sa patrie; aussi en Philadelphia, ou dans une autre capitale des etats unis peuve exercer Ses Sciences pour le bien des hommes libres.[1] Car vivre entre les hommes qui S'aiment ensemble comme des freres, qui ne connoissent pas plus l'esclavage, ces homms Servir pour leur avantage, c'etoit toujours mon desir passionné et est aussi a present la cause de ma Supplique. Si peut etre quelques indignes, qui des differents causes etoint contraints de quittér leur patrie, un noble congrés, digne de la plus grande venération, ont deja plusieurs fois incommodé avec des priers indiscrets, je prie, de ne me compter pas sous le meme nombre. Les lettres testimoniales d'un *Forster,* qui avec le Capitain Kok faisoit le tour en cinglant du Monde;[2] les lettres testimoniales d'un *Soemmering, Weidmann, Strack* et de mes autres docteurs, dont les nommes sont assez connues dans les Universités d'Angleterre, les lettres testimoniales de toute la faculté medicinale, tant sur mon Conduit, que Sur mes Sciences, et le patent du Doctorat, que j'ai reçu dans notre université, me garderont assez de ce Soupçon si jaurai le bonheure de recevoir une rescrit favorable. Avec plaisir je rendrai touttes cettes lettres testimoniales si je serois si heureux de me pouvoir rejouir de l'aide d'un Congres grand, et digne de la plus grande veneration.

S'il manquoit aussi dans ces provinces (qui doivent a votre Excellence tant de vrai fortune humaine) des hommes, qui par education et enseignement enrichissent le tresor publique en talents, Sciences, en eclaircissement de l'esprit, en gout sain, en diligence et industrié en passions des citoiens prudemment conduits: je connais ici un Professeur de l'université, dont les etudes per vingt ans etoint l'education selon les mellieurs principes, fondés sur la natur humain, et qui est dans une pratique continuelle. Cet homme a fait un plan complet, Sur les ecoles civiles, tant dans la paÿs plat, que dans les villes, pour les garçons et pour les filles: Sur les ecoles preparativs a l'universités, et Sur une ecole normale pour ÿ enseigner des maitres utiles; que cet homme avec mon assistence en quelques Sciences, realisoit, S'il etoit dans un etat, ou on favorisoit avec zele le bien humain, que, helas! dans notre patrie allemande et particulierrement dans un Archiepiscopat catholique (tant qu'on en écrit sur l'education) pourtant n'en attache pas de sitot, dont devoir le demande, d'ordonner l'education; et ce la, tant moins a present, ou on jette le mecontentement universel qui S'etende presque par toute l'Europe, Seulement Sur l'eclaircissment trop avancée; lorsque pourtant l'oppression trop impitoÿable Seulement en est la cause. Cet humaniste Solide dont j'ai fait mention, publieroit aussi des pieces convenables pour chaque classe des hommes utile. il appuÿoit l'imprimerie, et en generale il faisoit tout pour l'état des gens de profession, qu'on peut attendre dans cette egard de forces d'un homme, et en effet, tout cela ave⟨c⟩ des Sentiments pleins de Sincerité et de tollerance.

Si nous nous verrons si heureuse de reçevoir une reponse de votre Excellence nous trouverons peut etre des hommes en Philadelphia meme, qui ne pas moi, pourtant le dit humani⟨s⟩te connoissent bien, et en personne peuvent donner l'avis a votre Excellence, Sur les talents et le caractére de cet homme Soli⟨de⟩ Cependant je prie favorable indulgence, Si cette Suplique de couvre trop leur auteur allemande, qui n'a pas jamais eu la bonheure de pouvoir exercer cette langue en france meme. En attendant une reponse favorable, je reste continnuellement a votre Excellence votre tres-humble et très-obeis⟨sant⟩ Serviteur

Jean Francois Gergens
Medecin

S'il est permis d'osér encore une priére, nous demandons tres humblement; Si un curé catholique de Mayence qui s'appelle *Jean Frederic Koch,* reste a present de puis un an et demi a Philadelphia.[3] S'il se trouve sous le gouvernement de votre Excellence; celui vous peut enseigner sur l'état des Sciences, particulierrement Sur l'état de la faculté medicinale Sur notre Université.

S'il plait votre Excellence de nous faire le bonheure avec une reponse favorable: nous prions de signer votre rescrit gratieuse avec Suivante Inscription. A: Jean François Gergens Medecin praticien a Mayence: chez Monsieur *Forster* conseiller de la cour, et Bibliothecaire premier de l'université a Mayence.

ALS, DNA: RG 59, Miscellaneous Letters.

1. No response from GW to Gergens about whether or not the young doctor should immigrate to Philadelphia or some other state capital to practice medicine has been found.

2. Johann Georg Adam Forster (1754–1794) and his father, Johann Reinhold Forster (b. 1729), immigrated to England in 1766 and were asked to accompany Capt. James Cook on his second voyage to the Pacific Ocean in 1772. Georg Forster's account of this three-year cruise, *A Voyage around the World,* was published in 1777. He held professorships at several European universities during the late 1770s and 1780s before being named head librarian at the University of Mainz. James Cook (1728–1779) explored the Pacific Ocean on three separate occasions, in 1768–71, 1772–75, and 1776–79. During his travels Cook visited, among other places, the Antarctic icefield, Australia, New Zealand, and the Bering Strait.

3. Catholic priest Jean-Frederic Koch apparently was not living in Philadelphia at this time.

From Henry Knox

Sir. War-department, May 15th 1792.

I have the honor to inform you, that yesterday I received letters, from governor Blount, dated the 22'd of April, of more pacific appearance, than the one of the 14th of April to Doctor Williamson.[1]

Mr Shaw, and the Bloody Fellow, and other Cherokees who left this city the 19th of February, were on the 22'nd, within four miles of governor Blount; all well.[2] The said indians had generally been well treated, but sometimes alarmed by the folly and wickedness of the frontier people.

I have the pleasure to inform you, that the bearer of Blount's letters, brought the enclosed from major Hamtramck.[3] I trust, in God, it is the sure dawning of a general peace, north west of the Ohio.

General Putnam has not yet finished his Ohio business; but will probably to day—He, General Wayne, and the quarter master general, will, I expect, all depart this week.

The person who delivered Hamtramck's letter, informed me, that Lieutenant Jennifer was charged with letters from brigadier general Wilkinson, but that he had halted at Hagers Town for a day or two[4]—That brigadier general Wilkinson had established Fort St Clair, placed therein a garrison, and plenty of provisions; and returned uninjured to Fort Washington. I have the honor to be, Sir, with profound respect, Your most obedient Servt

H. Knox
Secy of War

LS, DLC:GW; LB, DLC:GW.

1. Gov. William Blount's letter to Knox of 22 April has not been identified. For Blount's letter of 14 April to Hugh Williamson, see Knox to GW, 12 May, n.1.

2. Leonard D. Shaw, who had graduated from the College of New Jersey in 1784, was appointed deputy agent to the Cherokee Nation in January 1792. Shortly after arriving in the Southwest Territory Shaw took a Cherokee wife. Increasingly estranged from Governor Blount, Shaw was charged with inebriety, and he was replaced in early 1793. The Cherokee chief Bloody Fellow (Nenetooyah; Iskaqua; Clear Sky) led the Indian delegation that arrived at Philadelphia in late December 1791. For the negotiations which followed their arrival, see Knox to GW, 17 Jan. 1792, source note.

3. John F. Hamtramck's letter to Secretary of War Knox, which was written at Fort Knox on 31 Mar. 1792, reads: "The 28th Instant I received a letter from

Lt Col. [James] Wilkinson who informed me of his appointment in the army and who directed me to send some agents to all the Belligerent Tribes of Savages, resident on the Wabash Illinois River, and on the Southeastern borders of Lake Michigan, which shall be done as speedily as possible.

"Since my last letter I had the honor of writing you, the Chiefs of the Eel River and of the Weya have been with me, their intention is to be at peace with the United States, and to have for its basis, certain articles of agreement, which I have made with them and the only ones I could find to be consonant to their wishes. This negociation having taken place previous to my receiving the orders of Lieut. Col. Wilkinson, will I suppose be found sufficient without sending to them—however if it should be found necessary for them to go to Fort Washington, they soon can be informed of it—From Col. Wilkinson I expect to receive farther directions on that point. The Peankishaws the only nation remaining on the Wabash, who have not yet been with me have been prevented by the death of their King, on his way to Fort Knox and the Nation having no Prince Royal to succeed to the Crown have been employed for a long time in the election of a Monarch whenever that is done, which will be in about a week, I expect to see them when I will probably have an opportunity of securing their friendship—Indeed I have very little doubt of their adopting the measures of the others—Altho the Indians did not show a disposition to return to war, I found it was necessary to guard against their joining those of the Miami, who will no doubt give them very pressing invitations in the spring—this could not be done without some engagements on both sides which I have the honor to inclose. I hope Sir they will be acceptable, I have done for the best, and all that could be done. It is difficult for me to give you any assurance of their sincerity—if they are sincere, it is from no other motive but to get back their prisoners—however—it may be very easy after this to keep them in a pacific State, and to prevent them from joining those who are hostile, this can be effected by some acts of generosity towards them—for if our Government does not make them presents they will go to the British, who will be glad to see them and who will supply them amply—I asked the two chiefs of Eel River who were with me, and who are neighbours to the Miamis if the British had given any presents to the Indians last summer—their Answer was—Yes my father, the Goods were in large heaps like stacks of Hay—do you get Arms and ammunition also? We get every thing but big Guns. If you had done so and if your people had not told the Indians that their lands belonged to you[,] you would have had no war—I have been informed by some Indians that a number of Merchants with Goods from Michlemackinac were in the prairies towards the Illinois River trading with the Indians—Indeed I am sure some of them have been on the Wabash and undersold our Merchants and there is now in this village a quantity of goods from that place and New Orleans which consequently has paid no duty to the United States—The Laws of this Territory or the laws of the United States have made no provision to prevent it, to the great detriment of those merchants who buy their goods in the United States and cannot sell so cheap. But the worst evil of all is a number of Villains in this Village who keep the Indians continually drunk. there is so much difficulty and ceremony to find them out that not one of them has yet been punished since the civil government has taken place, and the most fatal consequences may be expected if it continues—for the Indians, who will sell all their peltrys for liquor will find themselves and families naked in the spring and having no means to procure ammunition or other necessaries will go to war for plunder—the only possible way to prevent this abuse would be to prohibit all spiritous liquors to be brought into the place without permission from the commanding Officer, and if only one or two Men were intrusted to sell or keep liquor in his house, it would be a very easy thing to prevent the Indians from getting drunk—Such measures may possibly be contrary to the principles of a republican Government, but it is not less necessary in this place in our present situation of affairs—Civil Law is an admirable institution any where except on a frontier situated in the center of an Indian Country and in a time of War—before the civil authority took place, I was well acquainted with every thing that passed in the village. No Indians came in—No person gave them lodging without my knowledge, few of them got drunk in comparision to what it is now All persons and strangers coming into the village were obliged to report themselves, by which means I received every intelligence.

"The Governor [Arthur St. Clair] sensible of the necessity of such regulations, has by proclamation and militia orders provided for its continuance, but I am sorry to say that no part of it is put in execution neither is it in my power at present to enforce it.

"All the information I could obtain from the chiefs who were with me, was that all the Indians of the Lakes intended to go to war early in the spring and that their Women and Children were to be supplied with provisions by Capt. [Alexander] McKee the British Agent for Indian affairs—they also informed me that the pieces of Cannon lost on the 4th of November last, were left on the ground, that a large party of Indians intended to keep at a small distance from the place to attack any body who should come to take them off—that the number of the Indians against us last action had been about 1500—that we were then about four good days march from the Miami and on the waters of the Wabash, and that the loss of the Indians had been very inconsiderable.

"Another circumstance which may not be amiss to inform you of is that two Indians of the tribes taken prisoner last year went from here to Fort Washington last summer on a visit to their friends—there they saw the Chickasaw Indians who were on the expedition with us, who told them, that it was a folly for the Indians of the lakes, to be at war with us, that they themselves had been a long time in arms against the White people, but they at last found it their interest to live in peace with them—that their nation and the Choctaws would join the Americans to go against them if it should be necessary. these circumstances were reported by the above two Indians who returned to their Nation the last autumn, and came up the river with me. This appears to have struck the Indians with such a panic that it has reached the Miami who I am informed would make peace with the United States, if they had an opportunity.

"As it is necessary to permit some merchants to go into the Indian Towns, I have made choice of a few, who have entered into a bond of one thousand dollars, and to whom I have given licence for six Months—On this head I expect to receive some directions from the Governor, to whom I have wrote on the subject—The getting of firewood for the garrison has become very difficult, we are obliged to go at so great a distance for it, that it keeps the men on a constant fatigue, this together with some other inconveniencies we lay under by being so near the Town, would render it adviseable to move the Garrison, further up the River.

"The Governor in my instructions directs me to try to obtain the consent of the Indians for the establishment of a Garrison at the Eel River or the Weya—I have not yet found matters sufficiently Ripe to make the proposition but I believe that some presents would remove every difficulty that might exist.

"Since my writing the above I have received a letter from Colonel Wilkinson who directs me to send a couple of Spies to the Miami in order to get intelligence of the disposition of the Indians—I have engaged two confidential Indians who are to set off immediately and to return sometime in May. . . . P.S. We have on hand for about Six Months provision but the Indians who are every day in the Garrison consume some of it, and it is unavoidable" (DLC:GW).

Hamtramck also enclosed "Articles of certain engagements passed at Fort Knox at Vincennes between John Francis Hamtramck Esquire Major of the 1st United States Regimt on the one part and the Chiefs of different tribes of Indians on the Wabash on the other part with the following Conditions," dated 14 Mar. 179[2], which read: "1st That as Major Hamtramck has not sufficient power to conclude a treaty of peace with the Indians of the Wabash, he shall immediately inform the great Chief of the United States, that it is the sincere desire of the Indians here represented to bury the hatchet forever and to establish a lasting peace and friendship with the United States.

"2dly That measures may be speedily taken to conclude a solid and everlasting treaty of peace between the Wabash Indians and the United States and that the treaty shall be held at Vincennes.

"3dly That the United States shall confirm to the Indians the lands they legally claim and that no part shall be taken from them, but by a fair purchase and to their satisfaction.

"4ly The Indians here represented solemnly promise on their part, that no more hostilities or depredations shall be committed by them on any of the Citizens of the United States.

"5ly That they will at all times give notice to the commanding Officer of Fort Knox or other Garrison of any designs which they may know to be carried on by any nation of Indians or any individual whatever against the interest or prejudicial to the United States.

"In Testimony whereof" Hamtramck, Capt. Erskurius Beatty, Ens. Ross Bird, and Lt. Abner Prior signed for the United States; Kickapooquaigh, Atchenewaugh, Contomaumgaugh, Awpaighchenecaugh, Pullaaswaigh, Chacowaatagh, and La Poussiere made their marks for the Weya Indians; and Peankeunshaw and Checunememshaw made their marks as representatives of the Eel River Indians.

An additional "Provisional Article," which was attached to the document and signed by the same individuals, reads: "As the Kickapoos of the Weya have left that Country and gone on the Illinois River, and are not represented with us in council

"We the Chiefs of the Eel River and Weya Indians farther agree that in case the said Kickapoos should return on the Wabash we shall use our endeavours to bring them to the above mentioned measures or otherwise to drive them out of the Country" (DLC:GW). John Stagg, Jr., attested on 15 May 1792 that the "foregoing are true copies from the originals."

4. Daniel St. Thomas Jenifer of Allegany County, Pa., who had served as a sergeant major in the levies of 1791, was appointed a lieutenant in the U.S. Army in March 1792. After killing William Pitt Gassaway in a duel in March 1793, Jenifer was dismissed from the service.

From Thomas Jefferson

Dear Sir Philadelphia May 16. 1792.

The day after your departure I received from a mister Greene, a merchant now at N. York, through a third person, the following communication "that he had had very *late* advices from Spain *by way of the Spanish islands,* to this effect, that war with France was inevitable, that troops were marching from all quarters of the kingdom to the frontiers, & that 50. sail of the line had been commissioned."[1] this was permitted to be mentioned to me, but, for particular reasons, to no other person. I suppose the particular reasons were some mercantile speculation founded on the intelligence: perhaps it may be to buy up all our flour. we have London news to the 1st of April, and nothing of this is mentioned. I have a letter from Colo. Humphreys of March 18. which says nothing of it. I am in hopes therefore the only effect will be to get us a good price for flour or fish: this being our lookout, while the success of the speculation is that of the adventurer. you will recollect that we had learned the death of the emperor of Marocco after a battle in which he was victorious. the brother opposed to him it seems was killed in the same action, and the one, Muley Islema, who had been so long in the sanctuary, is proclaimed emperor. he was the best character of the three, and is likely to be peaceable. this information is from Colo. Humphreys. the Queen of Portugal is still in the same state. Wyllys does not pronounce her curable, tho' he says there is nothing which indicates the contrary. he has removed from her all her former physicians.[2] mister Madison has favored me with some corrections for my letter to mister H. it is now in the hands of the Attorney general, and shall then be submitted to

Colo. Hamilton. I find that these examinations will retard the delivery of it considerably. however delay is preferable to error.[3] mister Pinkney is engaged in going over such papers of my office as may put him in possession of whatever has passed between us & the court he is going to. I have 100. olive trees, and some caper plants arrived here from Marseilles, which I am sending on to Charleston, where mister Pinkney tells me they have already that number living of those I had before sent them. I have the honor to be, with sentiments of the most perfect respect & attachment, Dear Sir Your most obedt & most humble servt

Th: Jefferson

ALS, DNA: RG 59, Miscellaneous Letters; ALS (letterpress copy), DLC: Jefferson Papers; LB, DNA: RG 59, George Washington's Correspondence with His Secretaries of State; LB (photocopy), DLC:GW.

1. GW had departed for Mount Vernon on 10 May 1792. On the following day Jefferson received a letter from William Vans Murray, dated 9 May, passing along information he had received from the New York merchant William Green. War between France and Spain did not formally break out until March 1793, however.

2. For David Humphreys's letter to Jefferson of 18 Mar., see *Jefferson Papers,* 23:293. Despite the best efforts of Dr. John Willis, Maria I continued her descent into insanity. She was removed from the Portuguese throne in 1792.

3. For the background to Jefferson's letter to George Hammond of 29 May, see GW to Jefferson, c.5–6 Mar. 1792, source note and note 2. For the text of the letter, which represented the U.S. government's response to the long list of supposed American contraventions of the Treaty of Paris of 1783 presented by Hammond on 5 Mar., see ibid., 551–613. Jefferson, who had completed a draft of the letter by mid-May, submitted it to the other members of the administration for their consideration. GW expressed his approval of the letter in late May shortly after returning to Philadelphia from his visit to Mount Vernon (see Jefferson to James Madison, 1 June 1792, *Jefferson Papers,* 24:10).

From Bouscat

Sir, la goyave [Guadeloupe Island] 17th May 1792

He who has the honor to write to you is a young Frenchman who arrived about six[1] months ago in the Island of Gaudeloupe. Brought up in the Romish Religion, smitten with the charmes, the morality and the truths of the Evangelists, with the excellence and dignity of Priesthood, his disposition was soon formed for a state so august & so sublime. Free to follow his vocation, he prepared to receive the order which would irrevocably engage him in the service of the Alter, when the national Assembly usurped[2] the exclusive power of putting down the Pope & the Council, and exacted an oath repugnant to the conscience of a man just, & jealous of the title of a true & faithful Catholic.[3] By this illegal, & even tyrannical decree he was turned aside from his purpose, and saw himself thrown far away from that state after which he had so ardently sighed.

But, Sir, that which yet adds weight to his misfortune is the extreme indigence in which the Revolution has plunged his family. Deprived of a small Ecclesiastical Benefice, which was, however, a support & a resource to this family—without estate—without an income—reduced to groan under the cruel lot which oppresses the authors of his being, and impatient, nevertheless, to soften their misfortune, he hastened to commit himself to the fury of the waves, to go afar from his unhappy country to seek & obtain succour for them. Vain hope!

An European who arrives in America (West Indies) is incapable of holding a place in the government, he must have a knowledge of agriculture & the manufacture of Sugar, and, moreover, must suffer a continual degradation, and the total loss of his Physical Powers, the effects of frequent sickness occasioned by the heat of the climate.

A place of this description is the only one, Sir, that a young French ex-abby has been able to find & occupy; but this place, besides its trifling advantage, deprives him of the two greatest enjoyments, *that of comforting his parents,* and *following his literary pursuits.*

Beneficience, the virtue dear & precious to your heart, is this day, Sir, invoked & laid claim to, either to see accomplished the first wish of his heart, *that of succouring his family,* or to be able to cultivate letters & the sciences, which have become necessary to his moral existance.

The Title generally odious to the French,[4] and the quality of a stranger in the government of the United States, does not permit him, Sir, to form the smallest apprehension of the favourable reception of his demand. Yes, Illustrious President! fortified by the too cruel truth of the considerations which he has exposed to you—by an enthusiasm sacred to humanity—and by the spirit of fraternity & justice which has constantly ruled & directed your heart, the young emigrant dares to hope that his petition will obtain from you the wished for reception.

But whatever may be the decis[i]on with which you may please to honor it, Sir, it shall be precious to him under any form[5]—and he will be among the first to offer you the homage of profound respect & lively gratitude with which he shall have the honor to be all his life Sir, Your most humble & Obedt-Sert

Bouscat

Translation, DNA: RG 59, Miscellaneous Letters; ALS, DNA: RG 59, Miscellaneous Letters. The French text of the ALS appears in CD-ROM:GW.

1. As Bouscat wrote "dix" on the ALS, it is clear that he had arrived at Guadeloupe ten months before, not six.

2. The remainder of this phrase is more accurately translated as: "the powers exclusively vested in the Pope and the Councils."

3. In July 1790 the French Constituent Assembly passed the Civil Constitution of the Clergy, which reduced the number of bishops to eighty-three by assigning one diocese to each department, declared that bishops and parish priests were to be elected, and began paying the clergy's salaries out of state funds. Because a large portion of the French church resented and opposed its subordination to the state and the reduction of the pope's jurisdiction to spiritual matters, in November 1790 the Assembly ordered the clergy to swear an oath declaring their loyalty to the constitution, which implied their acquiescence to the reorganization of the church. Those who did not take the oath were to be removed immediately from their ecclesiastical offices.

4. This phrase is more accurately translated as: "The generally odious title of 'Frenchman.'"

5. No reply from GW to Bouscat has been found.

From Gimat

Sir, Sainte Lucie [1]8[1] May 1792

The remembrance of the kindness which your Excellency shewed me when I had the honor of serving under your orders, gives me great hope that one of my friends, a man of rare and distinguished merit, will obtain your good will & deserve Your esteem, during the stay which he proposes to make in North America, whether he goes for the re-establishment of his health, which cannot support the warm climate of the Antilles—the temperate climate of the north will re-establish it without a doubt. Permit me, Sir, likewise to beg your attention for a young man, Mr de

Courville, whose parents are my particular friends in this Colony.

I pray your Excellency to pardon the liberty which I have taken in recommending to you M.[,] Made Raphel[2] and M. de Courville, to whom I am very much attached. Their intention is to fix themselves in the State of Maryland where the rigour of the climate during the winter is more supportable to an inhabitant of the Antilles, than it would be more to the North.[3]

I perceive that I shall myself shortly have need of the same Climate. It is in that happy country where I have passed the most pleasant days of my life that I hope to restore my health which has been much injured in the scorching county which I inhabit.

If I should be so happy as to be able to render any service to your Excellency, whether in my own Government, or in the other french Antilles, you ought to be persuaded of the lively pleasure which I should take in convincing you of my zeal in doing whatever might be agreeable to you, and of the respectful sentiments with which I have the honour to be Your Excellency's Most humble & most Obedt Servt

Gimat.

Translation, in Tobias Lear's hand, DLC:GW; ALS, DLC:GW. The French text of the ALS appears in CD-ROM:GW.

Jean-Joseph, chevalier de Gimat (1747–1793), who served as an aide-de-camp to Lafayette during the Revolutionary War, was appointed a lieutenant colonel in February 1778 and was promoted to colonel in November of that year. After being wounded at the Battle of Yorktown in October 1781, Gimat returned to France, where in the spring of 1782 he was named colonel of the regiment of Martinique in the French Antilles. He also served as governor of the island of Saint Lucia, a post which he held from 1789 until he was displaced for his royalist sympathies in early June 1792. Almost exactly one year later, while commanding a corps of 1,000 émigrés invading Martinique under the protection of a squadron of English warships, Gimat was mortally wounded.

1. In his translation Tobias Lear mistakenly dates Gimat's letter the "8th" of May. The ALS gives the correct date: "18 May 1792."

2. The ALS, which reads "M, Mad[am]e raphel," indicates that both Raphels intended to immigrate to the United States.

3. Etienne Raphel (1754–1811), who had been serving as procurator general on the island of Martinique, and his wife, Jeanne Elizabeth Fressenjat Raphel (b. 1771), immigrated to Maryland in 1792 and settled at Frenchman's Bay at the mouth of the Gunpowder River. Whether or not Courville immigrated to the United States at this time has not been determined.

From Thomas Jefferson

Dear Sir Philadelphia May 18. 1792

Since I wrote you the day before yesterday, I have recieved a letter of Mar. 25. from Colo. Humphreys informing me that the Queen of Portugal was considerably better: as also mentioning the death of the emperor of Germany. what effect this last event will have on the affairs of Europe, cannot be foreseen, the character of the successor being absolutely unknown. he is 24. years of age. one would conjecture that if he has any dispositions to war, he would think a little time necessary to get his election passed in form, to see if the troubles within his dominions quieted by his father would be likely to break out or not &c. and that this would hold him back one campaign. still this event renders peace less certain, as the character of his father was so decidedly pacific, that one might count on that.[1] there seems to have been a magnificent story current in London for the three or four last days of March, of the capture of Seringapatam, & Tippoo Saib great slaughter &c. but on the 1st of April the date of the latest paper which the vessel brings (she is from Glasgow) it had died away to a *hum,* raised by Stockjobbers who wanted to sell out. it did in fact raise East India stock 2. or 3. per cent. still it was not fallen into entire discredit as appears by some paragraphs and consequently cannot be decidedly pronounced untrue perhaps the contradiction of it was the counter-hum of those who wanted to buy in.[2] I have the honour to be with great & sincere respect & attachment Dr Sir your most obedt & most humble servt

Th: Jefferson

ALS, DNA: RG 59, Miscellaneous Letters; ALS (letterpress copy), DLC: Jefferson Papers; LB, DNA: RG 59, George Washington's Correspondence with His Secretaries of State; LB (photocopy), DLC:GW.

1. For earlier reports of the death of the Holy Roman Emperor Leopold II and the accession of Francis II, see Lafayette to GW, 15 Mar., n.1, and Gouverneur Morris to GW, 17 Mar., 6 April 1792.

2. For the background to the British offensive against Tippoo Saib's capital of Seringapatam during the Third Mysore War on the Indian subcontinent, see Gouverneur Morris to GW, 18 Sept. 1790, Thomas Jefferson to GW, 1 May 1791, and note 2, Tobias Lear to GW, 1 May 1791, GW to Robert Sinclair, 6 May 1792, n.1.

From John Sinclair

Sir Whitehall London. 18th May 1792

Among the other respectable characters, to whom I take the liberty of sending the inclosed papers, it is impossible for me not to request General Washington's acceptance of a copy.[1]

It would give me, Sir, particular pleasure, to understand, that they are fortunate enough to meet with your approbation.[2]

The objects to which they relate, are great and important, and, I flatter myself, the plans therein recommended, will be thought intitled, to the cordial co-opperation and support, of every real friend to the interests of society. I have the honour to be, with great esteem & respect, Sir—your most obedient & very humble Servant

John Sinclair

ALS, PHi: Dreer Collection.

John Sinclair (1754–1835) of Caithness, Scotland, who had been educated at Edinburgh and Glasgow in the 1760s, served in Parliament 1780–1802 and 1807–11, and he sat on the British board of agriculture 1793–98 and 1806–11. Between 1792 and GW's death in 1799, the two men exchanged many letters, and Sinclair continued to send GW statistical reports and agricultural surveys compiled and published under the auspices of the agricultural board (see Griffin, *Boston Athenæum Washington Collection,* 89–95, 183).

1. Although the enclosures, which GW in his response to Sinclair of 20 Oct. 1792 referred to as a "Pamphlet & papers," have not been identified, they were probably the same works that Sinclair sent Thomas Jefferson on 18 May: *Specimen of the Statistical Account of Scotland* (Edinburgh, 1791) and *Prospectus d'un ouvrage intitulé: Analyse de l'état politique d'Écosse, d'après les rapports des ministres de chaque paroisse . . .* (London, 1792) (see *Jefferson Papers,* 23:524). Neither work was in GW's library at the time of his death, however.

2. GW expressed his approval of Sinclair's efforts in his letter of 20 Oct. 1792.

To Charles Carter of Ludlow

Dear Sir, Mount Vernon, May 19th 1792.

Your letter of the 30th ultimo was on its way to Philadelphia whilst I was on my journey to this place—owing to which I did not receive it until it reverberated—this must be my apology for not giving the receipt of it an earlier acknowledgment.

It would give me pleasure to receive your Son into my family, if it could be made tolerably convenient to me—or if any advantage was likely to result from it to the young Gentleman himself. I was in no *real* want even of Howell Lewis, but understanding that he was spending his time rather idly, and at the same time very slenderly provided for by his father, I thought for the few months which remained to be accomplished of my own servitude, by taking him under my care, I might impress him with ideas, and give him a turn to some pursuit or other that might be serviceable to him hereafter;[1] but what that will be I am at present as much at a loss to decide as you would be—for as the heads of the different departments have by law the appointment of their own Clerks[2]—are responsible for the conduct of them—are surrounded always with applicants—and, I presume, have their own inclinations and friends to gratify: I never have, in a single instance, and I am pretty sure I shall not now begin, recommending any one to either of them.

My family, now Howell is admitted into it, will be *more* than full, and in truth *more* than is convenient for the House, as Mr Dandridge (a Nephew of Mrs Washington's) is already one of it. and but one room for him, Howell and another person to sleep in, all the others being appropriated to public or private uses.

If your Son Charles is of age, and it should be yours and his own inclination to pursue a military course—I would, if any vacancy should happen (at present there is none) in one of the Regiments endeavour to place him therein.[3] You will perceive I have made age the condition—the reason is, it is established as a rule in the War Office to appoint none knowingly, that are under it. My best respects to Mrs Carter. I am &c. &c.

Go: Washington.

LB, DLC:GW.

1. For the appointment of Howell Lewis to GW's official "family," see GW to Betty Washington Lewis, 8 April, Howell Lewis to GW, 24 April, which is printed as a note to Betty Lewis to GW, 19 April, and Betty Lewis to GW, 14 May 1792.

2. Section 2 of "An act for establishing the salaries of the Executive Officers of Government, with their assistants and clerks" of 11 Sept. 1789 reads in part: "That the heads of the three departments . . . shall appoint such clerks therein respectively as they shall find necessary" (*Annals of Congress,* 1st Cong., 2233).

3. For Charles Landon Carter's desire to study medicine, rather than entering on a military career, see Charles Carter to GW, 26 May 1792.

From Henry Knox

Sir War department May 20. 1792

I have the honor to inform you that the Pittsburg mail which arrived on friday last did not bring any information of further indian incursions.[1]

Contrary to my expectations yesterday I received a letter from General Brooks declining his appointment.[2]

I have not received any answer from General Hull to the invitation given him to repair to this City in case of Brooks non acceptance. Indeed as he lives out of Town, it could not be well expected until tuesday next. I Shall again write him by Tomorrows post.[3]

The Quartermaster Genl and Genl Putnam will not be in readiness to set out until tuesday or Wednesday, and General Wayne by thursday or friday.[4]

The recruits by returns, and estimation amount probably to about 850. I have the honor with perfect respect to be sir Your most obedient Servant

H. Knox

ALS, DLC:GW; LB, DLC:GW.

1. Knox is referring to Friday, 18 May 1792.

2. For the background to John Brooks's appointment as a brigadier general, see Memorandum on General Officers, 9 Mar., n.8, and GW to the U.S. Senate, 9 April. Brooks's letter declining the appointment has not been identified.

3. Knox wrote to Gen. William Hull on 6 May 1792 and again on 20 May. Hull, who on 17 May had responded to Knox's first letter by saying that he needed a few more days to make up his mind, wrote Knox on 20 May declining the appointment (see Knox to Hull, 6, 20 May, and Hull to Knox, 27 May, NNGL: Knox Papers).

4. According to this timetable James O'Hara and Rufus Putnam would set out on 22 or 23 May and Anthony Wayne on 24 or 25 May 1792.

To James Madison

My dear Sir, Mount Vernon May 20th 1792.

As there is a possibility if not a probability, that I shall not see you on your return home; or, if I should see you, that it may be on the Road and under circumstances which will prevent my speaking to you on the subject we last conversed upon;[1] I take the liberty of committing to paper the following thoughts, & requests.

I have not been unmindful of the sentiments expressed by you in the conversations just alluded to: on the contrary I have again, and again revolved them, with thoughtful anxiety; but without being able to dispose my mind to a longer continuation in the Office I have now the honor to hold. I therefore still look forward to the fulfilment of my fondest and most ardent wishes to spend the remainder of my days (which I can not expect will be many[2]) in ease & tranquility.

Nothing short of conviction that my derilection of the Chair of Government (if it should be the desire of the people to continue me in it) would involve the Country in serious disputes respecting the chief Magestrate, & the disagreeable consequences which might result therefrom in the floating, & divided[3] opinions which seem to prevail at present, could, in any wise, induce me to relinquish the determination I have formed: and of this I do not see how any evidence can be obtained previous to the Election. My vanity, I am sure, is not of that cast as to allow me to view the subject in this light.

Under these impressions then, permit me to reiterate the request I made to you at our last meeting—namely—to think of the proper time, and the best mode of anouncing the intention; and that you would prepare the latter.[4] In revolving this subject myself, my judgment has always been embarrassed. On the one hand, a previous declaration to retire, not only carries with it the appearance of vanity & self importance, but it may be construed into a Manœuvre to be invited to remain. And on the other hand, to say nothing, implys consent; or, at any rate, would leave the matter in doubt; and to decline afterwards might be deemed as bad, & uncandid.

I would fain carry my request to you farther than is asked above, although I am sensible that your compliance with it must add to your trouble; but as the recess may afford you leizure, and I flatter myself you have dispositions to oblige me, I will, without apology desire (if the measure in itself should strike you as proper, & likely to produce public good, or private honor) that you would turn your thoughts to a Valadictory address from me to the public; expressing in plain & modest terms—that having been honored with the Presidential Chair, and to the best of my abilities contributed to the Organization & Administration of the government—that having arrived at a period of life when the private Walks of it, in the shade of retirement, becomes necessary, and will be most pleasing to me; and the spirit of the government may render a rotation in the Elective Officers of it more congenial with their ideas of liberty & safety, that I take my leave of them as a public man; and in bidding them adieu (retaining no other concern than such as will arise from fervent wishes for the prosperity of my Country) I take the liberty at my departure from civil, as I formerly did at my military exit,[5] to invoke a continuation of the blessings of Providence upon it—and upon all those who are the supporters of its interests, and the promoters of harmony, order & good government.

That to impress these things it might, among other things be observed, that we are *all* the Children of the same country—A Country great & rich in itself—capable, & promising to be, as prosperous & as happy as any the Annals of history have ever brought to our view[6]—That our interest, however deversified in local & smaller matters, is the same in all the great & essential concerns of the Nation. That the extent of our Country—the diversity of our climate & soil—and the various productions of the States consequent of both, are such as to make one part not only convenient, but perhaps indispensably necessary to the other part; and may render the whole (at no distant period) one of the most independant in the world. That the established government being the work of our own hands, with the seeds of amendment engrafted in the Constitution, may by wisdom, good dispositions, and mutual allowances; aided by experience, bring it as near to perfection as any human institution ever aproximated; and therefore, the only strife among us ought to be, who should be foremost in facilitating & finally accomplishing such great & desirable objects; by giving every possible support, & cement to the Union. That however necessary it may be to keep a watchful eye over public servants, & public measures, yet there ought to be limits to it; for suspicions unfounded, and jealousies too lively, are irritating to honest feelings; and oftentimes are productive of more evil than good.

To enumerate the various subjects which might be introduced into such an Address would require thought; and to mention them to you would be unnecessary, as your own judgment will comprehend *all* that will be proper; whether to touch, specifically, any of the exceptionable parts of the Constitu[t]ion may be doubted. All I shall add therefore at present, is, to beg the favor of you to consider—1st the propriety of such an Address. 2d if approved, the several matters which ought to be contained in it—and 3d the time it should appear: that is, whether at the declaration of my intention to withdraw from the service of the public—or to let it be the closing Act of my Administration[7]—which, will end with the next Session of Congress (the probability being that that body will continue sitting until March,) when the House of Representatives will also dissolve.[8]

'Though I do not wish to hurry you (the cases not pressing) in the execution of either of the publications beforementioned, yet I should be glad to hear from you generally on both—and to receive them in time, if you should not come to Philadelphia until the Session commences, in the form they are finally to take. I beg leave to draw your attention also to such things as you shall conceive fit subjects for Communication on that occasion; and, noting them as they occur, that you would be so good as to furnish me with them in time to be prepared, and engrafted with others for the opening of the Session.[9] With very sincere and Affectionate regard I am—ever Yours

Go: Washington

ALS, NNPM; ADfS, NN. Madison docketed the ALS: "G. Washington Mt Vernon May 20. 1792 with the answer of J.M. & notes of a conversation on the subject May 5. 1792." Below the docket Madison wrote "see letters of J.M. on file."

1. Madison left Philadelphia for his home, Montpelier, in Orange County, Va., during the last week of May 1792. For GW's recent discussion with Madison in Philadelphia, their chance meeting along the road during GW's return trip from Mount Vernon, and GW's hand delivery of this letter at that time, see Madison's Conversations with Washington, 5–25 May 1792.

2. At this place on the draft manuscript, GW first wrote "which may not be many" within parentheses. He then struck out "may not" and inserted the phrase "I can not expect will" above the line.

3. At this place on the draft manuscript, GW first wrote "unsettled state of" before striking out that phrase and inserting "divided" above the line.

4. For GW's original request, see Madison's Conversations with Washington, 5–25 May 1792. For Madison's draft of GW's Farewell Address, see Madison to GW, 20 June 1792, and the enclosure to that document.

5. For GW's "military exit," see his Circular to the States, 8–21 June 1783 (LS, NNPM).

6. At this place on the draft manuscript, GW first wrote "recorded" before striking out that word and inserting "ever brought to our view" above the line.

7. In the end GW issued his Farewell Address, which is dated 19 Sept. 1796, a couple of weeks before the election of 1796, not as the final act of his administration (ADS, NN).

8. Although both the House and Senate adjourned on 2 Mar. 1793, the Senate reconvened for a special one-day session two days later to witness the inauguration of the president, hear his brief remarks, and attend to a few other matters (*Annals of Congress,* 2d Cong., 666–68).

9. For GW's earlier enlistment of Madison's aid in drafting his speech for the opening of Congress, see Madison's Conversations with Washington, 5–25 May 1792. For the final version of GW's address, see GW to the U.S. Senate and House of Representatives, 6 Nov. 1792.

To Hannah Fairfax Washington

Dear Madam, Mount Vernon May 20th 1792

To the variety & importance of public business which presses upon me towards the close of the Session of Congress, and which leaves not a moment to attend to my private concerns, You will have the goodness to impute this late acknowledgment of the receipt of your obliging favor of the 9th of April.

Permit me now, my dear Madam, to offer my best thanks for your kind attention to the request contained in my former letter, and for the information which you have been so good as to furnish me with relative to the genealogy of the family of Washington.

I return herewith the Will of Lawrence Washington agreeably to your desire.

Mrs Washington received with much pleasure your kind remembrance & affectionate regards, and would, were she here (where I am[1] for a few days only) return the same with much sincerity—to which permit me to add the best wishes and ardent prayers for your happiness of Dear Madam Your Affecte and Obedt Servt

Go: Washington

ALS, owned (1992) by H. K. Thompson, Hornell, N.Y.; Df, ViMtV; LB, DLC:GW.

1. In both the draft and the letter-book copy this phrase reads "where I am come for a few days only."

From Alexander Hamilton

Sir, Philadelphia May 21st 1792.

I returned here yesterday from New Ark, & find that nothing material has occurred in my absence.[1]

There is nothing new except what is contained in the papers, and what I doubt not has been announced to you from the War Department—the Convention between Hamtramck and certain Tribes on the Wabash.[2] With the most perfect respect and truest attachment, I have the honor to be &c.

Alexr Hamilton.

LB, DLC:GW.

1. Hamilton, who had gone to Newark, N.J., to attend a meeting of the Society for Establishing Useful Manufactures, had left Philadelphia on 13 May 1792.

2. For Maj. John F. Hamtramck's agreement with the Wabash Indians of 14 Mar. 1792, see Henry Knox to GW, 15 May, n.3.

To Thomas Jefferson

Dear Sir, Mount Vernon, May 21st 1792.

I have had the pleasure to receive your letter of the 16t[h] inst. I sincerely hope that the intelligence which has been communicated to you of a War between France and Spain being inevitable, is not founded in truth.[1]

It is my intention to commence my Journey to Philadelphia on Thursday next.[2] I shall stop in George Town one day, and proceed on from thence without further delay, unless my horses should require rest, some of which got foundered and lame on the journey to this place. With very sincere regard, I am, Dear Sir, Your affecte & Obedt Servt

Go: Washington

LS, in Tobias Lear's hand, DLC: Jefferson Papers; Df, in Lear's hand, DNA: RG 59, Miscellaneous Letters; LB, DNA: RG 59, George Washington's Correspondence with His Secretaries of State; LB (photocopy), DLC:GW. Jefferson's docket indicates that this letter was received on 24 May.

1. Earlier this month William Vans Murray had sent Jefferson intelligence that he had received from the N.Y. merchant William Green of a coming con-

flict between France and Spain (see Murray to Jefferson, 9 May, *Jefferson Papers,* 23:488–89).

2. GW is referring to Thursday, 24 May.

To Henry Knox

Dear Sir, Mount Vernon, May 21st 1792.

I have received your letters of the 12th & 15th insts. with their enclosures. From the tenor of Mr Seagrove's letter I am in hopes that the business of running the line &c. will be amicably accomplished, notwithstanding the unfavorable curcumstances which have occurred. When I passed through George Town, Mr Ellicot informed me that a letter from his brother, dated at the Rock Landing the 19th of April, gave unfavourable intelligence of the business—that two Indians having been detected in Stealing horses at Green Court-House, one was killed, and the other so severely whipped as to have died in consequence of it—that a party of the Cowettas (to whose tribe these Indians belonged) had taken revenge by killing two white men—that the Chiefs of the Nation had sent Orders to the Rock landing for such of the Indians as might have assembled there to return home, and that a party which had arrived at that place had actually gone back[1]—and further observd, that from the appearance of things he did not beleive the line would be run.

The letter from Mr Seagrove being dated two days after that from Ellicot and giving a more favorable complexion to the matter than his, I am in hopes that our affairs in that quarter will yet come to an amicable & mutually agreeable conclusion.

I am pleased with the intelligence contained in your letter of the 15th with respect to the information received from Governor Blount and from Major Hamtramck. I trust that the arrival of the Bloody fellow & other Cherokees in their nation will have been attended with good effects towards the interest of the United States.

I most sincerely hope that the communications from Major Hamtramck may be a prelude to a general peace with the hostile Indians, and I cannot help thinking that it carries with it that appearance.

I intend setting out for Philadelphia on Thursday next[2]—shall stop one day in George Town, and proceed on from thence as expeditiously as my horses (some of which got foundered & lame on the journey to this place & have not yet recovered) will permit me to do. With sincere regard I am Dear Sir Your Affect. & Obet St.

Df, in Tobias Lear's hand, DLC:GW; LB, DLC:GW.

1. For more information about these revenge killings, see James Seagrove to GW, 21 April 1792.

2. GW left Mount Vernon on his return trip to Philadelphia on Thursday, 24 May.

From Madame Bobindesorolles

Sir, Philadelphia 22d May 1792.

At a moment when the French are accomplishing a Revolution which has raised a flame in their Colonies, insomuch that part of the Inhabitants of St Domingo are obliged to abandon their possessions,[1] I find myself one of the most unhappy among them. My husband & [son][2] having been disappointed in embarking in the Vessel with me, the affliction into which I am thrown, and the sickness which I experience do not permit me, Sir, to go out and make my respects to you. I find myself obliged to wait the arrival of my husband & [son][3] in your States before I can acquit myself of that duty. We are Inhabitants of Cul du Sac, A Quarter of Port au Prince, and we consider ourselves peculiarly happy, amidst these unfortunate circumstances, to have been able to land in a country where peace & true liberty reign. The French ⟨a⟩re too precipitate in their movements—they substitu[t]e words for actions—It is not possible in a Country such as St Domingo to adopt the new Government—The Society & Climate are totally different from those of France. We are afflicted at the prospect of the ancient Colony if such tutelary men as You, Sir, do not extend their ⟨h⟩and to it, without which all is lost. I have with me my sister Madme Dérulney who is also an inhabitant of Cul du Sac, and who waits too for her husband, and laments as well as myself her misfortunes & dispairs of being able to render her respects to you. With the most respectful Sentiment I am Sir Your most Obed. & humble Se[rvan]t

Bobindesorolles

Translation, in Tobias Lear's hand, DNA: RG 59, Miscellaneous Letters; ALS, DNA: RG 59, Miscellaneous Letters. The French text of the ALS appears in CD-ROM:GW.

1. For the background to the slave uprising of August–September 1791 on the island of Saint Domingue and the resulting exodus of members of the French planter class from that Caribbean colony, see Samuel Wall to GW, 16 Sept., n.1, Charles Pinckney to GW, 20 Sept., n.1, and Ternant to GW, 22, 24 Sept. 1791.

2. Tobias Lear mistranslated the French word *fils* as "daughter."

3. Lear again mistranslated the French word *fils* as "daughter."

Court Judgment

[Dumfries, Va., 22 May 1792]

At a Court held at Dumfries the 22d day of May 1792.

George Washington Esqr. Pl[ainti]ff against Adam Stuart, Thomas Montgomerie, Cumberland Wilson & George Mason; Dfts	In Debt

Judgment for 1576 Sterling, with interest from the 4 January 1772. 'till paid—& the Costs. Cr. for £3.3.0, Maryland Currency & 25:4—Sterling pd 2d July 1774—& all payments to be allowed the Dofts which shall be made to the satisfaction of James Keith, before or at the next Court.

Same Plff agst Same Dfts	In Case

Judgment for 748:17—Current money, and Costs—£65:2:2, by consent of the Plff, released. Execution to be stayed 'till April next.

D, DLC:GW.

For the background to this document, specifically the difficulties GW and the other executors of Thomas Colvill's estate had encountered in their attempt to secure the money due from the purchasers of Colvill's Merryland tract, see Thomas Montgomerie to GW, 24 Oct. 1788, source note.

From Thomas Jefferson

Dear Sir Philadelphia May 23. 1792.

Since my letter of the 18th we have had no confirmation of the capture of Tippoo Saib,[1] nor of a fable current since that of the massacre of the king of France. this last was current in Philadelphia two or three days, and had the merit I believe of being raised here, as no source for it could ever be found. letters of Mar. 1. & 16. from mister Barclay at Gibraltar contradict the death of Muley Ishem, but confirm that of the emperor Yezid: he supposes it rather probable however that Selima (the best of them) will continue emperor. should there be a division of the empire between him & Ishem, he shall have to visit both. he was about to proceed immediately, considering the crisis sufficiently over to justify his visiting Selima. between the victory obtained by Yezid & his death, which was two weeks, he put to death upwards of twenty thousand persons in cold blood, without respect to age or sex. he gave up the Jews to plunder: and in the pillage, little discriminated, which took place, Francis Chiappe lost his whole property.[2]

I inclose a letter I wrote two days ago, which being long and not on subjects of news, can be read at your best leisure.[3] I have the honour to be with the most perfect attachment & respect Sir your most obedt & most humble servt

Th: Jefferson

ALS, DNA: RG 59, Miscellaneous Letters; ALS (letterpress copy), DLC: Jefferson Papers; LB, DNA: RG 59, George Washington's Correspondence with His Secretaries of State; LB (photocopy), DLC:GW.

1. For the defeat of Tippoo Saib and the capture of his capital, Seringapatam, during the Third Mysore War, see GW to Robert Sinclair, 6 May, n.1.

2. For calendared versions of Thomas Barclay's letters to Jefferson of 1 and 16 Mar., see *Jefferson Papers,* 23:174, 285–86.

3. For the enclosed letter, see Jefferson's second letter to GW of this date.

From Thomas Jefferson

Dear Sir Philadelphia May 23. 1792.

I have determined to make the subject of a letter, what, for some time past, has been a subject of inquietude to my mind without having found a good occasion of disburthening itself to you in conversation, during the busy scenes which occupied you here. perhaps too you may be able, in your present situation, or on the road, to give it more time & reflection than you could do here at any moment.

When you first mentioned to me your purpose of retiring from the government, tho' I felt all the magnitude of the event, I was in a considerable degree silent. I knew that, to such a mind as yours, persuasion was idle & impertinent: that before forming your decision, you had weighed all the reasons for & against the measure, had made up your mind on full view of them, & that there could be little hope of changing the result. pursuing my reflections too I knew we were some day to try to walk alone, and if the essay should be made while you should be alive & looking on, we should derive confidence from that circumstance, & resource if it failed. the public mind too was then calm & confident, and therefore in a favorable state for making the experiment. had no change of circumstances supervened, I should not, with any hope of success, have now ventured to propose to you a change of purpose. but the public mind is no longer so confident and serene; and that from causes in which you are no ways personally mixed. Tho these causes have been hackneyed in the public papers in detail, it may not be amiss, in order to calculate the effect they are capable of producing, to take a view of them in the mass, giving to each the form, real or imaginary, under which they have been presented.

It has been urged then that a public debt, greater than we can possibly pay before other causes of adding new debt to it will occur, has been artificially created, by adding together the whole amount of the debtor & creditor sides of accounts, instead of taking only their balances, which could have been paid off in a short time: That this accumulation of debt has taken for ever out of our power those easy sources of revenue, which, applied to the ordinary necessities & exigencies of government, would have answered them habitually, and covered us from habitual murmurings against taxes & tax-gatherers, reserving extraordinary calls, for those extraordinary occasions which would animate the people to meet them: That though the calls for money have been no greater than we must generally expect, for the same or equivalent exigencies, yet we are already obliged to strain the *impost* till it produces clamour, and will produce evasion, & war on our own citizens to collect it and even to resort to an *Excise* law, of odious character with the people, partial in it's operation, unproductive unless enforced by arbitrary & vexatious means, and committing the authority of the government in parts where resistance is most probable, & coercion least practicable. They cite propositions in Congress and suspect other projects on foot still to increase the mass of debt. They say that by borrowing at ⅔ of the interest, we might have paid off the principal in ⅔ of the time: but that from this we are precluded by it's being made irredeemable but in small portions & long terms: That this irredeemable quality was given it for the avowed purpose of inviting it's transfer to foreign countries. They predict that this transfer of the principal, when compleated, will occasion an exportation of 3. millions of dollars annually for the interest, a drain of coin, of which as there has been no example, no calculation can be made of it's consequences: That the banishment of our coin will be compleated by the creation of 10. millions of paper money, in the form of bank bills, now issuing into circulation. They think the 10. or 12. percent annual profit paid to the lenders of this paper medium are taken out of the pockets of the people, who would have had without interest the coin it is banishing: That all the capital employed in paper speculation is barren & useless, producing, like that on a gaming table, no accession to itself, and is withdrawn from commerce & agriculture where it would have produced addition to the common mass: That it nourishes in our citizens habits of vice & idleness instead of industry & morality: That it has furnished effectual means of corrupting such a portion of the legislature, as turns the balance between the honest voters which ever way it is directed: That this corrupt squadron, deciding the voice of the legislature, have manifested their dispositions to get rid of the limitations imposed by the constitution on the general legislature, limitations, on the faith of which, the states acceded to that instrument: That the ultimate object of all this is to prepare the way for a change, from the present republican form of government, to that of a monarchy of which the English constitution is to be the model. that this was contemplated in the Convention, is no secret, because it's partisans have made none of it.[1] to effect it then was impracticable; but they are still eager after their object, and are predisposing every thing for it's ultimate attainment. so many of them have got into the legislature that, aided by the corrupt squadron of paper dealers, who are at their devotion, they make a majority in both houses. the republican party, who wish to preserve the government in it's present form, are fewer in number. they are fewer even when joined by the two, three, or half dozen anti-federalists, who, tho they dare not avow it, are still opposed to any general government: but being less so to a republican than a monarchical one, they naturally join those whom they think pursuing the lesser evil.

Of all the mischiefs objected to the system of measures before-mentioned, none is so afflicting, and fatal to every honest hope, as the corruption of the legislature. as it was the earliest of these measures it became the instrument for producing the rest, & will be the instrument for producing in future a king, lords & commons, or whatever else those who direct it may chuse. withdrawn such a distance from the eye of their constituents, and these so dispersed as to be inaccessible to public information, & particularly to that of the conduct of their own representatives, they will form the most corrupt government on earth, if the means of their corruption be not prevented. the only hope of safety hangs now on the numerous representation which is to come forward the ensuing year. some of the new members will probably be either in principle or interest, with the present majority. but it is expected that the great mass will form an accession to the republican party. they will not be able to undo all which the two preceding legislatures, & especially the first have done. public faith & right will oppose this. but some parts of the system may be rightfully reformed; a liberation from the rest unremittingly pursued as fast as right will permit, & the door shut in future against similar commitments of the nation. Should the next legislature take this course, it will draw upon them the whole monarchical & paper interest. but the latter I think will not go all lengths with the former, because creditors will never, of their own accord, fly off entirely from their debtors. therefore this is the alternative least likely to produce convulsion. But should the majority of the new members be still in the same principles with the present & shew that we have nothing to expect but a continuance of the same practices, it is not easy to conjecture what would be the result, nor what means would be resorted to for correction of the evil. true wisdom would direct that they should be temperate

& peaceable. but the division of sentiment & interest happens unfortunately to be so geographical, that no mortal can say that what is most wise & temperate would prevail against what is more easy & obvious? I can scarcely contemplate a more incalculable evil than the breaking of the union into two or more parts. yet when we review the mass which opposed the original coalescence, when we consider that it lay chiefly in the Southern quarter, that the legislature have availed themselves of no occasion of allaying it, but on the contrary whenever Northern & Southern prejudices have come into conflict, the latter have been sacrificed & the former soothed, that the owers of the debt are in the Southern & the holders of it in the Northern division; that the Antifederal champions are now strengthened in argument by the fulfilment of their predictions; that this has been brought about by the Monarchical federalists themselves, who, having been for the new government merely as a stepping stone to monarchy, have themselves adopted the very constructions of the constitution, of which, when advocating it's acceptance before the tribunal of the people, they declared it insusceptible; that the republican federalists, who espoused the same government for it's intrinsic merits, are disarmed of their weapons, that which they denied as prophecy being now become true history: who can be sure that these things may not proselyte the small number which was wanting to place the majority on the other side? and this is the event at which I tremble, & to prevent which I consider your continuance at the head of affairs as of the last importance. the confidence of the whole union is centered in you. your being at the helm, will be more than an answer to every argument which can be used to alarm & lead the people in any quarter into violence or secession. North & South will hang together, if they have you to hang on: and, if the first corrective of a numerous representation should fail in it's effect, your presence will give time for trying others not inconsistent with the union & peace of the states.

I am perfectly aware of the oppression under which your present office lays your mind, & of the ardor with which you pant for retirement to domestic life. but there is sometimes an eminence of character on which society have such peculiar claims as to controul the predilection of the individual for a particular walk of happiness, & restrain him to that alone arising from the present & future benedictions of mankind. this seems to be your condition, & the law imposed on you by providence in forming your character, & fashioning the events on which it was to operate: and it is to motives like these, & not to personal anxieties of mine or others who have no right to call on you for sacrifices, that I appeal from your former determination & urge a revisal of it, on the ground of change in the aspect of things. should an honest majority result from the new & enlarged representation; should those acquiesce whose principles or interests they may controul, your wishes for retirement would be gratified with less danger, as soon as that shall be manifest, without awaiting the completion of the second period of four years. one or two sessions will determine the crisis: and I cannot but hope that you can resolve to add one or two more to the many years you have already sacrificed to the good of mankind.

The fear of suspicion that any selfish motive of continuance in office may enter into this sollicitation on my part obliges me to declare that no such motive exists. it is a thing of mere indifference to the public whether I retain or relinquish my purpose of closing my tour with the first periodical renovation of the government. I know my own measure too well to suppose that my services contribute any thing to the public confidence, or the public utility. multitudes can fill the office in which you have been pleased to place me, as much to their advantage & satisfaction. *I,* therefore, have no motive to consult but my own inclination, which is bent irresistably on the tranquil enjoyment of my family, my farm, & my books. I should repose among them it is true, in far greater security, if I were to know that you remained at the watch, and I hope it will be so. to the inducements urged from a view of our domestic affairs, I will add a bare mention, of what indeed need only be mentioned, that weighty motives for your continuance are to be found in our foreign affairs. I think it probable that both the Spanish & English negociations, if not completed before your purpose is known, will be suspended from the moment it is known;[2] & that the latter nation will then use double diligence in fomenting the Indian war. With my wishes for the future, I shall at the same time express my gratitude for the past, at least my portion in it; & beg permission to follow you whether in public or private life with those sentiments of sincere attachment & respect, with which I am unalterably, Dear Sir, Your affectionate friend & humble servant

Th: Jefferson

ALS, DLC:GW; ALS (letterpress copy), DLC: Jefferson Papers.

1. See, for instance, Alexander Hamilton's speech of 18 June 1787 to the Convention in which he says: "As to the Executive, it seemed to be admitted that no good one could be established on Republican principles" and that the "English model was the only good one on this subject" (Madison, *Notes of Debates in the Federal Convention,* 135).

2. For the background to the negotiations with Spain, which held out the prospect of opening the Mississippi River to U.S. trade, see Jefferson to GW, 22 Dec. 1791, source note. For the recent negotiations between the U.S. and Britain concerning the fulfillment of their mutual obligations under the Treaty of Paris of 1783 and the possibility of a commercial treaty between the two nations, see GW to Jefferson, c.5–6 Mar., source note and note 2, and Jefferson to GW, 16 May 1792, n.3.

From William Davies Shipley

Sir Llanerch Park near St Asaph [Wales] May 23d 1792

I hope you will forgive the Liberty I take in transmitting to you my late Father's works, which I have been induced lately to publish.[1]

The high Esteem & Veneration I well know the Author entertained for both your private & public Character, added to the near Relation which much of the Contents bears to that glorious Cause which had ever his warmest Wishes, And which he lived to see so nobly vindicated (principally thro' your Exertions) will I trust excuse my Presumption.

That you may long enjoy the Fruits of your honorable & honest Labours, & live to see your Country attain that complete State of National Prosperity & Happiness to which she seems so rapidly approaching, is the sincere Wish of, Sir, Your most faithful & Obedt humble Servt

W. D. Shipley

P.S: I am sorry to observe the Printing is shamefully incorrect—but the mistakes are in general so glaring that the Reader will immediately rectify them.

ALS, DLC:GW.

The Rev. William Davies Shipley (1745–1826), dean of St. Asaph, was the eldest son of the Rev. Jonathan Shipley (1714–1788), bishop of St. Asaph, a longtime friend of Benjamin Franklin and the Adamses, who in June 1786 had performed the marriage of Abigail Adams (1765–1813) and William Stephens Smith. Before the Revolutionary War, Jonathan Shipley had gained popularity in the colonies for his vigorous denunciation in the House of Lords of England's American policies. GW owned a copy of Shipley's much-cited pamphlet *A Speech Intended to Have Been Spoken on the Bill for Altering the Charters of the Colony of Massachusett's Bay,* which was published in London in 1774 (Griffin, *Boston Athenæum Washington Collection,* 182).

1. Jonathan Shipley's *Works* (London, 1792) was in GW's library at the time of his death (ibid., 500).

From B. Francis

Sir Boston, May 25. 1792.

A person who has been sometime in America, takes the liberty to address you on the subject of Metals.

The want of Metals in a country inhabited by an ingenious and diligent people, must greatly retard their progress in manufactures, and operate as a check upon their population. The enquiry after the existence of the ores of the useful metals, in the United States has not, to my knowledge, ever been prosecuted in such a manner, and by such means, as to prove that they are, or are not, to be met with, in situations convenient for working to effect, and in such quantity as to promote their production.

If the analogy which is found to prevail throughout the greater parts of Nature holds good in the Continent of North-America, we may reasonably expect from its great extent; its mountains, vallies, springs of water impregnated with minerals, and the metals which without much seeking for are already found, that not only the useful metals, but fossils that are the basis of several extensive manufactures, or of so much service to agriculture, or use in medicine, maybe discovered of almost equal benefit to the States as a view of Silver or Gold. By analogy in this case, I do not mean that, because the continent of Europe produces the useful *fossils,* the same precisely maybe expected from the bowells of America, but I mean that the uniformity discovered to predominate in the arrangement of the *strata* throughout the continent

will convey my idea much better. —
1
2
3
4
5
This drawing represents a section of the surface of the Earth, to the depth

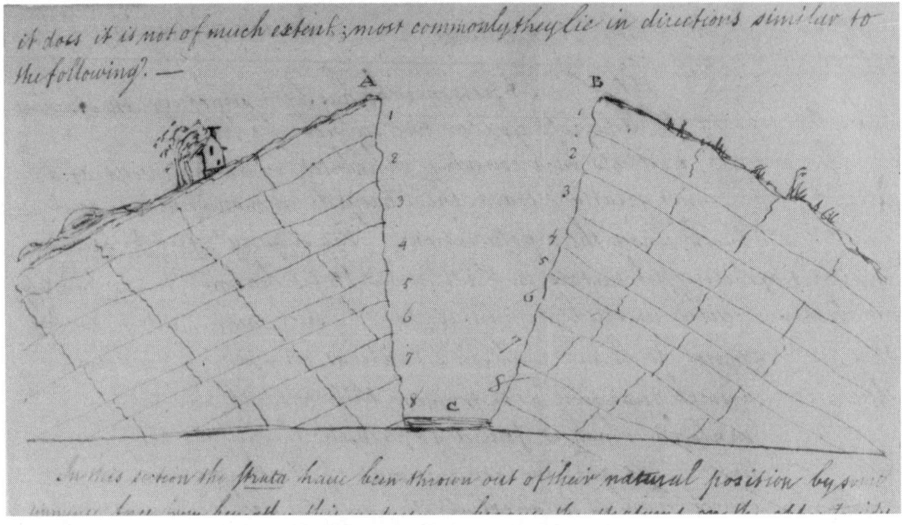

it does it is not of much extent; most commonly they lie in directions similar to
the following. —
A
B
C
In this section the strata have been thrown out of their natural position by some

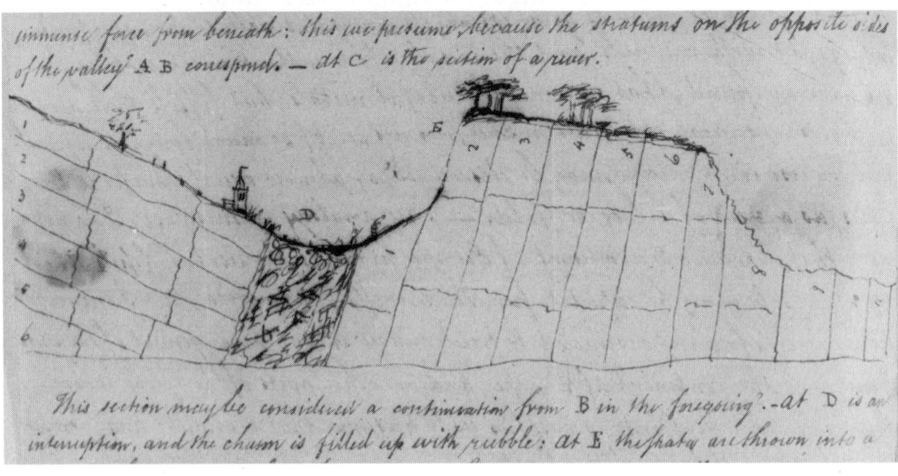

immense force from beneath: this we presume, because the stratums on the opposite sides
of the valley A B correspond. — At C is the section of a river.
D
E
This section may be considered a continuation from B in the foregoing. - At D is an
interruption, and the chasm is filled up with rubble: At E the strata are thrown into a

Fig. 1. B. Francis's sections of the Earth's strata, 25 May 1792. (National Archives, Washington, D.C.)

of Europe, and on other parts of the Globe where they have been dug into, qualifies us to presume, that a similar arrangement prevails over all parts of the Earth.

The most natural position of the *strata* of our Globe, is that which the Solid parts of any mixture would take if left to subside viz. Horisontal: But the following representation will convey my idea much better.[1] This drawing represents a section of the surface of the Earth, to the depth of five strata, their *natural* position; they are generally found of various thickness, and may also be distinguished by their productions. This position seldom occurs, and when it does it is not of much extent; most commonly they lie in directions similar to the following.[2]

In this section the *strata* have been thrown out of their natural position by some immense force from beneath: this we presume, because the stratums on the opposite sides of the valley A B correspond. At C is the section of a river.

This section maybe considered a continuation from B in the foregoing.[3] At D is an interruption, and the chasm is filled up with rubble: At E the strata are thrown into a position almost perpendicular. By comparing these representations with the rocks and mountains of any country, or with accurate engravings of such prospects, it will appear that the recognition of any particular *stratum* will be no difficult matter to a mineralist. It will hence also appear, That an acquaintance with the construction and arrangement of the external parts of the Globe, is indispensably necessary in all extensive subterraneous researches.

Metals seem to have an origin very different to the rocks in which they are found. This appears, not only from their greater specific gravity, but also from their not being imbedded in their substance but in their fissures, or between their laminæ.

Did my circumstances qualify me to gratify an inquisitive disposition, I should with great pleasure commence an enquiry into the arrangement, construction & produce of the *strata* in the United States. I am persuaded such a research would not only open a ⟨*illegible*⟩ of new Ideas, but if properly conducted would enable the country to judge of its subterranean resources, would be a good foundation for its natural History, would promote Industry, the study of chymistry, and the prosecution of Manufactures. But as the restraints I labour under will deny my attempting it while they exist, I have presumed to address this to you,

Sir, with a tender of my services, in case Such an enquiry should appear to merit your patronage & encouragement;[4] & am, Your most obedt Servt

B. Francis.

P.S. My Business will occasion my going to New-York in about fourteen days, where I shall continue sometime,[5] and where a Letter addressed to me at the Post-Office will be sure to come into my hands.

ALS, DNA: RG 59, Miscellaneous Letters.

1. See fig. 1, section 1.

2. See fig. 1, section 2.

3. See fig. 1, section 3.

4. On 22 June 1792 Thomas Jefferson, replying to Francis on behalf of the president, wrote "that the subterranean riches of this country not yet explored are very great, but the exploring the mineral kingdom, as that of the vegetable & animal, is left by our laws to individual enterprize, the government not being authorised by them to interfere at all: consequently it is not in the power of the President to avail the public of the services you are pleased to tender in this line" (DLC: Jefferson Papers).

5. Francis was in New York when he next wrote GW on 27 Oct. 1792.

From Charles Carter of Ludlow

My Dr Friend Acadamy [Fredericksburg, Va.] May 26th 92

Your favor of the 19th came to hand last even. I am much obliged by your kind offer, of a Commn upon a vacancy, but that Life is entirely out of his line my Son has been from early Youth, inclined (indeed) devoted to Study in which (good Judges) say he has for his age made, a tolerable progress. he is now studying Physick, under Doctor Wellford,[1] and intends to Philadelphia, in september, to attend the Lectures during the Winter he wished to have been in your Famy supposing, that he coud have devoted, the evenings to his particular pursuit, as he was told, the fare part of the day woud be only required believe me I am satisfied, you wd with pleasure, have reced him, had it been convenient. I am happy to hear you enjoy a good state of Health, and hope you found yr Farms, in a prosperous way. it gave me pleasure to hear, you had taken, my Young Friend under yr care, and hope it will turn out, to his advantage. Be pleased to present my compts to yr Lady in which Mrs Carter joins yr Aff. Friend & Much Obligd Hbe St

Chs Carter

ALS, DLC:GW.

1. Dr. Robert Wellford (1753–1823) was born in England and came to America with the British army during the first year of the Revolutionary War. On 13 June 1778, according to GW's aide-de-camp John Laurens, "A Party of The Enemy was out . . . and in returning Left a Mr Welford formerly Surgeon in their Service—this Gentleman made himself disagreeable to the British officers, by his humanity to our wounded—and was obliged to resign—he has taken an opportunity of becoming a Willing prisoner to a People whose sentiments are congenial with his own" (John Laurens to Henry Laurens, 14 June 1778, *Laurens Papers,* 13:457). Wellford established a medical practice first in Philadelphia and later, during the early 1780s, in Fredericksburg, Virginia. In 1794 he served as director of the medical department during the expedition to suppress the Whiskey Rebellion.

From Samuel Lawrance

Esteemed Friend Springfield [Mass.] 5 mo. 27 1792

We would have thee stir the people up to peace for War shall cease, as is declared of by Enoch the Prophet in that prophecy mentioned by Christopher Love a little before his execution[1] it being the time Prophece'd of by Isaiah wherein Nation should not lift up Sword against nation neither should they learn War any more.[2] We would have thee following this peace embrace the principale held forth by George Fox asserting that the way to obtain salvation and Eternal life was to receive the Lords immediate teaching by his Spirit in the iner Man,[3] And as thee imbraces this looking that the Salvation of the mortal Soul entirely depends on receiving this teaching and not grieving this teacher thee will be lead not, only into one but into all truth, and thee will have a testimony againsts Wars and fightings and will be lead to promote the kingdom of peace For there are some of that Scociety called Quakers whom the Lord has rejected they having run their rase in Iniquity and will soon be cutt of by the persecution foretold By Byshop Usher,[4] And he will call others in who will faithfully bear a testimony for this principle and exclude Wars and fightings from the Kingdom of Christ which was promised to be such that Swords Should be beaten into Plowshares and Spears into pruning hooks[5] which kingdom We shall now fully bring in as amply as is sett forth Rev. 11. Chap. 15., in which the Kingdoms of this world will be the Kingdoms of the Lord and his Christ, for Nation shall not lift up Sword against Nation neither shall they learn war any more. And we would have Thee faithfuly study peace and not learn war any more that Thee may be an example to such as would follow us in the kingdom of peace for the fulness of the Gentiles has come in and We shall have to gather the Indians who are the of[f]spring of Abraham, of the rase of the Jews, who where to be gathered as declared by the Apostle Rom. 11.

The same Apostle in writing to one of the Churches in that day shews them that the day of Christ (that is the end of the World), should not come unless there came first a pulling away and the man of Sin be revealed the son of pardition who opposeth and exalteth himself above all that is called God or that is worshiped, We say that all which is called God or that is Worshiped is come and has been opposed and exalted above that unknown before preluditary Sin to the end of the World, spoken of Thes 2. Chap. 3.4. verse having been committed in these days whe[re]in Men now live which claims the momentious attention of all, And the Friends we say are stained with it, yet this should not lessen the esteem of any for that principle which we have above commended to thee, for had they followed the dictates of the Spirit of Truth They would have not only been preserved out of this Monstrous Iniquity; but out of all Evil.

May thee having knowledge of these things walk wisely for that persecution above spoken of will come And may thee fully discharge thy duty, and yet walk Christian like towards all Men that the stain of this monstous iniquity may not lie at thy door; and yet none may stigmatize the[e] with being a persecutor.

I have been consered to communicate of these things to thee, and have sent thee enclosed a Pamplet of my writing,[6] may thee place the highest confidence in what is therin declared, stedfastly believg the things spoken of that government therin mentiond, and that the day of final decition to all men is approa[c]hing with steps as near as is therein declared and that all may confine their views as to the conserns of this life within the compass of 30 or 40 years—Thy Friend in Christ Our name in this Flesh

Samuel Lawrance

P.S. Please to give the reading of the pamplet to as many of thy Friends as would incline to read it[7]—I have wrote to some of the Sovereyns of Europe and enclosed a pamplet in my letters to them please to excuse my bad writing farewell.

ALS, DNA: RG 59, Miscellaneous Letters.

1. Shortly before his execution for plotting against Oliver Cromwell's English Commonwealth, the Puritan minister Christopher Love (1618–1651) said that "the Revelation by St. John and the prophecy which St. Jerome copied off, and translated out of the Hebrew language, as was written on Seth's pillar, in Damascus; which pillar is said to have stood before the flood, and was built by Seth, Adam's son and written by Enoch the prophet," revealed that in 1805 "God will be universally acknowledged by all: Then a general reformation and peace, when the people shall learn war no more. Happy is the man that liveth to see this day" (Christopher Love, *Prophecies of the Reverend Christopher Love: and His Last Words on the Scaffold* [Norwich, Conn., 1795], 7–8).

2. See Isa. 2:4.

3. George Fox (1624–1691), the founder of the Society of Friends, opposed established religious conventions, scriptural authorities, and creeds and favored a reliance on divine inspiration.

4. Lawrance apparently is referring to the lecture given by the Anglo-Irish prelate James Ussher (1581–1656) at Christ Church in 1603 in which he predicted, on the basis of Ezek. 4:6, the passage of God's judgment in forty years.

5. Lawrance is quoting from Isa. 2:4.

6. Lawrance's pamphlet has not been identified.

7. No evidence has been found indicating that GW passed on Lawrance's pamphlet to anyone.

From Samuel Davidson

Sir George Town 28 May 1792.

Sensible of the multiplicity of important business which must necessarily occupy your attention, I would not presume to trespass thus on your time, did not events of the first importance to my own welfare and happiness, compel me however painful, to apply to you as the source from whence alone relief can flow, a knowledge of your disposition to render impartial Justice, inspires me with the confidence, to state a few facts.

Soon after your proclamation establishing the permanent residence of Congress on the Potowmac appear'd I became a purchaser of property in the now City of Washington to the amount of £6000, to effect which purchase I have involved nearly my all, add to this, I prevailed with an only Brother in this country—the father of a numerous family—to become an Adventurer in that enterprize to the amount of £4500. these speculations during the Administration of Major L'Enfant, had promised us great advantages, in so much that during that period 'twas in our power to have disposed of them at a very handsome advance. It is a very melancholy fact, of very general credence, that since that unhappy Secession, the property in the city has become of little or no value, arising as I concieve from the total incompetency of the present Commissioners to a due and energetic execution of the duties of their office—the individual and private character of the present Commissioners is undeniably amiable and respectable, but not having had the education and habits of men of business, they certainly are totally disqualified to conduct operations of so extensive and complex a nature, which requires not only constant and unremitted attention, but all the energy and spirit of the most active mind, to every Proprietor the fact comes home with peculiar force, that since the conducting the business has devolved on the Commissioners alone, all public confidence in the object is lost, the Proprietors retrospect its late situation in comparison with its present, with the most poignant sorrow, since they now perceive a total abatement of disposition in individuals to speculate in the property, this distressing fact from whatever cause it may arise has excited the most serious apprehensions in the mind of every friend to the business—affairs thus situated and having embarked the greater part of my Property in the new City, I am alarmed for my own fate, I have been restrained from expressing my sentiments until the present moment from considerations of respect to you and in the wish and expectation that some change ere this moment would have taken place which might have cherished those hopes with which in the first instance I was inspired.[1]

It is probable my character may have been pourtrayed to you in an unamiable point of view, by the tongue of malice, respecting a refusal to Mr Ellicott to cut a ditch through my land, a wish to stand justified to you induces me to detail a few particulars relative to that transaction: when Major L'Enfant was here clothed with authority, he requested me to dig clay in one of the Public Streets and observed it would be of service to the Public, he pointed out the spot the most proper and I accordingly at my own expence employed Men to turn it up, with an intention of building a House in the City while I was in the execution of this work and under the impression that my authority was good, I received a laconic and mandatory letter from the Commissioners replete with all the airs of the most dictatorial authority commanding me to desist and a subsequent one threatening me with most rigorous prosecution in the federal court if I did not comply, having my feelings thus wounded by the insolent manner in which I was treated I have felt myself perfectly justified in the refusal of a request from them, reasonable in itself and which on another occasion I should have chearfully acquiesed in.[2]

As daily and repeated complaints are made by the Proprietors against the measures of the Commissioners, a sense of justice to their own characters as well as an anxiety for the interests of the city induces them to collect a few of the facts on which they found their complaints and which in a few days will be forwarded to you, in the most perfect confidence that as far as they can be substaintiated you will give them the attention they may deserve.[3]

Throwing myself on your candour to pardon the freedom I have taken in thus addressing you, I remain with sentiments of the greatest respect. Sir Your most obedt hum. Servt

Sam: Davidson

ALS, DNA: RG 59, Miscellaneous Letters; LB, DLC: Samuel Davidson Papers.

1. On 9 Mar. the proprietors of the Federal City wrote to George Walker protesting Pierre L'Enfant's dismissal (see Kite, *L'Enfant and Washington,* 168–69). On the same date thirteen of the proprietors, including Samuel Davidson, wrote L'Enfant expressing their dismay at his ouster and hoping that "some mode of accommodation may be devised, to admit of your return" (ibid., 170).

2. David Stuart and Daniel Carroll wrote Davidson on 27 Mar.: "In riding through the City of Washington, this Morning we observed some Clay thrown up in one of the public Streets and on enquiry were informed it was done by your directions—It is with Pain, we feel ourselves compelled in the discharge of our duty to counteract the inclination of any of the proprietors, but we expect it will be a sufficient justification, for our interference, and inducement for your desisting to observe that the Streets are the property of the public and ought not to be invaded" (DNA: RG 42, Records of the Commissioners for

the District of Columbia, Letters Sent, 1791–1802). Davidson responded that same day: "the Clay you allude to, was turned up by my orders; at the request of a Gentleman, whom I then considered your equal in Authority, and now your Superior in Judgement. I have only to observe that, as soon as I can make it convenient, I shall proceed to make Bricks of that Clay—in the mean time—you may take your remidy" (DNA: RG 42, General Records, Letters Received, 1791–1867). On 12 April the commissioners informed Davidson "that if you do proceed, we shall take measures to have a suit instituted against you in the Federal Court" (DNA: RG 42, Records of the Commissioners for the District of Columbia, Letters Sent, 1791–1802).

3. No such letter of grievances from the proprietors of the federal district to GW has been found.

From Lefebvre

à Monsieur Newbury Port [Mass.] ce 28 may 1792

Supplie humblement Dominique Damphoux Demonié Ecuyer Et sieur de Vachier ancien officier des troupes dètachèes de La marine, habitant De L'isle gouadeloupe Disant Monsieur qu'Etant accablé D'infirmités et ne pouvant Se donner Par lui même son Nécessaire ni S'habiller que par Le Secours de Ses Domestiques, Cet etat maL'heureux obligea Le Suppliant De Passer à Newbury Port Le 5 du mois de juillet Lannée Derniere avec Deux Domestiques Esperant De trouver Du soulagement En cette contrée. il fut trompé dans cette attente. & Se trouve toujours afflige De même; Ce qui L'oblige de repasser à La gouadeloupe. et au moment de mon Embarquation mon nêgre germain S'est evadé, En m'enlevant une petite male avec Du linge Pour Son usage—Dont Pour ces même articles je me trou⟨v⟩e Debiteur Envers un marchand de cette Ville. En outre Du tabac que j'avois don⟨n⟩é a mon autre Domestique, il veut Se prevaloir Sois Disant des privileges attachées En cette contrée Disant qu'il Est libre par les Loix D'ici[1] mais Le Suppliant saddrèsse monsieur à Vous pour reclamer votre justice afin que Vous Donniez Des ordres Pour que ce même nêgre soit arrêté et Embarquer Pour La Pointe à Pître. Parceque Le Suppliant ne croit pa⟨s⟩ que les Loix d'ici puissent valloir Pour des habitants Etrangers que ne viennent que pour Sétablire & amenent des Domestiques Pour Son service.[2] Le Suppliant Est persuade Monsieur De toute Vôtre equitté & justice En pareil Cas Surtoût Dans L'etat maL'heureux ou il se trouve: & ne cessera de faire des

Voeux au Ciel Pour La Conservation & La Prosperité De Votre personne Pour monsieur Damphoux demonié

Lefebvre

ALS, DNA: RG 59, Miscellaneous Letters. Tobias Lear's docket on the reverse of this letter reads: "From Monsr Lefebre requesting the President to order restitution of two slaves to be made to him, who had been liberated in Massachts. 28th May 1792."

1. Massachusetts's constitution of 1780 had been interpreted by state judges during the early 1780s as abolishing slavery in the Commonwealth (Moore, *History of Slavery in Massachusetts,* 200–223). By 1784, according to Thomas Jefferson, there were no slaves in Massachusetts "but those who remain in voluntary slavery. The laws have given them all freedom if they require it" (*Jefferson Papers,* 7:339). In order to prevent a massive influx of fugitive slaves, however, the Massachusetts general court resolved in March 1788 that "no person being an African or Negro, other than a subject of the Emperor of Morocco, or a citizen of some one of the United States . . . shall tarry within this Commonwealth, for a longer time than two months." Those who tried to stay longer were to be incarcerated, and if they persisted in their desire to remain in Massachusetts, they were to be whipped (Moore, *History of Slavery in Massachusetts,* 228–29).

2. No reply from GW to Lefebvre has been found.

From Harriot Washington

Mt Vernon May 28 1792

I now take up my pen to write to my dear Uncle, I hope you arrived safe in Philadelphia, and at the time you exspected, If my dear Uncle finds, it convenient to give me a guittar, I will thank you if you will direct it to be made with key's and string's both, as they are easier to lear[n] to play on, and not so easy to be out of order, but if one with key's, is dearer than without, I shall be much obleiged to you for one with string's, I should not trouble you for a guttar, if I was not certain that I could learn myself, every person that I have asked say's that It is the easiest instrument to learn on that is, and any body that can turn a tune, can play on a guittar, but Mrs Bushrod Washington, has been so kind as to offer to teach me if I could not learn myself.[1]

If you please to give my love to Aunt Washington Nelly and Washington. I am My dear Uncle Your affectionate Neice

Harriot Washington

ALS, ViMtV.

1. On 27 June, GW paid $17 "for a guitar for Miss Harriot Washington" (Decatur, *Private Affairs of George Washington,* 273).

From Thomas Jefferson

Sir
Philadelphia May 30. 1792.

It is my duty to suggest to your attention that in the act of the late session of Congress for making certain appropriations, is a clause enacting that a sum of 50,000 D. in addition to former provision be appropriated to defray any expence which may be incurred in relation to the intercourse between the U.S. & foreign nations, and to add that the public service will be advanced by having that sum ready for your orders as speedily as may be conveniently effected.[1] I have the honour to be with the most perfect esteem & respect Sir Your most obedt & most humble servt

Th: Jefferson

ALS, DNA: RG 59, Miscellaneous Letters; ALS (letterpress copy), DLC: Jefferson Papers; LB, DNA: RG 59, George Washington's Correspondence with His Secretaries of State; LB (photocopy), DLC:GW; copy, DNA: RG 59, Domestic Letters.

1. Jefferson is referring to section 3 of "An Act making certain appropriations therein specified" of 8 May 1792 (*Annals of Congress,* 2d Cong., 1387). At GW's command Tobias Lear transmitted a copy of Jefferson's letter to Alexander Hamilton on the following day and asked Hamilton to "let the President know when the sum mention'd in the enclosed Letter will be conveniently ready for his order" (DLC:GW). Hamilton responded to Jefferson on 29 June that he thought it "convenient to draw on the Commissioners in Holland for the sum which is required. . . . I therefore propose . . . that the Treasurer draw bills, in your favour, for a sum in guilders equal to fifty thousand dollars; that you give him an acknowlegement for these bills, as a purchase for the use of your department; promising to pay the amount when you shall be furnished with money for that purpose from the Treasury, pursuant to the abovementioned Act" (Syrett, *Hamilton Papers,* 11:606–7). The next day GW authorized Hamilton to borrow the required sum from "any body or bodies politic, person or persons whomsoever" (see GW to Hamilton, 30 June 1792).

From Alexander Hamilton

[Philadelphia] 31st May 1792.

The Secretary of the Treasury has the honor to inform the President of the Unit'd States that the place of Keeper of the Light house on Thatcher's Island in the State of Massachusetts has become vacant by the death of Mr Hustin. The following persons are respectably recommended—Joseph Sayword—Henry White—Samuel Hustin, son of the deceas'd Keeper, and—[ ] Rowe. The first is strongly recommended both by the Collector of Boston and the Collector of Gloucester.[1] The latter has also recommended Captn Rowe.

LB, DLC:GW.

1. For the appointment of Samuel Houston, Sr., as keeper of the lighthouse on Thatcher's Island, see Hamilton to GW, 3 Jan. 1790. On 14 Mar., Boston collector Benjamin Lincoln informed Hamilton of Houston's death and recommended Capt. Joseph Sayword as "by far the best qualified" to be his replacement. "He is an old master of a vessel, is a good pilot himself & will carry on to the Island one or more of his Sons who are also well acquainted with the coast. . . . I am informed that Capt Sayward could have obtained every certificate he wished had he been a candidate for the office in the first instance but he was not. The people rather sought him than he the office" (Syrett, *Hamilton Papers,* 11:132–33). On 2 June, Tobias Lear wrote Hamilton from Philadelphia to inform him "that the President approves of Joseph Sayword to be Keeper of the Lighthouse on Thatcher's Island, in the State of Massachusetts—vice Houstin deceased" (DLC:GW).

From Joachim Jacob Brandt

Sir, Philada, June 2d, 1792

The Legislature of the Union during their last sitting passed two Acts (which you were pleased to approve) for affording relief to persons disabled in the service of the United States in the War with Great Britain a defect in the first respecting its operation was the cause why a second or Act Supplementary was enacted[1] & therefore it is that being One of the description considered in the Acts alluded as well as Numbers of others who are at present in a situation little above want; that is a state of dependance and uncertainty. that I now humbly presume to address you that you may be pleased to point out some mode by which we may hope for a speedy relief and that we may be informed thereof as conveniently as may be[2] and which consistent with your Characteristic goodness and Justice will be affording relief to the distressed; and that you may continue to preside over us long and with your usual Philanthropy We humbly & sincerely pray.

Signed in behalf of himself & divers others
Joachim Jacob Brandt

ALS, DNA: RG 59, Miscellaneous Letters.

1. Brandt is referring to "An Act to provide for the settlement of the claims of widows and orphans, barred by the limitations heretofore established, and to regulate the claims to invalid pensions" of 23 Mar. and "An Act providing for the settlement of the claims of persons under particular circumstances, barred by the limitations heretofore established" of 27 Mar. 1792 (see *Annals of Congress,* 2d Cong., 1346–49).

2. The claims act of 23 Mar. 1792 provided that every applicant for a pension attend "the Circuit Court of the district in which they respectively reside . . . in person, except where it shall be certified by two magistrates that he is unable to do so," for its evaluation of the merits of their case. The court, "in case in their opinion the applicant should be put on the pension list," would then transmit its certification to the secretary of war for his review. In those "districts wherein a Circuit Court is not directed by law to be holden, the Judge of the District Court shall be, and he hereby is, authorized to exercise all the powers given by this act to the respective Circuit Courts. And it shall be the duty of the Judges of the Circuit Courts, respectively, during the term of two years from the passing of this act, to remain at the places where the said Courts shall be holden five days at the least, from the time of opening the sessions thereof, that persons disabled as aforesaid may have full opportunity to make their application for the relief proposed by this act" (ibid., 1347). For the judicial outcry against the provisions of this act, see Caleb Brewster to GW, 15 Mar., n.4, Edmund Randolph to GW, 5 April, U.S. Circuit Court Judges for N.Y. to GW, 10 April, and enclosure, GW to the U.S. Senate and House of Representatives, 16, 21 April, U.S. Circuit Court Judges for Pa. to GW, 18 April, and James Iredell and John Sitgreaves to GW, 8 June, and note 6. Sections 2–4 of the act of 23 Mar. were repealed on 28 Feb. 1793 by "An Act to regulate the claims to Invalid Pensions" (ibid., 1436–37). No reply from GW to Brandt has been found.

To Thomas Jefferson

[Philadelphia, 2 June 1792][1]

I wish more favorable explanations than I expect, from your interview with the British Minester.[2]

AL, DLC: Jefferson Papers.

1. Jefferson's docket indicates that this letter was "recd June 2. 1792."

2. For the diplomatic exchange between Jefferson and British minister

George Hammond concerning the nonexecution of various provisions of the Treaty of Paris of 1783, see GW to Jefferson, c.5–6 Mar., source note and note 2, and Jefferson to GW, 16 May, n.3. Hammond, who on this date wrote a brief response to Jefferson's list of grievances of 29 May, could not meet with the secretary of state in person until the following day. For Jefferson's notes of his inconclusive conversation with Hammond of 3 June 1792, see *Jefferson Papers,* 24:26–33.

To Béhague

Sir, [Philadelphia, 3 June 1792]

I have received the duplicate of the polite letter which you did me the honor of writing to me on the 28th of may 1791.[1] The first has not reached my hands.

The obliging[2] manner in which you express your wishes to prove the sincerity of your attachment to the United States by keeping up and encouraging the treaty of amity which unites France and America, merits the acknowledgements of the good citizens of this Country, as well as the protection which you mention to have given to the American Vessels on the coast of the Isle of Belle Isle, where you commanded in the late war.

The Constitution of the Society of the Cincinnati does not permit the President to decide on the qualifications for admission into that Society. He can only grant diplomas to such as may have been admitted in confo[r]mity to the general Institution.[3] And in order to be better informed of the pretensions of foreign Officers for admission, power was given to the Count de Rochambeau, the Marquis de la Fayette and the Count d'Estaing to admit such as should appear to have well-grounded pretensions, to wear the Insignia of the Order; and the Certificate of those gentlemen being[4] transmitted to the Secretary of the Society[5] (which office is now filled by General Knox) will entitle the person to whom it is granted to a Diploma. With sentiments of due consideration I have the honor to be, Sir, Your most Obedt Servt

Go: Washington

LS, in Tobias Lear's hand, PHi: Dreer Collection; Df, in Lear's hand, DNA: RG 59, Miscellaneous Letters; LB, DLC:GW.

An undated note written in another hand in the left-hand margin of the first page of the LS reads: "This letter from Genl Washington was transmitted to me confidentially during the civil Commotions then existing in the French Windward Islands. The Governor Genl (Behague) had been driven by the Revolutionists from the Island of Martinique. This letter therefore retained by [Consul] F[ulwar] Skipwith."

Jean-Pierre-Antoine, comte de Béhague (1727–1813), who had served in the French army from the early 1740s until 1776, was named commandant of Belle-Île, France, in October 1777. In August 1790 he was appointed to command the troops forming in France to pacify the French Windward Islands. Arriving at Martinique in March 1791, Béhague acted quickly, some said despotically, to put down the rebellion there. Denounced in the National Assembly by deputies from Martinique in December 1791, he was replaced in early June 1792. Upon learning of Louis XVI's downfall, Béhague went over to the émigré princes and the British. In 1793 he assisted the British in their attempt to retake Martinique from the French. In the fall of that year, Béhague traveled to London, and five years later he was named commander of the émigrés' army of Brittany.

1. The translation of Béhague's letter to GW of 28 May 1791 written at Fort Royal, Martinique, reads: "Being appointed to the general government of the Windward Islands, his Majesty chose me, at the same time, to command the sea & land forces which the National Assembly had decreed, by a law of the 8h of december last, to re-establish tranquility in this part of America.

"I shall be much flattered if, under these circumstances, I can prove to the United States over which your Excellency presides, and particularly to you, Sir, how much I have it at heart to keep up and encourage the treaty of amity which unites us.

"Your Excellency will see by the Manuscript, to which I have joined the homage of one of my memorials on the Colonies, that I have not been the last to signify that desire. The approach of that period to which I have restored the late M. [Jean-Frédéric Phélypeaux, comte] de Maurepas, and the events which have been the consequence, will put your Excellency in a situation to judge of the influence of this manuscript.

"It is upon this consideration, Sir, as well as for the constant services which I have been so happy as to render to American Vessels against the Guernsey Cruisers, which never ceased to trouble their navigation on the coast of the Isle of Belle Isle, where I commanded last war, that M. de la Fayette has authorized me to be decorated with the insignia of the Cincinnati, expecting that the United States would readily grant me the honor of a Diploma in conformity to his letter, of which I join a copy. . . . P.S. M. de Pressineaux, an officer of the highest distinction, and who fought, during the whole of the last war in the cause of the United States, begs me to address to you his memorial on the same subject. I beseech your Excellency to take his request into serious consideration. I shall participate in the acknowledgement.

"It is to the Consul of the United States of America for the French Antilles [Fulwar Skipwith], that the first of my letters to your Excelleny has been confided I beg the acceptance of the memorial which accompanies this, as well as that which accompanied my first dispatch" (translation, DNA: RG 59, Miscellaneous Letters; LS, DNA: RG 59, Miscellaneous Letters).

2. At this place in the draft manuscript, Lear first wrote and then struck out the words "offer of your services."

3. At this place on the draft manuscript, Lear wrote and then struck out "Meetings of the Society." He then wrote "Institution" above the line.

4. Lear's first draft of the remainder of the letter, which he subsequently struck out, reads: "laid before the General meeting of [the Society] will enable the Society to judge of the propriety of such admissions—and the Diplomas of such as are admitted are laid before the President by the Secretary of the Society for his signature."

5. At this place on the draft manuscript, Lear first wrote "Genl Meeting." He then struck out these words and wrote "Society" above the line.

Henry Knox to Tobias Lear

[Philadelphia] 3 June 1792. Asks Lear "to inform the President of the United States that I propose to avail myself of his permission to go to New York by the early stage tomorrow Morning, and to return on thursday or at furthest on friday evening next."[1]

ALS, DLC:GW; LB, DLC:GW.

1. Knox's journey north apparently was a business trip. On Thursday, 7 June, Knox wrote his wife, Lucy Flucker Knox, from New York: "Here I am yet. But I hope to get away tomorrow—most certainly my public business is suffering. Upon the fullest consideratio⟨n⟩ of the subject I have agreed with Mr [William] Duer to relinquish all claims to the eastern [Massachusetts] purchases, provided he shall on or before the first day of March next give me *real or personal security to my approbation or public stock* . . . 37500 Dollars or *fifteen thousand pounds New York Curry* divided into three equal installments" to be paid over the next three years. In a postscript Knox added that his wife should "Remember however the Agreement with Duer *is a* secret" (NNGL: Knox Papers). On the following evening, 8 June, Knox wrote his wife from Elizabeth, N.J.: "I am here on my return having staid longer than I expected—I finished my business in New York agreably to the plan I mentioned whether it will be productive time will discover—If the first payment shall be made in time all may be well—every thing will therefore depend on that point" (NNGL: Knox Papers). Knox returned to Philadelphia by 14 June (see Knox's letter to his daughter Lucy, 14 June 1792, NNGL: Knox Papers). For the background to Henry Knox's land speculations, see Knox to GW, 21 Dec. 1788, n.1.

From Jacob Read

Sir Charles Ton So. Carolina 3rd, June 1792

Mr Hugh Rose of this State will do himself the honour of paying his Respects to Your Excellency and delivering this Letter[.] I pray leave to present him to Your Excelly as a Gentleman of worth and fortune.

As my brother in Law and also a Cousin German by birth I

cannot be indifferent to Mr Rose's Reception or happiness on his present tour[.] I have therefore taken the Liberty of presenting Mr Rose to you sir as my friend and a Gentleman in Whose Welfare I am particularly interested.

Mrs Rose who is my Sister will not fail of paying her Respects to Mrs Washington if they have the good fortune to find Your Excellency & family in Philadelphia.

I pray You Sir to do me the favour to present Mrs Reads' and my own most Respectful Compliments to Mrs Washington with our Sincere acknowledgements for her politeness & Attention when in New York. With the most Respectful Esteem and Regard I am Your Excellency's Most Obedt Humle Servt

Jacob Read

ALS, DLC:GW.

From Ann McCrea

Hounerd Sir, Philada June 4th 1792

In my Distresed Situation I Make Bold to Call on you for a Little Help, your Houner May Rest assur'd Nothing But want Induces me, the Reason of me Being in this town my Son Left me with an Intention of Coming here but was took Sick in Wilmington, me Hearing of his Sickness Came Imediately to See him a few Days after I Came there He to my Sorrow Died, Left me there friendless and Moneyless, I wish to go Home to Dumfrees, I hope your Hounerd wount think hard of me for Making So Bold, I am, with the greates Respect Your Very Humble Servt

Ann McCrea

ALS, DLC:GW.

Although it has not definitely been ascertained that GW gave money to McCrea to assist her in her journey back to Virginia, he did on this date give one dollar to "a poor woman with 6 children going from N. York to Balti[mor]e" (Decatur, *Private Affairs of George Washington,* 265).

John Stagg, Jr., to Tobias Lear

[Philadelphia] 4 June 1792. Forwards "in the absence of the Secretary of War[1] . . . the enclosed letter from Governor Blount; which I request you will please to lay before the President of the United States."[2]

ALS, DLC:GW; LB, DLC:GW.

John Stagg, Jr. (1758–1803), of New York, who had risen to the rank of major in the Continental army during the Revolutionary War, was appointed a clerk at the War Department in March 1786, and by 1792 he had been promoted to the position of chief clerk. Stagg served in that capacity throughout the remainder of GW's two presidential administrations.

1. For the reasons for Knox's absence, see the secretary of war's letter to Lear, 3 June 1792, n.1.

2. The letter which Southwest Territory governor William Blount wrote to Knox from Knoxville on 5 May 1792 reads: "Enclosed are copies of my letters to the chiefs of the Chickasaws and Choctaws, of the 27th of April, by a person who will certainly overtake Messrs. [James] Robertson and [Anthony] Foster before their departure from Nashville. I shall again write them in such terms as shall appear to me proper, under the change of circumstances that have taken place, and shall invite them to meet me at as early a day as the information I have received will warrant an expectation of the arrival of the goods.

"I beg you to assure the President, that I never shall order any part of the militia into service, only in cases of imminent danger; and I beg leave to remark in the present, I did not order them out until many murders had been committed, although Virginia, our next neighbor, with a less exposed frontier, and without a single murder committed since the 27th of August, had called out two full companies. I have not heard of any murders committed on our frontiers, since that of the 5th of April. . . . The proposed meeting at Coyatee, of the chiefs, to hear the report of the Bloody Fellow and associates, from Philadelphia, has not yet taken place; but I am informed it is now intended to be held in twelve days." Blount concludes his letter with a long discussion of horse stealing by the Creeks and by Indians and whites in combination and the consequent raising of tensions along the frontier (*ASP, Indian Affairs,* 1:265).

From David Stuart

Dear Sir, G: town 4th June 92

I cannot but think it necessary that you should know, that Bowles's brother, John, who passed through this town last winter on his way to his Brother, returned a fiew days ago[1]—A Gentleman who had some conversation with him, as he passed through here, tells me, he informed him, that he staid about a fortnight with his brother; and then went to the Bahama islands: from thence he came to Norfolk, and now intends to go to Kentucky; after staying a fiew days with his friends near Hagar's town. I am Dr Sir, with the greatest respect, Your Obt Serv.

Dd Stuart

P:S: his rout from here, was through Baltimore.

ALS, DNA: RG 59, Miscellaneous Letters.

1. John Bowles, a younger brother of William Augustus Bowles, later settled in Washington County, Maryland. He represented that county in the state house of delegates from 1804 until 1813, in 1815–16, and in 1820–21. For GW's opinion of what should be done about John Bowles, see GW to Stuart, 9 July 1792.

From G. E. Butler

[5 June 1792][1]

The humble Address of E. Butler In all humility Sheweth that he and Family is Distress'd to the lowest By having his house and all Burned by the Indians to whom shou⟨ld⟩ the Distress'd apply to leave the same to Commiseration of the Protector of your Contry who by whome the same is redress'd, Your Compliance ⟨*mutilated*⟩ Most Renown'd ⟨*mutilated*⟩ In Duty Bound will eve⟨r⟩ ⟨*mutilated*⟩

G. Ed. Butl⟨er⟩

N:B. I am reso[l]ved to die in the just Cause of the loss of Genll Butler and my Two Children, If your Excellency Confers on a person posessed of Marshal notions a Commison I shall sett out Intantainously.[2]

ALS, DNA: RG 59, Miscellaneous Letters.

1. This letter, which is docketed "From Mr G. E. Butler June 1792," is filed in DNA: RG 59 under 5 June 1792.

2. No response from GW has been found.

From the Commissioners for the District of Columbia

Sir. George-Town 6th June 1792

We enclose you a Copy of a Section of our Act of the Assembly of Maryland, passed at the last session, the Treasurer, as we are informed, has about 24,000 Dollars now in Hand, we shall be obliged to you for your Order, as the late Demands has been so heavy that it is proper to lodge more Money in our Treasurers hands[1]—There is a Ballance of 5746 Maryland Currency yet to receive on the Virginia Donation for the first Year[2]—we are sir with the highest Respect Yours &c.

Th. Johnson
Dd Stuart
Danl Carroll

LB, DNA: RG 42, Records of the Commissioners for the District of Columbia, Letters Sent, 1791–1802.

For the acts of the Maryland and Virginia legislatures providing, respectively, $72,000 and $120,000 for the construction of public buildings in the Federal City, see Daniel Carroll to GW, 22 Jan. 1791, John Eager Howard to GW, 22 Jan. 1791, and Beverley Randolph to GW, 15 Feb. 1791, n.1.

1. For GW's order for this purpose, see GW to Thomas Harwood, 11 June 1792.

2. The D.C. commissioners wrote Gov. Henry Lee on 6 June asking when they might expect the balance of the first installment of Virginia's donation to the Federal City. Lee replied from Richmond, Va., on 29 June: "I have submitted your letter of the 6th of June to the Council of State. The executive are very desirous of enabling you by every means in their power to forward the important work committed to your care and lament that it is not practicable to ascertain the Periods at which you may expect payments of the contribution of this Commonwealth, in as much as they are occasionally called on for advances of money in the protection of the frontiers, which object demands a preferential attention. The balance of the first instalment is nine thousand Dollars one moiety of which is now subject to your order, and the remaining moiety will be paid as soon as in our power, nor shall any unavoidable delay interrupt your receipt of the monies arising under the second instalment" (DNA: RG 42, General Records, Letters Received, 1791–1867).

From Rodolph Vall-travers

May it please Your Excellency! Rotterdam, June 6th 1792.

The Packet, with instructive Materials, collected from the Academies of Berlin, Leipzig, Petersburg and Hamburg, in Aid of Mr John Churchman's, your ingenious Countryman's, Labors, towards an experimental very interesting Theory of magnetical Motions and their Variations, transmitted to Your Excellency, by Captn Bell, from Hamburg, in March 1791.[1] having been kindly received & forwarded to that worthy Gentleman, by Tobias Lear, Esqe your Exccy's Secretary, the 10th of Septembr following, to his very great Joÿ: I now take the Liberty, to have again Recourse to the same secure Channel of Your generous Protection, in conveying this new Packet of further important Materials, towards the same Doctrine; collected during a Twelvemonth's Stay in these Parts; in Behalf, not only of my indefatigable Friend, but of Navigation & philosophical useful Investigations in general, from the first Characters of the Age, in Point of solid mathematical Knowledge.[2] A third Packet, not less valuable, shall get ready in the Course of this Summer, & be transmitted the same, with Your Excellency's kind Leave & Approbation.[3] The present is entrusted to the special Care of my much esteemed Friend, Mr Chrn Maÿer, agent to Mr Adrn Valck of Baltimore, sailing back on Board the good Ship, Wackzamkeed, commanded by Captn Tys Van Haas, with a Cargo of about 400. Passengers, chiefly Germans, bound to Philadelphia; followed with an other Cargo of the Same, of about 300. more, shipt off to New-York, on Board the Rodolph & Elizabeth, Captn Jürgens Commander, both from this City; This Accession of industrious Emigrants is, in great Measure, owing to the patriotic Zeal & Activitÿ of Mr Mayer, from whose Talents your prosperous Commonwealth is likely to derive many further Benefits.

I hope, Your Excellency has received long ago, my Letter of July 21t 1791. from this Place, along with my Manuscript Work, collected from Mr Eshelscrown's german Materials, furnished me, when at Hamburg, entitled: *The present political & mercantile State of all the chief European Settlements in East India in 3. Vols. 4°. 1789–1790;*[4] entrusted to the Care of Captn Folger, of Baltimore, a Relation of my deceased great Friend, Dr Benjn Franklin; who, I hear, arrived safe in August following. He promised me, to deliver my Manuscript to Yr Exccy in Person; and to dispose of it, agreable to your kind Commands; when found of some public Utility to that important Branch of your extensive Trade & Navigation. Yr Exccy's Silence, as well as his, concerning this Object, on which I have bestowed much Time and Labor, make me anxious about its Fate.[5] I am equally ignorant of the Fate of a 3d Letter of mine to Yr Excy conveÿed by Captn Stuart of Baltimore, last ÿear, on the 1t of Augt inclosing Six Copies of mÿ german Publication and Dispersion of Dr Franklin's Instructions sent me to Vienna, from Paris, & advice to all those, who propose to Settle in N. America; which I got inserted, from Time to Time, in various Almanacks, Newspapers, and other periodical Works throughout Germany; the good Effects of which still continue to be sensibly felt. Capn Wm Dolliver of Boston, bound from this Place to Savannah, in Georgia, with his Brig, the Massachuset, took Charge of a further Letter to your Excellency, dated Novr 19th 1791; containing a Series of Objects, in which I am still ambitious to signalize my Sincere Veneration & Attachment to the Service of your confederate Union;[6] ever since my first Acquaintance with Dr Bn Franklin, as Fellow-Member of the roial Society in London, 35. Years ago; and afterwards with yr worthy Patriot, H. Laurence Esqe yr unfortunate Predecessor in the Presidency of your States in Congress; with both whom I had the Honor to correspond, ever since.

All these; besides my several Letters to the learned, encouraging Societies of your Continent, with Offers of interesting literary Communications, to promote every Branch of useful Knowledge & Industry, to the utmost Stretch of mÿ small power and Sphere of Action; remaining unnoticed: it wd argue the highest Degree of Presumption in me, were I to flatter myself with any further Hopes of mÿ wellmeant Tenders having been acceptable.[7]

Nor will the Narrowness of my present Fortune, greatly impaired by mÿ manÿ liberal Sacrifices, together with mÿ advanced Age, permit me now, to repair to N. A. to reside there some Time, & to recieve your Commands & Instructions in Person, without some adequate Aid & Compensation: Great as my Desire is, to be an Eye-Witness of that flourishing State of public Felicity, of which Yr Excellcy has been, & please God! will long continue to be, the chief Promoter and Support.

Mr Short's Destination, as your public Minister to this Republic, having, I hear, been changed to a particular Service at the Court of Spain and good Mr Dumas's unhappy Situation at the Hague, obnoxious to the Court from his Attachmt to the french Interest, and quite Sunk by the Weight of his Sufferings in Body & Mind, having it no longer in his Power, to be of actual Service to his Principals, in this important Station, wou'd willingly accept of my Assistance in his Functions, were I duely authorised to relieve him.[8] The present general Strugle, between Liberty & Despotism, affords no indifferent Matter of Contemplation to yr happy Commonwealth, even as a peaceable Spectator of all the inhuman Horrors of so bloody a Contention.

Tho' nine Years more advanced in Age, than Your Excellence, I feel myself, as ardent as ever, to exert every Ability in mÿ Power, in the Execution & faithful Discharge of whatever Commands Yr Exccy shall be pleased to intimate to Your Excellence's Most sincerily devoted humble Servant

Rodolph Vall-travers.

ALS, DLC:GW.

1. See Vall-travers to GW, 20 Mar. 1791, and the notes to that document.

2. The packet that accompanied Vall-travers's letter of 6 June has not been identified, but on 15 Oct. 1792 Tobias Lear forwarded the "letter and papers" intended for John Churchman to William Barton "as it appears that in case of Mr Churchman's absence from home they are to be left" in his care (DNA: RG 59, Miscellaneous Letters).

3. Whether or not a third packet for transmission to Churchman was sent to GW in the summer of 1792 has not been determined. The next extant letter from Vall-travers to the president is dated 12 Nov. 1792.

4. For more information on Adolph Eschelcrown and his work on the East Indies, see Vall-travers to GW, 21 July 1791, and note 2.

5. Although Capt. Frederick Folger arrived in Baltimore in September 1791, he did not send Vall-travers's letter and its enclosure to GW until early February 1792 (see Vall-travers to GW, 21 July 1791, source note and note 2).

6. GW had received at least one and perhaps both of these letters. For Vall-travers's letter to GW of 1 Aug. 1791, see Vall-travers to GW, 21 July, nn.2–5. For his letter of 30, not 19, Nov. 1791, see Vall-travers to GW, 21 July, n.5, and 19 Nov. 1791 (letter-not-found entry), n.1.

7. In early 1792 GW had referred Vall-travers's letters of 15 Nov. 1789, 20 Mar., 21 July, 1 Aug., and 30 Nov. 1791 to Thomas Jefferson, who replied to Vall-travers for the president on 2 April 1792 (see *Jefferson Papers*, 23:366–67). Notwithstanding the lack of encouragement he received, Vall-travers wrote at least seven more letters to the president between the winter of 1792 and the spring of 1796.

8. Vall-travers never received either aid to allow him to come to America or an appointment from GW. For information about William Short's diplomatic appointment to the Spanish court, see GW to the U.S. Senate, 22 Dec. 1791, source note, 11 Jan. 1792, and The Controversy over Diplomatic Appointments to Great Britain, France, and the Netherlands, c.3 Jan. 1792, editorial note.

To the Commissioners for the District of Columbia

Gentlemen, Philadelphia June 8th 1792

The bearer of this, Mr James Hoben,[1] was strongly recommended to me by Colo. Laurens and sevral other Gentlemen of So. Carolinia when I was there last year, as a person who had made architecture his study, and was well qualified not only for planning or designing buildings, but to superintend the execution of them. He informs me that he intends to produce plans of the two buildings next month agreeably to the advetisement of the Commissioners,[2] and is now on his way to view the ground on which they are to stand. I have given him this letter of introduction in order that he might have an opportunity of communicating his views & wishes to you, or of obtaining any information necessary for completing the plans. But as I have no knowledge of the man or his talents further than the information which I recd from the Gentlemen in Carolina you must consider this letter merely as a line of introduction for the purposes mentioned.[3] With estem & regard I am Gentlemen Yr most Obed. Se[rvan]t.

Df, in Tobias Lear's hand, DNA: RG 59, Miscellaneous Letters; LB, DNA: RG 42, Records of the Commissioners for the District of Columbia, Letters Sent, 1791–1802; LB, DLC:GW.

1. James Hoban (c.1762–1831), who was born and educated in Ireland, moved to the United States shortly after the Revolutionary War and settled briefly in Philadelphia before moving to Charleston, South Carolina. During his career as an architect, he designed South Carolina's first statehouse in Columbia and the President's House in the Federal City, and he served as supervising architect of the U.S. Capitol. Hoban also commanded a company of militia in the federal district.

2. "An Advertisement for the President's House," which was drafted by Thomas Jefferson in March 1792, offered "A Premium of 500 dollars, or a Medal of that value . . . to the person who before the 20th. day of July next shall produce . . . the most approved plan . . . for a President's house to be erected in" the Federal City (*Jefferson Papers,* 23:227–28).

3. On 17 July, in GW's presence, the commissioners awarded Hoban first prize in the competition to design the President's House, and on the following day they hired him to supervise the execution of his design (see Commissioners for the District of Columbia to GW, 19 July, and GW to the Commissioners, 23 July 1792).

From James Iredell and John Sitgreaves

Sir, Newbern, North Carolina, June 8th 1792.

We the Judges now attending at the Circuit Court of the United States for the District of North Carolina, conceive it our duty to lay before you some important observations which have occurred to us in the consideration of an act of Congress lately passed, entitled, "An Act to provide for the settlement of the claims of widows and Orphans barred by the limitations heretofore established, and to regulate the Claims to Invalid Pensions."[1]

We beg leave to premise, that it is as much our inclination as it is our duty, to receive with all possible respect every act of the Legislature, and that we never can find ourselves in a more painful situation than to be obliged to object to the execution of any, more especially to the execution of one founded on the principles of humanity and justice, which the Act in question undoubtedly is. But however lamentable a difference in opinion really may be, or with whatever difficulty we may have formed an opinion, we are under the indispensable necessity of acting according to the best dictates of our own judgement, after duly weighing every consideration that can occur to us, which we have done on the present occasion.

The extreme importance of the case, and our desire of being explicit, beyond the danger of being misunderstood, will, we hope, justify us in stating our observations in a systematic manner. We therefore, Sir, submit to you the following.

1. That the Legislative, Executive and Judicial Departments are each formed in a seperate and independent manner, and that the ultimate basis of each is the Constitution only, within the limits of which each department can alone justify any act of authority.

2. That the Legislature, among other important powers, unquestionably possess that of establishing Courts in such a man-

ner as to their wisdom shall appear best, limited by the terms of the Constitution only, and to whatever extent that power may be exercised, or however severe the duty they may think proper to require, the judges, when appointed in virtue of any such establishment, owe implicit and unreserved obedience to it.[2]

3. That, at the same time, such Courts cannot be warranted, as we conceive, by virtue of that part of the Constitution delegating *Judicial power,* for the exercise of which any act of the Legislature is provided, in exercising (even under the authority of another Act) any power not in its nature *Judicial,* or if *Judicial* not provided for upon the terms the Constitution requires.

4. That whatever doubt may be suggested, whether the power in question is properly of a judicial Nature; Yet inasmuch as the decision of the Court is not made final, but may be at least suspended in its operation by the Secretary of War if he shall have cause to suspect imposition or mistake; this subjects the decision of the Court to a mode of revision which we consider to be unwarranted by the Constitution;[3] for tho' Congress may certainly establish, in instances not yet provided for, Courts of appellat Jurisdiction, yet such Courts must consist of Judges appointed in the manner the Constitution requires, and holding their Offices by no other tenure than that of their good behaviour, by which tenure the office of the Secretary of War is not held, and we beg leave to add, with all due difference, that no decision of any Court of the United States can, under any circumstances, in our opinion, agreeable to the Constitution, be liable to a revision or even suspension by the Legislature itself, in whom no Judicial power of any kind appears to be vested, but the important one relative to impeachments.

These, Sir, are our reasons for being of opinion as we are at present, that this Circuit Court in the execution of that part of the Act which requires it to exercise and report an opinion on the unfortunate cases of Officers and Soldiers disabled in the service of the United States. The part of the act requiring the Court to sit five days for the purpose of receiving applications from such persons we shall deem it our duty to comply with, for whether in our opinion such purpose can or cannot be answered, it is we conceive an indispensable duty to keep open any Court of which we have the honor to be Judges, as long as Congress shall direct.[4]

The high respect we entertain for the Legislature, our feelings as men for persons whose situation requires the earliest as well as the most effectual relief, and our sincere desire to promote, whether Officially or otherwise, the just and benevolent views of Congress so conspicuous on the present as well as on many other occasions, have induced us to reflect whether we could be justified in acting under this act personally in the Character of Commissioners during the Session of a Court; and could we be satisfied that we had authority to do so we would chearfully devote such part of our time as might be necessary for the performance of the service. But we confess we have great doubts on this head. The power appears to be given to the Court only, and not to the Judges of it;[5] and as the Secretary at War has not a discretion in all instances, but only in those where he has cause to suspect mistake or imposition, to with-hold a person recommended by the Court from being named on the Pension list; it would be necessary for us to be well persuaded we possessed such an authority before we exercised a power which might be a means of drawing money out of the public Treasury, as effectually as an express appropriation by law[.] We do not mean, however, to preclude ourselves from every deliberate consideration whether we can be warranted in executing the purposes of the Act in case an application should be made.

No application has yet been made to the Court or to ourselves individually, and therefore we have had some doubts as to the propriety of giving an opinion in a case which has not yet come regularly and judicially before us. None can be made more sensible than we are of the necessity of Judges being in general extremely cautious of not intimating an opinion in any case extrajudicially, because we well know how liable the best minds are, notwithstanding their utmost care, to a bias which may arise from a preconceived opinion, even unguardedly, much more deliberately given: But in the present instance, as many unfortunate and meritorious individuals whom Congress have justly thought proper objects of immediate relief, may suffer very great distress even by a short delay, and may be utterly ruined by a long one, we determined at all events to make our sentiments known as early as possible, considering this as a case which must be deemed an exception to the general rule upon every principle of humanity and justice; resolving however, that so far as we are concerned individually, in case an Application should be made, we will most attentively hear it, and if we can be convinced this opinion is a wrong one we shall not hesitate to act accordingly, being as far from the weakness of supposing that there is any reproach in having committed an error, to which the purest and best men are sometimes liable, as we should be from so low a sense of duty as to think it would not be the highest and most deserved reproach that could be bestowed on any men (much more Judges) that they were capable, from any motive, of persevering against conviction in apparently maintaining an opinion which they really thought to be erroneous.

We take the liberty to request, Sir, that you will be pleased to lay this letter before the Legislature of the United States at their next Session[6]—and Have the honor to be &c.

James Iredell—one of the Associate Judges
of the Supreme Court of the U.S.
John Sitgreaves—Judge of the U.S.
for the North Carolina Dist.

LB, DLC:GW; copy, Nc-Ar: James Iredell, Sr., Papers.

1. For more information about this act, which was passed on 23 Mar. 1792, see Caleb Brewster to GW, 15 Mar., n.4; *Annals of Congress,* 2d Cong., 1346–48. For the protests against its provisions made by various federal judges, see Edmund Randolph to GW, 5 April, U.S. Circuit Court Judges for New York to GW, 10 April, and enclosure, GW to the U.S. Senate and House of Representatives, 16, 21 April, and U.S. Circuit Court Judges for Pennsylvania to GW, 18 April 1792.

2. Iredell and Sitgreaves are referring to article 1, section 8 of the U.S. Constitution, which gives Congress the right to establish judicial tribunals inferior to the U.S. Supreme Court.

3. Section 4 of the above-mentioned act of 23 Mar. gave the secretary of war the power "to withhold the name of such applicant from the pension list, and make report of the same to Congress at their next session" if he had "cause to suspect imposition or mistake" (ibid., 1348).

4. Iredell and Sitgreaves are referring to section 3 of the act in question (ibid., 1347).

5. All of the references in section 2 of this act are to the "Circuit Court" or to the "Court." Section 3 explicitly mentions "the powers given by this act to the respective Circuit Courts." Only in districts "wherein a Circuit Court is not directed by law to be holden" was "the Judge of the District Court" to act in its stead (ibid.).

6. For GW's submission of Iredell and Sitgreaves's letter to Congress, see GW to the U.S. Senate and House of Representatives, 7 Nov. 1792; see also ibid., 611, 671–72. On 28 Feb. 1793 Congress passed "An Act to regulate the

claims to Invalid Pensions" which, among other things, repealed the second, third, and fourth sections of the act of 23 Mar. 1792, assigned investigative duties to "the Judge of the district in which such invalids reside" instead of the circuit court, and eliminated the secretary of war's right unilaterally to review the judges' decisions (ibid., 1436–37).

From Samuel and Elizabeth Willing Powel

Friday 8 June 1792

The Speaker of the Senate of Pennsylvania will have the Honor to wait on the President of the United States and Mrs Washington on Thursday next.[1]

Mrs Powel has the Pleasure to present her respectfull Compliments to them and to express her Regrets that she cannot have the Honor of dining with them upon that Day.

L, ViMtV.

Samuel Powel served as Speaker of the Pennsylvania senate from 1792 until 1793.

1. The following Thursday was 14 June 1792.

From Thomas Jefferson

[Philadelphia] June 9. 92.

Th: Jefferson, with his respects to the President, incloses him a letter from mister Rittenhouse on the subject of procuring a house for the mint.[1] mister Rittenhouse thinks the house in 7th street can be bought for 1600.£. it is probable that none can be rented under £150. and this sum would pay the interest and sink the principal of 1600£ in 15 years. the outhouses will save the necessity of new erections, and there is a horse mill, which will save the building one for the rolling mill: so that on the whole Th: J. concurs in opinion with mister Rittenhouse that it will be better to buy this house; and submits the same to the President.[2] a plan of the ground & buildings is inclosed.[3]

Mr Rittenhouse thinks the appointment of a Chief coiner & Engraver (in one office) necessary to prepare the proper machines for coining copper. he thinks Voight perfectly equal to the duties of the coiner.[4] he is no engraver himself, and it is therefore proposed that he shall consider the cost of engraving dies as a charge to be deducted from his salary of 1500. Doll. he has not been consulted on this point. he is willing to accept the appointment, & to retire from it of course on the arrival of any successor whom we shall import from abroad.[5]

AL, DNA: RG 59, Miscellaneous Letters; AL (letterpress copy), DLC: Jefferson Papers; LB, DNA: RG 59, George Washington's Correspondence with His Secretaries of State; LB (photocopy), DLC:GW.

1. The enclosure probably is David Rittenhouse's letter to Jefferson of 8 June 1792, which has not been found by the editors of the *Jefferson Papers* (see Summary Journal of Letters, DLC: Jefferson Papers).

2. For GW's agreement with Jefferson and Rittenhouse on the necessity of purchasing a house for the Mint, see GW to Jefferson, this date.

3. The enclosed plan has not been identified.

4. For Henry Voigt's application for the office of chief coiner, with which he enclosed a recommendation from Rittenhouse, and his appointment to that position, see Voigt to GW, 13 April, and notes.

5. Voigt served as chief coiner of the U.S. Mint from July 1792 until his death in 1814.

To Thomas Jefferson

Dear Sir, [Philadelphia] Saturday June 9th 92

I am in sentiment with you & the Director of the Mint, respecting the purchase of the Lots & Houses which are offered for Sale in preference to Renting—as the latter will certainly exceed the Interest of the former.

That all the applications may be brought to view, & considered, for Coining &ca; Mr Lear will lay the letters and engravings before you to be Shewn to the Director of the Mint.[1] I have no other object or wish in doing it than to obtain the best. Yrs &ca

Go: Washington

ALS, NNGL.

1. For David Rittenhouse's appointment of Henry Voigt as chief coiner of the U.S. Mint in July 1792 and GW's approval of that decision, see Rittenhouse to GW, 9 July, printed in GW to Jefferson, 9 July, n.1, and GW to Rittenhouse, 9 July 1792.

From Arthur Young

Sr Bradfield Hall [England] June 9. 92.

I beg leave to present your Excellency with a book I have published; & to request that you will pass over the first half of it & read only the second. The age is so frivolous that if a work contain only a subject of importance it has but little chance of attention unless it proceed from a genius of the first class, and this circumstance induced me to publish some rubbish to tempt people to the plough.[1]

When America sees the work that is made with the corn trade in France, she may bless herself at being governed by more enlightened legislators.[2] I have the honour to be With the Greatest Respect Your Excellency's Much obliged & Devoted St

Arthur Young

ALS, MH.

1. Two copies of Young's *Travels, during the Years 1787, 1788, and 1789. Undertaken More Particularly with a View of Ascertaining the Cultivation, Wealth, Resources, and National Prosperity, of the Kingdom of France* (Bury St. Edmund's, England, 1792; London and Bury St. Edmund's, 1794) were in GW's library at the time of his death (Griffin, *Boston Athenæum Washington Collection,* 231–32).

2. Young says in his book that the French government's apprehension about the grain supply, proclamations against its export, ordinances regulating its sale, restrictions on its transportation from province to province, and laws against speculation all tended to erode public confidence, raise the price of grain, and bring on famine conditions unnecessarily (see the two-volume 1794 London edition, 1:488–98, 625).

To Lafayette

My dear Sir, Philadelphia June 10th 1792

In the revolution of a great Nation we must not be surprized at the Vicissitudes to which individuals are liable; and the changes which they experience will always be in proportion to the weight of their public character; I was therefore not surprised, my dear Sir, at receiving your letter dated at Metz which you had the goodness to write me on the 22d of January. That personal ease & private enjoyment is not your primary object I well know, and until peace & tranquility are restored to your Country upon permanent & hononorable grounds I was fully persuaded, in my own mind, that you could not be permitted long to enjoy that domestic retirement into which you had fondly entered.

Since the commencement of your revolution our attention has been drawn, with no small anxiety, almost to France alone; but at this moment Europe in general seems pregnant with great events, and to whatever nation we turn our eyes there appears to be more or less cause to beleive, that an important change will take place at no very distant period. Those philanthropic spirits who regard the happiness of mankind are now watching the progress of things with the greatest solicitude, and consider the event of the present crisis as fixing the fate of man. How great! How important, therefore, is the part which the actors in this momentous scene have to perform! Not only the fate of millions of the present day depends upon them, but the happiness of posterity is involved in their decisions.

You who are on the spot cannot, I presume, determine when or where these great beginnings will terminate, and for us, at this distance, to pretend to give an opinion to that effect would at least be deemed presumptious. We are however anxious that the horrors of war may be avoided, if possible, and the rights of man, so well understood & so permanently fixed, as while despotic oppression is avoided on the one hand, licentiousness may not be substituted for liberty or confusion take place of order, on the other. The just medium cannot be expected to be found in a moment, the first vibrations always go to the extremes, and cool reason, which can alone establish a permanent & equal government, is as little to be expected in the tumults of popular commotions, as an attention to the liberties of the people is to be found in the dark Divan of a despotic tyrant.

I assure you, my dear Sir, I have not been a little anxious for your personal safety, and I have yet no grounds for removing that anxiety; but I have the consolation of beleiving that if you should fall it will be in defence of that cause which your heart tells you is just. And to the care of that Providence, whose interposition & protection we have so often experienced, do I chearfully commit you & your Nation, trusting that he will bring order out of confusion, and finally place things upon the ground on which they ought to stand.

The affairs of the United States still go on in a prosperous train. We encrease daily in numbers & riches, and the people are blessed with the enjoyment of those rights which can alone give security and happiness to a nation. The war with the Indians on our western frontier will, I hope, be terminated in the course of the present season without further effusion of blood; but, in case the measures taken to promote a pacification should fail, such steps are pursued as must, I think, render the issue by the sword very unfavorable to them.

Soon after the rising of Congress I made a journey to Mount Vernon, from whence I returned but a few days ago, and expect (if nothing of a public nature should occur to detain me here) to go there again some time next month with Mrs Washington and her two little grand children, where we shall continue 'till near the next meeting of Congress.[1]

Your friends in this Country are interested in your welfare & frequently enquire about you with an anxiety that bespeaks a warm affection. I am afraid my Nephew George, your old aid, will never have his health perfectly re-established, he has lately been attacked with the alarming symptom of spitting large quantities of blood, and the Physicians give no hopes of a restoration unless it can be effected by a change of air, and a total dereliction of business (to which he is too anxiously attentive[2] he will, if he should be taken from his family & friends, leave three fine child:—viz.—two Sons & a daughter—the eldest of the boys he has given the name of Fayette to and a fine looking child he is).[3] Hamilton, Knox, Jay & Jefferson are well & remember you with affection—Mrs Washington desires to be presented to you in terms of friendship & warm regard, to which I add my most affectionate wishes & sincere prayers for your health & happiness—and request you to make the same acceptable to Madm. lafayette & your children. I am—&ca &ca

G.W.

DfS, in Tobias Lear's hand, DLC:GW; LB, DLC:GW.

1. GW, who briefly had visited Mount Vernon in mid-May, left Philadelphia on 11 July for a more extended visit that would last into the fall of 1792.

2. The remainder of the text within the parentheses is in GW's hand.

3. For more information about George Augustine Washington's battle with tuberculosis, see G. A. Washington to GW, 26 June, and source note, 7 July, GW to Alexander Hamilton, 29 July, and GW to Henry Knox, 15 Aug. 1792. The three children of G. A. and Frances (Fanny) Bassett Washington were Anna Maria (1788–1814), George Fayette (1790–1867), and Charles Augustine (b. 1791).

From Gouverneur Morris

private

My dear Sir, Paris 10 June 1792.

Altho I have been above a Month in this City I have not been able untill within a Day or two to make up my Mind as to the Sentiments of the Person mentiond to you in mine of the twenty first of March, or rather I could not obtain that Certainty which was needful before I could properly mention them to you. I can now venture to assure you that *by coming into Office he has not chang'd his Sentiments.*[1]

My former Letters have mention'd to you the Indiscipline of the french Armies, and the public Prints will give you such Facts on that Head as may tend to making up in your Mind a solid Judgment as to future Events[.] The first Step towards Bankruptcy has already been made by extending to seventeen hundred Millions the Sum of Assignats which may be in Circulation. A further Extension must take Place in a few Days. The Powers combin'd against France have it therefore in their Choice to wear her out by a War of resources or dash into the Heart of the Country. This last will best suit with their own Situation but I do not think they will advance before the Begining of August.[2]

Your Letter to the King has produc'd a very good effect. It is not relish'd by the Democrats who particularly dislike the Term *your People* but it suits well the prevailing Temper which is monarchic.[3] The jacobine Faction approaches to its Dissolution, as you may perceive by its Agonies. In fact the Deliberations are so absurd & so extravagantly wild that they daily furnish new Arms to their Enemies. You will perceive at a Glance that this is not a Moment for making commercial Treaties[.] I shall however do all which I can without seriously compromising our *future Interest.* I am ever most truly yours

Gouvr Morris

ALS, DLC:GW; LB, DLC: Gouverneur Morris Papers.

1. In his letter to GW of 21 Mar., Morris had written that his use of this phrase in a later letter would mean that French minister of foreign affairs Charles-François du Périer (Duperrier) Dumouriez remained committed to destroying the Jacobin and other political clubs and bringing about a change of government in France.

2. An army comprised of Prussians, Hessians, and French émigrés under

the command of Karl Wilhelm Ferdinand, duke of Brunswick (1735–1806), invaded France on 19 August. Brunswick's forces were repulsed at Valmy on 20 Sept. and retreated toward the Rhine River.

3. The versions of GW's letter to Louis XVI of 14 Mar. 1792 in English use the words "your nation" twice, "your Kingdom" once, and "yourself, your family, and people" once (copy, DLC: Jefferson Papers; LB, DNA: RG 59, Credences). It is the French translation that includes the objectionable phrase "vôtre peuple" (Arch. Aff. Etr., Cor. Polit., Etats Unis, 36).

To Thomas Barclay

Sir Philadelphia June 11. 1792.

Congress having furnished me with means for procuring peace, and ransoming our captive citizens from the government of Algiers, I have thought it best, while you are engaged at Marocco, to appoint Admiral Jones to proceed to Algiers, and therefore have sent him a commission for establishing peace, another for the ransom of our captives, and a third to act there as Consul for the U.S. and full instructions are given in a letter from the Secretary of state to him, of all which papers, mister Pinkney now proceeding to London as our Minister Plenipotentiary there, is the bearer, as he is also of this letter.[1] it is sometime however since we have heard of Admiral Jones, and as, in the event of any accident to him, it might occasion an injurious delay, were the business to await new commissions from hence, I have thought it best, in such an event, that mister Pinkney should forward to you all the papers addressed to Admiral Jones, with this letter, signed by myself, giving you authority on receipt of those papers to consider them as addressed to you, and to proceed under them in every respect as if your name stood in each of them in the place of that of John Paul Jones.[2] you will of course finish the business of your mission to Marocco with all the dispatch practicable, and then proceed to Algiers on that hereby confided to you, where this letter with the commissions addressed to Admiral Jones, and an explanation of circumstances, will doubtless procure you credit as acting in the name & on the behalf of the United States, and more especially when you shall efficaciously prove your authority by the fact of making, on the spot, the payments you shall stipulate. With full confidence in the prudence & integrity with which you will fulfill the objects of the present mission, I give to this letter the effect of a commission & full powers, by hereto subscribing my name this eleventh day of June one thousand seven hundred & ninety two.

Go: Washington

LS, in Thomas Jefferson's hand, NjP: de Coppet Collection; L (letterpress copy), in Jefferson's hand, DLC: Jefferson Papers; copy, DNA: RG 233, Second Congress, 1791–1793, Records of the Office of the Clerk, Records of Reports from Executive Departments; copy, DNA: RG 59, Instructions to Diplomatic Officers, Instructions, 1785–1906; copy, DNA: RG 46, Third Congress, 1793–1795, Records of Executive Proceedings, President's Messages—Foreign Relations. The copy in DLC: Jefferson Papers is a letterpress imprint of the LS without GW's signature.

1. For the background to this document, see GW to Thomas Jefferson, 10 Mar., and note 3, Conversation with a Committee of the U.S. Senate, 12 Mar., Jefferson to GW, 1 April, and note 1, Jefferson's Memorandum on a Treaty with Algiers, 10 April, and source note, and GW to the U.S. Senate, 8 May (third letter), and note 2. For Secretary of State Jefferson's long letter to John Paul Jones of 1 June 1792, see *Jefferson Papers,* 24:3–10. The American naval hero John Paul Jones (1747–1792), who had been living in Paris since 1789, died on 18 July 1792 before Jefferson's instructions reached him.

2. On 7 Aug., Thomas Pinckney wrote Jefferson of his sorrow "to see the death of our late gallant naval officer Paul Jones announced in the papers. . . . I shall take the earliest opportunity of writing to Mr. B[arclay]" (ibid., 282–83). Because of his inability to find a reliable courier, however, Pinckney did not forward the papers to Barclay until mid-November 1792 (ibid., 600–601, 736–37). Barclay died suddenly from "an inflamation of the lungs" shortly after receiving Pinckney's packet (ibid., 25:86).

To Thomas Harwood

Sir, Philadelphia June 11th 1792.

Be pleased to pay to Thomas Johnson, David Stuart and Daniel Carroll Esqrs., Commissioners of the Federal District, or to their order, or to the order of any two of them, Twenty four thousand Dollars in part of the sum given by the Assembly of Maryland towards defraying the expences of the public buildings within the said District.[1]

G: Washington

LB, DLC:GW.

1. For the background to this letter, see the Commissioners for the District of Columbia to GW, 6 June, and note 1. The D.C. commissioners received

their payment from Harwood on 3 July 1792 (DNA: RG 42, Records of the Commissioners for the District of Columbia, Proceedings, 1791–1802).

From Richard Potts

sir Frederick Town [Md.] 12 June 1792

Finding it very inconvenient to attend the Circuit and district Courts of the United States from this place so remote from the seats of those Courts, and considering it material to the interests of the United States That the Residence of the Attorney should be nearer the Scenes of Business, I am induced to give up my appointment as Attorney for the District of Maryland, and beg that this may be received as my resignation thereof—Permit me to assure you that I entertain a just sense of the honour conferred by that trust reposed in me, and am led to this step by a sense of duty, after experiencing that I cannot discharge the duties of that station with advantage to the public, without a change of Residence that present circumstances would not justify. With Sentiments of the highest Respect I have the honour to subscribe myself Your obedt Servant

Richard Potts

ALS, DNA: RG 59, Miscellaneous Letters. The postmark on the cover of this document reads: "BALT June 21."

Richard Potts (1753–1808), a lawyer in Frederick, Md., served in the Md. house of delegates 1779–80 and 1787–88, the Continental Congress in 1781, and the Md. convention that ratified the U.S. Constitution in 1788. He was U.S. attorney for Maryland 1789–92, chief judge of the fifth judicial circuit 1791–93 and 1796–1801, a U.S. senator 1793–96, and an associate justice of the Maryland court of appeals 1801–4.

From Thomas Jefferson

[Philadelphia] June 14. 1792.

Th: Jefferson with his respects incloses to the Presiden⟨t⟩ two letters recieved yesterday from mister Morris.[1] he had sent the Observations of mister Keith to mister Rittenhouse, wi⟨th⟩ a note for his consideration. Th: J. incloses the Note wit⟨h⟩ mister Rittenhouse's answer for the perusal of the Presiden⟨t⟩ if he thinks them worth the time.[2]

P.S. the Proces-verbal accompanying mister Morris's lette⟨r⟩ has appeared in our newspapers, exactly translated.[3]

AL, DNA: RG 59, Miscellaneous Letters; LB, DNA: RG 59, George Washington's Correspondence with His Secretaries of State; LB (photocopy), DLC:GW. The mutilated text on the edge of the manuscript page is supplied in angle brackets from the letter-book copy.

1. For the relatively brief letters Gouverneur Morris wrote to Jefferson from London on 6 and 10 April 1792, see *Jefferson Papers,* 23:382–83, 392–93.

2. On 14 Jan. 1792 George Skene Keith had sent GW a critique of Jefferson's advocacy of the rod-pendulum as a standard of measure. After receiving Keith's comments from GW, Jefferson wrote David Rittenhouse on 8 June that Keith's "language is so lax, that it is difficult to know with precision what idea he means to express. . . . What does he mean by saying that the difference between the cubic foot proposed by Th: J. and the English cubic foot (which Th: J. had stated to be 1/14 as Mr. Skene does) 'is a monstrous error?'" On 11 June, Rittenhouse replied to Jefferson that Keith "has indeed expressed himself so very loosely that it is not easy to say what he intended. One thing however is clear, that he meant to depreciate the Rod-pendulum; and this he has done in a manner that does no credit to his Candour or Abilities. . . . I think I never saw so much *no meaning,* so ill expressed and in so few lines as his paper contains" (see ibid., 24:44–45, 64–66).

3. The "Proces-verbal" enclosed in Gouverneur Morris's letter to Jefferson of 10 April 1792 was a report of the assassination of Gustav III of Sweden. It was published in the *National Gazette* (Philadelphia) on 14 June.

From William Claiborne

Sir, Richmond June 15th 1792

My Son Ferdinand Leigh Claiborne has a great desire to become a Millita[r]y Man, and has been honord with a Letter from The Govr of Virga & Colo. Carrington in his favor, which Letters, with the Recommendation of my freind The Honr. Samuel Griffin I beg leave to refer your Excellencey to, for his Character[1]—I think it Necessary for me to say that it is with my Consent & indeed wish, that he makes an Application for an Appointment—& Should he be so Luckey as to gain his wishes I trust he will make a Valuable Officer—I have the honor of being personally Acquainted with your Excelly. But least you May have forgotten me I beg leave to inform you that I am the Son of Nathl Claiborne who lived upon Pamunkey River in Kg William and if you can provide for my Son, I shall Esteem it a favor Done.[2] Sir, Yr Mo. Obt very hblest

Wm Claiborne

ALS, DLC:GW.

1. Although the recommendations from Col. Edward Carrington and Samuel Griffin have not been identified, Gov. Henry Lee wrote GW from Rich-

mond, Va., on 15 June that he could not "resist the importunity of several respectable gentlemen to ask your attention to Mr Ferdinand Leigh Claiborne a youth of genteel manners and good character, and who is desirous of entering into the army. I am well assured that applications of this nature ought to be presented to the secretary of war, but on this occasion I have been obliged to deviate from the general will in compliance with the solicitation of Mr Claibornes friends" (DLC:GW).

2. Nathaniel Claiborne (died c.1756) of Sweet Hall, Va., operated a ferry on the Pamunkey River during the 1750s where GW sometimes crossed on his way to Williamsburg (see Memorandum, 15–30 May 1755, n.4). Ferdinand Leigh Claiborne (d. 1815) was appointed an ensign in the U.S. Army in February 1793, and he was promoted to lieutenant in the spring of 1794 and captain in October 1799. He resigned from the service in January 1802. During the War of 1812 Claiborne led a force of Mississippi volunteers.

To Thomas Jefferson

Dear Sir [Philadelphia] Friday 15. June 1792

When Artizans are imported, and criticism is at Work, the inducement is greater to obtain those who are *really* skilful: for this reason, if Mr Pinckney should not readily meet with those who are unequivocally such; or, if there is a chance of getting better in France than in England, I think it would be well to instruct him to correspond with Mr Morris on this Subject with a view to obtain the best.[1] I should be mortified to import men not more understanding in the business of Assaying, Engraving & Coining than those who are already among us. Yours. &ca

Go: Washington

ALS, DLC: Jefferson Papers.

1. On 11 June, Jefferson had written to Thomas Pinckney from Philadelphia that "We shall have occasion to ask your assistance in procuring a workman or two for our mint; but this shall be the subject of a separate letter." On 14 June, Jefferson asked Pinckney to "endeavor, on your arrival in Europe to engage and send us an Assayer, of approved skill, and of well attested integrity, and a Chief-coiner and Engraver, in one person, if possible." Jefferson's postscript to the latter letter, which he apparently wrote after receiving GW's letter of 15 June, reads: "Should you not be able to procure persons of eminent qualifications for their business in England, it will be proper to open a correspondence with Mr. [Gouverneur] Morris on the subject and see whether he cannot get such from France. Next to the obtaining the ablest artists, a very important circumstance is to send them to us as soon as possible" (*Jefferson Papers,* 24:63, 74–76).

From Henry Lee

My dear President Richmond June 15th 1792

When I was in Norfolk I heard of your passing thro Baltimore on a visit to Mt Vernon, and flattered myself with being enabled to pay my respects to you, but on my return I heard of your departure for Philada.[1]

This happiness I must hope for on a future day.

In the mean time permit me to occupy a few moments of your time.

You cannot have forgotten a declaration which you made at your own table just before your acceptance of the arduous station you enjoy, which then sunk deep into my head and never can be eradicated, viz. that a frank communication of the truth to you respecting the public mind, would be ever received as the highest testimony of respect & attachment.[2]

Often have I wished to have presented you with evidence of my affection & devotion in conformity to the above declaration since your return to public life, but presuming that you might derive ample information from others, and distrusting my own enquiry and observations I have heretofore silenced my desire.

Nor indeed for the same reasons should I now commence the task did it not appear to me indispensably necessary, for if the information be accurate, you are deceived & abused by those in whom you place the highest confidence, and consequently your own character as well as the public interest may be submitted to derogation and injury—what one minister may have done on one occasion, may extend to all occasions and to all ministers.

You cannot be a stranger to the extreme disgust which the late appointment to the command of the army excited among all orders in this state, whether the same be just or not, is immaterial at present, or whether taking into view all the circumstances of the case a better appointment could have been made is by no means the object of my enquiry.[3]

The event was the subject of general conversation; during which period Col. Darke visited Richmond, and of course became a party in the opinions & communications given on the occasion. What he said to me was in my judgement necessary to you, and I took the liberty to write to Col. Darke requesting him to commit to paper the conversation between us the previous day.

This he did and I enclose it for your perusal.[4]

I thought it proper to send you the original, altho the hand writing is Rather obscure, least a copy might in any degree change the meaning of the communication.

If Col. Dark is right it follows clearly that in a very important matter to yourself & the community, one of your officers exerted himself to encrease certain difficultys which obstructed the execution of your own wishes, instead of endeavoring to remove them, acting in obedience to his own desire rather than follow the decision of his superior.

If your ministers dare thus to do, you must be subject to hourly impositions, and the national concerns will be regulated by their and not your judgement.

I have not nor shall I lisp a word of this communication to the gentleman whom it concerns—For yourself only it is intended.

It is not in my power to ascertain whether the same be true or not; you can readily distinguish this fact. Col. Darke is a man of truth and honor and he speaks positively.[5]

You will I trust, be the event as it may impute my conduct to the motives which produce it, respect, & attachment to yourself—personally I do not feel on the occasion, only that I can not dissemble the gratification which the opinion you was pleased to express of my talents afforded, and indeed I am candid to declare that I prefer such a testimonial, to the office itself to which I might have been appointed.[6] I have the honor to be dear sir with the most affectionate respect & attachment your h: sert

Henry Lee

ALS, DLC:GW.

1. GW left Philadelphia for Mount Vernon on 10 May and apparently began his return trip to the U.S. capital on 24 May 1792.

2. GW repeated his desire for Lee to provide him with "every information that will enable me to . . . investigate with more accuracy the characters of public men—or the utility of public measures" in his letter to Lee of 30 June 1792.

3. For the appointment of Anthony Wayne as a major general in the U.S. Army and as commander of yet another punitive expedition against the hostile Indians on the northwest frontier, see GW to the U.S. Senate, 9 April 1792. The Senate approved Wayne's nomination on 11 April (*Executive Journal,* 1:119).

4. William Darke's letter to Henry Lee of 12 May 1792 reads: "In answer to your Letter Concerning the Conversation I had the honor to have with the president, as it was not of a private nature—as far as it related to you, I will Give as Good an account as my Memory will alow—as it Could not be the presidents desire that I Should not. he Mentioned you as Commander in chief of the Army Spoke much in favour of your abilitys in So Respectful a maner that I thaught you would Certainly have bean apointed, he indeed Said Something of your Rank in the late Continantal Army—and asked me if I would Serve Should you be apointed to the Chief Command—which question I did not answer though I Confess I think I Should—but being so destressed in mind for Reasons that I need not Mention to you I did not Give his Excelency an answer, but Intended to do it before I left town, which I did not knowing he was Much ingaged in business of importance I was in doubts he would think I intruded, at the Same time was determined if you had bean apointed to have Gone with you and Given you what Little assistance I was Capable of—or indeed any other of my aquaintance that I thaught equal to that Grate and important trust. The Secretary at war Said Somthing to Me Concerning My excepting of Some apointment I told him I first wanted to know who would Command the Army and Said Somthing of you and Some other—[Henry Lee noted at this point: "Two conversations with the secretary of war; the first of which he urged the objections to my rank, persuading Col. Dark that he could not in honor serve under me the second conversation the same idea was pressed & the information given as to my appointment"] he let me understand Some time after, that he thaught I could not Serve with you with propriety, honour or words to that purpose—but that you would not be apointed—this I confess I thaught Genl Knox might be mistaken in, as from what I heared from the president I had a Right to Expect you would, I most Sincerely wish you had I would have bean with you, even if I had not bean apointed to any Command" (DLC:GW).

5. For GW's dismissal of the allegations of misconduct brought against Secretary of War Knox by Darke in his letter to Lee of 12 May, see GW to Lee, 30 June 1792.

6. For GW's evaluation of Lee's abilities as a soldier, particularly in regard to Indian warfare, see Thomas Jefferson's Memorandum of a Meeting of the Heads of the Executive Departments, 9 Mar., and Memorandum on General Officers, 9 Mar. 1792.

From Thomas Chittenden

Sir— Williston [Vt.] June 16th 1792

The unprovoked insult lately offered to this, and the united government by the commanding officer of a british Garrison within the jurisdiction of the united States; is so flagrant a breach of the Laws of Nations, and the late treaty with great Britain; that

I feel myself under obligations to give you the earliest information of it. I have inclosed you sundry affidavits, to which I refer you for the particulars. Inclosed also is a copy of my Letter to the Governor of Canada of the 16th instant.[1] As soon as I receive an answer I shall without loss of time, communicate it to you, together with such other circumstances as may hereafter come to my knowledge.[2] I am with the greatest respect your Excellencys very humble servant

Thoms Chittenden

ALS (retained copy), Vt. Chittenden noted at the bottom of the manuscript page that this was a "True copy from the Original." His docket reads: "Copy of my Letter to the president of the U. States. June 16th 1792."

1. Thomas Chittenden (1730–1797), who had served as governor of Vermont since 1778, with the exception of the 1789–90 term, agreed in May 1792 to the organization of a town government at Alburg, a few miles away from the disputed post of Pointe-au-Fer, N.Y., and just south of the Canadian border. As the British had for some time before the spring of 1792 claimed jurisdiction over Alburg and had prevented Vermont from effectively controlling the area, the stage was set for conflict. In early June, British soldiers stopped a Vermont deputy sheriff and two justices of the peace from carrying out their duties in Alburg, an act which ignited the crisis. For Chittenden's letter to acting Gov. Alured Clarke (c.1745–1832) of Lower Canada of 16 June, see Walton, *Vermont Records,* 4:458–59. For the enclosed affidavits, see ibid., 465–70.

2. Governor Chittenden next wrote GW on 16 July 1792. For more information about this diplomatic imbroglio, see Thomas Jefferson to GW, 5 July, n.1, 6 July, n.1, and GW to Jefferson, 7 July, n.2.

Henry Knox to Tobias Lear

[Philadelphia, 16 June 1792].[1] Asks Lear "to submit the enclosed letter from Genl Chapin, to the President of the United States.[2] Capt. Brant will be here by tuesday, at furthest, in the judgement of the express who has just arrived."[3]

ALS, DLC:GW; LB, DLC:GW.

For the reasons for Joseph Brant's delay in visiting Philadelphia, see GW to Knox, 25 Feb., source note and note 1, Timothy Pickering to GW, 21 Mar., and Knox to GW, 22 April 1792, n.3.

1. Although the dockets on the ALS and the letter-book copy both read 17 June 1792, Knox wrote "Saturday Morng" at the bottom of the ALS, indicating that this letter was written on 16 June.

2. Israel Chapin's letter to Knox has not been identified.

3. The "judgement" of the express notwithstanding, Knox was forced to write Lear again on Wednesday, 20 June, to inform him that "Captain [Joseph] Brandt will be here to morrow. I have made arrangements for his reception—Colonel [Thomas] Procter and Major [John] Stagg will meet him at Bristol with four of the City horse—upon his arrival 13 Guns" (DLC:GW). Knox informed Lear on the next day that "Capt. Brant and myself will have the honor to wait on the President at 12 oClock today—The President can then arrange any other day he shall judge proper" (DLC:GW; because the ALS of Knox's letter to Lear of 21 June was mistakenly docketed as having been written on Tuesday, 26 June 1792, both the ALS and the letter-book copy of this letter in DLC:GW are filed under that date).

To Thomas Jefferson

Dear Sir, [Philadelphia] June 17th 1792.

The Attorney General will, I presume, draw the Deed for the Lot for the Mint. The purchase of it, I approve of.[1]

If you can aid me in answering the queries of Mr Young, contained in his letter enclosed, I would thank you[2]—I wish to write to him by Mr Pinckney.[3]

Is not fish Oil one of the things that will claim the particular attention of Mr Morris?[4] Yrs &ca

Go: Washington

ALS, DLC: Jefferson Papers.

1. For GW's approval of the purchase of a house and lot for the use of the U.S. Mint, see GW to Jefferson, 9 June.

2. GW enclosed a copy of Arthur Young's letter to him of 18 Jan. 1792. For Jefferson's response, see Notes on Arthur Young's Letter to George Washington, 18 June 1792, printed in *Jefferson Papers,* 24:95–99.

3. On 23 June, Thomas Pinckney left Philadelphia for London to assume his position as U.S. minister to the Court of St. James.

4. For the duties levied by the French National Assembly on whale oil and the restrictions placed on its importation in March 1791, see Lafayette to GW, 7 Mar. 1791, Gouverneur Morris to GW, 9 Mar. 1791, and GW to Lafayette, 28 July 1791. Jefferson apparently did not consider the matter of much moment. On 16 June 1792 he wrote in a postscript to his letter to Gouverneur Morris: "I have said nothing of our whale oil, because I believe it is on a better footing since the Tariff than before" (*Jefferson Papers,* 24:89).

Tobias Lear to Alexander Hamilton

United States [Philadelphia] 18 June 1792. Transmits by GW's command for Hamilton's inspection "a letter from John Ritchie, Inspector of the 2d division in Maryland, to the President."[1]

LB, DLC:GW.

1. Neither Ritchie's letter to GW nor any reply from GW or Hamilton to Ritchie has been found.

To Arthur Young

Sir, Philadelphia June 18[–21] 1792.

Your letter of the 18th of Jany was received about a fortnight ago. For the Annals which you have had the goodness to send me, I pray you to accept my thanks. No directions having accompanied the second sett, and presuming they were intended for the Agricultural Society in this City, I have, in your name, presented them to that body.[1]

As far as it is in my power, I will endeavour to solve the doubts which are expressed in your queries, contained in the above letter. and first—"Labour is so slightly touched on, that I know not how to estimate it."

The information on this, as well as on other points of my last communication, was given in transcripts of the letters I had received in answer to certain queries, hastily submitted, to some intelligent Gentlemen of my acquaintance, in the States of Pennsylvania, Maryland & Virginia.[2] If therefore the article of labour was not sufficiently enlarged upon, or, if there appeared too great a diversity in the price of this article, in that of land, and of other things, to be easily reconciled and understood; you must ascribe the inconsistency, or omission, to that cause; & to the habits, & value which is set on these things in the different States, and in different parts of the same State.

South of Pennsylvania, hired labor is not very common, except it be at harvest, and sometimes for cutting grass. The wealthier farmers perform it with their own black Servants, whilst the poorer sort are obliged to do it themselves. That labour in this Country is higher than it is in England, I can readily conceive. The ease with which a man can obtain land, in fee, beyond the

Mountains—to which most of that class of people repair, may be assigned as the primary cause of it. But high wages is not the worst evil[3] attending the hire of white men in this Country, for being accustomed to better fare than I believe the labourers of almost any other Country, adds considerably to the expence of employing them; whilst blacks, on the contrary, are cheaper: the common food of them (even when well treated) being bread, made of the Indian Corn, Butter milk, Fish (pickled herrings) frequently, and meat now and then; with a blanket for bedding: In addition to these, ground is often allowed them for gardening, & priviledge given them to raise dung-hill fowls for their own use. With the farmer who has not more than two or three Negros, little difference is made in the manner of living between the master & the man; but far otherwise is the case with those who are owned in great numbers by the wealthy; who are not always as kind, and as attentive to their wants & usage as they ought to be; for by these, they are fed upon bread alone, which does not, on an average, cost more than seven dollars a head pr Ann. (about 32/ Sterling).

From these data, in aid of my last communications, you will be able to form an idea of the cost of labour in this Country.[4] It varies, however, in the different States as I have already observed, and sometimes in the same State; but may be said to vibrate with white men, between ten & fifteen pounds—and for black men between Eight and twelve pounds sterling pr Ann., besides their board. No difficulty, I should conceive, would be found in obtaining those of either description on the terms here mentioned; but I do not advance this with certainty, not having been in the habit of hiring any, myself, for several years past. Blacks are capable of much labour, but having (I am speaking generally) no ambition to establish a *good* name, they are too regardless of a *bad* one; and of course, require more of the masters eye than the former. Formerly, I have given to *skilful* & *careful* Cradlers, a dollar a day during harvest; which was a sixth more than the usual price; but then, I knew the men, & that they would oblige themselves to cut *clean,* and lay *well,* four acres of Wheat a day (if it did not stand very heavy on the ground)—or, if I prefered it, they would cut by the Acre paying them at the rate of a dollar for every four acres. There are men who will rake & bind as fast as the Cradlers will cut the grain, but to do this is deemed hard work, and when done, entitles them to Cradlers wages. These people eat three times a day (once perhaps of milk) and are allowed a pint of spirits each man. A Barn floor, with straw & a blanket, serves them *at harvest* for lodging.

When I observed in a former letter that, "all our labour was performed by Negros" I must have alluded to the custom in Virginia—the State in which I then lived, & from which I wrote;[5] but my last communication to you, was on a more extensive Scale, comprehending the practices, & prices of Pennsylvania & Maryland, as well as different parts of Virginia; which (latter) is a state of great extent—differing much in its products and culture.

The English Statute acre is the measure by which we have hitherto bought & sold land; and the price of land, as handed to you in my last, includes buildings, fences, arable, meadow, in short the improvements of every sort appertaining to the tract, on which they are placed. To a stranger at a distance, this aggregate mode, of estimating the value of a farm is, it must be confessed, dark, & unsatisfactory; but to the parties present, who see & examine every thing, & judge for themselves, it is quite immaterial. The *Seller* warrants the title, & quantity which he sells; and both form an opinion of the total worth of the premises. It rarely happens, however, that buildings & other improvements are estimated by the purchaser at near what they cost the Seller, especially on *old* farms which have been a good deal worked; the received opinion being, that fresh land without improvements, is more to be desired than worn, & much abused land is with such as are usually found thereon; but this is to be considered as a general, not an invariable rule; for the better & more attentive farmers keep their farms in high order, and value the improvements accordingly.

Never having been in England, I ought not to hazard an opinion, or attempt a comparison between the Soil of that Country & this, in their virgin & unimproved State; but from what I know of the one, & have heard of the other, I should decide in favor of the latter at a distance from the Sea-board; which from the highlands of the Neversink (in East Jersey) to Florida inclusively, is flat; and with but few exceptions, sandy, and generally of mean quality. From the falls of the Rivers to the Mountains—which is generally from Sixty to 100 miles—and above the latter—except the craggy hills & mountains which lye between the Eastern & Western waters; the best lands are to be found. They are strong, and after having been used, & abused in a shameful manner, will, with a little repose, get covered with white clover. The upper Country is healthiest also.

You seem surprised, and no wonder, to hear that many of our farmers—if they can be so called—cultivate much ground for little profit; because land is cheap, and labour is high; but you will remember, that when I informed you of this fact, I reprobated at the sametime both the practice & the principle. The history however of it, is this—a piece of land is cut down & kept under constant cultivation—first in Tobacco & then in Indian Corn (two very exhausting plants) until it will yield scarcely anything; a second piece is cleared & treated in the same manner; then a third—& so on until probably, there is but little more to clear. When this happens, the owner finds himself reduced to the choice of one of three things—either to recover the land which he has ruined, to accomplish which he has perhaps neither the skill, the industry, nor the means; or to retire beyond the Mountains; or to substitute quantity for quality, in order to raise something. The latter has been generally adopted; and with the assistance of horses, he *scratches* over much ground, & seeds it, to very little purpose as you may suppose, & have been informed; for I presume an English farmer would bestow more labour on *one* acre by deep & frequent ploughings, besides the dressings he gives to the land, than the other does on *five* acres. It is but justice however to Pennsylvania, to declare that her husbandry (though not perfect) is much better; and her crops proportionably greater. The practice above mentioned applies more particularly to the Tobacco States which, happily, are yielding more and more every year to the growth of Wheat, and as this prevails the husbandry improves. Instances could be enumerated, and where no extraordinary dressings or management has been used, of land yielding from thirty to forty bushels of Wheat pr acre, that *has been* very much exhausted.

Your mode of calculating the taxes of this Country, being unusual *with us,* I may not accurately understand; and as the Virginia method was, if I recollect rightly, detailed in my former accounts,[6] I know not how to give you a more distinct idea of them than by exhibiting the items of the specific charges on every species of taxable property—viz.—on Land, Negros, Stock &ca. This, as it respects an estate in Virginia with which I am very well acquainted, I am enabled to do, & will do. We have a Road tax besides but it is light, and in most of the States paid by a contribution of labour, which rarely exceeds two days in the year, for each male labourer. Dutiable articles is a distinct tax, the quantum of which depends upon the consumption, and the consumption upon the disposition of the consumer: with the aid therefore of the Laws (which I sent you)[7] every man can calculate, better than I am able to do for him, the amount of his own expenditures in this way. An additional duty, or excise, was imposed last Session;[8] and this being now sent, will, if I am not mistaken (with what was mentioned in my former communication) bring *every tax, direct, & indirect,* to your view, to which property, in this Country, is subjected; either by the general government, or the laws of the States of Pennsylvania, Maryland & Virginia, to which the observations have been confined.

Beef, & other meats; Grain of all sorts, and flour; Butter; Cheese; and other things in quantities to make them an object; are always, I conceive, in demand; and are sought after by the purchasers. The Sale of lesser articles, at a distance from market towns, may, sometimes, stick on hand; but rarely, I believe forego a Sale if they are worth the transportation.

Sheep thrive very well in the middle States, though they are not exempt from diseases—and are often injured by dogs; and more so as you approach the Mountains, by Wolves. Were we to use horses less, and Oxen more, on our farms (as they do in the New England States) we should, unquestionably, find our account in it; yet, strange as it may seem, *few* are in the practice of the latter—and *none* push the raising of Sheep to the extent they might, and ought to do. The fact is, we have, in a manner, every thing to learn that respects neat, and profitable husbandry.

Bakewells breed of Sheep[9] are much celebrated, and deservedly I presume; but if entrusted to a common Bailiff (or what with us is called an Overseer) would, I should apprehend, soon degenerate for want of that care & attention, which is necessary to preserve the breed in its purity. But, the great impediment is, the British Statutes. These discourage men of delicasy in this Country from attempting what might involve the Master of a Vessel in serious consequences if detected in the breach of them.[10]

Others however, less scrupulous, have attempted to import English Rams with Success, and by this means our flocks in many places are much improved—mine for instance, 'though I never was concerned directly nor indirectly in the importation of one, farther than by buying lambs which have descended from them. the average weight of the fleeces being 5 lbs.

Our modes, system we have none—are so different from yours—generally speaking, and our business being carried on so much within ourselves, so little by hiring, and still less by calculation, that I frankly confess to you, I am unable to solve your query respecting Sheepwalks—or how many sheep an acre of Woodland pasture would support.

I shall have pleasure at all times as far as I possess the means, or can command them, to give you every information that can contribute to your *own* satisfaction, or that of *a friend*; but I am so thoroughly persuaded of my inability to throw new lights upon any branch of husbandry in a Country where it is so well understood as in England; and, that anything I could write to you on that subject, would only serve to expose the defective practice of my Countrymen, & be considered as the beacon of our ignorance, that I am disenclined to see any production of mine in a work, where so much useful information is conveyed to the public, as is to be found in your Annals of Agriculture.[11] With very great esteem I am Sir Your Most Obedt Servt

Go: Washington

P.S. June 21st. I have not yet received the account of taxes I promised you, and for which I had written to Virginia; but I will send it by the first conveyance after its arrival.[12]

This letter goes by Mr Pinckney Minister from the U. States to the Court of London, through which channel I recommend any letters you may favor me with to pass, who being detained a day or two longer than was expected, by the Vessel in which he is to embark,[13] has given me an opportunity of asking Mr Jefferson (who is well acquainted in the South Western parts of Virginia, near Charlotsville)—and Mr Peters (one of the best farmers in the State of Pennsylvania, about Six miles from this City) to give me there sentiments on the several queries contained in your letter.[14] These you ⟨will find enclosd herewith in their own words. On applying to Colo. Hamilton for the statement mentioned in

Mr Peters' letter he put into my hands, together with the statement, several communications which were made to him last year by some of the most respectable farmers in this part of the Country in consequence of an application from him for information on certain points respecting Farms, And as they appeared to contain some matters worth attention I had them copied, and they are also enclosed.[15] Mine, & each of theirs, are written without any previous consultation, & may be considered (my Estate in the Neighbd of which I am best acquainted lying about midway between theirs) as the opinions of men living, North, South, & in the centre of the District of which an acct was given to you in my communications of the 4th[16] of Decr last.⟩

ALS (incomplete), PPRF; ADfS, DLC:GW; LB, DLC:GW. The mutilated portion of the postscript is supplied within angle brackets from the draft.

1. For Young's earlier requests that GW forward volumes of his *Annals of Agriculture* to the Philadelphia Society for Promoting Agriculture, see Young to GW, 1 Feb. 1787, 25 Jan. 1791.

2. See GW to Young, 5 Dec. 1791, and its enclosures: Circular on the State of American Agriculture, 25 Aug., Thomas Hartley to GW, 24 Sept., Thomas Johnson to GW, 10 Nov., and David Stuart to GW, 18 Nov. 1791.

3. At this place in the draft manuscript, GW first wrote "circumstance" before striking out the word and inserting "evil" above the line.

4. For GW's "last communications," see GW to Young, 5 Dec. 1791.

5. In November 1787 GW had written Young from Mount Vernon that "I am not able to give you the price of labour as the land is cultivated here wholly by slaves, and the price of labour in the Towns is fluctuating, & governed altogether by circumstances" (GW to Young, 1 Nov. 1787).

6. For the information on taxation in the Commonwealth of Virginia that GW previously had sent to Young, see David Stuart to GW, 18 Nov. 1791, which GW enclosed in his letter to Young of 5 Dec. 1791.

7. GW had enclosed a volume containing the "taxes of the General Government . . . found in the Revenue laws" in his letter to Young of 5 Dec. 1791.

8. GW is referring to "An Act concerning the Duties on Spirits distilled within the United States" of 8 May 1792 (see *Annals of Congress,* 2d Cong., 1374–79).

9. Agriculturalist Robert Bakewell (1725–1795) of Leicestershire, England, was famous for developing a breed of sheep that combined high-quality meat with a long, coarse coat.

10. For over a century England had tried to restrict the exportation of live sheep, rams, and lambs and raw wool. Young had been involved in the opposition to the most recent effort to limit the export of such items, the Wool Bill of 1788 (see H. B. Carter, *His Majesty's Spanish Flock: Sir Joseph Banks and the Merinos of George III of England* [London, 1964], 41, 44; Young to GW, 1 July 1788, and note 1).

11. For Young's request that he be allowed to publish GW's views on agriculture and GW's reluctance to give his permission, see Young to GW, 1 July 1788, 19 May 1789, 18 Jan. 1792, and GW to Young, 4 Dec. 1788, 5 Dec. 1791. Young did not publish his agricultural correspondence with GW until after the president's death.

12. For GW's account of taxes on "an estate in Virginia with which I am very well acquainted," see GW to Young, 2 Dec. 1792.

13. Thomas Pinckney departed Philadelphia on 23 June, sailed from New Castle, Del., two days later, and reached London on 3 Aug. 1792 (see Alexander Hamilton to William Short, 23 June, Syrett, *Hamilton Papers,* 11:554; Frances Leigh Williams, *A Founding Family: The Pinckneys of South Carolina* [New York, 1978], 297).

14. For GW's request for information from Thomas Jefferson and Richard Peters, see GW to Jefferson, 17 June, and to Peters, 20 June 1792. For Jefferson's response to GW's inquiry, see *Jefferson Papers,* 24:95–99. For Peters's response, see Peters to GW, 20 June 1792.

15. Among the documents that GW enclosed in this letter were Richard Peters's letter to Alexander Hamilton of 27 Aug. 1791; Peters's account of four nearby farms; Henry Wynkoop's letter to Hamilton of 29 Aug. 1791; Wynkoop's estimate of average annual agricultural production in Bucks County, Pa.; John Neville's letter to Hamilton of 27 Oct. 1791 and its enclosure; John Beale Bordley's letter to Hamilton of 11 Nov. 1791; Bordley's account of a farm in Talbot County, Md. (Syrett, *Hamilton Papers,* 9:114–18, 123–27, 419–20, 490–93); Thomas Jefferson's Notes on Arthur Young's Letter to George Washington, 18 June 1792 (*Jefferson Papers,* 24:95–99); and Richard Peters's letter to GW of 20 June 1792.

16. Although both the draft and the letter-book copy read "4th," GW's most recent letter to Young was dated 5 Dec. 1791.

From Alexander Hamilton

Treasury Departmt June 19th 1792.

The Secretary of the Treasury has the honor to submit to the President of the Ud States a provisional Contract entered into between the Superintendent of the Delaware Lighthouse and Abraham Hargis[1] for sinking a well for the accomodation of that Light house; together with a report of the Commissioner of the Revenue on the subject, & some explanatory statements.[2]

The Secretary has delayed this communication under an impression that the allowance was excessive, and with a hope that something better might be done: but reputable workmen who have been consulted appear to be of opinion that the charge is not unreasonable, and no other person has been found disposed to undertake at a lower rate. More from the latter circumstance, than a conviction that the terms are not less moderate than they ought to be, the Contract is now submitted. The approbation of it may be qualified by a reservation that if all the materials mentioned in the Estimate B are not used in the work, a proportional deduction shall be made from the sum stipulated.[3] This, it is represented, will be agreed to by Mr Hargis.

Alexder Hamilton
Secy of the Treasury.

LB, DLC:GW.

1. Abraham Hargis apparently served as keeper of the Delaware lighthouse throughout GW's presidency (see Hamilton to GW, 18 June 1790; *JPP*, 344–45).

2. Tench Coxe's letter to Hamilton of 28 May enclosed a contract "for the digging and building of a well for the Use" of the Delaware lighthouse and discussed "the causes of the extraordinary expence" (see Syrett, *Hamilton Papers*, 11:449).

3. At GW's command Tobias Lear wrote Hamilton on 22 June transmitting "the Contract made with Abraham Hargis for sinking a Well for the accomodation of the Delaware Lighthouse, which has received the President's approbation, qualified in the manner suggested in the Secretary's Letter of the 19th inst." (DLC:GW). Also on 22 June, Hamilton sent Lear "a letter from Mr [William] Al[l]ibone, which contains some explanations respecting the well at Cape Henlopen; to be communicated to the President" (DLC:GW). For Allibone's letter to Tench Coxe of 25 May, see Syrett, *Hamilton Papers*, 11:544. Hamilton forwarded the contract to Coxe on 23 June, and Coxe communicated the president's approval to Allibone in writing on 25 June 1792 (ibid., 545, 549).

To James Anderson (of Scotland)

Sir, Philadelphia June 20th 1792.

I had the pleasure a few days ago to receive your letter of the 28t[h] of September, enclosing a letter from the Earl of Buchan, and accompanied with some seeds of the Sweedish Turnip, or *Ruta Baga*.[1] At the same time I received from Mr Campbell, a bookseller in New York, *six* volumes of the *Bee*, which he informed me were transmitted by your directions.[2] In your letter you mentioned having sent the *four* first volumes of the Bee, and the Earl mentions in his that he has sent me *a sett*. I therefore concluded that the six vols. which I have received are those mentioned by his Lordship, and especially, as the pamphlet on wool, by Sir John Sinclair, which you observed in your letter accompanied the books which you sent, was not with those which I received. I mention these circumstances in order, that if there is any mistake in the transmission of the books, it may be set right. I feel no less grateful, Sir, for your polite attention, whether the books which I have received be those sent by yourself or by the Earl. I must beg your acceptance of my best thanks for the Sweedish Turnip seed, and the particular account which you were so good as to give me respecting it⟨.⟩ As I have spent great part of my life (and that not the least pleas⟨ing)⟩ in rural[3] affairs I am always obliged by receiving such communications or novelties in that way as may tend to promote the system of husbandry in this Country.

When you first determined upon publishing the *Bee,* the Earl of Buchan had the goodness to transmit to me the plan[4] of the work, with which I was much pleased, and from the answe⟨r⟩ which I then gave to his Lordship's letter; I have considered myself as a subscriber to the publication, and must beg to be informed to whom or in what manner I shall cause payment to be made for it.[5]

I have not yet had it in my power to peruse those volumes of the Bee which I have received, but I promise myself much entertainment & information from them; for the extensive & liberal ground upon which you appear to have undertaken the work must make it interesting to the good citizens of every Country, and for your complete success in it you have my best wishes. I am Sir, with proper consideration, Your most Obed. Ser.

Df, in Tobias Lear's hand, DNA: RG 59, Miscellaneous Letters; LB, DLC:GW. The mutilated letters along the edge of the manuscript page are provided in angle brackets from the letter-book copy.

1. The letter that James Anderson wrote GW from Edinburgh on 28 Sept. 1791 reads: "I send inclosed a letter from the Earl of Buchan [of 15 Sept.] to your excellency.

"I have also the honour to transmit along with it a copy of the four first volumes of the *Bee,* which are all that are yet published of that periodical Work—of which I humbly request your acceptance, as a small testimony of respect from a lover of mankind to one of their principal benefactors.

"I intended to have done myself this honour, at the conclusion of the former volumes; but, from a consciousness of the work having fallen so far below my own wishes and expectations, in the execution, (owing to a variety of discouraging circumstances in a beginning work, with which it would be impertinent to trouble you) I declined it—nor should I now have so far presumed on your goodness, had I not been urged to it by Lord Buchan, who has been a liberal contributer to this work, and some other respectable persons in this country, whose advice I consider as a law to me. One merit, at least, it can claim that of being seriously intended to benefit my fellow creatures, without respect to persons. And if it shall continue to have the circulation it has hitherto obtained, I flatter myself it may become, in several respects beneficial.

"I embrace this opportunity of transmitting to you a few seeds of the Swedish Turnip, or *Ruta Baga,* which I can promise are of the true sort, being saved by myself. It is a new plant here, and possesses the singular quality of retaining its firmness, suculence, and other qualities even till its seeds be perfected—We consider it in this country as a particularly valuable acquisition, as it affords us the *certainty* of having succulent food for our cattle in the spring when all others may fail—It is probable it may not prove so great an acquisition in America as here—But for milch cows in the spring, it is probable that it may even with you have its use—Please observe that it does not grow to so large a size as some other turnips—and never grows large on *a light* soil. It thrives best on a damp spungy mold, which is to be found in low places where the sediment of water has been deposited—whose specific gravity is small, and which is only fitted to produce a few kinds of useful plants that are cultivated by the farmer—It grows also very well on a rich clayey soil tending to damp—fortunately for its culture on such soils it admits of being transplanted as readily as a colwort plant. It may be sown about the middle of May and transplanted in june—Some seeds however ought to be reserved for a later sowing lest these plants should run to seed.

"I use the freedom also to send a copy of a pamphlet on wool by Sir John Sinclair—and have only to add on that subject, that the *Shetland* wool, has been found, upon trial, since the writing of that pamphlet to be possessed of qualities still more valuable than was then suspectd.

"It would give me much pleasure, if in my humble line I could prove in any respect serviceable to you or any of your friends, or in any way contribute to promote the interests of your countrymen here—If such thing should occur, you may at all times command my services" (PHi: Gratz Collection).

2. On 12 May, New York City bookseller, stationer, and printer Samuel Campbell wrote GW: "I lately received from Dr Jas Anderson of Edinburgh, with orders to forward to Your Excelly, a copy of His publication called the Bee, and a small bag of Swedish turnip seed; which I now forward, & hope they will be safe delivered" (DNA: RG 59, Miscellaneous Letters). For more information about James Anderson and the *Bee, or Literary Weekly Intelligencer,* see Buchan to GW, 27 Mar. 1790, n.1.

3. Lear first wrote the word "agricultural" at this place on the manuscript. He then struck out that word and replaced it with "rural."

4. Lear first wrote and then struck out "& purpose" at this place on the manuscript.

5. For Buchan's letter informing GW of the *Bee,* see Buchan to GW, 27 Mar. 1790. For GW's reply, which did not include a request that he be enrolled as a subscriber to the publication, see GW to Buchan, 30 June 1790. During the

next two years, Anderson continued to send GW volumes of the *Bee,* and GW repeatedly requested that he be informed to whom he was to make payment. After receiving six guineas from GW in 1794 for the fifteen volumes he had received, Anderson informed GW that he had intended the volumes to be a gift (see Anderson to GW, 6 Dec. 1794, DLC:GW).

To the Earl of Buchan

My Lord, Philadelphia June 20 1792

I presume you will, long before this reaches you, have received my letter of the first of May, in answer to the honor of your Lordships favor of the 28th of June, by Mr Robinson.[1] In that letter, I have stated, that the reason of my having so long delayed acknowledging the receipt of it, was a wish that the portrait, which you were pleased to request, should accompany the letter.[2]

It was not till the 10th instant that I had the honor to receive your Lordships second favor of the 15th of September which was enclosed in a letter from Doctr James Anderson, and accompanied with *six* volumes of the Bee.[3] These were forwarded by a Bookseller at New York, who mentions his having received directions from Doctr Anderson to transmit them to me.[4]

I must therefore beg your Lordships acceptance of my warmest thanks for this additional testimony of your politeness. Considering myself as a subscriber to the *Bee* I have written to Doctor Anderson to know in what manner I shall pay the money, that it may get regularly to[5] his hands.[6]

With sincere prayers for the health & happiness of your Lordship—an⟨d⟩ gratefully impressed with the many mark⟨s⟩ of attention which I have received from you—I have the honor to be with Great esteem Your Lordships Most Obedient Serv⟨t⟩

Go: Washington

ALS, PPRF; Df, in Tobias Lear's hand, DNA: RG 59, Miscellaneous Letters; LB, DLC:GW; copy, MHi: Miscellaneous Collection. The mutilated text along the edge of the manuscript is supplied in angle brackets from the draft.

1. In both Lear's draft and the letter-book copy this name is correctly written as "Robertson."

2. For Archibald Robertson's portrait of GW and its transmission to Buchan, see the frontispiece to this volume, Robertson to GW, 21 April, and notes 2 and 3, and GW to Buchan, 1 May 1792, and note 1.

3. For James Anderson's letter of 28 Sept. 1791, see GW to Anderson, 20 June 1792, n.1.

4. At this place in the draft manuscript, Lear wrote: "and Dr Anderson observes in his letter to me, that he had sent the *four* first volumes of this work. On comparing these accounts I presume I am indebted to your Lordship for those which I have received, as you mention to have sent me *a sett,* and more especially as Dr Anderson says that he has sent with the Bee, a pamphlet on wool by Sir John Sinclair, and there was no such pamplet accompanying the books which have come to my hands." While making revisions to the draft, GW struck out this passage. For the bookseller Samuel Campbell's transmission of a package of papers and seeds from Anderson to GW, see GW to Anderson, this date, n.2.

5. On the draft manuscript Lear first wrote "Dr Andersons hands, and shall accordingly request his information on this matter." GW later struck out the phrase and inserted "his hands."

6. See GW to Anderson, this date, and note 5. On 2 Feb. 1800 Buchan wrote on the reverse of the ALS of GW's letter: "I had presented to the General some volumes of Dr James Andersons Bee & mentioned to him that I proposed to write some papers for that periodical work which might have a Scope toward the United States. So attentive was this great and good man to the most minute circumstances that five Guineas accompanied this letter for Dr Anderson as a subscriber to his Paper."

From John Ely

Dear sir Say Brook [Conn.] 20th June 1792

Be Pleased to Permitt me once more Mr President, to ask your Indulgent Reflection for a Moment on the Situation of a man whose Feelings are Extreamly Injured when his Fondness for his Country Induced him to Exert every Nerve for her Releif (Perhaps to a Fault) uppon Principal as well as Duty not Doubting that Goverment would Distribute Equal Justice at the Close of the War.[1]

Yet after 7 Years Persuit by Humble & Dutifull Petitions found my Self Disappointed. Frequent And Repeated Committes have been appointed all of which Reported that my Claim was a Just & Meritorious Claim[.] The Secretary of war also made a Very Particular Report Stateing most Clearly to Congress that my acting as a Physician to the Prisoners was Intirely Distinct from Official Duty & that I aught to be Paid as a Regimental Cirgeon Dureing the time I acted as such. Yet after all my Petition was Negativd in the Senate.[2]

Yet sir I have this agreable Reflection that I have Contributed to the relif of the Sick & wounded Prisoners and in some measure have Prevented a Very Heavy Debt which must have accrewd, & must have been Paid—this Service was not only Done with Great Fategue & Resque of Life But with Great Expence for an Induvidual. without a Horse without Money Yet a Tour to be Performd, almost Every Day for the Best Part of 4 Years into 4 Differant Townships which was absolutly Performd by me sometimes on foot & Sometimes on Horseback to the Tune of 3 & 4 Dollars pr Day to Visit the Sick & wounded Officers on Long Island. and I Beg Leave Further to State that no Expence has arisen Dureing the war in Consiquence of Sickness among the Prisoners on Long Island But that I have Defrayd, Except a Small Bill of a Certain Doctr Bambridge a Refugee Physician[3] and I Belive for One Patient Only he Charged £60 which Mr Skinner Refused to Pay Since which a Suit at Law was Commincd & the Money Recoverd, with additional Expence. these Facts are made Manifest by the Testimony of Colo. Boudenott Baty & Skinner[4]—I have Therefor Only to Regrett that Ruin as to my Property has in fact Taken place in Consiquence of the accumelated Debts Contracted for the above Purpose, and my Children Drove from a Decent Patrimony and to seek an asulum in the wild of America & my self at 55 years of age Obligd, to work Double tides for Soport, this I do with Health Thank god & a Degrea of Chearfullness. I aught However to have added that Part of my Property was Burned, by the Traitor Arnold. and that it being on an Island Said to be without the Limitts of this State by which means I am Prevented from Receveing Relief by the State which has been afforded to Other Sufferers within its Limitts.

But Mr President it is Sugested to me that the Committee from the Senate Soposd the State of Connecticutt had made me full Compensation for my Services, to which I Beg to State that in a Settlement with the State of Connecticutt they Paid me in Paper the Prime Cost of the Medicens Only accor[d]ing to a Bill amounting to £150 S[terling] Money they also allowd me Sundry Sums for Extra Expences while on Command Previous to my Captivity (viz.) Expences to the Northern Army when Visited wt. the Small Pox &ca, But Sir I Never asked the State for nor Did I Ever receive a Farthing as a Compensation for any Service I Rendered the Prisoners while in Captivity or for Horse hire or Other Expences in Performing Sd Service. This will appear by the Testimony of Colo. Cook & Colo. Chester who were of the Committee when I Settled wt. the State Colo. Cook was soon after a Member of Congress and Presented my Petition to the same while Every matter was fresh in Memory.[5] I Pray now to ask the President if it is not Reasonable that my Expences aught at Least to be Paid. I am wt. Great Respect Your Obt Humble Servt

John Ely

ALS, DNA: RG 59, Miscellaneous Letters.

1. Ely apparently is referring to his letter to GW of 25 Dec. 1789, which covered an earlier letter to GW of 26 Oct. 1780 (DLC:GW).

2. For Ely's petitions for relief, which were not settled by Congress until 1833, thirty-three years after his death, and for Henry Knox's report in his favor, see Ely to GW, 25 Dec. 1789, n.2.

3. Absalom Bainbridge (1743–1807), who had graduated from the College of New Jersey in 1762, practiced medicine in Maidenhead, N.J., until about 1772, when he moved to Princeton. He joined the British army in 1776 during its advance through New Jersey and relocated the next year to Long Island, N.Y., where he served as a surgeon to the British forces for the remainder of the war. His property in New Jersey having been confiscated, Bainbridge went to Britain after the Revolutionary War to seek compensation for his losses. Successful in that endeavor, he returned to New York City by 1790.

4. Abraham Skinner, who had been captured by the British at the Battle of Germantown in October 1777, was exchanged in June 1778. By July 1779 he was commissary of prisoners at Goshen, N.Y., and in September 1780 Congress appointed him commissary general of prisoners.

5. Joseph Platt Cooke (1730–1816), who had been a member of the Connecticut assembly, a justice of the peace, and a militia colonel before the Revolutionary War, served in a military capacity until 1778, when he resigned his colonelcy. He sat in the state house of representatives in 1776, 1778, 1780–82, and 1784 and in the Continental Congress in 1784–85 and 1787–88. John Chester (1748–1809) had been appointed colonel of a Connecticut state regiment in June 1776.

To Thomas Forrest

Sir, Philadelphia June 20th 1792.

The publication which you had the politness to send me last fall, intituled, "Proceedings relative to Ships tendered for the Service of the United East India Company," reached my hands some time in April; And lately I have been favored with your voyage from Calcutta &c.[1]

These marks of attention are received with gratitude, and merit my best thanks, which I beg you to accept for you[r] very great politness. I am, Sir, with proper consideration Your most Obedt Servt.

Df, in Tobias Lear's hand, DNA: RG 59, Miscellaneous Letters; LB, DLC: GW. Lear's draft was addressed to "Capt. Thomas Forrest Grafton Street—London."

After serving briefly in the Royal Navy, explorer, navigator, and author Thomas Forrest (c.1729–c.1802) spent most of his career in the employ of the East India Company. Having been stationed almost continuously in the Indian Ocean since the early 1750s, he published extensively about the weather, sailing routes, and geography of the region.

1. On 14 Nov. 1791 "Capt. Thomas Forrest Author of the Voy. to New —— [Guinea]" wrote GW from "London Grafton Str[ee]t near Fitzroy Chaple" to send "his best Respects to Mr Washington and . . . a late publication which will give his Excellency a deal of Information" (DLC:GW). Forrest's *Proceedings relative to Ships Tendered for the Service of the United East-India Company, from the First of January, 1780, to the Thirty-First of March, 1791* (London, 1791) and his *Voyage from Calcutta to the Mergui Archipelago, Lying on the East Side of the Bay of Bengal* (London, 1792) were both in GW's library at the time of his death (Griffin, *Boston Athenæum Washington Collection,* 71, 82–83).

From Thomas Jefferson

[Philadelphia] June 20. 92.

Th: Jefferson, with his respects to the President, incloses him a publication by mister Knox an Under-secretary of state in England, who seems to have been the true parent of the British system with respect to our commerce. he asks the favour of the President to read the paper No. 18—page 60—as it shews the expectation of what would be done on our part, & an acknolegement of the injury it would do them, could we enforce it. papers 12. & 13. are also interesting: but not so pointedly so.[1]

AL, DNA: RG 59, Miscellaneous Letters; LB, DNA: RG 59, George Washington's Correspondence with His Secretaries of State; LB (photocopy), DLC:GW.

1. William Knox (1732–1810) was British undersecretary of state for American affairs between 1770 and 1782. In 1789 he published in London a two-volume work entitled *Extra Official State Papers . . . by a Late Under Secretary of State.* Knox's "paper No. 18," while supporting the placement of restrictions on U.S. trade with the British West Indies, concludes that a trade war with the Americans would be very damaging to British commerce. In "papers 12. & 13" Knox argues that the United States's role in the British economy should be that of a mere supplier of raw materials and that once Britain and Canada could adequately supply the needs of the British West Indies, trade between the United States and those islands should be cut off.

From Thomas Jefferson

[Philadelphia] June 20. 1792.

Th: Jefferson has the honor to inform the President that the Director of the Mint has occasion for a sum of money for the following purposes.

	D[ollars]
for the house purchased 1600.£ Pensylvania[1] or	4266.66
for about 15. tons of copper to be procured.	abt 5000.
on account for workmen &c.	733·34
	10,000.

making in the whole ten thousand Dollars.[2]

AL, DNA: RG 59, Miscellaneous Letters; AL (letterpress copy), DLC: Jefferson Papers; LB, DNA: RG 59, George Washington's Correspondence with His Secretaries of State; LB (photocopy), DLC:GW.

1. On 16 June, David Rittenhouse wrote Jefferson that he had "bargained with the owner for the House and Lot on Seventh Street, between Arch and Market Streets, of which you saw the Draught for the Use of the Mint. The price £1600. in Cash, Pennsylvania Currency" (*Jefferson Papers,* 24:89).

2. For GW's approval of this transaction, see GW to Jefferson, 9 July, and note 1, and GW to Rittenhouse, 9 July 1792.

From Henry Knox

Sir War department June 20th 1792.

I have the honor to submit to your consideration a letter to Andrew Moore Esq. upon the appointment of some Ensigns in the Rifle Companies raising in the South Western parts of Virginia, and also a conditional appointment to Richard Chandler as an Ensign.[1]

This Gentleman is well recommended to Mr Jefferson, and also in a letter from Captain Ballard Smith to me—He is stated to Mr Jefferson as a person who most probably can raise a number of good rifle Men.[2] I have the honor to be with the highest respect Your most obed. Servant

H. Knox

LS, DLC:GW; LB, DLC:GW.

On this date Tobias Lear, at GW's command, returned "to the Secretary of War the enclosed letters which have been submitted to the President" and informed him "that the President has no objection to the footing upon which the appointments mentioned in these letters are placed, altho at the same time the President observes that he thinks Captn [James] Stephenson's Company is upon ground different from the others" (DLC:GW).

1. Knox's letter to Andrew Moore has not been identified. Richard Chandler (d. 1801) wrote Jefferson on 18 Nov. 1792 that when he had applied in "June in Person to Genl. Knox, Secretary of War, for an appointment in our Foedral Army thare was no Vacancey but [he] was promised the first that might happen" (*Jefferson Papers,* 24:630–31). Chandler was appointed an ensign in the U.S. Army in May 1794, and he was promoted to lieutenant in July 1798. He served as a paymaster from July 1795 until December 1801.

2. Jefferson had received written recommendations of Chandler from Hugh Rose, on 15 May, and Thomas Bell, on 4 June (see ibid., 23:500–503, 24: 24). Ballard Smith's letter to Knox has not been identified. Ballard Smith (d. 1794), who had risen to the rank of lieutenant during the Revolutionary War, was appointed a captain in the U.S. Army in June 1790, and he was promoted to major in June 1792.

From Henry Lee

My dear Sir Richmond June 20[t]h 92

I beg leave to make known to You the bearer hereof Mr Williams a portrait painter.[1]

This gentleman is an American citizen, is of good character and is considered as possessing great natural talents in his line.

Of the last fact I am too inadequate a judge for to venture my own opinion.

He has a singular solicitude to be permitted to take your portrait and therefore has asked from me a letter of introduction.

If his execution thereof, shall in any degree equal his anxiety on the occasion, he will do honor to himself—I confess I am interested in his success as he has promised to present the portrait to the C[ommon] Wealth in case it should be a good one, by which means we shall have the gratification of beholding daily the semblance of our beloved and illustrious Countryman.[2] With the most respectful and affect. attachment I have the honor to be ever your ob. Sert

Henry Lee

ALS, DLC:GW.

1. William J. Williams (1763–1828) was a member of Masonic Lodge No. 22 of Alexandria, Virginia.

2. For GW's negative reply to this letter, see GW to Lee, 3 July.

From James Madison

Dear Sir Orange [Va.] June 20th 1792

Having been left to myself, for some days past, I have made use of the opportunity for bestowing on your letter of the 20th Ult: handed to me on the road, the attention which its important contents claimed.[1] The questions which it presents for consideration are 1. at what time a notification of your purpose to retire will be most convenient. 2 what mode will be most eligible. 3 whether a valedictory address will be proper and adviseable. 4 if both,[2] whether it would be more properly annexed to the notification, or postponed to your actual retirement.

The answer to the 1st question involves two points, first the expediency of delaying the notification; secondly the propriety of making it before the choice of electors takes place, that the people may make their choice with an eye to the circumstances under which the trust is to be executed. On the first point, the reasons for as much delay as possible are too obvious to need recital. The second, depending on the times fixed in the several States, which must be within thirty four days preceding the first wednesday in December, requires that the notification should be in time to pervade every part of the Union by the beginning of November. Allowing six weeks for this purpose, the middle of September or perhaps a little earlier, would seem a convenient date for the act.

2. with regard to the mode, none better occurs than a simple publication in the newspapers. If it were proper to address it through the medium of the general Legislature, there will be no opportunity. Nor does the change of situation seem to admit a recurrence to the State Governments which were the channels used for the former valedictory address.[3] A direct address to the people who are your only constituents, can be made I think most properly through the independent channel of the press, through which they are as a constituent body usually addressed.

3. on the third question I think there can be no doubt that such an address is rendered *proper* in itself by the peculiarity and importance of the circumstances which mark your situation; and *adviseable*, by the salutary and operative lessons of which it may be made the vehicle. The precedent at your military exit, might

also subject an omission now to conjectures and interpretations which it would not be well to leave room for.

4. The remaining question is less easily decided. Advantages and objections lie on both sides of the alternative. The occasion on which you are *necessarily* addressing the people, evidently introduces most easily and most delicately any *voluntary* observations that are meditated. In another view a farewell address, before the final moment of depàrture, is liable to the appearance of being premature and awkward. On the opposite side of the alternative, however, a postponement will beget a dryness and an abridgment in the first address, little corresponding with the feelings which the occasion would naturally produce both in the author and the objects; and though not liable to the above objection, would require a resumption of the subject apparently more forced; and on which, the impressions having been anticipated & familiarised, and the public mind diverted perhaps to other scenes, a second address would be received with less sensibility and effect, than if incorporated with the impressions incident to the original one. It is possible too, that previous to the close of the term, circumstances might intervene in relation to public affairs or the succession to the Presidency, which would be more embarrassing, if existing at the time of a valedictory appeal to the public, than if subsequent to that delicate measure.

On the whole my judgment leans to the propriety of blending together the notifying and valedictory address; and the more so as the crisis which will terminate your public career may still afford an opportunity, if any intermediate contingency should call, for a supplement to your farewell observations. But as more correct views of the subject may produce a different result in your mind, I have endeavored to fit the draught inclosed to either determination. You will readily observe that in executing it I have aimed at that plainness & modesty of language which you had in view, and which indeed are so peculiarly becoming the character and the occasion; and that I have had little more to do, as to the matter, than to follow the just and comprehensive outline which you had sketched.[4] I flatter myself however that in every thing which has depended on me, much improvement will be made, before so interesting a paper shall have taken its last form.

Having thus, Sir, complied with your wishes, by proceeding on a supposition that the idea of retiring from public life is to be carried into execution, I must now gratify my own by hoping that a reconsideration of the measure in all its circumstances and consequences, will have produced an acquiescence in one more sacrifice, severe as it may be, to the desires and interests of your country. I forbear to enter into the arguments which in my view plead for it; because it would be only repeating what I have already taken the liberty of fully explaining:[5] But I could not conclude such a letter as the present without a repetition of my anxious wishes & hopes, that our country may not, in this important conjuncture be deprived of the inestimable advantage of having you at the head of its councils. With every sentiment of respect & affectionate attachment, I am, Dear Sir, your most Obedt freind & Servant

Js Madison Jr

ALS, NN: Washington Papers, Farewell Address Box; ALS (copy), DLC: Madison Papers.

1. By happenstance, GW had encountered Madison on the road on 25 May 1792 while returning to Philadelphia from Mount Vernon (see Madison's Conversations with Washington, 5–25 May 1792).

2. The ALS copy in the Madison Papers reads "requisite or adviseable. 4. if either."

3. Madison is referring to the valedictory Circular to the States that GW sent to the various state governors between 8 and 21 June 1783 (LS, NNPM).

4. GW had provided Madison with an outline of the tone and content he desired for his Farewell Address in his letter of 20 May 1792.

5. See Madison's Conversations with Washington, 5–25 May 1792.

Enclosure
Madison's Draft of the Farewell Address

[c.20 June 1792]

The period which will close the appointment with which my fellow citizens have honoured me, being not very distant, and the time actually arrived, at which their thoughts must be designating the citizen who is to administer the Executive Government of the United States during the ensuing term, it may conduce to a more distinct expression of the public voice, that I should apprize such of my fellow citizens as may retain their partiality towards me, that I am not to be numbered among those out of whom a choice is to be made.

I beg them to be assured that the Resolution which dictates this intimation has not been taken without the strictest regard to the relation which as a dutiful citizen I bear to my country; and that in withdrawing that tender of my service, which silence in my situation might imply, I am not influenced by the smallest deficiency of zeal for its future interests, or of grateful respect for its past kindness; but by the fullest persuasion that such a step is compatible with both.[1]

The impressions under which I entered on the present arduous trust were explained on the proper occasion.[2] In discharge of this trust I can only say that I have contributed towards the organization and administration of the Government the best exertions of which a very fallible judgment was capable. For any errors which may have flowed from this source, I feel all the regret which an anxiety for the public good can excite; not without the double consolation, however, arising from a consciousness of their being involuntary, and an experience of the candor which will interpret them. If there were any circumstances that could give value to my inferior qualifications for the trust, these circumstances must have been temporary. In this light was the undertaking viewed when I ventured on it. Being, moreover still farther advanced into the decline of life, I am every day more sensible that the increasing weight of years, renders the private walks of it in the shade of retirement, as necessary as they will be acceptable to me. May I be allowed to add, that it will be among the highest as well as purest enjoyments that can sweeten the remnant of my days, to partake, in a private station in the midst of my fellow citizens, of that benign influence of good laws under a free Government, which has been the ultimate object of all our wishes, and in which I confide as the happy reward of our cares and labours. May I be allowed farther to add, as a consideration far more important, that an early example of rotation in an office of so high and delicate a nature, may equally accord with the republican spirit of our constitution, and the ideas of liberty and safety entertained by the people.

(If a farewell address is to be added at the expiration of the term, the following paragraph may conclude the present).

Under these circumstances a return to my private station according to the purpose with which I quitted it, is the part which duty as well as inclination assigns me. In executing it I shall carry with me every tender recollection which gratitude to my fellow citizens can awaken; and a sensibility to the permanent happiness of my Country, which will render it the object of my unceasing vows and most fervent supplications.

(Should no further address be intended, the preceding paragraph being omitted, the present address may go on as follows).

In contemplating the moment at which the curtain is to drop for ever on the public scenes of my life, my sensations anticipate and do not permit me to suspend, the deep acknowledgments required by that debt of gratitude which I owe to my beloved country for the many honors it has conferred on me, for the distinguished confidence it has reposed in me, and for the opportunities I have thus enjoyed of testifying my inviolable attachment by the most steadfast services which my faculties could render. All the returns I have now to make will be in those vows which I shall carry with me to my retirement and to my grave, that Heaven may continue to favor the people of the United States with the choicest tokens of its benificence; that their Union and brotherly affection may be perpetual; that the free constitution which is the work of their own hands, may be sacredly maintained; that its administration in every department, may be stamped with wisdom and with virtue; and that this character may be ensured to it by that watchfulness over public servants and public measures, which on one hand will be necessary to prevent or correct a degeneracy; and that forbearance, on the other, from unfounded or indiscriminate jealousies which would deprive the public of the best services, by depriving a conscious integrity of one of the noblest incitements to perform them; that in fine, the happiness of the people of America, under the auspices of liberty, may be made compleat, by so careful a preservation, and so prudent a use of this blessing, as will acquire them the glorious satisfaction of recommending it to the affection, the praise, and the adoption of every nation which is yet a stranger to it.

And may we not dwell with well grounded hopes on this flattering prospect; when we reflect on the many ties by which the people of America are bound together, and the many proofs they have given of an enlightened judgment and a magnanimous patriotism.

We may all be considered as the children of one common country. We have all been embarked in one common cause. We have all had our share in common sufferings and common successes. The portion of the Earth allotted for the theatre of our fortunes, fulfils our most sanguine desires. All its essential interests are the same; whilst its diversities arising from climate from soil and from other local & lesser peculiarities, will naturally form a mutual relation of the parts, that may give to the whole a more entire independence than has perhaps fallen to the lot of any other nation.

To confirm these motives to an affectionate and permanent Union, and to secure the great objects of it, we have established a common Government, which being free in its principles, being founded in our own choice, being intended as the guardian of our common rights and the patron of our common interests, and wisely containing within itself a provision for its own amendment, as experience may point out its errors, seems to promise every thing that can be expected from such an institution; and if supported by wise councils, by virtuous conduct, and by mutual and friendly allowances, must approach as near to perfection as any human work can aspire, and nearer than any which the annals of mankind have recorded.

With these wishes and hopes I shall make my exit from civil life; & I have taken the same liberty of expressing them, which I formerly used in offering the Sentiments which were suggested by my exit from military life.[3] If, in either instance, I have presumed more than I ought, on the indulgence of my fellow citizens, they will be too generous to ascribe it to any other cause than the extreme solicitude which I am bound to feel, and which I can never cease to feel, for their liberty, their prosperity and their happiness.

ADf, NN: Washington Papers, Farewell Address Box; ADf (retained copy), DLC: Madison Papers.

1. In the margin beside this paragraph on the draft at NN, Madison wrote and then apparently tried to erase a note that reads: "Should this address be considered as the final one, the paragraph here in brackets may as well perhaps be omitted, the sentiments being afterwards brought into view in another form."

2. See the final version of GW's First Inaugural Address, 30 April 1789.

3. For GW's "exit from military life," see his Circular to the States, 8–21 June 1783 (LS, NNPM).

To Richard Peters

Dear Sir, Philadelphia June 20th 1792

Excuse my giving you the perusal of a letter that is tinctured with compliment. Pass these over, and solve the queries & doubts of the author;[1] and you will much oblige Yr Obedt Servt

Go: Washington

ALS, PHi: Dreer Collection.

On the cover of this letter, GW wrote: "Expecting Mr Peters might be in Town, this letter was sent to Colo. [Francis] Johnston's; not finding him there, & the Ship by which the P—— means to write to Mr Y—— on the point of Sailing (say saturday [23 June]) he sends it to him in the Country." Peters's country estate was six miles from Philadelphia. Francis Johnston (1748–1815), who had served in the Pennsylvania conventions of 1774 and 1775 and had risen to the rank of colonel in the Continental army during the Revolutionary War, had been appointed receiver general of Pennsylvania in 1781. He was still serving in that capacity at this time.

1. GW apparently forwarded to Peters his letter to Arthur Young of 18–21 June, which included GW's observation that Peters was "one of the best farmers in the State of Pennsylvania." For Peters's attempt to answer Young's queries, see his letter of this date.

From Richard Peters

Dear Sir Belmont [Pa.] June 20. 1792

I shall be happy if I can assist in solving Mr Young's Queries;[1] but the Time will not admit either of Accuracy or the Combinations necessary to form the Average of Labour, Building & Improvement applicable to the State at large. From Mr Y's Calculations, formed I presume upon Communications from you, I am surprized to find that the Prices of Labour & Quantity of Product are, in a great Degree, similar to those of this State; tho' You seem to have confined yourself to Virginia & Maryland.[2] I mean the Labour & Wages of Hirelings for as to Slaves I have but a very imperfect, & you a perfect Knowledge of what concerns their Value, Expence & Labour.

1. Our Wages for Hirelings by the Day are commonly 2/ in Winter, & 2/6, 9 Months in the Year for common Days-Work on a Farm & every Thing found as to eating & drinking—The same Man will hire & find himself at 3/ & 3/6 ℔ Day—For a Reaper 3/ to 3/9 & found & the same for cutting Grass—Reaping by the Acre I have never had done under 5/ but the Price generally 7/6 the Labourers finding Themselves—Neither Reaper or Mower will on an Average do more than ¾ an Acre. Mowers ℔ Day are allowed here a pint of Rum or other Spirits ℔ Day—a vile & unnecessary Practice. Reapers have as much as they choose perhaps three half pints ℔ Day but this Practice is yearly diminishing. When I say that a Reaper or Mower will do ¾ of an Acre I mean of a common Crop for in heavy Grain or Grass, such as a good English Crop, no Labourer here will reap or mow above half an Acre. As to mowing, or what we call cradling, Grain, we pay a Man 5/ to 6/ ℔ Day & found, & the Days Work about the same with Mr Young's Statement viz. 2 or 2½ A[cre]s ℔ Day. Mowing ℔ Acre 5/ to 6/ & a pint of Rum. Laboure[r]s find themselves Food.

2. The Hire of a Waggon 4 Horses & Drivers from 15/ to 20/ ℔ Day.

3. The yearly Hire of a good Labourer in Pennsilvania I think 60 Dollars or £22, 10 Currency & found, Cloathing excepted.

4. As to the Quantum of Labour to be commanded for Pay I know not how to answer. Many who have small Farms either on Rent or their own Property can spare a Portion of their Time to assist their Neighbours for Hire. The Class of People merely Labourers is not very numerous & by no Means Stationary or collected. The independent Situation they can place themselves in by removing to the Frontiers is the Cause of the Scarcity of Labourers in the settled Parts of the State. Nor is the Demand for Labour so regular as to detain unconnected Labourers in any Spot. Whether the considerable Improvements we are about undertaking by Roads & Canals will operate so as to attract Labourers from other States or from Europe in Hopes of constant Employment is yet problematical. If these Works employ none but our own People the Price of Labour will encrease on the Farms[.] There is no Doubt but that the Rates of Labour are & will for a long time continue to be higher than they are in England—Our People live better than those of the same Rank in

Life in any Part of the World. The Employer pays for the Habits of the Hireling who not only eats & drinks well when provided for in Addition to his Wages but out of his Wages *must* (if he has one) provide for his Family according to the Custom of the Country. Even an English Labourer who lives better than one in any other Part of Europe would be astonished at the Fare of one in America[.] I do not believe Mr Young much mistaken when he says that the Rate is comparatively 100 ℔ Cent higher than in England; & the Habits of living are as much the Cause of it as the Easiness of the Passage over the Mountains. I am not displeased as a Citizen at this Circumstance, tho' as a Farmer it is against my Profit. Some Things might be retrenched, but I am happy when I know that our common People are better fed & cloathed than in any other Part of the World.

5. The Prices of Land are so extremely various that there is no fixing an Average. The Situation & Improvement always add to Value. Knowing so little as our Farmers do of the Means of renovating Land the longer they are cleared the less valuable for the most Part they are. I gave to Col. Hamilton an exact Account of the Debtor & Creditor of four Farms in my Neighbourhood taken from the Knowledge I have of the general Circumstances of this Part of the Country. The Result is very unfavourable to the Characters of our Farmers. Be pleased to ask Col. H. for it as I have not a Copy.[3] I believe Col. H. who in some Project he had, sent for Information to all Quarters could most easily give Satisfaction in this Point. Mr Y. does not know that in Parts where there are no Slaves the Farmer & his Family do the greater Portion of the Work of their Farms within themselves. This is the Reason why they can get forward & live well. If Calculations were made of every thing being hired few Farms in Pennsilvania would clear a Farthing. A Man here saves Money by a Crop of 10 Bushells & in England he would perish under it. There he rents & hires—here for the most Part the Farm is his own & he hires little or none at all.

The Products of *Wheat* can be all sold

—Barley not in great Quantities our People not being as fond as they ought to be of Beer.

—Rye—may encrease in Demand by domestic Distillation—at present it is no great Object

Butter—Fluctuating—but all may be sold now produced.

Beef—a good Article & when we know better how to cure it for Exportation will encrease in Demand.

Mutton—No Sale for any great Quantities. For some Time hence this will not be a great Sheep Country. The dryness of our Seasons burn up the Pasture for a great Part of the Year—we keep too many Dogs who destroy them. & our Country is much intersected with Mountains inhabited by Wolves which cannot be extirpated. It is a profitable Article so far as you can extend it but no great Capital can be employed in it & if the Bussiness was more extensively carried on the Profit would be reduced to Nothing. Our long Winters are inimical to Sheep—they render the keeping expensive & subject the Animal to numberless Disorders. We can have no succulent or green Forage—Turnips are out of the Question our Snows & severe Weather destroy or cover them, nor is their Culture certain—I have tried the English Sheep which were degenerate & stand the Climate but badly. As to Fleece it is but scant, 3 lb. ⅌ Sheep being rather an Overcalculation. Wool is now in some Demand but I have known it unsaleable. I hope Manufactures will continue to encrease the Demand but the Prospect of this is distant. Mr Y's Calculation upon Waste Land might be well enough if the Circumstances before stated as to Sheep did not forbid our going extensively into them. Sheep have most Enemies where there could be most Range for them; & they require Care as well as Range. I know none who have tried the Sheep Business that have suceeded. Folding is very well—but it requires Labour & the Sheep crouded together here have often perished. I cannot ascertain how many an Acre will support for none are kept within my Knowledge but in small Numbers & as a Variety in a Farmers Stock. They are close Feeders & destroy Pasture prodigiously.

Excuse me, Sir, for this hasty & imperfect Sketch. I should have gone more deeply into the Subject had the Time You allot permitted. Unless one could find, as it is in England, the Business carried on in different Branches systematically it is difficult to make Calculations or even Observations generally applicable. Few People here do all their Business by hiring & some scarcely hire at all. The Race of Tenantry is miserable indeed. I am with the greatest Respect Your obedt Servt

Richard Peters

Should you think of any particular Point I would be pleased to mention it. I will pay particular Attention to it. Mr Young's Letter would require a very extended Discussion.

ALS, DLC:GW.

1. For Arthur Young's queries about the condition of agriculture in the United States, see Young to GW, 18 Jan. 1792.

2. For GW's communication of information about agriculture in the United States to Young, see Circular on the State of American Agriculture, 25 Aug. 1791, and GW to Young, 15 Aug., 5 Dec. 1791, and 18–21 June 1792.

3. Peters soon found a copy of the investigation of four nearby farms that he had sent to Alexander Hamilton on 27 Aug. 1791, and he forwarded it to GW (see Peters to GW, 22 June 1792). GW already had requested and received a copy from Hamilton, however (see GW to Arthur Young, 18–21 June). It is printed in Syrett, *Hamilton Papers,* 9:116–18.

From John Hazelwood

Phila. June 21st 1792

Sir in the Year 1776 By order of your Excellency I fitted four fire ships In the City of New York, for which I never had Any Compensation.[1] as I was sent by your self to Poughkepsie to fitt a Boom & Chain to be put a Cross the North River &c., it being too late when I returnd to Apply as our Army were retreating from Long Island & there being so much to Attend to That I thought it improper.

I now wish to have it settled as Congress have takein Off their limitation Acts but as it will be necessary to have some proof I hope your Excellency will give me a line certifying that I fitted them[2] which favour shall ever be Acknowledged by your most Obt & Very Humbl. Sevt

John Hazelwood

ALS, DNA: RG 59, Miscellaneous Letters.

1. There was apparently little validity to this claim. Hazelwood, who had been appointed to command a squadron of fire rafts by the Pennsylvania council of safety in late December 1775, was paid a salary and reimbursed for fitting out and servicing these vessels by that body on 12 April, 10, 21 June, 28 Aug., 2, 23 Sept., and 7 Oct. 1776 (see *Naval Documents,* 3:286, 4:789, 5:456, 669, 6:338, 658, 967, 1154). At the request of the N.Y. convention but apparently with the knowledge and approval of both GW and the Pa. council of safety, Hazelwood fitted out another vessel and sailed to Poughkeepsie, N.Y., in the summer of 1776. Although the N.Y. convention told Hazelwood to apply to

GW if he needed money or assistance, it later voted to pay him $300 for his trouble and expense (ibid., 5:1244, 6:307). On 10 Oct. 1776 the Continental Congress resolved that Hazelwood, along with several others, be paid "their whole account of their charge for preparing six sail of fire ships at New York, and their expences going to, in, and coming from, New York to Philadelphia" (*JCC,* 6:865). When Hazelwood applied to GW on 22 Mar. 1790 for a federal appointment, he did not mention that he had not been properly reimbursed for his services, only that "he was sent by the [Pennsylvania] Council of Safty to New-York to Form some fire Rafts & Ships which he performed."

2. Hazelwood is referring to "An Act providing for the settlement of the claims of persons under particular circumstances, barred by the limitations heretofore established" of 27 Mar. 1792, which says "that every such officer, soldier, artificer, sailor, and marine, having claims for services rendered to the United States in the Military or Naval Departments, who shall exhibit the same for liquidation at the Treasury of the United States, at any time during the said term of two years, shall be entitled to an adjustment and allowance thereof on the same principles, as if the same had been exhibited within the term prescribed by the aforesaid resolutions of Congress" (*Annals of Congress,* 2d Cong., 1348–49). No letter from GW to Hazelwood certifying the latter's claims has been found.

To Gouverneur Morris

(Private)

My dear Sir, Philadelphia June 21st 1792

Since writing to you on the 28th of January, I have received your several favors of the 27th Decr from Paris—4th of Feby, 17th & 21st of March, and 6th & 10th of April from London. I thank you very much for the interesting and important information contained in several of these letters, particularly that of the 4th of Feby. If the last article, of which it is comprized, should, in your judgment, require an acknowledgment, I shall rely on your goodness to make it in suitable & respectful terms. You can be at no loss to discover the paragraph to which I allude.[1]

The plot thickens, and developement must have begun—but what the final issue will be, lyes too deep for human ken. I will hope for the best, without allowing myself to wander in the field of conjecture, for the result.

Your letters, though exceedingly interesting in point of information, require but little to be said, in the way of reply. The accounts given therein will be treasured up, to be acted upon as circumstances will warrant, and as occasions may present. One thing, however, I must not pass over in silence, lest you should infer from it, that Mr D—— had authority for reporting that, the United States had asked the mediation of Great Britain to bring about a peace between them and the Indians.[2] You may be *fully* assured, Sir, that no such mediation *ever* was asked; that the asking of it *never* was in contemplation; and, I think I might go further & say, that it not only never *will* be asked, but would be rejected if offered. The U. States will never have occasion, I hope, to ask for the interposition of that Power, or any other, to establish peace within their own territory. That it is the wish of that government to intermeddle, & bring this measure to pass, many concurrent circumstances—(small indeed when singly considered) had left no doubt on my mind before your letter of the 6th of April came to hand—what is there mentioned of the views of Mr P——[3] as well as of the assertions of Mr D—— is strong as, "proof of holy writ" in confirmation thereof. The attempt has, however, in its remotest movements, been so scouted as to have retarded, if it has not entirely done away, the idea. But I do not hesitate to give it to you as my *private,* & decided opinion, that it is these interferences, and to the underhanded support which the Indians receive (notwithstanding the open disavowal of it) that all our difficulties with them proceed. We are essaying every means in our power, to undeceive these hostile tribes with respect to the disposition of this Country towards them; and to convince them that we neither seek their extirpation, nor the occupancy of their lands (as they are taught to believe) except such of the latter as have been obtan'd by fair treaty, & purchase, bona fide made, & recognized by them in more instances than one. If they will not, after this explanation (if we can get at them to make it) listen to the voice of peace, the sword must decide the dispute; and we are, though very reluctantly, vigorously preparing to meet the event.

In the course of last winter, I had some of the chiefs of the Cherokees in this City, and in the Spring I obtained (with some difficulty indeed) a full representation of the Six Nations, to come hither. I have sent all of them away well satisfied; and fully convinced of the justice & good dispositions of this government towards the Indian nations, *generally.* The latter—that is the Six nations, who, before, appeared to be divided, & distracted in their Councils, have given strong assurances of their friendship;

and have resolved to send a deputation of *their* tribes to the hostile Indians with an acct of all that has passed, accompanying it with advice to them, to desist from further hostilities.[4] With difficulty, *still* greater, I have brought the celebrated Captn Joseph Brandt to this City, with a view to impress him also with the equitable intentions of this government towards *all* the nations of his colour. He only arrived last night, and I am to give him an audiance at twelve this day.[5]

Nothing has yet been hinted on this side the water, to any of the Officers of government, of the other matter mentioned in your letter of the 6th of April; though suspicions of it have been entertained.[6]

Knowing from the letters of the Secretary of State to you, that you are advised in all matters of public concern, and will have transmitted to you the Laws as they are Enacted, and the Gazettes as they are published, I shall not trouble you with a detail of domestic occurrences.[7] The latter are *sur*-charged, and *some of them* indecently communicative of *charges* that need evidence for their Support.

There can be but few things of a public nature (likely to happen in your line, requiring to be acted upon by this government) that may not be freely communicated to the Department to which it belongs; because, in proceeding thereon, the head of the department will, necessarily, be made acquainted therewith. But there may, in the course of events, be other matters—more remote in their consequences—of the utmost importance to be known, that not more than one intermediate person would be entrusted with; *here,* necessity as well as propriety will mark the line—Cases not altogether under the controul of necessity,[8] may also arise, to render it advisable to do this, and your own good judgment will be the best director in these cases. With much truth & Affection I am always—Yours

Go: Washington

Be so good as to give the enclosed letter a safe conveyance to Mr De la Fayette.[9]

ALS, NNC; ADfS, DLC:GW; LB, DLC:GW.

1. In the last paragraph of his letter to GW of 4 Feb., Morris had written that the king and queen of France wanted GW to know that they disapproved of recent developments in French diplomacy.

2. For Henry Dundas's report that the United States wanted Britain to mediate a peace with the hostile Indian nations, see Morris to GW, 6 April.

3. Morris's letter to GW of 6 April does not mention William Pitt's views on the subject of British mediation.

4. For the recent visit of the chiefs of the Five Nations to Philadelphia, see Timothy Pickering to GW, 21 Mar., and notes 2 and 3, GW to the Five Nations, 23 Mar., and source note, to the U.S. Senate, 23 Mar., and Henry Knox to GW, 1 April 1792.

5. For Joseph Brant's long-delayed visit to Philadelphia, see GW to Knox, 25 Feb., source note and note 1, Pickering to GW, 21 Mar., and note 1, Knox to GW, 22 April, n.3, and to Tobias Lear, 16 June 1792, and note 3.

6. Morris wrote GW on 6 April about Dundas's claim "that the treaty made long since by Sir William Johnson seemed to be the proper Ground on which *to fix a Boundary* between the United States & the Indian tribes."

7. For Thomas Jefferson's letters to Morris of 23 Jan., 10 Mar., 28, 29 April, and 16 June 1792, see *Jefferson Papers,* 23:55–57, 248–50, 467–69, 472–73, 24:88–89.

8. In the draft and letter-book copy, this phrase reads: "*here,* necessity as well as propriety, will confine you to a point. Cases *not altogether* under the controul of necessity."

9. See GW to Lafayette, 10 June 1792.

To George Skene Keith

Revnd Sir, Philadelphia June 22d 1792.

I have received your letter of the 14th of January together with the copies of a pamphlet on Weights, Measures and coins which accompanied it.

On the 7th of may I acknowledged the receipt of your letter dated July 1st[1] 1791, and its enclosure, which did not get to my hands 'till some time this spring.[2]

I have now to request that you will accept my thanks for this further mark of politness and attention in sending me this additional number of your tracts, as well as for the manuscript which accompanied them.[3] The subject of your book is of high importance to society in general, and particularly so to the commercial[4] world. If an uniformity of weights and measures could be established upon a proper foundation through the several nations of Europe and in the United States of America, its advantages would be great indeed: And so important is the object that we ought not to lose sight of it, altho' it may not be attained at the present moment.

I have caused the letter to Mr[s] Barclay, and one of the pamphlets, to be sent to Easton agreeably to your request. I am, Revnd Sir, Your most Obedt Servt

Go: Washington

LS, in Tobias Lear's hand, CCC; Df, in Lear's hand, DNA: RG 59, Miscellaneous Letters; LB, DLC:GW.

1. On the draft manuscript Lear mistakenly wrote "5th."

2. Keith had enclosed a copy of his *Tracts on Weights, Measures, and Coins* (London, 1791) in his letter to GW of 1 July 1791. GW's acknowledgment of 7 May 1792 had been made by his secretary Tobias Lear (see Keith to GW, 1 July 1791, n.2).

3. Keith had enclosed a handwritten critique of Thomas Jefferson's advocacy of the rod-pendulum as a standard of measure in his letter to GW of 14 Jan. 1792. For Jefferson's ill-tempered answer to the points Keith raised in his paper, see Jefferson to GW, 14 June, and note 2; see also *Jefferson Papers,* 24:44–45, 64–66.

4. At this place on the draft manuscript, Lear wrote and then struck out "parts of the."

To Edward Newenham

Dear Sir Philadelphia 22d June 1792

I have now before me your letters of the 9th of January & 12th of february, to which it will not be in my power to reply so fully as my inclination would lead me to do if I had no avocations but those of a personal nature.

I regret exceedingly that the disputes between the Protestants and Roman Catholics should be carried to the serious and alarming heigth mentioned in your letters. Religious controversies are always productive of more acrimony and irreconcilable hatreds than those which spring from any other cause: And I was not without hopes that the enlightened and liberal policy of ⟨the present⟩ age would have put an effectual stop to contentions of this Kind.

The present appears to be an eventful moment in Europe. The declaration of war by France against the King of Hungary[1] will probably soon discover what part the several nations in Europé will take; but when or where those agitations which now shake that quarter of the glo[b]e[2] will terminate is beyond the ken of human wisdom.

Notwithstanding our local situation & political circumstances guard us against an interference in the contests betwe⟨en⟩ the European powers; yet we cannot be indifferent as to the issue of a business in which the happiness of so many millions of our fellow creatures[3] is involved. We have had nothing from France since the declaration of War, but are waiting with no small degree of anxiety for further intelligence which may enable us to form some *conjecture* on this momentous business.

I am happy in being able to inform you that the affairs of this country are still going on in a prosperous train. The ha[r]vest through the several States, so far as I have been able to extend my enquiries, promises to be abundant for the quantity sown, and it is said by those who are well acquainted with the subject, that there has never been a year in which so much land has been cultivated in grain, particularly Wheat, as in the present. I paid a visit to Mount Vernon immediately on the rising of Congress,[4] and was much pleased to find the appearance of crops of my own farms much more flattering than I had known them for many years past, and the country, generally, exhibited the face of plenty. An insect, called the Hessian fly, has made its appearance and done some mischief in parts of this State, Delaware & Maryland; but the destruction occasioned by this enemy will bear but a very trifling proportion to the whole crop of the Country, and I am informed that its ravages, where it has been found this year, are far less than those committed by the same insect some years ago.[5] An investigation of the natural history & progress of this insect is now taking place, in order to see if some effectual measures cannot be fallen upon to prevent its devastations. As it is a subject deeply interesting to every individual in the community I flatter myself that such enquiries & communications will be made respecting it as will lead to its extirpation.[6]

Mrs Washington unites with me in sincere wishes for the health & happiness of Lady Newenham & yourself. I am, with great esteem, Dear Sir, Your most Obedt Sert.

Df, in Tobias Lear's hand, DNA: RG 59, Miscellaneous Letters; LB, DLC:GW. The mutilated text is supplied in angle brackets from the letter-book copy.

1. Upon the death of his father, Leopold II, Francis II had been crowned king of Hungary and Bohemia and Holy Roman Emperor.

2. Lear mistakenly wrote the word "glove" at this place in the draft.

3. In the letter-book copy this word is transcribed as "citizens."

4. GW left Philadelphia for Mount Vernon on 10 May and apparently be-

gan his return trip on Thursday, 24 May 1792 (see GW to Henry Knox, 21 May).

5. For earlier damage to American wheat crops caused by the Hessian fly (*Phytophaga destructor*), see Arthur Young to GW, 19 May 1789, n.2, Samuel Powel to GW, 9 Dec. 1789, GW to Powel, 15 Dec. 1789, and Tobias Lear to GW, 5 June 1791. For its infestation of the crops around Philadelphia in 1793 and at Mount Vernon in 1794, see GW to Anthony Whitting, 19 May 1793 (ALS, DLC:GW), to William Pearce, 2 Nov. 1794 (ALS, ViMtV).

6. In the spring of 1791, Thomas Jefferson proposed to the American Philosophical Society that it appoint a committee "to collect materials for forming the natural history of the Hessian fly, the best means of preventing or destroying it &c." (Jefferson to Charles Thomson, 20 April 1791, *Jefferson Papers,* 20:244–45). The committee, which Jefferson chaired and which also included Thomson and doctors Benjamin S. Barton, James Hutchinson, and Casper Wistar, soon began the slow process of soliciting, receiving, and analyzing information about the Hessian fly. For Jefferson's own studies of the Hessian fly, see the editorial note to The Northern Journey of Jefferson and Madison, and Jefferson's Notes on the Hessian Fly, 24 May–18 June 1791 (ibid., 20:445–49, 456–62).

From Richard Peters

Dear Sir Philada June 22d 1792

I was ashamed to send you so hasty & desultory a List of Observations on Mr Young's Letter & on Reflection I find I have not paid sufficient Attention to some material Parts of it.[1] By the Desire I had of speedily complying with your Request I have in a great Degree defeated the Object of the Trouble you were pleased to take in making it. It will however be now too late to do anything more, as it would be of no Use to you by the present Opportunity, if indeed it would be at all useful in any Case. I will promise to be more attentive should I again be honoured with a similar or any other Request from you.

I have found & send you a Copy of the Letter & Statement I mentioned to have sent to Col. Hamilton[2]—This Statement is not conjectural as I consulted the Owners of the Farms I made the Subject of it. They were mortified at the Result, tho' they could not find Fault with the Estimate. They consoled themselves that they could live, & that they never went into minute Calculations. They all agreed that a Farmer never counted upon Interest of Capital & that striking this out of the Account & giving them their Maintenance as some Compensation for their Labour personally—the Thing was well enough. I am with sincere Respect & Esteem Your obed. Servt

Richard Peters

ALS, DLC:GW.

1. For Peters's "List of Observations on Mr Young's Letter," see Peters to GW, 20 June 1792.

2. For Peters's letter to Alexander Hamilton of 27 Aug. 1791 and its enclosure, see Syrett, *Hamilton Papers,* 9:114–18.

From James Smith

Dear Sir Hull, Old England. June 22. 1792

I take the liberty of sending these few lines to you togather with my kind love hoping they will find you in a comfortable state of health & the best of happiness Sir, though I am an entire strainger to your person yet not so to your Name, caracter, & encreasing Fame, these are not confined within the bounds of America Ever since I read (in Gordon's History of the united States[1]) of your patriotism and steadiness in the war, the honourable peace you were instrumental in procuring for the States; togather with the wholesome laws that are established among you I have found a particular affection toward your person and that part of the globe where you dwell and should be happy in coming to see you & afterwards to settle in some part of your Country—But to give you a short Detail of my pedigree & employment, Sir, I am the Son of a Farmer in the west of Yorkshire a young Man, that is unmaried. I have been a short time at an Academy near Halifax and am now entering upon the work of the christain ministry, in the independant connection, which Sect prayed to God for your prosperity & sucsess in the time of the war and greatly applaud your disintrested conduct since the peace. Sir, I have a strong desire to come over to your Country, could I obtain a promise of your patronage & favour, (upon condition of my being an honest man & good citizen) it would be a very great inducement towards my leaving Britain, and my friends, to come over to America Sir, having the greatest confidence in you[r] fidelity I have sent these few lines to you in order that I might know whether my coming to America will be a prudent step and to be informed whether I can meet with incouragement, or not. Sir, if I meet with encouragement, I purpose coming to see you (and I shall be very happy in it) the next Summer please let me have your thoughts upon the subject, as soon, as you can. Sir, I shall be very glad to hear of your age, and the state of your health after the various fatigues you have passed through. Sir, publick affairs are going on but roughly in Britain, as Mr paine asserts, goverment is looking one way, and the people another, and this is the reason why I wish to be made a member of your commonwealth by settling in some part of it. Sir, without vanity I can say that I have a love to America, to her Soil, and to her law, but I cannot say so of Old England because I look upon it that some remarkable troubles are awaiting her and ready to burst forth. I understand that great disturbances are likely to break forth at London The Bill for the abolition of the Slave is likely to be thrown out by the House of Lords, which will be very much contrary to the voice of the nation.[2] Indeed Sir, they are behaving towards the Dissenters in a very proud & imperious manner which I am rea⟨*mutilated*⟩ think in the end will produce some very ⟨*mutilated*⟩ consiquences, because I believe they are possess⟨ed⟩ of the same spirit for liberty which their Brethren in America are possessed of and shewed themselves so active in defending in the war. Sir Mr paine has lately published his 2 volume on the rights of man which is called by the King & his ministry a nefarious work that militates against their honour. It is reported they are prosicuting the printer, as printing a libel—I hope Mr paine will keep out of the British Dominions for the future if he do not, the higher powers will certainly put him to Death for they are already Drinking Damnation to paine, to his works, & his principles, whilst others greatly admire them.[3] I am, Sir, yours affectionately

James Smith

N.B. P. Direct to me—at Mr Murrow's Linen Draper. Barrow—Lincolnshire—To be left at Mr Rodes, Stationer, Market, Hull. old England.[4]

ALS, DLC:GW.

1. For more information about William Gordon's *History of the Rise, Progress, and Establishment of the Independence of the United States of America: Including an Account of the Late War; and of the Thirteen Colonies, from Their Origin to That Period* (London, 1788) and GW's interest in the work, see Gordon to GW, 24 Sept. 1788, and notes, 28 Oct.–1 Nov. 1788, 16 Feb. 1789, 20 Feb. 1790, and GW to Gordon, 25 Feb. 1791.

2. Although William Wilberforce, Thomas Clarkson, and their allies continued to advocate emancipation, Parliament did not abolish the slave trade until 1807.

3. Thomas Paine, who fled to France in the summer of 1792, was convicted in absentia in December for publishing part 2 of *Rights of Man*.

4. Smith wrote a similar letter to GW on 28 Dec. 1792, but he apparently never received any reply from the president.

To Henry Laurens

Dear Sir, Philadelphia June 24t[h] 1792

The enclosed letter came to my hands agreeably to its direction; but on opening it I found it was addressed to & intended for you, and that the superscription, directing it to me, was probably a mistake in the writer;[1] I have therefore transmitted it to you, and am, Dear Sir, with very great regard Your most Obedt Servt.

Copy, in Tobias Lear's hand, DNA: RG 59, Miscellaneous Letters; LB, DLC:GW.

1. The enclosed letter has not been identified.

Letter not found: from Anthony Whitting, 24 June 1792. On 1 July, GW informed Whitting that "Your letter of the 24th Ulto came duly to hand."

From John Downing

St Christophers [Island, West Indies] June the 25th 1792

When I consider for a Moment the Importance of the Personage I am about to address My Pen is arrested As it were by some Invisible Power, and on the other side, I am Urged to this by an Impetuous Youth of 17 who has devoted his Future Life to the Profession of Arms; He encourages Me by Saying: Do not fear That General Washington, the Model Cincinnatus, will Receive Your offer of your Youngest Son with Disdain or contempt; His Excelency knows the Value of an Old officer too Well, So to do; It is Reported from all Quarters that the United States have not Yet been able to Reduce the Savages, you must Remember when I was much Younger, how Eager I was (with their own Weapon the Tamnyhock) to engage with one of 3, who Set upon you when you Refused them Rum; In Vain, I Reply; That the States of America never Can Want Officers or Soldiers to Repress the Insults of those Savages But will Surely conquer them; The Service of America is the next Service to that of My own country, & the one I could Wish My Son, it is a Noble Field for Abilities & Indistry, falling then under the Weight of My Sons Ardor, I offer him to The Service of the States, & I Have no doubt But he will Deserve, As far as an Individual Can do, every Encouragement He may Meet with, I am Convinced he will prove a Brave Soldier, And a Faithful Citizen to that State that Attaches his gratitude; Will your Excelency Excuse My offering at a line more, whereby your time so preciouse must be the longer taken up; The first time I ever Saw America Was at the Expedition of Louisbourgh,[1] Since which time I have been over most of it, & often Wished to End My days in it; In 33 Years Service, I have Now a company of Artillery and Am at this time Stationed on the West India Station. I Have the Honor to Be Your Excelency's most Obedeint and very Respectful Humble Servant

John Downing
Captn British Artillery

ALS, DNA: RG 59, Miscellaneous Letters.

GW replied to Downing from Philadelphia on 20 Oct. 1792: "The warm & earnest manner in which you have recommended your son, in your letter to me of the 21st of June, for an appointment in the American Army, makes me regret the necessity I am under of informing you, that I see no prospect of the young Gentleman's wish being gratified in this respect; for so numerous & so respectable are the applications for military appointments from our own citizens that scarcely one in four of these can be gratified, and to grant that to a foreigner which is claimed by so many of our own citizens, unless under some very peculiar circumstances, might be styled not only unjust, but impolitic. I am therefore persuaded, Sir, that you will receive this matter in its true light, and be assured that I have a proper sense of the respectable manner in which you mention this Country, as well as of the polite expressions towards myself which are contained in your letter" (Df, DNA: RG 59, Miscellaneous Letters; LB, DLC:GW).

1. Downing apparently is referring to the expedition of Gen. James Wolfe against the fortress of Louisburg on Cape Breton Island in the spring and summer of 1758. It surrendered on 27 July after a siege of nearly two months.

From Alexander Hamilton

Treasury Departmt June 26. 1792.

The Secretary of the Treasury has the honor respectfully to submit to The President of the United States a Report of the Commissioner of the Revenue on the Subject of a certain Pier to be erected in the River Delaware, in lieu of one previously established there which was carried away by the Ice at the breaking up of the River in the last Spring.[1]

After the best examination which the Secretary has had in his power, he submits the Contract provisionally entered into between The Superintendant of the Delaware Lighthouse &c. and Thomas Davis and Thomas Connaroe Junior, as the best thing practicable. He begs leave to add that the erection of the Pier prior to the ensueing Winter is of the most material importance to the Navigation of the River.[2]

Alexander Hamilton

LB, DLC:GW.

1. Superintendent William Allibone reported "the entire loss & destruction of one of the Piers at mud Island" to Hamilton on 13 Mar. 1792. Three days later Allibone informed Hamilton that "From a view of the Prices and estimates of Building Peirs heretofore with some allowance for the General advance of Wages, I am of Opinion that it will require an appropriation of not less than two thousand Dollars" to construct a new pier. Commissioner of the Revenue Tench Coxe on 20 June transmitted the contract to Hamilton and reported on the reasons for the high cost of replacing the destroyed pier (see Syrett, *Hamilton Papers,* 11:129, 135, 531).

2. At GW's command Tobias Lear wrote Hamilton on 28 June in order "to return to the Secretary of the Treasury, a contract, with his approbation subjoined, between the Superintendant of the Delaware Lighthouse &c. and Thomas Davis & Thomas Connaroe Junior for erecting a Pier in the River Delaware in place of one which was carried away by the Ice on the breaking up of the River last Spring" (DLC:GW). On the following day Hamilton forwarded the approved contract to Tench Coxe "in order that the business may be proceeded upon" (ibid., 606). Thomas Davis was a wharf builder from the Southwark district, a suburb on the southside of Philadelphia. Thomas Connaroe (Conaroe; Conrow), Jr., whose father of the same name had also been involved in the repair of piers on the Delaware River, lived at Springfield Township, Burlington County, N.J., in 1793.

From George Augustine Washington

Honor'd Uncle Berkley County [Va.] 26th June 1792

When I left Mount Vernon it was my intention to have returned there about this time, but three days detention on the road in consequence of bad weather, and ill health since my arrival here will procrastinate my return a week longer than I had determen'd when I set out—On my way up I increased my

Cold and Cough very much and a disagreeable hourseness attended it—which so much disorderd and weakned me as to produce disagreeable apprehensions, but my cold for three or four days having considerably deminished and my strength increased, gives me hopes that with prudence it may pass off without any serious consequences—I hope that by remaining here a week longer and paying proper attention to my health that I shall be able to return, and better than when I set out—I have felt much anxiety at being absent from Mount Vernon at so busy a season, and having been informd by Fanny that my Children & several of the family have been very unwell increased my anxiety to return, but the state of my health being such as to render me incapable of business thought it advisable to continue here a little longer in the attempt to regain it[1]—My Father who is in better health than he has been for several years desire with the family to be kindly rememberd to You and my Aunt—My tenderest affe⟨c⟩tions attend You both & the Children and good wishes[2] for Mr & Mrs Lear & the family and believe me to be with the strongest attachment—Your sincerely affectionate Nephew

Go. A. Washington

ALS, CSmH.

George Augustine Washington long had been beset by failing health. For his illness during the summer and fall of 1791 and his trip to Berkeley Springs, Va. (now W.Va.), to restore his health, see G. A. Washington to GW, 1 Aug., n.8, GW to Lafayette, 10 Sept. n.3, to John Dandridge, 2 Oct., and to Tobias Lear, 2 Oct. 1791. For his visit to New Kent County, Va., during the winter of 1791–92 for the same purpose, see Anthony Whitting to GW, 15–16 Jan. 1792. For GW's recognition that G. A. Washington required "a change of air" and rest if he ever was to recover his health, see GW to Lafayette, 10 June 1792.

1. For George Augustine Washington's continuing battle with tuberculosis, see G. A. Washington to GW, 7 July, GW to Alexander Hamilton, 29 July, and to Henry Knox, 15 Aug. 1792.

2. G. A. Washington inadvertently wrote "wisheses" on the manuscript.

From David Jenkins

Sir, Philada, June 27th 1792

The subscriber who now takes the liberty to address you was in the year 1755 a Lieutenant in the 44th Regmt in the British service under the command of Gen. James Abercrombie, and in Colonel Gage's regiment;[1] but was under the necessity of selling his commission on account of bodily infirmities; and being afterwards reduced to indigent circumstances has been employed for some time past in teaching a school, Of this last source of subsistence he has lately been deprived by a severe stroke of the Palsy; he is therefore under the necessity of returning to his native country where he has a competence depending sufficient to support him and his family comfortably[.] Being therefore under the necessity of applying to the genorisity of my present countrymen I was advised, by several Gentn both in Virginia and Pennsylvania, to make my case known to your Excellency in hope of sharing that liberality which has often been exerted in relieving the unfortunate and distressed[2]—Your friendship in this respect will much oblige Sir, your Excellencies most obedient humble servant

David Jenkins

ALS, DNA: RG 59, Miscellaneous Letters.

1. Maj. Gen. James Abercromby (1706–1781), who had been appointed commander of the 44th Regiment on 13 Mar. 1756, arrived in Albany, N.Y., as second in command of the British forces in North America in June of that year. He was recalled in the fall of 1758, however, following a disastrously unsuccessful attack on Fort Ticonderoga. Thomas Gage (1721–1787) was lieutenant colonel of the 44th Regiment during the campaign leading to Gen. Edward Braddock's defeat on 9 July 1755. Having been promoted to major general in 1761, Gage served as commander in chief of all British forces in the American colonies between 1763 and 1775.

2. On this day GW gave $5 "to a man by the name of Jenkins who says he was a Lieut. in Genl Braddock's troops" (Decatur, *Private Affairs of George Washington,* 275).

From Alexander Hamilton

Treasury Departmt June 28th 1792.

The Secretary of the Treasury respectfully submits to The President of the United States the copy of a Report of this date from The Commissioner of the Revenue, on the subject of certain provisional contracts, which have been entered into for the stakeage of certain waters in North Carolina.[1] He sees no cause to doubt the reasonableness of these Contracts. The higher rate of that for Neuse River is sufficiently accounted for by a longer term of time. They will hereafter include an entire year.[2]

Alexander Hamilton
Secy of the Treasury.

LB, DLC:GW.

1. Hamilton is referring to Tench Coxe's evaluation of "three contracts for Stakeage in the rivers and Bays of North Carolina from the port of Beaufort inclusively to the northern part of Albemarle sound" (see Coxe to Hamilton, 28 June 1792, in Syrett, *Hamilton Papers,* 11:583).

2. On 30 June, Tobias Lear wrote Hamilton at GW's command in order to transmit to him "three Contracts entered into for the stakage of certain waters in North Carolina, which have been submitted to the President of the United States & have received his approbation" (DLC:GW). Hamilton returned the contracts to Coxe that same day (ibid., 607).

Henry Knox to Tobias Lear

[Philadelphia] 28 June 1792. Asks Lear to submit to GW "the enclosed letters from Governor Blount, Mr Allison and Judge McNairn, and others, by which the train of affairs with the Cherokees will be discovered."[1]

LS, DLC:GW; LB, DLC:GW.

1. On 16 May, Southwest Territory governor William Blount wrote Knox that he agreed with the secretary of war that a post should not be established at the mouth of Duck Creek; that it was uncertain when the treaty goods would arrive at Nashville; that the Indians would not be at Nashville before mid-June; and that he had further frontier atrocities to relate. Two boys "of the name of Wells. one about eight the other ten years of age were picking strawberries near their fathers door in his view when the Indians six in number came up to them tomahawked & scalped them & went off without making further attempts on the family—Judging from the place where these boys were killed [Campbell's Station] suspition falls on the Cherokees or Creeks. There is no instance of the no[r]thern tribes having killed so low down nor within less than Eighty Miles." Blount closed his letter with an extract of a letter from Andrew Pickens of 28 April which reads in part: "While a part and that the ostensible ruling part of a Nation [the Cherokee] affect to be at & I beleive really are for peace & the more active young men are frequently killing People & stealing horses it is extreamly difficult how to act—The People even the most exposed would prefer an open War to such a situation, the reason is obvious a man would then know when he saw an Indian he saw an Enemy & be prepared & act accordingly" (Carter, *Territorial Papers,* 4:150–52). The letters from David Allison, Judge John McNairy, and others have not been identified.

To Thomas Jefferson

[Philadelphia, 29 June 1792][1]

I am grieved to find that Mr Short was, on the 22d of April, without his Comn & Instructions[2]—and that Mr Morris was not then in Paris.[3]

AL, DLC: Jefferson Papers.

1. Jefferson's docket on the cover of this letter and his Summary Journal of Public Letters (DLC: Jefferson Papers) record that GW's note was received on 29 June.

2. For the appointment of William Short and William Carmichael to negotiate outstanding differences between the United States and Spain, see GW to the U.S. Senate, 11 Jan., Jefferson to GW, 18, 22 Mar., and GW to Jefferson, 25 Mar., 28 April 1792. Jefferson wrote at the bottom of the manuscript page: "it proved afterwds that the ship carrying the instructions was wrecked." Duplicate papers were prepared and sent, but they did not reach The Hague until mid-November 1792. Short left The Hague in mid-December 1792 and arrived at Madrid in early 1793.

3. Gouverneur Morris left Paris on his trip to London on 22 Jan. and did not return to the French capital until 6 May 1792.

To Samuel Powel

Dear Sir, [Philadelphia] June 29th 1792.

I feel much obliged by your kind offer of one of the tubs of Grape Vines from Madeira. If the remaining two contain plants enough to answer your own purposes, I will accept it with thankfulness; but let me entreat you not to disoblige yourself in order to accomodate me.[1]

A Vessel will sail in a few days for Alexandria, by which I shall send sundry parcels to Mount Vernon.

Mrs Washington unites with me in compliments & best wishes for Mrs Powell & yourself—and with grt esteem & regard I am—Dear Sir Yr Most Obedient and Affectionate Servt

Go: Washington

ALS, ViMtV.

1. It is not known whether Powel renewed his offer and delivered to GW "one of the tubs of Grape Vines from Madeira."

Letter not found: from Anthony Whitting, 29 June 1792. GW wrote to Whitting on 4 July that "Your letter of the 29th Ulto came to my hands yesterday."

To Alexander Hamilton

[Philadelphia, 30 June 1792]

For carrying into execution the provisions of the third section of the Act intitled, "An Act making certain appropriations therein specified,["] passed the Eighth day of May in this present year.[1]

I do hereby authorise you the said Secretary of the Treasury in the name and on the credit of the United States to borrow of any body or bodies politic, person or persons whomsoever the sum of Fifty thousand Dollars; and to enter into such Agreements for the reimbursement thereof as shall be needful and proper; hereby promising to ratify whatever you shall lawfully do in the premises.[2]

In testimony whereof I have hereunto subscribed my hand at the City of Philadelphia the thirtieth day of June in the year One thousand seven hundred and ninety two.

G: Washington

LB, DLC:GW.

1. Section 3 of this act required that "a sum of fifty thousand dollars, in addition to the provision heretofore made, be appropriated to defray any expense which may be incurred in relation to the intercourse between the United States and foreign nations" (*Annals of Congress,* 2d Cong., 1387).

2. For the background to this document, see Thomas Jefferson to GW, 30 May, and note 1. On 30 June, Hamilton informed William Short, the U.S. minister at The Hague, that as a result of Hamilton's proposal to Jefferson of the previous day, a "bill has been drawn in favour of the Secretary of State on our Commissioners [in Holland] for One hundred and twenty three thousand, seven hundred and fifty Guilders," the equivalent of $50,000 (Syrett, *Hamilton Papers,* 11:609).

To Henry Lee

(Private)

Dear Sir, Philadelphia 30th June 1792.

Your favor of the 15th came duly to hand, but at a time when I was much engaged with the Secretary of State in dispatching Mr Pinckney to the Court of London—and in considering other business of importance.

I shall repeat in this letter what I have declared to you on a former occasion—vizt—that wishing to promote the public weal, & to make justice and impartiality the lines by which to walk, to accomplish this, every information that will enable me to work on so solid a basis, or which would enable me to investigate with more accuracy the characters of public men—or the utility of public measures, cannot fail of being acceptable to me, whilst I have any thing to do with either—particularly the latter.[1]

Having premised these truths, I shall add, on the subject of your letter, that[2] I can no more condemn G[eneral] K[nox] on the evidence of Colo. D[arke']s letter to you, than I am disposed to go into a *full* vindication of his conduct against the implications which are contained in that Letter[3]—When assertion stands against assertion, recourse must be had to collateral circumstances to come at the truth, or the preponderating weight, but these are not necessary in the instance before us, for it will not be unfair to Declare, that the conduct of Colo. D—— is uncandid, and that his letter is equivocal. He acknowledges in it, that when *I* asked if he would serve, if you should be appointed to the chief command, that he gave no answer; but does not, in any part of his letter tell you what answer he gave G.K. to the same question; unless you take the following for one, when he was applied to, to know if he would accept of an appointment "I told him I first wanted to know who would command the Army, and said *something of you, and some other*" but are these equivocal expressions to be placed against the positive declaration of the other? especially too, when Colo. D—— in relating the conversation which passed between himself & me, has mistaken both the substance and tendency of it; For you may be assured, Sir, I never mentioned your name, or the name of any man living to him as one who was in the smallest degree fixed on, for the command. The Secretary at War, himself, was unacquainted with the final decision when Colo. D—— left this City. The truth is, I never was more embarrassed in[4] any appointt—& the object of my conversation with the latter was to learn the public sentiment as far as it could be obtained from him, with respect to this matter; And to questions of this tendency he said he had heard Morgan, Scott and yourself mentioned on his Journey through, and from Kentucky to his own house—&, if I understood the significancy of things not expressed he compd himself—I took an occasion *then,* to observe, that I conceived few men were better qualified for such a command than you were & asked if he thought your junr Rank in the late Army would be an objection[5] with those who had been your Seniors in it to serve under you—his reply (when a little pushed by bringing the case home to himself for I wanted to draw an explicit declaration from him) was, that he believed it would be an unpleasant, or agrating thing or words to that effect—but the manner, more than the expression throughout the whole of the conver[satio]n which was after dinnr and when we were alone led me to conclude that it would not be relished by him. What his real intentions might be at that time—when he was speaking to G.K.—or lastly to you no one but himself is master of.

I have no hesitation in declaring to you that the biass of my inclination was strongly in your favor; but, that the result of my enquiries—direct & indirect—of Military, and indeed of other characters (who were well disposed to see you in nomination) was, that if you were appointed to the Command it would be vain to look for Senior Officers to act subordinately; or if they consented, it would be so grudgingly as, more than probably, the seeds of Sedition would be coeval with the formation of the Army; such being the nature of Military pride.[6] Admitting this then One of two things would inevitably have followd either—an army composed of discontented materials, or of junr characters, the first might be attended with fatal consequences—the other (however excellent the Officers might be) if any disaster shoud befal the [army] it would instantly be asscribed to the inexperience of the principal Officers in stations to which they had never been accustomed; thereby drawing a weight upon my shoulders too heavy to be borne. This was my *own* view of the subject; & the principle upon which I acted not, be assured, because G.K. was of this, or of that opinion. The fact, I sincerely believe is, that he was as much puzzled as I was, to fix on the first Officer, under the circumstances that existed.

How far the appointment of G[eneral] W[ayne] is a popular, or an unpopular measure is not for me to decide. It was not the determination of a moment, nor was it the effect of partiality or of influence; for no application (if that in any instance could have warped my judgment) was ever made in his behalf from any one who could have thrown the weight of a feather into his scale but because, under a full view of *all* circumstances he appeared most eligable[7]—To a person of your observation & intelligence, it is unnecessary to remark that an appointment which may be unpopular in one place, or with one set of men, may not be so in another place or with another set of Men and vice versa—and that to attempt to please every body is the sure way to please nobody—of course the attempt would be as idle as the executn wd be impracticable—G.W. has many good points as an Officer—and it is to be hoped that time, Reflection, good advice and above all, a due sence of the importance of the trust which is committed to him, will correct his foibles, or cast a shade over them. With estm & Regd I am &ca

G. W——n

AL[S] (incomplete), sold by The Rendells, Inc., "The Presidents," item no. 17, catalogue no. 150 (1980); ADfS, DLC:GW; LB, DLC:GW. The Rendells' catalogue only reproduces the first page of the AL[S].

1. For Lee's reference to "a declaration which you made at your own table just before your acceptance of the arduous station" of president, see Lee to GW, 15 June 1792.

2. The remainder of the transcription of this letter is taken from the draft.

3. For William Darke's letter of 12 May to Lee, see Lee to GW, 15 June, n.4.

4. At this place on the draft manuscript, GW first wrote "puzzled by" before striking out these words and inserting "embarrassed in."

5. At this place on the draft manuscript, GW wrote and then struck out the phrase "to or in our designs."

6. For GW's recognition that Lee's relatively junior rank during the Revolutionary War would prevent many senior officers from serving under him, see Thomas Jefferson's Memorandum of a Meeting of the Heads of the Executive Departments, 9 Mar., and Memorandum on General Officers, 9 March.

7. For the recent appointment of Anthony Wayne as a major general in the U.S. Army and as commander of a further expedition against the hostile northwestern Indians, see Thomas Jefferson's Memorandum of a Meeting of the

Heads of the Executive Departments, 9 Mar., Memorandum on General Officers, 9 Mar., Henry Knox to GW, 1 April, n.1, GW to Knox, 4 April, and note 1, and GW to the U.S. Senate, 9 April 1792. The Senate approved Wayne's nomination on 11 April (*Executive Journal,* 1:119).

To John Francis Mercer

Sir, Philadelphia June 30th 1792.

I little expected that I should have had occasion, at this time (after the pointed assurances you gave me more than three years ago, of discharging what was due to me, fully) to remind you that I have received only Three hundred and eighty pds of the balance; and to ask what I am to expect from you in future.[1]

I delayed from day to day while you were in this City (until it was too late) to apply to you on this Subject, in hope, and expectation that you would not have left town without mentioning it yourself.

Before I apply to the Executors of Colonels Tayloe & Thornton who were Securities for the money loaned to your deceased father, John Mercer Esqr., I will await the Receipt of your answer to this letter[2] which I hope will be given as soon [as][3] you can make it convenient.

It has been of little avail hitherto, to inform you of the causes of my want of this money; although, in more instances than one, I have done it with the utmost truth and candour: nor should I say any thing further to you on this head now, were I not in a manner compelled to declare, that from an occurrence which did not exist before I have a call upon me for a considerable Sum, in a few months; against which it is *indispensably necessary* that I should be provided.[4] I am—Sir Your Most Obedt Servt

Go: Washington

ALS (letterpress copy), NN: Washington Papers; LB, DLC:GW.

1. For the background to this letter, see GW to James Mercer, 18 Mar. 1789, and note 1, 4 April 1789, and to John Francis Mercer, 5 April 1789. In May 1791 the estate of James and John Francis's father, John Mercer, still owed GW £908.15.11½ (Ledger B, 221). The account was finally settled in April 1793 when GW accepted a tract of 519 acres in Montgomery County, Md., from John Francis Mercer (Ledger C, 4).

2. Mercer's reply to GW of 10 July has not been found. For GW's displeasure at the information contained in Mercer's response, see GW to Mercer, 23 July 1792. GW apparently had been considering applying to the executors for the

estates of John Tayloe and John Thornton (d. 1777) for some time. On 9 May, Edmund Randolph had written to GW, apparently in response to an inquiry by the president: "After revolving the affair of Mercer's debt, I can see no reason for distrusting my opinion of this morning. The original securities cannot be absolved. You have done no act, expressly directed to this object; and the receipt of partial sums from John or James Mercer cannot possibly affect your primary title. I take the liberty of recommending, that the notice, which you purpose to give, should be addressed not only to Colo. Tayloe's executors, but also to Colo. Thornton's. Altho' a recovery must probably be had in the first instance against the former, yet they will have a right of contribution against the latter; and therefore the latter ought to [be] apprized of the danger" (DLC:GW).

3. This word is supplied from the letter-book copy.

4. For this prospective call upon GW for money, see GW to Mercer, 23 July 1792, n.3.

To John Greenwood

Sir, Philadelphia July 1st 1792.

Your letter of the first of May and the box which accompanied it came safe, and duly to hand on the eve of my departure for Virginia;[1] which is the reason why I have not acknowledged the Receipt of them sooner.

The contents of the latter (with the alterations which were necessarily made) answered very well—and enclosed you have, in Bank notes, twenty dollars, the sum I have usually sent you,[2] but if it is insufficient let me know it and more shall be forwarded by Sir Yr Obedt Hble Servt

Go: Washington

ALS, AU-M.

1. Although Greenwood's letter to GW of 1 May has not been found, the box that he enclosed apparently contained a set of dentures that GW had sent to Greenwood for alterations and repair. GW left Philadelphia for Mount Vernon on 10 May. For more information about GW's dentures and his dealings with Greenwood, see GW to Greenwood, 16 Feb. 1791, and notes, and Greenwood to GW, 10 Sept. 1791, and note 1.

2. On 16 Feb. 1791 GW had sent Greenwood $20 for a new set of false teeth "and the repairs of the old ones, and, etc."

To Anthony Whitting

Mr Whiting, Philadelphia July 1st 1792.

Your letter of the 24th Ulto came duly to hand,[1] and I am glad to find by it that you have had *some* rains though not as *much* as has fallen in these parts—and that your Crops are deriving the benefit of them. If the Corn is standing, & alive, I do not, on account of its backwardness, despair of a Crop; if you are able to keep it clean, & the ground well pulverised; which I hope will be the case.

It is much my wish that the swamps at both places may be got fully into Corn;[2] if for no other reason than that of working the grd to destroy the wild growth, to pulverize, and to level it. I wish also that No. 2 at Dogue Run may have all the missing hills of both Corn & Potatoes made good; the first with early Corn, and the latter with any kind of Potatoes you may have, or can get. Without this I shall not ascertain a fact I was very desirous of knowing.

I am very glad to receive so favorable an Account of your Wheaten prospect, although it be touched with the Rust, and not filled so well as might be wished: and I am much pleased at your beginning harvest so soon, notwithstanding the prognostic's of the Farmers around you—I am satisfied there is more utility, & less danger & loss in doing it, than if it had been delayed until their ideas had made it fit for the scythe or Sickle.

In my last I suggested to you a wish that the Brickyard inclosure might be sown with Buck-wheat & grass seeds; and these wishes are not changed. If the Buckwheat will not kill the grass that is sown with it, it will certainly shade, protect & keep it moist at a time when the hot Sun would be very apt to injure it—Turnips in my opinion will not answer well in that ground—first because they will not come off in time for fall sowing of the grass—and secondly, because they are considered as a very exhausting Crop when they are not fed off.

I expect, if nothing happens more than I know of at present, to set out for Mount Vernon about the twelfth of this month:[3] previous to my arrival, I desire you will have the Well by the Kitchen thoroughly cleaned, by some professional people; and while they are about it that they may be well attended, as you know accidents frequently happen in this work, by the noxtious effluvia that sometimes arise in these places; I would not have any of my own people descend into it: The same persons, or some other skilful ones might be employed to sink the Well directly opposite to the centre of the green house, but just within the Brick yard Inclosure So as not to interfere with the Road. This well is to be walled with the Bricks that are making, and which ought to be exceedingly well burnt—& none used for that purpose that are not so—The diameter after it is walled should be, in the clear, five feet; for the purpose of admitting a frame at the bottom that is necessary for a new mode of drawing Water—but if the Well could be sunk I would not have it Walled up (for the reason above) until I arrive. It will take about 200 bricks for every foot the Well is deep, & not less than 60 feet depth ought to be calculated upon; this would require 12,000 hard bricks; and to obtain them 15,000 ought to be made, and so disposed of in the kiln as to insure their being well burnt—about 50,000 of the common Bricks will be sufficient for the purposes for which they are intended.

The Ferry and French's Plantations were not noticed in the last weeks Report.[4] I am—Your friend &ca

Go: Washington

ALS, ViMtV.

1. This letter has not been found.

2. On GW's 1793 map of his Mount Vernon farms, he indicates the existence of swamps near the mill and at Muddy Hole farm (see *Papers, Retirement Series,* 4:460–61). GW had tried for several years to reclaim the swamps (see George Augustine Washington to GW, 14 Dec. 1790, n.4, GW to Whitting, 4 Sept. 1791).

3. GW left for Mount Vernon on 11 July (see Tobias Lear to Thomas Jefferson, 11 July 1792).

4. Whitting's farm report has not been found.

From Alexander Hamilton

[Philadelphia] 2 July 1792. Encloses "the sketch of a letter to be written by Mr Lear to Mr Langdon."[1]

LB, DLC:GW.

1. For the appointment of Woodbury Langdon as one of the commissioners to settle the accounts between the United States and the individual states for

the expense of the Revolutionary War, see GW to the U.S. Senate, 23 Dec. 1790. For the acts of Congress regarding the settlement of these accounts, see "An Ordinance for settling the Accounts between the United States and Individual States" of 7 May 1787 (*JCC,* 32:262–66, 34:502), "An Act for settling the accounts between the United States and individual States" of 5 Aug. 1789, and "An Act to provide more effectually for the settlement of the accounts between the United States and individual States" of 5 Aug. 1790 (*Annals of Congress,* 1st Cong., 2214, 2357–59).

Tobias Lear's letter of 2 July 1792 to Langdon reads: "I am commanded by the President of the United States to inform you, that it is indispensably necessary you should without delay repair to the seat of the Government, to prosecute, jointly with your Colleagues the business of your office as Commissioner. It being of great and real importance that the settlement of the public accounts should be brought to a close as speedily as possible, and, as in order to this, it is essential, that it should be pursued with diligence and perseverance, I am further instructed by the President to say, that if any circumstances in your situation should be incompatible with your immediate and steady attendance it is proper you should resign the Office: For however he should regret the necessity of a change, at such a stage of the business, which could not fail to be attended with inconvenience, he must regard this as a less evil than frequent interruptions of its course, by absences of the Commissioners" (DNA: RG 59, Miscellaneous Letters). Langdon did not resign his position, however. He and his fellow commissioners submitted their final report to GW in June 1793.

From Henry Knox

Sir War department 2 July 1792

I have the honor respectfully to submit to your consideration certain principles for the formation of the four sub Legions, and for the arrangeme⟨nt⟩ of the commissioned officers thereof.[1]

And also in case of a reduction of any of the new troops that the officers should be reduced by Lot. I have the honor sir to be with perfect respect Your humble Servant

H. Knox

ALS, DLC:GW; LB, DLC:GW. The mutilated text is supplied in angle brackets from the letter-book copy.

1. On 13 July, Knox sent Anthony Wayne "the arrangement of the Officers to the four Sub Legions, the principles of which were approved by the President of the United States" (Knopf, *Wayne,* 32). For the text of Knox's "Organization of the Army in 1792," which he communicated to the House of Representatives on 27 Dec. 1792, see *ASP, Military Affairs,* 1:40–41.

From Thomas Jefferson

[Philadelphia] 3 July 1792. Submits "the translation of a letter from Messrs Viar & Jaudenes, with the draught of an answer he proposes to them, & a letter to the Governor of Georgia. he incloses also a translation of the papers which accompanied the letter he received."[1]

AL, DNA: RG 59, Miscellaneous Letters; LB, DNA: RG 59, George Washington's Correspondence with His Secretaries of State; LB (photocopy), DLC:GW.

1. For Josef Ignacio de Viar and José de Jaudenes y Nebot's letter to Jefferson of 26 June and its enclosures, see *Jefferson Papers,* 24:129–31. On 3 July, Jefferson wrote Viar and Jaudenes to inform them that he had forwarded their message "on the subject of the robbery [of five Negro slaves] supposed to have been committed within the territory of Florida by three citizens of the state of Georgia" to GW and "that due enquiry shall be immediately made into the transaction, and that every thing shall be done on the part of this government which right shall require, and the laws authorise" (ibid., 156). On this date Jefferson also sent Gov. Edward Telfair of Georgia a copy of Viar and Jaudenes's letter and wrote that he was "persuaded that nothing will be wanting on your part to satisfy the just expectations of the government of Florida on the present occasion" (ibid., 155–56). Edward Telfair (c.1735–1807) held a variety of state and local offices before and during the Revolutionary War. He served as a delegate to the Continental Congress in 1778 and 1780–82, supported the ratification of the Constitution, and served as governor of Georgia in 1786 and 1790–93.

From Thomas Jefferson

[Philadelphia] 3 July 1792. Encloses "to the President a letter just recd from Colo. Humphreys."[1]

AL, DNA: RG 59, Miscellaneous Letters; LB, DNA: RG 59, George Washington's Correspondence with His Secretaries of State; LB (photocopy), DLC:GW.

1. The enclosed letter from David Humphreys, U.S. minister to Portugal, to Jefferson of 3 May 1792 concerned the recent assassination of Gustav III of Sweden, "fresh tumults in Turin between the Students and the Artificers," the slowness of Queen Maria I's mental recovery, and the glut of wheat and corn on the Portuguese market that was depressing the price American importers could charge for these items (*Jefferson Papers,* 23:480–81).

From Thomas Jefferson

[Philadelphia] 3 July 1792. Submits "to the President a letter to mister Van Berckel on the subject of the infraction of the privileges of his house by a constable."[1]

AL, DNA: RG 59, Miscellaneous Letters; LB, DNA: RG 59, George Washington's Correspondence with His Secretaries of State; LB (photocopy), DLC:GW.

1. For Dutch minister Franco Petrus Van Berckel's letter to Jefferson of 25 June complaining about the invasion of his residence and the arrest of his domestic servant Frederic Gitt by the Philadelphia constable Elihu Meeker and Attorney General Edmund Randolph's letter to Jefferson of 26 June giving his opinion of the matter, see *Jefferson Papers,* 24:125–29. The letter to Van Berckel that Jefferson submitted to GW on this date is dated 2 July 1792. While admitting that "There could be no question but that this was a breach of [diplomatic] privilege," Jefferson informed Van Berckel that "from the circumstance of your Servant's not being registered in the Secretary of State's office, we cannot avail ourselves of the more certain and effectual proceeding which had been provided by an act of Congress for punishing infractions of the law of nations." Taking his cue from Randolph, therefore, Jefferson asked Van Berckel whether he preferred to settle the matter "By a warrant before a single magistrate to recover the money paid by the Servant under a process declared void by law" or "to indict the officer in the Supreme Court of the United States, with whom it would rest to punish him at their discretion" (ibid., 149–50). For Van Berckel's response, which enclosed a list of his domestic servants and left the decision about what to do in Jefferson's hands, see ibid., 157–58. Meeker was indicted by a grand jury at the Pennsylvania circuit court on 11 Oct. 1792. Fearful that Meeker's punishment would exceed the seriousness of the offense, however, Van Berckel shortly thereafter asked that the prosecution be dropped (Marcus and Perry, *Documentary History of the Supreme Court,* 2:320).

To Henry Lee

Dear Sir, Philadelphia July 3d 1792.

Your letter of the 20th Ulto was presented to me yesterday by Mr Williams—who as a professional man—may, or may not be for ought I know,[1] a luminary of the first magnitude. But to be frank, and I hope you will not be displeased with me for being so—I am so heartily tired of the attendance which from one cause or another has been given ⟨to⟩ these kind of people, that it is now more than two years since I have resolved to sit no more for any of them and have adhered to it, except in instances where it has been requested by[2] public bodies, or for a particular purpose (not of the Painters) and could not, without offence be refused.[3]

I have been led to make this resolution for another reason besides the irksomeness of sitting, and the time I loose by it—which is, that these productions have in my estimation, been made use of as a sort of tax on individuals by being engraved (and that badly) and hawked about or advertised for Sale. With very great esteem & regard I am Dear Sir Yr most Obt & Affe Servt

G. W——n

ADfS, DNA: RG 59, Miscellaneous Letters; LB, DLC:GW; copy, ViHi. The ALS, which was sold in New York City on 21–22 Jan. 1926 at an auction conducted by the American Art Association, has not been found (*American Book-Prices Current,* 32 [1926], 854). The mutilated text is supplied in angle brackets from the letter-book copy.

1. At this place on the draft manuscript, GW first wrote and then struck out the phrase: "be in his profession."

2. At this place on the draft manuscript, GW first wrote "the public" before striking out "the" and writing "public bodies."

3. Although declining to sit for William J. Williams on this occasion, GW allowed the artist to take his portrait two years later after receiving a request from Masonic Lodge No. 22 of Alexandria, Virginia. The resulting work, an unflattering piece showing an aged and unhappy GW wearing the costume, emblems, and insignia of the Masonic order, was completed in September 1794 (see Eisen, *Portraits of Washington,* 2:505–6). For an engraving of the portrait, see Charles H. Callahan, *Washington: The Man and the Mason* (Washington, D.C., 1913), frontispiece.

From William Carter, Sr.

Sir. [Richmond, 4 July 1792]

William Wray, a Youth of a Reputable Family, & a Nephew of mine by Marriage, having lived with me from August 1784. in Order to study Physick & Surgery, is now very desirous of entering into the Army with a View of serving his Country & improving himself in the practical Part of his Profession & wishes to be appointed a Mate under a Surgeon for that Purpose; But in Case there is no Vacancy for him in his proper Line He is desirous of being favoured with some Commission:[1] As I wish to be his Friend as far as lies in my Power to get him into the Army, where I have Reason to think from his Assiduity to Business & Attention to his Duty he may merit Preferment—He the said Will: Wray is young & healthy, of good natural Parts, & having given him a good Education: I do hereby certify that I think him capable & qualified for the above Purposes: And do now recommend him to the Favour and Freindship of your Excellency—Given under my Hand this 4th Day of July 1792.

William Carter senior
At Richmond—And Surgeon to the
Continental Hospital in Williamsburg
during the late War

P.S. Sir By my Desire Colo. Carrington enclosed a Copy of the above in a Letter to General Knox five or six Weeks ago:[2] But having received no Appointment, nor the least Inteligence of any Kind from the General, He (William Wray), is very unhappy indeed. And as he is so very desirous of getting some Commission in the Army I make free to address You on the Subject in his Behalf. I am, Sir, with all due Respect & Esteem your most obedient and very humble Servant

William Carter senr

ALS, DLC:GW.

William Carter, Sr. (1732–1799), of Richmond, Va., served as a Continental army surgeon in the southern department from July 1776 until the end of the Revolutionary War.

1. William Wray apparently never received a military appointment from GW.

2. The letter that Col. Edward Carrington wrote to Henry Knox in the spring of 1792 enclosing a recommendation from William Carter, Sr., has not been identified.

To Anthony Whitting

Mr Whiting, Philadelphia July 4th 1792.

Your letter of the 29th Ulto came to my hands yesterday[1]—and this answer to it will be in Alexandria on Friday; &, more than probable, will reach you before Monday.[2]

As you think it will be best to sow Lucern *alone,* in the Inclosure by the Stable; I am content that it should be so; and will send, or bring some seed, in aid of what you have, to stock it w⟨e⟩ll. The Brick yard Inclosure I would have sown *wholly,* or *partly,* as you may think best (for I do not recollect the quantity of g⟨ro⟩und in it) with B⟨uc⟩k Wheat & Clover; but with the latter it might be well perhaps to mix a little Timothy seed. The other part of that lot (if all is not sown in Buck Wheat) may be planted with Potatoes if you think they will be off in time for the Grass-Seeds.

You may proceed, in the manner you have pointed out, in getting out the Wheat in No. 6 at Dogue-Run; before you have finished which, I shall, I presume, be at home; if not, proceed as shall appear best in your own judgment with the Residue—but do not suffer mares that are with foal to be employed in this business, as it is very apt to make them cast their foals⟨;⟩ especially, if they are at all forward with them. I am Yr friend &ca

Go: Washington

P.S. If the ground that was ploughed in the Visto, leading to the white gates could be got in order in time, and sown with Buck wheat and Timothy, or Orchard grass, it would answr the dble purpose of a crop of the first, & laying it with the latter.

ALS, CtSoP: on deposit at the Beinecke Rare Books and Manuscripts Library, CtY. The text that appears within angle brackets has been damaged by the folding of the ALS manuscript.

1. Whitting's letter to GW of 29 June 1792 has not been found.

2. GW is referring to Friday, 6 July, and Monday, 9 July 1792.

From Thomas Jefferson

[Philadelphia] 5 July 1792. Encloses "a letter just recieved from mister Hammond, which will be difficult to answer properly."[1]

AL, DNA: RG 59, Miscellaneous Letters; LB, DNA: RG 59, George Washington's Correspondence with His Secretaries of State; LB (photocopy), DLC:GW.

1. British minister George Hammond's letter of 5 July to Jefferson reads: "I have the honor of submitting to your consideration copies of certain papers, which I have received from Canada. They contain information that some persons, acting under the authority of the State of Vermont, have attempted to exercise legal jurisdiction within districts now occupied by the King's troops, and have committed acts of violence on the persons and property of British Subjects residing under the protection of his Majesty's garrisons.

"At this period, when the grounds of the subsisting differences between our respective countries are become the subjects of serious and temperate discussion, I cannot but entertain the strongest confidence that the general government of the United States will entirely disapprove of the violent conduct observed by the State of Vermont upon this occasion, and will in consequence thereof adopt such measures as may be best calculated to prevent a repetition of it in future" (*Jefferson Papers,* 24:160). For a description of the documents that Hammond enclosed in this letter, see ibid. For an extended discussion of

Hammond's complaints, which centered around the organization of a local government for Alburg, Vt., located a few miles south of the Canadian border but in close proximity to the British-held post of Pointe-au-Fer, N.Y., and the legal proceedings brought by the state of Vermont against Patrick Conroy, a British official who had served as a justice of the peace there in the past, see ibid., 160–62. See also Thomas Chittenden to GW, 16 June, and note 1. For Jefferson's response to Hammond, see Jefferson to GW, 6 July, n.1.

Henry Knox to Tobias Lear

[Philadelphia] 5 July 1792. Asks Lear to submit "the enclosed important papers from Mr Seagrove" to GW.[1]

ALS, DLC:GW; LB, DLC:GW.

1. These enclosures have not been identified.

From James Seagrove

Sir Rocklanding Oconee River [Ga.] July 5 1792

The information, which I am about to give appearing to me of importance to the United States, I hope will plead my excuse for thus intruding on your moments of retirement.

In my dispatch of the 14th Ulto to the Secretary of War I promised to procure what information I could respecting a spanish Officer which General McGillivray mentions in his letter to me of the 18th of May, a Copy of which you have herewith.[1]

I find, on enquirey of the Indian Chiefs now with me, that this Spanish Officer is the same person that I have mentioned in my former letters as a Spanish resident or Agent, who had arrived from New Orleans and lived in a House of General McGillivray's at little Tallassie.

It remains no longer a doubt who this person is, and his business in the Creek Nation. His name is *Olivar* a Frenchman born a Captain in the Spanish Army, wears the Uniform of the Regiment of Leuiseana, sent by the immediate orders of the Barron Caron du Lette, Governor of New Orleans, as an Agent (or perhaps something more) to conduct affairs in the Creek Nation.[2]

It would appear by the Stile of General McGillivrays letter to me, that this Spanish Agent had just arrived and that he was a Stranger to him or his business, this was not the case, for it is well known and I can produce unquestionable proofs that he had then been several months at McGillivrays own house at little Tallassie. the general took much pains in sending for a number of Chiefs and introduced this Spaniard to them as their *great friend* who was come to live among them, and to do great things for them. It can also be made appear that the general was riding about the Country with this Spaniard at the time when By his engagements he ought to have been with me.

I have not a doubt but that the arrival of this spanish Agent was in Consequence of a preconcerted plan between McGillivray and the spaniards on his visit last winter to their possessions and that Captain Olivar, is to be his successor in the Creek land. For you must know that the general is again gone with nearly the whole of his property into New Orleans, and I doubt whether he returns, certain it is that he hath engaged to attend the Spanish treaty, with the Indians at Pensacola in September next.

As soon as General McGillivray quit the nation Captain Olivar, threw of[f] all Mask, by calling meetings in the Towns, and directing what the Indians should, and should not do. He in the most public and positive manner forbids them parting with a foot of land to the United States, and also forbids their running the boundary line between them & Georgia, and positively tells the Indians not to have any thing to do with the Americans,[3] It is said by several persons (but I cannot vouch for the truth of it) that he has gone so far in the upper Towns as to advise the Indians turning out against our people on the Western Waters, I think this not improbable, for about ten days past he had the impudence to come into the lower Towns, and give out public Talks, advising the Indians not to come near me, & on no account to run the line. This I have from persons who were present & heard him. I am happy in being able to inform you that he met a very cool receiption in the lower Towns. The Indians who had been with me had returned home and influenced their people so much in our favor that he found it convenient to make a speedy retreat to little Tallassie.

A Brother in law of general McGillivrays (a white man) who lives at Tallassie, of the name of Weatherford,[4] is now here who confirms what I have related of this Spanish Agent, & further says that he hath at McGillivrays house a quantity of Goods, which he distributes among the Indians—that he draws orders on Government in favor of all Indians going to Orleans, who received goods and Ammunition, which they bring up in boats and that they have a Constant intercourse in this way—that he has engaged in securing the Chiefs to attend the Treaty at Pensacola, that it was much talked of in the nation that one object of the spanish Treaty would be to obtain leave to erect Forts and establish garrisons on the Creek lands.

Those matters seem of so much moment—come so direct, and I beleive unquestionably true, that I have lost no time in giving you notice thereof.

I cannot account for this interferrence of the spaniards I some times think that Captain Olivar, cannot be supported by his Government in such doings, and that he is exceeding his instructions.

By the Secretary of Wars dispatch to me of the 30th of April, it would appear that a good understanding exists between the United States and Spain.[5]

In consequence of the secretary of Wars directions in the dispatch alluded to above—I wrote a line to the Governor of St Augustine in order to feel his pulse on the occasion, as well as to know from him, what they had done with Bowles, a Copy of our correspondance you have herewith.[6]

My communications to the Secretary of War of the 24th May together with my letter to General McGillivray of the 21st of the same month, and my talks to the Indians, I must pray your perusal of.[7]

I find that the Spanish Agent is on very friendly terms with Bowles successor in the Nation, a Man of the name of Wellbanks.

I cannot help expressing my fears to you, that the spaniards are playing a double game with us on the score of Mr Bowles, My Opinion is, that they will make him useful to their views, their very kind treatment of him, since he has been among them, cannot fail to create suspicion in the breast of any one as well acquainted as I am with Spanish want of linity to *actual prisoners* especially such as have offended against their government. Bowles hath not been confined by them, and it is a doubt with me, but what appeared a capture of him to us, was in fact a concerted plan with him, He is sent to spain but not in confinement, why send him there—sure the Governor of New Orleans or the

Captain general at the Havana, are possessed with powers equal to punishing or acquiting a Man of Mr Bowles character.[8] I fear there is some dark & dangerous business in contemplation among those people. I fear General McGillivray is not faithful to the United States, and I have my su[s]picions that if any mischief is abruing he is deeply engaged in it, I never expect he will come forward as an active character in the field, he wants spirit, and this is the reason of his placing Olivar, in his stead, and of his withdrawing to the spaniards as an asslum, Olivar is represented to me as a Man of good address, who speaks the French, Spanish and English languages equally well.

I fear the reason of McGillivrays not meeting me, and his not forwarding the business of the Treaty made at New York, as well as his evasive conduct to all the pressing arguments made use of to him by the Secretary of War, and myself arrose from preconcerted plans with his Spanish and English friends, and not from any real opposition the Indians made thereto.

Agreeable to my instructions I have laboured very hard to replace this *ungreatful Man* in the confidence of his countrymen, which he had lost from his duplicity, and want of resolution, I fear I shall be censured by the Indians who are our friends for my Zeal in his behalf, I assure you that nine out of ten of them now dispise him and seldom mention his name but with disrespect.

I concieved it my duty to have Major Call, the commander of the Federal troops, & Mr Ellicott the surveyor present at my communications with the Indians in order that they might witness the situation of Matters and act accordingly.

It is truly disagreeable to me but duty to you impells me to mention, that this once valuable Officer hath resigned himself to so continual a state of intoxication with strong liquors, as to render him totally incapable of acting or even judging of what is proper in the line of his duty[.] I have already hinted this to the Secretary of War and referred him to the Officers who went from this for further information.[9]

Notwithstanding the untoward State the Creek nation is represented to be in by General McGillivray I think I can venture to assure you, that I shall be able to keep them from breaking with us, if not restore them to order and get all matters settled with them. I hope you will see the necessity of my having it in my power to supply them occasionally. you are too well acquainted with the nature of Indians for me to say more to you on this head as well as the precarious situation of those people at present.

In the execution of these as well as in any other matters you are pleased to commit to my care I can only say that fidelity & industry in me Shall not be wanting.

I have left open the Secretary of Wars dispatches for your persual, Should any thing further offer of consequence I shall forward it by express. I have the honor to be &c.

James Seagrove

LB, DNA: RG 107, Office of the Secretary of War, Letters Sent and Received, 1791–1797; copy, DNA: RG 46, Second Congress, 1791–1793, Records of Legislative Proceedings, Reports and Communications Submitted to the Senate; copy, DLC: Jefferson Papers; copy, DNA: RG 233, Third Congress, 1793–1795, Records of Legislative Proceedings, President's Messages; copy (extract), DNA: RG 59, Instructions to Diplomatic Officers, Instructions, 1785–1906; copy (extract), DNA: RG 46, Third Congress, 1793–1795, Records of Executive Proceedings, President's Messages—Foreign Relations.

1. Alexander McGillivray's letter to Seagrove of 18 May reads in part: "a Spanish officer has actually arrived, and tells the Indians that he has orders to prevent them from running the line, or doing any other business with the Americans, and invites them to a meeting, in September next, at Pensacola" (*ASP, Indian Affairs,* 1:302). Seagrove's letter to Henry Knox of 14 June reads in part: "The story of the Spanish officer I do not put faith in; it can hardly be possible that the Spanish nation would interfere in such business, especially as we seem to be on good terms with them. . . . I shall make it my first business to ascertain the story of the Spanish officer, which you shall have without delay" (ibid.).

2. Francisco Luis Hector, baron de Carondelet, the Spanish governor of Louisiana and West Florida, appointed Lt. Pedro Olivier as Spain's agent to the Creek Nation in February 1792. Carondelet instructed Olivier to "interfere by all possible means with the execution of the" 1790 Treaty of New York between the United States and the Creeks; to convince the southern Indian tribes that the Americans "are aiming, since their independence, at nothing less than the annihilation of all the Indian nations of this continent, in order to take possession of their lands"; and to persuade the Creeks that their "own preservation and that of their children urges them to draw near Spain, who has so disinterestedly protected them, and who is ready to defend them if they will conclude a defensive alliance with the Cherokee, Choctaw, and Chickasaw nations, obligating themselves to be guarantors of the lands and possessions of all" (Carondelet to Olivier, 30 Mar. 1792, in Kinnaird, *Spain in the Mississippi Valley,* 3:21–22).

3. For further information about Pedro Olivier's activities at this time, see Knox to GW, 28 July, n.4.

4. Charles Weatherford, one of Alexander McGillivray's brothers-in-law, ran

packhorses between Pensacola and the Creek Nation and served as a Spanish informant (Caughey, *McGillivray of the Creeks,* 103, 212).

5. Secretary of War Knox's letter to Seagrove of 30 April has not been identified.

6. Seagrove's letter to Gov. Juan Nepomuceno de Quesada y Barnuevo of 13 June reads in part: "I find that [William Augustus] Bowles hath occasioned great feuds among those unfortunate people [the Creeks], and that his designs were eventually hostile. But, as he is now removed, (I hope never to return) I hope the nation will soon be restored to a state of tranquillity. There are, however, several of Bowles' white associates still in the nation, endeavoring to mislead the Indians. Some of these white wretches have lately advised the savages to commit depredations on your government. . . . The principal agent of Bowles that is now in the nation, is a man of the name of Willbanks. . . . I shall be happy in a line from you, before my departure, with an account of Mr. Bowles's present situation and prospects, together with any other information you may see fit" (*ASP, Indian Affairs,* 1:303). Quesada's reply of 14 June reads in part: "I am clear, that, since the late war, various white men, of desperate fortunes, remained in, or continue going to, and coming from, the Indian nation, who, without a real attachment to, or perhaps being authorized by, any Power, have dedicated themselves (and continue to do so for their own private views, or for pure mischief's sake,) to work up the savages against Spaniards and Americans. It is very probable that Bowles aimed at something more, but he certainly assumed the character of principal in his projects. I have always considered him to be a mere tool of other persons. All I know at present of this adventurer is, that he was sent a prisoner from Apalacha to New Orleans, from thence to the Havana, and from that lately to Spain" (ibid.).

7. For an extract of Seagrove's letter to Knox of 24 May, which describes the strength of Bowles's party, the extent to which McGillivray had been discredited as a leader, Pedro Olivier's influence within the Creek Nation, and an attack on an American settlement south of the Cumberland River, among other things, see ibid., 296. Seagrove's letter to McGillivray of 21 May includes a plea that if "the feuds which distract your country unfortunately increase so as to endanger your remaining in the nation, and that you determine on a temporary removal, I would by all means advise its being to the United States, for reasons which must be obvious to you" (ibid., 298–99).

8. Seagrove's fears that the Spanish were playing "a double game" with regard to Bowles were unjustifiable. Bowles spent the next three years in various Spanish prisons before being exiled to the Philippines in 1795.

9. For more information about Richard Call's descent into alcoholism, see Knox to GW, 9 July 1791, and Seagrove to GW, 21 April 1792. In the latter letter Seagrove says that Michael Rudolph, John Mills, and Moses Porter would be able to give the president additional information about Call's intemperance.

From Thomas Jefferson

[Philadelphia] 6 July 1792. Submits to GW the draft of a letter from Jefferson to George Hammond.[1]

AL, DNA: RG 59, Miscellaneous Letters; LB, DNA: RG 59, George Washington's Correspondence with His Secretaries of State; LB (photocopy), DLC:GW.

1. GW replied to Jefferson later this date: "The enclosed will, I think, throw the labouring Oar upon Mr H—— & is approved of accordingly" (ALS, DLC: Jefferson Papers). Jefferson's final version of his letter to George Hammond of 6 July reads: "I have the honor to acknolege the receipt of your letter of yesterday with the papers accompanying it, and will immediately lay them before the President of the U.S. But not being acquainted with the situation of Caldwell's manor [Alburg, Vt.], at which it is said that an officer of Vermont has distrained some cattle and that [British] Capt. Savage rescued a part of them, I shall be glad to be enabled to inform the President whether this Manor is on the North or South side of the 45th. degree [the boundary line between the United States and Canada]. If your information ascertain's this point I will thank you for a communication of it" (*Jefferson Papers,* 24:164). For the legal proceedings against the British official Patrick Conroy, including the seizure of his cattle, see ibid., 160. Hammond responded to Jefferson later this day: "I have no information as to the precise situation of Caldwell manor; but from a variety of circumstances I am inclined to believe that Caldwell manor either is situated near to, or forms part of, the town of Alburgh, which town, though on the south side of the 45th degree of latitude, is under the protection and jurisdiction of the district of Point au fer, now occupied by his Majesty's garrison" (ibid., 164–65). For the background to this exchange of letters, see Thomas Chittenden to GW, 16 June, and note 1. For the administration's official response to Hammond's complaints, see GW to Jefferson, 7 July, n.2.

From Winthrop Sargent

Cincinnati County of Hamilton and Territory of the United States North west of the River Ohio.

Sir, July the 6th 1792.

I do myself the honour to transmit by Major Vigo, a copy from the public records of the Territory of the United States, north west of the river Ohio, to the 30th of June inclusive.

The long absence of two of the judges from the Government, has prevented the adoption of laws for more than the six months last past, which is considered and lamented as a very great misfortune to the territory.[1]

Since closing my official communications sir, Major Vigo has presented to me the enclosed petition from the people of Vincennes which I beg leave to lay before Congress.[2]

Observing that the petitioners are generally in very indigent circumstances—much attached to the United States, and that the whole expense of resurveying their ancient possessions, *will,* by an estimate of the surveyor, amount to about one thousand dollars.

With every sentiment of the highest respect, I have the honour to be Sir, Your most obedient, and most devoted servant,

Winthrop Sargent

LB, DNA: RG 59, Territorial Papers, Northwest, 1787–1801.

On 27 Oct., GW received this letter and its enclosures, which included copies of the letters Sargent wrote as secretary of the Northwest Territory during the first half of 1792 (see Tobias Lear to Thomas Jefferson, 28 Oct. 1792, DNA: RG 59, Miscellaneous Letters).

1. Sargent is referring to the extended absence of judges George Turner and John Cleves Symmes from the Northwest Territory. It was not until the fall of 1792 that Secretary of State Thomas Jefferson wrote on behalf of the president to Turner and to Gov. Arthur St. Clair "to bring this circumstance to your notice, not doubting but that the public exigencies of your Office will overweigh in your mind any personal inconveniencies, which might attend your repairing to that Country" (Jefferson to Turner, 9 Nov., to St. Clair, 10 Nov. 1792, *Jefferson Papers,* 24:604–5).

2. On 27 Nov. 1792 the House of Representatives read a copy of this letter and a "petition of a number of inhabitants of St. Vincennes, on the Wabash, praying that the resurvey of their lands, directed by a late law, may be made at the public expense," both of which it referred to a committee composed of Samuel Livermore, Frederick Augustus Conrad Muhlenberg, and George Leonard. On 31 Dec. the House considered the committee's report, resolved that the resurvey "be made at the expense of the United States," and asked that a bill "be brought in, pursuant to the said resolution." The bill, which was presented to the House of Representatives on 7 Jan. 1793, passed in the House on 6 Feb. and in the Senate on 13 February. GW signed "An Act to repeal part of a Resolution of Congress of the twenty-ninth of August, one thousand seven hundred and eighty-eight, respecting the inhabitants of Post Saint Vincents" on 21 Feb. 1793 (*Annals of Congress,* 2d Cong., 728–29, 768–69, 801, 863, 1431; *Journal of the Senate,* 5:55).

From Mason Locke Weems

[6 July 1792][1]

Sensible that it ever affords a heartfelt pleasure to your Excellency to promote the happiness of Mankind, and knowing how eminently Almighty God has put it into your power to Advance the Welfare of the Citizens of *these States,* I take the liberty of Solicting Your excellency's Patronage to a Work which is evidently and most *happily* calculated to enlarge the Reign of Piety and Virtue among that Class of Citizens (I mean the *Great*) whose Examples have the weightiest Influence on the Manners of the Community. I am endeavoring to give the Public, a large Edition of the Celebrated *Doctor Blair's Sermons,* in which, Just Sentiments, a Glowing Piety, and Amiable Affections are set forth in such Elegant & harmonious Language as to be read with considerable Avidity by those very Persons who woud reject Other Discourses of equal Piety but unhappily destitute of their *external* Grace and Ornament.[2] It was suggested to me that were your *excellency* & Some Other Leading Characters in Philadelphia to Shew a good will to this Work it might greatly Augment & Accelerate its Progress. I brought Letters to his Excellency the Governor,[3] to Mr Morris Mr Barclay &c. &c. Some I have presented. Mr Morris not only patroniz'd by Subscription, but Voluntarily Offerd his Interest with his Friends—had Doctor Wm Smith or the British Consul[4] been at home, Shd perhaps been *introduced* to your Excellency, as I happen to be related to those Gentlemen. Tho' I *was once* introduced to your Excellency by Doctor Craik. Shoud your Excellency think well to patronize & encourage this extensively Diffusive way of propogating these Valuable Discourses You will find that Mr Morris has left a Chasm Just above his Signature and for that purpose, I told Mr Morris that Doctor Craik had introduced me to your Excellency some Years ago at M. Vernon.[5] he Observd "it was unnecessary to get any further introduction." With Sentiments of the highest Veneration I remain Your excellency's Friend & Well Wisher

Mason L. Weems.

ALS, PHi: Gratz Collection; ALS (photocopy), DLC:GW.

Mason Locke Weems (1759–1825) was born in Anne Arundel County, Md., raised in England, and ordained an Anglican priest in 1784. He returned to the United States in that year to serve as rector of All Hallows Parish at South River in Anne Arundel County. In later years Weems supported his wife and ten children by serving as a preacher and bookseller and as the author of numerous moral essays and biographies. His 1800 biography of GW was one of the earliest to be written.

1. This letter is docketed in part, "6th July 1792."

2. In 1795 Weems sent GW a copy of Hugh Blair's *Sermons. To Which Is Pre-*

fixed That Admired Tract, On the Internal Evidence of the Christian Religion (Baltimore, reprinted for Weems, 1792–93), which "you were so good as to patronize; and for which you paid" (DLC:GW). It was in GW's library at the time of his death (Griffin, *Boston Athenæum Washington Collection,* 503).

3. Thomas Mifflin (1744–1800), who had served as a member of the Continental Congress 1774–75 and 1782–84, major general in the Continental army during the Revolutionary War, Speaker of the Pennsylvania house of representatives 1785–88, and president of the state's supreme executive council 1788–90, was governor of Pennsylvania 1790–99.

4. Phineas Bond (1749–1815), who had graduated from the College of Philadelphia in 1766 and had worked as a lawyer before having his property seized and his professional life disrupted during the American Revolution because of his Loyalist sympathies, was appointed British consul at Philadelphia and commissary for commercial affairs in North America in April 1786. He served in that capacity until the beginning of the War of 1812.

5. GW noted in his diary entry for 3 Mar. 1787 that "Revd. Mr. Weems, and yg. Doctr. Craik who came here [to Mount Vernon] yesterday in the afternoon left this about Noon" (*Diaries,* 5:112).

To Thomas Jefferson

Saturday [7 July 1792][1]

Pray send me Mr Hammond's communications to you on thursday & your letter to him in answer;[2] and let me see you at Eight 'Oclock this Morng. Yrs

G.W.

ALS, DLC: Jefferson Papers.

1. Jefferson's docket indicates that this note was received on Saturday, 7 July 1792.

2. For British minister George Hammond's letter to Jefferson of Thursday, 5 July, see Jefferson to GW, 5 July, n.1; for Jefferson's response of 6 July, see Jefferson to GW, 6 July, n.1. On 9 July, Jefferson wrote Hammond two letters. In the first letter Jefferson gave as the reason for the delay in providing the administration's answer to the British complaint that he "could not be assured of expressing to Mr. Hammond, in conversation, sentiments which should be really those of the government until there should have been a consultation on them; and that consultation has been retarded by particular accidents till this morning" (*Jefferson Papers,* 24:202). In his second letter Jefferson expressed his regret "that while the grounds of difference between our respective countries are under amicable discussion, any circumstances should arise on either side, which might excite questions of still greater delicacy or tend to disturb or imbarrass the course of the discussion. We have no information on our part of the facts which are the subject of your letter of the 5th. but the Governor of

Vermont [Thomas Chittenden] will be immediately applied to for such information, on the receipt of which no time shall be lost in taking thereon those measures which shall appear proper." Jefferson assured Hammond "of our sincere dispositions to cultivate harmony on our borders and a friendly understanding in general between the two nations" and said that the "present imbarrassment, arising so unexpectedly, is a proof how important it is to hasten to a conclusion the general settlement of our rights" (ibid., 202–3). In his letter to Governor Chittenden of this date, Jefferson asked for the needed information and emphasized "that no measures be permitted in your state, which, by changing the present state of things in districts where the British have hitherto exercised jurisdiction, might disturb the peaceable and friendly discussion now in hand, and retard, if not defeat, an ultimate arrangement" (ibid., 200; see also Jefferson to Chittenden, Hammond to Jefferson, and Jefferson to Hammond, all 12 July, ibid., 218–21). For the background to the Alburg controversy, see Chittenden to GW, 16 June, and note 1.

From Thomas Jefferson

[Philadelphia] 7 July 1792. Sends "a recommendation of a candidate for keeping the lighthouse at Cape Henry."[1]

AL, DNA: RG 59, Miscellaneous Letters; LB, DNA: RG 59, George Washington's Correspondence with His Secretaries of State; LB (photocopy), DLC:GW.

1. The enclosure was a recommendation of John Waller Johnston written by David Meade Randolph of Presque Isle, Va., on 30 June and addressed to Jefferson (DLC:GW). Although Alexander Hamilton, on 22 Sept., and Jefferson, on 8 Dec., forwarded additional recommendations of Johnston to the president (both DLC:GW), Johnston apparently never received an appointment from GW.

From John Kean

Sir Philadelphia July 7th 1792.

The Commission with which I have this day been honored is a mark of your approbation highly grateful to me—I shall endeavour by my actions to merit & preserve it.[1]

My present occupation will not permit me to appropriate to the expediting this business so much of my time as I could wish & the nature of the service may require; but no exertion shall be wanting on my part so far as my time will allow to facilitate the exertions of my Colleagues to bring the business to as speedy a conclusion as the nature of the case will admit of.[2] With sentiments of the most exalted esteem I have the honor to be sir Yr Obt Servt

John Kean

ALS, DNA: RG 59, Miscellaneous Letters.

1. For Kean's attempt on 31 Oct. 1791 to resign as one of the commissioners to settle the Revolutionary War accounts between the United States and the individual states because of his appointment as cashier of the Bank of the United States and GW's successful effort to dissuade him from that course, see GW to Kean, 10 Nov. 1791, and source note. The "Commission" Kean is referring to is the agreement that he continue to serve as one of the commissioners settling Revolutionary War accounts.

2. The commissioners submitted their final report to GW in late June 1793, and GW forwarded it to Congress in early December of that year (see Commissioners for Settling Revolutionary War Accounts to GW, 29 June 1793; *Journal of the House,* 6:19).

From George Augustine Washington

Sulpher Springs Berkley County [Va.]
10 Miles from my Fathers

Honor'd Uncle July 7th 1792

I wrote You the 24th Ulto that I had contrary to my fixed resolution of returning to my Mount Vernon in a fortnight been tempted to procrastinate the time—from the flattering hope of benefiting my health,[1] which is really so precarious that I am at a loss what to say about it—I am some times for three or four days tantalized with a belief that I am geting better but by the slightest cold (which with all the prudence I can use am very subject to) my indisposition is increasd—not experiencing that advantage which I had flatterd myself with and anxiously wishing to return I had determind t⟨o⟩ do it but have been over rooled by the advise of a Physician in this County whose skill I have confidence in, to delay my return for a short time, and by the effects of this water which he doubted not I should find beneficial, as he did not think my disorder consumptive and if it was should the waters disagree with me I might desist in the use of it—my complaints are complicated, my head which is frequently and severely disorderd is I apprehend either rheumattic or nervous, for which complaints this spring has been found very advantageus—I came here yesturday and unless I here some unfavorable accounts from Mt Vernon (which I hope will not be the case) mean to continue a fortnight if I find I am like to benefit from it—I very reluctantly consente⟨d⟩ to a longer absence and nothing short of the desireable object I am in persuit of would tempt me—if I can only regain a tolerable share of health I promise myself much satisfaction from Yours and my Aunts return to Mt Vernon—No conveyance offering immediately to Philadelphia I forward this by a Gentleman to Frederick Town to be put in the Post Office at that place—I feel a constant concern for the health and happiness of Yourself my Aunt & the Children and believe me to be with the most unbounded attachment Your truely affectionate Nephew

Go. A. Washington

I beg my good wishes to be offerd to Mr & Mrs Lear the Gentlemen of Your family my Cousins Geo: & L: Washington.

ALS, ViMtV.

For the background to George Augustine Washington's bouts of ill health during the early 1790s and their continuance throughout the summer of 1792, see G. A. Washington to GW, 26 June, source note and note 1.

1. G. A. Washington's previous letter to GW was written on 26, not 24, June 1792.

From Alexander Hamilton

Treasury Department July 8. 1792

The Secretary of the Treasury has the honor respectfully to submit to the President of the United States the inclosed Contract between the Superintendant of the Delaware Lighthouse &[c]a and Benjamin Rice, for the making of two Mooring chains for the use of the Beacon boats on the River Delaware, together with sundry papers relating thereto. The object appears to be a necessary one, & the terms comparatively good. The amount of the Expence will be Four hundred & twenty Dollars. All which is humbly submitted.[1]

Alex. Hamilton
Secy of the Treasury

LB, DLC:GW.

1. On 10 July, Tobias Lear wrote Hamilton at GW's command to inform him that the president approved of the contract (DLC:GW).

To Thomas Jefferson

[Philadelphia] July 9th 1792.

Pray draught a proper answer to the enclosed,[1] approving of what the Director of the Mint has done, and is about to do; and requesting an estimate of the money which will be wanted to enable him to proceed in the business of Coining agreeably to what he proposes.

Go: Washington

ALS, DLC: Jefferson Papers.

1. The enclosed letter from David Rittenhouse to GW of this date reads: "Tho' a long continued state of ill health has left me little relish for the usual pursuits of Interest or Ambition, I am nevertheless extremely sensible of the honour you have done me by appointing me, unsollictted, Director of the Mint. Having by the advice of my friends determined to accept that office, for the present, I think it my duty to give every assistance in my power to the business, and have taken the Oath of office required by law.

"On consulting the Secretary of State I find that some of the Officers for the Mint are still expected from Europe. This will occasion further delay, as least as to going generally into Coining. But as small money is very much wanted we think proper, in the mean time, if Your Excellency approves of it, to Coin some Copper Cents & half Cents, and likewise small Silver, at least Dismes & half Dismes. I have purchased, on Account of the United States, a House and Lot which I hope will be found Convenient for the Mint, but considerable alterations must be made, and some small new buildings erected. I have likewise engaged Mr [Henry] Voight to act as Coiner, and he has several workmen now employed in making the necessary Engines, and preparing the Dies. A quantity of Copper will be wanted; perhaps 15 Tons might be sufficient, and Measures for procuring it ought to be immediately taken, and for these several purposes some money will be required.

"I shall be happy in receiving your Excellency's approbation of these preparatory Steps, together with such further directions as You may think proper to give" (DNA: RG 59, Miscellaneous Letters).

To David Rittenhouse

United States of America [Philadelphia, 9 July 1792]

Having had under consideration the letter of the Director of the mint of this day's date, I hereby declare my approbation of the purchase he has made of the house and lot for the mint, of the employment of mr Voight as Coiner, of the procuring fifteen tons of copper, & proceeding to coin the cents and half cents of copper & dismes & half dismes of silver: and I leave to his discretion to have such alterations and additions made to the buildings purchased as he shall find necessary, satisfied that under his orders no expence will be incurred which reason & necessity will not justify: and I desire that he will make out an estimate of the sums of money which will be wanting for these purposes & of the times at which they will be wanting, in order to enable the treasury to make arrangements for furnishing them with convenience.[1] given under my hand this 9th day of July 1792.

Copy, in Thomas Jefferson's hand, DNA: RG 59, Miscellaneous Letters; LB, DLC:GW.

Earlier on 9 July, Jefferson had sent GW "two forms of approbation of the proposals of the Director of the mint. that which would be to be signed by the President himself would probably be most satisfactory to the Director, but might be liable to the objection of drawing the President into the details of business with a greater number of officers of government. this on the other hand would sometimes shorten business. the President will decide and make use of which he pleases" (DNA: RG 59, Miscellaneous Letters). The unused version of Jefferson's draft was written as a response to Rittenhouse from the secretary of state (DLC: Jefferson Papers).

1. For Rittenhouse's "Estimate of immediate Expenditures for the Mint" and the payment of the entire $10,000 as a lump sum, see GW to Alexander Hamilton, 10 July 1792.

To David Stuart

Dear Sir, Philadelphia July 9th 1792.

Although I did not acknowledge the receipt of the letter you wrote to me some time ago respecting Bowl[e]s, I was not unmindful of the contents:[1] but upon consulting[2] some Professional Gentlemen I was informed that his being brother to the noted Bowls was not, without some overt act of his own, sufft to lay hold of him.

If nothing more happens than I am aware of at present, I shall leave this City on thursday, with Mrs Washington and the Children for Mount Vernon; and if the weather is tolerable, and ourselves and horses keep up, I shall be, I expect, at George town on Monday or tuesday of the week following.[3]

I shall bring with me, or send on if I am likely to be delayed, the plans for the public buildings which were sent (I believe) by the Commissioners, to Mr Jefferson; but, if none more elegant than these should appear[4] on, or before the 16th instt the exhibition of Architecture will be a very dull one indeed.[5] My best wishes to Mrs Stuart & the family—& I am—Dear Sir Yr Obedt & Affecte Hble Servt

G. W——n

ADfS, DNA: RG 59, Miscellaneous Letters; LB, DLC:GW.

1. Stuart had informed GW in his letter of 4 June of the visit of William Augustus Bowles's brother John to Georgetown.

2. At this place on the draft manuscript, GW wrote and then struck out the phrase: "advising with some of the gentlemen learned in the Law."

3. GW left Philadelphia on the afternoon of Wednesday, 11 July. He was in Georgetown during the first part of the following week (see GW to Thomas Jefferson, 17 July, to the Commissioners for the District of Columbia, 8 June, n.3).

4. At this place on the draft manuscript, GW wrote and then struck out the phrase: "it matters not."

5. On 6 June the D.C. commissioners sent Jefferson "for the Presidents view, a Draft for the Capitol by Wm. [Philip] Hart of Taney Town, and an imperfect Essay of Mr. [Abraham] Faw. These are all we have yet received" (*Jefferson Papers,* 24:36). On 5 July the commissioners informed Jefferson that "We have received several plans for the public Buildings, which we had prepared to send forward; and expect several more will be presented; but as we have just heard, from the Presidents Steward, that he may be expected here, by the 15th Instant; we shall . . . retain them for his inspection and choice here" (ibid., 159).

To Alexander Hamilton

[Philadelphia] 10th July 1792.

Estimate of immediate Expenditures for the Mint.[1]

	Dollars.
Price of the House & Lot, to be paid on executing the Conveyance	4266.⅔
15 Tons of Copper, suppose 16 Cents ℔ lb.	4800.
Repairs of the Buildings, Workmen's wages &c.	933.⅓
Dollars	10,000.

David Rittenhouse

United States [Philadelphia] 10th July 1792

The Secretary of the Treasury will cause to be paid to the Director of the Mint, Ten thousand Dollars for the purposes above specified.

G: Washington

LB, DLC:GW.

1. For the background to this document, see GW to Thomas Jefferson and GW to David Rittenhouse, both 9 July 1792. For Rittenhouse's earlier estimate of the funds needed by the U.S. Mint, which also totaled $10,000, see Jefferson to GW, 20 June (second letter).

Jefferson's Conversation with Washington

July 10. 1792.

My lettre of [ ] to the President, directed to him at Mt Vernon, had not found him there, but came to him here.[1] He told me of this & that he would take an occasion of speaking with me on the subject. he did so this day. he began by observing that he had put it off from day to day because the subject was painful, to wit his remaining in office which that letter sollicited. he said that the declaration he had made when he quitted his military command of never again acting in public was sincere.[2] that however when he was called on to come forward to set the present govment in motion, it appeared to him that circumstances were so changed as to justify a change in his resolution: he was made to believe that in 2 years all would be well in motion & he might retire. at the end of two years he found some things still to be done. at the end of the 3d year he thought it was not worth while to disturb the course of things as in one year more his office would expire & he was decided then to retire. now he was told there would still be danger in it. certainly if he thought so, he would conquer his longing for retirement. but he feared it would be said his former professions of retirement had been mere affetation, & that he was like other men, when once in office he could not quit it. he was sensible too of a decay of his hearing perhaps his other faculties might fall off & he not be sensible of it. that with respect to the existing causes of uneasiness, he thought there were suspicions against a particular party which had been carried a gre⟨at⟩ deal too far, there might be *desires,* but he did not believe there were *designs* to change the form of govmt into a monarchy. that there might be a few who wished it in the higher walks of life, particularly in the great cities, but that the main body of the people in the Eastern states were steadily for republicanism as in the Southern. that the peices lately published, & particularly in Freneau's paper seemed to have in view the exciting opposition to the govment.[3] that this had taken place in Pennsylvania as to the excise law, according to information he had recd from Genl Hand that they tended to produce a separation of the union, the most dreadful of all calamities,[4] and that whatever tended to produce anarchy tended of course to produce a resort to monarchical govment. he considered those papers as attacking him directly, for he must be a fool inde[e]d to swallow the little sugar plumbs here & there thrown out to him. that in condemning the administration of the govment they condemned him, for if they thought there were measures pursued contrary to his sentiment, they must conceive him too careless to attend to them or too stupid to understand them. that tho indeed he had signed many acts which he did not approve in all their parts, yet he had never put his name to one which he did not think on the whole was eligible. that as to the bank which had been an act of so much complaint, until there were some infallible criterion of reason, a difference of opinion must be tolerated. he did not believe the discontents extended far from the seat of govment. he had seen & spoken with many people in Maryld & Virginia in his late journey.[5] he found the people contented & happy. he asked however to be better informed on this head—if the discontent were more extensive than he supposed, it might be that the desire that he should remain in the government was not general.

My observations to him tended principally to enforce the topics of my lettre. I will not therefore repeat them except where they produced observations from him. I said that the two great complaints were that the national debt was unnecessarily increased, & that it had furnished the means of corrupting both branches of the legislature. that he must know & every body knew there was a considerable squadron in both whose votes were devoted to the paper & stockjobbing interest, that the names of a weighty number were known & several others suspected on good grounds. that on examining the votes of these men they would be found uniformly for every treasury measure, & that as most of these measures had been carried by small majorities they were carried by these very votes. that therefore it was a cause of just uneasiness when we saw a legislature legislating for their own interests in opposition to those of the people. he said not a word on the corruption of the legislature, but took up the other point, defended the assumption, & argued that it had not increased the debt, for that all of it was honest debt. he justified the excise law, as one of the best laws which could be past, as nobody would pay the tax who did not chuse to do it. with respect to the increase of the debt by the assumption I observed to him that what was meant & objected was that it increased the debt of the general govmt and carried it beyond the possibility of paiment. that if the balances had been settled & the debtor states directed to pay their deficiencies to the creditor states, they would have done it easily, and by resources of taxation in their power, and acceptable to the people, by a direct tax in the South, & an excise in the North. still he said it would be paid by the people. finding him really approving the treasury system I avoided entering into argument with him on those points.

AD, in Jefferson's hand, DLC: Jefferson Papers.

1. Jefferson is referring to his second letter to GW of 23 May 1792.

2. GW is referring to his Circular to the States of 8–21 June 1783 (LS, NNPM).

3. For more information about Philip Freneau and the *National Gazette,* see Anonymous to GW, March 1792, n.3.

4. GW had nominated and the Senate had confirmed Edward Hand as one of Pennsylvania's three excise inspectors in early March 1792 (see GW to the U.S. Senate, 6 Mar. [third letter]).

5. GW had left Philadelphia for Mount Vernon on 10 May and after a brief visit apparently began his return trip on 24 May 1792.

Tobias Lear to Henry Knox

United States [Philadelphia] July 10th 1792

By the President's command T. Lear has the honor to return to the Secretary of War the enclosed letters from Governors Lee & Telfair which have been submitted to the President, and to inform the Secretary that the President requests that any answer to these letters which may require his inspection, may be submitted to him by twelve o'clock tomorrow, as he intends setting out for Virginia in the afternoon.[1]

Tobias Lear
Secretary to the President
of the United States.

ALS (retained copy), DLC:GW; LB, DLC:GW.

1. The letters from governors Edward Telfair of Georgia and Henry Lee of Virginia to the secretary of war that Knox had forwarded to the president for his consideration have not been identified. It is not clear whether GW received drafts of Knox's replies to Telfair and Lee before leaving for Mount Vernon on the afternoon of 11 July.

Letter not found: from John Francis Mercer, 10 July 1792. In his letter to Mercer of 23 July, GW referred to "Your favor of the 10th."

Letter not found: from Alexander Spotswood, 10 July 1792. On 23 July, GW wrote Spotswood a letter in which he mentioned "your favor of the 10th."

From Thomas Jefferson

[Philadelphia, 11 July 1792][1]

Th: Jefferson with his respects to the President sends him a letter to received by which he will perceive that mister Blodget has deposited with the two Boston banks 10,000 Doll. subject to the draught of the Commissioners.[2]

also two proof sheets of the city: recd from Boston.[3]

AL, DNA: RG 59, Miscellaneous Letters; LB, DNA: RG 59, George Washington's Correspondence with His Secretaries of State; LB (photocopy), DLC:GW.

1. The dockets on the autograph letter and the letter-book copy both indicate that this note was written on 11 July 1792.

2. For the enclosed letter, see Samuel Blodget, Jr., to Jefferson, 25 June 1792, in *Jefferson Papers*, 24:119–20. For more information about Blodget's loan proposal, see GW to the Commissioners for the District of Columbia, 6 Mar., and note 7, Jefferson to GW, c.21 Mar., and note 2, and GW to Jefferson, 21, 30 Mar., and 3 April 1792.

3. Harrison Gray Otis, the bearer of Blodget's letter to Jefferson, also had delivered "four first Impressions of the City of Washington, from the plate executed by your order" by Samuel Hill of Boston (ibid., 119–20). For earlier attempts to have a plan of the Federal City engraved by M. Pigalle, see GW to Tobias Lear, 2 Oct., n.5, and Lear to GW, 6, 9, 11 Oct. 1791. For the revision of Pierre L'Enfant's original draft by Jefferson and Andrew Ellicott, see GW to Jefferson, 15, 28 Feb. 1792; see also the editorial note, "Fixing the Seat of Government," ibid., 20:63–69. For the employment of Hill as the engraver of a *Plan of the City of Washington in the Territory of Columbia, Ceded by the States of Virginia and Maryland to the United States of America* . . . (Boston, 1792), see GW to Jefferson, 4 Mar., and notes 3 and 4, to the Commissioners for the District of Columbia, 6 Mar. 1792, n.8; see also the editorial note, "Fixing the Seat of

Government," and Blodget to Jefferson, 20 April, 3 May 1792, ibid., 20:68–69, 23:437, 479–80.

Tobias Lear to Thomas Jefferson

[Philadelphia] July 11t[h] 1792

The President of the U.S. informs the Secretary of State that he has retained one of the proof Sheets of the federal City, and returns the others with the letter from Mr Blodget, which the President thinks had better be sent to the Commissioners by the mail, which will certainly reach G. Town on Monday.[1] The President's Cavalry are in such order that he cannot say with any precision when he shall reach that place; he however, wishes the Secretary to mention to the Commissioners that he sat out this afternoon; but being incumbered with lame and sick horses it is uncertain when he will be at George-Town.[2]

The President observes that the soundings of the River & Branch are not noted either in this or the other proof sheet, which he thinks would be very satisfactory & advantageous to have done.[3]

AL, DLC: Jefferson Papers.

1. Jefferson immediately dispatched Blodget's letter to the commissioners for the District of Columbia (*Jefferson Papers,* 24:212). GW expected that letter to reach Georgetown by Monday, 16 July.

2. At GW's command Bartholomew Dandridge wrote Gabriel P. Van Horne from Baltimore on 14 July "that one of the Presidents horses, which had been sick previous to his leaving Philada, was so far reduced & tired by the time he reached Bush-town that the President was under the necessity of leaving him at that place in care of Mrs [Elizabeth] Stiles. The P——nt requests the favor of you, to enquire, & as soon as the horse is able to travel that you will contrive to send him to Alexa.—either by driving him in one of your Stage Coaches (as he is a carriage horse) or by causing one of your Stage Drivers to lead him. The President will willingly pay any expence which may attend the sending the horse to Alexa." (DLC:GW). GW arrived at Georgetown by 17 July (see GW to Jefferson, that date).

3. Jefferson wrote to Blodget on 12 July: "the soundings are not in the sheets you send me. I have written to the Commissioners recommending to desire Mr. [Andrew] Ellicot, if they were not in the original, to insert them in one of these proof sheets and forward it to you that they may be put into the plate" (*Jefferson Papers,* 24:218). Unfortunately Jefferson had been sent prints, not proof sheets, and the engraving plate was already on its way to Philadelphia (ibid., 20:17–18, n.46).

Letter not found: to James McHenry, c.11 July 1792. McHenry wrote GW on 17 July that he had received GW's letter, noting: "It has the Philadelphia post mark of the 11th."

From John Churchman

Bank Street Baltimore July 14th 1792.

J. Churchman presents his compliments to the President of the united States, having lately received several Letters from Baron Vall-Travers, in which one is mentioned to be sent by Captain Folgier, which has not come to hand, Understanding that Captain Folgier delivered some Letters last Spring to the President from the Baron,[1] J.C. would be very glad to know, in any way the least troublesome, whether any one came for him at that time, he could never think of troubling the President on this occasi⟨on⟩ if the Baron had not heretofore written to him under cover directed to the Presiden⟨t⟩ he begs leave to add that he informed Vall-Travers what he had in charge.[2]

AL, DNA: RG 59, Miscellaneous Letters.

1. On 6 Feb. 1792 Capt. Frederick Folger of Baltimore had forwarded to the president Rodolph Vall-travers's letter to GW of 21 July 1791 and its enclosures.

2. At GW's behest Bartholomew Dandridge replied to Churchman on this day "that the President cannot recollect the precise times that letters from Baron Vall Travers have come under cover to him for Mr Churchman; but the President is very certain none ever came which were not forwarded to Mr Churchman" (DNA: RG 59, Miscellaneous Letters). For Vall-travers's use of the president as a means to get letters and other materials to Churchman, see Vall-travers to GW, 20 Mar., 21 July 1791, and Tobias Lear to Churchman, 10 Sept. 1791.

From Henry Knox

Sir War Department, July 14th 1792.

The last post which left Pittsburgh on the 6th instant, brings information of entire tranquility on the frontiers.

General Wayne has desired to know what conduct he is to pursue relative to the Small pox—that disorder being at Pittsburgh.

I have informed him that it would be improper to innoculate at this time as well on account of the warm season of the year, as the crisis of affairs.

The Returns of additional Recruits are enclosed.[1] I have the honor to be with the most perfect Respect Your hume servant

H. Knox

LS, DLC:GW; LB, DLC:GW.

1. On 9 July 1792 Knox had sent GW a detailed "Schedule of the" 1,599 "Recruits actually marched and ordered to march from the respective rendezvous" (DLC:GW). In the enclosed return Knox reported that a further 73 recruits had arrived by 14 July, making a grand total of 1,672 soldiers present and accounted for (DLC:GW).

From Tobias Lear

Sir, New York July 15th 1792

I have the honor to inform you that we arrivd here last evening after a pleasant journey from Phila. and shall sail for Providence in about an hour. I have thought it best, & upon the whole most œconomical to take a water carriage to Providence.

The principal object in troubling you with a letter at this time is to mention that while I was on board the Packet this morning engaging a passage I met with Colo. Stevens of this place & in the course of conversation upon general subjects he made enquiry respecting the federal City, and from thence took occasion to observe that he had been applied to to superinte[n]d the new manufacturing town to be built in Jersey, but he did not think the compensation offered (2000 dols. / per Annum) a sufficient object to induce him to leave his business in this place; and at the same time observed that a business of this kind was peculiarly suited to his genius & inclination & that he should not have hesitated one moment about accepting the offer made him if the compensation p⟨*mutilated*⟩ equalled his p[r]esent business. He asked if a person was engaged to superintend the public works to be carried on at the city, in the place of Major L'Enfant, I told him I did not know of any one who was absolutely engaged.[1]

I have just mentioned this conversation, Sir, that if a person of

Colo. Stevens' character shoud be wanted for the purpose of superintending the works at the City, your thoughts might thereby be called to him, as otherwise he might not occur—His fitness you are able to judge of from your Knowledge of him during the war.[2]

Mrs Lear & our little boy are in good health and unite with me in respec[t], gratitude, and Sincere prayers for the health & happines of yourself, Mrs Washington & the family. With truth & sincerity I have the honor to be Sir Your most obedt & grateful Servt

Tobias Lear.

ALS, DNA: RG 42, General Records, Letters Received, 1792–1797.

Lear, who had doubted as recently as mid-June that he would be able to visit New England this summer, left Philadelphia on 12 July to gauge popular support for GW's reelection, find a teacher willing to set up a school in the U.S. capital to educate GW's step-grandson, and as he wrote Benjamin Lincoln in early September 1792, "to establish my mother . . . in a situation where she may reasonably expect to spend the remainder of her days in a comfortable & independent manner" (Brighton, *Checkered Career of Tobias Lear,* 104–6). Lear and his family returned to Philadelphia on 7 October. For the other letters exchanged between GW and Lear during the latter's tour of New England, see Lear to GW, 21 July, 5 Aug., 23 Sept., 7 Oct. 1792, GW to Lear, 30 July, 21 Sept., 1 Oct. 1792.

1. After Pierre L'Enfant's resignation the D.C. commissioners appointed Andrew Ellicott to head the surveying department. In the summer and fall of 1792, Ellicott and his assistants made a survey of the boundary of the federal district and began laying out the Federal City.

2. GW forwarded Lear's letter to the D.C. commissioners on 23 July with the comment that Ebenezer Stevens was apparently "a Sober, honest & good tempered man—Very industrious—Fertile in invention & resources—and great at execution." Nothing came of Stevens's application, however.

From Edward Newenham

Dear Sir, Bellchampe [Ireland] 15 July 1792

Permit me, in the warmest manner, to Introduce to yr Excellency, Mr Anderson, who, together with all his Family have been my most Zealous friends upon all occasions.

Encouraged by the rising Prosperity of the United States, joined with the Principles of its Government, he has turned a good part of his Property into *ready money,* & intends to settle, with his Children, in some one of the States; he goes first to Philadelphia, & will there have the Honor of paying you his respects, in order personaly to see the MAN, whom he always admired.[1]

He is not fixed, whether he will enter into the Mercantile Line, or become a purchaser of Land; that depends on the advice he gets; he has neither Connections or Acquaintance in America, & Since, the Death of my Ever respected & Dear Freind Doctor Franklin, I have none, but your Excellencey to recommend him to, which I take the Liberty of doing it—He is of a respectable Private Family here & has always maintaind the best of Characters.

Lady Newenham joins me in Sincere Respects, & fervent wishes for yours & Mrs Washingtons health & happiness. I have the Honor, to be, with perfect Respect & Esteem your Excellencys most obt & most Hble Servt

Edward Newenham

ALS, DLC:GW.

1. GW replied to Newenham on 20 Oct. 1792 that he had "received yours of the 15th of July introducing Mr Anderson," but he did not indicate whether or not he had met him personally.

From Giuseppe Ceracchi

Sir Amsterdam 16 july 1792

No man is happier then I'm in this moment, for I rely feel a trù satisfactory honor in addressing the President of the Unit. Stat's.

I shall communicate this sensetion to my Cildren, they shall learn to pronounce General Washingtons' name with the highst admiration, and shall, inspire the desire to addresse personaly the Hero of America universily admired trowout the world.

My worth being to little, I have nothing to offer but the greatfull sentiments end veneretion with which I'm Sir your most obt end most Humble Servt

Joseph Ceracchi

ALS, DLC:GW.

On this day Ceracchi also wrote Martha Washington: "Besides the generality of Gentilmen, all the Ladyes in Oland are ravished at the sight of my model that rappresents General Washington, what dignity they sais, what solidity shows in his mind. happy must be the Lady that posseses his heart. In this occasion Madame I feel the graet advantage of indolging my self, I informe the Ladyes of the high end Eminent Caracter of the Person to which I have the honnor to dedicate my perfait Estime end Respectes" (DLC:GW). For the terra-cotta model that Ceracchi executed from life in the winter of 1791 or the early spring of 1792, see Ceracchi to GW, 31 Oct. 1791, source note.

From Thomas Chittenden

Sir, Vermont Williston July 16th 1792

Before this time I conclude you have recived my Letter of the 16th of June Incloling Sundry affidavits relaletive to the abuses lately offred this as well as the united Stats by the officers & Soldiers Stationed at Point au farr togeather with a Copy of my Letter to Leiut. Governor Clarke upon the Subject.[1]

I now have the Honor to Transmit to your Excellency a Copy of Governor Clarke's answer to me I shall make no Commints upon the equivocal and evasive manner in which it is written.[2]

as I was Sensible that the Conduct of this garrison might Involve questions of national Importance and desarve a national discursion I took the earliest oppertunity of transmiting to your Excellency the Information I had recived upon the Subject, but as the Injury was more immediately felt by the Citizens of this State I Consider my Self Justifiable in requsting of the Commanding officer at Quebec an Explanation of So new and unprecedented abuses from that Quarter Imprest with the Idea that what had been don was without his order or approbation. I Submit to your Excellency how fair I have acted prudant in this Bisness or what futher or differant measures I Should have taken.

I thint it my duty further to observe that Alburgh is a tongue of land Seperate from the main land Canted Point a fer by the waters of Lake Champlain. Containing abought Sixteen Thousand acres and is from three to Ten mils distant from the garrison it contains between Sixty & Seventy heads of famileys Including abought five Hundred Souls.

A part of the Settlers possessed the Land as an old french Seignory the other part as a grant under the authority of the State of Vermont. the formor Settlers finding their Title Invalid and wishing to avail themselvs of a Title under vermont in order to Secure to them Selvs the reward of their toils Assimbled with the other Inhabitance and Easily in the munth of June organized as a Town agreeably to the Laws of this State and took the Necessary oaths to Intitle them Selvs to the privilege of free men and citizenship, within this State—and are—(a few only excepted) Solicitous not only to be protected but Governed by the Laws of this & the united Stats at the Last Session of the legislature in this State Two Justises ware appointed residunt at Alburgh who ware Soon after Sworn in to office. previos to their appointment the Inhabitance had not been the Subjects of any civil Government but the place had been too much a randizvous for outlaws and fugitives from Justice as their views are now meritorious it is to be hoped that every attempt to defeat them will meet its deserved recompence. I have the Honour to be your Excellencys very Hbl. Servt

T.C.

Copy, Vt.

1. For Governor Chittenden's letter to Alured Clarke of 16 June and the affidavits that he enclosed in his letter to GW of that date, see Walton, *Vermont Records,* 4:458–59, 465–69.

2. Acting governor Clarke's letter to Chittenden of 5 July reads in part: "Your representation leading to Questions beyond the sphere of my Trust, and being unaccompanied with the Proofs to be expected with Complaints of that kind, I can only give command for the Investigations to be obtained here on a Subject of such Importance to the Peace of the Border" (ibid., 460).

From Alexander Hamilton

Sir, Philadelphia July 16. 1792.

I have the honor to enclose a Resolution of the Commissioners of the Sinking Fund of the 16th inst:, for your consideration and approbation.[1]

My absence from Town and hurry after my return, prevented the making of the arrangement before you left this place.[2] I shall hope to receive your determination previous to the day which limits the receiving of proposals, as the purchases must be made within the month. Nothing else new has occurred since your departure.

With perfect respect & the truest attachment, I have the honor to be &c.

A: Hamilton.

LB, DLC:GW.

1. The commissioners of the sinking fund met on 13 July and resolved that as "there are, at their disposal, certain sums of money, arising from the funds assigned by law . . . That the said sums of money be applied, within the time limited by law, to the purchase of the several kinds of stock, at the lowest prices, pursuant to the directions of the law, and according to the rates prescribed in the last resolution of this Board, concerning such purchases. . . . That Samuel Meredith, Treasurer of the United States, be the agent for the foregoing purpose; that he receive sealed proposals to any amount; that he prefer the lowest offers; that he have regard, as far as may be, to the purchasing of equal proportions of the several kinds of stock; and that he advertise to receive proposals until the 28th of July, instant, inclusively" (*ASP, Finance,* 1:237).

2. Hamilton had attended a meeting of the Society for Establishing Useful Manufactures in Newark, N.J., on 4–7 July 1792. GW had left Philadelphia for Mount Vernon on 11 July.

From James Gibbon

Sir Petersburg, Virga July 17th 1792

Coll Carrington as Supervisor of the district of Virginia having been obliging enough to suggest to me the resignation of Coll Newton as Inspector of the th4 Suvey and that twas his intention to recommend me to succeed him—I have taken the liberty, in aid of his good offices in my behalf to trouble you with my own application[.] Having already acted under the Supervisors orders it is left for him to say how far I may be Entitled to yr favour in this case.[1]

The office of Surveyor of the port I have held with a hope that some compensation adequate to its duties wou'd have offerd in ⟨*illegible*⟩ tho I've heretofore been disappointed in this I'm not altogether without hope that a proper representation will yet effect it.[2]

As the duties of Inspector of the th4 Suvey and that of Surveyor of the customs are in a great degree combin'd and I belive in no instance incompatible so I shall feel myself happy if you Sir shou'd think proper to combine them[3] in the instance of him who is with very great respect Yr Oblig'd Humb. Servt

J. Gibbon

ALS, DLC:GW.

1. No written recommendation from Col. Edward Carrington to GW concerning James Gibbon's appointment as inspector of the fourth survey has been found.

2. Gibbon was appointed surveyor of the port of Petersburg, Va., in August 1789, and in March 1792 he became port inspector (see GW to the U.S. Senate, 3 Aug. 1789, 6 Mar. 1792 [third letter]; *Executive Journal,* 1:14, 104). For Gibbon's earlier request that he be appointed to a more remunerative post, see Gibbon to GW, 24 Jan. 1790.

3. GW did not accede to this request. On 19 Nov. 1792 he nominated Gibbon inspector of the fourth survey, and the Senate consented to Gibbon's appointment two days later (ibid., 125–26).

To Thomas Jefferson

Dear Sir George Town July 17th 1792

I am extremely sorry to find by the enclosed letter that the affairs of France put on so disagreeable an aspect.[1]

As I know it is your intention to proceed immediately on, I will not ask you to call at Mt Vernon now but hope it is unnecessary to say that I shall be glad to see you on your way going or Returning.[2] I am sincerely & Affecy Yrs

Go: Washington

ALS, DLC: Jefferson Papers. Jefferson docketed the ALS as having been received at Georgetown on 17 July 1792.

1. GW's enclosure has not been identified.

2. Jefferson briefly visited Mount Vernon on his journey to Monticello and on his return trip to Philadelphia (see GW to Jefferson, 23 July, and Jefferson's Conversation with Washington, 1 Oct. 1792).

From Carl Heinrich Kreppelin

Amsterdam, 17 July 1792. Encloses a letter from Professor Kilsberger of Mainz, who wishes GW to send him news of his brother through Kreppelin.

ALS, in German, DNA: RG 59, Miscellaneous Letters. This letter apparently was neither translated for nor acted upon by GW.

From James McHenry

Sir. Fayetteville [Md.] 17 July 1792.

The letter you did me the honor to write which I had not received when I had the honor to see you was handed me the day after. It has the Philadelphia post mark of the 11th and was they tell me overlooked by the post-master here or rather his assistant when my letters were called for. I thought it proper to mention this particular to you that the cause of its detention might not be misunderstood.[1]

I have now to request of my dear General, that he will on his return devote one day to *Baltimore town,* and that sometime before, you will be so kind as to let me know the day we may look for you. The merchants who have a sincere love and attatchment for you wish very much to give you a public dinner, which might perhaps be contrived without occasioning much delay, if you could arrange your stages so as to reach us early in the forenoon.[2]

Mrs McHenry begs to be presented to Mrs Washington. We both hope that the remainder of your journey was without accident and wish you that repose and happiness in your favorite Mount Vernon, to which you are so well intitled. I have the honor to be Sir, sincerely & affectionately[3] Yours

James McHenry

ALS, DLC:GW.

1. This letter has not been found. McHenry apparently saw the president while GW was on his way to Mount Vernon for a visit that would last until October 1792.

2. For GW's reply to McHenry expressing his willingness to "spend a day in Baltimore on my return to Philadelphia, if time & circumstances would permit" and his dislike of "formal & ceremonious engagements," see GW to McHenry, 13 August. For the Baltimore merchants' renewed request that GW stop in their city, see McHenry to GW, 25 Sept. 1792. GW and Martha Washington spent the night of 10–11 Oct. in Baltimore on their return to Philadelphia (*Baltimore Evening Post and Daily Advertiser,* 11 Oct. 1792).

3. McHenry mistakenly wrote "affectionalely" at this place on the manuscript.

From Eelko Alta

Sir Rauwerd [The Netherlands] July 19th 1792

for some time ago I observed in the *Patriotic Museum* a communication given by Mr Brissot concerning the œconomical transactions of your Excellency at your Country Seat, and also your attachment for agriculture and more particularly to that branch thereof, which is my principal Study. this encreassed the respect which I nourished towards you, contemplating You as the General of the United States, who so gloriously Resigned that Station, because Your Excellency gave thereby the exemple to people (who by the assistance of divine Providence are in debted to you for their liberty and independence) how to use and to cultivate their free land. this induced me to address your Excellency more so as I observed in Said communication, that your Excellency intended to give a *Specimen of artificial Pasturages, Seldom to be found in your country, and necessary as often the Cattle are in Want of pasturing*: which last article is not to be done but only to Separate a certain quantity of Pasturing from the general one by means of ditches or Small canals and to make Hay, which will be easily done by your Excellency through a number of negros, provided a Sufficient number of mowers can be obtained, which class of men come from Hanover & Oldenburg yearly to this Province of Friesland—and who in the expectation of a tolerable living would be easily engaged by me on the requisition of your Excellency, for I am apprehensive that the art to mow, is not well understood in America, and it is not only required to mow but more particularly to mow well, but all this will be explained more at large by the Rules to be laid down by me, which not only have in View to direct how to make artificial Pasturing, but also to improve the new made, this Subject having been my particular Study and by following my exemple and advice, is arrived to a great perfection in friesland, Since about fifty years also elswhere, even in Holland (were they do not cultivate the artificial pasturages according to the methode of friesland) and undoubtly in England as I am informed; but this may be otherwise, for I have never Seen the treatise of the renowed English Agriculturer *Arthur Young* on agriculture, notwithstanding this gentleman is known to me to be a Skillfull man out of the correspondence with my friend Trappe a Russish gentleman, who travelling to cultivate the knowledge of agriculture has been acquainted with him, and finishing his letter to me concluded with the Words of his friend A. Young Vive l'agriculture, but my view is to offer Your Excellency my Services in case it should met with your approbation, and could be of use to the People of America, to write a short and plain treatise on this Subject, to be translated either here or in america according to your choice in to the English language and to be published. but as every land can not be treated in the Same manner, I am desirous to know the Soil & the nature thereof of Your artificial Pasturages, and of all that Sort of land which may or can be appropriated thereto, that is, if it is of Clay, soft or hard clay, fenny or Sandy and the latter if entirely Sandy or mixed, for of the Sandy Dry and hard Soil is not much to be expected, and will in all probability not be necessary in Such an extensive Country, I am also to know if the water can run freely through ditches or canals towards the River which is absolutely necessary, and if there are meadows or low land were the water is to be removed by means of water mills, So as we have a number in our Country and which land is verry fruitfull; finally how many Rods Square contains an Acre (the measure by which the lands in america are Surveyed[).] If I had been acquainted two years ago with the genius of your Excellency for agriculture, and Artificial Pasturages I should perhaps have taken the liberty of addressing my Self at that time of tryal and Severity for me, for in the Year 1790—I have been deposed from my clergical office without any trial, through the arbitrary and despotic, power of the States of friesland only for writing a letter to one of the exiled Patriots, containing no politics. (from which despotic conduct no appeal could be had at that time, and no remedy is to be Expected in the present days), which Said office was my only dependence and furnished me a Revenue of 1000 guilder dutch Currency, which was to be raised from Pasturages which I partly used my Self, and which by my culture and industry were emproved more than one fourth part in Value—being thus deprived of my Station, nothing was to be done for me than to turn farmer, and to lease a farm, & outhouses for the Sum of thousand guilder annually, and of which I can not reap the profits by far, as I could from my former land, and my Situation being So much Confined that even here I would have fallen short, if not the generosity of Mr van Staphorst and other friends had enabled me, for which my gratitude shall ever last, and I requested this gentleman to transmit these presents the contents being known to him.

Although Your Excellency is at present at a distance from his country Seat, being the President of the United States, I trust I shall have not by these presents been displeasing to Your Excellency, and that I shall be honored with an answer,[1] I beg leave to recommend your Excellency and all his concerns to the protection and blessings of heaven, and subscribe myself with great Respect Sir Your Excellency's most obedient Servant

Eelko Alta,
forme[r]ly minister of the gospel
at Boasum in the Province of friesland
now living by the wittebrug
onder Rauwerd in friesland.

L, DLC:GW.

1. No written response from GW to Alta has been found.

From the Commissioners for the District of Columbia

sir George-Town 19th July 1792

Yesterday the Commissrs Contracted with Mr Hoben for his services by the year at 300 Guineas, his Draft and Attention may, be confined to the Palace or extended to other objects they may chuse. Doctor Stewart's uneasiness at the State of his Family occasioned his leaving us as soon as the most material of our Business was finished—This morning we went with Mr Hoben to the Seite of the Palace that he might lay out the foundation, the Plan, being much less than Majr L'Enfant's Design will not fill up to the diverging Points marked by the Stakes—This will necessarily occassion a Division of the Excess, on the two sides, or to recede the whole distance on one only, it does not seem, to create so much Embarrasment as might be expected, but as the work may go on without any waste of Labour till you will be here again we have left the Choice open to be made by yourself, on the Spot—Hobens Affairs requires his absence about a Month his return is expected to be as soon as he will be much wanted—After Docter Stewart left us we received a Letter and Draft from Judge Turner, there is something in it striking and agreeable to us, we send it for your Consideration—Lamphier's Plan is given up as impracticable, we have written to Ballet inviting him down to attempt Improvements,[1] Mr Turners too seems very capable of it—We still hope a little time may give you an Oppertunity of making a Choice to your Satisfaction—We are &c.

Th. Johnson
Danl Carroll

LB, DNA: RG 42, Records of the Commissioners for the District of Columbia, Letters Sent, 1791–1802.

For the background to the employment of James Hoban by the D.C. commissioners, see GW to the Commissioners for the District of Columbia, 8 June, and notes 1 and 3.

1. Robert Lanphier (1765–1856) of Alexandria, Va., was a son of the Irish immigrant carpenter and joiner Going Lanphier, whom GW had hired during the late 1750s and early 1770s to renovate the mansion house at Mount Vernon. The younger Lanphier, whose "Elevation for the Capitol" of 1792 is owned by the Maryland Historical Society, later worked in the Federal City as a carpenter, jeweler, and engraver. French émigré architect Stephen (Etienne) Hallet (1755–1825) drew five designs for the Capitol between July 1792 and March 1793. In the spring of 1793, the D.C. commissioners appointed Hallet to study the plan chosen for the Capitol, which had been drawn by one of his competitors, William Thornton, and to estimate the cost of its construction. Hallet's inability to get along with his superiors led to his discharge in November 1794, however.

To John Lewis

Dr Sir, Mount Vernon 20th July 92

I was in hopes the letter wch was written to you at my request, by my Nepw G. A: Washington—dated the 25th of March—wd have rendered a further application from me to you, on that subjt unnecessary[1]—but as he says, you have made no reply to it—as I Am informed that my power of attorney to you, was regularly recorded in Gates County No. Carolina & That Mr Cowper is making great improvement upon the land (which is an evidence that the bargain with him is closed & of course the money paid, as that was the condition of it) and, as you are upon the point of removing to Kentucky. I must, and do *insist positively* upon receiving my moiety of the money, which has been paid by Mr Cowper or any person in his behalf before you go—and to know how the ballance stands.[2]

You must be sensible, Sir, it was my opinion at the time you proposed to make sale of this land that the moment was not favorable for it—but, as the Affairs of your fathers Estate pressed, and my own[3] want of money was great, I consented to its being done;[4] but I cannot nor will not consent to lye out of my moiety of the Money that has been receid in payment. I am Dr Sir Yr obedt Hble Servt

G. W——n

ADfS (photocopy), ViMtV; LB, DLC:GW.

1. George Augustine Washington's letter to Lewis of 25 Mar. 1792 has not been identified.

2. For the background to the sale to John Cowper in mid-May 1791 of 1,093 acres in Gates County, N.C., which GW and Lewis's father, Fielding Lewis, had originally purchased in 1766, see GW to Cowper, 25 May 1788, to Lewis, 16 Sept., 8 Dec. 1788, Lewis to GW, 15 Dec. 1787, 7, 13 Dec. 1788, G. A. Washington to GW, 7 Dec. 1790, n.7, and Indenture with John Cowper, 17 May 1791.

Lewis responded to GW from Fredericksburg, Va., on 24 July: "I recd your favor by Howel [Lewis]. I cannot pretend Sir to exculpate myself for not having paid you your proportion of the money I received from Mr Cowper But the fact is I had executions against my property and body for Sevral hundred pounds on Account of having been Security for Mr William Thompson of this place, my property wou'd not sell. I made use of your money to extricate myself under the certainty as I expected in a very short time to be able to replace it. My Expectations of money were disappointed till very lately[.] I now have as much money as will pay the Amot Received. Coll William Fontaine is to pay £100 for Mr Cowper I shall go to him tomorrow on my return will come up or Send by Howell the money to you and will then render you an account of the Sale of the land. Mr Cowper has by no means complied with the payments agreed on. I aver to you I had little thought of going to Kentuckey before I made a Settlement with you[.] Indeed it is uncertain whether I ever go to that Country again. I woud ask your excuse for my conduct in this business Cou'd I conceive I merited it, but as I cannot by any means reconcile my behaviour to myself I dare not hope excuse. Beleive me Sir no transaction of my life ever gave me half the uneasiness this has done" (ViMtV). On 3 Oct. 1792 Lewis sent GW both a portion of the proceeds from the sale of the land and his account with John Cowper. For the difficulties that Cowper later had in making his payments on time, see GW's account with Cowper of 3 Oct. 1792 (DLC: GW) and his letters to Cowper of 26 Oct. 1793, 27 Jan., 9 Mar., 30 July, 4 Sept. 1794 (all LB, DLC:GW).

3. At this place on the draft manuscript, GW mistakenly inserted the word "own" between "and" and "my." The letter-book copy retains GW's original phrasing: "and own my want."

4. GW was mistaken about his reluctance to sell this piece of land. On 8 Dec. 1788 he had written Lewis that "I am as much in want of Money as your fathers Estate can be, and therefore will gladly dispose of the Carolina Land, if even a tolerable good price can be had for it." By 1794, however, GW's recollections had blurred to the point that he believed that "the land was disposed of con-

trary to my judgment, & given into, merely to accommodate the demands on" Fielding Lewis's estate and that the land "was in a manner given away, & without my consent" (see GW to Cowper, 9 Mar., 30 July 1794, both LB, DLC:GW).

From Henry Knox

Sir War department July 21st 1792

I have the honor to inform you that General Wayne in his letter of the 13th instant from Pittsburg says.

"There are no traces of hostile Indians to be discovered upon the borders of the frontiers—all is quiet—and the farmers are assiduously employed in harvesting their hay and grain which I hope they will effect in safety."

The advance of his troops had not then arrived—but I Estimate by the 28th he would have collected nearly five hundred—including Stakes horse.

Captain Mills will march a detachment from Trenton on the 23d of the following description.

Capt. Mills's company	Ensign Turners detachmt from	Massachusetts	34.
	Ensign Drakes	Connecticut	25.
	detachment from Philadelphia		36
			95.
Captain Guions Company			95.
Captain Rodgers's detachment Cavalry			40
			230

Captain Ballard Smith is marching from Richmond about one hundred and ten—Recruits.

Major Rudulph is ordered to muster and accelerate the recruits from Fredericksburg—Alexandria, Winchester and Hagers Town to the amount of Two hundred and fifty.

The four rifle companies raising on the South Western frontiers of Virginia—to wit—Thomas Lewis Howell Lewis Alexander Gibson & William Preston's have not succeeded greatly I estimate them at about two hundred at present—and they are ordered to repair to Point Pleasant at the mouth of the great Kenhawa.

As soon as a sufficient number of Recruits shall be assembled at any rendezvous they shall be marched.

I have the honor to enclose an extract of a letter from Brigr General Wilkinson of the 12th of the last Month.[1]

In addition to which I am informed by Mr Hodgdon who has arrived here, that Colonel Hardin and Major Trueman had gone forward with the pacific measures, but he did not recollect the date but I judge they left Fort Washington about the twentieth of May.

They were to proceed upon Harmers trace to a given point then to seperate—Hardin to St Dusky and Trueman to the Miami of Lake Erie.[2]

It would seem to be fair to conclude that the peace of the frontiers is owing to the pacific overtures.

That these overtures should succeed is devoutly to be desired—For if any Credit is to be given to the enclosed account signed by a Lieutenant Colonel Phillips, it will be difficult to keep the peace with the Creeks[3]—This is all I know upon the subject.

Major Gaither will depart the next week, and I will charge him most strongly to keep the peace.[4]

Major Sargent declines the office of Adjutant and Inspector assigning as a reason that the office is not attended with Rank He hints at a Brigadiers rank but I suppose he would be content with that of Lieutenant Colonel.[5]

I know not at present whom to suggest for his successor. If you should think of any suitable person for this important office, I humbly request that you would appoint him—Brigadier Wilkinson has arisen in my mind as the most suitable—his punctuality rank and activity combined would perhaps give more vigor to discipline than any other person—But I presume he would not accept the office to the prejudice of his command.

Two Captains have been ejected [from] the army at Fort Washington. for inebriety—One, Capt. McPherson was persuaded to resign—Captain Platt cashiered—I have transmitted the proceedings of the Court Martial to General Wayne for his approbation. I have the honor to be Sir—with perfect respect Your obedient servant

H. Knox
Secy of War

LS, DLC:GW; LB, DLC:GW.

Knox enclosed John Stagg's return "of the Recruits at the respective rendezvous" of 21 July, which reported that 1,672 recruits had arrived by 14 July and 62 more by 21 July, for a grand total of 1,734 (DLC:GW).

1. The enclosed extract of the letter that James Wilkinson wrote to Henry Knox from Fort Washington on 12 June 1792 reads: "The Savages have committed no act of hostilities since my last, other than pursuing and forcing back to Fort Hamilton, a scout, consisting of two rifle men, bound to the advanced posts with dispatches; in their flight these couriers lost a packet of letters, but as far as my knowledge extends they were un-important, and it is uncertain whether the enemy got possession of them or not.

"I have not heard one word of or from my messengers first dispatched to the Omee with pacific overtures, altho they have been out more then seventy days, nor have I received a tittle of intelligence from St Vincents, and I remain in the same state of ignorance, with respect to the issue of Colo. [John] Hardin & Major [Alexander] Truemans mission.

"My anxiety impresses my mind with apprehension for their safety, and tho' the event be doubtless equivocal, yet all my reasoning upon the subject, justifies the conclusion, that the enemy have actually been in deliberation upon the propositions for peace.

"My mounted infantry have commenced duty, and on the 17h instant I expect the mounted rifle men from Kentucky; these Corps will be employed in repeling the depredations of the enemy should any be offered; in protecting our hay cutters; and in escorting provisions to Fort Jefferson, which shall be pushed forward with exertion and without remission" (DLC:GW).

2. For the background to the peace mission of Alexander Trueman and John Hardin, see Thomas Jefferson's Memorandum of a Meeting of the Heads of the Executive Departments, 9 Mar., and Knox to GW, 1 April 1792, n.2.

3. The enclosed account has not been identified.

4. Henry Gaither recently had been appointed to command troops on the Georgia frontier (see GW to the U.S. Senate, 9 April 1792).

5. For Winthrop Sargent's nomination as adjutant general and inspector, see GW to the U.S. Senate, 9 April. After several other persons had declined to be considered for the post, GW nominated Michael Rudolph adjutant and inspector on 22 Feb. 1793. The Senate consented to his appointment the following day (see GW to the U.S. Senate, 22 Feb. 1793; *Executive Journal,* 1:132, 134).

From Tobias Lear

Sir, Portsmouth, New Hampshire, July 21st 1792.

I have the honor to inform you that we arrived here yesterday, and had the pleasure to find all our friends in good health. Our passage from New York to Providence was a very pleasant one, and performed in about 36 hours. We met with no accident during the journey, and were highly favored in the weather.

Agreeably to your directions I called upon Mr Morris before I left Philadelphia, and observed to him, that as you understood the house in which you lived was only engaged for two years, which term would expire on the first day of October next, you had ordered me to see him upon the subject,[1] and to learn from him whether he expected to remove into the house himself at the end of that time, or whether it was his intention that the President should occupy it until his present term of service expired. Mr Morris replied that no other idea had ever entered his mind, but that you should occupy the house as long as you might find it convenient or agreeable—that the reason of the term being limited to two years was from the full expectation that an house would, within that time, be provided by the State of Pennsylvania for the residence of the President; but as he found that the government house was not likely to be completed so soon as was expected, he was making alterations, for his better accommodation, in the house where he now lives. I further observed to him, that if he had any desire to return to his former dwelling, and the house which he now inhabits would be rented, you would readily give up the one which you now hold, and take the other; or if that was not to be rented, you would get the best accommodation you could elsewhere. He answered, that when the alterations now carrying on should be completed the house would be as convenient for him as the other, and even if that should not have been the case, he should never have entertained an idea of returning to his former residence so long as it might be agreeable to the President to occupy it.

As in the conversation with Mr Morris, I made use of the expression "until the President's present term of service expires"—he asked me if it was expected that any other more suitable house would be provided by that time, as he was confident the goverment house would not then be fit to occupy. I told him I did not know that any other would be; but that you had no occasion to look forward beyond the time for which you were elected, for accommodations of this nature. He then asked me if you had determined not to continue at the head of the government after the expiration of the present term. I told him I did not know that you had come to any determination on the subject; but that I knew full well if you followed your own wishes & inclination they would lead you to retire. He observed, that he knew himself that to be the case; but he hoped to God that the love of your Country & of mankind which had heretofore overcome in you every personal & private consideration, would still prevail, and that you would not give up the government & the Country to that fate which he clearly foresaw awaited them if you should determine to retire from the Chair. He thought the reasons for your continuing were, if possible, more strong than those which first induced your acceptance of the Office.

So far as I have had an opportunity of hearing any sentiment expressed on this subject it has uniformly agreed with the above. The rout by which I came hither and the little stop which I made in the several places th[r]ough which I passed afforded but little opportunity of hearing the opinion of many persons on this or other topics; but I found an eagerness of inquiry on this head, mixed with an apprehension of what might be the consequences of your retiring, which convinced me that it was considered as a matter of the first importance. The general idea seemed to be, to say nothing of the fatal effects expected from divisions & parties, that most of the important things hitherto done under this government, being, as it were, matters of experiment, had not yet been long enough in operation to give satisfactory proof whether they are beneficial or not, and that they could not under any other administration have the fair experiment which they would have under that which first introduced them.

I had the honor of writing a few lines from New York,[2] and shall not fail to write as often as anything may occur worth giving you the trouble of perusing it.

I was a little surprized to find that the Indian War is extremely unpopular in New England. I have not heard it mentioned by a single person who did not consider it as arising rather from a wish on the part of the United States to obtain lands to which they have no just claim, than as a war of necessity, as it really is. Whenever I have heard this subject introduced I have not failed to set the matter in its true light, and I flatter myself that I have convinced those with whom I have conversed on this head that the U.S. neither want nor have ever claimed an inch of land from the Indians which they have not obtained by fair treaty and honorable purchase. I was astonished to find that they had taken so little pains to make themselves masters of the subject before they condemned it—an idea had obtained that the war was unjust without any one having inquired into the matter far enough to give a single reason why it was unjust.

So far as I have had an opportunity of learning, I find the people this way very much in favor of the establishment of the Federal City. A report has been propagated, that it was on the decline & that some circumstances had retarded its progress and would probably totally defeat it; but I was pleased to find, that this report was very little regarded.

The crops of grain & grass are good, and the prospect of Indian Corn (which is 3 or 4 weeks more forward here than in Virginia) remarkably fine—The Country appears flourishing and the people prosperous & happy. In this town they are doing business to more advantage than they have ever done before since the revolution.

Mrs Lear & our little boy are well & less fatigued with the journy than could have been expected. Mrs Lear will have the honor of writing to Mrs Washington as soon as she gets a little settled from the confusion of the journey—and in the mean time she unites with me in sentiments of gratitude & respect for yourself & Mrs Washington, love to the Children & best regards to Major Washington & his lady and to Messrs Dandridge & Lewis.

With the most sincere & affectionate attachment & perfect respect I have the honor to be Sir Your most Obedient Servant

Tobias Lear.

ALS, DLC:GW.

For the purposes of Tobias Lear's visit to New England during the summer of 1792 and a listing of the letters exchanged between GW and Lear during the latter's sojourn there, see Lear to GW, 15 July, source note.

1. For the background to GW's rental of Robert Morris's house from the Corporation of the City of Philadelphia, see GW to Lear, 5 Sept., 27 Oct., 14 Nov. 1790, and Lear to GW, 4, 21 Nov. 1790.

2. See Lear to GW, 15 July.

From Alexander Hamilton

Private

Sir Philadelphia July 22 1792

I wrote to you on Monday last, transmitting a resolution of the Commissioners of the Sinking fund.[1] Nothing in the way of public business requiring your attention has since occurred.

There is a matter I beg leave to mention to you confidentially in which your interposition, if you deem it, adviseable, may have a good effect.

I have long had it at heart that some good system of regulations for the forwarding supplies to the army, issuing them there and accounting for them to the department of wa⟨r should⟩ be established. On conversing w⟨ith the⟩ Secretary at War, I do not ⟨find⟩ that any such now exists; nor have the intimations I have taken the liberty to give on the subject, though perfectly well received, hitherto produced the desired effect. The utility of the thing does not seem to be as strongly impressed on the mind of the Secy at War as it is on mine.

It has occurred to me that if you should think fit to call by letter upon the Secretary of the Treasury and the Secretary at War to report to you, the *system and regulations under which the procuring issuing and accounting for supplies to the army is conducted,* it would produce what appears to be now wanting. I submit the idea accordingly.[2] With the most perfect respect & truest attachment I have the honor to be Sir Your most Obed. & hum. serv.

A. Hamilton

ALS, DLC:GW; copy, DLC: Hamilton Papers. The mutilated text has been supplied within angle brackets from the copy in the Hamilton Papers.

1. Hamilton had last written GW on Monday, 16 July 1792.

2. Acting on Hamilton's suggestion, GW wrote Hamilton and Henry Knox on 1 Aug. requesting information about the regulations under which army provisions were issued and accounted for. Hamilton sent his report to GW on 10 August. Knox wrote GW on 7 Aug. that the "papers which you have been pleased to require shall be transmitted by the post of Monday next," 13 Aug. 1792. Knox's letter to GW of 11 Aug., which apparently covered his report, has not been found, however.

From Reuben Rowzee

Sir, Winchester [Va.] 22d July 1792

The Petition, which I had the honor to transmit you, by Mr R. Lewis about this time last year, signed by many worthy Gentleman, in the vicinity where I resided, on the subject of my deplorable situation, has never yet been finally answered. The Gentleman who was pleased to convey the memorial to you has never yet had it in his power, I have learned, to afford me those Communications, which could only palliate the miseries I have so long suffered through the wicked artifices of a man who I wished to serve. I hope in Heaven by this time you have considered the documents which I took the Liberty to send you; and that I may as soon as public convenience, and private leisure, will permit, receive an answer that will be decisive. Believe me Sir, candid, when I declare, that I cannot satisfy the claim, or even a part of it, without being incapable of answering for a violence, to my pitiless family, before a *just* and *almighty God,* from whose mercy only, I look and hope for a glorious, and happy immortality. If I were a single man, I could not hesitate one moment to part with my little all, to satisfy the debt, but such has not been the will of providence, and even under my present woful circumstances, I derive happiness, on the occasional interviews, I have with my children, in the surly walls of a loathsome prison. In the Course of human affairs, my residence in this world can not be very long, and rather would I consume the remaining span of my day in Captive misery, than for my poor children after I am cold in the Ground, to be obliged to beg the little, which nature does want, from door to door. Pardon, good Sir, this warm l[ett]r, it is the overflowings of a heart, of an old grey headed, affectionate Father. I will only pray your answer, as soon, as your absence from the necessary avocations of busy life will admit, and when your private business may be not importunate for your attention. I am with submissive Respect, Sir, Yr mo: obt Hble: s⟨*illegible*⟩

Reuben Rowzee

ALS, DLC:GW.

For more information about the judgment GW's agent Battaile Muse had obtained against Reuben Rowzee at the March 1790 session of the Frederick County court, Rowzee's imprisonment for debt in the spring of 1790, and his obstinate refusal to make a deal to get out of prison, see Muse to GW, 28 Nov. 1785, n.5, 20 July 1790, and note 5, and 22 Aug. 1791, and note 1.

To the Commissioners for the District of Columbia

Gentlemen, Mount Vernon July 23d 179[2][1]

Your favor of the 19th, accompanying Judge Turner's plan for a Capitol, I have duly received; and have no hesitation in declaring that I am more agreeably struck with the appearance of it than with any that has been presented to you. I return it without delay, because (among other reasons for doing it) Mr Turner wishes to receive it, in any event, immediately.

There is the same defect, however, in this plan as there is in all the plans which have been presented to you—namely—the want of an Executive apartment: wch ought, if possible, to be obtained. The Dome, which is suggested as an addition to the center of the edifice, would, in my opinion, give beauty & granduer to the pile; and might be useful for the reception of a Clock—Bell, &ca. The Pilastrade too, in my Judgement, ought (if the plan is adopted) to be carried around the simicircular projections at the ends; but whether it is necessary to have the elevation of the upper Storey 41 feet is questionable; unless it be to preserve exactness in the proportion of the several parts of the building; in that case, the smaller Rooms in that Storey would be elivated sufficiently if cut in two, & would be the better for it in the interior provided they can be lighted. This would add to the number of Committee Rooms of which there appears to be a dificiency: And quere, would not the section B in the North division of plan No. 2 be more usefully applied as a library than for the purpose it is designated?[2]

Could such a plan as Judge Turner's be surrounded with Columns, and a colonade like that which was presented to you by Monsr Hallet (the Roof of Hallet's I must confess does not hit my taste)—without departing from the principles of Architecture—and would not be too expensive for our means, it would, in my judgement, be a noble & desireable Structure. But, I would have it understood in *this* instance, and *always,* when I am hazarding a sentiment on these buildings, that I profess to have no knowledge in Architecture, and think we should (to avoid criticisms) be governed by the established Rules which are laid down by the professors[3] of this Art.

I think you have engaged Mr Hoben upon advantageous terms; and hope if his industry and honesty are of a piece with the specimen he has given of his abilities, he will prove a useful man & a considerable acquisition.[4] The enclosed Is handed to you, merely because it is my wish that you should be possessed of every information of the kind that comes to my knowledge.[5] The person therein mentioned (Stevens) was a Lieutt Colonel of Artillery during the War, and was (and for aught I know to the contrary, is) a Sober, honest & good tempered man—Very industrious—Fertile in invention & resources—and great at execution. He was, as I have been informed, bred a house Carpenter; but how well acquainted he may be with that business, or how far he may be able to carry on work in a masterly manner upon a grand scale, I have no data to decide upon. He is a native of Boston, but since the War has lived in New York, where he carries on the business of a lumber Merchant to (I believe) a considerable extent. With great esteem & regard I remain Gentlemen Yr most Obedt Servt

Go: Washington

ALS, DLC:GW; ALS (photocopy), DNA: RG 42, Photostatic Copies of Letters from Presidents of the United States to the Commissioners for the District of Columbia and Their Successors, 1791–1869; ADfS, DLC:GW; LB, DLC:GW; LB, DNA: RG 42, Records of the Commissioners for the District of Columbia, Letters Sent, 1791–1802.

1. Although GW wrote "1793" on the ALS manuscript, the draft and the two letter-book copies are all dated 23 July 1792. In addition, the letter-book copy in DNA indicates that this letter was received by the commissioners on 3 Aug. 1792.

2. No copy has survived of Judge George Turner's design of the Capitol, which he asked the D.C. commissioners to return to him in early October 1792.

3. At this place on the draft manuscript GW wrote "Mastrs" instead of "professors," a wording which is repeated in the DLC:GW letter-book copy.

4. For the background to the D.C. commissioners' employment of James Hoban in the Federal City, see GW to the Commissioners for the District of Columbia, 8 June, and notes 1 and 3, and Commissioners for the District of Columbia to GW, 19 July 1792.

5. GW enclosed Tobias Lear's letter to him of 15 July 1792, in which Lear recounts a conversation he had with Ebenezer Stevens concerning the latter's desire to be appointed Pierre L'Enfant's successor in the Federal City.

From David Humphreys

(Secret & confidential)

My dear Sir. Lisbon July 23d 1792

I take the liberty of writing to you again, after a considerable *interval*,[1] to assure you there can be *none* in my sentiments of affection & gratitude to you. At the same time, I enclose a Manuscript "Poem, on the National Industry of the U.S.," which, after you shall have done with it, if it should be so fortunate as to meet your approbation, I pray you will hand to Mr Lear, that he may have it printed according to the desire expressed in my letter to him by this conveyance.[2] As far as I can judge of my own heart, I conceived myself to have been animated by love of Country in writing the Poem. I own I have received pleasure in composing, however others may or not in perusing it. For it is not for me to decide how I have succeeded in the execution. I have endeavored to polish the versification as highly, as in any thing I have before written. The conceptions are mostly the result of observation. And the sentiments, I know, are such as comport perfectly well with patriotism & good morals. I wish never to write any thing but what is friendly to the cause of Humanity; I was glad to have an occasion of speaking well of the Polish new Constitution. The Characters, I think, are all just & particularly that of the Queen of Portugal, who cannot now be flattered by it. The contrast between the former & present character of the Portuguese; and the pernicious effects of Idleness visible here, & in Spain suggested several of the ideas. *But for this fact I question whether I should ever have written on the Subject.* How far that want of exertion among the People of those Countries is to be attributed to their Governments, I will not now pretend to say. The Poruguese (with whom I am most acquainted) were once a gallant & glorious Nation; and even now appear capable of being moulded into a very respectable form.

The natural advantages of this Country are much greater than its actual moral & political state would authorize one to conclude. But from the jealousy of the Government and the arbitrary nature of the Police, it is difficult to obtain true informations, as you will judge from the following fact. Soon after my arrival I endeavoured, by all justifiable means to get some insight into the real state of the Country. For this purpose I gave written questions to a few Persons, from whom I desired, in the paper itself, such answers as might be perfectly discreet, & not improper in any point of view. One copy of my questions had been translated into Portuguese by Jacob Dohrman our acting Consul, & put into the hands of a *foreigner* (but an *Inhabitant* here) whom I had no knowledge of, nor had ever seen. By some means the police came to the knowledge of what this Person had written on the present state of Portugal. He was taken up, put on board a vessel, & sent to France: where he has made a complaint of the treatment to the National Assembly. Another Person concerned with him in the matter, was apprehended & confined several weeks in Prison here. I was told by a Gentleman who was present, the Intendant on seeing the Papers said, "the Questions were those of a man of sense, & very proper to be asked by a Person in public Character . . . but that these People had been too free in some of their observations."

If I were better informed, the limits of a letter would allow me to give but a very imperfect particular Idea of the moral, political & economical state of the Kingdom. A short paragraph may however serve to give a general Idea as well as a long Dessertation. An unlimited monarchy, a Mad Queen, a foolish Prince-Regent, a weak Administration, an ignorant Laity, a bigotted Clergy & an existing Inquisition, are not able to prevent the *prosperity* of the Country. If left to itself what must it then be? Or what must have been its progress, if the late Prince of Brazil had lived to come to the Throne; and if he could have been aided by as able a Minister as the late Marquis of Pombal was?[3] But "the ways of Heaven are dark & intricate." Providence knows its own designs best.

Of the late Prince, I have, on good authority, heard so many facts, which indicated wisdom, goodness, & a tender regard for the happiness of the lowest of mankind, that I have little doubt he would of his own accord have assembled the long-neglected Cortez, & adopted a Constitution as favorable to liberty (at least) as that of Poland. Having learned to understand English by his own Industry, he read many of the best political works in the language. He expressed on many occasions the most manly & liberal sentiments with respect to Government. He was free from pride & affected reserve. And from his affability and condescension he was the delight of all who approached him. There is scarcely a man in the Kingdom who has any knowledge of, or has ever conversed with the present Prince. He appears to me to want sense. What he is, or may come to be, we know not. There is little, except his filial affection, that augurs very well.[4]

The late Marquis of Pombal was indeed a great man, & an able Minister. As a public Character his virtues & faults were all in extreme; for he had nothing of mediocrity about him. He had every thing to do. He began with things at the right end, for he put one foot on the neck of the Clergy, & the other on the Neck of the Nobility. And there he held them until the death of the King whom he served—when he was dismissed, retired to his estate, & underwent a kind of tryal, from the influence of his enemies. But he had the King's written mandate for every thing he did, so that his conduct stood unimpeachable. He died as he lived, haughty, independent & laughing at all his enemies could say of him. But the seeds of improvements he sowed in almost every Department are not yet dead. They are now bringing forth fruits, in spite of all the attempts of subsequent Ministers to root them up. This his enemies, to whom he was always severe, probably sometimes cruel & unjust, begin to allow. And I consider him, with all his imperfections on his head (which were neither few or small) as a Minister who has done more good to his Country than any other in Europe since the time of the immortal Sully.[5]

Notwithstanding the Prince of Brazil's character is known to so little advantage, & the Queen's natural goodness of heart is so evident; I believe her Malady was upon the whole a fortunate event to the Kingdom. Just before her incapacity was declared, the Priests were gaining such an ascendency, as gave thinking People the most gloomy apprehensions. Had not that event taken place, it is asserted on pretty good authority, there would have been an *Auto de Fe,* even so near the close of the 18th Century. The poor free masons & some little Offenders were sadly persecuted. And now that there are Subjects accused of atrocious crimes in the view of the Religion of the Country, I question whether anything will be done. There are now a number of young Gentlemen, of good family, Students of the University of Coïmbra, put into the Inquisition, for breaking into a nunnery & committing other rash actions.

In the articles I enumerated as impeding the natural & inevitable prosperity of the Kingdom, I did not mention the Nobility, because I meant to bestow a moment's notice on them. The Marquis of Pombal found them poor, proud & servile, but treacherous to such a degree that he could not employ them in offices of confidence. He gave the command of the Army, and of the Provinces to foreigners, for he knew in the last short war between Portugal & Spain,[6] the Nobility would willingly have sacrificed the Country, for the sake of sacrificing him. For other offices he chose all young men, & mostly from the middle class; he could not depend on those of rank, or advanced in age for the least thing. So low in Spirit were the commissioned, & even field Officers of the army degraded, when the Comte de Lippe took command of the Army, that it was no uncommon thing for them to be Servants in Noblemen's families, and occasionally attend as such at Table.[7] To overcome prejudices, & prepare the then rising Generation for future utility, the Marquis improved the University of Coïmbra by liberal Institutions, he induced a number of learned foreigners to become professors in it, and he established a great number of schools throughout the Kingdom. Many of the Nobility & others now coming on the Stage of life have profited by these Institutions. My former letters to the Secretary of State have announced great liberality of Individuals. Still the Nobility, (I speak of the generality, for there are among them some honorble exceptions) are by no means so good as they ought to be, though far less despicable than they were. Too many of them are still, insolent to their Inferiors, involved in debts, and cringing at Court to such a degree of baseness as is absolutely incredible. They literally perform the offices of menial Servants, & in addition to their common knee-Service in offering any thing to the Royal hands, they consider it as an infinite honor to be permitted to play Cards with the Royal Personage, though they are obliged to do it by remaining the whole time on their knees. They will learn better. The Nation in general are by nature docile, intelligent, patient & capable of improvement. There is a middle Class from which much is to be expected. Men in business are growing rich fast, & consequently of some weight & importance in the State. Foreigners have unintentionally taught them this. It is an indubitable fact, that the Merchants of the English & other Factories have, by taking Portuguese youths into their Compting houses as Clerks, taught the

Portuguese (within 20 years past) to do almost all their own mercantile business. But a few years ago, there was scarcely one commercial Portuguese House. Now several merchants of that Nation have made *princely* fortunes. Much of the private business of the Country, and all the public Contracts (formerly given to foreigners) have come into their hands. While the business of the foreign Factories has considerably declined.

This Country is not however ripe for any great or sudden Revolution, or for enjoying total liberty. Yet I see among all the Young People, particularly in the navy, the same Anglo-manie, the same rage for imitating the English, which in France preceded the Revolution. Many foreign Officers in this Service have told me no better subjects for Soldiers ever existed than the Portuguese. It will be the Policy of the Government to remain quiet, & to take no part in the measures which agitate almost all Europe.

The storm seems louring over Poland & France more than ever. The combination against Liberty is truly formidable. But I trust a good Providence will defeat it. The King of Prussia with 60,000 well-appointed Troops is certainly on his March against the French. I have this day written to our Minister at Paris, to the Marquis la Fayette, & to the Duke de Rochefoucault a *project* for diminishing the German Armies which may enter France.[8] It is by defraying at the national charge the expence of the passage to the U.S. of such Persons belonging to those Armies as shall chuse to transfer themselves to settle there. I believe the *plan* to be feasable and œconomical. It is so far at least not chimerical, that Addresses may be published, & facilities given for the execution of the measure without expence or risque. It will be fairly turning the weapon of Desertion against the Enemy. The experiment can cost nothing. And perhaps the very design being known to the Austrian & Prussian Cabinets may have some influence in deterring them from sending their Armies into France. If any good comes of it, I will solace myself with the conscious pleasure of having first made the suggestion.

Lord St Helens, the British Ambassador at Madrid, having been here a few days ago on his way to England, I was induced to make enquiries of him respecting the actual situation of Mr Carmichael's health & spirits. He informed me with frankness, yet in a delicate manner, that he considered Mr Carmichael on many accounts as an amiable & valuable Man; but that his health is ruined, & that (what is worse) he has addicted himself entirely to hard drinking. Lord St Helens added these words, "His breath smells as strong, even in a morning of Spiritous Liquor as any Sailor's I ever met with."[9] Disagreeable as the task is, a sense of duty obliges me to mention the circumstance precisely as it came to my knowledge: because it seemed necessary for the public good that you should know it. I never saw the Person in question intoxicated in my life. It is true he suffered miserably from depression of spirits. I was however in hopes the return of health, business, & amusement, would give new energy to those talents which appeared to be very capable of rendering service to the U.S. in the field where they are employed: but which seemed to have languished a long time merely for want of notice, & having something to do.

This letter is of such a nature that I shall destroy the Copy for fear of its falling into improper hands, & I beg leave to suggest to your discretion whether it may not be expedient to do the same with the original? I entreat, in all events, my best Compliments may be presented to Mrs Washington & the family; and that you will be assured, My dear Sir, that I am with every sentiment of attachment Your Most affe. friend & Obliged Servant

D. Humphreys

ALS, DLC:GW; ADfS, CtY: Humphreys-Marvin-Olmstead Collection.

Humphreys's draft, which is dated 4 July and which, in addition to being much shorter, differs significantly from his letter in its final form, reads: "As no one knows better than yourself, that, by indulging at times in fondness for the fine Arts, I do not neglect the duties of a public employment, I need make no apology in transmitting for your perusal 'a Poem on the national Industry of the U.S. of America.' No subject can be more worthy of their *attention*, or conducive to their *prosperity*. If then, Poetry can have a tendency to excite, the one, & promote the other, it ought to be considered but as patriotism under a different name. And if Poetry, resuming its antient chastity, should scorn to make use of a Mythology, once ornamental because believed true, now used as a substitute for genius where that is wanting, it may perhaps boast, like Liberty, a new triumph in a new World.

"It will be seen that this Poem was written in celebration of the sixteenth anniversary of Independence. That day is consecrated, not by an official Ordinance, but by the common consent of America, to festivity & thanksgiving. Although I am no friend to multiplying Hollidays, because they not only encroach upon the time of the industrious part of the Community, but serve to produce habits of idleness & vice: yet I am persuaded it would have an happy influence on the public mind, in augmenting our patriotism & philanthropy, to set apart, at least, four days in every year, for the expression of national joy & gratitude. Those days might also be usefully employed by our Militia, in reanimating so much of a military Spirit as shall be necessary for the defence of our Country & Constitution.

"Is there a Child in America, who ought not to be instructed in the great things which Heaven has done for us as a Nation? Can that instruction be received with more pleasant and forcible impression than on the annual return of those days, which constitute the most memorable periods of the American Revolution? Such are the 4th of July 1776, on which Independence was declared; the 3d of Sept. 1783, on which Peace was concluded; and the 30th of April 1789, when our Constitution was carried into effect. Had not the American People sufficiently demonstrated that the birthday of their President is a day which they delight to honour; I should, from motives of personal delicacy, have omitted to mention the 22nd of Feby 1732. In wishing, with the concurrent voice of Millions, many auspicious returns of that day, with the uninterrupted continuance of health & happiness for yourself; I have the honour to remain, With every sentiment of respectful attachment, My dear Sir, Your affectionate friend & Humble Servant" (CtY: Humphreys-Marvin-Olmstead Collection).

1. Humphreys had last written the president on 12 May 1791.

2. Humphreys's "Poem on Industry—Addressed to the Citizens of the United States" was published in Philadelphia in mid-October 1794.

3. Maria I of Portugal's eldest son, José (b. 1761), died from smallpox in 1788. Sebastião José de Carvalho e Mello, marquês de Pombal (1699–1782), who served as Portugal's chief minister for foreign affairs 1750–56 and as prime minister 1756–77, supported university reform, the reorganization of the army, the rebuilding of Lisbon following the earthquake of 1755, the persecution of the Society of Jesus, the stimulation of the national economy, and increased trade with India and Brazil.

4. Maria I's son João VI (c.1769–1826) assumed power in 1792 because of his mother's insanity. The French invasion of 1807 forced João, Maria, and their court to flee to Brazil. Having become king of Portugal upon Maria's death in 1816, João returned to Lisbon in 1821.

5. During the decade following his appointment as finance minister by Henry IV in 1598, Maximilien de Béthune, duc de Sully (1560–1641), reorganized the French financial system, replenished the national treasury, and supported various economic reforms and internal improvements.

6. Humphreys is referring to the brief conflict between Spain and Portugal in 1762 at the close of the Seven Years' War.

7. Wilhelm, Graf von Schaumburg-Lippe (1724–1777), a grandson of George I of England through an illegitimate line, was sent to Portugal in the summer of 1762 to shore up the Portuguese military; he stayed on afterwards to help reorganize the Portuguese army.

8. Louis-Alexandre, duc de La Rochefoucauld (1744–1792), was a member of the French Academy of Science and the Estates General of 1789 before the French Revolution. He later became president of the Department of Paris. In

September 1792 La Rochefoucauld, a nobleman, was lynched on the road to Paris. Humphreys sent his proposal to Gouverneur Morris, Lafayette, and La Rochefoucauld in mid-August 1792. Morris replied to Humphreys on 6 Dec. that "Before its Arrival the Duke de La Rochefoucault had perish'd and Monsieur de La Fayette had been obliged to fly. I therefore have not forwarded to him the Letter but still hold it subject to your Order. That for the Duc de La Rochefoucault I committed to the Flames" (Morris, *Diary of the French Revolution,* 2:534–36).

9. Alleyne Fitzherbert, Baron St. Helens (1753–1839), whose diplomatic career already had taken him by 1790 to Brussels, the court of Catherine the Great of Russia, Ireland, and The Hague, was dispatched to Madrid in May of that year to settle a trade dispute between Britain and Spain. He negotiated an alliance between the two nations in 1793 and returned to England in early 1794. In March, St. Helens returned to The Hague as ambassador extraordinary, and in 1801 he traveled to St. Petersburg, Russia, as Britain's representative to congratulate Tsar Alexander I on his accession to the throne.

To Thomas Jefferson

Dear Sir, Mount Vernon July 23d 1792

The friday after you left this place I received the enclosed dispatches from Governor Chittendon, of the State of Vermont.[1]

If you conceive it to be necessary, undr the circumstances which exist,[2] to write again to that Gentleman before he replies to your former letter on the subject[3] in dispute, you will, of course, take such measures thereupon as shall appear[4] proper under a full view of all circumstances.[5] With great esteem & regard I am—Dear Sir Your Obedt & Affecte Servt

Go: Washington

ALS, DLC: Jefferson Papers; ADfS, DNA: RG 59, Miscellaneous Letters; LB, DNA: RG 59, George Washington's Correspondence with His Secretaries of State; LB (photocopy), DLC:GW.

1. GW apparently received Gov. Thomas Chittenden's letter of 16 June and its enclosures on Friday, 20 July.

2. At this place on the draft manuscript, GW first wrote and then struck out the phrase: "in this case to be referred to me." He then started to write a phrase beginning "respecting the" but again struck out those words.

3. At this place in the draft, GW wrote and then struck out "of his complaint" before inserting "in dispute."

4. At this place on the draft manuscript, GW wrote and then struck out the word "right" before inserting "proper."

5. For Jefferson's letter to Governor Chittenden of 9 July, see GW to Jefferson, 7 July, n.2; *Jefferson Papers,* 24:200. On 12 July, Jefferson wrote Chittenden:

"I must renew my entreaties to your Excellency that no innovation in the state of things may be attempted for the present. It is but lately that an opportunity has been afforded of pressing on the court of Gr. Britain our rights in the quarter of the posts, and it would be truly unfortunate if any premature measures on the part of your state should furnish a pretext for suspending the negociations on this subject" (ibid., 218–19). On 30 July, Jefferson wrote GW that he thought it best to await Chittenden's response to his two letters. Chittenden apparently never replied to Jefferson's inquiries.

To John Francis Mercer

Sir, Mount Vernon July 23d 1792

Your favor of the 10th did not get to my hands until Saturday last,[1] although I sent to the Post Office regularly, every Post day since I came to this place for the lettrs wch I expected.

Your letter conveys no specific assurance of the time, or manner of discharging the bal[anc]e which is due to me. I am placed on no better, indeed on worse ground—than I stood years ago with respect to this debt; and you cannot have forgotten that these were my apprehensions, which I expressed to you upon more occasions than one. Why then should I be told at this late day after every endeavor on my part to accomodate matters to your convenience of your intention of offering all your property for sale when part of it ought to have been applied to my use years since? or to what purpose (for me I mean) is it that you should offer property for sale if the price set thereon will admit no purchasers, or if sold that the money is to be converted to other uses than for my benefit? The latter you must be sensible I know to have been the case and the other, as it respects negros which you offered to me formerly, & from other circumstances, I have no reason to disbelieve.

It is not from inclination, that I become acquainted with any Gentlemans circumstances, and far is it from my practice to investigate what he owes; but you must excuse me when I tell you, that I have heard enough of yours to give me some uneasiness, as well on your Acct as on mine. To two facts I shall glance. A Gentn in Phila., witht having the least Suspicion (I believe) how matters stood between you & me, was enquiring into the value of your Marlborough Estate; & through another channel I understd the reason was, that your debt to him was considerable; &

that, *that was the mean* by which he was to be securd. The other, is the Agency of Mr Montague who I know is determined to push the settlement of that business.[2] Others I have also heard of: but nothing, I beg you to be persuaded, Sir, but my own interest in the case, would have induced me to mention them to you. Hard indeed then would it be upon me if after twenty odd years endulgence & receiving *any thing,* and *driblets* as they were offered which dissipated (being unequal to my objects) as insensibly as the morning dew that I should be *still* postponed or put off with vague promises until perhaps, you & your property may have parted.

There can be no difficulty in settg *this,* or any other Acct where the debits & credits are regular, & the intentions of the parties are fair; and I am persuaded if you will be at the trouble of riding to this place, a few hours will ascertain the bal. which is due to me—or in case disagreement should arise on any point, it might be so stated as that an impartial Umpire might decide it for us witht trouble or lawsuits besides, I have at this place a number of letters, Papers, and the Mill Books, which might throw light upon things which to you may seem to want explanation, & cannot be had elsewhere—Other matters also might be more clearly explained, & better understd by oral conversation than is practicable by letter. I know of nothing (at present) that will call me from home soon, unless I should go to the New City the first day of next month; of which I gave the Commrs some, but no positive intimation. However, if you are inclined to comply with this request, & will name the precise day you will be here, I will not be from home.

I beg you to be assured, that it will be extremely irksome & painful to me to go into a Court of Justice for the recovery of what is due to me, & for which I have with very great inconvenien[ce] & disadvantage to myself waited so long; but it must be the case unless it can be averted by some measure wch possibly, may be adopted at the meeting wch is now proposed, & which it may be well for you to think on, previous thereto.

I have not yet been called upon legally to answer the complaint of Henshaw; but shall be ready to do it whenever it shall be found necessary or expedient[3] & for that purpose shall keep the Bill, & the answer which you have drawn until I either see you, or hear from you again. The answer as drawn misstated a fact[4] with respect to the power vested in Mr Lund Washington—The truth of that matter stands thus—The Sale as you have recited, was made in Novr 1774 on 12 months credit. In May following I went to the second Congress as a member thereof witht givg Lund Washn then or at any time thereafter powers fully expecting to return as soon as the business of the Session should close; but, being chosen to commd the Army, I proceeded to Cambridge and from thence—as soon as it became apparent to me that my absence from home was likely to be of much longer continuance than I had calculated upon—I wrote to Colo. Tayloe informing him thereof, & desiring him to[5] take the *sole* management of the trust which had been commitd to us jointly upon himself, as my situation would no longer permit me to pay any further attention to it—& because I should not consider myself responsible for any transaction subsequent to the Sale. previous to which he had thrown the whole burthen upon me & nothing remained for him to do but to appoint a Collector (if he did not chuse to be at the trouble himself[)], & he submit the money to the decision of the Court agreeably to the decretal Order.[6] What *he* did—or rather what he neglected to do, would be tedious to relate, & I presume can compose no part of my answer. and with respect to the particular instance of depreciation as stated in the answer, my memory is not furnished with the circumstance at prest. I am—Sir Yr most Obedt Hble Servt

G. W——n

ADfS (photocopy), ViMtV; LB, DLC:GW.

1. Mercer's letter to GW of 10 July, which had arrived on Saturday, 21 July, has not been found.

2. Edward Montagu (c.1720–1798), who had been the London agent for the Va. House of Burgesses between 1759 and 1770, later served as an attorney for George Mercer's English creditors.

3. Henshaw's complaint did not come before the Va. court of chancery until the spring of 1794 (see Bushrod Washington to GW, 22, 27 April [both ViMtV], GW to Bushrod Washington, 30 April 1794). In his letter to Bushrod Washington of 30 April 1794, GW wrote: "That Henshaw may have become a purchaser at the sale in 1774 on the terms, and to the amount set forth in the Bill, is highly probable. But I have no recollection of his ever having made a tender of payment to me at Cambridge, or of the conversation which he has stated; and conceive, if application had been made to me for the purpose mentioned, he would have recd an answer to the effect" that he should deal with John Tayloe (ALS [retained copy], ViMtV).

4. GW's first version of this phrase on the draft manuscript reads: "The

answer drawn (appears, from the Last rending I have given it) to have mistaken a fact and was to be rectified."

5. At this place on the draft manuscript, GW wrote and then struck out the words: "call for the Bonds."

6. For the reasons the money from the sale of November 1774 had to be submitted to the Va. court of chancery for its decision, see Tobias Lear to John Rutherfurd, 18 April 1792.

To Robert Morris

Dear Sir, Mount Vernon July 23d 1792.

This letter will be presented to you by Mr Jno. Augo. Spotswood, Son of General Spotswood. The enclosure, communicates the ideas of the father, and the wishes of the Son as fully as it is in my power to make them known to you; and when compared with the former letters from Genl Spotswood to me, which you have seen,[1] leaves nothing more for me to add on this subject than to say that your good Offices in behalf of the young Gentleman will oblige[2] the father, the Son & myself.

I have no knowledge of the young man, nor have I the least reason to distrust the character given of him by his father—but it is a fathers account—and you, better than I will know whether any, & what allowances are to be made for it.

Mrs Washington joins with me in a tender of best wishes for Mrs Morris yourself & the rest of the family. With very great esteem & regard I am—Dr Sir—Yr Most Obedt and Affect. Hble Sert

Go: Washington

ALS (photocopy), DLC:GW, ser. 9; LB, DLC:GW.

1. GW's enclosure has not been identified. Alexander Spotswood's letters to GW regarding a maritime berth for his son John Augustine Spotswood were written on 4 Dec. 1791, 14 Mar., and 10 July 1792 (not found).

2. At this place on the draft manuscript, GW wrote and then struck out the words: "all those of us."

To Alexander Spotswood

[Mount Vernon, 23 July 1792]

Mr Spotswood delivered me your favor of the 10th, on Friday last and I have given him a letter to Mr Morris of Philadelphia,[1] who, I persuade myself, will render him any service, which it may be in his power to do consistently. At all times, when you can make it convenient, I should be happy to see you at this place; & with my love to Mrs Spotswood,[2] in which Mrs Washington joins me.

Transcript of the ALS printed in the catalog of the auction of the library of Walter C. Janney conducted by William D. Morley, Inc., on 21 Nov. 1950.

1. John Augustine Spotswood delivered his father's letter to GW of 10 July, which has not been found, on Friday, 20 July 1792. GW's letter to Robert Morris is dated 23 July.

2. Elizabeth Washington Spotswood (1750–1814) was the eldest daughter of GW's half brother Augustine Washington.

From Alexander Hamilton

Sir, Treasury Departmt July 26. 1792.

Samuel Hobart, third Mate of the Cutter on the New Hampshire Station, has tendered his resignation and sent forward his Commission which I retain 'till your return not to encumber you with it at Mount Vernon. This occasions two vacancies, as to that Cutter, of first & third Mate. The Collector of Portsmouth recommends the second Mate, John Adams, for first Mate, and a Benjamin Gunnison, who has been a Master of a Vessel, as second Mate. From a conversation which I had with Mr Langdon, while here I believe the recommendation of the Collector well founded.[1]

The Captain of the Cutter, on the New York Station, informs that Mr Morris the first Mate has accepted an advantageous offer on board of an India-Ship. This leaves the Cutter without any other Officer than the Master, who, and the Collector of New York recommend Capt: Ashur Cook as first Mate, and one John Fenley as second Mate. Captn Dennis also mentions a son of the present Surveyor of New York for third Mate.

The keeping up in the Cutters their due complement of Officers and Men is now become interesting to the public service. As it will not be easy to obtain better lights, I am induced to submit as they stand the recommendations respecting the first and second Mates of each Cutter. As to the third Mate for the New York Cutter some further enquiry is necessary.[2]

Should you approve, and be without blank Commissions, it is

still desireable that I should be able as early as convenient to notify your determination. The persons will enter into service upon that notification and then Commissions can be antedated. With the most perfect respect and truest attachment, I have the honor to be &c.

Alexander Hamilton

P.S. May I be permitted to remind you of the vacancies in the Maryland Cutter, about which you intended to enquire on your way?[3]

LB, DLC:GW.

1. In response to Tench Coxe's note of 17 Dec. 1791 to Tobias Lear (DLC: GW), Lear wrote Thomas Jefferson on 19 Dec. that the president "wishes Commissions to be made out for the following persons as officers on board the Revenue Cutter on the New Hampshire station—vizt. John Parrott, first mate; vice [John] Flagg—declined. John Adams, second mate; vice Parrott—promoted. Samuel Hobart Junr third mate" (DLC:GW). For the collector of Portsmouth Joseph Whipple's recommendations, see Whipple to Hamilton, 7 Oct. 1791 and 30 June 1792 (Syrett, *Hamilton Papers,* 9:297–99, 11:610).

2. In his letter to Hamilton of 5 Aug., GW approved the appointments of Adams, Gunnison, Cook, and Fenley and agreed that further inquiry was needed before a third mate could be chosen for the N.Y. cutter.

3. For GW's inquiries into the vacancies in the Maryland cutter service on his way home to Mount Vernon, see GW to Hamilton, 5 Aug. 1792.

From James Seagrove

Sir Rock landing on the Oconee in Georgia 27th July 1792

I herewith send you a copy of what I had the honor of communicating to you on the 5th instant which I sent by express to Savannah to be forwarded from thence by Mr Habersham the Collector since that date I am not so happy as to receive a line from any of the public departments and as the Cloud in this Southern Country seems to thicken with matter interesting to you and the Union I must again trouble you with what information I have been able to collect since the above period.

In the first place you will find inclosed the Copy of a letter which I wrote Governor Telfair of Georgia and also the declaration of Charles Wethersford against a Col. Samuel Alexander of the Militia of Green County in this State which will in some degree convey to you the licentious ungovernable spirit of the people on this frontier and on how precarious a tenure we hold peace with the Indians—The refractory conduct of the frontier inhabitants of the upper part of this State is so notorious and so apparently determined to bring on a War with the Indians that all endeavours to preserve peace seems in vain.[1]

My motives for sending Governor Telfair the deposition against Alexander and writing him as you will please observe was that he should not plead ignorance at a future day of the Conduct of his Citizens and at same time to see what measures he would take to check such doings.

Was it necessary or would it answer any purpose I could have many very many of such testimonies taken. Scarcely a day passes but I have fresh instances of those frontier banditti's opposition to pacific measures and of their flying in the face of the General Government. To such lengths have matters got among them that they now consider the troops and servants of the United States who are placed among them nearly as great Enemies as they do the Indians and for no other reason than that they recommend moderation and a compliance with the laws of the land.

It is truly distressing that a few such vile characters should bring an oduim on the State of Georgia; For they are few comparatively speaking to the good people in the State, who are as forward as any in the Union to support federal measures. but the misfortune is that there is sufficient of those bad to involve the whole in great distress which will be the case should there be an Indian War.

Since my last to you which was pretty full on the subject of Spanish and Indian matters I have received many pieces of information, all tending to confirm me in the opinion that the Spaniards are acting as much to the injury of the United States as they possibly can, and that General McGillivray hath verified my predictions of him.

From every information which I can collect from White people and Indians there does not remain a doubt with me but that the Spaniards will if they possibly can involve the United States in a War with the four Southern Nations of Indians every exertion is making by the Spaniards and undue measures taking with the Savages to stir them up against us.

The enclosed testimony on Oath of James Leonard who appears to be a man of information and respectable decent manners will explain and open to you new matter of perfidy in spain as well as base Conduct in General McGillivray—Mr Leonard is a Stranger to me and in this Country—his appearance is much in his favour, he is a modest man, of few words, and seems actuated in this information by no other motive but to serve the United States. He is a Citizen of Massachusetts & lived at Beverly.

Mr Leonard's testimony being corroborated to me by a variety of Accounts and circumstances within my own knowledge that I am the more readily led to place confidence in it. He is now with me, and I have taken much pains in cross examining and sounding him on this information, but cannot find him defective, or any room for suspicion as to his veracity.[2]

That General McGillivray has all along been acting a Traitor's part by the United States. I have long suspected and hinted to you. To him alone are the United States to charge all the delays and confusions and irregularities which have taken place between them and the Creek Nation. He it is who hath impeded and prevented business being done with them—It is to him that Bowles owes his consequence—for certain it is that he was weak and wicked enough to believe (for several Months after Bowles[']s arrival in the Nation) that he came under authority from the British Government, and therefore underhandedly favoured him. Bowles had address enough to impose this belief on McGillivrays *director Mr Panton,* and they carried on the deception, with a view in the end, to injure Spain as well as this Country and to reastablish the English with the Creeks. This I have from one of McGillivrays own family who was let into the secret.[3]

McGillivray is now gone & I hope most sincerely never will return to the Nation; for so long as he has a say in their Councils the United States never will succeed with the Indians. He is an Enemy in his heart to our Country & measures & is now so totally under the influence & direction of Spain & Panton, that he cannot or dare not, serve the United States if he was so inclined. Upon the whole I think it fortunate that he has thrown off the mark, & taken himself out of the nation—his name will soon be dispised by the Indians—provided the Agents of America are allowed to speak freely to them. I can with confidence and truth say, that had not McGillivray been in the way, that I should, ere this, have had all matters agreeably situated between the United States & the Creeks. He has been a heavy clog on my endeavours—for instead of opposing him in his perfidious acts, I was using every argument to reinstate him with his Country who had penetration to see that he was acting a double part, & therefore they dispised him. I view and consider him as of very little consequence to the United States; there are men in the Creek Nation may be made much more useful, & of greater influence than ever he was.[4]

Should it be found that the Spaniards are acting as has been represented; & that you see fit to combat them in their own way: that is, make use of the Indians—I will engage to turn the tables compleatly on them. For you may rely, that the Indians are disposed to be our friends, notwithstanding the underhand unwarrantable doings of McGillivray & the Spaniards. The Spaniards it is well known they dislike, & would sooner join any nation then them. So that if I am allowed to Speak plainly to the Leading characters, and have it in my power to make them presents. I think I cannot only prevent them acting against us—but secure them to act as circumstances may require. I have allready taken measures to have two or three trusty fellows at The Treaty at Pensacola, from whom I shall hear what is done there. Tomorrow I shall set off for the head of St Mary's where I expect to meet *Kinnard* the principal active man in the lower Towns, with some other Chiefs, to give them their lesson before they go to Pensacola.[5] Allow me to mention the naked defenceless state of the So. W. frontier—not more than fifteen men there & those without even a Serjant to direct them. I have applied to Major Call to send one of the Company's now here to go to the head of St Mary's, but he does not find himself at liberty[6] in my opinion a respectable force on that frontier is necessary at this time.

Inclosed I send you an Anonymous letter which came enclosed to me from the Creek nation—it is directed to the Printer in Savannah. The writer of it I do not know, but it contains the received opinion & belief of all the white people in the nation—and many matters stated in it, are absolutely true.[7]

The situation of affairs in this quarter seem so very interesting that I do not think prudent to delay giving you information; and as the conveyances to me, are uncertain and danger of dispatches falling into improper hands, I have sent the Bearer James Jordan a very trusty young man who lives with me, & to whom you may committ the care of any Commands you may have to me. He has orders to wait your time for that purpose. I have sent also a letter I received from Timothy Barnard—it may afford you some information—as Bernard is a man to be depended on. I have left my letter to the Secretary of War open for your perusal.[8]

I shall continue my endeavours to discover what is going forward in the Nation as well as among the Spaniards & convey you notice. In hope of soon hearing from you with further power & instructions[9] I remain Your Most Obedient Most Devoted and Very Humble Servant

Js Seagrove

LB, DNA: RG 107, Office of the Secretary of War, Letters Sent and Received, 1791–1797; LB (photocopy), DNA: RG 46, Second Congress, 1791–1793, Records of Legislative Proceedings, Reports and Communications Submitted to the Senate; copy, DNA: RG 233, Third Congress, 1793–1795, Records of Legislative Proceedings, President's Messages; copy (extract), DLC: Jefferson Papers; copy (extract), DNA: RG 59, Instructions to Diplomatic Officers, Instructions, 1785–1906; copy (extract), DNA: RG 46, Third Congress, 1793–1795, Records of Executive Proceedings, President's Messages—Foreign Relations.

1. On 10 July, Charles Weatherford declared that Col. Samuel Alexander of Greene County, Ga., had told him: "We are determined" that the boundary line between the Creeks and the state of Georgia "shall not be run, unless the first articles of the treaty shall be complied with beforehand . . . [and] that they (meaning the people of the upper counties of Georgia) could, in seven days, raise one thousand men, who would, by force, prevent its being run, and break up the whole business" (*ASP, Indian Affairs,* 1:307). Seagrove had written in his letter to Georgia governor Edward Telfair of 18 July that Colonel Alexander was a man who had murdered Indians "in cool blood, and who was the principal cause (as your Excellency well knows) of involving the country in a long, bloody, and expensive war with the Creek Indians," and he observes that "if my labors are not counteracted by bad white people in this country, I have not a doubt of preserving peace" (ibid., 306–7).

2. James Leonard, a merchant who had plied his trade in New Orleans, Spanish Florida, and the Creek Nation during the previous two years, declared on 24 July that "from what he has seen, and came to his knowledge in the Spanish country, that the Spaniards are doing every thing in their power to engage the Indians in a war with the United States; not only the Creeks, but the other three nations, viz. the Choctaws, Chickasaws, and Cherokees. . . . That this deponent received undoubted accounts, before his quitting Tensa, that five Spanish regiments, said to contain between five and six hundred men each, had actually arrived as a reinforcement to the posts on the Mississippi, since the beginning of May last; and that many more regiments were expected from the Havana to that country. That very large quantities of artillery and stores had also arrived to the posts on said river" (ibid., 307–8).

3. For the background to William Augustus Bowles's intrigues against Alexander McGillivray in the Creek country from the summer of 1791 until Bowles was seized by Spanish authorities in late February 1792, see the Secret Article of the Treaty with the Creeks, 4 Aug. 1790, source note, enclosed in GW to the U.S. Senate, that date, "John A. Dingwell" to GW, 12, 16 Aug. 1790, "Dingwell" to Henry Knox or Tobias Lear, 17 Aug. 1790, the enclosures to Memorandum from Lear, 18 Aug. 1790, Knox to GW, 14 Nov. 1791, n.1, 26 Dec. 1791, n.1, and to Lear, 30 Nov. 1791, n.1. For William Panton's long-standing business interests in the region, see Knox to GW, 6 July 1789, n.1.

4. On 6 July 1792 Alexander McGillivray signed at New Orleans a treaty with the Spanish governor Francisco Luis Hector, Baron de Carondelet, guaranteeing the lands belonging to both Spain and the Creek Nation at the time of the 1784 Treaty of Pensacola and requiring Spain to furnish the Creeks "& their Ally's with ample, & sufficient Supplys of Arms & ammunition, not only to defend their Country, but even to regain their encroached Lands, should the Americans refuse willingly & peaceably to retire in the time pointed out [two months], or in case of the Creek Nation being unjustly attacked by any People whatever unprovoked" (Caughey, *McGillivray of the Creeks,* 329–30). McGillivray returned to Little Tallassie by 10 Aug. 1792 (ibid., 333).

5. For the background to the gathering of Indian chiefs at Pensacola in the fall of 1792, see notes 4 and 7 to this document and Seagrove to GW, 5 July, and note 2.

6. For earlier criticisms of Maj. Richard Call's intemperance and the impact it might have on his decision making, see Henry Knox to GW, 9 July 1791, and Seagrove to GW, 21 April, 5 July 1792.

7. The anonymous letter to the printer of the *Georgia Gazette* (Savannah) which was written by "A FRIEND TO JUSTICE" on 29 June 1792, reads in part: "Mr. [William] Panton has lately made a tour through the Upper Creeks to the Cherokees, and returned through the Lower Creeks to St. Mark's. He encouraged the Indians every where to oppose the Americans, and not give up their land; he particularly told the Creeks not to run the line. To back Mr. Panton, a Spanish officer has been sent into the Creeks; his talks are to the following purport, viz: Not to give up an inch of land nor run the line, and they should be protected in it; and that there was a large quantity of arms, ammunition, &c. for them at Pensacola, which he invited them to come and receive. He also told them, that, if any blood was spilled to let him know, and he would write to the King of Spain, who had soldiers enough, not far off, to assist them. . . . Talks to the same effect have been sent to the Cherokees, Chickasaws, and Choctaws, but we are happy to hear that neither his nor Panton's talks will be taken by the Chickasaws nor Lower Creeks, but treated with the contempt they deserve. Some of the Upper Creeks, we understand, approve of them." The author also asserts that Panton and Pedro Olivier were attacking Alexander McGillivray's reputation, that the Spanish were sending cannon up the Mississippi River for use against the United States, and that William Augustus Bowles "is gone to the court of Spain, to negotiate some business relative to a free port; he is allowed four dollars per day during his embassy; he is treated

with every mark of distinction, and not a prisoner, as has been industriously insinuated by Panton and his myrmidons" (*ASP, Indian Affairs,* 1:309).

8. Timothy Barnard served as deputy agent to the Creeks for several years during the first half of the 1790s, and he was one of the interpreters at the Treaty of Coleraine in 1796. His letter to Seagrove of 13 July, which includes all of the stock arguments about William Augustus Bowles, Pedro Olivier, and the calling of a meeting at Pensacola in the fall of 1792, hypothesizes that "there were some disputes on the Mississippi, between the Spaniards and Americans, about the land; that the Spaniards were afraid of the Americans, and that they wanted to get the Indians to fight the Americans first, to save themselves" (ibid., 309–10). Seagrove wrote Secretary of War Knox on 27 July that "if I am supported with goods and provisions to give [the Creeks], and allowed to act freely with them in gaining their friendship, that, notwithstanding every thing to the contrary, I will be able to keep the Creeks in peace with us, if not make them very useful" (ibid., 310).

9. Secretary of War Knox, after consulting with GW, Alexander Hamilton, and Edmund Randolph, replied on 31 Aug. to Seagrove's letters of 5 and 27 July (ibid., 259). Both Knox's letter and GW's shorter response to Seagrove of 4 Sept. apparently were delivered to Seagrove by James Jordan on 1 Oct. 1792.

From Jonathan Trumbull, Jr.

Sir Lebanon [Conn.] 27th July 1792

I have the honor to inclose, for your information, the Copy of a Letter which I have this day received from Mr Barclay—covering a Petition from the American Prisoners, now in Captivity at Algiers, a Copy of which is also transmitted herewith.[1]

This communication I beg leave to make to you Sir! as the only mean in my power, during the recess of Congress, which can afford me the hope of contributing to the relief of our suffering fellow Citizens, whose unhappy situation is so well pictured in their Petition. With the most perfect Respect & Regard I have the honor to be sir! Your most Obet & most hu. Servt

Jona; Trumbull

ALS, DNA: RG 59, Miscellaneous Letters; ADfS, NHi.

On 20 Aug., GW replied to Trumbull from Mount Vernon: "Your letter of the 26th Ulto enclosing one from Mr [Thomas] Barclay containing the petition of our prisoners in Algiers, came duly to hand. Every thing that my powers and means will enable me to do consistent with justice & policy shall not be wanting to the relief of these unfortunate captives. and I would fein hope they will not be ineffectually employed" (ALS, NNGL; ADfS, DNA: RG 59, Miscellaneous Letters; LB, DLC:GW). GW's mistake in referring to Trumbull's letter as being "of the 26th Ulto" can be traced to GW's docket on the letter, which reads in part, "26th July 1792."

1. Thomas Barclay's letter to Jonathan Trumbull, Jr., which was written at Gibraltar on 28 May 1792, reads: "I do myself the honor to inclose you a Petition which I received Yesterday from the American Prisoners at Algiers, who request in the most earnest manner that you will lay it before the House of Representatives" (DNA: RG 59, Miscellaneous Letters). The petition, which was written at Algiers on 29 Mar. 1792 and signed by Richard O'Bryen and twelve other American captives, reads: "That we were captured nearly Seven Years ago, by Cruizers belonging to the Regency of Algiers, while we were navigating Vessells belonging to Citizens of the U. States—That we were for a considerable time flattered with the expectations held up to us, that we would be redeemed from Captivity as soon as it could be done consistent with propriety, and the Interest of our Country—That to effect this redemption, Mr John Lamb was sent to Algiers on the part of the U. States, and that he entered into an agreement with the Regency of Algiers for our Ransom; in consequence of which the terms were recorded on the Books of the Regency—But Mr Lamb never returned to fulfill them by the payment of the ransom Money, 'tho he promised, in the name of the U. States, to do it in four Monthes[.] That we understand, several persons have since been employed to make enquiries, whether the ransom agreed upon by Mr Lamb might not be reduced—but all attempts of that sort have hitherto proved ineffectual—the Regency declaring that the Contracts made by the Agent on the part of the U. States ought to be discharged—That we were for some time supplied with such Sums of Money as served, together with the prospect of redemption held up to us, to alleviate, in some degree, the rigours of our Captivity—but those supplies have ceased for a considerable time; during which we have been reduced to the utmost distress—and we are compelled in a great measure to depend on the Charity of transcient people—That, owing to the melancholly situation to which we are reduced, one of us, James Harnett has been deprived of his senses, and is confined in a Dungeon—the rest remain destitute almost of all the necessaries of Life—And in this deplorable situation, we have resisted any temptations to enter into the service of the Regency—that might hereafter be attended with Repentance or Remorse—trusting in the Justice & Humanity of Congress, that we shall never be reduced to the necessity of abandoning our Country and our Religion.

"Your most humble Petitioners further pray, that you will consider what our sufferings must have been for nearly seven Years Captivity—twice surrounded by the pest [plague] & other contagious distempers—which has numbered Six of our Brother sufferers in the Bills of Mortality—And we, the unfortunate remnant remain employed on the most laborious Work—far distant from our friends, families & connections—without any real prospect or assurances of ever seeing them more.

"But we entreat that some attention will be paid to our situation—and that Congress will, before the whole of us perish, take such steps towards our being liberated, as in their Judgment shall appear right & proper—and Your most humble Petitioners will ever pray & be thankfull" (DNA: RG 59, Miscellaneous Letters). As Congress was not in session from May to November 1792, the petition was not read until 9 Nov. when it was "referred to the Secretary of State, to report thereon to the Senate" (*Annals of Congress,* 2d Cong., 613).

From Henry Knox

Sir War department July 28th 1792

Since the letter I had the honor of transmitting the 21st instant I have received a letter from Governor Blount dated the 4th instant.[1]

A meeting of the Cherokees at Estanaula had taken place which lasted from the 24th of June to the first of July at which the little Turkey and many other Chiefs were present but the Bloody Fellow and John Watts[2] whom the Governor in his former letter styled "*the Champions for peace*" were absent—But most of the others who composed the delegation were present.

The dispositions manifested were friendly—a number of chiefs were selected to protect the boats who were to pass down the Tennasee with the goods designed for the conference to be held with the Chickasaws and Choctaws at Nashville.

But the little Turkey expressed considerable dissatisfaction at the line towards Cumberland alledging it to be the hunting grounds of the four Nations to wit—the Creeks—Cherokees—Choctaws and Chickasaws.

It is to be observed that this Man is the most influential chief of the Cherokees, and that he was neither at the Treaty of Hopewell in 1785 or Holstein in 1791—I have had some doubts whether that part of the line was agreeable to the opinion of the Cherokees generally—and it really appears to me that something will yet be to be arranged on that subject.

Some Indians supposed to be Creeks have committed several murders at Nashville, and have wounded General Robertson and his Son.[3]

The Governor has had discretionary power to call forth such portions of Militia as he should judge expedient for the protection of the exposed parts of his government, and he has at different periods actually called for five companies of militia most of which are now in service.

The Governor expected the Chickasaws and Choctaws to meet him at Nashville about the 25th instant.

The Goods for the conference at Nashville left Holstein under the charge of Mr Allison the 3rd instant under a proper escort, besides the Indian chiefs before mentioned.

The Governor and General Pickens were to set out for Nashville on the 5th instant to cross Cumberland Mountains escorted by some horse which he called out for the occasion.

The Governor has transmitted the affidavits of two Men recently from the Creek Country, tending to prove the interference of the Spanish Agent to prevent the Creeks from running the line—and also of some parties of Creeks making depredations on the Cumberland Settlements.[4]

It would seem the Creeks consider the Cumberland settlers as intruders on the joint lands of the four Nations, and therefore they have a right to steal horses and in case of opposition to kill.

It is to be hoped the Governor may devise some measures to prevent the progress of those depredations and which lead to a general confusion and war with the Creeks and Cherokees—I shall write him by the way of Fort Pitt.[5]

No information yet of Colonel Hardin or Major Trueman[6]—General Wayne on the 20th gives information of some recent depredations by small parties on Ohio County.

About three hundred and twenty effectives of his troops had arrived.

The information of Recruits since the last Return is agreeable to the within.[7]

The desertions of the troops on the march are excessive—Out of about three hundred and fifty, nearly fifty deserted from Reading to Fort Pitt.

General St Clair has returned from the Western parts of this state I have intimated to him your desire of his repairing to his Government but he says it will be extremely inconvenient to him to do it as he has a law suit to be tried in September next—He seems to think that it would not be proper or necessary for him to be present at the Trial of Ensign Morgan—He is to deliver me his evidence in a week or ten days when I shall order Mr Morgan to join the Army for his trial.[8] I have the honor to be with the highest Respect Your most obed. Servant

H. Knox
Secy of War.

LS, DLC:GW; LB, DLC:GW.

1. See William Blount to Knox, 4 July, in Carter, *Territorial Papers,* 4:157–59.

2. John Watts (Kunoskeskee; Young Tassel) was one of the leading Cherokee chiefs.

3. Governor Blount wrote Knox on 31 Aug. that on 15 July two Americans were killed and one wounded "*On the road that leads from Nashville to Kentucky*" (*ASP, Indian Affairs,* 1:276). On 4 July, Blount wrote Knox: "On the 8h of June General [James] Robertson and his Son were wounded by Indians on his own plantation, himself shot through both arms, one broke and his Son through the thigh but both are on the recovery" (Carter, *Territorial Papers,* 4: 159). James Robertson (1742–1814) was appointed a justice of the peace for Davidson County, Southwest Territory, in December 1790, a brigadier general of militia in February 1791, and a U.S. agent to the Chickasaw Nation the following year.

4. Blount enclosed three affidavits in his letter to Knox of 4 July: those of James Ore, Ezekiel Abel, and Daniel Thornbury (see *ASP, Indian Affairs,* 1: 274–75). Ore said that he "was informed by a white man, who understood the Creek language, and one in whom this deponent had entire confidence, that the purport of Oliver's [Pedro Olivier] talk with the chiefs of the Creeks was, 'That the Spanish talk, the French talk, and the British, were all one; when was the day they asked them for land? But the Americans were still wanting their lands; and if they wanted ammunition and arms to defend their lands, come to them, meaning the Spaniards, and they should have them'" (ibid., 274).

5. See Knox to Blount, 15 Aug., in Carter, *Territorial Papers,* 4:162–64.

6. For the background to the peace mission of Alexander Trueman and John Hardin, see Thomas Jefferson's Memorandum of a Meeting of the Heads of the Executive Departments, 9 Mar., and Knox to GW, 1 April 1792, n.2.

7. Knox enclosed a return "of the Recruits at the respective rendezvous" of 28 July, which reported that 1,734 recruits had arrived by 21 July and 93 more by 28 July, for a grand total of 1,827 soldiers (DLC:GW).

8. John Morgan (1770–1819), who had been commissioned an ensign in the U.S. Army in May 1790, served as an aide to Gen. Richard Butler during Gen. Arthur St. Clair's expedition of 1791. Following the disastrous defeat of 4 Nov. 1791, St. Clair charged the deceased Butler with failing to inform him of the presence of a large force of Indians nearby on the night before the battle. Morgan's court-martial was brought on by a letter of condolence that he had written to Butler's widow in which he exonerated Butler and blamed St. Clair for the defeat. When this letter was published, St. Clair brought charges of slander and insubordination against Morgan. Morgan's court-

martial was convened at Anthony Wayne's headquarters a short distance south of Pittsburgh in August 1793, and he was found guilty and cashiered in December 1793.

To Alexander Hamilton

(Private & confidential)

My dear Sir, Mount Vernon July 29th 1792.

I have not yet received the new regulation of allowances to the Surveyors, or Collectors of the duties on Spirituous liquors;[1] but this by the bye. My present purpose is to write you a letter on a more interesting and important subject. I shall do it in strict confidence, & with frankness & freedom.

On my way home, and since my arrival here, I have endeavoured to learn from sensible & moderate men—known friends to the Government—the sentiments which are entertained of public measures. These all agree that the Country is prosperous & happy; but they seem to be alarmed at that system of policy, and those interpretations of the Constitution which have taken place in[2] Congress.

Others, less friendly perhaps to the Government, and more disposed to arraign the conduct of its Officers (among whom may be classed my neighbour & quandom[3] friend Colo. M.[4]) go further, & enumerate a variety of matters—wch as well as I can recollect, may be adduced under the following heads.[5] Viz.

First—That the public debt is greater than we can possibly pay before other causes of adding new debt to it will occur; and that this has been artificially created by adding together the whole amount of the debtor & creditor sides of the accounts, instead of taking only their balances; which could have been paid off in a short time.

2d—That this accumulation of debt has taken forever out of our power those easy sources of Revenue, which, applied to the ordinary necessities and exigencies of Government, would have answered them habitually, and covered us from habitual murmerings against taxes & tax gatherers; reserving extraordinary calls, for extraordinary occasions, would animate the People to meet them.

3d—That the calls for money have been no greater than we

must generally expect, for the same or equivalent exigencies; yet we are already obliged to strain the *impost* till it produces clamour, and will produce evasion, and war on our citizens to collect it, and even to resort to an *Excise* law, of odious character with the people; partial in its operation; unproductive unless enforced by arbitrary & vexatious means; and committing the authority of the Government in parts where resistance is most probable, & coercion least practicable.

4th—They cite propositions in Congress, and suspect other projects on foot, still to encrease the mass of the debt.

5th—They say that by borrowing at ⅔ of the interest, we might have paid of[f] the principal in ⅔ of the time; but that from this we are precluded by its being made irredeemable but in small portions, & long terms.

6th—That this irredeemable quality was given it for the avowed purpose of inviting its transfer to foreign Countries.

7th—They predict that this transfer of the principal, when compleated, will occasion an exportation of 3 Millions of dollars annually for the interest; a drain of Coin, of which as there has been no example, no calculation can be made of its consequences.

8th—That the banishment of our Coin will be compleated by the creation of 10 millions of paper money, in the form of Bank-bills now issuing into circulation.

9th—They think the 10 or 12 pr Ct annual profit, paid to the lenders of this paper medium are taken out of the pockets of the people, who would have had without interest the coin it is banishing.

10th—That all the Capitol employed in paper speculation is barren & useless, producing, like that on a gaming table, no accession to itself, and is withdrawn from Commerce and Agriculture where it would have produced addition to the common mass.

11th—That it nourishes in our citizens vice & idleness instead of industry & morality.

12th—That it has furnished effectual means of corrupting such a portion of the legislature, as turns the balance between the honest Voters which ever way it is directed.

13th—That this corrupt squadron, deciding the voice of the legislature, have manifested their dispositions to get rid of the limitations imposed by the Constitution on the general legislature; limitations, on the faith of which, the States acceded to that instrument.

14th—That the ultimate object of all this is to prepare the way for a change, from the present republican form of Government, to that of a monarchy; of which the British Constitution is to be the model.

15th—That this was contemplated in the Convention, they say is no secret, because its partisans have made none of it—to effect it then was impracticable; but they are still eager after their object, and are predisposing every thing for its ultimate attainment.

16th—So many of them have got into the legislature, that, aided by the corrupt squadron of paper dealers, who are at their devotion, they make a majority in both houses.

17th—The republican party who wish to preserve the Government in its present form, are fewer even when joined by the two, three, or half a dozen antifederalists, who, tho' they dare not avow it, are still opposed to any general Government: but being less so to a Republican than a Monarchical one, they naturally join those whom they think pursuing the lesser evil.

18th—Of all the[6] mischiefs objected to the system of measures beforementioned, none they add is so afflicting, & fatal to every honest hope, as the corruption of the legislature. As it was the earliest of these measures it became the instrument for producing the rest, and will be the instrument for producing in future a King, Lords & Commons; or whatever else those who direct it may chuse. Withdrawn such a distance from the eye of their Constituents, and these so dispersed as to be inaccessible to public information, and particularly to that of the conduct of their own Representatives, they will form the worst Government upon earth, if the means of their corruption be not prevented.

19th—The only hope of safety they say, hangs now on the numerous Representation which is to come forward the ensuing year; but should the majority of the new members be still in the same principles with the present—shew so much deriliction to republican government, and such a disposition to encroach upon, or explain away the limited powers of the constitution in order to change it, it is not easy to conjecture what would be the result, nor what means would be resorted to for correction of the evil. True wisdom they acknowledge should direct temperate & peaceable measures; but add, the division of sentiment & interest happens unfortunately, to be so geographical, that no mortal can say that what is most wise & temperate, would prevail against what is more easy & obvious; they declare, they can contemplate no evil more incalculable than the breaking of the Union into two, or more parts; yet, when they view the mass which opposed the original coalescence, when they consider that it lay chiefly in the Southern quarter—that the legislature have availed themselves of no occasion of allaying it, but on the contrary whenever Northern & Southern prejudices have come into conflict, the latter have been sacraficed and the former soothed.

20th—That the owers of the debt are in the Southern and the holders of it in the Northern division.

21st—That the antifederal champions are now strengthened in argument by the fulfilment of their predictions, which has been brought about by the monarchical federalists themselves; who, having been for the new government merely as a stepping stone to monarchy, have themselves adopted the very construction, of which, when advocating its acceptance before the tribunal of the people, they declared it insuceptable; whilst the Republican federalists, who espoused the same government for its intrinsic merits, are disarmed of their weapons, that which they denied as prophecy being now become true history. Who, therefore, can be sure they ask, that these things may not proselyte the small number which was wanting to place the majority on the other side—and this they add is the event at which they tremble.

These, as well as my memory serves me, are the sentiments which, directly and indirectly, have been disclosed to me.

To obtain light, and to pursue truth, being my sole aim; and wishing to have[7] before me *explanations* of as well as the *complaints* on measures in which the public interest, harmony and peace is so deeply concerned, and my public conduct so much involved; it is my request, and you would oblige me in furnishing me, with your ideas upon the discontents here enumerated—and for this purpose I have thrown them into heads or sections, and numbered them that those ideas may apply to the corrispondent numbers. Although I do not mean to hurry you in giving your thoughts on the occasion of this letter, yet, as soon as you can make it convenient to yourself it would—for more reasons than one—be agreeable, & very satisfactory to me.[8]

The enclosure in your letter of the 16th was sent back the Post after I received it, with my approving Signature;[9] and in a few days I will write to the purpose mentioned in your letter of the 22d both to the Secretary of War & yourself—At present all my business—public & private—is on my own shoulders, the two young Gentlemen who came home with me, being on visits to their friends—and my Nephew, the Major, too much indisposed to afford me any aid, in copying or in other matters. With affectionate regard I am always—Yours

Go: Washington

ALS, DLC: Hamilton Papers; ADfS, DLC:GW; LB, DLC:GW.

1. Hamilton enclosed the "new regulation of allowances" in his letter to GW of 30 July 1792. For the background to that document, see Proclamation, 4 Aug., and note 2.

2. At this place on the draft manuscript, GW wrote and struck out the following passage: "the Legislature, and which they say, the friends to the adoption of it when the enemies were opposing it in the several Conventions averred never could be admitted, or so tortured in that manner. The plea of expediency, or war necessity they say, ought never to be admitted but in the greatest and most pressing emergency and then, acts of indemnity & ratification ought immediately to follow." He then inserted the word "Congress."

3. The Latin word "quondam" means "at one time" or "formerly."

4. GW is referring to Col. George Mason.

5. For the background to this letter, see Thomas Jefferson to GW, 23 May (second letter), and Jefferson's Conversation with Washington, 10 July 1792. GW here repeats the points made in Jefferson's second letter of 23 May almost verbatim.

6. At this place on the draft manuscript, GW first wrote and then struck out the word "numerous."

7. At this place on the draft manuscript, GW wrote and then struck out the phrase: "the pros & cons of every subject."

8. Although Hamilton promised on 11 Aug. to send GW his answer to the president's questions by the "next Monday's Post," 13 Aug., he did not complete his work by that time. Hamilton mailed his lengthy response on 18 Aug. 1792.

9. For Hamilton's enclosure, "a Resolution of the Commissioners of the Sinking Fund," see Hamilton to GW, 16 July 1792, n.1.

From Alexander Hamilton

Sir, Treasury Department July 30. 1792.

I have the honor to transmit herewith sundry papers relative to an arrangement, which has been concerted between the Commissioner of the Revenue and myself, on the subject of compensation to the Officers of Inspection, in consequence of additional latitude given to The President of the United States by the Act of the last Session entitled, An Act concerning the duties on spirits distilled within the United States. This arrangement, founded on the best lights hitherto in the possession of the Department, is respectfully submitted to your consideration & disposal.[1]

More adequate compensations than those heretofore allowed (and which from necessity were restricted within narrower limits than were originally deemed proper) are essential to the effectual execution of the law. Many Officers wait the issue of a new arrangement to decide their continuance or non-continuance in Office.

The additions now proposed will, it is not doubted, leave the aggregate expence within the limits prescribed by law; the contingent items having been estimated largely for greater caution.

Intimations have been received that the non-execution of the Law in certain scenes begins to produce discontent in neighbouring ones, in which a perfect acquiescence had taken place.[2] This is natural, and implies a danger of a serious nature, if not timely obviated. The inadequateness of compensation, by preventing the acceptance of Offices, where the Law is least popular, is one of the causes of that non-execution. It is interesting that this cause be removed as a preliminary to the vigorous enforcing of the law in the delinquent scenes; which makes it desireable that a more competent arrangement of compensations should be adopted as speedily as shall consist with due consideration and your convenience. With the highest respect and the truest attachment, I have the honor to be &c.

Alexder Hamilton

LB, DLC:GW.

1. For the background to the preparation of the enclosed report of Hamilton and Tench Coxe and its issuance in early August, see Proclamation, 4 Aug. 1792, and note 2.

2. Daniel Huger, for instance, wrote Hamilton on 22–25 June "that during my Journey thro' Virginia, I learnt that it was customary with the North Carolinians to convey Large quantities of their distilled Spirits into that State, which, as privileged people, they Sold at a Cheaper rate than those of their Sister State could afford to do and of course had the preference" (Syrett, *Hamilton Papers,* 11:541–43). Edward Carrington informed Hamilton in mid-July of the "non execution of the Excise Law in N Carolina" (ibid., 12:83–85).

From Alexander Hamilton

Sir Philadelphia July 30th[–3 August] 1792

I received the most sincere pleasure at finding in our last conversation, that there was some relaxation in the disposition you had before discovered to decline a reelection. Since your departure,[1] I have lost no opportunity of sounding the opinions of persons, whose opinions were worth knowing, on these two points—1st the effect of your declining upon the public affairs, and upon your own reputation—2dly the effect of your continuing, in reference to the declarations you have made of your disinclination to public life—And I can truly say, that I have not found the least difference of sentiment, on either point. The impression is uniform—that your declining would be to be deplored as the greatest evil, that could befall the country at the present juncture, and as critically hazardous to your own reputation—that your continuance will be justified in the mind of every friend to his country by the evident necessity for it. Tis clear, says every one, with whom I have conversed, that the affairs of the national government are not yet firmly established—that its enemies, generally speaking, are as inveterate as ever—that their enmity has been sharpened by its success and by all the resentments which flow from disappointed predictions and mortified vanity—that a general and strenuous effort is making in every state to place the administration of it in the hands of its enemies, as if they were its safest guardians—that the period of the next house of representatives is likely to prove the crisis of its permanent character—that if you continue in office nothing materially mischievous is to be apprehended—if you quit much is to be dreaded—that the same motives which induced you to accept originally ought to decide you to continue till matters have assumed a more determinate aspect—that indeed it would have been better, as it regards your own character, that you had never consented to come forward, than now to leave the business unfinished and in danger of being undone—that in the event of storms arising there would be an imputation either of want of foresight or want of firmness—and, in fine, that on public and personal accounts, on patriotic and prudential considerations, the clear path to be pursued by you will be again to obey the voice of your country; which it is not doubted will be as earnest and as unanimous as ever.

On this last point, I have some suspicion that it will be insinuated to you, and perhaps (God forgive me, if I judge hardly) with design to place before you a motive for declining—that there is danger of a division among the electors and of less unanimity in their suffrages than heretofore. My view of this matter is as follows:

While your first election was depending I had no doubt, that there would be characters among the electors, who if they durst follow their inclinations, would have voted against you; but that in all probability they would be restrained by an apprehension of public resentment—that nevertheless it was possible a few straggling votes might be found in opposition, from some headstrong and fanatical individuals—that a circumstance of this kind would be in fact, and ought to be estimated by you, as of no importance—since their would be sufficient unanimity to witness the general confidence and attachment towards you.

My view of the future accords exactly with what was my view of the past. I believe the same motives will operate to produce the same result. The dread of public indignation will be likely to restrain the indisposed few. If they can calculate at all, they will naturally reflect that they could not give a severer blow to their cause than by giving a proof of hostility to you. But if a solitary vote or two should appear wanting to perfect unanimity, of what moment can it be? Will not the fewness of the exceptions be a confirmation of the devotion of the community to a character, which has so generally united its suffrages, after an administration of four years at the head of a new government, opposed in its first establishment by a large proportion of its citizens and obliged to run counter to many prejudices in devising the arduous arrangements, requisite to public Credit and public Order? Will not those, who may be the authors of any such exceptions, manifest more their own perverseness and malevolence—than any diminution of the affection and confidence of the Nation? I am persuaded, that both these questions ought to be answered in the affirmative; and that there is nothing to be looked for, on the score of diversity of sentiment which ought to weigh for a moment.

I trust, Sir, and I pray God that you will determine to make a further sacrifice of your tranquillity and happiness to the public good. I trust that it need not continue above a year or two more. And I think that it will be more eligible to retire from office before the expiration of the term of an election, than to decline a reelection.

The sentiments I have delivered upon this occasion, I can truly say, proceed exclusively from an anxious concern for the public welfare and an affectionate personal attachment[.] These dispositions must continue to govern in every vicissitude one who has the honor to be very truly and respectfully Sir Your most Obedt & hum. serv.

A. Hamilton

August 3d Since writing the foregoing I am favoured with your interesting letter of the 29th of July. An answer to the points raised is not difficult & shall as soon as possible be forwarded.[2]

ALS, DLC:GW.

1. GW left Philadelphia for Mount Vernon on the afternoon of 11 July (see Tobias Lear to Thomas Jefferson, that date).

2. For Hamilton's lengthy reply to GW's letter of 29 July, see Hamilton to GW, 18 Aug., and its enclosure, entitled "Objections and Answers respecting the Administration of the Government," which is printed in Syrett, *Hamilton Papers,* 12:229–58.

From Thomas Jefferson

Dear Sir Monticello [Va.] July 30. 1792.

I received yesterday the letter you did me the honor to write on the 23d inst. covering one from the Governor of Vermont. as the question Which party has a right to complain, depends on the fact Which party has hitherto exercised jurisdiction in the place where the seizure was made, and the Governor's letter does not ascertain that fact, I think it will be better to wait his answer to my two former letters in which he cannot fail to speak to that point.[1] I inclose a letter just received from Colo. Humphreys; as also one for the Commissioners of the federal territory from my self, covering one from mr Blodget.[2] the inhabitants of Culpepper are intent on opening a short and good road to the new city. they have had a survey of experiment made along the road I have so much enquired after, by Slate[3] run church, Champs' racepaths & Songster's tavern to George town, and they have reason to believe they may make it shorter by 20. miles and better than any of the present roads. this once done, the counties from Culpepper Southwardly will take it up probably, and extend it successively towards Carolina. I have the honor to be with the most perfect respect & attachment Dr Sir Your most obedt & most humble servt

Th: Jefferson

ALS, DNA: RG 59, Miscellaneous Letters; ALS (letterpress copy), DLC: Jefferson Papers; LB, DNA: RG 59, George Washington's Correspondence with His Secretaries of State; LB (photocopy), DLC:GW; copy, DLC: Jefferson Papers.

1. On 23 July, GW sent Jefferson Gov. Thomas Chittenden's letter to the president of 16 June and its enclosures, which included a copy of Chittenden's letter to the acting governor of Lower Canada, Alured Clarke, and affidavits taken from several residents of Alburg, Vermont. For Jefferson's letters to Chittenden of 9 and 12 July, see GW to Jefferson, 7 July, n.2, and 23 July, n.5; *Jefferson Papers*, 24:200, 218–19. Jefferson never received an answer from the Vermont governor. By the fall of 1792, however, the British had dropped their claim to jurisdiction over Alburg.

2. David Humphreys's letter to Jefferson of 21 May 1792 reports a shift of policy on the part of the Spanish government. It would no longer provide monetary support to opponents of the French Revolution, but it would send funds to the French court (ibid., 23:531–32). Jefferson's letter to the commissioners for the District of Columbia of 29 July covered a letter of 10 July from Samuel Blodget and a receipt for the engraved plan of the Federal City (ibid., 24:264).

3. In the letter-book copy this word is mistakenly transcribed as "State."

To Tobias Lear

⟨De⟩ar Sir, Mount Vernon July 30th 1792.

Your letter from New York came duly tó hand,[1] and I was glad to find you had got that far in safety. I wish the remainder of your journey may prove equally pleasant and prosperous. My journey was not of this sort, for after I had parted with the Coach horses I was plagued with those which succeeded them, the following day; and the sick mare, by a dose of Physic which had been administered the night I reached Chester, was so weakened, & failed so much, that she was unable to carry Austin any farther than Susquehanna: from thence she was led to Hartford and left—and two days afterwards gave up the ghost.

I found the face of the Country here, and on the Road this side Baltimore, much, very much indeed, parched by a severe drought; and the Corn in miserable plight; but the day & night we reached home there fell a most delightful & refreshing Rain, and the weather since has been as seasonable as the most sanguine farmer could wish; & if continued to us may make our Indian Corn crop midling—great it is hardly possible to be—so much was it in arrears when the Rains set in.

Great complaints were heard of the Hessian fly, and of the Rust or Mildew, as I travelled on; and in some places I believe the damage has been great; but I conceive more is said than ought to be, on this subject; and, that the Crop upon the whole will be abundent of Wheat: mine in quantity (and the quality is good) will, I expect, greatly exceed any I have made these several years past.

I found at George town many well conceived, & ingenious plans for the Public buildings in the New City: it was a pleasure indeed, to find—in an infant Country—such a display of Architectural abilities. The Plan of Mr Hoben, who was introduced to me by Doctr Tucker, from Charleston, & who appears to be a very judicious man, was made choice of for the President's House; and the Commissioners have agreed with him to superintend the building of it—& that of the Capitol also, if they should, hereafter, be disposed to put both under one management.[2] He has been engaged in some of the first buildings in Dublin—appears a master workman—and has a great many hands of his own. He has laid out the foundation which is now digging & will be back in a month to enter heartily upon the work. The Plan for the Capitol was not fixed on when I left George Town—two or three very elegant ones (among a great many others of less merit) had been presented—but the draughtsmen, not being there, a postponement became necessary to receive explanations.[3] The Bridge will be accomplished (it is said) by the time Specified in the Contract;[4] and every thing that could be put in motion before the Plans for the public buildings were fixed on, is in as much forwardness as could be expected—& will now, I have no doubt, advance rapidly.

As you did not mention your having spoke to Mr Morris about the house, I am under some apprehension that you omitted to do it; which will be unlucky. Give me an Acct of what I suggested to you as a matter for indirect enquiry.[5] All here are well, except the Major, whose situation I think is unpromising & precarious—growing worse[6]—they all join me in best wishes for Mrs Lear, yourself & the Child. I am Dr Sir Yr Affecte friend

Go: Washington

ALS, CSmH.

1. Lear had written to GW from New York on 15 July 1792.

2. For the hiring of architect James Hoban to supervise the construction of the presidential mansion in the Federal City, see GW to the Commissioners for the District of Columbia, 8 June, 23 July, and the Commissioners for the District of Columbia to GW, 19 July 1792. Hoban also was asked to oversee the building of the U.S. Capitol.

3. The search for a suitable design for the U.S. Capitol continued through the fall and winter of 1792. William Thornton's drawing was chosen in early April 1793 (see Harris, *Thornton Papers,* 1:238–39).

4. For a description of the stone bridge over Rock Creek and its construction, see GW to Thomas Jefferson, 21 Mar., n.1; see also GW to David Stuart, 8 April, and note 1, and Stuart to GW, 18 April 1792.

5. Lear, in fact, had spoken with Robert Morris before leaving Philadelphia about whether or not the president would be allowed to continue to use Morris's house in the capital after 1 Oct. 1792 (see Lear to GW, 21 July). Morris had informed Lear at that time that GW could use his residence as long as he wished.

6. GW's nephew Maj. George Augustine Washington was fighting a losing battle with tuberculosis (see GW to Lafayette, 10 June, G. A. Washington to GW, 26 June, and source note, 7 July, GW to Alexander Hamilton, 29 July, and to Henry Knox, 15 Aug. 1792).

From Henry Knox

Sir. War-department, July 31'st 1792.

It is with deep regret I transmit the enclosed paper;[1] the purport of which I have just received from Mr Morris.

The number of persons with Major Trueman—the time—and other circumstances—render the account, but too credible. It is probable something upon this subject will be received shortly from the Ohio.[2] I have the honor to be Sir, with the highest respect, Your most obedient servt

H. Knox
secy of War.

LS, DLC:GW; LB, DLC:GW.

1. Knox's enclosure has not been identified.

2. On 15 Aug. the *Pennsylvania Gazette* (Philadelphia) printed an "Extract of a letter, dated Buffaloe creek, July 19, 1792," which reads in part: "By a person who left Head Quarters, Fort Washington, the 11th ult. and arrived here on Wednesday last, we are informed, that Col. Harben [John Hardin], Major [Alexander] Trueman, and two others, were killed by the Indians a short distance from Fort Jefferson, on their way to the Indian towns, to invite them

to a treaty; this information was brought to Head Quarters by a party of men and an Indian from Post St. Vincent [Vincennes], two days before our informant left it; we also understand, that accounts have been received in this town, from Buffaloe creek, by the way of Fort Franklin, containing information similar to the above—(We most sincerely lament the loss of such valuable men as Col. Harden and Major Trueman, and would suggest the propriety of sending those members of Congress, who proposed, and so strenuously supported pacific measures to be adopted with the Indian nations, at this time, with the next message or invitation for a treaty.)"

To Alexander Hamilton

Sir, Mount Vernon, August 1st 1792

I learn with pleasure from the War Office, by the Secretary's last dispatches, that our Northwestern frontier is in a state of tranquility:[1] it may be construed into an indication that *some* of the messages which have been sent by Government have reached the hostile Tribes, and have occasioned them to deliberate thereon. Devoutly is it to be wished that the result may be favorable, both for themselves and the Ud States.

No expectation of this, however, ought to suspend, or in the smallest degree relax the preparations for War; but as War under any circumstances is expensive, and with such a long & rugged land transportation as the one by which we have to convey the supplies for the Army must, for the quantum of them, be extremely so. It behoves us to be as precise in all our arrangements—as œconomical in our provisions—as strict in our issues, and as correct in accounting for them to the War or Treasury Departments (as the case may happen to be) as possible. That I may know under what regulations these matters are, I have, by this days Post, written to the Secretary of War desiring him to report to me the mode which is pursued by his direction from thence, for providing, transporting, issueing & accounting for them. If the Treasury Department has an agency in any of these matters, I require a similar Report from thence also.[2]

Mr Kean by a Letter which I have received from him, accepts his renewed Commission for settling the Accounts between the United States, & the individual States;[3] which, please to say to him, gives me pleasure—and add, that any efforts he can make to bring this business to a speedy & happy issue, I shall consider as rendering an important service to the Union; because I view the closing of these Accots *speedily* as extremely essential to it's interest & tranquility. Let me know if Mr Langdon (the Commissioner) is returned to his duty?[4] and, in that case, when? I am &c.

G: Washington

LB, DLC:GW.

1. See Henry Knox to GW, 21 July, and note 1.

2. For Hamilton's suggestion that GW ask the War and Treasury departments to report to the president their procedures concerning the provisioning of the army, see Hamilton to GW, 22 July 1792, and note 2. Hamilton's report was written on 10 Aug. 1792. Henry Knox's report, which has not been found, was apparently dated Saturday, 11 August.

3. See John Kean to GW, 7 July, and note 1.

4. Hamilton wrote GW on 11 Aug. that he had communicated the president's wishes to Kean, "who promises every possible exertion," and that Kean's fellow commissioner Woodbury Langdon had returned to his post.

To Henry Knox

Sir, Mount Vernon Augt 1st 1792.

Your dispatches of the 14th & 21st Ult. came duly to hand, and it is probable the Servt who carries this letter to the Post Office, will bring me a third of this weeks date.[1]

I did not acknowledge the receipt of the first letter at an earlier date, because there was nothing contained in it which required a reply. And I am too little acquainted with the Authority under which Colo. Henry Karr detached Lt Colo. Philips—the cause—or the object of that detachment, to form so good an opinion of the propriety of the *measure* as it is easy for me to predict the probable consequences of it.[2] I hope Major Gaither has before this, embarked for that quarter, strongly impressed with the views of the general Government, & the disposition of it to preserve peace (if it can be done upon just & honorable ground).[3]

The tranquility, which (by your last accts handed to me) prevails on our No. Western frontiers gives me much satisfaction and affords a pleasing prospect that the exertions of government to bring the hostile Indian tribes into a pacific mood will not have been exercised in vain. This, however, is not to relax any preparation for a contrary event. Proceed as if war was inevitable: but do it, I entreat you, with all the œconomy which can result from system & good regulations. Our finances call for it, & if these did not, our reputation does. The supplies of an Army through so long, & rugged a land transport[at]ion must, under the best management, be expensive & our attention therefore ought to be proportionate—and that I may form some ideas of the former I desire you would Report to me the Regulations which you have adopted for providing, forwarding, & issuing of them, and the mode of having them accounted for to the depart. of War. I have written to the Secretary of the Treasury for similar information on these points so far as any of them may come within the purview of his department.[4]

Reiterate, in your letters to Genl Wayne, the necessity of employing the prest calm in disciplining, & training the troops under his command for the peculiar service for which they are destined—He is not to be sparing of Powder & lead (in proper & reasonable quantities) to make the Soldiers marksmen.[5]

There is no propriety that I can perceive in giving the Rank of Brigr to Majr Sergant—nor do I conceive that Genl Wilkenson would, or indeed ought, to relinquish his present commd. I have turned this mattr in my thoughts but as yet have not been able to hit upon a character to my mind for the Office of Adjutant General. I will think again, & again on the subject, & will inform you of the result.[6]

So long as the vice of drunkenness exists in the Army so long I hope, Ejections of those Officers who are found guilty of it will continue; for that and gaming will debilitate & render unfit for active Service any Army whatsoever.[7] I am Sir Yr Most Obedt Servt

G.W.

P.S. Would Majr Fish accept the Appointment of Adjutt General with the Rank of Lieutt Colo.? He strikes me as an eligable character. Colo. Posey also (who wants to be employed) might if ready at his pen[8] make a good one, for in other respects (& I do not know that he is deficient in this) he is said to be an excellent Officer.[9]

ADfS, DLC:GW; LB, DLC:GW.

1. On 5 Aug., GW informed Knox that he had received the secretary of war's letters of Saturday, 28 July, and Tuesday, 31 July 1792.

2. Col. Henry Karr, who had served as a captain in the Georgia militia during the Revolutionary War and had been wounded at Fish Dam Ford in November 1780, was a delegate from Greene County to the Georgia constitutional convention in the summer of 1789 (*Pennsylvania Gazette* [Philadelphia], 15 July 1789). GW is referring to information contained in an account signed by

one of Karr's subordinates, Lieutenant Colonel Philips, which was enclosed in Knox's letter to GW of 21 July but which has not been found.

3. Knox reported to GW on 7 Aug. that Maj. Henry Gaither would depart for the Georgia frontier within a few days. In his letters to GW of 21 July and 7 Aug., Knox writes that the preservation of peace would be Gaither's primary objective.

4. For the secretary of the treasury's suggestion that GW make this request of Knox, see Alexander Hamilton to GW, 22 July 1792, and note 2. Knox apparently dated his report to GW, which has not been found, Saturday, 11 August. Hamilton's report to GW on the same subject was written on 10 Aug. 1792.

5. Knox quoted this paragraph in his letter to Anthony Wayne of 7 Aug., which is printed at Knox to GW, that date, n.3.

6. For Winthrop Sargent's nomination as adjutant general and inspector, see GW to the U.S. Senate, 9 April. GW nominated Michael Rudolph to the position on 22 Feb. 1793, and the Senate consented to his appointment on the following day (see GW to the U.S. Senate, 22 Feb. 1793; *Executive Journal*, 1:132, 134).

7. Knox quoted this paragraph in his letter to Anthony Wayne of 7 Aug., which is printed in Knox to GW, that date, n.3. Knox had reported the dismissal of captains Mark MacPherson and John Platt from the army for drunkenness in his letter to GW of 21 July.

8. At this place on the draft manuscript, GW wrote and then struck out the words: "& capable also."

9. Nicholas Fish, on 7 Sept., and Thomas Posey, on 10 Oct., both declined the offer to be nominated as adjutant general and inspector of the U.S. Army (see Knox to GW, 7 Aug., n.6).

From Alexander Hamilton

Sir, Treasury Departmt 3d Augt 1792

I have the honor to enclose a letter from the Commissioner of the Revenue of the 25th of July, on the subject of a provisional Contract for the supply of the Lighthouse in New Hampshire; together with the Contract for your consideration & decision. I agree in the opinion expressed by the Commissioner of the Revenue.[1] With the most perfect respect and truest attachment, I have the honor to be &c.

Alexander Hamilton.

P.S. Inclosed you will be pleased to receive the Copy of a letter of 31st May, just received from our Commissioners at Amsterdam. It announces a further Loan of 3,000,000, of florins at 4 ℘ Cent.[2]

LB, DLC:GW.

1. On 25 July, Tench Coxe wrote Hamilton that the provisional contract "is precisely similar" to the preceding one, "which was grounded upon an Estimate of which an Extract is inclosed. The compensation to the keeper is as heretofore. The price of the Oil is uncommonly low, which however, I presume to be owing to the Use of an inferior species. An examination into this article of supply, as consumed in all the Lighthouses, appears necessary and will shortly be made. In the mean time no other doubt or Objections to the Contract now to be submitted, occurs" (DNA: RG 58, Letters of the Commissioner of the Revenue and Revenue Office, 1792–1809). GW signed the provisional contract and returned it to Hamilton "Under a blank cover" by 13 Aug. 1792.

2. The enclosed letter from the U.S. commissioners at Amsterdam to Hamilton of 31 May has not been identified. For Hamilton's authorization of the Holland loan of 1792, see Hamilton to William Short, 21 Mar. 1792, in Syrett, *Hamilton Papers,* 11:165. GW expressed his pleasure at the terms of the agreement in his letter to Hamilton of 13 Aug., and he ratified the loan early the following November.

From Henry Knox

Sir, War department August 4th 1792

By the letters of the 28th from General Wayne all was quiet on the frontiers.

Captain Hendricks left Buffaloe Creek on the 18th of June and others of the five Nations were to accompany him.[1]

A Mr McConnell a man of Credit has been in this city and left it without my seeing him, he left Fort Washington the first of July, he says the Indian prisoners, who were sent by the way of the Wabash to the hostile Indians had returned, and brought favorable reports of the disposition of the Indians for peace, excepting the Shawanese—and that Genl Wilkinson had written me fully upon the subject, but which I have not received.[2]

The accounts of the Recruits are not materially different from the last Return.[3] I have the honor to be with the highest respect Your most obedt servant

H. Knox
secy of War

LS, DLC:GW; LB, DLC:GW.

1. For the reasons for Capt. Hendrick Aupaumut's delayed departure from Buffalo Creek, N.Y., see Israel Chapin to Knox, 17 July, in Knox to GW, 7 Aug., n.5.

2. On the afternoon of 4 Aug., Francis Vigo arrived from Fort Washington bringing two letters to Knox from James Wilkinson. An extract of the first letter, dated 6 July 1792, reads: "Mr Vigo brings an account, that information had been received at St Vincents, by means of a savage, that a party of four men, in the neighbourhood of one of our posts, bearing a flag, had been intercepted and murdered by a party of shawanese—This account is involved in obscurity, and is somewhat inconsistent—As my first party consisted of three men, and Col. [John] Hardin had one only, and major [Alexander] Trueman two—But, as these last parties were to continue together until they reached the Pickawa (Old Town) on the Big Miami, and as the time when the murder is said to have been committed, corresponds with that of their departure from this post, I dread Sir, I very much fear, 'tis too true, and every prospect of peace would of consequence be extinguished, was it not for the silence of my confidential agents—I am at a loss how to interpret this silence, unless they may have been obliged to take a circuitous route to get back" (DLC:GW).

An extract of Wilkinson's second letter, also dated 6 July, reads: "Agreeably to my letter of the 21st ulto, I left this post on the evening of the 22d, and arrived at Fort Hamilton about noon the next day—a variety of arrangements relatively to the hay—the army—provisions and transport detained me at that post until the 24th in the morning, at which time I got in motion for Fort Jefferson, with a convoy of one hundred and twenty horses loaded with flour, under the escort of the Kentucky rifle corps.

"For the advantage of good food and water, I encamped that evening about six miles short of St Clair, and was at that post before seven o'clock the next morning—Here I met four militia rifle men, who had been engaged for the purpose and were occasionally employed as scouts and runners at and between the advanced posts—these men informed me, that about nine o'clock the preceding day, a large body of savages, had attacked a party of men who were mowing grass on a Prairie adjacent to Fort Jefferson—that being themselves a part of the guard ordered for the protection of this working party, they were cut off from the post and forced to retire to St Clair—that as they retreated they heard a heavy and continued fire of small arms and cannon, which they presumed to be an attack upon the Fort.

"I immediately ordered a subaltern and thirty men from the garrison of St Clair, to take charge of the convoy, and to move forward that day about six miles, there to wait my orders, and advanced myself with the rifle-horse men, in such a disposition, as guarded me against the enterprize of the enemy, and enabled me to feel his force (without committing myself) or to attack to advantage, as circumstances might direct—In the moment that I marched off, three horsemen arrived from Major [David] Strong, with a letter—The party which brought the letter informed me that the enemy were still in the neighbourhood of the post—This intelligence hastened my movements, but the necessary caution retarded my advance, and I did not reach it before sun-set.

"As Major Strong could give me no certain information of the Enemy, subsequent to the attack made upon the mowers (for they had not approached the garrison, altho' they fired a general volley after the affair was over) I conceived they had retired, and accordingly dispatched a runner, with orders to the officer who had charge of the convoy to move forward as soon as it was light, and for his greater security I detached a subaltern and twenty five men to meet him—The next morning before sun rise I ordered out the rifle men to take the track of the enemy, to pursue, overtake, and attack him if possible, under the necessary prudential restrictions—This corps composed, generally, of select woods men, returned in about two hours, and Captain [Daniel] Barbee who commands, reported that he could not discover, by what route the enemy had moved off, as they had seperated on the ground where they made the attack—The security of my convoy was the next object of my attention, and fearing the enemy meant to play me a trick—Mr Barbee was ordered to march to its protection, and the whole got up about noon, without molestation—In the mean time, a light scout of rifle men on foot, who had been sent out to seek further discoveries, returned and made report, that they had surprized one of the enemy, who dropt his pack (which they brought in) and escaped, and they gave the opinion, that the main body was encamped about three miles west of the garrison—Tho' doubting this information, I determined to ascertain the fact, and for this purpose I detached Capt. [Jacob] Kingsbury with fifty men from the garrison—the rifle horsemen and mounted infantry—But this party after a detour of several miles likewise returned without being able to make any discovery—Too much time had now elapsed to leave me a hope of coming up with the enemy, and it remained for me to ascertain, with all possible precision, the strength of the party—the route by which they had approached, and that by which they retired—To this end, I sent out a subaltern and twenty five rifle men to fall upon their back track, and trace it to the nearest encampment; and with the residue of the horse, I proceeded to the ground where the enemy had made the stroke upon the mowers—Here I soon discovered that they had pushed thro the prairie, which being extensive, and too soft for the horse, I dismounted twenty rifle men, and sent them across it to the nearest woodland where they immediately discovered the enemies trail, by which it was evident they had retreated, in the forenoon of the day, on which they made the stroke.

"The party employed in cutting and securing the hay, consisted of a serjeant, corporal and twelve, and for their protection I had annexed, to major Strong's command, a serjt and twelve of the mounted infantry, with the militia scout before mentioned—of these the serjeant and one of the infantry, two horsemen and one horse are certainly killed—the corporal and eleven of the infantry are missing, and three horses have been wounded—The enemy retired by the western margin of the Prairie, keeping a North course, and the rifle men who had been detached on the back track, in about four miles, fell in with the camp the enemy had occupied the night preceeding the attack, and from their fires and other demonstrations, it may be fairly concluded that their number was between eighty and one hundred, of which three were on horseback, one of these was dressed in scarlet—the rest of the party wore clean white shirts, and they butchered our dead with unexampled barbarity.

"But Sir, whilst we have been unfortunate at Fort Jefferson in our attempt to make hay, we have been much favored at Fort Hamilton, as we have now at that post at least one hundred Tons, cut and cured, and in quality little inferior to Timothy; and if I can secure that which is made and protect the prosecution of the measure, I shall with great facility be able to increase the quantity to 400 Tons, before the 20th of September: for this purpose I have increased the garrison, and have stationed the corps of mounted infantry under Lieutenant [Asa] Hartshorne in its vicinity" (DLC:GW).

3. Knox enclosed a return of the 1,827 "Recruits at the respective rendezvous" in his letter to GW of 28 July.

Proclamation

[Mount Vernon, 4 August 1792]

In pursuance of the powers and authorities vested in me by the Acts of Congress (of the 3d of March 1791. and the Eighth of May 1792.) relative to the duties on distilled spirits and to the collection there of,[1] the following alterations and additions to the arrangement of Offices and distribution of compensations made on the 15th day of March 1791. are hereby adopted and established.[2]

1st. The District of Maryland shall be divided into three Surveys. The first consisting of all the Counties on the western side of the Chesapeak Bay (except Montgomery, Frederick, Washington and Alleghaney)—namely Harford, Baltimore, Ann Arundel, Prince Georges, Calvert, Charles and St Mary's. The duties of the Inspector of this survey shall be performed by the supervisor. The second survey is to consist as at present, of the counties of Montgomery Frederick, Washington and Alleghaney. the duties of this Survey will continue to be performed by the Inspector thereto appointed. The third Survey is to consist of all the counties on the Eastern Shore of Chesapeak bay, namely Cecil, Kent, Queen Ann's, Talbot, Dorset, Worcester, Somerset, and Caroline; for which an Inspector will be appointed. The duties of this survey are to be performed by the Supervisor, until that appointment shall be made.

2. The Commissions to be allowed to the Supervisors and Inspectors of surveys shall be upon the whole amount of the duties collected within their respective districts and Surveys upon Stills, and spirits distilled in the United States, and which have or shall accrue after the last day of June 1792.

3. The Supervisors of New Hampshire, Connecticut, New-York, Vermont, New-Jersey and Pennsylvania shall each receive a commission on the said amount of the Revenue in their respective districts (excepting what accrued prior to the first day of July

1792) of one per centum, in lieu of the commission of one half per centum before all owed.

The Supervisor of Delaware shall receive a commission in manner aforesaid of two per centum in lieu of one per centum.

The Supervisors of Maryland, North Carolina, & South Carolina shall each receive a Commission in manner aforesaid of one and an half per centum in lieu of one per centum.

The Supervisor of Georgia shall receive a commission, in manner, aforesaid, of two per centum, in lieu of one per centum.

4. To the salaries of the following Supervisors there shall be additions as set against the names of their offices to commence on the first day of July 1792.

The Supervisor of Massachusetts an addition of 200 Drs per annum.

The Supervisor of Rhode Island	100.	[per annum]
The Supervisor of New York	100.	"
The Supervisor of Maryland	100.	"
The Supervisor of Virginia	200.	"
The Supervisor of South Carolina	100.	"

5. The compensation to the Inspector of the third survey of the District of Maryland, when appointed, shall be a salary of four hundred & fifty dollars ℔ annum & a commission of one per centum.

6. The compensation to the Inspector of the second survey of the District of South Carolina shall be a salary of Four hundred & fifty Dollars ℔ annum, and a commission of one per centum in lieu of his former compensation.

7. The Collectors of the Revenue shall be entitled to receive the following commissions upon the Revenue on Stills and distilled spirits by them collected; that is to say, upon the Revenue upon spirits distilled from foreign materials two per centum; upon the Revenue upon Spirits distilld from domestic materials and upon Stills employed on the said materials in Cities, towns or Villages, four per centum; and upon the Revenue upon Stills not in Cities Towns or Villages, five per centum.

8. There shall be allowed to the officers of Inspection who shall legally sign Certificates to accompany each Cask of distilled spirits and to the officers or other persons, who shall be authorised to mark the same, the sum of five Cents for each & every Cask of Spirits distilled in the United States, so marked and cer-

tified, to be divided between the officer or person who shall mark, and the officer who shall sign the Certificates for the same, if those duties shall be performed by different persons.

9. There may also be allowed to persons employed to guage Spirits distilled in the United States, the sum of two Cents and one half for each Cask so guaged, if the person thus employed shall be an Officer of Inspection authorised to mark the Casks containing the said spirits, or to sign Certificates to accompany the same. But if the person employed to guage such distilled Spirits be not an officer of Inspection authorised to mark or issue Certificates for the same, he may be allowed a sum not exceeding six cents for the service of gauging each Cask.

10. There shall likewise be allowed to the Collectors of the Revenue for measuring the capacity of each Still; and marking the still & head, according to Law, the sum of Fifty Cents.

11. The Supervisors of the several Districts shall be at liberty to allow to such of the Collectors of the Revenue, as, for the execution of the public service, it shall appear to them really necessary, so to compensate, a yearly sum over & above their other emoluments, not exceeding in a district the number of Collectors, nor the average or medium sum to each, or to the whole number, which are set against the same below.

that is to say—In New Hampshire the Supervisor may allow to 2 Collectors 50 Drs each.

In Massachusetts to 10 do 400. Dollars to be divided at discretion among them.

In Rhode Island	to	1.
In Vermont		2.
In Connecticut		4.
In New York		2.
In New Jersey		5.
In Pennsylvania		14.
In Delaware		3.
In Maryland		9.
In Virginia		24.
In North Carolina		14.
In South Carolina		8.
In Georgia		3.
	that is to	89.

Collectors 60 Dollars each, at an average or medium, to be di-

vided within each District at the discretion of the Supervisor.

12. There may be allowed to Eighty auxiliary officers of Inspection, to be appointed by the Supervisors in Counties wherein no Collector of the Revenue resides, a sum not exceeding twenty Dollars each for keeping an office to receive entries, issue Licences, and to perform such other services in aid of the Collectors as may be legally authorised and as they may be willing to execute for that compensation. Of these there may be,

in Rhode Island	1.
in New Hampshire	2.
in Massachusetts	10.
in Vermont	4.
in New York	10.
in Pennsylvania	5.
in Maryland	2.
in Virginia	20.
in North Carolina	11.
in South Carolina	10.
in Georgia	5.

13. There shall be allowed to the officers of Inspection & the persons employed to mark foreign distilled spirits, Wines and Teas, the sum of Five Cents for every Cask or package of the Merchandize above mentioned, which shall be legally marked and certified, to be equally divided between the officer signing the Certificate & the officer or person marking the Cask or package, if those duties shall be performed by different persons. Given under my hand at Mount Vernon on the fourth day of August 1792.

Go: Washington

LB, DLC:GW. This proclamation was submitted in an abstract to Congress (see GW to the U.S. Senate and House of Representatives, 22 Nov. 1792, and note 1).

1. See "An act repealing, after the last day of June next, the duties heretofore laid on distilled spirits imported from abroad, and laying others in their stead; and also upon spirits distilled within the United States, and for appropriating the same" of 3 Mar. 1791 and "An Act concerning the Duties on Spirits distilled within the United States" of 8 May 1792, in *Annals of Congress*, 1st Cong., 2384–2405, 2d Cong., 1374–79.

2. See Executive Order, 15 Mar. 1791, and GW to Alexander Hamilton, 15 Mar. 1791 (first letter). On 1 Nov. 1791 the House of Representatives asked Secretary of the Treasury Hamilton to report on the difficulties attending the

execution of the act laying duties on distilled spirits (ibid., 2d Cong., 151–52). On 6 Mar. 1792 Hamilton communicated his report, in which he wrote that the president needed "greater latitude" respecting the compensation paid to collectors of the duty and "that 7½ per Cent of the total product of the duties on distilled spirits, foreign as well as domestic, and not less will suffice to defray the compensations to officers and other expences incidental to the collection of the duty" (Syrett, *Hamilton Papers,* 11:105). "An Act concerning the Duties on Spirits distilled within the United States," which incorporated many of Hamilton's suggestions, was signed into law by GW on 8 May 1792. Section 16 of this act granted the president the additional latitude that Hamilton had requested by authorizing him "to make such allowances for their respective services to the supervisors, inspectors, and other officers of inspection as he shall deem reasonable and proper, so as the said allowances, together with the incidental expenses of collecting the duties on spirits distilled within the United States shall not exceed seven-and-a-half per centum of the total product of the duties on distilled spirits for the period to which the said allowances shall relate, computing from the time the act [of 3 Mar. 1791] . . . took effect: *And, provided, also,* That such allowance shall not exceed the annual amount of seventy thousand dollars, until the same shall be further ascertained by law" (*Annals of Congress,* 2d Cong., 1378–79). Commissioner of the Revenue Tench Coxe and Hamilton hammered out a "draught of a supplementary arrangement of the Business of the Revenue" and "the reasons in support of these supplementary regulations" in the late spring and summer of 1792 (see Coxe to Hamilton, 25 July, Syrett, *Hamilton Papers,* 12:85–98). Hamilton forwarded the result of their labors to GW on 30 July for his approval.

To Alexander Hamilton

Sir, Mount Vernon, Augt 5. 1792.

Since the date of my last dispatch to you of the 1st instant, I have received your Letters of the 26. & 30 ulto, and have affixed my signature to the arrangement of Compensations to the Officers of Inspection in consequence of additional latitude given to The President of the United States by the Act of the last Session, intitled "An Act concerning the duties on spirits distilled within the United States."[1]

I have done this on full conviction that the best information the nature of the case would admit, has been obtained at the Treasury to keep the aggregate within the limitations of the Law, & to proportion the Compensations to the services of the respective Officers; presuming also that it appeared essential (from a full view of circumstances, and the benefits likely to be derived from the measure, to the public) that an increase of the Officers of Revenue was really necessary; for I should be unwilling to add to the former establishment, unless the propriety of it was apparent. Unless the Attorney General should be of opinion that The President of the United States has power under the Act of March 1791. or the subsequent one of last Session, to appoint (in the recess of the Senate) an Inspector of the Survey newly constituted in Maryland, it must remain, as is proposed, under the immediate direction of the Supervisor.[2]

If, after these regulations are in operation, opposition to the due exercise of the collection is still experienced, & peaceable proceedure is no longer effectual, the public interest & my duty will make it necessary to enforce the Laws respecting this matter; & however disagreeable this would be to me, it must nevertheless take place.

The Collector was not at Baltimore when I passed through that place; but from the Naval Officer I learnt that the service wou'd sustain no loss by the resignation of the Master of the Maryland Revenue Cutter—that the first Mate was a more competent character, and that the general expectation was that he would be appointed to command it. That I might know how far the sentiments of others accorded with those of the Naval Officer, I requested the Supervisor (Mr Gale) to make enquiry & to inform me of the result; but not having heard from him since, the first Mate (his name I do not recollect) may be notified by you, of my intention to commission him Master so soon as I am provided with Commissions for that purpose—at present I have none.[3] The same may be given to John Adams as first, & Benjamin Gunnison as second Mate of the Revenue Cutter in New Hampshire: and to Ashur Cook first and John Fenley second Mate of the New York Cutter. The third Mate for the latter may remain for further enquiry & consideration.[4]

If your information with respect to the proposed characters for the Cutter in New Hampshire is not such as you can entirely rely upon, Mr Lear who is on the spot might afford you some aid in the investigation of them, or others.[5] I am Sir &c.

G: Washington

P.S. As I have neither time nor inclination to copy the enclosed, I would thank you for having a transcript of it made & sent to me.[6]

LB, DLC:GW.

1. For the "arrangement of Compensations to the Officers of Inspection," see Proclamation, 4 Aug. 1792. GW is referring to the additional latitude given him in section 16 of "An Act concerning the Duties on Spirits distilled within the United States" of 8 May 1792 (*Annals of Congress,* 2d Cong., 1374–79).

2. GW is referring to section 4 of "An act repealing, after the last day of June next, the duties heretofore laid on distilled spirits imported from abroad, and laying others in their stead; and also upon spirits distilled within the United States, and for appropriating the same" of 3 Mar. 1791 and section 17 of "An Act concerning the Duties on Spirits distilled within the United States" of 8 May 1792 (*Annals of Congress,* 1st Cong., 2384–2405, 2d Cong., 1374–79). Tench Coxe wrote George Gale, the supervisor of the revenue for the district of Maryland, on 20 Aug. that the "appointment of an Inspector for the third survey is defered only because the special power to appoint the Revenue Officers, vested in the President by the Act of March 3rd 1791 has expired, and this being a new office created by the President it is conceived that he cannot fill it by his ordinary power of appointment, which is applicable only to vacancies in pre-existent offices created by law occasioned by the Death &c. in the Recess of the Senate" (DNA: RG 58, Letters of the Commissioner of the Revenue and Revenue Office, 1792–1809). For the attorney general's judgment in a similar case, see Edmund Randolph's Opinion on Recess Appointments, 7 July 1792, *Jefferson Papers,* 24:165–67.

3. David Porter (1754–1808) of Boston served first as a Continental navy midshipman and later as a privateer captain during the Revolutionary War. In 1783 he moved his family to Baltimore, where he joined the merchant marine, and in 1792 he was first mate on the Maryland cutter *Active.* George Gale (1756–1815) of Somerset County, Md., served in the Maryland house of delegates for several terms, in the Maryland ratifying convention of 1788, and in the U.S. House of Representatives from 1789 to 1791. A Federalist, he was appointed in March 1791 to be supervisor of the revenue for the Maryland district and inspector of the first survey. Gale's letter of recommendation to GW, which is dated 4 Sept., arrived after GW had decided to appoint Porter master of the *Active.* On 13 Aug., Alexander Hamilton had written Otho Holland Williams, the collector at Baltimore, asking him to inform Porter of his appointment, which was to be effective 5 Aug. (Syrett, *Hamilton Papers,* 12:199; Tobias Lear to Thomas Jefferson, 26 Oct. 1792).

4. For the recommendations of Adams, Gunnison, Cook, and Fenley, see Hamilton to GW, 26 July 1792. For the appointments of Adams, Gunnison, and Fenley, see Lear to Jefferson, 26 Oct. 1792. GW appointed William Loring first mate of the N.Y. cutter, effective 15 Nov., and Caleb Stacey third mate, effective 6 Nov. (see Lear to Jefferson, 18 Dec. 1792).

5. For the reasons for Tobias Lear's trip to New England in the summer of 1792, see Lear to GW, 15 July, source note. Lear had arrived in Portsmouth, N.H., on 20 July (see Lear to GW, 21 July).

6. Hamilton enclosed a copy of this letter, which has not been found, in his letter to GW of 10 Aug. 1792.

To Henry Knox

Sir, Mount Vernon Augt 5th 1792

Since writing to you on the 1st instt Your letters of the 28th & 31st of July have come to hand. The latter, containing an acct of the fate of Majr Trueman, fills me with deep concern. The circumstances with which it is related (unless fabricated[1] to answer some purpose to us unknown) will not allow one to doubt the fact.[2] Nor do the Accounts from the Southward wear a much more agreeable aspect[3]—Every exertion therefore on the part of Government must be used to avert the evils of War which seem to be impending & if these are found to be impracticable then to meet the event with firmness & resolution as a mean to which I hope the Recruiting Officers will double their diligence to obtain the men & thier vigilance to prevent desertion. The latter is shameful, & call for vigorous pursuits & exemplary punishments.[4]

I hope & do earnestly exhort, the utmost attention on the part of General Wayne & the Officers under him, to fitt the men for the Service they are intended—It is indispensably necessary—and I beseech you to suffer no delay in forwarding the supplies which are necessary for the Army.

I wish Governor Blount may have been able to terminate the Conferences which he was to have had at Nashville about the 25. of last month with the Cherokees Chickasaws & Choctaws to the mutual advantage & satisfaction of all the parties concerned, but the difficulty of deciding between lawless Settlers & greedy (land) Speculators on one side, and the jealousies of the Indian Nations & their banditti on the other, becomes more & more obvious every day—and these, from the interference of the Spaniards (if the Reports we have be true) and other causes wch are too evident to require specification add not a little to our embarrassments.[5]

I flatter myself, Governor St Clair will not forget that there are duties which require his attention in the Territory committed to his care although his presence at the trial of Ensign Morgan may not be necessary or proper. But, if an important lawsuit claims his attendance in the State of Pennsylvania in September and it can be dispensed with in his Government, I would not wish to deprive him of the advantage of being present at the trial.[6]

The enclosed letter from People stiling themselves Oneidas or Onandagos came to my hands on friday last. It may not be amiss to make some enquiry into the matter. for oftentimes, it is more easy to prevent an evil, than to Redress it after it has happened.[7] I am Sir Yrs &ca

G.W.

ADfS, DLC:GW; LB, DLC:GW.

1. At this place on the draft manuscript, GW wrote and then struck out the words "with malicious intention" before inserting "to answer some purpose to us unknown."

2. See Knox to GW, 31 July, and note 2.

3. See Knox to GW, 28 July, and notes 3 and 4.

4. In his letter to GW of 28 July, Knox had described the number of recruits deserting on the march as "excessive."

5. Gov. William Blount wrote Knox on 31 Aug.: "On the 10th instant the conference with the Chicasaws and Choctaws ended, there was a very full representation of the former but not of the latter owing there is a reason to beleive to the Spanish influence. . . . During the conference General [Andrew] Pickens and myself received the strongest assurances of peace and friendship for the United States from both Nations and I believe they were made with great sincerity. The Cherokees as well as the Creeks commit depredations and deserve to be punished, that is, the young and unruly part of them for the Chiefs to a Man except *Double Head,* who was a Signer of the Treaty, I have great reason to believe most earnestly wish for peace & friendship" (Carter, *Territorial Papers,* 4:166). For the recent actions of the Spanish agent Pedro Olivier, see James Seagrove to GW, 5 July, and Knox to GW, 28 July, and note 4.

6. For Arthur St. Clair's Pennsylvania lawsuit and the court-martial of John Morgan for slander and insubordination, see Knox to GW, 28 July, and note 8.

7. Ten days later GW again referred to "the complaint exhibited by the Oneida's or Onandago's (I am not certain wch) against a trader that had been obtruded upon them; & committing the matter, & the regulation of the Trade with the first of these tribes, to the Govr" of New York, George Clinton (see GW to Knox, 15 Aug. 1792).

From Henry Knox

Sir War department Sunday 5th August 1792.

Yesterday afternoon Mr Vigo arrived here from Fort Washington, and brought dispatches from Brigadiers General Putnam and Wilkinson to the 9th of July, as will appear by the abstracts of Brigadr Wilkinson's letter of 9th July herein enclosed.[1]

I have the honor to enclose for your consideration General Putnams letter giving his opinion of the operations proper to be pursued—On this letter, I shall, by the next post, submit to your view some observations.[2]

The fate of poor Trueman is but too probably sealed and perhaps that of Hardin too.

General Putnam, in his letter of the 5th of July, which principally contains the same information as that mentioned in Wilkinsons letters, states it as his opinion that a treaty ought to be concluded as soon as possible with the Wabash Indians and presents be made[3]—Being firmly persuaded of the soundness of this opinion I shall direct the measure. It is more especially necessary as Mr Vigo informs me that the said Indians would not come even to Fort Washington much less to Philadelphia.

Brigadier Wilkinsons attention to all parts of his duty and his activity render him a great acquisition to the public.

A Banditti without any fixed residence consisting of about ten Cherokees thirty Creeks and fourteen Shawanese—Outcasts—from their respective tribes are perpetually committing depredations on the Cumberland settlements they have lately attacked a military station near Nashville and carried it twenty one men were killed or taken—But the friendly Cherokees compelled the said banditti to deliver up their prisoners amounting to Six—these are the same rascals probably who attacked Major Doughty in the Year 1789.[4] I have this information from Mr Vigo.

The necessity of the case will justify the measure of empowering Governor Blount to call out Sixty or one hundred mounted Riflemen to cut off if possible the said Banditti—He has that number at present in service. And as he has been empowered to retain in service as many as he shall judge proper; there can be no doubt but he will keep them up as long as necessary.[5] I have the honor to be with the greatest respect Your most obed. servant

H. Knox

LS, DLC:GW; LB, DLC:GW.

1. For the extracts taken from the two letters that James Wilkinson wrote to Knox on 6 July 1792, see Knox to GW, 4 Aug., n.2.

2. Rufus Putnam's letter to Henry Knox, which was written at Fort Washington on 8 July 1792, reads: "My letter to you of the 5th instant I gave into the hand of Mr Vego [Francis Vigo] at this place who is gone down to the rapids with an intent to proceed immediately to Philadelphia by the way of Lexington.

"The more I reflect on the subject the more I am convinced it will be best to proceed with the Indians on the Wabash and others in that quarter in the manner I have recommended in my letter above referred to and as far as possible detach them from the Councils and influence of the other Indians.

"But I think it will not be necessary and perhaps not proper to stipulate an annual allowance of Goods to be delivered to them until a purchase of land be made which I conceive ought not to be done (unless the proposition of selling be made by them) until the contest with the Shawanese and other hostile Nations is determined—For this is the argument made use of by our Enemies and the only one that prevailed with the Chippewas and many other tribes to join in the war and which is continually urged on the Western Indians as a motive to join in the confederacy—viz. 'The Americans are after your lands and mean to take them from you and drive you out of the Country.'

"I am informed from good authority that when the Delawares, Wyandots and Shawanese first invited the Chippewas and other tribes to join in the war—they answered 'For why should we go to war, we have no quarrel with the Americans, when our Father (meaning the King of Great Britain) was at War and called on us to join him against a set of rebellious Children, we did so, but our father has now made peace with those Children and there is now no reason why we should go to war against them it will be enough for us to go against the Americans when our father calls on us again, but you continued the Chippewas are always quarrelling with your neighbours it would be better for you to be at peace.' To this the Delawares &ca replied, 'That the thirteen fires were endeavouring to take their lands from them, that they challenged the whole country as their own that the thirteen fires had marked out to them a small tract for hunting Ground on which they could not live.' well says the Chippewas 'what is that to us the Americans have done us no harm and why should we fight for your lands you may fight yourselves for them and defend your Country there is reason that you should but we shall get nothing by it, if we join in the war, it is better that we mind our business and live in peace[']—To this the Delawares &c. could find no answer—until a British Emissary whispered in their ear 'Tell them that when the Americans have conquered you and got possession of your land, they will then take theirs from them also for that is their intention, and they never will rest until they have got the whole country.' Is that the case replied the Chippewas and other nations 'then we will fight too' and immediately agreed to assist in defending the country against the encroachments of the Americans.

"I have been the more particular in relating this Anecdote (which is a fact may be relied on) because it shows the reason why so many nations are drawn into the war against us—That it must be something more than merely the influence of British emissaries may be fairly argued from their being a greater number engaged in the present contest than the British government with all their arts and money were able to persuade to engage in their service (in the Western quarter) during the late war and what can be their motive but the fear of losing their lands or in otherwords that the Americans intend to take their lands from them without their consent, whenever they think proper agreeably to the doctrine of the Treaties at Fort McIntosh and the Big Miami.

"It is therefore in my opinion indispensibly necessary to convince the Western Indians as soon as possible that these suggestions are false: and since they are not willing at present to come to Philadelphia or even to Fort Washington they should be treated with at Vincennes as soon as possible.

"In confident expectation that a commission will be forwarded as soon as may be empowering Major [John Francis] Hamtramck or some other person to hold a treaty at Vincennes agreeably to the stipulation he has made for that purpose: A part of the Indian Goods here will with the prisoners, be forwarded to Fort Knox.

"Yesterday a Canoe going up the Ohio, with two Men a Woman and a Boy were attacked by the Indians, one of the Men was killed the other wounded the Boy taken and the woman escaped unhurt—this is another circumstance against my hearing from Hendrick [Aupaumut] in the way proposed—and with some, conclusive evidence that the grand Council is broke up with a determination of continuing the war—but I doubt this for there has not been time for the Chiefs that were at Philadelphia to council at Buffaloe Creek and arrive at the Tawa River by this time and I do not believe that the Council would break up before their arrival and those from Canada as no doubt they had information that they were coming—I am determined to send another speech to the belligerent tribes if I can persuade some of the Wabash Indians to carry it and engage to bring back an answer.

"I have several reasons for making this attempt. First if some bad men have murdered our messengers having the Presidents speech although the speech may be carried to the Council they may not consider it as properly coming before them and the Chiefs may be in doubt whether we will now receive a messenger from them or not, the arrival of a new speech will I think remove this doubt—altho I mention nothing of the rumour I have heard—Besides by a messenger of this sort I expect to ascertain the fact whether our messengers are murdered or not and also reduce the matter to a certainty whether they will let me speak to them or not.

"I propose remaining here for the present as it is uncertain whether any flag will arrive from the enemy or at what post they may come in and should Capt. Hendrick arrive at Fort Jefferson as proposed I shall have notice of it in thirty six Hours.

"But I suppose that after all rational means are used to accomodate this business by treaty we fail in the attempt, & that a continuance of the war is inevitable—pardon me Sir if unasked I offer a few sentiments on the subject.

"Mr [Thomas] Hutchins and others have said a great deal about the fine navigation of the Allegheney River and French Creek, the big Bever, the Cayahoka the Sioto and Sandusky with the Wabash and Tawa Rivers or the Miami of the Lake—And it is true they are all very fine Rivers and at certain seasons many of them afford plenty of Water to float Craft of very considerable burthen for a great distance, But the fact is that not one of them will serve any valuable purpose for transporting by water the baggage stores and provisions of an Army for any considerable distance, toward any object where Government can possible mean to point their force in any offensive operation even the Ohio at some seasons is difficult if not quite impenetrable in some parts—

therefore all considerable movements of an army between the Ohio and Lake Erie should be calculated to be by land.

"You will permit me to speak freely and I know you will not be offended my intention is to serve you by way of information and I write with the greatest deference.

"To establish a capital post at the Miami Village with a proper number of intermediate stations sufficient to secure a communication from Fort Washington to that place is undoubtedly an object to be persevered in and I think if the business is conducted in a prudent manner it may be effected with two thousand men without any hazard.

"But to stop there will by no means induce the Indians to treat it will rather be provoking than distressing to them nor will the frontiers receive any considerable protection thereby.

"My opinion is not to advance any farther in this quarter at present but to make arrangements for carrying a line of stations from the Mouth of the Big Beaver Creek on the Ohio to the Mouth of the Cayahoga on Lake Erie where I would erect a strong post here I would build such water craft as should be thought necessary to transport the army. I intended to make use of this way into the Tawa River as far as the rapids (about 14 Miles) or to such place as should be found most convenient for establishing a post there (for I will venture to pawn my reputation upon it if from the overtures now making the Indians are not brought to a treaty they never will[)] until you establish a post in the mouth of the Tawa River and prevent the British agent or his emissaries and Indians any more counselling there together (or in the Indian language put out their Council fire in this place) this is the place where every year the British Agent distributes the annual presents to all the nations far and near inhabiting the Country South of Lake Erie and Westward beyond the Miami village.

"While the army are employed in building the fort at Cayahoga provided they do not arrive there before the spring and preparing their Water Craft—the Western Army should proceed from Fort Jefferson and erecting proper stations by the way establish themselves at the Miami Village, The Indians seeing two armies advancing in opposite directions will probably be confused in their Councils they will consider the Country of the Wyandots, Delawares and Shawanese lost, their allies will most if not all withdraw themselves and the Delawares &c. sue for peace or quit their country or if that should not be the case, as they can never know when your army will move nor where it will strike they never can prevent them from landing and in a short time by intrenching secure themselves against ten times their number and should they still be obstinate yet will they not be able to prevent the two armies from establishing a line of communication from the Mouth of the Tawa River to the post at the Miami village.

"The security that such an arrangement will give to all the Country which will be thereby evinced as well as to the six Nations and the Inhabitants on Allegany River is very obvious.

"It has been the opinion of some that we should communicate with Lake Erie by the way of Presque Isle—but I am by no means of that opinion because the distance is much greater from Pittsburg (or from any part of the Alleghena River to which water carriage is always certain) to Presque Isle then from the mouth of Big Beaver to the Mouth of Cayahoga, and the Country from Pittsburgh to Presque Isle is much worse to make a road. Indeed from Big Beaver to Cayahoga the Country is very level and except about seven or eight miles is very dry and good for a Road while the other for the greater part of the way is bad hills and for 15 Miles very wet—besides the distance from Presqe Isle to the Tawa River is nearly double to that from Cayahoga. moreover if a post is made at Presque Isle there must be another at Cayahoga: for such is the Navigation of Lake Erie especially for some distance West of Cayahoga that boats in their passage Westward must always put into the Mouth of that River & wait a favorable time to pass the Rockey shore which in Hutchins Map is marked thus X.

"On the West bank of Cayahoga is a riseing ground or high bank from whence the country about is commanded as well as the extreem into the River, which is deep and navigable for Vessels of considerable burthen for several miles up.

"The route from the mouth of Big Beaver I expect will be best on the West side until we are two or perhaps, three, miles above Kishkuske then the road will cross at a good ford & turning Westward will cross the creek twice more, then leaving the Creek a little above salt springs. it will cross the Cayahoga about ten miles from its mouth & pass down on the west side. at all the crossings are good fords unless the water should be uncommonly high.

"The number of intermediate stations will depend on the distance they are from each other. allowing twenty miles to be a proper distance then four only will be required.

"I believe this to be the nearest & best route by which a communication can be opened between the Ohio river & Lake Erie without having regard to Water navigation, which whoever depends on will be deceived; Altho I doubt not but that at some seasons considerable advantage may be derived from water carraige on most of the rivers I have mentioned & the big beaver & Cayahoga may some times be made a good use of this way.

"The facts I have mentioned in this statement, I have from a Man of Judgment and undoubted veracity, who has had full Opportunity to examine the country not only on the route from big beaver to Cayahoga but has also travelled by many different roads from Pittsburg to Sandusky and detroit resided ten years among the Delawares is fully acquainted with all the streams that make a part of the Muskingam river as well as the southern Shore of Lake Erie and all the streams that fall into it between Cayahoga and Detroit.

"In some part of this route the country is open. in other parts are thickets of brush to be Cut out but the principle difficulty, is a swamp and wet ground for seven or eight miles, the greatest part of which must be causs[w]eyed, but I am told that lumber is plenty & handy, and if so one man will easily make one perch per day and allowing 640 men may be well employed at the work they will make this part of the road in four days. however if it should happen to be a dry fall it is doubtfull if one fourth part of the distance mentioned will require Bridging in the first movement of the army (when I speake of making a good road, I mean a Waggon road[)], there is now a Pack horse path to the whole distance which has been much used by traders and War parties.

"By this route all kinds of provisions except beef from Kentucky can be transported to the Miami village cheaper than thro' any other channell and from thence conveyed down the Wabash—or towards Lake Michigan, and into the upper part of the Illinoi Country, to supply any Garrisons which Government may think proper to establish in that quarter for the protection of the friendly tribes and the security of our trade with them, to this may be added the supply of the post at Detroit whenever we shall be in possession of it.

"If the proposition should meet with approbation measures for carrying it into execution cannot be too soon adopted for altho' the season will be too farr advanced before the event of the present overtures now making to the enemy is known, to admit of any offensive opperations of Consequence in this quarter, yet I concieve it will not be the case with respect to the plan I have proposed.

"I can see no objection against making an Establishment at the Big Beaver (where we have long had a small post[)] even while our negociations are depending.

"Under this Idea then I would propose the troops intended for the service as fast as they arrive at Pittsburg should be sent down to that place, that the works there be repaired and extended in a proper manner and Magazines of provisions forage &c. &c. &c. be collected for the expedition; This cannot probably be completed and the whole ready to move before October, and before that time I trust, it will be known whether we are to have a treaty with these fellows or not, if they shall agree to a treaty it is probable they will be as willing to hold it some where on the big beaver or at the mouth of Cayahoga as at any other place, and in that Case they can have no Objection to a road being made to transport the goods to Cayahoga.

"At all events when ever we make peace with them, and whatever we relinquish, in other respects, we must insist on establishing ourselves at Cayahoga for the purpose of supplying them with goods to be delivered there, or farther westward so that the work proposed at the big beaver will not be lost provided we come to a treaty & if we are to have no treaty we shall be ready to execute the plan by force, And in that case if we are ready to move by the first of October I think we may safely venture on the expedition for allowing Sixteen days to errect the four intermediate s[t]ations four to make the Causey and that we Cut our road and march five miles a day we shall reach Cayahoga in forty days, but I have no doubt but we shall be able to reach Cayahoga in half that time—About the time intended for the army leaving the post at Big beaver the enemy may be menaced from this quarter, and as they will not be alarmed at seeing you posted at Big-beaver, the Army will probably reach the Cayahoga before the enemy can possibly be in a situation to oppose them. at the same time a body of Volunteer militia might be encouraged to advance on Croffords route towards sandusky.

"The measure I beleive will be very populer with the people of Ohio County and all the Western part of Pennsylvania which will greatly facilitate the business—Forage for any number of horses may be brought to this place with little expence, and if the number of regular troops which may be raised by the time & spared for the purpose should be thought insufficient, I have no doubt but an ample supply of good rifle men, who live with in three days march of the spot would Voluntarily engage in the expedition.

"On the whole I have no doubt but we may without any unreasonable hazard establish ourselves at Cayahoga by the setting in of Winter and that by the first of May if not before a sufficient number of boats may be built for transporting the Army into the Ome [Maumee], or tawa rivers—But should the fall season prove unfavorable or any other unforeseen accident prevent our advancing to the Cayahoga this winter, yet if we can make our way good a part of the distance only, I think the object ought to be pursued as we shall be enabled thereby to commence our operations next year much earlier.

"Besides that, I think this is the best mode of carrying on the War, the sooner we show ourselves on the shore of Lake Erie, the better—such an Appearance will be a conviction to the Indians that many things which have been told them is false, and finding they have been imposed on in some things they will doubt the rest" (DLC:GW). For Knox's observations on Putnam's letter, see his letters to Anthony Wayne and to Putnam, both 7 Aug., at Knox to GW, that date, n.3. For GW's thoughts on Putnam's proposals, see GW to Knox, 13 Aug. 1792.

3. For the full text of Putnam's letter to Knox of 5 July, see Buell, *Putnam Memoirs*, 273–78.

4. William Blount wrote Knox on 31 Aug. that the banditti's attack of 26 June "*At Zeigler's Station, near Bledsoe's Lick, on the North side of Cumberland River*" left four Americans dead, four wounded, and thirteen as prisoners. "Of these prisoners, nine have been regained by purchase, made by their parents and friends, from the Cherokees, Shawanese, and Creeks, at the Running Water; of the four which remain, one is a Miss Wilson, now with the Creeks, the other three are negroes" (*ASP, Indian Affairs*, 1:276). For the attack on Maj. John Doughty's party in early 1790, see GW to the Chiefs of the Choctaw Nation, 17 Dec. 1789, source note.

5. On 15 Aug., Knox wrote to Governor Blount: "The five companies of Infantry and one of horse, you have ordered into service, if the companies are nearly full, would amount to a pretty formidable force. If sufficiently alert and active, it would seem to be a reasonable expectation, that they would intercept and chastise some of the banditti that have lately given your government so much trouble, and the south western frontiers of Virginia such serious alarms" (Carter, *Territorial Papers*, 4:163).

From Tobias Lear

Sir, Portsmouth [N.H.] August 5th 1792.

Since I had the honor of writing to you on the 21 ultimo nothing of a public nature has occurred in this quarter of sufficient importance to trouble you with an account of it. And being desireous of gaining all the knowledge of the sentiments of the people hereabouts respecting our public affairs, that I could obtain either personally or from the best information, I have delayed writing 'till this time in order that my account might be more full and accurate.

I have been careful to catch the observations of those who are considered men of information and influence in their respective States, with whom I have had an opportunity of being: and tho' they are various & sometimes opposite; yet I have found them generally concurring in these points—That more good has been felt in New England from the operations of the general government than its most strenuous supporters had promised—that none of those evils which its enemies foretold had come to pass—and that the people were happy and contented under it. But these observations were generally closed with remarking, that it was yet a government of experiment, and that it would be highly proper to see the *certain* effects of the Systems hitherto pursued, rather than change them for others which have not yet been tried. And that it might be well to stop, for a while at least, at the point where we now are, and not push further any matters which may now be disgusting to a part of the community until that which is done shall establish its utility beyond contradiction, or until circumstances may arise to render a further advance in those measures absolutely necessary.

This town has lately been visited by many strangers from different parts of the U.S. particularly from Massachusetts, and as I have been much with them in companies, I have had frequent opportunities of hearing their opinions, and what they said they conceived to be the opinion of their State or States upon several political points. Governor Hancock has been here for these ten days past accompanied by several respectable persons of his State, among whom were Mr Attorney General Sullivan and Colo. Orne, an influential Character in the politics of Massachusetts. Mr Gore, the Attorney for that District was also in town, tho' not of the Governor's party. From the political character & consideration of these Gentlemen it appears very likely that they express the sentiments of the several parties in that commonwealth with respect to the general Government. I have likewise met here Captn Spry of the British navy, Judge Burke & Mr Hazelhurst of South Carolina, Mr Hare of Philadelphia[1] and Dr Cutting.

On the subject of the ensuing election of President and Vice-President (which now begins to be much talked of) it seems to be generally beleived that Mr Adams will have nearly all the votes of the New England States for the office which he now holds. With respect to the Chief Magistrate but one idea prevails, but one sentiment is expressed. I have not even heard the question started—Whom shall we have if the present Chief Magistrate cannot be again prevailed upon to accept the Chair? For so strongly does the *necessity* of his continuance appear to be impressed on the mind of everyone that no other person seems ever to have been contemplated for that office.

I mentioned in my last that the people in this quarter were perfectly satisfied with the operations of the general government, and that the good effects of it were every day becoming more & more conspicuous.[2] I am now happy in being able to confirm this account from my own observations, so far as they have extended & from concurrent information. Ship-building, which is the principal employment of the Mechanicks in and about this place, and a primary object in Massachusetts, has encreased exceedingly within these two years, and the demand for Vessels is, notwithstanding, much greater at this moment than the supply. This is very justly imputed to the advantage which the laws give to our own ships over those of foreign nations:[3] and I am told there has scarcely been a cargo brought into New England for these twelve months past but what has been brought in American Vessels. Some, however, who are largely concerned in Navigation, still wish for a further extension of the laws with respect to foreign vessels; but those who are not immediately interested in that business, and are therefore perhaps better judges of the matter, think such an extension would be carrying the point too far & probably injure instead of benefit our Shipping. The other mechanic Arts keep pace with ship-building—Agriculture is not behind-hand in its extension and improvements—and a spirit of enterprize with respect to inland navigation—Roads—bridges &c.—seems to pervade this part of the Country. A circulating medium sufficient to give vigor & promptitude to all kinds of business adds new life to every pursuit. But some are apprehensive that the multiplication of Banks, for which there seems to be an insatiable rage, will ultimately throw such a quantity of paper into circulation as to produce much greater evils than would arise from the want of a sufficient medium: And many are of opinion that the issuing of bills from those Banks established under the authority of individual States militates with that clause of the Constitution of the United States which expressly restrains a State from issuing paper money.[4]

A few days ago the Skipper of a fishing vessel belonging to this port came to me and begged leave to relate a circumstance which happened to him and a number of other fishing vessels on the coast of Nova Scotia, which he conceived amounted to an infraction of the treaty on the part of the British.[5] He said the reason of his wishing to relate it to me was, that being informed that it would be proper to make the matter known to the President of the United States, and understanding that I was in this town he had called to communicate it to the President through me. I told him he had not chosen the proper Channel of communication for matters of this kind—that if he intended to bring it forward he must state the circumstances minutely in writing, supported by such testimony as might be proper to establish the fact, and transmit the same to the Secretary of State at Philadelphia. He thanked me for putting him in the right way and promised to pursue it:[6] but at the same time requested I would hear the story, which he related as follows.

["]That on his last fishing voyage, he, with a number of other fishing Vessels, went into the bay of Annapolis on the coast of Nova Scotia, to take with their seins some small fish for bait, a thing which they had always done since the Revolution (as well as before) without molestation, and conformably to the treaty; that they had scarcely come to anchor & got out their seins before a British Cutter came in—fired several shot at them, and ordered every vessel to get under sail and go out of the bay within ten minutes or she would sink them, and declaring that if ever they returned to that or any other of the bays on that Coast they should certainly be destroyed. This order they were obliged to comply with instantaniously, and by that means were prevented from obtaining bait, and consequently much injured in their Voyage."

I am emboldened, Sir, to make these communications to you

touching our public affairs, because you expressed a wish that I should do so, and to comply with your wishes or to be in any degree serviceable to you will always constitute one of the most pleasurable duties of my life.

I have been endeavouring to learn if a respectable and well qualified person can be obtained in this part of the Country to open a private School in Philadelphia, provided a sufficient number of scholars (not exceeding 12 or 15) should be found to make it an object worthy the attention of a suitable Character; and I have reason to hope I shall find such an one. Colo. Hamilton seemed to have it much at heart to establish such a school, and several other gentlemen favored the idea—and sure I am that unless Washington can be placed at such a seminary or changed from that tract in which he has hitherto been in Philadelphia, he & his friends will have cause to regret it as long as he lives.[7]

We intend leaving this place for Philadelphia the beginning of next month, and if we meet with no special delay shall probably reach that City about the 20th.[8]

I must beg the favor of being presented to Mrs Washington in terms of the highest respect & gratitude: to the Major & his Lady and the Gentlemen I tender my best wishes, and my love to the Children. In these Mrs Lear joins me, and begs your acceptance of her best respects. With the highest respect, & most sincere Attachment, I have the honor to be Sir, Your grateful & Obedt Servt

Tobias Lear.

ALS, DLC:GW.

For the background to Lear's trip to New England, see Lear to GW, 15 July, source note.

1. Aedanus Burke (1743–1802), who had risen to the rank of major in the S.C. militia during the Revolutionary War, was appointed an associate judge in 1778, served in the state legislature 1781–82 and 1784–89, and was elected chancellor of South Carolina in 1784 and to the state court of equity in 1799. Robert Hazelhurst was a Charleston merchant. Robert Hare, Sr. (1752–1812), was a well-to-do brewer who later served as Speaker of the Pa. senate 1796–1800.

2. See Lear to GW, 21 July 1792.

3. Lear apparently is referring to "An Act for laying a duty on goods, wares, and merchandises, imported into the United States" of 4 July 1789, which gave "a discount of ten per cent. on all the duties imposed by this act" to

American ships, and "An Act imposing duties on tonnage" of 20 July 1789, which taxed American vessels at six cents per ton, "all ships or vessels hereafter built in the United States, belonging wholly, or in part, to subjects of foreign powers, at the rate of thirty cents per ton," and "all other ships or vessels, at the rate of fifty cents per ton" (*Annals of Congress,* 1st Cong., 2183–86).

4. See U.S. Constitution, art. 1, sec. 10.

5. Article 3 of the 1783 peace treaty between Great Britain and the United States stipulates "that the Inhabitants of the united States shall have Liberty to take Fish of every kind . . . on the Coasts, Bays, and Creeks of all other of his Britannic Majesty's Dominions in America, and that the American Fishermen shall have Liberty to dry and cure Fish in any of the unsettled Bays Harbours and Creeks of Nova Scotia" (Miller, *Treaties,* 2:98).

6. Whether or not the unnamed "Skipper" pursued this matter has not been determined.

7. Upon returning to Philadelphia, Lear reported to GW: "I am happy to inform you that I found a person who is recommended by General [Benjamin] Lincoln & several other respectable Characte[r]s as being completely qualified in every respect to take charge of and superintend the education of a small number of boys, and who is ready to come on here & engage in that business as soon as he shall be informed that his services are desired" (Lear to GW, 7 Oct. 1792).

8. Lear and his family did not reach the U.S. capital until the morning of 7 Oct. (see Lear to GW, that date).

From Edmund Randolph

Dear Sir. Philadelphia August 5. 1792.

The inclosed letter has been delayed, longer than I intended. But whenever I have sat down to finish it, I have been unexpectedly interrupted. I trust, however, that it will reach you, before you shall have taken your definitive resolution.[1]

I have seen Fraunces thrice at the house; and he has informed me each time, that every thing was right.

Parties run high here in the choice of electors and representatives. The contest is now brought to such a point, that two opposite tickets, without any one name being the same in both, will be vehemently supported. I suspect, that Mr Fitzsimmons's election is very precarious. He certainly will miscarry, unless the old republican party should be found to be more numerous, than the old constitutional one. For, altho' the denominations are now lost, the members of them continue unchanged in their temper to each other.[2] The quakers seem to be undergoing a revolution in their friendship for governor Mifflin. They insinuate, that he roused the opposition of the people to the appointment of conferees for adjusting a ticket. I cannot ascertain, whether they have good grounds for their resentment.[3]

We are in hourly expectation of two arrivals from France; from whence we have received no intelligence later than the affair of Gouvion, as published in the gazettes.[4]

Mrs Randolph begs to be presented to Mrs Washington in the most respectful manner; and I always am, my dear sir, with a very affectionate attachment Yr obliged humble serv.

Edm: Randolph.

ALS, DLC:GW.

1. See Randolph to GW, this date (second letter).

2. Although Thomas FitzSimons of Pennsylvania was reelected to Congress in November 1792, he was defeated in his bid for a fourth term in 1794.

3. For Gov. Thomas Mifflin this matter was a serious concern, because he was a descendant of a prominent Quaker family of Philadelphia who had received substantial support from the Quakers during the gubernatorial election of 1790. Mifflin continued to serve as governor until 1799, however.

4. Jean-Baptiste de Gouvion (1747–1792), who had served as an engineer in America during the Revolutionary War, had risen to the rank of colonel in the French army by December 1787. During the French Revolution, Gouvion served as an officer in the Parisian national guard and as a deputy to the national legislative assembly in 1791–92. Having left the legislature in mid-April 1792, Gouvion was killed in action on 11 June 1792 while serving under Lafayette. Randolph probably is referring to a report printed on 4 Aug. in the *Gazette of the United States* (Philadelphia), which reads in part: "Some time since an account was published of the defeat of a detachment of M. la Fayette's army, under the command of M. Gouvion, on a foraging party, by an inferior force. That account is far from the truth. It appears that M. Gouvion was attacked by a superior force, but managed a retreat with great skill and success, having, notwithstanding the opposition he experienced, attained the object of his expedition, with little or no loss."

From Edmund Randolph

Dear sir Philadelphia August 5. 1792.

I have persuaded myself, that this letter, tho' unconnected with any official relation, and upon a subject, to the decision of which you alone are competent, will be received in the spirit, with which it is written. The Union, for the sake of which I have encountered various embarrassments, not wholly unknown to you, and sacrificed some opinions, which, but for its jeopardy, I should never have surrendered, seems to me to be now at the eve of a crisis. It is feared by those, who take a serious interest in the affairs of the U.S., that you will refuse the chair of government at the approaching election. If such an event must happen, indulge me at least in the liberty of opening to you a course of thought, which a calm attention to the fœderal government has suggested, and no bias of party has influenced.

It cannot have escaped you, that divisions are formed in our politics, as systematic as those, which prevail in Great Britain. Such, as opposed the constitution from a hatred to the Union, can never be conciliated by any overture or atonement. By others it is meditated to push the construction of fœderal powers to every tenable extreme. A third class, republican in principle, and thus far, in my judgment, happy in their discernment of our welfare, have notwithstanding mingled with their doctrines a fatal error, that the state-assemblies are to be resorted to, as the Engines of correction to the fœderal administration. The honors, belonging to the chief-magistracy are objects of no common solicitude to a few, who compose a fourth denomination.

The ferment, which might be naturally expected from these ingredients, does actually exist. The original enemies not only affect to see a completion of their malignant prophecies; but are ready to improve every calumny, to the disgrace of the government. To their corps are, or will be added in a great measure the mistaken friends of republicanism; while the favourers of the high tone are strenuous in the prosecution of their views.

The real temper, however, of the people, is, I believe, strictly right at this moment. Their passions have been tried in every possible shape. After the first tumult, excited by the discussion of the constitution, had abated, several acts of congress became the theme of abuse. But they have not yet *felt* oppression; and they love order too much, to be roused into a deliberate commotion, without the intervention of the most wicked artifices. They will, it is true, be told at the meeting of every state-legislature, that congress have usurped. But this, if unfounded, will be ascribed to the violence of those, who wish to establish a belief, that they alone can save the individual states from the general vortex, by being elected into the fœderal councils.

It is much to be regretted, that the judiciary, in spite of their apparent firmness in Annulling the pension-law, are not, what some time hence they will be, a resource against the infractions of the constitution, On the one hand, and a Steady asserter of the fœderal rights, on the other.[1] So crude is our judiciary System, so jealous are state-judges of their authority, so ambiguous is the language of the constitution, that the most probable quarter, from which an alarming discontent may proceed, is the rivalship of those two orders of judges. The main superiority of talents in the fœderal judges, (if indeed it were admitted) cannot be presumed to counterbalance the real talents, and full popularity of their competitors. At this instant too, it is possible, that the fœderal judges may not be so forgetful of their connection with the state-governments, as to be indifferent about the continuance of their old interest there. This, I suspect, has on some occasions produced an abandonment of the true authorities of the government Besides; many severe experiments, the result of which upon the public mind, cannot be foreseen, await the judiciary. States are brought into court, as defendants to the claims of land companies, and of individuals: british debts rankle deeply in the hearts of one part of the U.S: and the precedent, fixed by the condemnation of the pension-law, if not reduced to its precise principles, may justify every constable in thwarting the laws.

In this threatening posture of our affairs, we must gain time, for the purpose of attracting confidence in the government by an experience of its benefits, and that man alone, whose patronage secured the adoption of the constitution, can check the assaults, which it will sustain at the two next sessions of congress.

The fiscal arrangements will have various degrees and kinds of ill-humour to encounter. Objectionable as they were at first to myself in many respects; yet am I assured, that they cannot now be changed without a convulsion to public credit. Can any new project be suggested, free from blemish? Have not the clamors of the people concerning the assumption Subsided? Can any tax be substituted for the excise, without rekindling those very complaints, which the excise has generated, but which have now almost died away? If any thing can prevent machinations, like these, it will be a reverance for your official character; if any thing can crush them, it will be your negative.

Another of the efforts, meditated against the public debt, is to destroy its irredeemability. I sincerely wish, that this quality had never been given to it. But how can we tread back the ground, on which the European money-holders have been led into our funds? The injury to the U.S. can never amount to more, than the difference between the interest, which we pay, and some lower rate, at which perhaps we might borrow to discharge the debt. Borrow we must for such an object; since the sum, which we are free to wipe off according to our stipulation, is equal to our own present ability. And is this chance of advantage a sufficient temptation, on which to hazard our halffledged reputation? What would you say, Sir, if for this purpose a land-tax should be laid, by Congress which shall not take effect, unless the states should neglect to raise the money by their own laws? I think, it would soon be discovered, that such a measure would insensibly restore requisitions. These evils are also within the scope of your controul.[2] It will be a great point gained, that the judiciary Topics should be rendered as mild as possible. Such of them, as are likely to be most obnoxious, will in four years more be finished. The judges will be more cautious, with the eye of an independent executive, upon them. States and individuals will acquiesce in their judgments with more complacency, when they cordially believe that the existing executive watches over the public safety with impartiality.

The fuel, which has been already gathered for combustion, wants no addition. But how awfully might it be increased, were the violence, which is now suspended by an universal submission to your pretensions, let loose by your resignation. Those fœderalists, who can espouse Mr Clinton against Mr Adams, as Vice-President, will not hesitate at a more formidable game. Permit me, then, in the fervor of a dutiful and affectionate attachment to you, to beseech you to penetrate the consequences of a dereliction of the reins. The constitution would never have been adopted, but from a knowledge, that you had once sanctified it, and an expectation, that you would execute it. It is in a state of probation. The most inauspicious struggles are past; but the public deliberations need stability. You alone can give them stability. You suffered yourself to yield, when the voice of your country summoned you to the administration. Should a civil war arise, you cannot stay at home. And how much easier will it be, to disperse the factions, which are rushing to this catastrophe, than to Subdue them, after they shall appear in arms? It is the fixed opinion of the world, that you surrender nothing incomplete.

I am not unapprized of many disagreeable sensations, which have laboured in your breast. But let them Spring from any cause whatsoever, of one thing I am sure, (and I speak this from a satisfactory inquiry, lately made.) tho if a second opportunity shall be given to the people of shewing the⟨ir⟩ gratitude, they will not be less unanimous than before. I have the honor to be, dear Sir, with the most respectful affection Yr obliged ob. serv.

Edm: Randolph.

ALS, DLC:GW.

For the opinions of other members of GW's inner circle about the necessity for him to serve a second term as president, see Thomas Jefferson's Memorandum of Conversations with Washington, 1 Mar., Madison's Conversations with Washington, 5–25 May, Jefferson to GW, 23 May (second letter), Jefferson's Conversation with Washington, 10 July, and Alexander Hamilton to GW, 30 July–3 Aug. 1792.

1. For the outpouring of judicial opposition to "An Act to provide for the settlement of the claims of widows and orphans, barred by the limitations heretofore established, and to regulate the claims to invalid pensions" of 23 Mar. 1792, see Caleb Brewster to GW, 15 Mar., n.4, Edmund Randolph to GW, 5 April, U.S. Circuit Court Judges for N.Y. to GW, 10 April, and enclosure, GW to the U.S. Senate and House of Representatives, 16, 21 April, U.S. Circuit Court Judges for Pa. to GW, 18 April, Joachim Jacob Brandt to GW, 2 June, and James Iredell and John Sitgreaves to GW, 8 June, and note 6. Sections 2–4 of the act of 23 Mar. were repealed on 28 Feb. 1793.

2. The last four sentences of this paragraph originally were written as a separate paragraph and placed immediately above the paragraph beginning "Another of the efforts." Randolph, however, indicated his desired rearrangement of the text by writing two notes on the manuscript. In the margin next to the four sentences he wrote: "A. to come in after 'controul' on the other side," and in the margin next to the sentence ending "the scope of your controul," he wrote "A. See A on other side."

From Salamon Coer Bacri

Livorno [Tuscany], 6 Aug. 1792. Suggests that his family, because of its influence over and ties to the court of the Dey of Algiers, could assist in restoring peace between the United States and the Dey and in effecting the release of the American mariners held captive at Algiers. Bacri offers to advise the American plenipotentiary about how best to conduct his negotiations with the Dey so as to bring their discussions to a mutually satisfactory conclusion.

ALS, DNA: RG 59, Despatches from Consular Officers, Algiers. The Italian text of the original receiver's copy appears in CD-ROM:GW. The docket on the back of this letter, which is in Tobias Lear's hand, reads: "An Italian letter relative to redeemg The American Captives at Algiers &c.—Translated by the Secry of State—Octr 26. 1792."

Tobias Lear apparently transmitted Bacri's letter to Thomas Jefferson on 31 Oct., requesting that a translation be made and informing the secretary of state that "It was put into the President's hands by Mr [John] Swan[w]ick, who informs him that a vessel will sail for Italy tomorrow or next day, and if the enclosed letter is of a nature to require an immediate answer—this vessel presents an opportunity" (DLC: Jefferson Papers). Neither Jefferson's translation nor any written reply to Bacri from GW or Jefferson has been found, however. Bacri seems to have written GW again in early 1793 to offer "his services to redeem our Captives at Algiers & make a peace with that Regency for us" (*JPP,* 126). By the middle of the 1790s, Salamon Coer Bacri and his cousin Micaiah Coer Bacri, both of whom were members of a prominent Jewish mercantile house with branches in Italy and Algiers, were representing American interests with the Dey and supporting, through the provision of shipping and banking services, the United States's efforts to effect the release of the American captives (Barnby, *Prisoners of Algiers,* 243, 281–83).

From Richard Chichester

Newington [Va.] 6th Augt 1792.

Richard Chichester's Respectful Compliments to his Excellency George Washington Esqr., President of the United States of America, humbly Requesting his favour of Permission to hunt that Small Skirt of woods Just around the Tenement whereon William Gray lives, as his lameness &c. Renders it Impracticable to Amuse himself in that line, only, where there's a Road to Drive in A chair to the Stands—Which, if Permitted, Shall be Done without Injury to any Person Whatever.

AL, DLC:GW.

From George Muter

Sir Kentucky, Woodford County Augt 6th 1792.

I have served seven years, as chief Justice for the District of Kentucky, and I beleive I have given general satisfaction: but, in the appointments for the court of Appeals for our new state, I have been left out, & appointed for the court of Oyer & Terminer, which, if it continues agreeable to it's present establishment, will be of little consequence, and the judges will have little to do. The reason assigned for my being left out is, that, it would be improper the court of Appeals should consist of the judges of the former supreme court, on account of the appeals which may arise from that court to the present court of Appeals; but, as one of the former judges, is now a judge of the court of Appeals, & the other judges taken from the bar of the former court, & it is probable that, there will be but very few appeals, this is thought by some, not to be the true reason of my being left out.

As I wish to serve my country for a few years longer, and would in the present state of our affairs, prefer serving the united States, I am induced to offer you my services as judge of the Fœderal court, in this state, if mr Innes should resign, which it is probable he will do, as he is appointed the chief Justice of the court of Appeals.[1]

Should you think proper to appoint me judge of the Fœderal court, you may depend on my executing the duties of my office, with assiduity & integrity. I have the honour to be Sir Your most hle servant

George Muter

ALS, DNA: RG 59, Miscellaneous Letters.

1. Although Harry Innes was named chief justice of the Kentucky supreme court of appeals in July 1792, he declined the appointment and remained U.S. district judge for Kentucky until his death in September 1816. Muter served as head of the Kentucky court of oyer and terminer from 1792 until 1806.

From Henry Knox

Sir War department August 7th 1792

I have just been honored with yours of the first instant.

The papers which you have been pleased to require shall be transmitted by the post of Monday next.[1]

The communications last received from Fort Washington were such, that I thought it proper Major General Wayne should be possessed thereof by express in order to enable him to form a proper judgment of the measures to be pursued.[2]

I have the honor to enclose you copies of my letters of this date to Generals Wayne and Putnam.[3]

Any observations which you shall please to make thereon will be respectfully received.[4]

I have also the honor to enclose you copies of Israel Chapins letters of the 18 of July—He appears to have conducted with great propriety and zeal.[5]

I am inclined to believe Major Fish would not accept the Office of Adjutant General—I am not well informed how Coll Posey would answer for that office; but if his industry and talents at arrangements are equal to his character for bravery—he would be an acquisition to the service.[6]

Major Gaither will sail on Thursday or Friday—he has been detained for a vessel—his instructions will be pointed as to the preservation of the peace.[7] I have the honor to be Sir Your obedient Servant.

H. Knox

LS, DLC:GW; LB, DLC:GW.

1. See GW to Knox, 1 August. For the background to this request, see Alexander Hamilton to GW, 22 July 1792, and note 2. Knox apparently dated his report to GW, which has not been found, Saturday, 11 Aug., not Monday, 13 August.

2. For the intelligence that Knox had recently received from Fort Washington, see Knox to GW, 5 Aug., and notes 1, 2, and 4.

3. Knox's letter to Anthony Wayne, which was written at the War Department on 7 Aug. 1792, reads: "Having received, by the way of Kentucky, the dispatches herein enumerated from Fort Washington, and conceiving that the lowness of the Waters in the Ohio, mentioned in yours of the 28th Ultimo, may have prevented you from receiving similar intelligence, I have thought proper to forward copies for your information and consideration ℘ express.

"Comparing the information now transmitted with that from Newton contained in my last but little doubt can remain that poor [Alexander] Truemans fate is sealed—but I hope Colonel [John] Hardin may have escaped.

"Although two sets of Messengers (Hardin perhaps excepted) have thus been destroyed the hostile Indians may be possessed of the desires of the United States for peace—unless [Simon] Girty and such wretches dependent on the traders under the British auspices, may have concealed them.

"If Hardin should also be murdered our remaining hope for the hostile tribes to be acquainted with our pacific overtures must rest upon the Senecas, Captain Hendricks [Hendrick Aupaumut] Colonel Louis [Cook; Atoyataghroughta; Atyatoghhanongwea] and Captain [Joseph] Brant the Indians who were in this City for that purpose.

"I estimate that some of the above Indians are at the Glaize at present and perhaps most of them will be there in a few days—I should hope that considerable dependence may be placed on Captain Brant—He is well acquainted with the subject, and if his faithfulness in the cause he has undertaken, be equal to his intelligence, he will probably effect a treaty.

"Time will shortly disclose whether the murder of our messengers has been the premeditated act of the Council of the hostile tribes—the act of the Shawanese and other opposers of a peace or the effect of the blood thirsty disposition of individuals.

"I have enclosed you Brigadier General Putnams plan for carrying on the War—I feel exceedingly obliged to him or any other person for any plans ideas or even hints which they may think proper to offer[.] But every idea which he has brought forward has been weighed maturely by the President of the United States previously to the present arrangement. The result was that the Wabash and the Omie river of Lake Erie should be the boundary in case of progressing hostilities.

"If the propositions made by General Putnam were then relinquished for the present plan reasons for a perseverance therein multiply greatly. I shall therefore attempt to point out the exceptions to the Big Beaver and Cayahoga Route which occur to my mind:

"First Reasons of national policy will restrain (during the present negociations relative to the posts) all army arrangements on the lakes which might occasion collisions with the British inferior agents[.] This is a delicate point and is not therefore to be undertaken.

"Secondly. That in case of offensive operations a division of the probable efficient force would be such as to render the success problematical.

"Thirdly—No immediate object could be found for the operation of the said force moving by the way of Cayahoga—provided the information given by Captain Brant could be depended upon, to wit, that the Wyandots and Delawares have left San Dusky.

"Fourthly—That even if the foregoing reasons did not exist so strongly the advanced season would prevent the measure this year unless the motives were so powerful as to be a reason for the troops encountering all the hardships and danger of the late season as in the last campaign.

"Fifthly—A Post or Posts established at and below the Miami Village towards Lake Erie would it is presumed have the direct effect to make all the hostile Indians hitherto resident to the Eastward of the said Omie River as at Sandusky and other places remove to the Westward of the said River provided they have not already removed which is highly probable.

"The above Objections together with others arising from the necessity and propriety of continuing our advance from Fort Jefferson to the Miami Village are offered on Brigadier General Putnam's propositions for your consideration and remarks.

"The season of the Year is too far advanced, the number of the recruits too few and the undisciplined state of the army such, as to preclude any great expectations of all forward important movements this season.

"If the war is to progress the number of Recruits authorized by Law must be completed during the autumn and winter and every preparation by discipline and otherwise be made for the most forward and active operations as early in the ensuing spring as the waters and herbage will allow.

"Another conflict with the Savages with raw recruits is to be avoided by all means.

"I shall transmit these remarks to the President of the United States and his observations on the propositions of Brigadier Putnam and the objections herein stated shall be transmitted to you.

"You will judge from Brigadier General Wilkinsons letter of the propriety of forwarding him a respectable detachment of four or five hundred troops—The men designed for the Cavalry will of course be forwarded as they must be mounted there—but I pray you to give the proper orders that they be not prematurely hazarded.

"More Volunteers from Kentucky would be too expensive.

"In order that you may have all the information I possess on the subject of the navigation of the Big Beaver Creek and the route thence over to Cayahoga I enclose you the late Major [Jonathan] Hearts report upon that subject in consequence of instructions from me in the Year 1790.

"The letter of Brigadier General Putnam of the 9th of July relative to the establishment of a post on the Muskingum is referred to your judgment—If the Maps are to be depended upon a post at the place where Fort Lawrence stood, which was built in the Year 1764, would appear to have a good effect to protect Ohio and Washington Counties But whether it would be secure in itself unless the Garrison was very large, and whether it could be easily supplied are to be inquired into, and above all whether the division of force and the expence would be amply repaid by the benefits.

"I enclose you copies of the letters written to Brigadiers General Putnam and Wilkinson.

"It would be a species of injustice were it concealed that Brigadier General Wilkinson has afforded the greatest satisfaction by his Conduct, which has evinced the most indefatigable industry and zeal to promote the good of the service.

"I have this moment received the enclosed letter from Israel Chapin the Agent to the five nations—I transmit it to you as a new light upon the pacific overtures and the expectation which we may entertain of the agency of the Indians, independent of Captain Brant, who, I think will be at the Omie River of Lake Erie rather previous to the 20th instant.

"I am still of opinion and the more confirmed in it from Chapins letter that the Senekas with Captain [John] Jeffers' party ought not to be pressed to stay in service—their continuance may have bad effects.

"I shall from time to time communicate to you all the information which I shall receive relative to the objects of your command, in order that you may be enabled to take a comprehensive view of the subject and decide accordingly as the public interests shall direct.

"The President of the United States, in a letter received from him this day mentions 'Reiterate in your letters to General Wayne the necessity of employing the present calm in disciplining and training the troops under his command for the peculiar service for which they are destined—He is not to be sparing of Powder and lead (in proper and reasonable quantities) to make the Soldiers marksmen.'

"'So long as the vice of drunkenness exists in the army, so long I hope ejections of those officers who are found guilty of it will continue; for *that* and *gaming* will debilitate and render unfit for active service any army whatever[']" (DLC:GW).

Knox's letter to Rufus Putnam, which was also written at the War Department on 7 Aug. 1792, reads in part: "You will cultivate and make peace with the Wabash tribes to the utmost of your power, and you will judge how far your going to Post Vincennes, or any other place will facilitate the object—Extend your treaties with one tribe after another as far as possible, always subjecting them to the ratification of the President and Senate of the United States.

"The United States require no lands of the Wabash indians not heretofore ceded—Impress this idea upon all the tribes—Apply the goods at Fort Washington to the purposes of the said treaties.

"If it should so happen that in pursuance of your instructions you should have an immediate opportunity of repairing to the hostile indians you will appoint such time for assembling the Wabash tribes and all their connexions, as not to militate with the first object.

"I will endeavor to have more indian goods transported to Fort Washington, and I hope that an opportunity by a peace will be presen[te]d you of bestowing them to the benefit of the United States.

"I have communicated a copy of your letter of the 8th inst. to the President of the United States.

"The advancement of the public interest being the sole object of my pursuit and not the establishment of any particular opinion, I am sincerely obliged to you for the propositions relative to a different route by the Cayahoga.

"The Plan of operations was considered and approved by the President of the United States upon as full a view of all circumstances political as well as military which could be obtained at the time of decision.

"We are in a delicate situation politically with respect to th⟨e⟩ British government. There are existing circumstances of such a nature as to render it highly expedient to avoid all cases of a possible collision with that power—Were we posted on the margin of the lake and had therein a naval arrangement of the most diminutive size, the peace and dignity of the country might be committed to the discretion of a subalterns party.

"The President has therefore judged it prudent to keep at a distance from the lakes for the present—Hereafter arrangements similar to the one you proposed may be adopted. . . . I have also communicated to major general Wayne, your letter of the 9th, relative to a post on the Muskinghum, in order that he may take such measures thereon as he may judge proper.

"It will still be left to your discretion, when to deliver the prisoners—Brigadier General Wilkinson seems to think that most of them ought to be retained, to see what part their tribes will take.

"The enclosed letter is from General Israel Chapin, who is the Agent to the five Nations, and which I communicate to you as important information" (DLC:GW).

4. For GW's observations on this and several earlier letters from Knox, see GW to Knox, 13 Aug. 1792.

5. Israel Chapin wrote Knox on 17 July from Canandaigua, N.Y.: "Agreeably to the directions I received for the purpose, I set out for Buffaloe-Creek the ninth Ultimo. It was out of my power to dispatch Captain Hendrick, as soon as I could have wished. The Chiefs of the five nations at first peremptorily insisted on his waiting to accompany them and it was not without difficulties that they were induced to relinquish the point. After a Council which was protracted for several days they however gave their consent. He set out in a bark Canoe on the eighteenth with suitable attendants and provisions. It was the opinion of the Indians he would reach the place of destination in eight days. As I had possessed myself with all the information I expected I would have returned home after the departure of Captain Hendricks but the Chiefs would by no means consent to my leaving them while the treaty continued—And indeed I have not since been sorry, as I have reason to believe that my continuance has been the means of more perfectly reconciling the Anadaugas and Cyugas. The far greater part of both Nations have resided at buffaloe Creek ever since the late war. On my first arrival the principal chief of the Cyuaga Nation commonly known by the name of the *Fish Carrier* and indeed the whole of both nations were extremely disaffected, for the grounds of their disaffection, I must refer you sir, to, the speeches delivered me on the occasion which I ordered to be taken down in writing on the Spot, and transmit to you by this dispatch. After several conferences with the *Fish Carrier* in which I was greatly assisted by several chiefs who attended Congress he gradually relaxed in his severity and at last became perfectly friendly. A number of young Warriors had gone off in the Spring to join the hostile Indians. The Fish Carrier promised me that he would not only recall the party but would go in person to the Southern treaty and use every exertion to bring about a general pacification between Congress and the Southern Indians, that after he had been useful he would go and see General Washington and could then take him by the hand with confidence and pleasure, few Indians Chiefs have a more extensive influence than the fish Carrier, the alteration therefore of his sentiments could not but afford me the highest pleasure, I can only express it as my private wish that all his reasonable requests might be gratified.

"You have no doubt heard Sir that a number of Senecas were concerned with our people in cutting off a scout of hostile Indians. This event has occasioned a good deal of uneasiness among the five Nations. Their resentment is peculiarly excited against the Commander at Fort Jefferson. They say that contrary to the advice they received from Congress he has excited some of their thoughtless young men to strike the tomahawk into the heads of their brothers. That it has occasionned an uneasiness towards the whole of their nation and thrown obstacles in the way of their influence in favor of their friends.

"The Chiefs from Onida did not arrive during the Council I should otherwise have been able to have dispatched the Chiefs of the five Nations to the Southern treaty, previously to my leaving Buffaloe Creek two of the Massasioga Chiefs attended council with the five Nations—their appearance was perfectly friendly—The[y] expressed a wish to be made acquainted with our Great

Men[.] The Mohawks were sent for from the Grand River but as Captain Brant was absent and their principal Chief Sick they did not attend—Colonel Butler the Brittish Superintendant of the six Nations was also requested to attend. He came as far as the Garrison. The Commanding Officer would not permit him to proceed further[.] He however sent a speech to the Indians in which he told them they were in the right path and advised them to continue in it. I was visited by several Brittish Officers and Gentlemen from the settlement of Niagara, they behaved with a politeness that seemed nearly to approach to real friendship.

"On the whole every circumstance that respects the six Nations wears at present a most flattering appearance. The Chiefs that went to Congress are our Zealous friends, they particularly explained to the nations who convened for the purpose the speeches they had made and received while absent. The reception and treatment they received at Philadelphia, and I had the pleasure of observing that they meet with universal approbation.

"From the best intelligence I could procure the southern Nations rest in quiet except the Delaware and Shawanoes neither Can I learn that they at present have any thoughts of sending out war parties but are very attentive lest an enemy should surprize their Villages. The grand Council of Indian Nations are now convening at the Falls of the Big Miami. It is thought it will be the largest ever known, the Indians from Canada have been invited and are every day expected at Niagara. No offensive step will probably be taken until after the General deliberation and from the number of friends we shall have there, I am induced to expect a favorable issue.

"The five Nations manifested gratitude to Congress for their intention of erected Schools among them and providing them with Blacksmiths. I would however inform you Sir that it will be out of my power to do either except greater encouragement is given and if I may be permitted to give my private judgment if Congress would establish at present only one School to the West of Genesee River and endow it with a Stipend that would make it an object for a Gentleman of Character it might prove of infinite service both in conciliating the affections of the Indians and in laying a foundation for their civilization.

"I would wish, Sir, some direction how far I am to distribute to the Indians. I am continually surrounded by a Cloud of them since my appointment. They all expect to be fed from my Table, and made glad from my Celler, some instances too of Cloathing I have not been able to deny—I would Suggest the Idea whether a small store of Provissions and goods to be distributed on necessary occasions might not be a saving to the public" (DLC:GW).

On the following day Chapin wrote Knox: "My dispatches were made out and the post was waiting previous to the receipt of your last letter, I am able only to detain him to inform you in haste of the arrival of Captain Brant who is not in health but in good spirits. We have a regular conveyance from this to Albany once in two weeks. by the next post I will do myself the honor of answering particularly to your last favour" (DLC:GW).

6. Knox wrote Nicholas Fish on 29 Aug. offering to appoint him adjutant general of the U.S. Army (NNGL: Knox Papers), but Fish declined the offer on 7 Sept., writing: "At present my views are so detached from military pursuits,

that an appointment in that line, would not be in any degree desireable" (enclosed in Knox to GW, 15 Sept. 1792, DLC:GW). Col. Thomas Posey, who was later offered the position, declined it in mid-October (see Posey to GW, 10 Oct. 1792, DNA: RG 59, Miscellaneous Letters). GW nominated Michael Rudolph adjutant general and inspector on 22 Feb. 1793, and the Senate consented to his appointment the following day (see GW to the U.S. Senate, 22 Feb. 1793; *Executive Journal,* 1:132, 134).

7. Henry Gaither, who recently had been appointed to command troops on the Georgia frontier, intended to sail from Philadelphia either on Thursday, 9 Aug., or Friday, 10 Aug. (see also Knox to GW, 21 July, GW to Knox, 1 Aug. 1792).

To Richard Chichester

Sir, Mount Vernon Augt 8th 1792

On my return home I found your note of the 6th & Mr Whiting shewed me the letter you had written to him on the same subject the next day.[1]

When the first came to this place I was from home, & when the second was presented to me I was too much engaged to write myself, but desired Mr Whiting to inform you of my objections as I should do as soon [as][2] I had leisure.

I should feel no dis-inclination, Sir, to comply with your request could I be of opinion that any other than my domestic deer were to be found in the skirt of Wood you wish to drive—or that the probability of finding one of these did not greatly exceed that of rousing any other. I have about a dozen deer (some of which are of the common sort) which are no longer confined in the Paddock which was made for them, but range in all my woods, & often pass my exterior fence.

It is true I have scarcely a hope of preserving them long, although they come up almost every day, but I am unwilling by any act of my own to facilitate their destruction; for being as much affraid of Hounds (on which acct I parted with all mine) as the wild deer are—and no man living being able (as they have no collars on) to distinguish them whilst they are running from the wild deer, I might, & assuredly should have them killed by this means. For this reason as it can be no object since Mr Fairfax, I am informed, is unwilling to have his Woods at Belvoir hunted,[3] I am desirous of preserving mine. I am—Sir Yr Most Obedt Servt

Go: Washington

ALS (1996), NNMM, on deposit at NN; LB, DLC:GW.

1. Chichester's letter to Anthony Whitting of 7 Aug. 1792 has not been identified.

2. This word is supplied from the letter-book copy.

3. Upon his death in 1787, George William Fairfax bequeathed his Belvoir estate to Ferdinando Fairfax, the third son of his brother Bryan Fairfax.

To Francis Deakins and Benjamin Jones

Gentlemen, Mount Vernon Augt 8th 1792.

You are requested to fix a valuation on that part of Woodstock Manor in Montgomery County which shall be assigned as the part of Mrs Sophia Mercer, as soon as convenient to you; & should there be no division take place within three months from this date between the Legatees of the late Mr Thos Sprigg, you are requested to form your Estimate on the average value of the whole tract—in affixing a price you will estimate what the Land wou'd now sell for in ready money,[1] & should you differ in your opinions, you are requested to choose some third person who may determine as an umpire—in doing which you will much oblige Gentn yr hble Servants

George Washington
John Fs Mercer

L (retained copy), in Bartholomew Dandridge's hand, DLC:GW; LB, DLC:GW.

For GW's strongly worded suggestion that John Francis Mercer come to Mount Vernon to settle their accounts, see GW to Mercer, 23 July 1792. On this day GW also wrote and signed a memorandum, which reads: "that in settling the Accts of Mr John F. Mercer to this date, I have charged him with & have allowed in the same amount, One hundred & one pounds fifteen shillings, which by the Books kept by Mr Lund Washington for me, appear to have been money paid Mr James Mercer by Mr Washington" (DS, PHi: Etting Papers). Benjamin W. Jones, who was at this time the sheriff of Montgomery County, Md., later served as a rent collector for GW (see also GW to William Deakins, Jr., 13 Aug., William Deakins, Jr., to GW, 24 Aug. 1792, GW to Francis Deakins, 15 Jan., 5 Mar. 1798, Francis Deakins to GW, 24 Feb. 1798).

1. Sophia Sprigg Mercer (1766–1812), who had inherited Woodstock Manor from her grandfather Thomas Sprigg (1715–1781), married John Francis Mercer in 1785. Deakins and Jones sent GW their "Valuation of Mrs Sophia Mercers part of Woodstock Manor" on 20 Dec. 1792.

Bartholomew Dandridge to Robert Lewis

Sir, Mount Vernon 8th Augt 1792

Being in Richmond last week Mr P. Lyons jur, who does business for John Hopkins, Esqr. put into my hands for the President U:S. some public paper which had been funded by you some considerable time ago. He has requested of the Prest a rect which was given you at the time, for the Certificates; & the President, supposing it must be in your possession, directs me to desire you will forward it to him by the first safe conveyance that it may be returned to Mr Hopkins.[1] I am Sir Yr mo: Obt Servt

Bw Dandridge

ALS, ViMtV; LB, DLC:GW.

1. On 31 Aug., Dandridge wrote Peter Lyons, Jr., from Mount Vernon: "According to my promise when at Richmond, I now enclose to you a receipt obtained by Mr Robert Lewis from John Hopkins Esquire, for sundry Certificates belonging to Gen: Washington Esquire" (DLC:GW).

From the Supreme Court Justices

Sir, Philadelphia 9th August 1792.

Your official connection with the Legislature and the consideration that applications from us to them, cannot be made in any manner so respectful to Government as through the President, induce us to request your attention to the enclosed representation and that you will be pleased to lay it before the Congress.[1]

We really, Sir, find the burthens laid upon us so excessive that we cannot forbear representing them in strong and explicit terms.

On extraordinary occasions we shall always be ready, as good Citizens, to make extraordinary exertions; but while our Country enjoys prosperity, and nothing occurs to require or justify such severities, we cannot reconcile ourselves to the idea of existing in exile from our families, and of being subjected to a kind of life, on which we cannot reflect, without experiencing sensations and emotions, more easy to conceive than proper for us to express. With the most perfect respect, esteem, and Attachment, we have the honor to be, Sir, Your most Obedient and most humble Servants,

John Jay
William Cushing
James Wilson
John Blair
James Iredell
Thomas Johnson.

Copy, in Tobias Lear's hand, DNA: RG 46, Second Congress, 1791–1793, Senate Records of Legislative Proceedings, President's Messages; LB, DLC:GW. Tobias Lear attested on the manuscript of his copy that it was "A true Copy."

1. The enclosed copy of the "Representation" signed by the members of the U.S. Supreme Court reads: "That when the present Judicial arrangements took place, it appeared to be a general and well founded opinion, that the Act then passed was to be considered rather as introducing a temporary expedient, than a permanent System, and that it would be revised as soon as a period of greater leisure should arrive.

"The subject was new and was rendered intricate and embarrassing by local as well as other difficulties; and there was reason to presume that others, not at that time apparent, would be discovered by experience.

"The ensuing Sessions of Congress were so occupied by other affairs of great and pressing importance, that the Judges thought it improper to interrupt the attention of Congress by any application on the subject.

"That as it would not become them to suggest what alterations or system ought in their opinion to be formed and adopted, they omit making any remarks on that head; but they feel most sensibly the necessity which presses them to represent.

"That the task of holding twenty seven circuit Courts a year, in the different States, from New Hampshire to Georgia, besides two Sessions of the Supreme Court at Philadelphia, in the two most severe seasons of the year, is a task which considering the extent of the United States, and the small number of Judges, is too burthensome.

"That to require of the Judges to pass the greater part of their days on the road, and at Inns, and at a distance from their families, is a requisition, which, in their opinion, should not be made unless in cases of necessity.

"That some of the present Judges do not enjoy health and strength of body sufficient to enable them to undergo the toilsome Journies through different climates, and seasons, which they are called upon to undertake; nor is it probable that any set of Judges, however robust, would be able to support and punctually execute such severe duties for any length of time.

"That the distinction made between the Supreme Court and its Judges, and appointing the same men, finally to correct in one capacity, the errors which they themselves may have committed in another, is a distinction unfriendly to impartial justice, and to that confidence in the supreme Court, which it is so essential to the public Interest should be reposed in it.

"The Judges decline minute details, and purposely omit many considerations, which they are persuaded will occur whenever the subject is attentively discussed and considered.

"They most earnestly request that it may meet with early attention, and that the System may be so modified as that they may be releived from their present painful and improper Situation" (DNA: RG 46, Second Congress, 1791–1793, Senate Records of Legislative Proceedings, President's Messages). Tobias Lear attested at the close of the document that the above was "A true Copy." GW laid a copy of the justices' representation before Congress in early November (see GW to the U.S. Senate and House of Representatives, 7 Nov. 1792 [second letter]).

From William Barton

Sir, Philadelphia August 10th 1792.

You did me the honor, some time since, of accepting a printed copy of a paper of mine, which had been read before the American Philosophical Society. I now, Sir, take the liberty of offering for your acceptance the inclosed Supplement to that paper.[1] With sentiments of the highest respect, & most perfect attachment I have the honor to be, Sir, Your most obedt hble Servant

W. Barton

ALS, DLC:GW.

1. Although the supplement enclosed in this letter has not been found, a copy of Barton's *Observations on the Progress of Population, and the Probabilities of the Duration of Human Life, in the United States of America. Read before the American Philosophical Society Held at Philadelphia, for Promoting Useful Knowledge* (Philadelphia, 1791) was in GW's library at the time of his death (Griffin, *Boston Athenæum Washington Collection,* 19).

From Alexander Hamilton

Sir, Treasury Departmt Augt 10th 1792.

I have been duly honored with your Letters of the 1st and 5th instant. A copy of the latter is enclosed according to your desire.

You may depend upon it, Sir, that nothing shall be wanting in this Department to furnish all requisite supplies for the Army with efficiency & œconomy, and to bring to exact account all persons concerned in them as far as shall consist with the powers of the Department. Hitherto monies have been furnished to the War department, as they have been called for, for procuring all those articles which had not been objects of direct Contract with the Treasury. And I learn from the Secretary of War that every thing is in great maturity.

Under the former system, provisions and clothing were the only Articles which the Treasury had the charge of procuring; the receiving, issueing, & inspecting their quality belonged to the Department of War by usage.

The Act of the last Session, entitled "An Act making alterations in the Treasury and War Departments" prescribes that all purchases and Contracts for all Supplies for the use of the Department of War, be made *by or under the direction* of the Treasury Department.[1]

As much progress had been made in preparations for the Campaign, prior to the passing of this Act, by the Secretary at War, I thought it best to continue the business under his immediate care for some time—'till in fact all the arrangements begun should be compleated. It is now, however, determined that on the first of September the business of procuring all supplies will be begun under the immediate direction of the Treasury, upon Estimates and Requisitions from time to time furnished and made by the Department of War.

The arrangement which is contemplated for this purpose is the following—Provisions and Clothing will be provided as heretofore by Contracts made by the Secretary of the Treasury, pursuant to previous Advertisements. Articles in the Quarter Master's Department will be to be procured by him or his Agents or Deputies; for which purpose advances of money will be made to him directly, to be accounted for to the Treasury by him. Ordnance stores, Indian Goods and all contingent supplies will be procured by an Agent who will be constituted for the purpose with an allowance of Eight hundred Dollars a year in lieu of Commission. Accounts for his purchases in every case in which it can conveniently be done (which will comprehend the greatest number of cases) will be settled immediately with the Treasury and the money paid directly to the Individuals. In other cases, advances on Account will be made to the Agent, to be accounted for directly to the Treasury.

A leading object of this arrangment is to exempt the Officers, both of the War and Treasury Departments, from the ill-natured suspicions which are incident to the actual handling and disbursment of Public Money. None of the interior officers of either department, except the Treasurer, will have any concern with it.

The supplies of every kind will be delivered to the order of the Department of War. The issuing of them & the accounting for the issues (except as to provisions which are directly issued by the Contractors to the Troops & which are proved to the Treasury upon vouchers prescribed for the purpose) appertain to the Department of War. The Regulations, which have been adopted for the purpose, will no doubt be early reported to you by the Secretary at War; as well as those which have been concerted with the Treasury respecting the paying & accounting for the pay of the Troops.[2]

I beg leave to assure you that in the application of the general arrangement which you have adopted respecting the execution of the Act concerning distilled Spirits, the greatest attention will be paid to œconomy as far as the precautions of the Treasury can ensure it.[3]

I presume it to have been your intention that the opinion of the Attorney General should be taken as to the Power of the President to appoint the supplementary Officers contemplated during the recess of the Senate; which shall accordingly be done.[4]

It affords me much satisfaction to observe that your mind has anticipated the decision to enforce the Law, in case a refractory spirit should continue to render the ordinary & more desirable means ineffectual.[5] My most deliberate reflections have led me to conclude, that the time for acting with decision is at hand: and it is with pleasure, I can add, that an encreasing acquiescence is likely to render this course the less difficult in the cases in which an uncomplying temper may finally prevail.

I shall without delay execute your directions respecting the Officers of Cutters.[6] With the highest respect and the truest attachment I have the honor to be &c.

Alexander Hamilton

LB, DLC:GW.

1. Hamilton is referring to section 5 of "An Act making alterations in the Treasury and War Departments" of 8 May 1792 (see *Annals of Congress,* 2d Cong., 1383–86).

2. Hamilton had suggested on 22 July that GW request that both the secre-

taries of war and of the treasury report to him the regulations under which army provisions were being issued and accounted for. GW did so in writing on 1 August. Knox wrote GW on 7 Aug. that the "papers which you have been pleased to require shall be transmitted by the post of Monday next," 13 August. Knox's letter of 11 Aug. has not been found, however.

3. For the new arrangement of the excise service, see Proclamation, 4 August.

4. For the outcome of this exchange, see GW to Hamilton, 5 Aug., and note 2.

5. See GW to Hamilton, 5 August.

6. For the appointment of officers in the New Hampshire, New York, and Maryland cutter services, see Hamilton to GW, 26 July, and GW to Hamilton, 5 Aug., and notes 3 and 4.

From Alexander Hamilton

Sir Philadelphia Aug. 11. 1792

I have already written to you to go by this Post.[1] This is barely to inform you, that I have made the communication you desired to Mr Kean, who promises every possible exertion—and that Mr Langdon has been here about a fortnight.[2] With perfect respect & attachment I have the honor to be Sir Your obedient servant

A. Hamilton

P.S. I have made progress in certain answers; but shall scarcely be ready to send them before next Monday's Post.[3]

ALS, M. E. Saltykov-Shchedrin State Public Library, St. Petersburg, Russia.

1. For the secretary of the treasury's other letter "to go by this Post," see Hamilton to GW, 10 Aug. 1792.

2. See GW to Hamilton, 1 August.

3. Hamilton is referring to the questions GW raised in his letter of 29 July respecting the way the government of the United States was being administered. Having not completed his answers to the president's queries by the "next Monday's Post," 13 Aug., Hamilton mailed a lengthy reply to GW on 18 Aug. 1792.

Letter not found: from Henry Knox, 11 Aug. 1792. On 15 Aug., GW wrote Knox that "This morning your Letter of the 11th came to hand."

From Thomas Jefferson

Dear Sir Monticello [Va.] Aug. 12. 1792.

I have the honor to inclose you two letters lately recieved from mister Barclay.[1] under another cover also I send to the Commissioners, open for your examination, a plan for a Capitol from mister Blodget, which came by the last post. you will see, by that, the use of the paper of which I presented you a few sheets, Blodget's plan being on a sheet I had given him. it renders the use of a scale & dividers unnecessary.[2]

I had thought my self secure of a weekly conveyance of letters, by the establishment of a private post here, till the public one could get into motion. but of 4. post-days since my return, he has missed three. mister Davies is however endeavoring to procure a public rider.[3] we have had abundant rains since my return, which were necessary to bring on our corn. some appearances of weavil give us apprehensions for our wheat, and increase the wishes for a machine which would enable us to get it out within the months of July & August. I have the honor to be with perfect respect and attachment Dr Sir Your most obedient & most humble servt

Th: Jefferson

ALS, DNA: RG 59, Miscellaneous Letters; ALS (letterpress copy), DLC: Jefferson Papers; LB, DNA: RG 59, George Washington's Correspondence with His Secretaries of State; LB (photocopy), DLC:GW. The ALS cover is postmarked "RICHMOND Aug. 16."

1. For calendared versions of Thomas Barclay's letters to Jefferson of 17 and 28 May 1792, see *Jefferson Papers,* 23:519–20, 547–48. Barclay's first letter concerns the commercial consequences of the continuing struggle for the Moroccan throne. His second letter contains petitions from the American captives at Algiers and discusses Algerian military preparedness.

2. Samuel Blodget, Jr., on 10 July had sent Jefferson his "Plan for the Base and elevation of the Capitol," which has not been identified. The D.C. commissioners informed Blodget in late August of their rejection of his design (ibid., 24:205–6).

3. Augustine Davis, who had been editor of the *Virginia Gazette, and General Advertiser* (Richmond) since 1790, was at this time postmaster of Richmond and printer for the Commonwealth of Virginia.

To William Deakins, Jr.

Sir, Mount Vernon Augt 13th 1792.

The letter herewith enclosed is left open for your *private* perusal, and transmission.[1] Two motives prompt me to this measure—the first is, the christian name of a Mr Jones, high sheriff of Montgomery County, the person intended to be associated with your brother in the business referred to them in the said letter, was unknown to Colo. Mercer and myself: the second, that before his name should be inserted, I might be ascertained from some person in whom I could place confidence that Mr Jones is a gentleman of good character—not interested in fixing the price at more than the land would *actually* sell at for *ready money*; & who will decide impartially between Colo. Mercer & myself; for it is to be considered by these Gentlemen, that it is to all intents & purposes a ready money bargain.[2]

I made choice of your brother Colo. Francis Deakins, to say what the *Cash* price of the Land shall be. Mr Jones was the choice of Colo. Mercer, but his name by consent was to be withheld for the reasons above mentioned, as I had never heard of the Gentleman until he was brought forward on this occasion.

I do not wish to delay the insertion of his name until I hear from you: on the contrary, if in your opinion Mr Jones comes under the description I have required, I pray you to add his name to that of your Brother's, in the enclosed Letter, then seal, direct & forward it to the latter, that the business may be brought to a close as soon as it can be with convenience.[3] I am, Sir, &c. &c.

G: Washington.

LB, DLC:GW. The ALS of this letter, which was sold in New York City on 8 Dec. 1947 at an auction conducted by the Parke-Bernet Galleries, has not been found (*American Book-Prices Current,* 54 [1948], 572).

1. For the enclosed letter, see GW and John Francis Mercer to Francis Deakins and Benjamin Jones, 8 August.

2. William Deakins, Jr., wrote GW on 24 Aug. that his brother Francis Deakins thought Jones to be "an honest reasonable Man, & will Act with him to Value Mr Mercers land agreeable to your request" (DLC:GW).

3. Having determined Jones to be a man of character, William Deakins, Jr., inserted Jones's name, sealed the letter, and forwarded it to its intended recipients.

To Alexander Hamilton

Dr Sir, Mount Vernon Augt 13. 1792.

Under a blank cover, I returned signed the provisional Contract for the supply of the Lighthouse in New Hampshire.[1]

It is pleasing to find by the Letter from our Commissioners at Amsterdam, that the credit of the United States remains upon so respectable a footing in the United Netherlands.[2] I am Dr Sir, &c.

G: Washington

LB, DLC:GW.

1. On 3 Aug., Hamilton had forwarded to GW a provisional contract for the supply of the New Hampshire lighthouse with his and Tench Coxe's opinions of it (see Hamilton to GW, that date, and note 1).

2. For more information about the letter from the U.S. commissioners at Amsterdam to Hamilton of 31 May and the Holland loan of 1792, see Hamilton to GW, 3 Aug., and note 2.

To Thomas Jefferson

Dear Sir, Mount Vernon Augt 13th 1792.

Since my last to you dated the 23d of July, I have received the second epistle of Govr Chittendon, enclosing a copy of the Lieutt Governor[1] of Canada's letter to him; but as he does not in that letter acknowledge the receipt of the One which went to him from the Secretary of State's Office the motives which suspended an answer to his first letter still exist, unless[2] he has given the information required of him immediately to yourself; however, that you may have the whole matter before you, to answer when you are possessed of[3] all the facts which relate to the Subject, I forward the Governors last letter to me,[4] as I also do that from Colo. Humphreys to you, covered by yours of the 30th Ulto.[5] I am Dear Sir Yr Affecte

Go: Washington

ADfS, DNA: RG 59, Miscellaneous Letters; LB, DNA: RG 59, George Washington's Correspondence with His Secretaries of State; LB (photocopy), DLC:GW.

1. At this place on the draft manuscript, GW wrote and then struck out the name "Clarkes."

2. At this place on the draft manuscript, GW wrote and then struck out the

phrase "it has been forwarded." He then inserted the phrase "he has given the information required of him immediately" above the line.

3. At this place on the draft manuscript, GW wrote and then struck out the words "some information on." He then inserted the phrase "all the facts which relate to" above the line.

4. For Gov. Thomas Chittenden's second "epistle" and the enclosed letter from Alured Clarke to Chittenden of 5 July, see Chittenden to GW, 16 July 1792, and note 2. For Jefferson's letters to Chittenden of 9 and 12 July, see GW to Jefferson, 7 July, n.2, and 23 July, n.5; *Jefferson Papers,* 24:200, 218–19. For the correspondence between GW and Jefferson about whether the secretary of state should write Chittenden again before receiving a reply to his earlier letters, see GW to Jefferson, 23 July, and Jefferson to GW, 30 July. Jefferson never received a response from the governor of Vermont.

5. For David Humphreys's letter to Jefferson of 21 May 1792, see Jefferson to GW, 30 July, n.2; ibid., 23:531–32.

From Thomas Jefferson

Monticello [Va.] 13 Aug. 1792. Sends "the inclosed letters which the tardy movement of the Post did not bring to him till yesterday evening, a day later than he should have arrived."[1]

AL, DNA: RG 59, Miscellaneous Letters; AL (letterpress copy), DLC: Jefferson Papers; LB, DNA: RG 59, George Washington's Correspondence with His Secretaries of State; LB (photocopy), DLC:GW. The cover of this letter is postmarked: "RICHMOND Aug. 16."

1. The enclosures may have included the letters from Willink, Van Staphorst & Hubbard to Jefferson of 30 May, from F. C. A. Delamotte to Jefferson of 5 June, and from David Humphreys to Jefferson of 17 and 20 June, all of which Jefferson recorded in his Summary Journal of Public Letters as having been received on 12 Aug. 1792 (DLC: Jefferson Papers). For the text of the letter from Willink, Van Staphorst & Hubbard to Jefferson and abstracts of the others, see *Jefferson Papers,* 23:616, 24:34–35, 90, 102–3. GW returned the letters to Jefferson without comment on 23 August.

To Henry Knox

Sir, Mount Vernon Augt 13th 1792

My last to you was dated the 5th instt since which I have received your letters of the 4th 5th & 7th; & shall reply to such parts of them as appear to require it.

It is painful to find the Recruiting Service advancing so slowly as your last letters indicate. Endeavor to rouse the Officers who are engaged in this business, to fresh exertions. The unhappy fate of our Messengers is a lamentable proof of Indian barbarity; and a strong evidence of the bad dispositions of at least some of their tribes.[1] This ought to stimulate every nerve to prepare for the worst.

If the banditti, which made the successfull stroke on the Station near Nashville could be come at without involving disagreeable consequences with the tribes to which they respectively belong, an attempt to cut them off ought by all means to be encouraged;[2] an enterprize judiciously concerted, & spiritedly executed would be less expensive to the General government than keeping up guards of Militia which will always be eluded in the attack, & never be overtaken in a pursuit.

No measures should be left unessayed to treat with the Wabash Indians; nor can the Goods be better applied than in effectuating this desirable purpose; but I think a person of more dignified character than Major Hamtramck should be employed in the negotiation—No idea of purchasing land from them ought to be admitted; for no treaty, or other communications with the Indians have *ever* been satisfactory to them when this has been the subject. The principles, & general outlines of all these treaties ought to be given to the Negotiator, notwithstanding the right of disannulling is reserved to the Government—Illiterate people are not easily made sensible of the propriety, or policy, of giving a power, & rejecting what is done under it. These may be contained in Genl Putnams Instrns.

General Putnam merits thanks, in my opinion, for his plan, & the sentiments he has delivered on what he conceives to be a proper mode of carrying on the War against the hostile Nations of Indians, and I wish he would continue to furnish them, without reserve, in future.[3] But in the present instance, two reasons are so strongly opposed to the measure recommended by him as to render it unadvisable and dangerous one of which, the collision it might occasion, & the consequences thereof, in the pending negotiation with Gr. Britain he could not be acquainted with; the other, the inadequacy of our force to admit a division, & thereby running the hazard of being beaten in detail by encountering the enemies *whole* strength with part of our own are such as not to be overcome—The other reasons assigned by you are not without weight, but less in degree;[4] for Peace & War are now in balance[5] which will preponderate remains to be known—if the latter (which heaven avert) we must expect to encounter a powerful confederacy, & ought not to put anything to hazard which can be avoided by military[6] foresight.

I can form no judgment of the object or the propriety of establishing the Post on the Muskingham—mentioned in Genl Putnams letter to you of the 9th of July, as no copy of that letter has been sent to me;[7] equally unable am I to give any opinion on the Speeches and wishes of the Fish Carrier, as I know not the contents of them; 20 copies having accompanied the letter of General Chapin.[8]

General Wilkinson has displayed great zeal & ability for the public weal since he came into Service—His conduct carries strong marks of attention, activity, & Spirit, & I wish him to know the favorable light in which it is viewed.[9] With great esteem I am—Dr Sir—Yrs &ca

Go: Washington

ADfS, DLC:GW; LB, DLC:GW.

1. For the fate of the American peace envoys Alexander Trueman and John Hardin, see Knox to GW, 31 July, and note 2, 4 Aug., n.2, and 5 Aug. 1792.

2. For the recent attack on Zeigler's station near Nashville, see Knox to GW, 5 Aug., and note 4.

3. For Rufus Putnam's ideas about how the war against the hostile Indian nations should be conducted, see his letter to Knox of 8 July, which is printed at Knox to GW, 5 Aug., n.2.

4. For Knox's observations on Putnam's plan for the upcoming military campaign, see his letters to Anthony Wayne and Putnam of 7 Aug., which are printed at Knox to GW, that date, n.3.

5. At this place on the draft manuscript, GW wrote and then struck out the words "the scale but" before inserting "balance" above the line.

6. At this place on the draft manuscript, GW wrote and then struck out the word "human" before inserting the word "military."

7. Putnam's letter of 9 July to Knox suggests "the propriety of fixing a post Some where on the Muskingum River to be occupyed by about one Company of Musket men & two Companys Riffelmen. . . . they would be a great protection to Ohio County and Washington in Pennsylviania, as well as the Settlements on the Muskingum and the inhabitants on both Sides of the Ohio as far down as Bellevill" (Buell, *Putnam Memoirs,* 290–91). As he indicates in his letters to Wayne and Putnam of 7 Aug., Knox had forwarded Putnam's letter to Wayne for his decision on that date (see Knox to GW, 7 Aug., n.3).

8. For GW's receipt of more definitive information about the Fish Carrier's wishes, see Israel Chapin to Knox, 17 July, which is printed at Knox to GW, 7 Aug., n.5.

9. GW's opinion of James Wilkinson's qualities as a soldier was not quite as

positive as this letter suggests (see Thomas Jefferson's Memorandum of a Meeting of the Heads of the Executive Departments, 9 Mar., and Memorandum on General Officers, 9 Mar. 1792).

To James McHenry

(Private)

Dear Sir, Mount Vernon Augt 13th 1792.

Your letter of the 17th of July came duly to hand. I could, with pleasure, spend a day in Baltimore on my return to Philadelphia, if time & circumstances would permit; but it is not for me at this moment to say whether either would suit me; besides, I shall confess to you candidly, I have no relish for formal & ceremonious engagements, and only give into them when they cannot be avoided—among other reasons because it oftentimes—if not always—proves inconvenient to *some* of the party bestowing, if it is not to the party receiving the compliment of a public dinner—and is a tax which I am as unwilling to impose as many are to pay, if false delicacy would allow them to express their real sentiments.

If it should so happen that I can, conveniently, spend a day in Baltimore as I return it would give me pleasure to dine with yourself & a few other friends in a social way; & on this footing let the matter rest, as no previous notice of my coming is necessary in that case.

Having begun a letter to you, I will add something to it of a public nature. Mr Potts, the District Attorney of Maryland, has resigned that Office.[1] Who, in general estimation is best qualified to fill it?

Mr Robert Smith has been spoken of. Mr Hollingsworth has been mentioned. and Mr Tilghman and Mr Hammond have also been thought of,[2] but the two last living on the Eastern shore, and Baltimore being the theatre for the Courts, it might be inconvenient to both those Gentlemen to attend them; and the appointment no inducement to their removal. Which then of the other two would be most eligable? Would Mr Smith if the preference is given to him accept? or is there any other person more preeminently qualified than either of the Gentlemen I have named?[3] Your sentiments, freely given, on these enquiries will much oblige Dear Sir—Your Most Obedt & Affecte

Go: Washington

ALS, CSmH; ADfS, DLC:GW; LB, DLC:GW. The letter-book and draft copies are both dated 12 Aug. 1792.

1. For Richard Potts's resignation as Maryland district attorney, see Potts to GW, 12 June 1792.

2. Baltimore lawyer Robert Smith (1757–1842) declined GW's offer of the position of Maryland district attorney in the summer of 1792 (see GW to Smith, 31 Aug. 1792). Eastern Shore attorneys William Tilghman (1756–1827) and Nicholas Hammond (c.1757–1830) withdrew their names from consideration in the fall of this year (see McHenry to GW, 4 Oct. 1792 [first letter]). Tilghman, who served in the lower house of the Maryland legislature 1788–90 and in the state senate 1791–94, moved to Pennsylvania in the mid-1790s. He was appointed chief judge of the third judicial circuit in 1801, judge of the court of common pleas for Philadelphia and surrounding counties in 1805, and chief justice of the Pennsylvania supreme court in 1806. Hammond later served as president of the Farmers Branch Bank at Easton, Maryland.

William Vans Murray had recommended Baltimore lawyer Zebulon Hollingsworth (born c.1762) to GW in a letter dated 1 Aug.: "A long acquaintance with him enables to say that he is a man of integrity; & I conceive of parts exceedingly brilliant, with a knowledge of his profession which has raised his consequence at the bar, & increased his fortune. He is about thirty years of age & a marry'd man—An early, spirited & constant attachment to the government over which you, Sir, preside, has among other valuable qualities distinguished his merits as a good Citizen of America" (DLC:GW). GW nominated Hollingsworth on 19 Nov., and the Senate confirmed his appointment two days later (*Executive Journal,* 1:125–26).

3. On 16 Aug., McHenry provided GW with a written evaluation of these candidates and the name of another prospect for the position of Maryland district attorney.

Letter not found: from Edmund Randolph, 13 Aug. 1792. On 26 Aug., GW wrote Randolph "to acknowledge the receipt of your favors of the 5th & 13th instt."

To Henry Knox

Sir, Mo[un]t Vernon 15th Augt 1792.

This morning your Letter of the 11th came to hand, but I have not as yet had time to read, much less to consider, the enclosures therein contained.[1]

Mr Seagrove's dispatches of the 5th ulto enclosing a packet for you, was received at the same time; & about noon his other Letter of the 27th was brought to me by Express. The whole, as well those addressed to me, as the others directed to you, are sent forward under cover with this Letter by the Express who brought the last.

The extreme & dangerous illness of my Nephew (Major Washington, who has an affection of the Lungs, & for the last two or three days a violent & copious discharge of pure blood from them, by which he is so reduced as to be almost unable to speak)[2] together with the Letters & voluminous referrences accompanying them, places it out of my power at this moment, to pass any sentiment upon Mr Seagrove's Dispatches, by the bearer; but as far as my Memory & short notes will enable me to recollect the contents of them, it shall be done by the Post on Monday.[3]

My reason for forwarding of them without delay, is, that you may, previous to the receipt of any sentiments of mine, give the several matters contained in these despatches, & his former communications, the consideration they merit from a comprehensive & comparative view of the whole subject; & as some parts of it are of an important & delicate nature, it is my request that the Secretary of the Treasury would also consider them attentively; that the proceedings thereon, & answers thereto, may be the result of our joint & deliberate thoughts. If the Secry of State had been in Philada I should have called upon him also; for if Matters be as they are stated in Mr Seagrove's Letters & the enclosures accompanying them, our Affairs in that quarter are critically situated as they respect the State of Georgia & the southern Indians—& the Ud States and the Spaniards.

At present, however, I shall add nothing further on these topics; and with respect to your writing (as submitted in your letter of the 11th) to the *Governor* of Nw York concerning the complaint exhibited by the Oneida's or Onandago's (I am not certain wch) against a trader that had been obtruded upon them; & committing the matter, & the regulation of the Trade with the first of these tribes, to the Govr of that State;[4] I desire you to do in the premises as shall appear best under a full view of the circumstances, and the Laws relating to the arrangement of the intercourse with the Indians; for at present they are not enough in my mind to enable me to give any precise derictions concerning the Reference.

Who is Mr Rosecrantz?[5] and under what authority has he attended the Councils of the Indians at Buffaloe Creek? Subordinate interferences must be absolutely interdicted, or counteraction of the measures of Governmt—perplexity & confusion will inevitably ensue. No person should presume to speak to the Indians on business of a public nature except those who derive the authority, and receive their instructions from the War Office for that purpose. With esteem & regard I am Sir Yr Affecte

G. W——n

L (retained copy), in Bartholomew Dandridge's hand, DLC:GW; LB, DLC:GW.

1. For the background to this letter, which has not been found, see Alexander Hamilton to GW, 22 July 1792, and note 2.

2. For more information about George Augustine Washington's continuing ill health, see G. A. Washington to GW, 26 June, source note and note 1.

3. GW's letter to Knox commenting upon the information in James Seagrove's dispatches was written on Sunday, 19 Aug. 1792.

4. GW had first brought the Indians' complaint to the secretary of war's attention in his letter to Knox of 5 August.

5. On 27 July, Anthony Wayne had written Knox of "a Certain *Rosecrantz*—who I expect will accompany the *Legation* of the Five Nations to the Grand Council of the Hostile Indians, he speaks the Seneka, Delaware, & Shawanese Language's & has been promised a liberal reward, for bringing the earliest and most Authentick account of the result of their Councils & the real views & intentions of the Indians—, he appears to be in the Confidence of the corn planter" (Knopf, *Wayne,* 47–48). Nicholas Rosecrantz (Rosencrantz) later served as an interpreter and a soldier in the U.S. Army, being commissioned an ensign in May 1794 and promoted to lieutenant in May 1797. He was discharged from the service in June 1802.

Index